CADOGAN
*city guides*

KU-759-143

# PARIS

**Cadogan Books plc**
London House, Parkgate Road,
London SW11 4NQ, UK
guides@cadogan.demon.co.uk

Distributed in the USA by
**The Globe Pequot Press**
6 Business Park Road, PO Box 833, Old Saybrook,
Connecticut 06475–0833

Copyright © Dana Facaros and Michael Pauls 1997
Illustrations © Lyn O'Neill and Jeff Cloves 1997

Book and cover design by Animage
Maps © Cadogan Guides, drawn by Map Creation Ltd

Series editors: Rachel Fielding and Vicki Ingle
Editor: Dominique Shead
Proof-reading: Annabel Hall
Indexing: Isobel McLean
Production: Book Production Services
Printed and bound in the UK by Biddles Ltd

ISBN 1–86011–062–2
A catalogue record for this book is available from the British Library

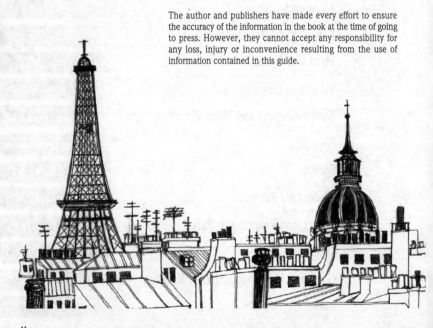

## About the Authors

Dana Facaros and Michael Pauls have written over 20 books for Cadogan Guides, including four on France. They live in a farmhouse in southwest France with their two children and assorted animals.

## Acknowledgements

A great big thank you, two sloppy kisses, three rousing cheers for Monsieur Andrew Gumbel whose impeccable hospitality on Boulevard Sébastopol made probing Paris a pleasure. Our much heartfelt appreciation to Michael Davidson and Brian Walsh for testing all the Paris bars, as well as for other technical assistance; special thanks to Old Nick out in Oregon—the provocative little book he sent helped us to put a bit of the devil in ours. Final thanks to Jackson and Lily.

The publishers would like to thank Animage for the design, Jeff Cloves for the extra drawings, Map Creation for the maps, Isobel McLean for indexing and Annabel Hall for proofreading.

## Please help us to keep this guide up to date

Despite the valiant efforts of the author and publishers to keep the guide up to date, standards in restaurants and practical details such as prices are liable to change. We would be delighted to receive any comments concerning existing entries or indeed any suggestions for inclusion in future editions or companion volumes. Significant contributions will be acknowledged in the next edition, and authors of the best letters (or e-mails) will receive a copy of the Cadogan Guide of their choice.

# Contents

## Museums 311–44

*Contents* vii

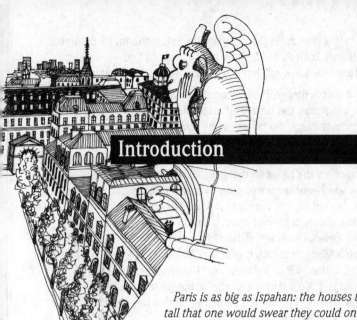

# Introduction

> *Paris is as big as Ispahan: the houses there are so tall that one would swear they could only be inhabited by astrologers. You can well imagine that a city built in the air, with six or seven houses built atop one another, is very populous; and when everyone descends into the streets, it makes a* bel embarras.

Montesquieu, *Lettres Persanes*

> *Qui regarde au fond de Paris a le vertige.*

Victor Hugo

And so Paris has been a wonder for nearly a thousand years, from the time when masons came to learn the magic numbers of Gothic architecture to the present day when we come to ponder the fearful symmetry of its latest geometric tricks—a pyramid of glass, a hollow cube, a sphere of a thousand mirrors.

Modern Paris is a bigger *bel embarras* than ever. Squeezed into one place are the brains, mouth, piggy bank and bossy-stick of a wealthy and talented nation that fondly regards itself as the most rational and sensible land on Earth; the *Ville Lumière* is France's collective dream, the vortex of all its vanity, its parasite and its shimmering showcase. The results are there for all to enjoy, for

Emerson's statement that 'England built London for its own use, but France built Paris for the world' is true in both senses: as a monumental show-off, but a generous and cosmopolitan one.

Like a cactus flower, Paris blooms only now and then, but when it does it captures the heart and mind like no other city can. In the last twenty years, the government has lavished billions on it to coax it into bud, and in many ways, Paris has rarely been more delightful: *nouvelle cuisine* is out of fashion, the new museums are spectacular, the plonk in the cafés is better, the street markets are more lavish and seductive than ever; even rear-platform buses are back. Best of all, the Parisians themselves have shed their grumpy postwar xenophobia and chauvinism to embrace the rest of the world. Besides all the Parisian things you do in Paris, you can also watch a Mongolian ballet, take in a film from Madagascar, attend an exhibition of Pacific Northwest Indian art, catch a concert of African jazz, do a tango, a samba or boogie to zouk from the Antilles, or sip Tibetan tea topped up with a lump of salty butter.

But don't worry; this book is no gushing tourist brochure (if that's what you want, they're free at the French tourist office). For Paris is a special case, precocious and exasperating, a shining light and dire warning, the city that 'changes faster', as Baudelaire sighed 150 years ago 'than a mortal heart'. Never destroyed by enemies or act of God, it has been perpetually devouring and re-creating itself over the past 200 years, a restless metamorphosis. After inventing so much of modern society and modern art in the 19th century, Paris is preening itself to become the 'culture pole of the 21st' (vanity has always been its worst sin). Yet at the same time its ruling technocrats are doing their best to turn the city, once so beloved for its earthy, spirited life, into an arty shopping mall, a spotless safety-tested playground for trendies and tourists. Paris may have already become the first capital to banish its muses to the suburbs. It's a battle for Paris' soul, and we worry, lest the City of Light itself become unable to cast a shadow. But even as you read these words, things could be changing. 'Paris is bored', they'd murmur in the 1800s—right before a revolution in art or in politics, or both.

# A Sentimental Dissection

'Paris Intra Muros is the same organism from top to bottom, from solid rim to rim ... You could lift it whole from a plate, like a nicely fried egg,' as John Gunther noted. It covers 86.8 sq km (33.5 sq miles), being slightly larger than Manhattan (not counting the recently annexed Bois de Boulogne and Bois de Vincennes). The population, 2,176,243, makes Paris denser than Manhattan—without the sky-scrapers. In contrast, Greater Paris covers most of the Ile-de-France region and counts around 8.5 million souls, triple the number in 1876.

Paris' first centre was the corner of Rue St-Jacques and Rue Cujas, where Roman surveyors laid out their *cardo* and *decumanus*. Since then the fried egg has spread out gradually and logically. The map shows its growth like rings on a tree trunk: the medieval walls (now the Grands Boulevards); the 18th-century Farmers-General wall (the next ring of boulevards) and the Thiers fortifications of the 1840s (the *Boulevards des Maréchaux* and present city limits). Since the Revolution, the city has been divided into 20 numbered *arrondissements*, spiralling outwards from the centre. Getting to know these is one of the first jobs of any new Parisian or visitor.

Paris is the biggest tourist destination in Europe; the two million play host each year to some 12 million tourists. It draws more Americans than Brits or anyone else, and it probably has more luxury hotels than any other city—also more outrageously expensive restaurants and shops. In French, the word for luxury goods is *articles de Paris*. The best ham is *jambon de Paris*; the best mushrooms *champignons de Paris* (in fact quite a few are actually grown here, in the endless tunnels under the city). If all the flowers are grown in Provence, here they are distilled into perfume. Paris is the top.

The rest of the French don't particularly care for their capital, no matter how jealous they may be of it. In Provence they call Parisians *les envahisseurs* (the invaders); an Occitan regionalist named Robert Escarpit dropped a memorable epigram when he called Paris 'the shop window of mediocrity that hides France'. Paris' heavy-handed predominance caused the cultural and economic backwardness of most other French cities; critics still moan about the 'French desert'—everything outside the city walls. Don't blame Paris; national governments run by provincials made it this way, while at the same time rarely ever permitting the city to control its own destiny. Historically, when it does govern itself it's usually during a revolution (Paris now has had limited self-rule since 1977). Twenty-five per cent of all the public employees in France live here—and they make a tremendous noise whenever anyone suggests decentralization, as happened when the socialists moved one of the *Grandes Ecoles* to Strasbourg.

Partly because of these, Paris is a city of strangers—only one in eight Parisians has even one Paris-born parent. In a sense Paris isn't a city, a real community at all, but a career stage—once you can move there, you've made it. Not everyone in Paris is a well-off government or corporate employee, or a student (though it often seems that way). Among those working in the city are huge numbers of immigrants (10% of the metropolitan population) who do all the city's dirty work—and, increasingly, run the small businesses. Add some 75,000 seamstresses, who help make the garment district around Rue Réaumur one of the liveliest parts of town; if they're over 30 and unmarried, they are the *Catherinettes* and wear big, silly hats on St Catherine's day. There are even some children(!) Having these seems to be coming back into style; last year the favourite names were Nicolas and Stéphanie. And don't forget the 13,976 professional cooks—almost three times as many as there are lawyers.

For all the high-tech fireworks of its new building projects, there's still much in Paris that seems preposterously quaint: the Académie Française, for example, or the ubiquitous 'keep off the grass' signs in the parks. But there are many other relics that seem wonderfully civilized, the sort of thing we go to Paris for: the *bouquinistes* by the Seine, the flower markets, the arcades around the Palais Royal, the politeness and decorum. Every tourist goes out for a stroll on the boulevards, even if the Parisians pay little heed to them anymore. The classic street furnishings—the trees, the Wallace fountains (donated by Richard Wallace, who left Paris a compensation for the art collection he removed to London) and the Morriss columns for theatre posters—are a symbol of Paris everyone knows.

Why those boulevards were built (*see* History, p.42) is not a pretty story. But it is a typical one. The posh, contented Paris of today is built on long decades of troubles (1789–1944), the like of which it had never seen, except perhaps in the 1400s, when—thanks to the English—Paris nearly disappeared. Maybe Paris' greatest talent is its way of making us forget there's blood on every stone here.

But we have hundreds of pages to go over all that. In the meantime, here are some more loose statistics to reflect on. Paris has a quarter of all the students, and a quarter of all the crime in France (which isn't very much). It has the highest divorce rates and accident rates. It has changed radically in the last thirty years to catch up with other modern capitals: in 1963 only 9% of homes had telephones (now 92%); only 49% had proper toilets and 62% a shower or bath (many more of these now). In this culturally mad city you will find Elysian Fields, a Mount Parnassus, a Campus Martius and a New Athens, along with about 900 free-standing statues—including 50 poets, 37 writers, five kings, five revolutionary leaders, two gardeners and one Sarah Bernhardt.

# The Pick of Paris in a Weekend

A hundred years or so ago, a weekend in Paris was synonymous with hanky panky. Of course it can still mean that (but you've bought the wrong guide; refer instead to the listings at the back of the weekly *Pariscope*). Otherwise, here are some subjective suggestions for the best way to spend a few days in and around the city:

**First-time visitors**: Most people would want to start by visiting Paris's ancient core and essential attractions: Ile de la Cité (Walk I)—with Notre-Dame and the Sainte-Chapelle—the Eiffel Tower, the Louvre, Montmartre, and Musée d'Orsay. For a taste of Paris at its best, you might consider one of the walks in the centre: the Marais (Walk II) on the right bank and St-Germain (Walk X) are two of the best for this. Take a boat ride along the Seine, browse at the *bouquinistes* along the quais, ride a bus with a back platform and, to complete the atmosphere, dine at one of the classic old *bouillons* like Chartier or Drouot if you're on a budget, or La Tour d'Argent or Lapérouse if you're not.

**Second-time visitors**: Have a look at the parts of the centre you haven't seen yet— Les Halles (Walk III), the Latin Quarter (Walk VIII) or the Opéra (Walk V), and the Palais Royal and the *passages* (Walk IV). St-Ouen flea market, Musée Rodin, Musée Cluny and its Lady and the Unicorn tapestries, maybe Père-Lachaise cemetery. To really get to know the city and its history well, a trip to the Musée Carnavalet is indispensible. Go and see a dance performance at the Opéra, or dance with your honey at Le Balajo. Eat in the Latin Quarter's brasserie Le Balzar or at La Coupole or one of the other classics up in Montparnasse.

**Third-time visitors**: Take the métro up to St-Denis, with its basilica and museum, or to the Mouffetard and the Jardin des Plantes (Walk IX). Find an obscure museum that fits some special interest, from television to crystal to Lenin to Louis Quinze chairs. There are still Guimard's Art Nouveau buildings in Passy and Auteuil, more fascinating cemeteries, the Sewers and the Catacombs. See a film at La Pagode or Studio 28 or the Grand Rex. Dine at Jacques Cagna or Au Pied de Fouet and have a glass of Paris red at the Café Mélac.

**Haven't-been-back-latelys**: Take in the *Grands Projets* if you haven't seen them: the Grande Arche, the Cité de la Musique, the new Louvre and Pyramid and glittering Louvre-Rivoli subterranean shopping centre, the newly refurbished Champs-Elysées, the Institut du Monde Arabe, the Opéra de la Bastille and the new Viaduc of arts and crafts shops along Avenue Daumesnil. Take a boat ride up the Canal Saint-Martin to La Villette. Have dinner at the Café Marly, listen to some jazz at the Hot Brass in La Villette, and take in a play at the Cartoucherie Théâtre du Soleil.

**Paris in the summer:** Summer, especially August, is notoriously the time not to visit Paris, at least if you want to see the city as it usually functions, with the streets full of Parisians (instead of 75% tourists) and all the shops and restaurants open. July, however, is a treat: the gardens are superb, especially the Bagatelle in the Bois de Boulogne, host to an annual international rose competiton. There are chamber music concerts in the Bagatelle's Orangerie and in Sainte-Chapelle, outdoor films, a jazz festival at La Villette, firemen's balls on the 13th and a parade down the Champs-Elysées and fireworks on Bastille Day. Take a Paris by bicycle tour (*see* p.9). Dine out one of the lovely terraces: the romantic Pavillon Montsouris or Le Pré Catelan.

**Nostalgic Paris:** Wander through the old residential streets of Montmartre, the Musée de Montmartre and Père-Lachaise and those off Rue du Faubourg Saint-Antoine in the Bastille quarter. Visit the Musée Carnavalet, the Musée de la Vie Romantique, the Edith Piaf museum. Dine at a classic *brasserie* like Bofinger or the Train Bleu in the Gare de Lyon, or at the Grand Véfour in the Palais Royal, and go and hear that old-time French music at Au Pied de la Butte.

**Exotic Paris:** Culturally Paris is so cosmopolitan you can pretend to be somewhere else altogether. Besides its displays of culture from around the world—the Musée des Arts d'Afrique et d'Océanie, Musée Guimet (when it reopens), the Musée de l'Institut du Monde Arabe, Musée d'Ennery, Musée de l'Homme, Musée Cernuschi—you can shop in the Chinese groceries in the 13th *arrondissement* or in the North African-flavoured market in Place d'Aligre; eat everything from Tibetan food at Tashi Delek, Macchu Pichu, or Baalbek, and take in some World Music at Le Divan du Monde and the New Morning, or the Chapelle des Lombards.

**Impressionists' Paris**: There are three major collections of Impressionists in the city where Impressionism was born: the Musée d'Orsay, the Marmottan and the Orangerie. Top it off with a pilgrimage to Giverny to see Monet's house and lovely gardens (the waterlillies bloom in July) and the museum of American impressionists. Dine on a struggling artist's budget at Aux Artistes or Des Beaux Arts.

**Medieval Paris**: Paris was hopping in the Middle Ages. Visit Chartres, Notre-Dame, Sainte-Chapelle, St-Eustache, the Tour St-Jacques, the cathedral of Saint Denis, and the fabulous medieval collections in the Musée de Cluny, as well as the smaller churches of Saint-Julien le Pauvre, St-Séverin and St-Nicolas. In March the churches host a festival of ancient music. Go to dinner and a show in the medieval dungeons at the Caveau des Oubliettes.

# Travel

*By Air*

## From the UK

All the best deals leave from London, as usual, but few can match the Chunnel-piercing Eurostar for price and convenience. Keep an eye peeled for special deals in the Sunday papers, *Time Out* and in the window of your local travel agent. Some of the cheapest options out are long-haul lines that stop off in Paris, but usually only once or twice a week. Travellers under 26 or students under 32 can pick up discounts at Campus Travel or STA (check your telephone directory for your nearest branch office).

## From Ireland

The best deals are often flight and accommodation packages. Pick up a list of firms from the French Government Tourist Office (*see* below).

## From North America

Paris, as a major transatlantic destination, often benefits in the airline price wars. There are a good dozen charter and cut-rate scheduled flight options; check the travel section of your Sunday paper. Agencies that have long had cheap flight options to Paris are: Uni-Travel, ✆ (800) 325 2222; Council Travel, ✆ (800) 223 7402; Access, ✆ (800) 825 3633; Discount Travel International, ✆ (800) 543 0110; or Last Minute Travel Club, ✆ (800) 527 8646. From Canada, there are decidedly fewer juicy options: Travel CUTS is a good place to start hunting for bargains (187 College St, Toronto, Ont., M5T 1P7, ✆ (416) 979 2406).

## From Australia and New Zealand

Those qualifying for a youth or student discount should contact their nearest STA office. Otherwise, flying by way of London or Amsterdam is usually the cheapest option, unless you can find a charter; ask your travel agent.

*transport from the airports*

You won't need to take a taxi from either airport. There are two of them: **Charles de Gaulle** (north of Paris), also known as **Roissy** from the suburb in which it is located, and **Orly** (south). Both terminals at Roissy are on the RER B line to central Paris (around 50F); Orly is linked every 4 to 8 minutes to RER B station Antony by an automatic métro, Orlyval (also around 50F). Orly is also linked by bus shuttle to central Paris RER C stations every 20 minutes (around 35F). Airport RER tickets include transfer on to the métros.

Both airports also have good bus services. From **Charles de Gaulle**: Air France buses run until 11pm, from the Air France terminal to Place Charles-de-Gaulle (Ave Carnot) or the slightly cheaper RATP (city) buses: no. 351 for Place de la Nation or no. 350 for the Gare du Nord. From **Orly**: Air France buses, from Air France terminal to the Invalides and Gare Montparnasse (36 Ave du Maine, until 11pm); RATP buses go to Place Denfert-Rocherau on the Left Bank. **Taxis** aren't the airport rip-off they are in some cities (about 200–250F to central Paris from either airport), but the other services are so good you should only consider a taxi if you have tons of baggage and can't handle it.

For your return trip, to be safe count on a train or bus taking an hour to reach either airport (it's usually slightly less).

### airline addresses in Paris

**Air France:** 119 Ave des Champs-Elysées, 75008, ✆ 01 44 08 24 24

**British Airways:** 12 Rue Castiglione, 75001, ✆ 01 47 78 14 14

**Air Canada:** 31 Rue Falguière, 75015, ✆ 01 42 18 19 20

**United Airlines:** 40 Rue Jean-Jaurès, 93710 Bagnolet, ✆ 01 49 72 14 14

**Delta Airlines:** 6 Pl des Vosges, 92052, ✆ 01 47 68 92 92

**Northwest:** 16 Rue Chauveau-Lagarde, 75008, ✆ 01 42 66 90 00

**American:** 109 Rue du Faubourg-St-Honoré, 75008, ✆ 01 42 89 05 22

**Aer Lingus:** 47 Ave de l'Opéra, 75002, ✆ 01 47 42 12 50

**Qantas:** 7 Rue Scribe, 75009, ✆ 01 44 94 52 00

## By Train

With the Channel Tunnel, it's only three hours on Eurostar trains to the Gare du Nord from London's Waterloo Station (is there poetic justice? Napoleon was the first to think of a channel tunnel, as a means of invading England). Fares are lower than planes; for information and booking, call ✆ (0345) 881881. For train information, contact the SNCF, ✆ 01 45 82 50 50.

## By Bus

The cheapest way to get to Paris is by bus; Hovercraft CitySprint from Victoria Coach Station in London to Paris takes about 8 hours, services by ferry slightly longer. Contact Hoverspeed reservations on (01304) 240241, or National Express Eurolines, 52 Grosvenor Gardens, London SW1, ✆ (0171) 730 8235 or (0990) 808080.

A car entering France must have its registration and insurance papers. If you're coming from the UK or Ireland, the dip of the headlights must be adjusted to the right. Carrying a warning triangle is mandatory; the triangle should be placed 50m behind the car if you have a breakdown. Drivers with a valid licence from an EU country, Canada, the USA or Australia don't need an international licence.

Prices on 'Le Shuttle' fluctuate according to the season; call ✆ (0990) 353535.

If you're not just visiting Paris, and plan to hire a car, look into air and holiday package deals to save money, or consider leasing a car if you mean to stay 3 weeks or more. Prices vary widely from firm to firm, and beware the small print about service charges and taxes. A couple of firms to try in the US are France Auto Vacances, ✆ (800) 234 1426 and Europe by Car, Inc, ✆ (800) 223 1516 or Renault, ✆ (800) 221 1052.

### Border Formalities and Visas

Visitors from the EU, US or Canada can enter France for up to 90 days; British visitors now need a full British Passport. If you plan to stay longer than 90 days, you're officially supposed to have the proper visa in your passport to apply for a *carte de séjour* (*see* Living in Paris). Other nationals must apply for a visa just to get in. Contact your nearest French consulate two or three months before leaving.

## Getting around Paris

### Maps

For detailed information the Michelin *Paris-Plan* (the little blue book) is indispensable: brilliantly conceived, a cartographical work of art. For day trips into the outskirts of the city, Michelin's green *Environs de Paris* no. 106 is the best.

### By Bus

The routes are a bit complicated—but get a map and use it. Riding the buses is much more fun than spending your vacation down in the dreary métro. This is especially true on the buses with back platforms; having a smoke out the back while houses and streets disappear behind you is one of the most serendipitous free pleasures Paris can offer. The killjoys did away with open platforms in the 1960s, but they are being revived by popular demand on some lines. Most buses on routes 20, 29, 75, 83 and 93 now have them. Other buses to ride just for fun are the 24, which cruises along the Seine (Left Bank side), and the little *Montmartrobus* (no number), which climbs from Place Pigalle up and down the steep streets of Montmartre. For bus info in English, call ✆ 01 40 46 42 12.

Enter at the front, leave at the rear; press the *arrêt demandé* button just before your stop. Note that **métro tickets are valid on buses too**, though you'll need more than one for long trips. A sign at the centre of the ceiling will tell you how many zones you're crossing and how many tickets you'll need to *oblitérer* in the machine next to the driver. Buses run very frequently—though service is reduced after 8.30pm and on Sundays.

*Noctambus*: the Paris night bus service can be useful, unless you live in the 7e or 16e. There are ten lines, all of which converge at Place du Châtelet from points around the edge of the city (map and information available from any information centre or métro stop). Buses generally run once an hour, from 1.30 to 5.30am, and each ride requires three tickets.

*Balabus*: Between 12.30 and 8pm on Sundays and holidays from April to September, the RATP's Balabus makes a tour of monumental Paris from the Grande Arche de La Défense to the Gare de Lyon. Price: only three métro tickets.

---

## By Métro

The métro is a godsend to disorientated visitors; not only quick and convenient for travelling, but its stations serve as easy reference points for finding addresses. It has its own special aroma and it recently became more democratic by dumping the first-class cars. Contrasts with the London underground are unavoidable. A ride in Paris costs less than half as much, and for that you get cleaner stations, faster service, fewer breakdowns, fewer fatalities—and staff a thousand times more helpful and courteous. Unlike London, with its offensive Big Brother propaganda about fare cheaters, the RATP would never think of treating its riders like criminals. You Londoners might give all this some thought while you're in Paris (not to mention you New Yorkers).

The only thing the world's least offensive underground service lacks is personality. Graphics and design are uninspired, and the ubiquitous white tiles lend a touch of clinical anaesthesia to your journey—maybe that's the idea; métro rides do seem to go by painlessly. Another minor complaint would be about the *direction* system. To find the right train, it isn't simply a matter of looking for 'northbound' or 'eastbound'. You'll need to look at the map, and see what's at the *end of the line*, in the direction you wish to travel. For example, if you wish to go north on the no. 7 line to La Villette, you're looking for a platform marked: *'Direction—La Courneuve 8 Mai 1945'*.

The buskers of all kinds and puppeteers who present entire skits between two stops add to the experience. Some métro stations have exhibits on art or the history of the locality: Louvre, Bastille (with part of the fortress' foundations built into the station), Hôtel de Ville, St-Denis-Basilique, Liège, St-Germain-des-Prés, Varenne. Some other stations have decorated platforms, such as the one at St-Michel with mosaics on the ceiling. One of the best métro thrills is to take Line 6 from La Motte-Picquet past the Eiffel Tower to Trocadéro, one of its few sorties above ground and over the Seine within the city limits.

Keep your ticket until the end, not only for spot checks, but because some of the bigger stations have automatic exit gates that gobble up the ticket. In parts of some stations, like the phenomenally complex Châtelet-Les Halles with more than 2km of passages, there are two of these in a row. So you'll spend the rest of your life down there, unless you ask an employee for a get-out-of-the-métro-free card, a *contremarque*. They're used to it.

## RER

The *Réseau Express Régional* is Paris' suburban commuter train system, run jointly by the SNCF (Société Nationale des Chemins de Fer Français) and RATP, so it's separate, but part of the system, and you can use métro tickets on it within the Paris boundaries. It can come in handy for getting across town fast, or for visiting places like the Musée d'Orsay or the Jardin du Luxembourg, where it has the closest station. From almost all the other stations, you can easily change onto the métro. The RER can also take you to Versailles or to the airports.

## RATP

The *Régie Autonome des Transports Parisiens* is the authority controlling the buses and the métro. Their main office is at 53 Quai des Grands-Augustins, **M** *St-Michel*. For recorded information (6am–9pm), call ✆ 01 43 46 14 14; for a human being you have to pay 3F a minute ✆ 08 36 68 77 14.

*Buying single 8F tickets is crazy*—always get a *carnet* of 10 (from any métro window or machine) for a 40% discount—good for buses too. Compared to transport fares elsewhere, this will seem ridiculously cheap, but if you're going to spend a lot of time in Paris and sit on public transport all day, you can do even better. Most Parisians carry the basic pass, good for buses, métro, RER and SNCF suburban trains. A weekly pass (*carte orange*) is 72F; a month is 243F. These are good for two zones only; for more zones the fee is higher; bring some passport photos when you apply. Note—these passes expire at the end of the week or month, so purchase them at the beginning of the period.

There is a special *Carte Paris Visite*, which is a rotten deal—you'll need to ride seven or eight times a day just to break even. A weekly *carte bus*, good for buses only, is priced according to how many sections it covers.

## By Taxi

There are 14,900 taxis in Paris and on the whole they're inexpensive, honest and competent, and a pleasure to ride. They'll get you to the station on time if it kills you both—it's a matter of honour—while forcing you to defend your government's policies, or telling you about their daughter's trip to Oklahoma City.

The Michelin *Paris-Plan* has all the city's taxi stands conveniently marked on the map with blue Ts. Radio taxis (☎ 01 42 41 50 50, ☎ 01 45 85 85 85, ☎ 01 49 36 10 10) can be especially helpful in rush hours, when cabs are hard to find. Fares are determined according to an arcane system, with three different base rates, corresponding to the three little fairy lights on top of the car, and those on the meter. There are extra charges for night trips, excess baggage, etc.

Taxis are required by law to: stop for you if the light on top is on (unless it's his last half-hour on duty); take you anywhere you want to go in Paris, or to Orly or Charles de Gaulle airports; follow whatever route you choose; accept all handicapped passengers; give you a receipt. Taxis are *not* required to: take animals; take more than three people; take an unreasonable amount of luggage; pick up passengers less than 50m from a taxi stand.

## By Car

This is absurd, of course. Parking is impossible everywhere in Paris, and battalions of the world's most elegant meter maids cheerfully await your every indiscretion. Paris tows away 1200 cars a day. Towing is privatized and something of a racket—they don't have to wait for an officer to call them, they just take what they want along the clearways (*axes rouges*). You can usually avoid this by leaving a person in the car. If you catch them in the act, demand that they call a policeman (a legal nicety); they don't want to wait and lose business, so they'll probably just move on.

Not even many luxury hotels have garages. Long-term parking in garages is exorbitant (one trick is to use the *Parcotrain* service of the SNCF, available at some main stations; even though you would have to buy a train ticket too, in some situations it's a good deal). Paris traffic gets a bad press—from the nationalistic British especially. Except on the abominable *Périphérique*, the always packed ring road, Parisians move at a serene and stately pace. Unlike New York or London, few motorists here will go out of their way to try and kill a pedestrian. Radar traps and spot checks are frequent. When oncoming drivers blink their headlights at you, it means the *flics* (cops) are waiting just up the road—the commendable custom of a gracious and civilized nation.

However civilized, the French do have alarmingly frequent lapses of judgement and attention—and an accident rate double that of the UK (and much higher than the US). The vaunted French logic and clarity breaks down completely on the asphalt. Go slowly and be careful. Never expect any French driver to consider the possibility of a collision. And remember the most important thing about driving in France: at intersections without signals, *the car on the right has right of way*. People forgetting this archaic rule cause the majority of accidents here.

### hiring a car

This too has its drawbacks: high rental rates and petrol. Unless sweetened in an air or holiday package deal, car hire in France is an expensive proposition (300F a day, including mileage for the cheapest cars). Petrol (*essence*) at the time of writing is on average 6F 20 a litre for super.

Forget the big chains. Though convenient and dependable, they're always the most expensive by far—over 200% more in some cases—and they wouldn't survive without tax-deductible business trippers. Some local firms that rent at reasonable rates are:

**SNAC:** 118 Rue de la Croix-Nivert, 15ᵉ ⓂFélix-Faure, ✆ 01 48 56 11 11
**Rual :** 78 Bd Soult, 12ᵉ, Ⓜ Porte-de-Vincennes, ✆ 01 43 45 52 20
**Dergi et Cie.,** 60 Blvd Saint-Marcel, 5ᵉ, Ⓜ Gobelins, ✆ 01 45 87 27 04

### By Bicycle

Fearless, experienced urban cyclists can hire bikes by half-day, day or week from:

**Dergi et Cie** (*see* above).

**Paris-Vélo**, 2 Rue du Fer-à-Moulin, 5ᵉ, Ⓜ Censier-Daubenton, ✆ 01 43 37 59 22, ✆ 01 47 07 67 45.

**Bicyclub SA**, 8 Pl Porte-de-Champerret, 17ᵉ, Ⓜ Porte-Champerret, ✆ 01 47 66 55 92.

**Paris Bike**, 83 Rue Daguerre, 14ᵉ, Ⓜ Denfert-Rochereau, ✆ 01 30 51 87 64. All terrain bikes rentals and city bike tours.

**Paris à Velo C'est Sympa!**, 9 Rue Jacques Coeur, 4ᵉ, Ⓜ Bastille, ✆ 01 48 87 60 01. Rentals and a variety of city bike tours.

**Continental Circus,** 2 Rue Brunel, 17ᵉ, Ⓜ Argentine, ✆ 01 47 74 45 70. For scooters.

### By Boat

The famous *bateaux-mouches* got their name (literally, fly boats), because the first ones were built in Lyon, on the Quai des Mouches. A part of the Paris tourist experience since the Universal Exposition of 1889, they have become victims of their own success, metamorphosing into floating bateaux-lasagnas, so wide that the arches of the Pont des Arts had to be rebuilt to let them through. The largest boat is equipped with a retracting wheelhouse to fit under the bridges. As we said, it's a tourist experience, with the recorded narration droning on in all the popular languages—and since the embankments are so high you won't really see very much. But it still can be fun. Most charge 40–50F for a 1-hour tour, and most also offer lunch and dinner cruises.

**Canauxrama**, ✆ 01 42 39 15 00. Reservation only for 3-hour tours of the Canal-St-Martin.

**Les Bateaux Parisiens**, ✆ 01 44 11 33 44, from the Port de La Bourdonnais, 7e, Ⓜ *Bir-Hakeim/Iéna*.

**Vedettes du Pont Neuf**, ✆ 01 46 33 98 38, from Sq du Vert-Galant, on the Ile de la Cité, Ⓜ *Pont-Neuf.*

**Vedettes de Paris**, ✆ 01 45 50 32 79, from the Port de Suffren, 7e, Ⓜ *Bir-Hakeim.*

**Bateaux-Mouches de Paris**, ✆ 01 40 76 99 99, from Pont de l'Alma (north side, 8e); this one has night tours in summer, and a very fancy dinner cruise for 500F.

Another line, La Patache, ✆ 01 42 40 96 97, goes from the Musée d'Orsay up the Canal St-Martin to La Villette, passing through old locks, and under tunnels (*see* Peripheral Attractions, p.360).

### By Helicopter

**Heli France**, ✆ 01 45 57 53 67; about 5500F an hour, but regrettably no place in Paris itself to land it.

### By Hot Air Balloon

The city won't let you float over the Eiffel Tower any more, but you can tour the surroundings of Paris; ring France Montgolfières, ✆ 01 40 60 11 23.

# Practical A–Z

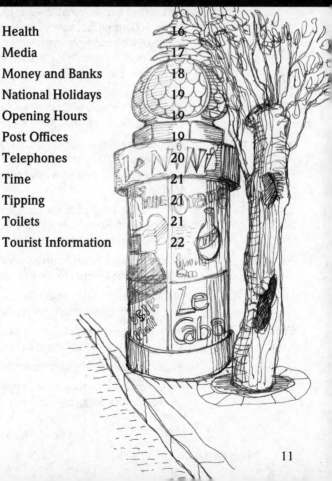

## Calendar of Events

Dates for nearly all the events listed below change every year. The central tourist office on the Champs-Elysées is the best source to check precise dates.

| | |
|---|---|
| March | *Festival des Instruments Anciens*, medieval, Renaissance and Baroque music, mostly in the city's churches. |
| Late March | International Festival of Women's Films at Créteil Maison des Arts; *Festival du Chien* dog show at Bercy; orchid show at Bois de Vincennes. |
| Late April | Waiters' race—8km circuit holding their trays, beginning and ending at the Hôtel de Ville; beginning of the *Foire de Paris* at the Porte de Versailles—the closest equivalent of the old St-Germain fair, with all kinds of new-fangled gadgets, food, wine and more—running through the first week of May. Also *Foire du Trône*, ancient traditional fun fair, Porte Dorée, Bois de Vincennes. |
| 1 May | Trade unions march and people buy sprigs of *muguet* (lily of the valley) for good luck, while the National Front rallies around the statue of Joan of Arc in Place des Pyramides. |
| Sometime in May | *Salon de Montrouge*, one of Paris' more intriguing annual art shows; *Marathon International de Paris*, 42km race from Place de la Concorde, which ends at the Hippodrome de Vincennes. |
| Mid-May | Five-day antiquarian fair in the Carré Rive Gauche, west of Rue des Saints-Pères. Late in May–June, French Open Tennis Championships at Roland Garros. |
| Pentecost | Dual pilgrimages by modern Catholics and traditionalist Lefèbvrites from Chartres to Sacré-Coeur. |
| Mid-June | International fireworks contest, in Chantilly; *Festival de Saint-Denis*, classical music concerts, through early July. |
| Late June | St John's Eve—fireworks show at Sacré-Coeur; *Fête du Marais*—jazz and classical music and drama. |
| 21 June | *Fête de la Musique*, free concerts across town. |
| Early July | *Festival de Saint-Denis*, classical music; *La Villette Jazz Festival*, 2-week long, big-name jazz fest at Parc de la Villette |

| 13 July | Firemen's feasts and balls in the neighbourhoods. |
|---|---|
| 14 July | Military parade on the Champs-Elysées; fireworks at Trocadéro; *Bastille Ball*, rollicking all-night gay party. |
| A few days later | End of the *Tour de France* in the Champs-Elysées. |
| September | *Fête de l'Humanité*, lively national Communist festival, in suburban La Courneuve; *Festival de l'Automne*, music dance and drama lasting until December. |
| October | FIAC—*Foire Internationale de l'Art Contemporain*—choice selections from galleries around the world. |
| First Saturday | Wine harvest in Montmartre—lots of good clean fun. |
| Mid-October | *20km de Paris* race, open to all and sundry—entries in past years have numbered over 20,000. |
| November | *Salon d'Automne*, major art salon in the Grand Palais. |
| 25 November | *Les Catherinettes*, women in the fashion trade who are over 25 and single, don outrageous hats—'*coiffer la Sainte-Catherine*'. |
| Christmas Eve | Midnight Réveillon feast—Parisians eat out and gorge like geese. Billions of oysters meet their maker. |
| New Year's Eve | Saint-Sylvestre, occasion for another ultra-rich midnight feast—in a week Paris downs 2000 tons of *foie gras*. |

## Climate and When to Go

The 18th-century Neapolitan Abbé Ferninando Galiani wrote of Paris: *'Bad, heavy air, poisonous water, an incredibly strange climate ... everything that does violence to the Neapolitan temperament'*. But, surprise: in a little climatic anomaly, Paris and its suburbs get slightly more sun and less rain than almost anywhere in northern France—hence all the sidewalk cafés, which seem almost Mediterranean to many of us, at least those of us not from Naples.

The worst months to visit Paris are September and October. Although the weather and light are beautiful, the city is packed to the brim with visitors and trade fairs. Winter can be soggy, cold and grey but the city's cultural life is in full swing, and there are fewer tourists. Paris in the spring can be meltingly romantic, warm and sunny or cool and drizzling but also crowded with tourists and visiting school groups. Summer is usually a bit hot but so many Parisians vacate in July and August the whole city slows down. Gourmets should note, however, that most of Paris' chefs take their holidays in August.

## Average Temperatures (in Fahrenheit/Centigrade)

Jan 48/9    Feb 47/8    Mar 50/10    April 60/16    May 62/17    June 74/24

July 77/25    Aug 78/26    Sept 69/20    Oct 62/17    Nov 54/12    Dec 45/8

## Consulates in Paris

**UK:** 16 Rue d'Anjou, Ⓜ *Madeleine*, ✆ 01 42 66 38 10

**Ireland:** 12 Ave Foch, Ⓜ *Etoile*, ✆ 01 44 17 67 00

**USA:** 2 Ave Gabriel, Ⓜ *Concorde*, ✆ 01 43 12 22 22

**Canada:** 35 Ave Montaigne, Ⓜ *Franklin D. Roosevelt*, ✆ 01 44 43 29 16

**Australia:** 4 Rue Jean-Rey, RER *Champ-de-Mars*, ✆ 01 40 59 33 00

**New Zealand:** 7 Rue Léonard-de-Vinci, Ⓜ *Victor Hugo*, ✆ 01 45 00 24 11

## Crime and Police Business

Nothing is likely to happen to you in Paris. For most Americans and British city-dwellers, in fact, coming here will be statistically less dangerous than staying at home. Streets are safe at night. There are a few good reasons for this: firstly, there is less widespread poverty and desperation here; secondly, the poor, and the criminals with them, are largely segregated out in the suburbs; thirdly, Paris is crawling with plain-clothes police, just as it was in the days of Louis XIV or Louis-Philippe—regular city cops, public transport cops, anti-dog-droppings cops, thirty-one flavours of cop in fact. But the ones to steer clear of are conspicuous enough: the boys in dark green with big sticks and patches that say **CRS** (*Compagnie Républicaine de Sécurité*). Their presence means you have stumbled into an area where a major demonstration is taking place (even in our peaceful times, these have lately averaged slightly less than one a day), or else a riot or revolution—even the most peaceful demonstrations can be followed by gangs of *casseurs* (vandals), looking for an excuse to raise some hell. Smile and follow the CRS's instructions, as they are uncouth and testy, and accountable to no one.

Besides the police, you will need to watch out for pickpockets, especially in the métro, in the flea markets (where everyone deals in cash), and wherever people are standing around to watch street performers (for instance, around Les Halles). Muggings are rare, but more common in the wealthier neighbourhoods (15e, 16e and 17e, among others), which are dead at night, and nobody's on the street. Car thefts, and thefts from cars (radios, etc.) are common.

Report thefts to the nearest police station—not a pleasant task, but the reward is the bit of paper you need for an insurance claim. If your passport is stolen, contact the police and your nearest consulate for emergency travel documents. By law, the police in France can stop anyone anywhere and demand ID; in practice, they only tend to do it to harass minorities, the homeless and scruffy, hippy types. If they really don't like the look of you, they can salt you away for a long time without any reason, on what is called *garde à vue*. You'll notice how nonconformists and marginal types *dress* conformist (or try to).

The drug situation is the same in France as anywhere in the West: soft and hard drugs are widely available, and the police only make an issue of victimless crime when it suits them (your being a foreigner just may rouse them to action). Smuggling any amount of marijuana into the country can mean a prison term, and there's not much your consulate can or will do about it.

## Disabled Travellers

A booklet called *Touristes Quand Même* is usually available in the tourist office, or write ahead to the Comité National Français de Liaison pour la Réadaptation des Handicapés, 30–32 Quai de la Loire, 75019 Paris. The city has an information office for the disabled in Place Mazas, 12ᵉ, ✆ 01 43 47 76 60, and has recently opened a **hotel** with complete facilities for travellers with disabilities: the Résidence Internationale de Paris, 44 Rue Louis-Lumière, 75020, ✆ 01 40 31 45 45, single 280F, or 30F in a four bed room. For **public transport**, there's the RER (but not the métro) and bus 20 linking the Gares St Lazare and Lyon by way of the Opéra, Place de la République and Bastille. All taxis are required by law to accept all handicapped travellers, whatever the circumstances. National museums offer the handicapped free admission.

## Electricity

The voltage is 220 and plugs have small round prongs; Brits will need only an adapter, Americans a voltage converter for any radios or appliances. The BHV department store on Rue de Rivoli, Ⓜ Louvre, has a good selection of such items.

## Gay Scene

Historically Paris has always been one of the most tolerant cities anywhere, especially in sexual matters—so tolerant, in fact, that the gay community has become a fairly integral part of Paris society. However, AIDS (*SIDA*)—which has hit Paris hard, with some 60 per cent of the national victims—has made the homophobes more vocal, but to a much milder degree than in Britain or the States. Most Parisians are only aware of their gay fellow citizens during the Bastille Ball, traditionally the biggest annual event in the gay calendar, with dancing and fun until dawn; or on a more sombre note, when there have been large demonstrations, usually motivated by ACT UP, to inform the public about AIDS and lobby for a greater commitment from the government in research funds—resulting in schemes like the 1-franc condom (*préservatif*).

The best place to find gay and lesbian literature is at *Les Mots à la Bouche*, 6 Rue Ste-Croix-de-la-Bretonnerie, 4ᵉ, with a large collection of gay and lesbian books and magazines, meeting rooms and exhibitions (Ⓜ*St-Paul*). This corner of the Marais is Paris' centre of gay-owned restaurants, bars and businesses (*see* under listings). The Centre Gai et Lesbien, 3 Rue Keller, Ⓜ Bastille, ✆ 01 43 57 21 47, has a full programme of meetings, discussions and social events. For women, another good address is the Maison des Femmes, 8 Cité Prost, 11ᵉ (but soon to relocate) ✆ 01 43 79 61 91 (Ⓜ *Faidherbe Chaligny*).

## Health

Local hospitals are the place to go in an emergency (*urgence*). If you need an ambulance and paramedic (SAMU), dial ✆ 15. Doctors take turns going on duty at night and on holidays—pharmacies will know who to contact, or else telephone *SOS Médecins*, ✆ 01 47 07 77 77, or *SOS Dentistes*, ✆ 01 43 37 51 00. If it's not an emergency, the pharmacies have addresses of local doctors, or you can visit the clinic at a *Centre Hospitalier*. Pharmacists are also trained to administer first aid, and dispense free advice for minor problems. Pharmacies open on a rota basis; Dhéry, 84 Champs-Elysées, ✆ 01 45 62 02 41, is open 24 hours a day.

Doctors will give you a brown and white *feuille de soins* with your prescription; take both to the pharmacy and keep the *feuille* for insurance purposes at home. British subjects who are hospitalized and can produce their E-111 forms will be billed later at home for the 20% of the costs that French social insurance doesn't cover.

Citizens of the EU who bring along their E-111 forms are entitled to the same health services as French citizens. This means paying upfront for medical care and prescriptions, of which 75–80% of the costs are reimbursed later—a complex procedure for the non-French. As an alternative, consider a travel insurance policy, covering theft and losses and offering a 100% medical refund; check to see if it covers your extra expenses in case you get bogged down in airport or train strikes. Remember that accidents resulting from sports are rarely covered by ordinary insurance. Canadians are usually covered in France by their provincial health coverage. Americans are plain out of luck; people with private insurance should consult their agent before setting off (don't expect much). There's some consolation for Americans in knowing that France is a civilized country, and that no one will die alone outside a hospital door (although the French are quite fastidious in asking about arrangements for payment).

**AIDS** *(SIDA)* **hotline**: ✆ 01 44 93 16 69, Mon, Wed, Fri 6–10pm.

**Crisis hotline:** SOS Help (bilingual), ✆ 01 47 23 80 80; 3–11pm.

**Drug problems** (including emergencies): the specialist is Hôpital Marmottant, 19 Rue d'Armaillé (17ᵉ, Ⓜ *Etoile*), ✆ 01 45 74 00 04.

**Poison hotline:** ✆ 01 40 37 04 04; 24 hours.

**Rape Crisis hotline** (free call): ✆ 0 800 05 05 95 95.

**Sexually-transmitted diseases**: free treatment is available at the Institut Prophylactique, 36 Rue d'Assas, 6ᵉ, ✆ 01 42 22 32 06.

Condoms are available in pharmacies and tobacconists, and now in machines in many métro stations. Pharmacists that speak English and can help match foreign prescriptions are Pharmacie Swann, 6 Rue Castiglione, 1ⁱᵉʳ, ✆ 01 42 60 72 96; British and American Pharmacy, 1 Rue Auber, 9ᵉ, ✆ 01 47 42 49 40.

## Media

**Newspapers:** Paris' first news kiosk opened in the Jardin des Tuileries in 1720, and since then the city has had an extraordinary variety of newspapers, including in the 1860s one called *La Naïade*, printed on rubber so dandies could read it in their morning bath. During the Siege of Paris (1870–1), thirty new papers were launched, and they never ran out of newsprint.

But the enterprising press barons' sheets of the last century somehow never evolved into newspapers as known in the US or Britain. The best, and one of the youngest, is probably the mildly left-wing *Libération*, the first editor of which was Jean-Paul Sartre. *Le Figaro*, owned by Robert Hersant, the French Murdoch, is bulldog-rightist, and very commercial, sometimes well written, sometimes repugnant. Parisian *intellos* (highbrows) love to hate it; it looks like an American paper, and has the same acid bite as the *Chicago Tribune* of the old days. *Le Monde*, an ambitious journal founded just after the liberation of Paris, is certainly the most French, lost in a baroque fog of verbiage that passes for profundity; real gems of erudition and wisdom appear in its pages, though finding them requires a lot of shovelling. *L'Humanité*, the Communist paper, used to be excellent, but has declined along with the party's fortunes. All the others are tabloid-quality. For politics, everyone reads the weekly *Le Canard Enchaîné*, with writing a little too colloquial and knowing for non-natives.

In English the *International Herald Tribune*, which is published in Paris and has more interesting articles about the city than most Parisian papers, is available everywhere; so are *USA Today,* the *European* and the quality British dailies. Also look for *Paris Free Voice*, a community newspaper from the American Church with reviews, cultural affairs and classifieds.

**TV** is a sorry mess of American retreads, game shows, French B-movies, and bicycle races. News reporting is equally bleak, though special reports and documentaries on Third-World (especially African) and environmental subjects can be exceptional. *TF1* churns out commercial, lowest-common-denominator programming (and is by far the most popular station). *France 2*, state-owned and once the class act of French TV, has recently lobotomized itself under market pressure, and now spins out lots of US-inspired trash—even its news has become a joke. *France 3*, also state-owned, is supposed to be an outlet for regional broadcasting, which never really happened—but still it occasionally comes up with an interesting show or classic film. *Canal Plus*, a slickly-run, scrambled pay-TV station offers recent movies and porn, and a chance for homesick anglophones to catch up the CBS nightly news at 7am (unscrambled). *La Cinquième* is another state station, devoted to educational programming; at 7pm it turns into *Arte,* an arty, highbrow German–French effort that produces something worth watching six nights out of ten. *M6* shows alternating music videos with reruns of *Bewitched* and *The Avengers*, known to the French as 'Leather Boots and Melon Hats.'

**Radio**: The band is crowded, mostly with teenage ear candy, or rather, teenage ear *bonbons* since Chirac's government decreed that 40% of all music every station plays has to be French. Some exceptions: *Radio Libertaire* (89.4), anarchist-run, alternative news and music; *Radio Beur* (98.2) and *Radio Maghreb* (94.0), North African; *Tropic FM* (92.6), a variety of real music, full of surprises; *Radio Latina* (99.0) and *FIP Paris* (90.4), some good jazz; *Radio Nova* (101.5), modern, kinky stuff; *Radio Classique* (101.1), classical, no commercials.

And not to forget the state-run dinosaurs: *France Info* (105.5) gives 24-hour news; *France Musique* (91.7) mixes one third classical and other music, and two-thirds commentary on it; *France Culture* (93.5) and *France Inter* (87.8) are also cultural, also mostly bla-bla.

## Money and Banks

The franc (abbreviated to F) consists of 100 centimes. Banknotes come in denominations of 500, 200, 100, 50 and 20F; coins in 20, 10, 5, 2, 1 and ½F, and 20, 10 and 5 centimes. You can bring in as much currency as you like, but by law you are only allowed to take out 5000F in cash. Traveller's cheques or Eurocheques are the safest way of carrying money, and the most widely recognized credit card is *Carte Bleue* (French *Visa*), which is accepted everywhere and will give you cash out of the automatic tellers with a PIN number.

Banks are generally open from 8.30–12.30 and 1.30–4; they close on Sundays, and most close on Saturdays as well. Exchange rates vary, and nearly all banks take a commission of varying proportions. Places that do nothing but exchange money (and this also applies to hotels and train stations) usually give the worst rates and take the heftiest commissions. It's always a good bet to purchase some francs before you go, especially if you arrive during the weekend.

**Lost credit cards:** American Express, ✆ 01 47 77 77 77; Visa, ✆ 01 42 77 11 90; Eurocard/Mastercard, ✆ 01 45 67 84 84; Diner's Club, ✆ 01 47 62 75 00.

## National Holidays

On French **national holidays**, banks, shops, museums and businesses close, but most restaurants stay open. These holidays are: 1 January, Easter Sunday, Easter Monday, 1 May, 8 May (VE Day), Ascension Day, Pentecost and the following Monday, 14 July (Bastille Day), 15 August (Assumption), 1 November (All Saints' Day), 11 November (First World War Armistice), and Christmas Day.

## Opening Hours

Normal opening hours in Paris are from 9 or 10 in the mornings to 7 or 8 in the evenings, Tuesday through Saturday. Smaller boutiques often take a couple of hours off for lunch. Note that many shops in Paris close on Sundays and Mondays, with the exception of *boulangers*, grocers (often open Sunday morning and Monday afternoon) and *supermarchés* (open Monday afternoon). Travelling food markets dwindle away at noon; most permanent street markets are open morning and afternoon, including Sunday morning but not on Mondays; markets selling clothes, art, antiques, etc., run into the afternoon.

## Post Offices

Until the 18th century, love letters in Paris were known as *poulets* because they were delivered by chicken sellers, who discreetly tucked the message by the wing. But even after *poulets* came by regular post, husbands were expected never to open letters (or chickens) addressed to their wives.

The modern French post office, the *PTT* or *Bureau de Poste*, is still distinguished by a blue bird on a yellow background. Post offices are open Mon–Fri 8am–7pm, and Sat 8am–12pm. You can purchase stamps in tobacconists as well as post offices. The **Main Post Office**, 52 Rue du Louvre, ⓜ *Les Halles* or *Louvre*, is open 24 hours (for phones, *poste restante* and telegrams, but not always for selling stamps). The office at 71 Ave des Champs-Elysées, ⓜ *George V*, stays open till 10pm, 8pm Sun. You can receive *poste restante* (general delivery) at any post office provided you give the office's address and postcode. Unless you know exactly where you're staying, it's easiest to have your letters addressed to the main office ('Poste Restante, 75001 Paris'); bring some ID to collect your mail.

*Postcodes*: In Paris all begin with 75, the departmental number; 75001 means the 1$^{ier}$ *arrondissement*, etc. Suburban codes begin with 92, 93, 94 95, etc.

## Telephones

Apart from bars where you can still find coin-operated *Point Phones*, all other public telephones in Paris have switched over to *télécartes*, which you can purchase at any tobacconist, métro or train station, or post office for 40F for 50 *unités* or 96F for 120 *unités*.

As of October 1996, all French phone numbers have ten digits, and all Paris ones begin with 01; if you're ringing from abroad, dial France's international code 33 and drop the first '0' of the number. For international calls from Paris, dial 00, wait for the change in the tone, then dial the country code (UK 44; US and Canada 1; Ireland 353; Australia 61; New Zealand 64), and then the local code (minus the 0 for UK numbers) and number.

The **easiest way to call collect** is to spend a few francs ringing the number you want to call and quickly give them your number in France, which is always posted in the box; alternatively ring your national operator and tell him or her that you want to make a reverse-charge call, *appeler en p.c.v.* You also need an operator in your home country to make **international calls by credit card**:

**UK:** 00 44 (BT), 00 944 (Mercury)
**Ireland:** 00 353
**US:** 00 11 (ATT), 00 19 (MCI), 00 87 (Sprint), 0013 (IDB Worldcom)
**Canada:** 00 16
**Australia:** 00 61 (Telstra), 002 061 (Optus)
**NZ:** 00 64

**Cheapest** times to phone: (all Paris time)

**Britain and Ireland**: weekdays 9.30pm–8am; Sat midnight–8am, 2pm–midnight; Sun all day.

**US and Canada**: any day 2am–noon; *highest rates* apply in effect Mon–Sat 2–8pm; at other times an intermediate rate applies.

**Australia and NZ**: any time *except* Mon–Sat 8am–9.30pm (sorry!).

Most post offices have public **fax machines** and offer free use of a *Minitel* electronic directory (alternatively dial ☎ 12—a free call—for a human operator; most speak some English). International directory assistance is 00 33 12 followed by the country code, but note that you'll have to wait for them to ring you back with your requested number. And, as anywhere else, remember that only billionaires and fools use the telephones in their hotel rooms.

**Police:** ✆ 17

**Fire:** ✆ 18

**First Aid/Ambulances (SAMU):** ✆ 15

*Horloge parlante* (time): ✆ 36 99

**Lost and found:** ✆ 01 45 31 14 80

**Electronic Wake-up service:** ✆ *55* plus the time you want to be wakened in four digits, followed by your phone number

**Weather in Paris:** ✆ 08 36 65 00 00

## Time

One hour ahead of GMT, six hours ahead of US Eastern Standard Time, nine ahead of California. Nine hours *behind* Sydney. Except during summer (daylight-saving) time of course, which begins in different countries on different dates and fouls up everything.

## Tipping

Almost all restaurants and cafés automatically add an extra 15% to the bill, and there's no need to leave any more unless you care to or in recognition of special service. The taxi man will be happy with 10%, the cinema usherette 2F.

## Toilets

That most fragrant and funky piece of Parisian street furniture, the sidewalk *pissoir* or *vespasienne* (named after the rough-edged Roman Emperor Vespasian, who collected urine to sell to fullers) has gone the way of the dodo, to be replaced by the ugly beige spaceship toilets of the Decaux Company. They cost 2F for 15 minutes of privacy, and are automatically sanitized after each user although sometimes they're out of order; delinquents make off with all the toilet paper.

Museums (except for the Natural History) have decent facilities, and you'll have to be very unlucky to find a café that hasn't improved on a hole-in-the-floor squatter ('worthy of Central Asia' was how George Orwell described the lavatory in the restaurant where he worked). In return for such luxury, though, you're more or less obliged to buy something or be sneaky. Train stations and fancier cafés with an attendant should be tipped 2F—though some attendants invent their own complex rate schedules. For all that, the reek in narrow alleys and *impasses* proves that not everyone feels like paying for a pee. If you're feeling nostalgic you can visit the last rusting *vespasienne* in Paris in Boulevard Arago, in front of La Santé prison, in the 14e.

## Tourist Information

The **main** office is at 127 Avenue des Champs-Elysées, ✆ 01 49 52 53 54, near the Arc de Triomphe, open daily 9am–8pm. Bilingual and helpful, the staff can help you find a hotel room, sell you a museum pass (*see* p.312), fill you in on events, and tell you about places to see in the Ile-de-France region. Other offices:

**Gare du Nord:** near the international arrivals area, ✆ 01 45 26 94 82

**Gare de Lyon:** ✆ 01 43 43 33 24

**Gare d'Austerlitz:** ✆ 01 45 84 91 70

**Gare de l'Est:** ✆ 01 46 07 17 73

**Gare Montparnasse:** ✆ 01 43 22 19 19.

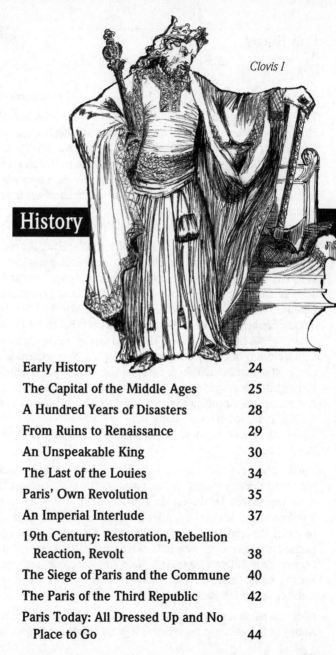

*Clovis I*

# History

# Early History

*The universe does nothing but pick up the cigar
butts of Paris.*

Théophile Gautier, 1865

The natural crossroads of northern France, Paris has been occupied since the earliest times; Stone-Age folk camped in Passy and Auteuil in the posh 16e, while Neolithic-era traders occupied the Ile de la Cité. The first inhabitants to leave their name were the Celtic **Parisii**, a fierce and warlike tribe who eventually settled down as boatmen on the the island, making a good living fishing and managing the river trade on the Seine. The Parisii's comfortable business was interrupted by the arrival of Julius Caesar in 52 BC. The Romans installed a garrison, and when the Parisii revolted a year later they were soundly thrashed.

Caesar mentions the capital of the Parisii in his *Gallic Wars*, but most likely it was nothing more than a simple jumble of wattle-and-daub huts. The Romans, however, knew a perfect site for a city when they saw one; the island, dividing the Seine in two, made it much easier to bridge. The Romans called their new colony **Lutetia**, from a Celtic word that meant something like 'mudville'. It did not grow quickly; northern Gaul was still a primeval frontier. But by the end of the 1st century AD, a true city had appeared. The island was left to the uncouth Celts, except for the building of a fortress and governors' palace at its western tip, and the new city, built of timber and Roman brick, took shape on today's Left Bank. Its main thoroughfare roughly followed the course of Rue St-Jacques; its modest forum, a low quadrangle containing a basilica and a temple, stood at the corner with Rue Soufflot, near the Panthéon. There were two large bath complexes (ruins of one can be seen under the Musée de Cluny), and an amphitheatre, excavated near Rue Monge.

Lutetia, with a population of some 10,000 in its palmiest days, was a quiet provincial capital through the imperial centuries. A rude break came in 256, when the town was sacked by the Franks and Alemanni, a prelude to the barbarian invasions of the 5th century. After these, however, Lutetia landed on its feet, becoming the capital of Clovis' new **Frankish Kingdom** *c.* 510. Christianity, the mandatory religion of the new state, was probably already present at an early date. Legends claim St Denis (*see* p.216, Walk VII Montmartre) arriving about 250; St Marcel, bishop in about 430, tamed a dragon that had been annoying the populace on the Left Bank.

Under the rest of the Merovingian kings, from 511 to 741, Paris kept its status; the **Abbey of St-Denis** was the dynasty's treasure house, and its place of burial. Their successors, the militaristic Carolingians, especially **Charlemagne** (768–814) were permanently on campaign, and preferred staying further east; Paris became something of a backwater, ruled by a count. This 8th–9th-century Paris was hardly a well-defined and compact town, but rather an agglomeration of distinct villages. At the centre, the old city on the island huddled around its castle and cathedral, with a cosmopolitan population that included a few Greeks, Britons, Syrians, Jews and Italians. New villages grew up around the 13 or so religious centres within two miles of the island. Some of these were important monasteries, such as St-Denis, St-Martin and St-Germain, others mere chapels. It was a custom in Merovingian times to build chapels along the main roads just outside a town; Ste-Geneviève, St-Germain-des-Auxerrois, and St-Merri began this way.

Within three decades of Charlemagne's death, Carolingian over-extension and bloody-mindedness had thrown their overnight empire into chaos. The **Vikings**, or Normans, first raided Paris in 845; they came back again in force in 856 and 861. In 885 they found the city somewhat better defended, but rather than accept such an affront they put the town under siege. **Count Eudes**, depending entirely on the city's own resources, held them off—the first time anyone had ever managed to do so. Eudes' heirs, the counts of Paris (later dukes), would for the next century be the most powerful lords of France. One of them, **Hugues Capet**, finally became its king in 987; his house was to reign uninterruptedly for the next 805 years.

## The Capital of the Middle Ages

The new French monarchs were merely first among equals; after the Carolingian collapse, local feudal powers were once again independent everywhere. But as dukes of Paris, the Capetian kings had a solid power base. 'France', in the 10th century, was hardly even a geographical expression. Such a thing as the 'French nation' was not even dreamed of; over the centuries the kings created one, with Paris at its core. The monarchy brought Paris prestige and the trappings of power, but the real achievements were the city's own: trade and commerce that made it the metropolis of northern Europe, its university, the intellectual centre of Christendom, and its Gothic architecture, not to mention its schools of painting, sculpture and music that created so much of the style of the Middle Ages.

Medieval Paris was divided into three parts: the Cité, home of the palace and cathedral; the university, on the Left Bank; and the busy, mercantile Right Bank. The **Latin Quarter** began its career in 1127, when nonconformist students expelled from the cathedral school of Notre-Dame settled in the relatively empty Left Bank. The teachings of Peter Abelard and his followers, hinting at a possible escape from Church dogma, started an intellectual revolution. The Left Bank filled up with eager scholars from all over Europe; an Englishman, John of Salisbury, is recorded complaining about the high rents in 1165. But by putting too much faith in Aristotle and not enough in common sense, the university condemned itself to senility by the 1300s; from that point it served scandalously as a tool of the kings and popes, the staunch upholder of religious orthodoxy.

The Paris of the merchants got its start in the same manner as the old *Parisii*: shipping on the Seine. The old Company of Boatmen from Roman, or perhaps even pre-Roman, times had amazingly survived through so many centuries, and became the foundation of the city's economy and government. Its boats are the inspiration for the trim ship that sails today across Paris' coat of arms—although some say that the narrow-tipped island itself, the Ile de la Cité, is the ship. This symbol also provides Paris with its motto, *fluctuat nec mergitur*: 'battered, but never sunk'. By 1141 trade had expanded so spectacularly that the boatmen and docks abandoned the island for Place de Grève on the Right Bank; about the same time the city's markets were being established at Les Halles. The new quarter soon became the most populous part of the city. The first guilds—not counting the boatmen—were also taking shape; the incorporation of the butchers, one of Paris' most powerful guilds for centuries afterwards, is recorded in 1146.

The first great royal benefactor of Paris was **Louis VII** (1137–80). **Notre-Dame** began to rise in his reign (1163), but the king's real contributions were of a more commercial nature, to help make the pennies jingle in a Parisian's purse: building the Place de Grève docks and a merchants' exchange near what is now Pont Neuf, and organizing the great **fairs** at St-Germain (Easter) and St-Lazare (All Souls').

A turning point in the history of Paris came in 1185. The chroniclers record Louis' son **Philippe-Auguste** (1180–1223) staring pensively for hours at something outside his palace window. That something was a great mountain of excrement, some of it undoubtedly the king's own, that had oozed and settled down into the public way, trapping carts, pedestrians and even horses; the sight of it, and perhaps the aroma, so moved the king that he not only had it removed, but also decreed Paris' first street-paving programme (on the bridges and five main streets only). Philippe-Auguste also built the first market buildings at **Les Halles**. He gave Paris a new wall, reflecting the considerable expansion of the city in the 12th century, and began the original, fortress-like **Louvre** to guard its western side. His reign, which saw the final victory over the Plantagenets, the annexation of much of southern France, and a considerable tightening of royal control over all aspects of life in France, was naturally a great boon to Paris. All the king's *baillis*, or prefects, for example, were required to build homes in the city, to which they had to come each year to report to the boss.

In the 1200s the momentum of growth continued. Paris' explosive economic expansion outstripped every other European city outside Italy. The city manufactured everything from luxury goods to armour, and it developed the first retail shops anywhere (interestingly, this trade began with books and art objects in the Latin Quarter). Organizing around itself the other cities and rich agricultural lands of the Ile-de-France, Paris created a giant, integrated economic unit, and supplied the economic power for its kings to spread their rule across what is now France.

An advanced economy naturally brought with it some advanced problems. The hordes of provincial country folk pouring into Paris to find a better life made the city an overcrowded inferno. Public health and sanitation were in a wretched state. Beyond that, the exploited workers were organizing. Their proto-union, the *alliance*, was just taking shape when the feltmakers walked out for Paris' first strike in 1250. In 1270 everyone went out—perhaps the Middle Ages' first general strike; they did it again in 1277.

From all accounts, these struggles were never as bloody as they might have been, perhaps owing to the influence of St Louis (**Louis IX**, 1226–70). This pious king, whose obsession with crusading greatly detracted from the good he could do his own kingdom, allowed Paris to set up its first free municipal government, under the direction of the guilds. And in the short time he did spend in Paris he made himself extremely popular, dispensing justice from under an oak in his palace garden on the island, or opening the palace and Sainte-Chapelle (his major architectural contribution) to the people for holidays and festivals.

Medieval Paris made its buildings in half-timber. In the 1100s they were mostly one or two storeys; a century later, they had shot up to four or five. The buildings hung over the streets, offering protection from the rain but also blocking out much of the light. Fountains being scarce, almost all the water was nasty sludge from the Seine—Paris' main street, crowded with boats and barges, where scores of millwheels turned and where the good wives washed their clothes. Water sellers carried it about the streets, and continued to do so up until the 1800s. As for garbage and sewage—don't ask. Paris' utter lack of concern for such things has given all medieval cities a bad reputation.

Urban life definitely had its drawbacks, but one cannot imagine that the Parisians were ever bored. Besides the throbbing street life, the taverns and ample opportunities for vices of all kinds, public entertainments were frequent: royal festivals, carnivals and the famous mystery plays, enacted on the steps of the major churches. Theatre, always out on the streets, also included secular subjects, folk themes such as the popular 'Dame Douce and the City of the Fairies'. Despite the opposition of churchmen, Parisians always loved to dance—in the 12th century country circle dances such as the *carole* were in fashion (every Sunday afternoon in St-Germain's meadow; bring your friends). One unexpected feature of medieval Paris was its public sauna baths. Paris today has five *hammams*, but in 1290 there were 27 of them. They had a bad reputation, partly because many were receptive to prostitutes, and partly because the Church always suspected that cleanliness was a vanity, if not downright heretical. Most were run by Jews, and they were probably an idea brought home by the crusaders, along with forks, poetry, underclothes, lutes, Persian fairy tales, table manners and many other useful things.

## A Hundred Years of Disasters

Paris began the terrible 14th century as by far the largest city in northern Europe, on a par with Venice and Milan; estimates of its population range from 80,000 to 200,000. It was a businessman's town, and its bourgeois élite had pretty much its own way—though labour troubles continued, with a strike in 1306 that turned into a full-scale rebellion. On the whole, business was bad; the kings were forced to call the **Estates General** four times in the first half-century, begging for cash.

Things got worse with the onset of the **Hundred Years' War**, and the English invasion in 1338. The routs at Crécy (1346) and Poitiers (1356), the latter resulting in the capture of King Jean, reduced much of France to anarchy; peasants and workers revolted in many places, while footloose bands of mercenary soldiers ravaged the country. Worst of all was the **Black Plague** (1348), which hit overcrowded Paris especially hard, carrying off over a third of the population.

The Estates General, looking across the channel to England, now began to demand a measure of real parliamentary control over royal policy and finances. Led by the Paris merchants' provost, **Etienne Marcel**, they refused any new taxes; Marcel seized control of the city and briefly held captive the dauphin (the future Charles V, while his father was captive in London), forcing him to sign a charter that would have set France along the road to parliamentary monarchy. In July 1358, however, Marcel was killed in a riot; the exiled dauphin re-entered Paris in triumph and revoked the charter—the turning point in French history that wasn't meant to be.

As king, **Charles V** (1364–80) ruled with caution and skill, regaining lost lands and reviving the shattered nation. In Paris, he rebuilt the Louvre and gave the Right Bank a new wall (the route of today's Grands Boulevards). In his day, the eye of the hurricane in the Hundred Years' War, the Marais was Paris' fashionable quarter; the king kept his court (and his famous menagerie) at the long-demolished Hôtel St-Pol.

In the 1380s, under mad Charles VI, chroniclers noted a surreal atmosphere, like a permanent deranged carnival. The entire decade was a painful succession of popular revolts and riots. In 1380 and 1382 the mobs were encouraged to pillage the Jews just to let off steam. Paris and France unravelled completely in the 1390s, as the king's brothers fought continuous little wars, scheming to succeed Charles while the English ravaged the countryside. It got worse. From 1390 to 1420, Paris lived under an almost continual state of siege, cut off from its hinterland and from commerce. Merchants went bankrupt; the poor often starved, and grass literally did grow in the streets. Between the factions Paris changed hands seven times in that period, each change accompanied by new massacres and atrocities.

By 1420, when the English finally marched in, Paris' misery was complete. One-third of the city's buildings were abandoned or completely wrecked, and possibly as many as three-quarters of its population had died or fled. Prostitutes that year were unusually cheap—you could have four for the price of an egg. Among the first measures of the Duke of Bedford, Paris' new English boss, were decrees of debt forgiveness and rent relief. Neither his well-meaning government nor the return of French rule (1436) brought improvement. Plagues returned four times between 1430 and 1450; wolves roamed outside the walls and occasionally crept inside by night to carry off a child. Why does France have so many lovely Renaissance châteaux in the Loire valley? Because Paris was a desolation, and for a long time few nobles, or even kings, could be induced to reside anywhere near it.

## From Ruins to Renaissance

Recovery was a long slow affair. The ethos of the medieval city was dead and cold, and not until the 1600s would a new Paris take form to replace it. It might never have recovered at all without government assistance. Kings issued decrees to repopulate the capital, offering cash grants at first, then offering freedom to killers and thieves if they would only consent to live there. One instructive example of how Paris got to be Paris is that in the 1400s Lyon became France's trade and financial centre—until the Parisians bribed the king to suppress that city's fairs in 1484.

By the late 15th century, France was back on its feet and making trouble for its neighbours. Charles VIII (1483–98), Louis XII (1498–1515) and François I (1515–47) all spent most of their time trying to gain control of Italy. But from the time of François I, instead of conquering Italy, the Renaissance Italians conquered France—with their art, music, poetry, clothes and cuisine. France had her own lights too—this was the age of Montaigne and Rabelais—and François founded the humanist Collège de France as a counterweight to the obscurantist Sorbonne. François and his son Henri II supported the showiest courts France had yet seen, in the royal palaces of the Marais and suburban digs such as Fontainebleau.

The Renaissance had definitely come to Paris—though hardly any memorable art or architecture was produced in the capital. The momentum of the Renaissance was continued by **Catherine de' Medici**, who along with her entourage brought so much to France from her native Florence. The Florentines claim Catherine introduced *haute cuisine* to France—though she is recorded as pigging out on Tuscan favourites like cockscombs and artichoke hearts, and then throwing up all over the Louvre. A sucker for any occultist crank who came to court, she practised voodoo and black magic, and had a way with poisons (*see* Walk III, p.151); yet she often showed real skill in managing a dangerous political situation after the death of Henri II. The most interesting thing about the queen is her desk, which after her death was found to have 200 secret compartments.

France's new plague was the **Wars of Religion** (1562–98), four decades of sporadic, nationwide civil war between Catholics and Protestants. Throughout the troubles, Paris stayed under the control of the crown and the Catholics. In 1572 a truce was agreed, and many of the principal Protestant leaders returned to the capital. Here Queen Catherine, fearing a loss of influence, arranged the **St Bartholomew's Day Massacre**, which took care of the moderate leaders and some 10,000 followers, and guaranteed another 26 years of war. For most of this time Paris was dominated by the Dukes of Guise, ambitious ultra-Catholics who wanted to be kings themselves, and kept the wars going when nearly everyone else wanted them to stop. Henri de Bourbon, King of Navarre and rightful heir to France, led the Protestant forces, besieged Paris and made it suffer before converting to Catholicism ('Paris is worth a Mass'); he ended the conflict with the 1598 **Edict of Nantes**, decreeing religious toleration. As **Henri IV** (1589–1610), he and his minister, Sully, did a lot for Paris, commencing an impressive building programme that included the Pont Neuf, Place Dauphine and Place des Vosges.

Henri ended his reign tragically, assassinated by a Catholic fanatic in Paris in 1610. His son, **Louis XIII**, took the throne at the age of 11. Louis' mother, fat and silly Marie de' Medici (immortalized by the incredible series of paintings by Rubens in the Louvre) controlled the government at first. In 1624 the weak-willed king was finally able to ease Mum out of power, with the help of his immensely capable and devoted minister, **Cardinal Richelieu**. Both king and minister died in 1642; they left France the strongest and most intelligently run state in Europe.

## An Unspeakable King

**Louis XIV** (1643–1715) became king at the age of five; the regent was his mother, Anne of Austria, and the minister was Richelieu's protegé, **Cardinal Mazarin**, whose father had been a Roman butler. Though corrupt to the core,

Mazarin did well by France in extremely perilous times, beating back a Spanish invasion, organizing the peace of Europe, and surviving the civil wars of the **Fronde** (1648). 'Fronde' means a slingshot, a children's toy; this name, which the people of Paris conferred on the affair, captures perfectly its lack of seriousness. In succession, the anachronistic and useless *Parlement de Paris*, the greedy nobility, and the long-oppressed bourgeoisie of Paris tried to take advantage of the child-king's weakness. Though briefly forced to flee Paris, Mazarin and the royal cause prevailed by 1661.

Young Louis, enjoying total, personal power over France and the French when he reached his majority in 1659, chose as his chief minister **Jean-Baptiste Colbert**. A relentless overachiever, Colbert assumed total control of the national economy and tried to reform everything, finally giving the peasants some relief, promoting the colonies in India and America, fighting corruption and setting up impressive state-controlled industries such as the Gobelins in Paris. None of the money Colbert made for Louis was able to rest in the king's pocket for long. As Louis grew older, his conceit and ambitions ballooned to incredible proportions, disturbing the peace of Europe for almost 50 years. Three long and inconclusive wars were followed by a really big one, the War of the Spanish Succession (1700–13), in which the nations of Europe at last combined to stand up to French aggression.

Meanwhile, at home, Louis had put an end to the factionalism of the nobles once and for all. Following the example of Henri IV, he simply lavished money upon them, bribing them to spend all their time at court, where he could hold the chits for their gambling debts. Turning the entire ruling class into complaisant, mincing lapdogs, while unattractive, at least ensured unity and civil peace. But surrounded by these noble sycophants—some 10,000 of them—Louis rapidly lost all touch with reality. Perhaps he never really believed himself to be the Sun incarnate, warming and illuminating this poor planet all by himself, but he did act the part, every hour of every day, and seemed to enjoy it. The bottom line for all this is simple: imagine the expenses of this court, and the insane new playpen that Louis built for it at Versailles, and then throw in the costs of the wars—France nearly went bust again.

Colbert, unwittingly, had done almost as much damage as Louis. His autarkic policies, meant sincerely to aid French business by stopping imports, and his absurdly minute regulations, covering every facet of business down to the length of workers' lunch hours, had helped wreck both trade and agriculture. By the end of Louis' long reign, the desperate crown was literally selling workers the right to work, with expensive licensing laws, while misery was widespread and terrible famines gripped town and country alike. As if this wasn't enough, Louis also destroyed

Henri IV's religious compromise. The Edict of Nantes was revoked in 1685, and torture and prison, or exile, became the lot of Protestants once more.

Louis' reign was rough on Paris, despite an ambitious building programme that included Place Vendôme and Place des Victoires, the Louvre colonnade, the Invalides and the Grands Boulevards. After the Fronde, Paris lost its last vestiges of self-government. Colbert's economics slightly favoured the city's middle class, but while prominent bourgeois could attain high office, and even noble titles, the overwhelming majority were hard pressed by high taxes and bad policies. As for the poor, the wars of the Fronde had left Paris with some 40,000 unemployed and homeless. To Louis, this was a matter for the police. The luckier ones escaped to starve on their own; the unfortunates got dragooned into the new workhouses, such as the Salpêtrière, where they could starve while performing slave labour for Colbert's new industries.

One disadvantage in grinding the poor was making thieves not only more numerous but also more rapacious. In the time of Louis XIV, muggers were not satisfied with your purse; they'd have your shoes and clothes too, along with your underwear if you were wearing any. **Nicolas de la Reynie**, the king's capable chief of police, had 800 boys on the street, looking dapper in their blue uniforms with silver stars. But they couldn't be everywhere in an unlit city of half a million, full of dark cul-de-sacs.

And if the crooks didn't get you, you were at least sure to step in something, or have something splash on your head; sanitary conditions had not improved an iota since the Middle Ages, and if anything they had worsened. La Palatine, writing in the 1660s, records the smell of rotting meat and fish in every street, and 'crowds of people pissing everywhere'. The king's household set the example; it was noted that underneath every balcony of the Louvre was a steaming heap of *ordures et immondices*. All this was La Reynie's business—everything was his business. This unsung hero from Limoges, who took the job in 1667, was a sympathetic fellow who often managed to protect poor Parisians from the whims of the king, and he probably did more for Paris than anyone in its long history: besides initiating the first street lighting (at least when there was no moon, a penny-pinching custom that lasted until the 19th century), he forced landlords to build latrines, widened streets, forbade the carrying of swords and canes, paved the quays of the Seine, required shopowners to sweep the streets in front of their doors, and closed down the *asiles*, noble properties that were off-limits to the police and became the haunts of robbers and predatory beggars, such as the famous 'Cour de Miracles'.

One problem even La Reynie could not solve was traffic. Deserted by night, by day most streets were a permanent traffic jam—the *Embarras de Paris*, as in the title of one of Boileau's satires. Streets were still of medieval proportions, the largest only 25ft wide. The majority of Parisians, cramped into minuscule tenement flats, lived on the streets most of the day; shopkeepers piled their goods out into them, and the huge iron shop signs (you can see some artistic examples in the Musée Carnavalet) crowded the centres, knocking off the hats of horsemen riding by. The little channel of free space in the middle had to accommodate pedestrians, horsemen, flocks of animals being driven to the butchers around the Châtelet, *fiacres* (horse cabs), wagons full of hay, firewood and food, sedan chairs, and—worst of all—the carriages, whose numbers increased dramatically in the 1600s. The traffic code was simple and concise: noblemen drove on whichever side of the street pleased them, and everyone else was required to give way. In 1662 Paris' first public transport appeared, financed by the scientist and philosopher Blaise Pascal. The first line went from the Bastille over the Ile de la Cité to the Luxembourg, and four others soon joined it. But lack of speed, and the arrogance of the nobles, who could chase all the other passengers off and then refuse to pay, drove the service out of business in 1677.

One striking feature of life under the Louies was the utter tedium of it all, even in Paris. By the 1500s the riotous festivals and entertainments of medieval Paris had been stamped out by pious prudes. In the 1600s this trend continued. Under the stingy Bourbons, royal fêtes were nothing compared to those of the old days, and the old religious festivals of the people withered into mere processions. Everyone gambled; Louis encouraged it at court to keep the parasites occupied, and enormous sums changed hands almost every day. Poorer folk had the royal lotteries, bowling and the new craze—cards. The first cafés appeared in 1643, but they did not become popular until 1669, when the Turkish ambassador, in search of a decent cup of java, introduced them to the upper classes.

The oppressive dullness certainly extended to culture. Under the close watch of Louis XIV's spies and censors, the French learned that frivolity and submission were the only safe paths to travel. Stifled by royal patronage and regulation, the plastic arts degenerated to mere interior decoration and regime propaganda. Parisians were impassioned for the theatre (including Lully and the first French operas), and Louis' reign had the great Molière to light up the stage, but by the 1680s, with the king under the influence of his hypocritically pious mistress, Madame de Maintenon, theatre's liberties were severely curtailed. The first periodicals appeared in the late 1600s, although these offered little more than court gossip and government-supplied puffery (opening a *Mercure Galant* at random, one reads: 'Ladies, you are right to learn to play tric-trac. Everyone plays it at court and in Paris, because it is a game of nobility and distinction …').

In all, Louis XIV's and Colbert's cultural policies were to prove more damaging, and longer lasting, than their failures in politics and economics. Frenchmen learned not to speak the truth, but to please. They learned that appearance, in this fallen world, was everything and content nothing. French cultural life up to this day has rarely escaped this nihilistic morass of mind control and well-polished conformity. The strangest fruit of this sad phenomenon is the myth of Louis XIV, and the imaginary 'Golden Age' of French civilization—the *Grand Monarque* and the *Grand Siècle*. For generations of proud Frenchmen, the alternatives to perpetuating this shabby lie were unthinkable.

## The Last of the Louies

Another century, another Louis. **Louis XV**, the *Roi Soleil*'s great-grandson, ascended the throne in 1715, at the age of five; this time the regent was the Duke of Orléans, who allowed Paris a refreshing interlude of Edwardian decadence after the Victorian coma of the 'Great Reign'. The regent fell for John Law's speculative schemes (*see* p.155), and the bursting of his 'Mississippi Bubble' (1720) nearly bankrupted the entire nation. When Louis XV began to reign in his own right, his people called him *le bien-aimé*, the well-beloved. Unfortunately, no. XV turned out to be a lethargic fool, who allowed France to be governed by flouncing favourites and court ladies, most notably the famous Madame de Pompadour (who gets a bad press, but was really the best of the lot).

France was stirring. This was the age of the salons and the **philosophes**: Voltaire, Diderot, Montesquieu and the rest, importing English political thought and common sense to the continent. The ills of France were discussed endlessly: the incredible privileges of the useless and all-devouring nobility and Church, the economic oppression of every productive element of society, and the total lack of justice, fairness and basic political rights. The solutions were obvious, but any hope of reform depended on the king, and he was not about to permit it. At home, discontent was slowly coming to the boil; abroad, France was losing colonial empires in America and India to Britain during the Seven Years' War (1756–63). Louis really did say '*après moi, le déluge*'. It was obvious. When the *bien-aimé* died in 1774, curses and rotten vegetables followed his coffin to St-Denis. Voltaire died four years later, regretting the coming Revolution he would not live to enjoy.

Under **Louis XVI** (1774–92) the last years of the *ancien régime* in Paris mixed progressive reforms with comical anachronisms. On the one hand, the removal of the stinking charnel house of the Innocents, the decision eventually to demolish the Bastille (both in 1786), and the clearing of the last buildings and shops from the bridges; on the other, something foolish almost beyond belief, the **wall of the**

**Farmers-General** (1784). The Farmers were *tax* farmers. For centuries, rich men had purchased this office from the kings. The crown expected a certain sum from a province, and anything the Farmers collected over that, they could keep. The Ile-de-France Farmers convinced the king to build an expensive new wall around Paris—not for defence, but so that they might better collect duties on goods entering the city. *Le mur, en murant Paris, rend Paris murmurant*, went a current joke. And it should be no surprise that this wall was one of the major causes of what came to pass in 1789.

## Paris' Own Revolution

Times were bad. By 1789, after a few disastrous harvests, the price of bread reached 4 *sous* a pound, while the average worker's daily wage was 16. But one can't help feeling some slight sympathy for **Louis XVI**, grandson of no. XV, blessed with a lack of brains and a chronic indecisiveness that would cost him his head. On the one hand he was aiding the American revolutionaries and encouraging excellent ministers such as Turgot (1774–6) and the Swiss banker, Jacques Necker (1777–81, 1788–91). On the other he allowed his fawning courtiers to convince him never to permit these ministers to push through real reforms. By 1789 the state's financial situation was desperate; Louis, having failed miserably on his own, made the fatal step of doing what every Frenchman demanded—he called the Estates General. They met at Versailles on 5 May 1789, for the first time since 1610. Accounts put off for 179 years are about to be settled:

**20 June.** The Third Estate, stymied in reform attempts by the noble and church delegates, swear the 'Tennis Court Oath', declaring themselves the **National Assembly** and promising not to break up until they give France a constitution.

**12 July.** Paris mobs sack customs barriers on the Farmers-General wall.

**14 July.** Taking of the Bastille; Parisians form militia, commanded by Lafayette.

**November.** Churches and monasteries confiscated (they had covered one eighth of the area of Paris).

Significantly, the Revolution that was gathering momentum was not really France's, but Paris'. After the capture of the Bastille, Parisian radicals invented the tricolour, taking Paris' own red and blue, and adding the white of the royal flag (Lafayette's idea). Then in 1790:

**17 July.** Louis visits Paris, and is forced to accept a tricolour cockade before crowds at the Hôtel de Ville.

**4 August.** Nobles and clergy in the Assembly renounce their privileges and feudal rights.

Now the Assembly went to work. The declaration of the Rights of Man was voted, along with a liberal constitution for France. Louis and his family attempted to flee Paris in June 1791, and were kept from then on almost as prisoners, in the Tuileries. Meanwhile, the *émigrés*, reactionary nobles who had fled France, were conspiring with foreign governments to overthrow the Revolution. The king was now obviously on their side.

**June–July 1792.** War with Austria and Prussia.

**10 August.** People of Paris take the Tuileries and imprison the royal family in the Temple. Paris government replaced by radical **Commune**.

**2 September.** Massacres of suspected traitors in Paris prisons.

**22 September.** New *Convention Nationale* declares France a republic.

**20 January 1793.** Louis XVI guillotined.

The end of the House of Capet was as pathetic as could be imagined. Louis XVI, 'Citizen Capet', stood dumbfounded at the tribunal; noticing a plate of rolls on the judges' desk, he forgot all about having been king and could not concentrate on any of the questions put to him. Finally, in tears, he blurted out: 'Please, sir, might I have one of those rolls?' Just before his appointment with the National Razor he is reported to have put away sixteen pork chops.

**March.** After military defeats, dictatorial **Committee of Public Safety** is set up to manage the national defence (which it does brilliantly), along with a Revolutionary Tribunal to ferret out traitors.

**2 June.** Paris Commune, controlled by the radical Jacobin faction, seizes the Convention and arrests the moderate faction, the Girondins.

In **September**, the **Terror** begins, egged on by the thoroughly insane, scrofulous Marat, a doctor-turned-journalist screaming for blood, and managed by the 'Incorruptible' **Robespierre**, a provincial lawyer who read too much Rousseau and had demented fantasies of returning mankind to a state of perfect virtue and innocence, and who was now virtual dictator of France. After Marat's assassination by sweet Charlotte Corday in July, the Terror really went to work; Robespierre sent to the guillotine moderate patriots such as Danton for spite, and *ancien régime* celebrities such as Marie Antoinette and 'Philippe-Egalité' (the Duke of Orléans who built the Palais Royal, and who had become a demagogic revolutionary) just for fun. After some 2500 heads had rolled, not counting thousands more in the provinces, some courageous members of the Convention arrested Robespierre and his henchmen; the Terror ended with his execution on 27 July 1794. This episode is often overemphasized. Much more importantly, the Revolution was working; it was successful on the battlefields, and it had righted its own excesses.

The Convention's new constitution provided for government by a five-man executive, the **Directoire**. By 1797 the mood of the nation had changed considerably. Reaction was in the air, and a royalist party began to manoeuvre semi-openly. In Paris few cared for politics after such a glut of it; the working people who had supported the Commune were silent, battered by rampant inflation, and still without the right to vote. A powerful class of *nouveaux riches* had grown up, profiting from the wars. Throughout the Revolution the city had never neglected fashion; ladies dressed in bold, revealing dresses and hairdos in the style of ancient Greece; now the young people of Paris went completely over the top in affected dress and manners, with flirting girls called *merveilleuses*, in great floppy hats and see-through blouses, and fops with heavy corkscrew canes and giant monocles called *incoyables* (really *incroyables*, but the cult was famously too lazy ever to pronounce its r's). In such an atmosphere the divided and ineffective Directoire could command little authority or respect.

## An Imperial Interlude

The victorious army had both authority and respect, and its most able general, **Napoleon Bonaparte**, had already saved the Republic from a royalist revolt in Paris (*see* Walk V, p.187). Having beaten the English at Toulon, and conquered northern Italy from the Austrians in a campaign against overwhelming odds, he was the man of the hour. With his brother Jérôme as speaker of the national legislature, and his ally, the intriguer Siéyès, in control of the Directoire, the road was prepared for a coup that many clever politicians found desirable; like the German conservatives in 1933, they were sure they could 'handle' their man. On 9 November 1799, Napoleon bullied the legislature into leaving Paris for St-Cloud, where his troops were, the better to 'protect' its members. There he put an end to it, and to the freedom of France. Napoleon's control was solid enough for him to declare himself Emperor in 1804.

The precedents for turning France into a totalitarian, militaristic state had already existed—thanks to Louis XIV and the tradition of tight, centralized control that had been in force ever since. As long as Napoleon was winning, and loot and art flowed into Paris, there was little need for a heavy hand. The real oppression came after 1810, when the economy was in disarray and the cemeteries were starting to fill up. Eight new state prisons, meant for political dissenters, had just opened when the game was up in 1814. Napoleon had big plans for Paris; he once mused how someday he would force every king on earth to build a palace in his capital, where they would come once a year to do him homage. The Arc de Triomphe, the Madeleine and the colonnaded Rue de Rivoli survive to give a small taste of how Paris would have been rebuilt if the Emperor had had his way.

The last battle, excepting the comical postscript of the Hundred Days, was fought under the heights of Montmartre on 30 March 1814. The next day the Russian Tsar and King of Prussia paraded down the Champs-Elysées, the first time foreign troops had occupied Paris since the Hundred Years' War. Paris was saved from a sacking by Tsar Alexander and the discipline of the Russian army; the Prussians, understandably, had wanted to have a little fun.

## 19th Century: Restoration, Rebellion, Reaction, Revolt

The Revolution had shaken France so thoroughly, and created so many opinions and so many grudges, that no regime of whatever stripe could govern impartially and effectively. The rest of the century would be an impossible search for consensus and legitimacy; from 1790 to 1875, the Gallic banana republic/empire/monarchy lived through 13 regimes and 17 constitutions.

The new king imposed by the allies was Louis XVI's old gouty brother, **Louis XVIII** (1814–24): 'partly an old woman, partly a capon, partly a son of France and partly a pedant'. Napoleon's veterans sat around in the cafés on half-pay, playing cards: whenever they played a king they referred to it as 'pig of clubs' or 'pig of hearts'. But France as a whole was content, and Louis had become mellow enough through long years of exile not to exact too much revenge, even permitting a charter (not quite a constitution) and a parliament. His successor was the third and youngest of the brothers, **Charles X** (1824–30). As Count of Artois he had been the head of the *émigrés*, and the most reactionary of the lot, the proverbial Bourbon who 'learned nothing and forgot nothing'. A stupid man, running an unjust and backward government, Charles was begging for another revolution; when he tried to gut the charter, he got it, in July 1830. Once again, it was Paris' show, a movement of journalists, secret political societies and Napoleonic veterans who seized the Hôtel de Ville, won over the troops, and tossed out the Bourbons once and for all, in the revolt of the '**Trois Glorieuses**', named after the three glorious days 27–29 July.

The new king was **Louis-Philippe** of the Orléans branch of the family. Son of Philippe-Egalité, he had fought briefly in the Revolutionary army and later ended up teaching French in Boston. The 'bourgeois king', in his drab coat that became the prototype for the international businessman's uniform of today, entrusted government to gradgrinds like the liberal Guizot, with his message to the poor: *enrichissez-vous!* (get rich). The rich alone had the right to vote, while the workers were rewarded with laws more oppressive than anything the Bourbons ever dreamed of, such as the 1838 decree forbidding them even to discuss politics. Paris was packed with police spies to enforce it; anyone who didn't quite agree with the divine necessity of capitalist entrepreneurship got a one-way ticket to Devil's Island. After Guizot, the premier was **Adolphe Thiers**, a feisty bantam rooster from Marseille who became the model for Balzac's ambitious provincial, Rastignac. He completed the Arc de Triomphe, as a sop to Napoleonic loyalists, and effected some major improvements: mandating primary education and building France's first railways.

But after 18 years, with old Guizot back in power, no one but the industrialists could be found to support the increasingly corrupt and weak regime. A provocative Washington's Birthday dinner in Paris started the 'Revolution of Contempt' on 21 February 1848. The next day students and workers occupied the Place de la Concorde; Louis-Philippe soon abdicated, and the **Second Republic** was proclaimed. The winner of the first presidential elections turned out to be Napoleon's nephew **Louis-Napoleon** (as one old veteran put it: 'How could I fail to vote for this gentleman, I whose nose froze at Moscow?'). Louis made a coup three years later and declared himself 'Emperor Napoleon III', sending some 26,000 political opponents off to the prison hulks in 1851 alone.

The emperor's wife, the fiery Spaniard, Princess Eugénie, was a good rider, an ultra-rightist paragon of ambition, and entirely too good-looking. She wore the Koh-i-Noor diamond in her tiara, and Louis on her bracelet; the new emperor who had previously written a book called *The Extinction of Pauperism* now found himself pampering a court of *nouveaux riches*, and presiding over a vulgar orgy of conspicuous consumption unmatched since Louis XIV's court at Versailles. The first 'fashion houses' attained prominence, and the first department stores were built (Au Bon Marché, 1852), feeding the idea of Paris as the 'city of luxury'. More than ever before, Paris had to be the showcase and symbol of an unloved regime, with the first of the great Expositions (1867), grandiose new monuments such as the Opéra, and the total replanning of the city by Napoleon III's prefect of the Seine, **Baron Georges Haussmann**.

Since the first Napoleon, radical, dangerous Paris had been deprived of any sort of self-government. Louis-Napoleon and Haussmann had ambitions for the city, and determined once and for all to make Paris safe for tyranny. The people of Paris had made three revolutions in 59 years, so the people of Paris must be removed. They were—some 200,000 of them, evicted to form new and even more dire slums in Belleville, Ménilmontant and other eastern quarters where the police hardly ever dared to travel. Horsemeat became popular about 1865—not because anyone liked it, but because it was the only meat three-quarters of Parisians could ever afford. The 'other Paris' spent 90% of its wages on wretched housing and rotten food; those wages were falling far behind inflation, and child mortality was at an all-time high.

The Paris of privilege went over the top. Celebrity whores, the *grandes horizontales* such as Cora Pearl, went for as much as a million francs a night. The theatres and cafés had never been so brilliant (or at least so well dressed); the boulevards booming with shiny black carriages were the envy of the world. Culturally, the tyranny rewarded kitsch and held talent in suspicion. Fashionable hack writers and salon painters earned wealth and acclaim, while the real thing—poets such as Baudelaire and painters such as Courbet and Manet—were constantly looking over their shoulders for the police.

## The Siege of Paris and the Commune

But by the end of Napoleon III's reign, the glitter was fading fast. The 1870 **Franco-Prussian war** was no contest; on 30 August Paris received a telegram from one of the commanders at Sedan: '*Nous sommes dans un pot de chambre et nous y serons emmerdés*', which is exactly what happened. By 3 September, under woefully incompetent leadership, most of the surrounded army had surrendered, including the emperor himself. Paris republicans, many freshly out of prison, organized a Committee of National Defence. By 19 September the city was surrounded by Prussian troops.

But Paris did not care to fall. Under Louis-Philippe, Adolphe Thiers had begun a ring of fortresses around the city that made it almost impregnable to a 19th-century army. And the city of luxury was moving with skill and determination, raising a citizens' militia and converting city industries to make guns and ammunition. All France was galvanized when one of the new leaders, **Léon Gambetta**, escaped the city for Tours in a balloon, bound to organize the resistance and enroll new forces in the unoccupied zones; Garibaldi came from Italy to help. In Paris, people ate sawdust-laced loaves, and then the horses and the animals in the zoo, and finally tracked down even the cats and rats in the sewers. Balloons and microfilm-carrying carrier pigeons were the city's only contact with the outside world.

The Prussians defeated the new makeshift armies in the south, but Paris held; the city was incensed when a self-proclaimed government at Bordeaux—led by none other than old Adolphe Thiers—signed an armistice. Wilhelm II was proclaimed kaiser of the new German Empire in Versailles' Hall of Mirrors, and his army was allowed a parade through the city it couldn't capture. Sullen Parisians stared silently at the Germans all down the Champs-Elysées. At one point Bismarck found himself alone and surrounded by an angry crowd on the Place de la Concorde; he disarmed them with panache, pulling out a cigar and asking if anyone had a light. After the Germans left, women came out to scrub the streets where they had marched. Officials of the old regime, if recognized on the street, were liable to be strung up or bound and dumped in the Seine. The National Guard and the citizens met in a monster rally at the Place de la Bastille, some 300,000 strong, murmuring of 1792, 1830 and '48. Paris was in a bad mood.

Thiers' government, now installed in Versailles, moved rapidly to disarm the city. When a detachment tried to confiscate the cannon on the heights of Montmartre, the National Guard resisted, killing two generals. Between 18–28 March 1871, the city's leaders declared the **Paris Commune**, a name that recalled the brave days of Etienne Marcel and the Revolution of 1789. The Commune wasn't at all communist, as its opponents have always claimed; its biggest demand was for a free municipal government, and its reason for existing was to assuage the shame that Napoleon III and Thiers had brought on France, and to assure that no new clownish tyrant would arise to replace the old one. As one army officer who fought bravely for the Commune put it: 'I have a horror of this society which has just sold France with so much cowardice.'

However, the Commune *was* foolhardy, dilettantish and totally inept. In the beginning the Communards were stronger than Versailles, and with the sympathetic risings that were taking place all over France, particularly in Marseille, they might well have made a real revolution. Instead its leaders dithered, arguing endlessly about pie-in-the-sky reforms and issuing manifestos while Thiers raised new troops. The Germans, who still occupied the areas east of Paris, enjoyed the whole show through their binoculars, and released thousands of French prisoners to give Thiers a hand. When the Commune did try to take Versailles, the badly led and untrained National Guard practically routed itself. Now the balance was turned. Versailles began bombarding the city in mid-April, causing tremendous damage in the *beaux quartiers* of the west.

**Bloody Week**, the taking of Paris, began on 21 May when an officer noticed that one of the main forts southwest of the city wasn't being defended, a typical Communard oversight. Troops poured into the city, meeting barricades at every important street corner. Resistance was effective in many areas, especially in Montmartre, defended courageously by a Women's Battalion under the poetess-revolutionary Louise Michel, and on the Left Bank, where there were columns led by two battle-hardened Polish radicals named Dombrowski and Wroblewski. Now the army that had been so badly embarrassed by the Germans began to take its revenge—against its own people. Chief organizer of the bloodbath was a ranking general, the Marquis de Gallifet. He, among others, initiated Versailles' policy of shooting all prisoners and suspects, men, women and children alike. The Communards in response began to shoot hostages, including the archbishop.

Paris was burning; whether due to Versailles shells or Communard arsonists, hundreds of buildings went up in flames, including the Tuileries Palace and the Hôtel de Ville. The working class of Paris, knowing they could expect no quarter, set up the last desperate barricades around the Belleville *mairie*. On 27 May, the last 150 fighters to surrender were lined up against the wall of the Père-Lachaise cemetery and shot.

Some 20,000–25,000 Parisians were killed in the fighting, or massacred afterwards. Another 20,000 spent a year or more in prison hulks or camps in French Guiana. Tens of thousands more fled the city forever. Entire quarters had been devastated; Thomas Cook was organizing special 'Ruins of Paris' tours. For over a year, little was done to rebuild—mostly due to the lack of tradesmen. In 1872 there was hardly a plumber or a roofer left in Paris, and the alleys of Belleville seemed populated solely by widows. Ironically, by driving up wages, the fight improved conditions significantly for the working people who were left.

## The Paris of the Third Republic

In the 1880s Paris was rebuilt—the regime that had destroyed it now naturally had to make its capital pretty again; Baron Haussmann's projects were completed just as he planned them. Republican prefects worked hard to bring Paris the benefits of modern technology; scores of new schools and hospitals were built, the métro was begun, and Paris moved into the urban vanguard in everything from street lighting to garbage disposal.

The 1890s, the *belle époque*, was great fun, a continuous carnival for anyone in Paris with a few *sous* to get in. Circuses and funfairs were everywhere—with the old merry-go-rounds you can still see around the city; more exotic entertainments included the first cinema, begun by the Lumière brothers in 1895 in a café on the Boulevard des Capucines. The Third Republic put on the best shows of all: the *Expositions Universelles* (*see* Topics, p.51). The Fair of 1889 gave Paris its definitive modern trademark, the **Eiffel Tower**, while 1900 supplied the Grand Palais and the Pont Alexandre III.

During the **First World War**, Paris did more than simply keeping up the boys' morale. At the beginning, in the autumn of 1914, it looked as though the Germans might break through; the government had already decided to flee to Bordeaux when Joffre's troops saved Paris in the 'Miracle of the Marne'—made possible by the famous ride of the Paris taxis, carrying up to the front the reserves that turned the tide. Late in the war Paris came under the fire of the Zeppelins and the Big Bertha howitzer; these were ineffective, though they provided an unsettling look into the wars of the future.

The victorious French hosted the peace conference at Versailles, but Paris was looking poor and a little bedraggled. Its low rents and bonhomie in the Twenties made it the perfect setting for Americans fleeing from Prohibition, racial prejudice and normality: Hemingway, Fitzgerald and Gertrude Stein shared an extremely lively decade with the modernist painters and the Surrealists, while Josephine Baker and jazz invaded the night clubs and Picasso painted stage backgrounds for Diaghilev's Ballet Russe. The Depression put a stop to such carrying on, and the Paris of the Thirties, marked by constant strikes, demonstrations and occasional street fights, simply wasn't much fun.

In May 1940, while the Nazi tanks were smashing through France's defences, a pathetic fatalism took hold of the city. The government quickly fled to Bordeaux, declaring Paris an open city; the Parisians were not startled to hear it, since half of them had already scrammed, blocking the roads and making any hope of a last defence even more unlikely. The Germans marched into town on 14 June; Hitler came to visit soon after, to drive the vacated streets patrolled by his soldiers. With Albert Speer, he was carefully touring the monuments, looking for ideas for his planned rebuilding of Berlin (his favourite was Garnier's Opéra). He stopped once to pose for the cameras, looking pensive at the tomb of his original, Napoleon.

Under the **occupation**, Parisians relearned to ride bikes and puzzled over ration cards, but on the whole daily life went on with eerie normality—the squalid death-in-life captured by the film *The Sorrow and the Pity*, the reality that French governments since the war have worked so hard to deny. Few occupied nations offered so many happy quislings. For every Parisian who worked in the Resistance, another joined the fascist militias; police and bureaucracy assisted efficiently in deporting democrats and Jews to the death camps. Celebrity collaborators included most stars of stage and screen (Maurice Chevalier, Arletty, Yvonne Printemps), journalists and intellectuals.

Liberation came two months after the Normandy invasions in 1944; Eisenhower's army graciously stepped aside to let the French under General Leclerc be the first to enter Paris, on 24 August. The last week of the occupation had been dramatic enough. Resistance units came out of the sewers and catacombs to assume control of many Paris neighbourhoods, and policemen barricaded themselves inside the Préfecture on the Ile de la Cité, bravely holding off German attacks for a week.

Hitler, besides his other character flaws, turned out to be a very bad loser, ordering his military commander to blow Paris to smithereens. The commander was General Dietrich von Choltitz, and fortunately for Paris he was one of those few Germans who didn't just follow orders. He maintained a delicate balancing act for days, lying to Berlin and to the Gestapo spooks in Paris, while secretly negotiating a surrender. Hitler was demanding 'Is Paris burning?' down the phone while Allied troops were moving into German headquarters in the Hotel Meurice. After the war the city made von Choltitz an honorary citizen. On 26 August came the military parades, and de Gaulle's triumphal entry into the city. War correspondent Ernest Hemingway liberated the Ritz bar, while Parisians settled occupation scores: girls who had been too friendly with the Germans got shaved heads, and were paraded through the streets with swastikas gouged into their skins.

## Paris Today: All Dressed Up and No Place to Go

The postwar era found Paris grumpy and out of sorts. Culturally, the city was dead indeed; art's avant-garde had moved to New York, while intellectual life revolved around the grim cult of the Stalinist-existentialist Sartre. The *nouvelle vague* cinema, a celebration of incoherence and ennui, captured the spirit of the times as well as the revolving-door governments of the Fourth Republic, or the grey technocrats and nervous priggishness of the Fifth. Under de Gaulle, Culture Minister André Malraux tried to revive some civic spirit, illuminating monuments at night, and forcing landlords to clean grimy building façades; at the same time government planners moved purposefully to get Paris ready for modern times—Les Halles was eliminated, as a vestige of the old and 'obsolete', while the towers of Maine-Montparnasse and La Défense, the new motorways such as the *périphérique* and endless miles of suburban tower blocks were built to proclaim their vision of the future.

Many Frenchmen, especially the leftists and old Resistance members, had hoped for a freer, more modern society in the postwar era. Instead—in politics and culture, in the factories and in the schools—they suffered under systems as regimented and undemocratic as ever. Following the 19th-century pattern, a long slow boil was followed by a sudden, unexpected eruption. It began, of course, in Paris, in **May '68** with the students' occupation of the university; within a week it was nationwide, spreading to *lycées*, to every other sort of school and institution, and most significantly to industry. As many as nine million workers went out on strike. For one delirious month it seemed that France would really change; the government counterattacked skilfully, however, using its total control over the television and radio to manipulate opinion, staging monster rallies of the silent majority in Paris, and finally winning a smashing victory in parliamentary elections in June.

De Gaulle and the state had prevailed, but France would never be the same. The president himself would resign within a year, after losing an important referendum. A trend for greater democracy, openness and decentralization has been making slow headway in many facets of society ever since. The year 1977 brought a novelty: a measure of **self-government** for Paris, accorded by the state for the first time since the Middle Ages. The right-wing RPR (the old Gaullist party) rapidly assumed control not only of the office of Paris mayor, but initially won all 20 *mairies* in the city's *arrondissements*. Paris' well-off, conservative population, and its centuries-old tradition of subjection to the state, has created a situation where politics *per se* scarcely exists (in some *arrondissements*, the fascist National Front often wins more votes than the Socialists). **Jacques Chirac**, who became mayor in 1977, made the city his rock-solid power base in his quest for the presidency. Chirac's friends point out that he made Paris run like a Swiss watch: efficient services, cleanliness, comprehensive planning, and plenty of culture and amenities. His opponents note his close ties to building and real-estate interests, which devastated huge areas of the city under Chirac's rule.

Undoubtedly the most important phenomenon of the postwar years has been the near-total gentrification of Paris proper, and the consequent schizophrenic division between the rich, privileged centre and the gritty, neglected suburbs run by the Communists or Socialists. Paris' upper classes have effected their Final Solution; excepting the tourists, they now have the city almost entirely to themselves. If Paris makes any contributions to culture in the coming decades, they may well come from the suburbs rather than the moribund centre; out in the *terra incognita* beyond the *périphérique* are the university branch of Nanterre, a stronghold of the 1968 revolt, some of France's most innovative theatre and dance groups, and a new subculture of *négritude* and French rap that is transforming popular music. Politically, the suburbs are stirring; a hopeless, futureless atmosphere of degradation, racism and marginalization is causing increasingly frequent disturbances—and a few all-out riots. The past decade of supposedly socialist rule, ignoring the suburbs and their people while lavishing billions worth of ornaments on the centre, has made distrust and despair complete. A serious explosion in coming years is not out of the question.

The problems of the suburbs, though, are still of little interest to Paris and its eternal *classe politique*. Just before he died, François Mitterrand confessed that he had really been a man of the right all along. His control of the Socialist Party provides a perfect example of how this small clique, made up of old schoolboys from the *Grandes Ecoles*, has been able cynically to manipulate French public life with the all-important goal of keeping itself on top. Mitterrand's two terms as president (1981–95) were a high time for the *classe politique* and for Paris. Determined to leave his mark on the city, Mitterrand inaugurated his **Grands Projets**—the Louvre redevelopment, the Grand Arche at La Défense, a new Bibliothèque Nationale, Bercy, the Bastille Opera, among others. Paris, and Mayor Chirac, had little to say about them.

Apart from these, the Mitterrand era will probably be remembered best for corruption—political sleaze nearly on an Italian scale, though managed with more decorum (when you see France's most popular television newsman solemnly interviewing a former cabinet minister, you might not be aware that both are recently convicted criminals). The booty was shared by all parties, and by the *classe politique*'s allies and schoolmates in business. France does have an independent judiciary, and a few courageous judges have been doing great work cleaning up the mess. Already scores of politicians and businessmen have received suspended sentences and fines; a few actually are doing time. The scandals are still coming out, notably in Paris. Here Chirac himself, along with Prime Minister Alain Juppé and new Paris mayor Jean Tiberi, were caught using city-owned housing for their own benefit; so far the politically-controlled state prosecutors have refused to issue indictments against such luminaries. Countless millions of francs have disappeared into thousands of pockets, and into the accounts of the political parties. In any case, the time of the *Grands Projets* is over. The till is just plain empty.

The pampered Paris of today, beyond doubt the best-scrubbed and shiniest Paris ever, is a bigger drain on the French taxpayer's pocket than Louis XIV's Versailles. It creates little and absorbs all. It talks and talks. It drinks less good red wine than Coca-Cola. But culturally and psychically, its shortcomings are hardly a result of lassitude or complacency. On the contrary—Paris is always thinking, always reading, always ready to try something new. The 1990s are not going to be anything like the brilliant 1890s, but if the last two hectic centuries of this city's career are any indication, anything can happen: the only thing that ever remains constant in Paris is change.

# Topics

# The All-Parisian Feast

Parisians are the urban heirs of the ancient Greeks, to whom man's proper abode was the sacred, man-made *polis*; any eccentric who wanted to see nature could just walk outside the walls (and stay there). Until Baron Haussmann planted his leafy boulevards and little *squares* all over Paris, the city hardly had a weed to call its own. No Parisian ever noticed the lack. To the medieval bourgeois, country life meant the serfdom his grandparents had escaped from. To the nobleman in the age of the Louies, it was a place to go hunting if the weather was nice. After Haussmann, Paris boosters bragged they had more trees than any city in the world, a preposterous claim often repeated in the press and books to this day. In fact Paris can't approach the tree totals of places like Kalamazoo or Milton Keynes. Paris and Nature simply do not mix.

Like every dog and every citizen, every tree in Paris has an identification number, and they only go up to 150,000 (one for every 14 people, or every three dogs). The city's ecologists keep close tabs on all of them, worried that the politicians and their developer friends will cut them down when no one is looking. The tallest is a plane tree on Avenue Foch, at 140ft; the prize for the one with the largest circumference goes to another plane in the Parc de Monceau, some 22ft around. Other flora is sparse indeed. A naturalist named Bouly de Lesdain, trapped in the city during the German occupation, could find nothing better to do than make a study of the mosses and lichens in the Tuileries—he identified only 18 species, including those growing on the *vespasienne* in the Place de la Concorde.

But it wasn't always like this. In the Ice Age woolly mammoths lived on the heights of Belleville and Montmartre. They came down to the Seine for a drink along a track that is now Rue St-Denis, the road down which kings would later enter Paris after their coronations. The fossil skeleton of a rhinoceros has been dug up near St-Germain-des-Prés. In the Middle Ages, thousands of cows, pigs and sheep trundled down every main street every day—the politically powerful Butchers' Guild enjoyed life in the exact centre of Paris. Pigs were allowed to roam as useful scavengers, until one day when *un diable d'un porc* went after the horse of King Louis VI's son Philippe, which resulted in the death of an heir to the throne. After that the only pigs tolerated belonged to the monks of St Antoine, who had some ancient privilege on the subject. Their porkers, never more than 12 in number, had the freedom of Paris as long as they wore bells around their necks. They were called the 'privileged pigs'.

The food chain of today's Parisian ecosystem (not counting the numerous humans, who go to restaurants or buy frozen *coq-au-vin* at the Monoprix), has at its summit some 90 kestrels (*faucons crécerelles*), who live on the towers of Notre-Dame and other tall buildings; they chiefly dine on the abundant sparrows, but the ornithologists who study the feather-balls they regurgitate from atop the Eiffel Tower say they also pick up quite a few escaped canaries. The other predator in town is the barn owl (*chouette effraie*), which haunts the Tuileries and Père-Lachaise cemetery by night. Hunting is good; Paris is estimated to have as many rats as people, and some six million mice. The rest of the *dramatis personae* includes a few magpies and tits, ducks on the Seine, weasels in inexplicable abundance, occasional squirrels and hedgehogs in the parks, and great tribes of bats who flit home each morning to the SNCF's stations and tunnels.

And not all the Americans in Paris wear expensive running shoes and hang out in the 8e. American muskrats were raised in France in the 1920s for fur; a few escaped, and these serene and adaptable animals have now thoroughly colonized the Paris sewers. Muskrats are occasionally seen ambling down the Canal St-Martin at night, looking for frogs or crayfish.

The point of all this is to propose an all-Parisian dinner, something nobody has considered since the siege of 1871, when not even the sewer rats were safe. It would be difficult to round up but not impossible. For starters, Canal St-Martin *écrevisses*. For the main course, catch yourself a 'city squab'—many of Paris's pigeons are tasty, dark-coloured *pigeons bisets*, whose ancestors escaped from the many *pigeonniers* around the city. Find a dessert you can make with Parisian honey, reputed to be very good; the park office at the Jardins du Luxembourg, where the hives are, sells it, when available, for a healthy 50F a kilo. Wine will be no problem. Try the plonk grown on the rooftop of the 9e's firehouse, and sold by the firemen for charity—or, even better, *Château Mélac*, which grows in the rain gutter of Mélac's café on Rue Léon-Frot (11e), and is squeezed between the waitresses' toes in a festive *vendange* each September; 'It is undrinkable', the owner modestly notes. Or else, there's the *pipi de chat* made in the last survivor of Montmartre's vineyards. In the old days, they had a song about it:

> *C'est le vin de Montmartre,*
> *Qui en boit pinte en pisse quatre.*

## Baudelaire and Hugo, Progress and Spleen

> *One can simultaneously possess a special genius and be a fool. Victor Hugo proves that to us well—the Ocean itself is tired of him.*
>
> Baudelaire

The Chinese curse, 'May you live in interesting times', fell upon Paris's two great poets of the 19th century, Victor Hugo (1802–85) and Charles Baudelaire

(1821–67). It was also the only thing the two had in common. Hugo consumed life whole—the noble and the grotesque, injustice and poverty, politics and religion—until he himself swelled up bigger than life. Where ennui, inertia and ill health oppressed Baudelaire, Hugo possessed the literary and sexual energy of a volcano. No poet since has enjoyed such popular idolatry, and it's a sobering lesson for anyone disgusted with today's crass commercialism to learn that in the 19th century you could buy Hugo ink or 'Soap of the Muses' with Hugo's picture, or a gas lamp in the form of Hugo's head with the inscription: 'He beams his rays through all of nature and becomes a sun for the human race.'

Certainly as the man who saw Notre-Dame as a giant 'H'—a projection of his own name—he was the perfect poet laureate for a city whose deadly sin is vanity. After all, Hugo's Paris novels were powerful enough to influence real life: *Notre-Dame de Paris* (1831) led directly to the restoration of the collapsing cathedral while *Les Misérables* (1862) inspired many readers to fight for social justice in the ill-fated Commune (Hugo, rather than join them, slunk off to Belgium).

The poet–city relationship was symbiotic. Paris could always count on Hugo to trumpet *le mot juste* for every occasion, from the city's first Exposition in 1855 ('Progress is the Footstep of God!') to the introduction for an 1867 guidebook to Paris ('A coach passes flying a flag; it comes from Paris. The flag is no longer a flag, it is a flame, and the whole trail of human gunpower catches fire behind it.') During the Prussian siege, Hugo tried to shame Bismarck for his impudence in trying to capture the French capital: 'It is in Paris that the beating of Europe's heart is felt. Paris is the city of cities. Paris is the city of men. There has been an Athens, there has been a Rome, and there is a Paris ...' When André Gide was asked to name France's greatest poet, he made his famous reply: 'Victor Hugo—alas!' Gide acknowledged Hugo as the supremely gifted craftsman, an incomparable virtuoso, but one whose unfailing lack of vision responded to the momentous changes of the 19th century by smothering them in words.

Like Hugo, Baudelaire wrote best about Paris, but it might as well have been a city from another planet, the ever tantalizing, ever changing urban hell of the 19th century. Baudelaire was the first to understand the collapse of the age-old relationships between the individual and society (*see* The Vertigo of Modernism, below); his Tableaux Parisiens in *Les Fleurs du Mal* and the prose poems in *Paris Spleen* have lost none of their evocative, disturbing power.

Baudelaire stands in an urban literary tradition that began with François Villon, Montesquieu and Diderot. It was updated during the Revolution by Louis-Sébastien Mercier, who wandered the streets of Paris by day, gathering material (*Tableau de Paris* and *Nouveau Paris*), and Restif de la Bretonne, who took the night shift (*Les Nuits de Paris*), two innovative figures who have never really had their due even in

France. Both wrote their sharp, detailed observations in sets of fragmentary sketches, a new form to fit a new age.

As 19th-century Paris convulsed from one upheaval to the next, the search for meaning from the streets was continued by the elusive Gérard de Nerval; his *Les Nuits d'Octobre* was inspired by Restif, but Nerval enriched what he saw with images from the dream world, forays into the subconsciousness that presage the Surrealists' exploration of Paris's mysteries: Louis Aragon's masterpiece, *Le Paysan de Paris* (1926), André Breton's *Nadja* (1928), written in the footsteps of Nerval, or Philippe Soupault's *Les Dernières Nuits de Paris* (1928) with its evocative epigram: 'To choose is to grow old.' And closer to our own time are Henry Miller's Paris books, and the Italian Giovanni Macchia's *Les Ruines de Paris* (1988), evoking the perpetual destruction, the slow, sweet apocalypse of this Sodom and Gomorrah on the Seine.

But it was Baudelaire the opium smoker, the *flâneur* outside the pale, a man clawed apart by the paradoxes within himself, who 'saw the elephant', as heroin addicts say when the drug wears off and leaves a vision of naked reality. What makes Baudelaire compelling reading today is that his 'elephant' is still with us. While Hugo gushed over progress with a capital P, Baudelaire pondered in the very same year, 1855, 'whether [humanity's] indefinite progress might not be its most cruel and ingenious torture; whether ... shut up in the fiery circle of divine logic, it would not be like the scorpion that stings itself with its own tail—progress, that eternal desideratum that is its own eternal despair!'

But poets, unlike progress, come to an end. When Hugo, 'the sun for the human race', had his supernova, he was given the biggest funeral in Paris's history. Black crêpe was hung over the Arc de Triomphe; two million people filed past his coffin; and the church of Sainte-Geneviève was converted once and for all into the Panthéon to become his last resting place. Baudelaire, in contrast, doesn't even get his own name over his modest grave in Montparnasse cemetery: you have to look under 'Aupick', the name of the stepfather he hated.

## The Compulsive Exhibitionist

As cities go, Paris has long been the champion show-off. From the Middle Ages to the Revolution, it drew crowds from all over Europe to its trade fairs, especially the annual luxury fair put on by the abbots of St-Germain. The first modern public exhibition was organized by the Directory in 1798. But when Britain astounded the world with the Crystal Palace in the Great Exhibition of 1851, an upstaged France had to respond.

Louis-Napoleon, who had just taken over the country, quickly formulated the

Gallic riposte. Set in the undeveloped land between the Champs-Elysées and the Ecole Militaire, the 1855 Exhibition turned out a poor imitation of the London show, a pastiche of ugly Second Empire glass and iron pavilions. Queen Victoria came to visit (the first British monarch since the Hundred Years' War) and was very polite. The French made a special effort to promote their art, and visitors were similarly polite about the halls of big canvases of Ingres and Delacroix. The thing that really excited the crowds was a new invention—silver plate.

Undismayed, the Parisians tried again in 1867. Again, consumer goods were the Exhibition's *raison d'être*: there was everything from Sèvres porcelain to locomotives. Adolphe Sax had a stand to promote his new saxophone, and the star of the Prussian exhibit was the advanced Krupp cannon, which Bismarck would soon be using on Paris itself. Still, a good time was had by all, and Paris decided to make fairs a habit, hosting one every 11 years or so. The next show, in 1878, was even bigger and better, the first modern, truly international Exposition—even Japan and China put up small pavilions. The telephone and phonograph were crowd favourites, along with the Statue of Liberty's head (the only part Bartholdi had finished) and, most amazing of all, a machine that manufactured ice. With a main pavilion on the Champ de Mars almost a half-mile long, the French government had spared no expense to impress; after the traumas of 1870–71, it was imperative to show the world that France was back on its feet.

Progress was the religion of the 19th century, and the World Fairs were its holy shrines. A German scholar once called the Paris fairs *Gesamtkunstwerke*—'total works of art', like Wagnerian opera; they were the ultimate spectacle, combining technology, nationalistic pageantry, art and music, fantasy architecture, fashion and exoticism, business and pleasure. Even the radical socialists loved them; no matter what your politics, the Expositions offered a glimpse of a richer, faster future, full of colour and light and delightful mechanical toys.

The one in 1889 was bigger still. Queen Victoria boycotted this one, as did many other monarchs—it commemorated the centenary of the Revolution. Later, they regretted missing it. The star was the Eiffel Tower, but just as impressive was the colossal glass Galerie des Machines, sadly demolished later. To match the Tower, engineers drilled a thousand-foot well into the Trocadéro gardens; visitors went down in elevators to the mysterious quarries and tunnels of underground Paris.

The 1900 version was perhaps the height of the phenomenon. Although Paris was sparking major revolutions in art that year, the Exposition organizers were blissfully unaware of it; architecturally, they retreated from the modernist triumphs of 1889 back to a tired, overripe eclecticism. But everyone loved it—no Fair before or since made so much money. Over the main gate, a voluptuous naked statue of the Fairy Electricity welcomed everyone in to a wonderland of technology: some of the first commercially available cars, a huge wall of constantly changing coloured electric lights, a 330ft version of that recent American invention, the Ferris wheel. The Tsar sent Eskimos, Cossacks and carpet weavers from Bokhara; the English, as before, sent their latest models of artillery and the Prince of Wales. The Germans spent more than everyone else put together, and angled for the biggest space in every category of industrial exhibit.

Paris missed its date with 1911, but the 1925 *Exposition des Arts Décoratifs* proved a fitting showcase for the creative Paris of the '20s—and gave the world the term 'Art Deco'. In 1931 the government sponsored a lavish *Exposition Coloniale*, a celebration of imperialism in the Bois de Vincennes, which included a replica of the Angkor Wat temple in Cambodia. Parisian Exhibitionism went out with a whimper in 1937, a half-hearted affair doomed by the malaise of the times and infighting between the Popular Front government and its rightist enemies. But crowds came to see television, Picasso's *Guernica*, Georges Simenon in a glass cage cranking out an Inspector Maigret detective novel in a week, and the Pavilion of Asbestos, the Wonder Mineral, where visitors were invited to immerse themselves in a roomful of the stuff. The most formidable pavilions belonged to Germany and the USSR, grim monsters bristling face to face next to the Seine. In just two years, the monsters would make a pact to divide up Europe; in three, one would be occupying Paris.

The myth of Progress, and the Parisian urge to show off, would never be the same. Paris hasn't tried one since, and the other postwar Expositions around the world have all been notably lacking in inspiration—where Paris a century ago created the Eiffel Tower for a centrepiece, in 1992 Seville could offer only a big orange.

## Lighter than Air

'All the merit of Paris is in its air,' wrote Louis-Sébastien Mercier in 1781. Air does seem to have a remarkably buoyant quality in Paris, a champagne effervescence that toys with gravity and lightens the wit; ideas and fashions rise and float over the city before dissipating into the mists of time; windbags in positions of power keep the city's culture and politics from ever coming down to earth.

Innately airy and pumped up with French derring-do, Paris was a natural to pioneer communion with the sylphs. The first known Parisian birdman was the eccentric Marquis de Bacqueville, who in 1742 made it halfway over the Seine in a prototype of a sailplane before crashing into a floating laundry barge, a landing so discouraging that the Marquis fought anyone who dared to mention the incident again. The next attempt had to wait until 1783, when the brothers Montgolfier, after remarking on how their shirts puffed up when they dried them by the fire, released their first balloon at Annonay in June. As soon as the news hit Paris, public subscription raised funds for a similar experiment, released two months later from Place des Victoires by physicist Jacques Charles. It floated all the way to Le Bourget, where peasants, thinking the gasbag was a monster, shot it down, tied it to a horse's tail and dragged it across the fields in triumph. Despite similar risks, two months later Paris launched the first-ever humans to leave the earth, Pilâtre de Rozier and the Marquis d'Arlandes, who sailed 300ft over Paris from Château de Muette to Butte-aux-Cailles. The crowd that met them tore their clothes off in its enthusiasm. Two weeks later Jacques Charles launched the first hydrogen balloon from the Tuileries and stayed aloft for two hours. 'But what use could it ever have?' one spectator wondered aloud. 'Of what use is a newborn baby?' retorted another, named Benjamin Franklin.

The 'firsts' continued apace: in 1791 Parisians in Parc de Monceau witnessed history's first parachute jump—at 1000 feet, from a balloon. In 1793 the armies of the Revolution made the first military use of balloons, to carry messages over the heads of their astonished enemies. In 1797 the first man on horseback went up in a balloon over Paris; it made the horse's nose bleed. In the next century, balloon ascents were used to raise funds for charity, Greek independence and other good causes. Amazing spectacles were performed by the first lady *aéronautistes*, especially the daring Madame Blanchard (wife of the first balloonist to cross the Channel), who in 1819 ascended over Paris in a balloon laced with a crown of fireworks; the bag ignited and she perished like a shooting star.

In the 1850s, as Victor Hugo thundered inspiration from the sidelines ('The holy ship ... the vertiginous shout of exploration!/It races, shadow, light, chimera, vision!'), Paris even debated setting up a balloon public transport system in which balloons, guided by steel cables, would be pulled along high wires over the city by steam engines. For no one had yet invented a way to steer a *montgolfière*, much to the sorrow of the besieged Paris of 1870, when daring balloon escapes over the Prussian lines captured the world's imagination. One balloon continued on haplessly all the way to Norway; another, by an extraordinary coincidence, crashed into a house in Brittany where the aged mother of the general in charge of Paris's defence was praying 'for a sign from heaven that her son might save France'. Yet not one of the 65 balloons launched was ever able to return to Paris (the only news from outside came via pigeons, on microfilm).

The Commune had barely fallen in 1871, when Paris had a preview of the future: next to the burnt shell of the Tuileries palace, 21-year-old Alphonse Pénaud flew 20 metres in a *planophore*—the first heavier-than-air machine to get off the ground (if only just). Pénaud also designed a helicopter and a delta-winged plane—so that everything will be ready, he wrote, when someone invents the engine to make it run.

Parisians themselves would make few other innovations in flight, but the city's enthusiasm never waned. In 1901 the Brazilian Santos-Dumont won a 100,000F prize for steering a dirigible from St-Cloud to the Eiffel Tower; the rapturous welcome Paris gave Lindbergh in 1927 is legendary. But it was the success of the Wright brothers in America that led one Parisian, Jules Romains, to predict: 'This autumn that gave birth to aviation like a miracle, makes one wonder if it's still worthwhile to dig (the métro) underground, at the cost of so many millions … when it's evident that by 1918, at the very latest, a good half of Paris's traffic could be made in airplanes'.

## Manet, or Blinded in the City of Light

*We are led to Believe a Lie*
*When we see not Thro' the Eye*
*God Appears & God is Light*
*To those poor Souls who dwell in Night,*
*But does a Human Form Display*
*To those who Dwell in Realms of Day.*

William Blake, *Auguries of Innocence*

In 1818 French physicist Nicéphore Niepce invented photography, but the slow exposure time of the film required the camera's subjects to pose with their eyes closed. Eyeballs were drawn in later—hence the curious impression that our ancestors went about with strange, bulging stares.

Yet those bulging stares could be as blind as cave fish, especially when looking at art. The blindness, or rather visual illiteracy, of the Paris public in response to Edouard Manet's *Déjeuner sur l'Herbe* and *Olympia* (now both in the Musée d'Orsay) led to national scandals in the 1860s that seem incredible today. Critics compared the fascination of *Olympia* to that of corpses in the morgue; her skin was dirty; she was a female gorilla. Manet was accused of purposely inflicting indecent pictures on a morally upright Paris (remember, this was the sorry age of Napoleon III) as a ploy to gain notoriety. Manet became so paranoid that he fought a duel over the work. He was so universally despised that in 1866 Zola lost his job as art critic at *L'Evènement* for daring to prophesy that 'M. Manet's place is reserved in the Louvre … it is impossible—impossible, you hear—that one day M. Manet will not triumph and crush the timid mediocrities that surround him'.

Like many artists of the period, Manet was inspired by photography; in his youth he invented a technique of oil painting inspired by the effects of over-exposed photographs. He painted directly 'Thro' the Eye' as Blake wrote. 'If our works have a character that makes them seem like a protest,' Manet wrote in the 1863 catalogue for the Salon of the Refusés, 'that is the result of sincerity, since the artist is only trying to render his impression.' Although the first to paint Impressionist scenes from everyday life, and to imitate the instantaneous effects of photography (as in his *Les Courses à Longchamp*), Manet cared little for subject matter and never injected any emotion into his work. He was what critics call a 'painter's painter', fascinated with the ineffable space between light and shadow.

Unlike many revolutionaries who followed, Manet never meant to provoke or challenge the Parisians. Son of a well-off bourgeois family in Paris, he was born to please: a handsome charmer with a ready laugh, his studio was often crowded with society ladies. Manet longed to be accepted by the public, to win the Salon prize his followers disdained—but not at the price of compromising his art. After 1879, the year when his arch-enemy Albert Wolff, critic of *Le Figaro*, finally admitted in print that Manet had pointed the way to others, Manet responded by standing up with his arms extended like a signpost whenever he saw Wolff. In 1881 he finally won a second-class medal at the Salon, achieving his life's goal and paving the way for the public acceptance of the Impressionists, Manet's followers, into the 'Realms of Day'. Two years later he would be dead, at the height of his power; his last major painting, that uncanny scene of Paris nightlife called *Le Bar des Folies-Bergères* (now in London), was painted from a wheelchair.

Art critics have found in *Olympia* the first nude in 400 years (since Lucas Cranach's *Venus*) to portray a naked woman honestly, clean of the accumulated crust of the Academic conventions; after the initial shock, the painting opened the eyes of Paris to a new literacy in seeing. Some were better students than others. In 1890 the Louvre only accepted *Olympia* as a gift after lengthy negotiations, and only hung it in 1907, after Clemenceau intervened to make Zola's words come true.

## No Dog Poo, Please, We're Parisians

In 1992, when Jacques Chirac was still mayor, a remarkable brochure appeared in every Parisian's mailbox. It was a full-colour comic book, printed at enormous expense by the City of Paris and devoted to the adventures of a dog named Archibald. We may assume Archibald to be of English extraction, not only from his name, but for his excruciating good manners and the fact that he wears a monocle. His purpose, which he accomplishes with aplomb, is to instruct less well-bred French dogs and thoughtless French humans on the importance of canine cleanliness. At the end of the story, Archibald puts to shame a dog named Rex, who only does it in the gutter when he feels like it. Then he helps his dog-sitter meet a nice girl with a poodle.

On the back of the brochure are the 'Ten Commandments of the Tidy Parisian Dog', as well as a helpful puppy chart to tell you how many *besoins liquides* and *besoins solides* your infant will be producing daily. For all dogs, the city recommends 'Always associate acts with words. Show him where to do it, while saying to him "*Tes besoins!*"' The city provides the number for its special 'Hello Cleanliness' hot line, in case we have any further questions. Finally there is the Parisian Dog's Motto: 'Me, I do it where I'm told to do it'.

Who could fail to be impressed by the inexhaustible cleverness and resources of the Paris government? They are indeed getting serious about misplaced *besoins*. A trained Dog Poo Squad of a hundred undercover agents stalks the streets of Paris day and night. They travel in pairs, and when they spot an anti-social dog owner they move in, flashing their *Propreté de Paris* ID cards and serving malefactors with fines of 600F and up. The *Propreté* doesn't fool around, as even the casual visitor will notice. Their fluorescent green-clad legions can be seen scouring the streets at any hour. Besides washing out 1650 miles of gutters daily, they have fleets of small green vans equipped with scrubbers, and even vacuum-equipped green motorcycles that weave in and out of pedestrian traffic on the pavements, frightening elderly ladies and children as they suck up offending gum wrappers and cigar butts.

This is neurosis on a Swiss scale, and rather startling in a city where, only a few decades ago, a man could feel himself lord of all he surveyed as he eased his load against any Parisian wall. Paris simply decided to become the cleanest metropolis on earth, and by all accounts it has succeeded (closest competitor: Pyongyang, North Korea). If Edith Piaf, who never, ever, washed her feet, returned to walk the streets of Paris, would the *Propreté* track her down and vacuum her up into a green van?

Pampered Paris has money to burn for such whims—the sanitation budget last year was over 11. 5 *billion* francs—as well as for *Grandes Arches*, pyramids, art exhibitions of spray-can graffiti, gadgets built into the street that catch motorists who go through red lights, even a 100-page official colour monthly (called *Paris, le Journal*; strangely enough, most of the advertisers seem to be paving contractors). All this while strapped working-class suburbs lack money for basic services. But what's bothersome is not the obscene amounts France lavishes on its overindulged Babylon, but the way they spend it. The tidiness mania is just a minor manifestation of France's old evil genius—the urge to control everything, to rationalize, sanitize, homogenize, to stamp out all traces of diversity and spontaneity, and make the city an expanded version of some cadaverous bourgeois parlour in the 7e. The Bourbons gradually stifled Paris's medieval bonhomie, its street life and popular festivals; Napoleon III and Haussmann wiped out the old Ile de la Cité, and swept the poor out of Paris's centre. De Gaulle and Pompidou took care of the markets at Les Halles, and governments since have fostered the total gentrification of the entire city. Pity poor Jacques Chirac, an ambitious man—they left him nothing to do but mop up dog pies. Now that he's moved on to the Elysée Palace, the fever seems to have subsided; the green machines are less in evidence, and on some streets you'll have to watch your step once more.

## Sleazy Serge

> He was probably le Petit Prince ... and became, in face of
> the tragic reality of life, a touching Quasimodo.
>
> Brigitte Bardot

Even the most flighty American tourist in Paris on 2 March 1991 sensed something was amiss. Glum looks and solemn murmurs filled the cafés; tearful crowds and journalists milled in Rue Verneuil. And then the tourist understood. Paris was mourning one of its own: alackaday, Serge Gainsbourg had kicked the bucket—the ice bucket, in his case. Then perhaps the tourist looked blank, and the Parisians attempted to jog the old memory bank. Who could forget Serge's hit songs and films—Bardot in hot pants straddling a bike in *Harley-Davidson*? Or *Bonnie and Clyde* with BB as Bonnie and sulky Serge as Clyde? Or perhaps Jane Birkin in the 1968 heavy-breather with the dingaling melody called *Je t'aime ... moi non plus*? Or perhaps his *Lemon Incest*, the video filmed with Serge lying (albeit clothed) in bed with his pubescent daughter Charlotte?

Like the cigarettes and booze that stole Serge from his adoring public, French pop music should have a health-warning label. But Serge's mind-boggling success wasn't altogether the result of his songs, or his loopy *franglais* lyrics (although once on television he simply belched and farted along to the music) but rather his role as king of insults, the great *provocateur*, the obscene drunk, the old rogue who burnt a 500F note on television ('not many of you can afford to do this,' he commented with a twinkle). His best mate Jane Birkin helped him create his scruffy image: ill-shaven, dishevelled hair, cigarette dangling from his lips, rumpled scout shirt and jeans. Serge had ears you could hang pianos from, but vacant singers and starlets found him an irresistible Svengali.

In Paris, the best poets and writers have traditionally been bad boys, from François Villon, a murderer and thief who barely escaped the scaffold, to Rabelais, who spent his life dodging a Sorbonne-sponsored *auto-da-fé* for heresy. Old Paris had a grand old tradition of *chanson* drinking clubs with names like The Society of Peeing Cats or The Liberated Squirrels, each wittier than the next and liable to be closed down for cutting too close to the quick. For Serge's direct role model, however, we have to race ahead a few centuries to Aristide Bruant, the celebrated *chansonnier* of Montmartre's cabarets in the late 1880s and '90s. Bruant was a shrewd businessman: he had a trademark stage costume (as seen in Toulouse-Lautrec's posters), and was the first to make a fortune from insulting the Parisians, who came from all over town to be bullied and lambasted as mugs, pigs, camels and worse. For all that, Bruant was a real poet; he updated Villon's slangy ballads to create a new genre of French song, a kind of sung poetry performed, according to one critic, with 'the most cutting voice, the most metallic voice I have ever heard; a voice of rioting and the barricades ... an arrogant and brutal voice which penetrated your soul like the stab of a switchblade into a straw man'. Bruant's songs also opened the eyes of the bourgeois to the homeless and jobless, the prostitutes and pimps and the *apaches* and toughs who end up at the guillotine, and Paris's 'little people'.

Bruant had many followers: Yvette Guilbert, Edith Piaf, Jacques Prévert, Juliette Greco—and even Serge in his way, without poetry or sincerity, but a lot of flab, cynicism and shock for the sake of shock. For the time being, Paris can't provide much better. A deeply conformist culture needs its Quasimodos and court jesters and, as sleazy as Serge was, Paris misses him. And so far, at least, he has no successor to tease it, to burn its banknotes, to belch in its face. You can pay homage to the great man with a cabbage (don't ask why), a cigarette offering or a scribble ('Serge, we will smoke together in paradise') at the shrine that has grown up around the door of his last address, 5 Rue Verneuil.

## The Vertigo of Modernism

> *It was as though in Paris Europeans saw a disease creeping into all their lives, and yet could not avert their gaze from the sick patient.*
>
> Richard Sennett, *The Fall of Public Man*

The disease is Modernism, bringing with it the disorientation of rapid, unending change. Most of us late Moderns have learned to cope with it, after almost two centuries of being whirled about on its berserk merry-go-round. But consider the plight of those present at the creation—in Paris, the 'capital of the 19th century', where much of the New first appeared, and where the disruption and turmoil were the greatest.

The protagonists of Modernism appear in the 18th century: the (for lack of a better word) bourgeoisie, the people who were starting to enjoy riding their first carriages on the Grands Boulevards, who were importing new machines from England, studying science, reading and writing Paris's first newspapers. As someone wrote at the time: 'They knew they were different, but not exactly what they were'. They argued about politics in the Palais Royal gardens, and from there they surged out to storm the Bastille and change history for us all.

Forty years later, under Louis-Philippe, the 'Bourgeois King', Paris belonged to them. Things were definitely starting to pop. There were more Parisians than ever, traffic was booming, machines of all kinds appeared. Crowds formed to demonstrate, or to watch hucksters selling gadgets, to watch balloon ascents, circus parades and every sort of new entertainment. The first railways were initiating Parisians into the allure of speed. By day Paris streets had become cramped pages of shop signs and advertising messages; by night gas lighting turned them into incredible fairy scenes.

With new dreams and new opportunities came new dangers, phenomena that, as we look back on them, seem almost occult. Mere things, for example, were starting to take on a life of their own. Shopkeepers such as Aristide Boucicaut, who founded the first department store in 1852, invented the tricks of modern merchandising, using advertising and displays to invest cheap, machine-made goods with an aura by associating them with aristocracy, or with some imagery of youth or exotic desirability or 'good taste'. Overwhelmed, Parisians were the first to slide down the slippery road of defining themselves by what they possessed.

Before department stores, these numinous idols were displayed in the arcades, another Parisian invention. Walter Benjamin, the mad philosopher of Modernism, was obsessed with Paris's arcades, the 'first consumer dream worlds', now obsolete and become fossils, or ghosts. He compared their entrances to 'the places one was shown in ancient Greece that descended into Hades'. (Visit them today, and you'll find them venerable, quiet and rather charming rest-homes for the commodities of yesteryear: antique toys, old books, music boxes, hand-made pipes).

Not only things but people, too, were becoming commodities, a bizarre equation that begins with a simple matter of clothes. Mr Sennett's remarkable book, quoted above, notes how prior to the Revolution people's rank and station in life could be guessed by their clothes—wives of artisans, for example, were forbidden to wear the same sort of frock or bonnet as wives of craft masters. Now all that was gone, and in a city doubling in size every two decades, other people had become 'unknown quantities'—a mystery, perhaps a threat. Paris had become a city of strangers.

At the same time, writers such as Balzac and Flaubert were creating the modern novel. With their careful descriptive writing, they reinforced what people were learning in everyday life: that every item of dress, every quirk of behaviour, every gesture might be a sign charged with hidden meaning. Not surprisingly, Parisians started to become quite self-conscious.

One result was that Paris, even more than London, invented the Victorian age. In the 1840s, city dress suddenly became more drab (and uglier) than ever before. While provincials still loved colour and style, Parisian men began to dress all alike: like undertakers, copying Louis-Philippe and his black suit. On the streets, in the theatre, they were learning to conduct themselves with a rigid, unflinching discipline. They were trying to hide themselves—from each other, and perhaps from Balzac. Women, reduced to chattels by the regressive Napoleonic code, suffered much worse: now came the time of whalebone corsets and other deforming costumes, of female hysteria and constipation, of paranoia about virginity and purity. In 1857 Charles Worth opened the first fashion house and invented the fashion model; women learned to imitate mannequins, and to display themselves as commodities just like the goods in the windows of the *Bon Marché*.

On the stages of old Paris's theatre district, the 'Boulevard du Crime', melodrama was king, with displays of emotion and passion never before imagined; Frédérick Lemaître (the actor portrayed in *Les Enfants du Paradis*) was its greatest practitioner. In the whirl of the cities, an uncontrollable and quite nasty genie had slipped out of its bottle. Its name was *personality*, its currency *feelings*. The repressed crowds were ready fairly to worship anyone like Lemaître who was somehow free to express this powerful new force. For music, Parisians flocked to see dramatic showmen such as Liszt and Paganini. In politics, a poet-politician like Lamartine could briefly hold back the flood of the 1848 revolution by insulting and shaming the crowds, making them know that he 'felt' more, suffered more than they. But this new idea of political charisma would not be perfected until the next century—in Germany.

Other politicians and theorists, drawing on Paris's revolutionary heritage, invented the myth of 'the people', a collective sort of 'personality' that would also later be perfected elsewhere—in Russia. It did 19th-century Paris, and France, little good. As the poet of the new era, Baudelaire, once said: 'By modernity I mean the ephemeral, the contingent', and though he meant opinions and fashions in shop windows he could just as well have been talking about French politics. Through the century, rotten regimes rose and fell while the clocks in the railway stations ticked on; what seemed tyranny, viewed from any one moment, is revealed as slapstick anarchy as we look back over the century as a whole.

More and more people were pouring into Paris all the time, cannon fodder for modernity's confusions: 25,000 slaughtered by their own army in 1871, a dozen times that from cholera, typhoid and other diseases of the slums. But more always came in to take their places, as Paris grew into a city of two million. Paris's soul and its symbol was in its streets, in the hurly-burly of all these people striving, winning, failing or just getting by, birthing a new world and a new culture as they struggled to come to grips with the incoherence around them. The street, their stage, spawned Balzac's *flâneur*, the passive, impotent observer of the crowd who had learned the basic tenet of the new city—'look, but don't touch'—the grandfather of the lost souls in Kafka and in *Death of a Salesman*. But the street also created new life, new possibilities; among its masses were revolutionaries in politics, art and ideas. These Parisians began to express themselves in the *belle époque* of the 1890s, blowing off Victorian steam and creating modern art, in a decade when glorious, disorderly creative urban life was at its height.

After the shock of the First World War, many began to have doubts about modernism and the unfathomable forces it unleashed. Anti-modernism turned modernism's tools on itself, and it was inevitably concerned with social control: whether fascism or communism—or psychoanalysis, with its emphasis on 'adjusting' and conformity—or modern architecture. One turning point came on 1 October 1924, when a vain young Swiss architect who called himself Le Corbusier went for a walk on the Champs-Elysées, and was nearly run down by the cars. In his own account of the event, at first he was saddened, recalling happier days when 'the streets belonged to us'. But then (in a typically modernist flash of contradiction) the architect suddenly changes his mind, choosing to identify himself with the brute power of mechanized civilization. 'Architecture or revolution,' he wrote; 'Revolution can be avoided'. To do that, 'We must kill the street!' People were to be locked up in tower blocks, 'machines for living': humbled, overawed, kept apart, made to fear. In architecture—as once in clothes—very often that which appears to be the cutting edge of modernism is really its defeat.

Perhaps a clue to modernism's future will be found in Paris. The city is getting itself ready for the climax, symbolized by the big clock in front of the Pompidou Centre, ticking off the seconds left until the new millennium, and by the *Grands Projets* of the 1980s, and by former Minister of Culture Jack Lang's efforts to inseminate culture artificially. But are these really a new stage in the New, or the end of it, where the dynamism and ephemerality of modernism are frozen into architectural museum-pieces, into state-controlled spectacles overseen by the Sub-Minister of Rock'n'Roll?

# Art and Architecture

# Art in Paris

Since the Renaissance, Paris has dominated the art of France and often even the art of Europe. The city's great social upheavals of the 19th century were translated by Paris artists into a tremendous revolution in the arts that, after decades of ridicule and mudslinging, toppled the staid reactionaries of the salon and Académie as irrevocably as the Bourbons. Today, instead of controversy in the plastic arts, there's a ten-ton load of patronage and encouragement from the Ministry of Culture—but, alas, very little art.

This has all been very frustrating for Mitterrand and his ex-Minister of Culture, the earnestly hip, popular and well-intentioned Jack Lang. No one expects much from the Beaux-Arts establishment any more, but Lang was so keen not to miss a beat from any quarter that he even put his seal of approval on Paris's spraypaint teenage graffiti, *le tagging*, until the *taggeurs* responded by spattering the elegant, showcase Louvre métro stop with their work. This often tragicomic imbalance between patronage and substantial results began after the Second World War, when Paris saw the avant-garde slip away to New York, and even, horror of horrors, to London. Paris wants it back, and Mitterrand (and Mayor Jacques Chirac) have spent billions to create once and for all the new Europe's undisputed Capital of Culture. If money can't buy you love, it can at least get you a mighty big dish of culture.

The French concept of culture as a responsibility of the state is a throwback to Louis XIV and his mastermind, Colbert: art gave a regime its prestige and was certainly far too important to leave to chance or natural evolution or artist's whim (the very same attitude that kings, emperors and presidents have always had about the city of Paris itself). One begins to suspect that the current government artmongers still smart over the rampant tackiness of the Third Republic, which not only failed to recognize the last batch of French geniuses but also actively mocked and disparaged them while paying through the nose for salon schlock. But what has the Fifth Republic nurtured? In the 1940s Jean Dubuffet, the philosopher of *art brut*, saw which way the wind was blowing when he declared that nothing at all is more unfavourable to real art than the idea of 'culture', which bridles and paralyses the imagination. Or, as Sanche de Gramont wrote in 1969, in *The French*: 'When the state considers that taste and style fall within its jurisdiction and links culture to the preservation of national values, it does not create, it embalms'.

On the positive side, no one can deny that Jack Lang's initiatives have brought all the arts closer to the average Parisian. If, like truffles, painting and sculpture stubbornly resist cultivation, at least the treasures that Paris possesses have never been better embalmed, housed in some of the most exciting museums in the world; since Mitterrand's election, attendance has soared.

## Middle Ages

The first Parisian artists were monk-illuminators of medieval manuscripts. Like their brethren throughout Europe, they had inherited the Byzantine tradition of portraying holy figures in a stiff, stylized manner to emphasize their otherworldliness. In the 13th century, when the new Gothic cathedrals created a demand for vast expanses of stained glass, artists adopted pictures from the illuminators, although their styles became freer and more natural, at least when not portraying saints (the best work is at **Chartres, Sainte-Chapelle, Notre-Dame** and **St-Denis**). The windows, in turn, inspired the brilliant illuminators of the Paris School during the reign of St Louis (1226–70).

When the Capetian kings made Paris their capital, the artists in their courts held the same rank as servants (*peintre et valet de chambre du roi*), and they were expected to design buildings, pagents, tapestries, books, chairs, chess pieces and anything else the king might fancy (*see* **Musée de Cluny**, p.241). As the court expanded, royal artists began to specialize, while the king's favourite painter was elevated to *premier peintre du roi*. The system remained intact to the Revolution.

By the 14th century, the university and court had sufficiently enhanced wealth and literacy in Paris for a new breed of artist, unattached to Church or nobleman, to live by selling painted books or accepting commissions (Jean Pucelle's *Bréviaire de Belleville* (1320s) in the **Bibliothèque Nationale**). The same century saw Paris's first invigorating contact with Italian painting by way of the papal court in Avignon, where Florentine and Sienese trecento styles were translated into a fairy-tale style known as International Gothic. The old Louvre was decorated with frescoes of flowery meadows and hunting scenes, while French sculptors, equally inspired by what they saw in Avignon, produced their delightful smiling, swivel-hipped figures of the Virgin, so popular that many were exported to Italy itself (*see* figures at the **Musée de Cluny**, p.241 and **Notre-Dame**, p.104).

In the lull in the Hundred Years' War before Agincourt, the French nobility went on an art buying spree that their *peintres-valets* couldn't satisfy. Flemish artists arrived to fill the gap, introducing their precise, detailed style (as seen in the few French paintings that have come down—among the best are the Louvre's *Portrait de Jean le Bon* and the *Parlement de Narbonne*). The most extravagant patron of the period was Charles VI's uncle, Jean Duc de Berry, who wrung every penny he could out of his domains to build castles filled with art. When Charles went mad, the Duc de Berry governed Paris, where his rapacious tax collectors caused riots—but helped pay Flemish painters to produce the enchanting *Très Riches Heures du Duc de Berry* with its scenes of medieval Paris (now in Chantilly's **Musée Condé**).

In 1391 painters in Paris had become important enough to be granted their own corporation, the *Maîtrise* or Guild of St Luke. Like all Paris guilds, it established exclusive rules and restrictions: apprentices at the age of 11 or 12 would spend five years learning under a master, then work for him as a *compagnon* before applying to join the *Maîtrise* by presenting a diploma work (the *chef d'oeuvre*). If accepted, the new master had the right to show and sell his work in Paris. 'Pirates' who tried to show or sell their art were prosecuted and often had their works destroyed. But there were ways of getting around the humourless Maîtrise: by working inside the walls of St-Germain-des-Prés abbey or by purchasing from the money-hungry Crown the right to be a *valet de chambre*.

## The Renaissance and the School of Fontainebleau

The little that has come down from the 15th century continues to show a strong Flemish influence: in court painter **Jean Fouquet** (*c.* 1420–75, author of the Louvre's remarkable, melancholy *Portrait of Charles VII*, and the *Livre d'Heures d'Etienne Chevalier* at the Musée Condé), and in the so-called Maître de Moulins employed by the Bourbons (*Ste-Madeleine et une Donatrice* in the Louvre and *Charles II Bourbon* at the Musée Condé.)

In 1497, Charles VIII's invasion of Italy brought back a number of paintings to Paris, beginning a taste for Italian art that became insatiable in the king most responsible for bringing the Renaissance to France, François I. François wanted not only the art, but the artists too: most notably Leonardo da Vinci, who died in the king's arms at Amboise in 1519 and, in 1528, painters Rosso Fiorentino and Francesco Primaticcio and sculptor Benvenuto Cellini to decorate his new château at **Fontainebleau**.

Rosso and Primaticcio were Mannerists, who elongated the limbs and bodies of their figures to give them a stylish elegance. Athough little survives of their original decorations (thanks to Louis-Philippe, who had them repainted by hacks), their stuccoes and the scheme of the painted panels remain to show the origins of the elegant long lines, clear colours and erotic tastes that figure in the **School of Fontainebleau**. In sculpture, the school's greatest master was **Jean Goujon** (1490–1561), whose Mannerist tendency was tempered by a study of the antique casts that adorned Fontainebleau's gardens (works in the **Louvre**, the *Fountain of the Innocents* and in the courtyard in the Ecole des Beaux-Arts). In painting, the earliest Fontainebleau style is epitomized in **Jean Cousin the Elder**'s only known work and one of the first French nudes, *Eva Prima Pandora*, in the Louvre; masterpieces from the later school include *Gabrielle d'Estrées in her bath* at the Musée Condé.

François I was also the first king to sit for many portraits, setting a fashion that few subsequent aristocrats failed to imitate, as the never-ending galleries at Versailles attest. François got not only the first, but some of the best portaits, from the Flemish Humanist **Jean Clouet** (1486–1540); his talented son **François Clouet** (1510–72) performed the same role in the courts of Henri II and Charles IX (both in the Louvre).

## The Age of Big Louies, or Art as Narcotic: the 17th century

The massive rebuilding of Paris in the 17th century created a tremendous demand for art of all kinds. Henri IV had at least made it easy to find the talent by converting the Long Gallery of the Louvre into lodgings and studios for artists. Patrons, however, continued to regard them as their servants, and imposed on them not only the subject matter but their own taste. Unfortunately their taste demanded only works that were pleasing, decorative and pretentious, and few paintings done in Paris offer more than a slight, vacuous charm. The greatest French painters of the day, Claude Lorrain and Nicolas Poussin, fled Paris like the plague and spent most of their lives in Italy. Louis XIII and Richelieu were as sweet as pie to Poussin when he returned briefly to Paris, and even put a comfortable house and a cask of the finest wine at his disposal—but Poussin still hightailed it back to artistic freedom in Rome, where he died.

So Louis XIII was stuck with the insipid Simon Vouet (1590–1649) for his **premier peintre du roi**. A decade spent in Italy taught Vouet the tedious, affected manner of religious painting then current; his secular manner, as in the classical scenes in the **Palais du Luxembourg**, hovers dangerously near the chocolate box. All the court artists who followed—Le Sueur, Mignard and Lebrun—painted in his workshop. **Eustache Le Sueur** (1616–55), the least affected of the lot, can still charm, as in the decorations from the Hôtel Lambert (in the Louvre).

The greatest artist to work in Paris under Louis XIII was Rubens, in town to do the queen-sized scenes of Marie de' Medici's flagrant life for the Palais de Luxembourg (now in the Louvre). Some of his Flemish and Dutch assistants stayed behind in St-Germain-des-Prés and sold their popular genre scenes at the St-Germain fair. They influenced a notable set of non-court painters to tackle similar everyday subjects, especially the **Le Nain brothers**—Antoine, Louis and Mathieu. The best was Louis (1593–1648), whose *Repas de paysans* in the Louvre attains a realistic nobility, void of the genre elements beloved by the Dutch. An even greater realistic artist was **Georges de La Tour** (1593–1652), whose solemn figures sculpted by darkness and candlelight are the most distinctive of the period. But Louis XIV's opinion of the Flemish and realist painters was well known: *'Enlevez-moi ces magots'* (get these apes away from me).

Meanwhile, artists of the Maîtrise, good Frenchmen as they were, were complaining that their monopolistic racket was threatened by artists who purchased their status from the king. In response, the king founded the *Académie royale de peinture et de sculpture* in 1648 to govern his artists. The Académie lay dormant until 1661, when the indefatigable Colbert took over its direction. Colbert believed that art had but one purpose: to enhance the glory of his master, Louis XIV, and France. To make the propaganda credible, but also to contain the high cost of luxury imports and make France into an art-exporter, Colbert demanded that the Académie dictate the highest standards to painters and sculptors, and to the weavers and furniture-makers at the the newly established Gobelins, assuring both quality control and political correctness. Astute flattery in the right places by **Charles Lebrun** (1619–90) earned him the position as the Académie's first director-dictator, and in 1675 he issued the magnificently flatulent Académie's Rules for Great Art, or the *Tables de Préceptes*. Lebrun then antagonized artists of the Maîtrise by declaring that only Académie members were allowed to teach (it was a considerable source of income), and he made all students study religious history, antiquity, mythology and moral instruction. The result of vast sums of money and Lebrun's bullying tactics produced an art organization unique in Europe, a stable of highly skilled artists and craftsmen on call to decorate a palace or whip up an opera set for the king's next do.

At the same time Colbert and Lebrun were snapping up paintings and sculptures for the royal collection (in the Louvre since 1681, where the academicians could study them). Starting with works left by François I, the two busy bees added the rich collections of Cardinal Mazarin and Fouquet (the *Surintendant des Finances* who had inspired Versailles before Louis XIV imprisoned him for life—*see* Vaux-le-Vicomte, p.479), and those of every other collector who just happened to go bankrupt. Colbert also made known the fact that the king welcomed presents, and Louis himself won twelve Poussins in a tennis match from the Duc de Richelieu. By

1709, 2400 pictures were stashed in the Louvre, giving it a considerable head start in the art race (London's National Gallery had 38, when founded in 1834).

And just what did the Académie produce for Louis according to their Préceptes? Glorious pageants for the Roi Soleil, scores of Gobelins tapestries, classical statues in the gardens of the Tuileries and Versailles and, essential for the proto-totalitarian state, public propaganda statues of Louis by Coysevox and G. Coustou to remind Parisians who was boss—even when they went to pray at Notre-Dame (their unveilings were the only occasions that brought Louis back to Paris after his move to Versailles). Lebrun, *premier peintre du roi*, spent his last 12 years directing the decoration of Versailles, painting the tedious Hall of Mirrors' ceiling on the glory of Louis. Lebrun's arch rival, **Pierre Mignard** (1610–95) was chiefly a portrait painter (see his *Molière* and *Cardinal Mazarin* at the Musée Condé) but was also chosen by the Queen Mother to paint 200 figures in her dome at Val-de-Grâce—a feeble copy of the holy circuses in the domes of Rome. Mignard refused to join the Académie—until Lebrun died, when he took over as its director. In the latter part of Louis XIV's reign, the chief painters were also portraitists: **Hyacinthe Rigaud** (1659–1743), who painted the Louvre's famous *Louis XIV at the age of 62*, as a pompous old poof in a miniskirt and high heels; and **Nicolas de Largillière** (1656–1746), who had a lighter, more shimmering touch that fitted in nicely with the spirit of the next century.

## The 18th Century: Rococo to Neoclassicism

Louis XIV's reign ended with a whimper of constipated religious art, and the echoes of Madame de Maintenon's footsteps in Versailles as she checked each Gobelins tapestry to make sure garments had been sewn over the nude figures. The old tyrant of tedium was still warm in the grave when Paris released all its pent-up frivolity in a wild orgy of indulgence and fun. Although Louis XIV had had to melt down his silver furniture to pay for his wars, Paris's financiers were rolling in money. The Regency launched the fashion for *rocaille*, or Louis XV Rococo, with an abhorrence of straight lines and love of decorative foliage and shell shapes that soon spread all over Europe. The first and finest painter to capture its whimsical spirit was **Antoine Watteau** (1684–1721). Watteau was the first original artist working in Paris (instead of Rome), patronized by the bourgeoisie and selling his work through dealers. When he was accepted into the Académie, it was as its first *peintre des fêtes galantes*, of courtship parties in the park; Watteau had translated the graceful, idle, twilit Venetian world of Giorgione into the parks outside Paris belonging to his wealthy patrons. Watteau's world is exquisite but ephemeral and tinged with melancholy, as if aware that he and the society he painted were doomed. The Louvre has his masterpiece, *L'Embarquement pour l'Ile de Cythère*; in the Revolution, David's students amused themselves by throwing spitballs at it, hating it for its lack of grandeur, realism, virtue and history, and the absence of the almighty individual—precisely the reason why Watteau appeals today.

Through the engravings of his works, Watteau exerted a mighty influence on the French decorative arts of the 18th century and he had a hundred imitators, most notably **Nicolas Lancret** (1690–1734) and **Jean-Baptiste Pater** (1696–1736), although their *fêtes galantes* often sink into mere genre scenes of pretty revellers. More solid bourgeoisie genre subjects typified the canvases of **Jean-Baptiste Chardin** (1699–1779), one of the most popular artists at the Académie's salons. In 1750 his public was dismayed when he abandoned figure painting to study in formal structure and composition in still life, works that form an essential link from Dutch *trompe-l'oeil* still lifes and Cézanne.

As Italian Baroque influences waned, the Académie reformulated its Rules for Great Art into a muddle-headed new doctrine called the Grand Manner in History-Painting (which included mythological and allegorical scenes). History painting was the only subject with prestige, and when painters such as Watteau and Chardin were admitted to the Académie they were given a lower rank; the top painting prize, the *Prix de Rome* was only given to the most convoluted historical tableaux, annually cooked up by Académie drudges. In 1734, when the Académie decided to exhibit the works of its members in public salons, room was made in the Louvre by shipping the old masters in the royal collection off to Versailles. It wasn't long before painters began to lower their lofty classical standard to please an ill-educated public (which, exposed to art only once every two years, not surprisingly focused on the most sensational or familiar subjects). A new being, the art critic, was born to help people talk about what they saw. One of the first was Diderot, whose favourite painter was the deplorable **Jean-Baptiste Greuze** (1725–1805) but only because his paintings offered edifying moral tales.

Besides Chardin, one of the great stars of the first salons was **Maurice-Quentin de La Tour** (1704–88), whose lively pastel portraits were inspired by the Paris visit of Venetian pastellist Rosalba Carriera. De La Tour was the favourite of that great trend-setter of the day, Madame de Pompadour (see his portrait of her in the Louvre), who also favoured **François Boucher** (1703–70), the most stylish, decorative painter of his time, whose luscious nudes and light, mythological fancies were designed for Rococo interiors and look like silly fluff on solemn museum walls. He knew his art had nothing to do with Michelangelo or Raphael, and he warned **Jean-Honoré Fragonard** (1732–1806) off them when Fragonard was about to depart for Rome. Fragonard heeded, and inherited his position as the chief decorative painter of the day, with an added touch of Watteau lyricism in his earliest works. Watteau also inspired *tableaux des modes*, engravings of people in fashionable costumes and the *estampes galantes* that evolved into intriguing Norman Rockwellish records of everyday life in Paris. **Louis-Léopold Boilly** (1761–1845) was a master of the genre. During the Terror, he found out he was about to be guillotined for his risqué works; he saved himself by beginning a *Triumph of Marat* just before Robespierre's prude squad reached his studio.

But Rococo flew too much in the face of the basic Parisian taste for balance, classical harmony and right angles for it to endure for very long; even as she patronized Boucher, La Pompadour's interest in the excavations at Pompeii (she sent her brother to Italy to study Greek and Roman architecture in 1749) pioneered the new, more classical style known as 'Louis XVI'. Painters of antique ruins such as **Hubert Robert** (1733–1808) filled the new Louis XVI interiors; **Jean-Antonine Houdon** (1741–1828) supplied the cool, elegant statues. As for portraits, two of the leading artists were, for the first time, women: **Elisabeth Vigée-Lebrun** (1755–1842), Marie Antoinette's favourite portraitist at Versailles (although her best work is *Madame Lebrun and her daughter* in the Louvre) and **Madame Labille-Guyard** (1749–1803), a friend of Robespierre, a more realistic artist and a feminist who fought to abolish the Académie's quota system for women and its ban against women teachers.

## The Revolution and Napoleonic Art

As the Revolution approached, Paris was full to bursting with hack painters: the salons had generated a huge market for low genre scenes, which encouraged even the most modestly gifted to take up the brush. Because only Académie artists could show at their own salon, outsiders complained that there was nowhere in Paris to expose their works, and in 1791 the National Assembly opened the salon to all, bringing in a flood of art—3000 paintings alone in 1795. The leading painter and art dictator of the Revolution, **Jacques-Louis David** (1748–1825), closed down the Académie's salon the next year and opened up a carbon copy called the Académie des Beaux-Arts. It held competitions for neoclassical patriotic pictures like his own, evocations of austere civic virtue, modelled on a ludicrous fantasy of ancient Rome. He led the government's nationalizing of art from royal palaces, churches (at least the bits that somehow escaped the anti-clerical fury of the sansculottes) and the châteaux of the émigrés. Another artist, Alexandre Lenoir, rescued sculpture (sometimes at the risk of his life, as at the Sorbonne) and during the Revolution opened the first public museum of French monuments.

In 1804 Napoleon made himself Emperor and mandated a new *style Empire* to decorate his residences (easily said but not well done—the Revolution had decimated the great art and craft organization Colbert had founded, so most Empire decorative work was shoddily made). Empire was the last hurrah of the neoclassical style begun by Madame de Pompadour, and was often employed in political propaganda far more repugnant and vile than even Louis XIV's. The best works are touched with the first whispers of Romanticism, as in the works of portrait painter **Pierre-Paul Prud'hon** (1758–1823; *Portrait de l'impératrice Joséphine*) and the works of sculptor **François Rude** (1784–1855) on the Arc de Triomphe. Napoleon found a willing toady in David (who had previously been Robespierre's), and gave him the task of recording the great moments of his career (*Le Sacre de Napoléon I* in the Louvre).

Besides imitating Louis XIV's use of art to sanctify tyranny, Napoleon shared his mania for the prestige of sheer accumulation. Advised by David and the Romantic chronicler of his triumphs, **Antoine-Jean Gros** (1771–1835), he cleaned out a number of Italian collections and even stripped Venice's San Marco of its famous horses as a prize for Paris; he booted the artists out of the Louvre and made it the Musée Napoléon, displaying his booty side by side with the ex-royal and now national collection. But thanks to the little hoodlum, all the artists and art-lovers in Paris could freely go to study the Grand Masters—a crucial first step for the artistic revolutions that were to follow.

## Early 19th Century: The Miasma of the Salons

At first the 19th century seemed to be a return to normality. The allies made the French return all the paintings Napoleon had nicked, and the embarrassing blank walls became the venue of the new salon of the Académie des Beaux-Arts. Only David was absent, having gone into exile in Belgium with the fall of his master. Without him to keep the Académie on the straight and narrow, his neoclassical doctrines quickly degenerated to a philistine grand manner of nice smooth surfaces, nudes and drapery. The return of the Bourbons encouraged historical subjects from the courtly golden days when kings were still fashionable, a mishmash indulgence in nostalgia called the *style troubadour*.

With David's departure, the chief artist remaining in Paris was his singularly irregular student, **Jean-Auguste-Dominique Ingres** (1780–1867), who after tossing off a few high-kitsch Napoleonic propaganda pieces went off until 1820 to Italy, where he studied the Mannerists' distortion of the figure. His serpent-backed *La Grande Odalisque* (in the Louvre) was accused of being 'Gothic' (i.e. quirky and individual) but he scored successes with his historical *troubadour* paintings. In Paris, in the rising tide of Romanticism, he found himself the pedantic standard-bearer of classical tradition, and for 27 years he kept his arch rival Delacroix out of the Académie.

The Romantic movement founded in Germany and England came to Paris only after the prolonged neoclassical hangover of the Revolution and Napoleon. Romanticism soon manifested itself in painting; being encouraged to crank out 'Gothic' scenes made artists think about of the old medieval spirit of freedom and individuality. Nor was it long before painters discovered that they, too, had plenty of lofty feelings to express, and they sought out subjects that they could respond to and paint emotively. The 1819 salon was shocked by its first Romantic painting, a barnburner called the *Radeau de la Méduse* (now in the Louvre) by **Théodore Géricault** (1791–1824), not only for its emotional qualities but for Géricault's charged topical subject—a shipwreck, caused by official negligence.

In 1822 **Eugène Delacroix** (1798–1863), putative son of Talleyrand, made his salon debut and quickly became the leader of the Romantics. Like Géricault he painted topical subjects that moved him; his *Liberty Guiding the People* (in the Louvre), the best-known image of the people of Paris at their barricades, was painted after the revolution of 1830. Considered as an incitement to riot, it was hidden away until the Exposition of 1855, when its image of a bourgeois gent in a top hat next to a worker seemed safely impossible.

Delacroix was also the only artist remembered today to receive some of the juicy public commissions initiated in 1814 by the Préfect de la Seine and the city of Paris to decorate churches stripped bare in the Revolution. Nearly all Paris's churches have at least a few murals—Delacroix did a chapel of St-Sulpice that Seurat greatly admired. The best of these commissions are mere interior decoration; the worst, by Ingres' dunce **Hippolyte Flandrin** (at St-Germain-des-Prés and Ste-Chapelle), are eyesores.

The Romantic emphasis on the emotions and the individuality of the artists was at odds with the conformism and solid virtues of Paris's bourgeois, and created the image of the artist as a bohemian, an eccentric outside respectable society. One group of painters—led by **Théodore Rousseau** (1812–67), and inspired by the 17th-century Dutch tradition, a desire to return to nature and the rising middle-class demand for landscapes—went off to paint in Barbizon, a hamlet in the Forest of Fontainebleau. But the greatest landscape painter of the day was **Camille Corot** (1796–1875), whose allowance from his middle-class parents allowed him to paint for 16 years before selling a single canvas. As lyrical as his landscapes are, Corot was the first painter inspired by photography (as in his famous, fluffy, grey foliage); by mid-century, when the Académie and salon public had tacitly accepted the fact that the best an artist could do was mimic the camera, Corot was extremely popular, and artists were instructed to paint in his style, in various tones of grey.

'Paint what your eyes see' became the slogan of the realist painters who followed, although the first exponent, **Gustave Courbet** (1819–77), was even more

Romantic and formal in vision than Corot, carefully composing his pictures to improve on what his eyes actually saw. Courbet's declarations that his own judgement and appreciation of his art was all that mattered infuriated the salon and its public. He was persecuted as a 'dangerous socialist' and when his works were rejected at the Expositions of 1855 and 1867, Courbet set an example for future outsiders by putting on one-man shows at his own expense; after serving as chief art agitator in the Commune he died in poverty and exile. Two other distinctive artists working outside the pale were **Honoré Daumier** (1808–79), a painter of Goyaesque vision known only for his cartoons in his lifetime, who also died in poverty, and **Charles Méryon** (1828–64), Baudelaire's friend, whose dark water-colours and drawings of a haunted, sinister Paris, alive with spirits, gargoyles and swarms of black birds, are a world in themselves, the obverse of the Paris of *Les Enfants du Paradis*. At the end of his life, Méryon became convinced that the police were after him and refused to leave his bed, threatening to shoot anyone who came near.

After the 1855 Exposition, the salon, ever more bloated, moved out of the Louvre into the huge Palais de l'Industrie, exposing the public to even more paintings that flattered its debased taste while pretending to uphold the traditions of French civilization. Napoleon III became the new sugar daddy of the arts, his reign introducing new heights in titillating nudes (see the Musée d'Orsay's works by Bouguereau and Cabanel), although it was the less offensive sculptor **Jean-Baptiste Carpeaux** (1827–75) who caused an outcry with his dancing girls at the Opéra. After the Commune, the Third Republic took over the reins of patronage, leaving Paris a collection of enormous photograph-inspired historical scenes by **Jean-Paul Laurens** and **Meissonnier**, artists who lived like princes. The most distinctive painter to enjoy official favour was **Pierre Puvis de Chavannes** (1824–94) who looked back further than any, to *quattrocentro* frescoes, adopting the forms and use of colour of the pre-Raphaelites (see the Hôtel de Ville, Panthéon and Sorbonne).

After Courbet, the salon next declared war on **Edouard Manet** (1832–83), who, like Corot, had suffecent means to withstand the thundering hostility his works provoked. When the salon jury of 1863 turned out so blatantly conservative that Napoleon III permitted a *Salon des Refusés*, Manet made Paris howl with outrage at the unclassical naked women in his *Déjeuner sur l'herbe*; his *Olympia* (1866) incited terrible derision (*see* Topics, p.55). Although Manet concentrated on undogmatic everyday subjects such as horse races and café life, his vision was, like Corot's, inspired by photography; it was his bold new technique, his novel but masterful handling of paint that offended the smoothies in the salon—and made him the idol of the Impressionists.

# Impressionism and Beyond: Paris Gives Birth to Modern Art

In 1874, in the studio of the photographer Nadar on Boulevard des Capucines, the *Société anonyme des artistes* held their first exhibition—yet another protest against exclusion from the salon. What set it apart from other protest shows were the artists exhibiting: **Degas, Renoir, Pissarro, Morisot, Sisley** and **Monet**. Monet's painting of a sunrise entitled *Impression: Soleil Levant* inspired the satirical paper *Charivari* to call the whole group **Impressionistes**—a name the painters adopted for their next seven exhibitions. The Impressionists were not as interested in the realism of photography as in the science behind it, the discovery that colour completely owes its existence to light. Influenced by Manet's undogmatic realism and painting technique, they made it their goal objectively to record what their eye saw in an instant. The Impressionists have been aptly compared to a group of scientists in a laboratory; each followed his individual research and offered a colourful vision of the new, modern Paris of the boulevards, as well as old French favourites: landscapes and pretty women. Unlike previous salon rebels, the Impressionists were born to be happy, and thanks to perceptive dealers such as Durand-Ruel their works achieved critical acceptance by the 1880s—although soreheads at the salon made sure that the state never gave them any commissions, or spent any money to purchase their works; one bequest to the state in the 1890s was rejected for containing too many Monets and Cézannes. Nearly all the magnificent paintings in the Musée d'Orsay are later gifts.

Impressionism became the benchmark that painters measured themselves against for the rest of the 19th century. Some of the most original artists committed the heresy of leaving Paris altogether: Gauguin, Emile Bernard and others moved to Pont-Aven and called their pictures 'Impressionist-Synthetist'. They exhibited them in a café just outside the 1889 Universal Exposition, shocking the mouldering salon (again) by claiming to portray their own innermost souls. Cézanne went home to Provence to work on structure, selling a few canvases (by size) through the Parisian colour dealer 'Père' Tanguey (whose portrait by Van Gogh is in the Musée Rodin). Artists who remained, or who were drawn to Paris, included **Georges Seurat** (1859–91), the most scientific of the postimpressionists, who invented pointillism to bring a new classical structure to art, 'to make Impressionism something for the museums'. In 1884 he took part in the founding of the *Salon des Indépendents*, open to all; those exhibiting included **Henri de Toulouse-Lautrec** (1864–1901), whose portraits of Montmartre and Paris's underworld have so powerfully affected the way the world looks at Paris, and **Henri Rousseau** (1844–1910), the first and greatest of naïve painters. At the same time, the expressive Romantic **Auguste Rodin** (1840–1917) was shaking sculpture awake from its stale neoclassical doldrums, causing furious controversies with his powerful, often radically distorted works—especially his *Balzac* on Boulevard Montparnasse.

In the 1890s the blithe Gay Paree of the *belle époque* was also the capital of *fin-de-siècle* decadence. Artists began to pour into the city, attracted by the *succès de scandales* of the Impressionists and postimpressionists (and the commercial success some were beginning to enjoy), while even the poorest could join in the bohemian life of the Latin Quarter and Montmartre, where studios, food, sex, wine, hashish and absinthe were cheap. Bourgeois taste remained as philistine as ever (even Baedeker's guide in the early 1900s suggested the historical murals at the Hôtel de Ville and the salon as the best of Paris's contemporary art), while dilettantes searched for ever more rare, exotic and exquisite stimulation—as in the works of **Gustave Moreau** (1826–98), who painted mythologies from his imagination, and in the followers of the Pre-Raphaelites, after Burne-Jones scored a big success in the 1889 Exposition. Most interesting of all are the works of **Odilon Redon** (1840–1916), who painted from his pre-Freudian dreams, and was much admired by Mallarmé and the Symbolists, although Redon declined to accept any labels.

An unfortunate side effect of the 'decadents' with their languid maidens and ambiguous sexuality is that they tainted a genuine renaissance in European design known in France as Art Nouveau. A revolt against the pseudo-historical architecture and interiors then popular in France, the aim of Art Nouveau was to create something completely new for the new century, to harmonize with the industrial age and to foster the collaboration of artists working in different media. Best known for its long flowing line, inspired by plants and the geometry of natural growth, Art Nouveau's complete devotion to craftsmanship put prices out of reach of the masses, and it never caught the popular fancy; after Oscar Wilde's trial, the Parisians looked askance at anything that recalled drooping lilies. The little success Art Nouveau had in Paris was mostly thanks to a German dealer in Oriental art named Siegfried Bing, who first introduced Japanese prints to Van Gogh and, inspired by Tiffany in New York, began to promote vases by **Gallé**, curvilinear furniture by Prouve, Vallin and Majorelle, and the virtuoso creations of **Lalique**, whose intricate, fairy-like jewellery, often in the form of dragonflies or beetles, delighted Sarah Bernhardt. La Bernhardt also loved to be depicted on the flattering Art Nouveau posters of **Alfons Mucha**, a Czech book illustrator living in Paris. On a larger scale, Maxim's (in 1899) and several cafés were decorated in the style, but Art Nouveau only reached the average Parisian thanks to Hector Guimard's métro entrances.

# 1900–40: Art Capital of the World

Among the poor bohemians living in Paris at the turn of the century were three painters inspired by the intense, pure colours of Van Gogh and the decorative Nabi group that grew up after Gauguin. **Henri Matisse** (1869–1954), **André Derain** (1880–1954) and **Maurice de Vlaminck** (1876–1958) first became known to the Paris public at an exhibition in 1905, when a critic labelled them Wild Beasts, or **Fauves**, for their uninhibited use of colour. Although Fauvism only lasted another three years, it was the first great avant-garde movement of the century and, as Matisse said, the one that made all the others possible.

The next movement followed quickly on its heels and lasted longer. In 1907, two hungry artists in Montmartre, admirers of the recently deceased Cézanne, **Pablo Picasso** (1881–1973) and **Georges Braque** (1882–1963), formulated Cubism, which liberated form in the same way that the Fauves liberated colour. Picasso and Braque aimed to depict the permanent structure of objects, and not the transitory appearance of the moment, by showing them from a number of angles at the same time. Championed by the poet Apollinaire, Cubism went through two distinct stages before the war: Analytical Cubism, up to 1912, where the forms are predominately geometric and colours muted, and from 1912 to the First World War, Synthetic Cubism, with stronger colours, greater sense of decoration, and the use of random elements such as newspaper clippings that eventually developed into collages. This second stage was originated by **Juan Gris** (1887–1927) who, like Picasso and Braque, also designed stage sets and costumes for Diaghilev's Ballet Russe.

In 1910 **Robert Delaunay** (1885–1941) painted his vibrant Cubist paintings of the Eiffel Tower, and two years later went a step further from the austere Cubism of Picasso, Braque and Gris to a lyrical style of brightly coloured, non-representational abstraction the poet Apollinaire called Orphism. Delaunay's closest follower was his Russian wife, **Sonia Delaunay** (1885–1979), who continued experimenting with bright colours and abstract forms. Orphism had a strong influence on German Expressionism and Italian Futurism, if little in Paris.

Other influences came as refugees from Eastern Europe found studios in La Ruche, the beehive-shaped pavilion salvaged from the 1900 Exposition, moved to Montparnasse by a mediocre, kind-hearted sculptor named Alfred Boucher who charged little or nothing to his impoverished 'bees'. La Ruche alumni make an impressive list, beginning with the Romanian **Constantin Brancusi** (1876–1957). In Paris since 1904, he was at first influenced by Rodin before abandoning naturalism altogether in 1907, carving simplified forms in stone to the point of abstraction; his wood sculptures evoke the powerful mysticism of Romanian folk art and inspired others to explore more fully the material they worked with (see the Atelier Brancusi at Beaubourg). Another gift to Paris from Eastern Europe was the Ukrainian **Osip Zadkine** (1890–1967), who took the multi-faceted aspect of Cubism to create powerful, expressive works, characteristically pitted with hollows and cavities (Musée Zadkine). **Marc Chagall** (1887–1985), with his dreamy Russian-Jewish paintings, brought figurative painting into the avant-garde, while the Lithuanian **Chaim Soutine** (1893–1943), through his thick, powerful use of paint, became one of the greatest Expressionist painters in Paris and had a strong influence on Francis Bacon. Another artist drawn to Montparnasse was **Modigliani** (1884–1920), whose linear, elongated figures are reminiscent of Botticelli.

Meanwhile Parisian **Marcel Duchamp** (1887–1968), who made the tradition of shocking the bourgeoisie a goal in itself, was causing the biggest outrage of all outrages at the 1913 Armoury Show (New York's introduction to modern art) with his *Nude Descending a Staircase*. In 1915 he outraged the public even further with his 'ready-mades'—everyday items such as toilet seats displayed as art to challenge the typical attitudes towards taste. His anti-art ideas had followers on both sides of the Atlantic: **Dada**, founded in Zurich in 1915, arrived in Paris after the war when **Picabia** and **Tristan Tzara** announced the fact to Gertrude Stein, one of the most perceptive avant-garde art critics and buyers in Paris (Ms Stein, however, wasn't going to have any part of anyone else's nonsense). The Dadaists made it their business to shock and scandalize in the good old Paris tradition, with events such as *The Vaseline Symphony*. In a cross-cultural exchange, American **Man Ray** (1890–1976), inspired by Duchamp in New York, moved to Paris, where his 'Rayograms' (making photographs without a camera) endeared him to the Dadaists.

In 1924 a new manifesto announced that Dadaism was dead and a new movement with deeper aims, known as Surrealism, would take its place. As its theoretician, André Breton, explained it, Surrealism was 'to resolve the previously contradictory conditions of dream and reality into an absolute reality, a super-reality'. The police had to be called to stop the riots at the first Surrealist show in 1925: exhibitors included Man Ray, Picasso, the Catalan **Joan Miró** (1893–1983) and **Max Ernst** (1891–1976); in 1929 the group was joined by **Salvador Dalí** (1904–89) whose knack for self-publicity made him the most famous and controversial member of the group. This was also the period when **Maurice Utrillo** (1883–1955) began to enjoy his first success for scenes of his native Montmartre, which he painted as therapy for a lifelong drink problem; self-taught, Utrillo is especially known for his handling of space and perspective. He was encouraged by his mother, **Suzanne Valadon** (1867–1938), who began as a painter's model for Renoir and Degas, and later achieved her own vigorous personal vision in Fauve colours.

## Postwar Paris

After the occupation, the Paris art scene reflected the grey, postwar malaise. Everyone seemed to be leaving for sunnier shores: Matisse had deserted for Provence in the 1920s, and was followed by Picasso and Chagall (although the latter returned to paint the ceiling of the **Opéra** in 1964). In the 1940s the explosion of Abstract Expressionism of de Kooning, Pollock and Rothko in New York stripped Paris of its position in the avant-garde, leaving the galleries in St-Germain to display the weary imitative abstract *école de Paris*. In 1965 the Ministry of Culture hoped to renew the success of La Ruche (which is still used by artists) by constructing a bland, new Cité Internationale des Arts near the Hôtel de Ville, though the results have been minimal.

The most important noises of the time were made by the anti-artists, such as **Jean Dubuffet** (1901–85), who engaged in open warfare with France's culture czars; in his art he rejected professional technique in favour of spontaneity and authenticity, which he called *art brut* (raw art), inspired by his collection of the works of children, prisoners and the insane. In the early 1960s a playful group of artists known as the Nouveaux Réalistes emerged, inspired by the everyday items presented as art in the style of Duchamp's 'ready-mades' and by a disgust for contemporary culture: **Niki de Saint-Phalle** (b. 1930), **Jean Tinguely** (1925–92), Bulgarian-American **Christo** (b. 1935), **César** (b. 1921), **Ben** and **Arman** (b. 1928) gave Paris in the 1980s some of its most important (and amusing) monuments. The current scene is best expressed in the thick, peeling layers of gallery posters on the walls of cafés and on billboards, each representing an exhibit with its own glittering *vernissage*, each discussed avidly for a moment before the next poster is pasted on top in an eternal search for the new.

# Architecture

*Paris is the only vast city with beauty imposed on her.*

Paul and Percival Goodman, *Communitas*

## The Parisian Style—Gothic

Nothing significant remains of Roman or Merovingian Paris. In the 12th century the city must have been packed with sumptuous churches and monasteries— though northern French Romanesque has little of the delight or high artistry of buildings in the south. In Paris's few surviving works (St-Germain, apse of St-Martin-des-Champs), you might even detect a touch of conscious classicizing.

The city's most famous secular Romanesque building, the lost 'Maison des Piliers' with its columned porch, seems to have been a serious attempt to re-create the Roman manner.

Many minds and hands contributed to the technological revolution of Gothic architecture, but the worthy Abbot Suger of **St-Denis** gets the credit for actually erecting the first building (1130–44). Suger wrote that he wanted to 'make what is material immaterial', a fine medieval sentiment, and Gothic builders did it with an amazing array of new advances: the pointed arch, bearing more weight than the old round ones, flying buttresses to restrain the outward thrust of a wall, complex vaulting to roof over large areas, stained glass and rose windows to give the new churches an undreamed-of sense of openness and lightness. A Gothic church *participates in the day*; the sun passing around its windows in its daily course creates a constantly shifting pattern of light and shadow. Its unprecedented and delicately balanced height, the product of both reason and passion, seemed to medieval Christians a mirror of the soul's striving towards God. Gothic cathedrals were meant as a microcosm of creation, including a little of heaven and a little of earth. Their decoration, in sculpture and glass, has a place for everything, from mundane affairs like the zodiacal signs and the farmers' 'labours of the months' to the more profound mysteries of Scripture. Unlike anything built before or since, they are works that one can spend a lifetime deciphering.

The first Gothic work in Paris proper was **St-Pierre-de-Montmartre** (1134); **Notre-Dame** was next, in 1163, and **St-Julien** on the Left Bank came three years later. Soon every town in the Ile-de-France was building one, and the style spread outwards from there to all of Europe.

The word 'Gothic', for what could be called Pointed, or French Classical, or 'Ile-de-France', is a term of disparagement invented by Raphael and the philistines in the 1500s, reflecting their Renaissance enthusiasm that was purposefully blind to all the ideas of medieval civilization. But in the 19th century, when romantics such as Viollet-le-Duc were trying to escape the mind-forged manacles of academic French architecture, they came to view Gothic as an aesthetic of freedom and individualism. It makes a fond fantasy, but nothing could be further from the truth. Gothic is *par excellence* the architecture of system and authority, controlled by the doctors of the Church; its beauty is the beauty of a civilization that had faith in itself, that balanced and measured all creation to reflect its beliefs.

**Sainte-Chapelle**, begun by St Louis in 1245 to house the precious relics he had brought back from the Crusades, is Gothic at the height of its power and sophistication: a small, simple building with walls over two-thirds glass, one so bright and full of colours it seems less a mere building than a spiritual vision. Because of the

Hundred Years' War and the long depression that followed, relatively little of medieval secular architecture survives: two beautiful, heavily restored mansions—the **Hôtel de Cluny** (1496) and the **Hôtel de Sens** (1475)—the **Conciergerie** and the 14th-century castle at **Vincennes**.

France continued and evolved its Gothic tradition as late as the 1600s. In the 14th–15th centuries it may be called **Flamboyant Gothic**, from the flame-like traceries in windows and sculptural decoration; **St-Germain l'Auxerrois** is a fine example. The last Gothic churches in Paris are clumsy bastards, half-medieval and half-Renaissance, with no sense that these two styles might be incompatible; buildings such as **St-Eustache** (1530–1640) have a certain charm nonetheless.

## A Renaissance Lost

With the Hundred Years' War came desolation and a national crisis of confidence; France wasn't quite in the mood for art in the *quattrocento*. The first truly Renaissance works in Paris were the **Fontaine des Innocents** and the **Cour Carrée** of the Louvre. An Italian would have said he was glad the French were finally catching on, but that the Louvre was a little over the top; Pierre Lescot's and Jean Goujon's ornate but harmonious Cour Carrée was nevertheless ahead of its time, and must have been closely studied by Baroque Italians. French noblemen were starting to build new Renaissance *hôtels particuliers* in the fashionable Marais, such as the 1544 **Hôtel Carnavalet**, now Paris's city museum.

## French Baroque and Academicism

Confidence most definitely returned with that excellent king, Henry IV. The Parisians bolted out of the gate with two remarkable compositions in the 1610s, the first of the *places royales* (squares built as a unified architectural ensemble, and usually dedicated to the ruling monarch): the **Place des Vosges** and the **Place Dauphine**. Claude Vellefaux, architect of the Place des Vosges, also built the 1607 **Hôpital St-Louis** in the same vein. Combining details from the Renaissance style-books with a French taste for brick, pitched roofs and gables, it could have been the birth of a lovely national style.

But France was still in a mood for imitation, and as before the new influences came from Italy. French Baroque, especially in Paris, is a trivial affair. The Counter-Reformation Church was promoting a new wave of religious building; with **St-Paul-St-Louis** in the Marais (1627) began the fashion for tepid reworkings of Roman architecture, and Italianate domes began springing up all over town (**Val-de-Grâce**, church of the **Sorbonne**). Where the Church had no hand, there could be interesting experiments, such as the pure and severe **Abbaye de Port-Royal**, begun in 1626 for Parisian Jansenists. In secular buildings, imported Baroque translated into a more restrained, more French manner; its leading exponents were François Mansart (additions to the **Hôtel Carnavalet**) and Louis le Vau (**Hôtel Lambert**, much of **Versailles** and the **Institut** on the left bank of the Seine, 1661). Italian landscape gardening was adapted to French tastes by André Le Nôtre (gardens at the **Tuileries**, **Vaux-le-Vicomte** and **Versailles**; his frigid compositions are the perfect symbol for a supercilious age that thought nature only existed to be improved upon.

Louis XIV and Colbert had long worked towards a total control of the arts, to ensure conformism and glorification of the regime. A turning point came in 1671, when they founded *Académies* of art and architecture to monopolize training in both fields. At the same time French architecture was reaching a strange sort of climax with the long postponed completion of the **Louvre**. In the beginning Louis and Colbert had called upon the King of Baroque himself, Gianlorenzo Bernini, to design the monumental façades that would surround the Cour Carrée. Bernini's foreign ideas and arrogance caused endless disputes; finally his plans were abandoned and the project was entrusted to Claude Perrault. The result, surprisingly, was a revelation, a remarkably original colonnade that has had a tremendous influence over everything built since in France, and many other countries too. Another strikingly original work of the same period was Libéral Bruant's proto-Rococo **Hôtel des Invalides** (1670).

Ten years later, however, Bruant's work was spoiled by the intrusion of a huge church by Louis XIV's pet architect, Jules Hardouin-Mansart; the **Dôme des Invalides** is an aimless, entirely derivative pile that the French to this day celebrate as one of the high points of their architectural achievement, perhaps because of its great size and gilded dome (Hardouin-Mansart can't really be blamed; he was merely a very successful social climber who took credit for work done by his staff— which explains how his name can be attached to a truly fine work, the **Grand Trianon** palace at Versailles). Another sign of the academic rot setting in was the **Observatory** (1668), also by Perrault. Here, the architect insisted so strongly on following contrived rules of aesthetics that the result was almost unusable by the astronomers.

Thanks to Louis and the tastemakers, French architecture was locked on a slippery slope to disaster. The new academic servitors of the state produced lifeless pastiches of classical columns and pediments, combined with traditional French rooflines and fenestration, the most famous example of which is the king's stupendous garden-folly at **Versailles**. The greatest absurdities began to appear in the 18th century: the church of **St-Sulpice** (rebuilt 1719–40) and above all Jacques-

Germain Soufflot's **Panthéon** (1755), also originally a church. One French critic has called this 'the first example of perfect architecture'. Yet it has no elements not borrowed from elsewhere, no coherence of the elements, not even the faintest notion of proportion or symmetry. Soufflot, like Hardouin-Mansart, was a salon conversationalist, not an architect; his Panthéon can barely stand by itself, and is closed to the public today while engineers try to save it.

Soufflot also distinguished himself by destroying much of the interior of Notre-Dame (besides knocking down part of the central portal, he took out most of the original windows and paving, whitewashed the walls and melted down the medieval altarpiece). This was only the most outrageous crime of an age that saw Paris's churches restored in the worst possible taste, wrecking more of the city's medieval heritage than the Revolutionary mobs would ever achieve. Not until the 1850s and Viollet-le-Duc would Paris even consider caring for its finest buildings.

## Neoclassicism

Ironically both St-Sulpice and the Panthéon were harbingers of an 18th-century reaction against the tastefully vacuous work of the Sun King's reign. The previous century was entirely 'neoclassical' in spirit, but by some corruption of language that term has come to mean the heavy, austere style that appeared in the *ancien régime*'s last decades. Still in the academic straitjacket, though influenced by the *Philosophes* and, above all, Rousseau, architects attempted an even more direct copying of ancient Greek and Roman forms, and found it somehow liberating.

The beginnings of this trend produced a good deal of dross, and two remarkable successes. First, Jacques-Ange Gabriel's **Place de la Concorde** (1755–75), not so much for the architecture as for a revolution in French planning—from a tightly-packed, introspective city to the expansive, horizontal and tree-lined Paris of today. Second was Claude-Nicolas Ledoux's 47 **barrières** for the new Farmers-General wall around the city. All are simple as pie, playfully recombining classical domes, cylinders, colonnades and pediments in such a way that each was a little demonstration exercise in itself, and each referred to all of the others. Only four survive (Place de la Nation, Place de Stalingrad, Parc de Monceau, Place Denfert-Rochereau) but you will see views of the others in the Carnavalet and other Paris museums.

Neoclassicism, appropriate to an age that strove for virtue, continued through the Revolution (when little was built), through Napoleon and into the restoration. Under Napoleon it reached its climax, with grandiose projects like the colonnaded **Rue de Rivoli** (1802), meant as a parade route for triumphal armies, the **Bourse** (A. T. Brongniart, 1808), the **Madeleine** (1806) and the **Arc de Triomphe** (1806).

# A Revolution in Iron

The creation of the Ecole Polytechnique in 1794 created a new sort of academicism, entirely separating the engineering side of architecture from the artistic. From then on, to learn architecture you had to attend the Beaux-Arts, the proud bastion of academicism. It was a fatal mistake. Paris, far ahead of any other European city, was on the verge of beginning a new architectural age, using durable, versatile iron and glass to make buildings fit for the Industrial Revolution and the new century dawning. As it is, Paris is full of brilliant works, daring and dazzling in the time when they were built, an achievement that everyone but the Parisians appreciates and honours today.

Glass roofs were being put up over narrow shopping streets as early as 1776; the first proposal for a purpose-built, glass light court came in 1780; someone had the idea of enlarging the Bibliothèque Nationale by covering its courtyard in this way, but Louis XVI's debt-ridden government could not find the funds. Revolution and war interrupted progress, though iron bridges like the Pont des Arts (1803) and the Pont d'Austerlitz (1806) appeared; the first of the **passages**, or arcades, were probably built in the 1790s (the Passage du Caire in the Sentier, the oldest survivor today, dates from 1799). Economic recovery in the Bourbon Restoration brought a mania for arcade building; the 1820s saw beautifully appointed ones such as the **Galeries Colbert–Vivienne** and the **Véro-Dodat**. Precursors of the modern department store, the *passages* numbered some 130 in 1840; only about a score of them remain today.

Other uses for iron and glass included churches, such as the graceful neo-Gothic **Ste-Clotilde** (1846), and more fittingly greenhouses (the **Serre du Jardin des Plantes**, 1830) and the railway stations, prime symbols of the Industrial Revolution that tried to marry the new technology to traditional French monumental architecture; the two that stand out are the Gare d'Orsay, by Victor Laloux (1900) and the Gare de l'Est (F. A. Duquesnay, 1847). The most surprising application—in libraries—was supplied by the visionary architect Henri Labrouste. His first experiment, the **Bibliothèque Ste-Geneviève** was but an exercise for one of Paris's greatest masterpieces, the main reading room of the **Bibliothèque Nationale**, an enormous, soaring ceiling of lovely intersecting domes, perching on the slenderest of iron columns.

Other architects came to realize the great potential for covering all sorts of spaces economically with iron, from the utilitarian market pavilions of **Les Halles** (Victor Baltard, begun 1851) to airy fantasies such as the all-glass **Jardin d'Hiver** in the Champs-Elysées. Both were among 19th-century Paris's most beloved landmarks and both have been demolished.

# Napoleon III and Haussmann: the Remaking of Paris

> *... nothing so sad as this immense rearrangement of stones by the hands of despotism, without social spontaneity. There is no more gloomy symbol of decadence. As Rome fell more deeply into its death-throes, its monuments sprang up more numerous and more gigantic. It was building its tomb, making itself beautiful for death.*
>
> Auguste Blanqui, a leader of the Commune

Few dictators anywhere have had such a will to build and transform, but then few dictators required people to address them as 'Emperor'. Louis-Napoleon knew nothing of this city where he had never lived before 1848, but to aid him he found a brilliant and forceful native Parisian named Georges Haussmann, whom he made Prefect of the Seine department, the post that had almost total control over every-thing in Paris. Much of their work was badly needed, almost philanthropic: sewers, gas mains, water supplies, new schools and several of the city's parks. When they were done, Paris was as up to date as any city in the world.

But another aspect of their plans for Paris proved a little harder to swallow. To facil-itate traffic, to enrich the unsavoury swarm of speculators that buzzed about the imperial throne, and to get the poor out of sight and out of mind, central Paris was nearly obliterated by a gargantuan programme of slum clearance and road building—Boulevards Sébastopol, St-Germain, St-Michel, de l'Opéra, Haussmann, among many others (the Prefect took care of himself; as Madame Haussmann once ingenuously remarked at a dinner party: 'It seems whenever we find a new house the government buys it to build a boulevard!'). No accommodation was made for the 200,000 or so displaced poor, who ended up in the new toadstool slums and shantytowns of the East End. And Haussmann showed absolutely no consideration for Paris's past; one of his most wanton crimes was the destruction of 80 per cent of the Ile de la Cité, the city's ancient heart.

Architecturally, it was the heyday of the Beaux-Arts, with eclectic regime show-pieces like the tasteless completion of the Louvre and Charles Garnier's mammoth **Opéra**. But just as modern technology was enrolled to support Napoleon III's tyranny, it had to do the same for his art. Garnier, like Soufflot, was no architect, and he never could have made this marble pile stand by itself—iron girders hidden under the frippery do the job.

## The Last Golden Age: 1870–1914

Recovery from the disasters of 1870–1 was slow, but by the 1880s the Third Republic was fostering good architecture once more. The 1889 Exposition was the apotheosis of iron, producing not only the **Eiffel Tower** but also the incredible **Galerie des Machines** (400m long), demolished in 1910. The tower is a magical apparition: a symbol for Paris, for its century, for all of modern industrial civilization—a building with no purpose, an ornament, yet one that delights everyone and makes intellectuals discuss and contemplate endlessly. By 1900, when Art Nouveau was beginning to flower, official architecture had lapsed back into eclecticism; a work such as the colonnaded, glass-roofed, lavishly decorated **Grand Palais** may seem to you magnificent or silly or both.

Sensuous, extravagant **Art Nouveau** seems a perfect match for the Paris of the *belle époque,* but in fact the style always met with a cool reception in a town still dominated by the Beaux-Arts. Many restaurants and cafés (like Maxim's) to this day have conserved their Art Nouveau decors, but as for buildings there are only a few choice works of Hector Guimard. Greatly influenced by Gothic restorer Viollet-le-Duc and his rediscovery of organic forms in architecture, Guimard is famous for

*29 Avenue Rapp*

his **métro entrances**, most of which are now gone. He also did some singular apartment blocks in the 16e: the **Castel Béranger** and others on Rue La Fontaine, **142 Avenue de Versailles** and **122 Avenue Mozart**. His Left Bank counterpart, Jules Lavirotte, similarly adorned the 7e: **Square Rapp** and **29 Avenue Rapp**.

Art Nouveau did have a big influence on another new feature of the Parisian scene—department stores. Since **Au Bon Marché** of 1876, these had been in the forefront of modernism, with huge light courts and grand staircases. At the turn of the century they accepted Art Nouveau in a big way; you can see what has survived at the wonderful **Samaritaine** and the **Galeries Lafayette**. This era also produced some surprises only tangentially related to Art Nouveau, including two unique churches: **St-Jean-de-Montmartre** (1894), with lattice-work arches of reinforced concrete, and **Notre-Dame-du-Travail** in Montparnasse (1891), a workingman's church with boldly exposed girders and rivets. Architects after 1900 put up some splashy buildings on **Rue Réaumur**, a busy street of the publishing and textile trades that would look entirely at home in Chicago (especially the block at no. 124, by Georges Chadanne, 1903).

## The 20th Century: From Classicism to the *Grands Projets*

Instead of carrying bravely on with modernism, however, Parisian architecture rapidly decayed into a heavy, tedious classicism—Louis XIV without the frills, as exemplified in the work of Auguste Perret (Théâtre des Champs-Elysées, 1911, Mobilier National at the Gobelins, 1931), and in the 1937 Exposition (Palais de Chaillot). After all the activity and successes in the last century, Paris has had almost nothing to contribute to the 20th. Even examples of important non-Parisian architects are few and uninspiring: the UNESCO building (1958) behind the Ecole Militaire, by Marcel Breuer, Pier Luigi Nervi, and Bernard Zehrfuss; a pavilion at the Cité Universitaire by Lúcio Costa (1959). There is a clutch of buildings, mostly houses, by the Swiss apostle of hypermodernism, Le Corbusier, austere buildings with large window areas (Villas Roche-Jeanneret, Square du Docteur-Blanche; Salvation Army Hostel, Rue Cantagrel).

Much more interesting than any of these are Le Corbusier's plans for Paris. So much did this man (and many of his contemporaries) hate the city, with its freedom and disorder, that he wanted to wipe it off the map. He submitted proposals for the never-built **Voisin Project** meant to create a new axis between the Gare Montparnasse and the Seine; most of the Left Bank was to be destroyed, and replaced with tidy rows of tower blocks. Paris's élite saved the Left Bank for itself, but after the Second World War it imposed Le Corbusier's totalitarian vision on hundreds of thousands of Parisians, 'rehoused' in some of the grimmest suburban concrete wastelands—wastelands constructed not by the bad intentions of politicians, or lack of funds, but entirely as a result of the messianic arrogance of men like Le Corbusier. Occasionally this sort of thing has sneaked inside the Paris boundaries, as in the redevelopments at Belleville or the Front de la Seine.

It was a good thing Paris had neither money nor ambition for much building up to the 1970s. Architects were still being trained almost exclusively in the Beaux-Arts until 1968, guaranteeing a maximum of conformity and an allergy to creativity. This shows best in the huge office project of **La Défense**, begun in 1958, though most of the large buildings are from the 1970s. Site planning has been notably unadventurous and unattractive, while the buildings themselves show the heavy influence of corporatist American firms such as Skidmore-Owings-Merrill. Paris suffered in many ways in the 1970s, from the destruction of Les Halles to the Right Bank expressway championed by President Pompidou, which turned one side of the Seine into a traffic chute. But the steadfast modernist Pompidou also stood Paris on its ear with Richard Rogers and Renzo Piano's **Pompidou Centre**, a controversial, high-tech structure that has won fans even among traditionalists.

With the 1980s and President François Mitterrand, both Paris and its tutelary state were desperate to make up for so much lost time. Thus the Pharaonic era of the *Grands Projets*: the **Grande Arche** at La Défense, the **Bastille Opéra**, the **Grand Louvre** renovation that includes I. M. Pei's Pyramid, the Science Park at **La Villette**, the museum conversion of the **Gare d'Orsay**, all by foreign architects. Frenchmen have been charged with designing the **Ministère des Finances** in Bercy and, biggest of all, the unfinished **Bibliothèque Nationale**. For a glimmer of optimism on the state of French architecture, the building that won the widest acclaim in the 1980s was Jean Nouvel's marvellously elegant **Institut du Monde Arabe** (1987) on the Left Bank. The same architect is preparing plans for a new cylindrical skyscraper at La Défense, meant to be the tallest in the world—but after years the plans are still on hold, and it may never get built.

## The Walks

Parisians invented the idea of walking the streets as an urban art form in the 19th century, and invented a verb for it: *flâner*, to stroll without any real purpose but to see and be seen. Sidewalk cafés were developed for sitting flâneurs to linger peacefully in the eye of the hurly burly urban hurricane. The essential was to go slow, to savour; in the 1840s it was considered elegant to walk one's pet tortoise.

If you've brought your tortoise, you'll have to multiply the walking times we've given by 300. But do take the lesson to heart: take your time. The city of light and fashion is self-consciously a spectacle, it is made to be looked at and admired, sometimes very arrogantly and pompously along its perspectives and *axes*; sometimes on a much more intimate, subtle scale—a cobblestoned courtyard, a cul-de-sac strung with ivy. Each of the eleven walks in this book hopes to reveal a different aspect of Paris, and only two—St-Germain and Expositions—are real bunion busters; but keep the latter in mind in stormy weather because it has half of Paris' museums, and the Invalides and Napoleon's tomb somehow come into their own in gloom rain and thunder. That is, if you haven't already visited Paris' primary indoor attractions: the Louvre, Musée d'Orsay, or La Villette's Science City.

Save Monday or Tuesday, when most museums close, for Walk I, historic Ile-de-la-Cité (Notre-Dame, the Conciergerie and Ste-Chapelle stay open), or for a stroll down memory lane in bohemian Montmartre (Walk VII), or through the *passages* (Walk IV). Wednesday through Saturday are best for: Walk III, Les Halles, the old Paris of merchants and markets (and the Pompidou Centre is open and not overly crowded); the Latin Quarter (Walk VIII) and nearby Jardin des Plantes/ Mouffetard (Walk IX), which look empty without the students; Walk V, the Opéra, the modern Paris of glitter, fashion and outrageous buildings. Sunday, when Parisian traffic dies down to a whimper (but the museums are packed), is a good time to explore the narrow streets of St-Germain and people-watch in the Luxembourg gardens (Walk X) or visit the 17th-century aristocrat quarter of the Marais and the modern yuppie fief of the Bastille (Walk II).

The Paris that refused to be squeezed into walks—the flea markets, La Villette, the Bois de Boulogne and Bois de Vincennes, Guimard's Art Nouveau buildings, St-Denis, most of the east end, Montparnasse and a quirky array of museums—will be found kicking about in the Peripheral Attractions section (*see* pp.345–80), arranged clockwise from the southwest fringes of the Right Bank around to the shadow of the Eiffel Tower.

**Start:** Ⓜ *Pont-Neuf*

**Walking time:** *less than an hour, but reckon on at least three to see Notre-Dame, Sainte-Chapelle and the Conciergerie.*

# I: Ile de la Cité and Ile St-Louis

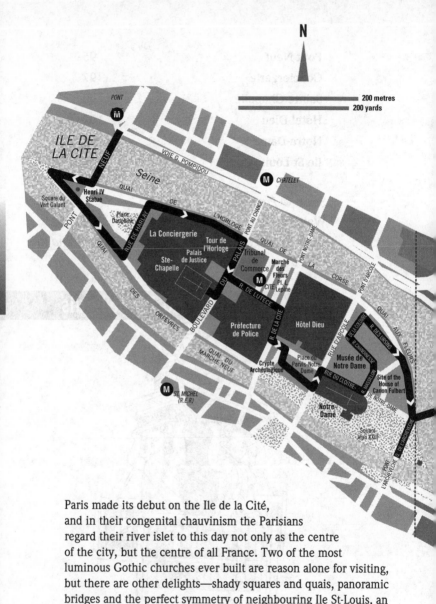

Paris made its debut on the Ile de la Cité,
and in their congenital chauvinism the Parisians
regard their river islet to this day not only as the centre
of the city, but the centre of all France. Two of the most
luminous Gothic churches ever built are reason alone for visiting,
but there are other delights—shady squares and quais, panoramic
bridges and the perfect symmetry of neighbouring Ile St-Louis, an
island-village of the *haute bourgeoisie*, concocted by 17th-century
speculators and architecturally little changed since. Over the

centuries institutions of law and health have gobbled up the rest of insular Paris—the Conciergerie, the infamous 'Ante-chamber of the Guillotine', the courts, the police and Paris' oldest hospital, the Hôtel-Dieu. But the sirens of their black marias and ambulances are whispers compared to the cacophony that used to rattle the Seine's bosom, when these were the most densely populated narrow lanes in Paris, and Parisians swarmed to hear the ballad singers on Pont Neuf or events like the *concert miaulique*, performed by 20 cats stuffed into a clavichord. On a Sunday morning, you can hear a distant echo of the old din in Place Lépine's twittering bird market.

## I: Ile de la Cité and Ile St-Louis

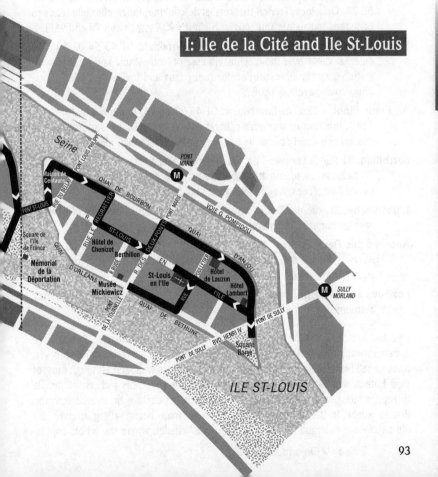

*If you do this walk in the morning, there are quite a few good spots for lunch near the end of it, on the Ile St-Louis; any of these would be a better bet than the touristy places around Notre-Dame.*

**Taverne Henri IV**, 13 Pl du Pont-Neuf, ✆ 01 43 54 27 90. Ancient, amiable wine bar in a Louis XIII building, where the Ile's lawyers feast on wines from Burgundy, *tartines*, charcuterie, boar sausage from Quercy; ask owner Robert Cointepas about Georges Simenon's last day on earth. Lunch around 100F (closed Sun).

**Au Rendez-vous des Camionneurs**, 72 Quai des Orfèvres, ✆ 01 43 54 88 74. Delicious, French-truckers'-style cooking; lunch clientele tends to be judges, journalists and cops; at night it's 90% gay (menu 78 and 95F).

**Brasserie de l'Ile Saint-Louis**, 55 Quai de Bourbon, ✆ 01 43 54 02 59. Has external views over the magnificent apse of Notre-Dame and a bar-view of a stuffed stork; an institution for rugby fans and lovers of old-fashioned *choucroute*; average 150F.

**Au Franc Pinot**, 1 Quai de Bourbon, ✆ 01 43 29 46 98. In a house dating from 1640, this former seamen's cabaret now offers the most serious food on this walk; ground floor wine bar; bargain gourmet lunch menu at 175F.

**Berthillon**, 31 Rue St-Louis-en-l'Ile. Queue up here for the best ice cream in Paris: 70 flavours, including an absolutely luscious chocolate (afternoons only; closed Mon, Tues, August and school holidays).

**L'Ilot Vache**, 21 Rue des Deux-Ponts. Lovely, old-fashioned and full of flowers, with an honest 120F menu that usually includes lots of seafood.

**Auberge des Deux Ponts**, 7 Rue des Deux-Ponts. The budget choice on the Ile St-Louis, with a 68F lunch menu that could include anything from onion soup to moussaka.

**Les Fous de l'Ile Saint-Louis**, 33 Rue des Deux-Ponts, ✆ 0143 25 76 67. Trendy tearoom, sometimes with live music; also a 75F lunch menu.

---

Like Rat and Mole in *The Wind in the Willows*, the 3rd-century BC Parisii were always messing about in boats, and they naturally found a river island a convivial place to call home. The Romans had a soft spot for it as well, and although most of their Lutetia was on the Left Bank, the palace of the governors and central temple to Jupiter stood here. When Clovis made Paris his capital, he moved into the Roman palace. In the 9th century, when the Normans began sailing up river, the old palace was enlarged to make the Cité Paris' citadel, where the whole population could take refuge. In 1194 Richard the Lionheart did his bit to make the Cité an administrative centre when he defeated Philippe-Auguste at Fréteval and burned all his archives; henceforth kings always kept copies of documents in the Palais de Justice. The kings remained in the palace until the 14th century, when Etienne Marcel's revolt suggested that living cheek by jowl with the fierce Parisians was no longer safe. Once they moved out to the Right Bank they rarely looked back, although the Cité remained Paris' administrative and religious centre, in the midst of the popular quarter described so vividly in Hugo's *Notre-Dame de Paris*.

If the revamping of the Ile de la Cité begun by Louis-Philippe and continued by Haussmann were 'progress' in any sense, then the Aztecs who queued up to have their hearts cut out by their priests were all the better for the operation. Extracting the dense medieval quarter from around Notre-Dame was especially cruel; 25,000 people who lived on a hundred colourful tiny streets were banished to the eastern slums, and although you can now see the cathedral from further away than ever, it will never look right without its proper setting, sad as a lone jewel in an empty box. Like the City of London and Wall Street, the area is dreary by day and deserted at night. Between the Conciergerie and Notre-Dame, only three huge buildings have replaced hundreds of houses, sixteen churches, three priories, docks and ware-houses, a prison, the Jewish ghetto, a hospital and a famous nest of prostitution called the Val d'Amour, the 'Valley of Love'.

> *From the métro, cross over to the Cité on the **Pont Neuf**, the longest and oldest bridge in Paris, but ever 'new' for its pivotal role in the city's urban evolution; in 1985 Christo paid it the ultimate 20th-century homage by wrapping it in white nylon.*

By the late Middle Ages, the ancient umbilical bridges tying the mother island to the banks of the Seine had become eternally jammed with traffic, and on 31 May 1578 the cornerstone for a new bridge was laid by Henri III. Like many master-pieces, it was born in tears; the eyes of the pontifex-king were noticeably red, having that very day buried two of his favourite 'Mignons', Quélus and Maugiron, who had self-destructed in a jealous duel; Parisian wags were quick to dub the new bridge the 'Pont aux Pleurs'. It was completed in 1605, and although often restored, retains its original form—minus Henri III's elaborate two-storey *Pompe de la Samaritaine* behind the second arch from the right bank, which drew water for the Louvre and Tuileries gardens. Before the advent of public fountains, the Pont Neuf marked the downstream limit where the city's 20,000 water carriers could legally draw water in the summer, but even then it was vile stuff, 'dirty, nasty, Ditch of a River', as visitor William Cole put it in 1765. The pump's memory lives on in the name of the department store (*see* p.170), and in the relief of the Samaritan woman at the well, one of the personnages and grotesques that decorate the Pont Neuf as seen from the river. Others portray the pickpockets, charlatans and tooth extractors who harangued, amused and preyed on the passing crowds. For throughout the 17th century, the bridge was *the* place to see and be seen in Paris: 'Pont-Neuf is in the city the way the heart is in the body, the centre of movement and circulation', wrote Mercier in his *Tableau de Paris*. When the police sought a suspect, they would post an agent on the Pont Neuf, and if after three days they failed to spot their man, they presumed he wasn't in Paris. A big attraction was the singers of satirical and anti-government ditties (the Pont Neuf was the only place where they were tolerated). Strollers could hire parasols at either end of the bridge, a sybaritic touch that shocked foreign visitors.

The Pont Neuf had the first raised pavements in Paris, a much appreciated innovation in the mucky era when *décrotteurs* (shoe and stocking de-turders) did a brisk business. It was also the first bridge without houses or shops, and opened up a view down the length of the Seine that enchanted Parisians and initiated the city's fetish with rearranging itself to form perspectives. Henri IV set the trend by incorporating the bridge in his new Place Dauphine (*see* below).

> *Little did the king suspect that his new Place Dauphine would be closed off on the Pont Neuf corner with his own memorial: the bronze equestrian **statue of Henri IV**, erected shortly after his assassination.*

The original figure of Henri was only half as good as that of his horse (presented to his widow Marie de' Medici by the great Tuscan sculptor Giovanni da Bologna). But artistic considerations never troubled the sleep of the mob of 1792, who smashed the horseman to bits. The next generation regretted their parents' fury, and in 1818 erected a new smiling Henri, recycling the bronze from the statue of Napoleon they had toppled off the Vendôme column. One worker in the foundry refused to see any humour in this salvaging of idols and secretly deposited Napoleonic propaganda and a statuette of the little emperor in the belly of the horse. Under the Second Empire the bronze horseman became the domaine of shoeshines, who moonlighted as clippers of the newly-fashionable poodles.

> *Steps from behind the statue lead down to the **Square du Vert-Galant**, the leafy prow of the Ile de la Cité.*

The Vert-Galant, or 'gay old spark' was a fond nickname for Henri IV, the most Parisian of kings and one whose incessant skirt-chasing endeared him to his subjects as much as his conversion to Catholicism. The weeping willow at the tip, trailing into the river, is traditionally the first tree in Paris to burst into leaf. The Square affords good views back to the Pont Neuf and its overdiligently restored carvings, and ahead to the **Pont des Arts** (1803), one of the first, and most elegant, iron bridges built in France. You can embark for a tour of the Seine's other bridges on a **vedette du Pont Neuf**, moored at the north end of the square.

In the Middle Ages, the Square was the tip of a muddy islet called Ile de Juif, a favourite place for burning Jews and witches, and used on 12 March 1314 for the execution of Jacques de Molay, the Grand Master of the Templars. Before going up in smoke, de Molay cursed his accusers, Pope Clement V and Philippe le Bel, and predicted (accurately) they would follow him to the grave within a year. As you go back up the stairs, note the **plaque** on the side of the bridge.

*Continuing from here along the south bank of the island, the curve of Paris' left thigh, as it were, is traced by the serene, bench-lined **Quai des Orfèvres**.*

This was originally a long wisp of an island connected to the Ile de la Cité in the 1300s; in the 1700s it was lined by the jewellers who gave it its name. One of them made the diamond necklace that embroiled the silly Marie-Antoinette, who would have surely been proved innocent in her lifetime had Georges Simenon's famous Inspector Maigret (office at no. 36 Quai des Orfèvres) handled the case.

*Turn left at the next corner, Rue de Harlay, which leads into the triangular **Place Dauphine**.*

After the Templar barbecue, the Ile de Juif was joined to Ile de la Cité and made into a royal garden; in 1607, Henri IV allowed Achille de Harlay, president of the Paris *Parlement*, to convert it into a square named after the dauphin, the future Louis XIII, on condition that he make it a set architectural piece like Place des Vosges. The design, a triangle of identical houses of brick and stone with façades facing both the square and the river, has been sorely tried over the centuries: the east side was demolished in the 19th century to set off the pompous façade of the Palais de Justice, and only houses nos. 14 and 16 preserve something of their original appearance. Gone too are the charlatans, including the famous Tabarin, inspiration for Molière's *Fourberies de Scapin* and father of all snake-oil showmen and modern commercial advertising; from 1624–34 Tabarin and his accomplices would amuse passers-by with skits of doctors and patients, or present plays in which the hero was duped—for the lack of a miracle drug, which was naturally offered for sale at the end of the performance.

Now it is quiet, a leafy triangle in the cold stone officialdom that has usurped the Cité. It has always seduced lovers of Paris, although it took surrealist André Breton to analyze the exact nature of Place Dauphine's charm: 'It is, without any doubt, the sex of Paris which is outlined in this shade.'

*As it was, the queen ended up, as you should, along the north bank of the island, or Quai de l'Horloge, at the **Conciergerie** (open, beyond the metal detectors, Apr–Sept 9.30–6.30, Oct–Mar 10–5; adm (joint ticket with Ste- Chapelle available); guided tours at 11 and 3pm).*

To set the mood for a building known as the 'Antechamber of Death', the first of three round towers you pass along the quay is the **Tour Bonbec** (1250), or 'babbler', where prisoners presumed guilty were put to the question, their memories jogged by the rack, the water torture (forced ingurgitation of hornfuls of water) or the boot (made of iron, in which pieces of wood were wedged). Justice could be swift; a trap door under the prisoners' feet waited to pitch them into an oubliette lined with razor-sharp steel spikes; the Seine washed their mangled bodies away.

The Conciergerie wasn't always so grim. In its first, 4th-century, incarnation it was the palace of Lutetia's Roman governors, a favourite retreat of Emperor Julian the Apostate. There was something of the proto-Parisian in Julian: his feckless attempt to bring back the old gods seems to have been less a serious belief in Zeus and Co. than a matter of *bon goût* and distaste for the clumsy Christian art of the day. Clovis requisitioned the palace *c.* 500, and established the Frankish monarchy within its walls; in 987 Hugues Capet moved in, and it stayed in the family for the next 800 years. As the kings grew wealthy, their palace grew ever more splendid, so that by the time Richard the Lionheart came to call on Philippe-Auguste, it resembled a fairy-tale miniature in the Duc de Berry's *Très Riches Heures*. The concierge after whom this section of the palace is named was no gimlet-eyed drab in dressing gown and slippers, but a powerful lord, appointed by the king to judge misdemeanours and help pay the royal bills by collecting the rents of the 200 boutiques on the ground floor.

In 1358, Etienne Marcel's partisans stormed the palace and assassinated the kings' ministers as the Dauphin Charles V stood helplessly by. It was a lesson in the vulnerability of the royal person in Paris that subsequent French kings forgot only at their peril; the immediate result was that Charles V ordered the construction of the less central and better fortified Louvre. Abandoned by the kings, the palace evolved into Paris' seat of justice and its prison. The concierge's job evolved as well: instead of boutiques he collected rent for cells and beds. In 1914 the Conciergerie became a public monument.

As you enter the first room, the Gothic **Salle des Gardes**, note the first pillar to your left. The capital is carved with scenes from the lives of Héloïse and Abelard, culminating in the scene of Héloïse clutching like a giant lollipop the part of her lover they were both to miss sorely (*see* below). Architecturally, the highlight of the Conciergerie is the adjacent room, Philippe le Bel's **Salle des Gens d'Armes** (1314), or guardroom, one of the largest Gothic halls ever built (229ft by 91ft). The spiral stair offered rapid access to the Throne Room above (now the Salle des Pas-Perdus); a passage under the stair leads to a **kitchen** (1350) built by Jean le Bon, with four enormous chimneys to placate the massive appetites of the royal household.

A grille separates the Salle des Gens d'Armes from a corridor called the **Rue de Paris**, named after 'Monsieur de Paris', a euphemism for the executioner during the Revolution. Here the poorest prisoners, unable to pay the price of the cell, slept on straw. A large percentage of the guillotine's more illustrious fodder passed through the dreary **Galerie des Prisonniers** just beyond: Marie Antoinette (whose cell has been reconstructed), Danton, Desmoulins, Charlotte Corday and St-Just. All would have their collars torn and hair cut in Paris' grimmest **Salle de la Toilette** before boarding the tumbrils. Upstairs are other reconstructed cells, a room listing the 2780 people condemned in Paris during the Revolution, the chapel where the unlucky Girondins feasted their last night on earth, and near the chapel a plaque marking the spot where Robespierre (whose favourite coat colour gave him the nickname of the 'seagreen incorruptible') spent his last hour in agony, with a jaw shattered from a failed suicide attempt, taunted by those who feared him only the day before; 'Yes, Robespierre, there is a God', one of his former colleagues commented drily as his head went plop in the basket.

> *From the Conciergerie, continue along the Quai to the square **Tour de l'Horloge**. In 1371 Charles V erected the first public clock in Paris here; later centuries joked that it ran 'comme il lui plaît', but though the innards have had to be replaced several times, it ticks on. The bridge here, the **Pont au Change**, was last rebuilt in 1639 and was originally lined with houses five storeys high, headquarters for financial wheeler-dealers in the days before the Bourse. Turn right onto the Boulevard du Palais for the **Cour du Mai**, the main entrance to the Palais de Justice.*

The Palais de Justice's façade conceals the Mercière, or gallery of shops that linked Sainte-Chapelle to the palace and provided, like the Conciergerie, rent money for the royal pocket. Although the name of the Cour du Mai recalls the May Day celebrations of Paris' lawyers, who in days of yore frisked merrily around a tree (a custom revived briefly with the Revolution's liberty trees) the courtyard is more sombrely remembered as the Conciergerie's loading dock, where the gorged tumbrils rumbled away to the clicking knitting needles of a hundred Madame Defarges.

> *To the left of the Cour du Mai's gate, pass through more metal detectors to visit a part of the Palais de Justice just as dazzling as the Conciergerie is grim: **Sainte-Chapelle** (same opening hours as Conciergerie).*

'There's a sucker born every minute,' said the great circus entrepreneur Barnum, who in a former incarnation must have lived in the Holy Land, bamboozling French crusaders into spending their hard-plundered cash on old bits of wood and bones. If all the existing pieces of the True Cross were refitted together, the result would be the size of a California redwood. The Crown of Thorns (one of several) was sold, miraculously intact, to Baudouin, 'Emperor of Constantinople', who had to pawn it to the Venetians. In 1239 St Louis redeemed it for 135,000 *livres*, and there was still enough change left in his purse to pick up other holy real McCoys (now all in Notre-Dame), including the staff of Moses, several drops of the Virgin's milk, Judas' lantern, the sponge dipped in vinegar, and the front half of John the Baptist's head, which was found by the French in the abandoned palace of the Caesars when they sacked Constantinople in 1204. Louis spent considerably less for the construction of this chapel.

You might say he got his money's worth. The cliché in every art book is that Gothic buildings *aspire*, in grace, lightness and height. Sainte-Chapelle, the ultimate Gothic building, has *arrived*. Here, as at Notre-Dame, you will lose any notion you might have had about the Middle Ages being quaint and backward. Every inch declares a perfect mastery of mathematics and statics, materials and stresses. To put it briefly, the upper chapel is nearly 65ft high, and almost three-quarters of its wall area is glass. Unlike the case with most of the great cathedrals, here we know the architect's name: Pierre de Montreuil. Not only did he design Gothic's master-piece, but he got it up in only thirty months and built it so well that not a single crack has appeared since the chapel was finished in 1248.

Sainte-Chapelle has an unusual plan, somewhat like a beaver lodge: the important part, the spectacular **upper chapel**, can only be entered from below, up a spiral stairway tucked in a corner of the **lower chapel**. As you go in, there's a clue as to why this double-deck arrangement was necessary—a flood marker from 1910 on one pillar shows how the Seine reached almost 6ft on this low-lying part of the island. Palace servants heard Mass in the lower chapel; the tombs belong to clerics of the 14th–15th centuries, and the painted decoration is 19th century.

Emerging from the narrow stair into the upper chapel is a startling, unforgettable experience. The other cliché in the books is that Sainte-Chapelle is a 'jewel box' for Louis' treasured relics; this too is entirely apt, even understated. Awash in colour and light from the tall windows, the chapel glitters like the cave of the Forty Thieves. The glass is the oldest in Paris (13th century), though much was restored a century ago according to the original designs. Of all the great French glass cycles, this one makes the most complete and concise 'picture Bible'. Almost all the major stories in both Testaments are represented:

On the **first bay** (from the entrance): *left*, Book of Genesis, including Adam and Eve and Noah's Ark; *right*, the Window of St Louis, comparing his relic-collecting with St Helen's discovery of the True Cross.

**Second bay**: *left*, Exodus, the life of Moses; *right*, David and Solomon.

**Third bay**: *left*, Laws of Moses; *right*, Book of Esther.

**Fourth bay**: *left*, Books of Deuteronomy and Joshua, Israel's wanderings in the desert; *right* Books of Judith and Job (underneath is King Louis's private oratory).

In the seven windows of the **apse**, from left to right: (1) Book of Judges, including the story of Samson; (2) Book of Isaiah and 'Tree of Jesse' (genealogy of Christ); (3) Life of the Virgin, the early life of Christ; (4–central window) the Passion; (5) John the Baptist; (6) Book of Ezekiel; (7) Books of Jeremiah and Lamentations.

And opposite the apse, in the **rose window**, the Book of Revelations.

Even when all the restoration is done, the chapel will never be quite as luminous as in St Louis' time. The windows on the left side are noticeably darker, because the philistines of the Paris *Parlement* built an extension of the law courts right up against them in the 18th century.

The atmosphere of the chapel is heightened by the lavish use of gold paint and the deep-blue ceiling painted with golden stars. This was part of the restoration, but in Louis' time it was probably much the same; this sort of heavenly decoration, fitting the Gothic sensibility so well, reached France in the 13th century, either from Italy or its original home, Byzantium. Beneath the glass are 12 *statues of the Apostles*; many are reconstructions, but the originals are wonderfully expressive works. The crosses they bear are 'consecration crosses', recalling the custom by which a bishop, when consecrating a church, would mark crosses on 12 of the pillars, to symbolize that the Apostles were the 'true pillars of the Church'. Above the statues are rare niello-work scenes of their martyrdoms.

On 19 May, St Yves's day, a Mass is celebrated in Sainte-Chapelle for the souls of all the lawyers who died during the year. St Yves, their patron, was a 14th-century ecclesiastical judge from Brittany who gave up his office to help the destitute. Before the Revolution he had his own chapel in Rue St-Jacques, next to a college for poor Breton scholars. Despite his obvious piety, the legend goes that St Peter refused to let Yves past the Pearly Gates because he was a lawyer, so he sneaked in. Peter ordered him out. 'Only if a bailiff serves me an expulsion order signed by a judge,' countered Yves. Peter combed heaven, but, unable to find any members of the legal profession there, was forced to let Yves stay.

> Before leaving the Palais de Justice compound, ascend the grand stair in the Cour du Mai and turn right for the hallowed, double-naved hall that represents the more run-of-the-mill Parisian lawyer's loftiest attainment, the **Salle des Pas-Perdus** *(open Mon–Fri 9–6)*. Balzac called it the 'cathedral of chicanery', where the law was 'spiders' webs that let the big flies pass through while the little flies get stuck'.

Originally the Great Hall of Philippe le Bel, the hall was rebuilt in 1871 and given its name, Pas-perdus (missteps) as a constant warning that it takes but one false step here to ruin a career (there's another Salle des Pas-Perdus in the stock exchange). In the afternoon, you can study the stride of lawyers flapping by in their raven gowns, especially around the **Première Chambre Civile**. This was originally St Louis' bedroom, and then the seat of Paris' *Parlement*, and during the Revolution, Fouquier-Tinville's Tribunal that sentenced over 2000 people to death in less than a year. The ornate ceiling was rebuilt in the style of Louis XII. To the right of its entrance, note the monument to the barrister Berryer—in the company of a tortoise, symbolizing the speed of justice.

> *Cross Boulevard du Palais for Rue de Lutèce, passing on the right the* **Préfecture de Police**, *where a plaque tells how, just before the Liberation of Paris, the police barricaded themselves inside and held off a bloody German assault (with tanks) for a week. Rue de Lutèce runs into* **Place Louis-Lépine**, *where a flower market offers a haven of dewy green fragrances in the desert of offices. The orchid stalls (in the first barn, off Rue de la Cité) are definitely worth a detour, or else you can get a 10ft potted palm as a souvenir of Paris. On Sunday mornings a bird market takes over, a tradition dating back to the birds sold in the Middle Ages on the Pont au Change. Paintings were sold along the bridge nearest here, the* **Pont Notre-Dame**, *of so mediocre a quality that 'peintres du pont Notre-Dame' was a term of disparagement.*

> *From the flower market, turn right on Rue de la Cité: the massive bulk to your left is the current incarnation of Paris' oldest hospital, the* **Hôtel-Dieu**, *founded in 660 by bishop St Landry.*

Despite the very best of intentions, the Hôtel-Dieu was for centuries a ripe subject for horror and black humour even beyond the borders of France. Patients could count on food and spiritual comfort, but until the 18th century, medical ignorance ensured that few who checked in ever checked out again. Financed by the revenue from hundreds of farms and houses in the Ile-de-France, private donations and a tax on theatre tickets, the hospital could hold up to 4000 patients. They were fed by kitchens equipped with spits able to roast 1200 pounds of meat at one time and served by a staff of selfless, utterly overwhelmed Augustinian nuns and a rotation of four priests always on duty to administer the last rites. Up until the 17th century there were never more than eight doctors and often as few as two for the entire hospital. Although they developed a knack for setting fractures and removing gallstones, they had less luck with amputations (performed without anaesthetic, in sight of all the patients). The beds of the Hôtel-Dieu were notorious for breeding disease and promiscuity, each designed for four to six people lying top to bottom; in the famine of 1692–3, 12 patients were squeezed into each bed, not to mention the four sprawled up on the canopies. At least their sheets, changed weekly, were as clean as the times could make them, thanks to the touching devotion of six nuns, the *petites lavandières* who spent every day of the year from 4am to 7pm up to their knees in the frigid Seine. Such was the daily rush to clear out the beds for new arrivals that attendants sometimes dumped invalids who had merely fainted into the cemetery carts, and more than once the funerals were interrupted by indignant protests from the pile of corpses.

> *Follow Rue de la Cité and turn left into the **Place du Parvis-Notre-Dame**.*

In the Middle Ages, the miracle plays and mystery plays put on by the confraternities were one of the major public entertainments. Often they were held here, where the magnificent porch of the cathedral could serve as 'Paradise', a word that over the centuries got mangled into *Parvis*. In those pre-Haussmann days, the Parvis was only a quarter the size it is now, and strollers down the web of lanes that once twisted here would marvel at the sudden sight of Notre-Dame looming up impressively before them. Note the bronze arms of the city and compass rose encrusted in the Parvis: this is Point Zero, the *umbilicus* of France from where, theoretically, all the national roads begin, and all distances are measured.

> *To the right of the Parvis, where the Hôtel-Dieu originally stood, French schoolchildren make a beeline to a 19th-century swashbuckling **statue of Charlemagne**, who with his great moustaches could pass for the blacksmith in Astérix. Traced in the Parvis is the former route of Rue Neuve de Notre-Dame, laid out by Louis VII in the 12th century. When new, this was the widest street in Paris—all of 21ft across. If you want to see what was underneath it, go down to the **Crypte Archéologique du Parvis-Notre-Dame** (open daily 10–6.30, till 5.30 Oct–Mar; adm; discount ticket with the towers of Notre-Dame available).*

What was begun as an underground car park in 1965 had to become a museum when the excavations revealed the 3rd-century wall of Lutetia, traces of Roman and medieval houses, 17th-century cellars, the Merovingian cathedral that preceded Notre-Dame, and foundations of the 1750 Enfants Trouvés, or foundlings hospital, where unwanted children were left on a revolving tray. The archaeological work is faultless, and the foundations are labelled and explained with fastidious care, helping visitors to sort out easily this 3-D puzzle of stones covering over 1500 years of history. But in truth there simply isn't much to see down here.

> *The Parvis today is one of the great tourist magnets of Europe, with eternal swarms of folk in silly hats moping about and videotaping the cathedral, as if they expect it to start dancing. A few will probably bump*

*into you as you gaze up at the gargoyles and the kestrels diving around the towers of the 'parish church of France', **Notre-Dame** (open daily 8–7 pm. Part or all of the cathedral will occasionally be closed for services; there are guided tours of the cathedral in English, Wed at noon. In French, daily exc Sun at noon, daily exc Sat at 2.30, also Thurs, 6pm).*

## Notre-Dame: Creation

This site has been holy ever since Paris was Lutetia, when a temple to Jupiter stood here (part of an altar, discovered in 1771, is in the Musée Cluny). In the 6th century, under Childebert, a small church was erected on what is now the Parvis, dedicated to the Virgin, St Etienne and St Germain. Sacked by the Normans in 857, it was quickly reconstructed but on the same scale, hardly large enough for the growing population of the Cité. A proper cathedral had to wait for Maurice de Sully, who became bishop of Paris in 1160; he raised the funds in spite of St Bernard, who preached jeremiads against such a worldly undertaking.

Cities all over France were beginning great cathedrals, soaking up plenty of money that had formerly gone to finance monastic empires like Bernard's. Notre-Dame came along on the crest of the wave; its architecture was destined to become the consummate work of the early Gothic, the measuring stick by which all other cathedrals are measured, and judged either a bit green or a bit overripe. Because it was in Paris, the cosmopolitan centre of learning, Notre-Dame had a considerable importance in diffusing Gothic architecture throughout Europe; for over two centuries its construction site was a busy, permanent workshop, through which passed the continent's most skilled masons, sculptors, carpenters and glassmakers. Plans changed continually, as new ideas and new problems came up. The first masters, responsible for the basic design, remain unknown. Later masters included Pierre de Montreuil, architect of the Sainte-Chapelle, who contributed most of the side chapels, the crossings and the Porte Rouge.

By 1302 the works were complete enough for Philippe le Bel to open France's first Estates General, or national parliament. Henry VI of England was crowned here in 1430; seven years later Charles VII was present at a solemn Te Deum to celebrate the retaking of Paris from the English. French coronations commonly took place at Rheims; the next one here would not come until 1804, the pompous apotheosis of Emperor Napoleon, brilliantly captured in the famous propaganda painting by David. According to Rabelais, the cathedral even played a part in the naming of Paris: his giant hero Gargantua, on a tour of the city, was so plagued by busybodies ('For the Parisians are such simpletons, such gapers and such feckless idiots that a buffoon, a pedlar of indulgences, a mule with bells on its collar or a fiddler at a crossroad will draw a greater crowd than a good preacher of the Gospel') that he sat on the towers of Notre-Dame and declared he would 'give them some wine, to buy my welcome. But only in sport, *par ris*. With a smile, he undid his magnificent codpiece and, bringing out his John Thomas, pissed on them so fiercely that he drowned two hundred and sixty thousand, four hundred and eighteen persons, not counting women and small children'.

During the Revolution, the Parisians had first trashed Notre-Dame, wrecking most of its sculptures; then they decided to demolish it. A few subtle voices stood up for its 'cultural and historical value' and the cathedral was saved to become the 'Temple of Reason', where Reason's goddess, a former dancer, held forth. But while Notre-Dame could still be filled with crowds for political or religious pageantry, little upkeep had taken place for centuries. The building was literally falling to bits, its statuary eroding away, when Victor Hugo, with his novel *Notre-Dame de Paris*, contributed immeasurably to a revival of interest in the city's medieval roots. Serious restoration work began in the 1840s.

Eugène Viollet-le-Duc, a man who spent his life trying to redeem centuries of his countrymen's ignorance and fecklessness, worked the better part of two decades on the site. His approach to restoration, especially to repairing the damage from the Revolution, was not scientifically perfect, but still far ahead of its time. Viollet-le-Duc's workshops produced original sculpture, attempting to capture the spirit of what had been destroyed or damaged instead of merely copying it. Since his time, Notre-Dame has continued to mark the important events in Paris' history, up to the celebrations of the liberation on 26 August 1944, when a mysterious sniper took pot shots at de Gaulle.

## Façade

No one in the 18th century is ever recorded as having said a kind word about Notre-Dame, but the men of the Enlightenment could well have taken a lesson in form from the cathedral's powerful **façade**, a marvel of visual clarity and symmetry, as disciplined as a Napoleonic army and rather more graceful. To see this façade as it was intended, remember that, as with the temples of ancient Greece, originally all the statues and reliefs of a Gothic church were painted in bright colours. The statuary begins at the level of the rose window: *Adam and Eve*, on either side of the rose, and the *Virgin flanked by angels*. Below these, running the length of the façade, is a row of 28 *kings of Judah and Israel*, the ancestors of Jesus. By the 1700s, popular belief held them to be kings of France, and all got their heads knocked off during the Revolution. A royalist surreptitiously buried them in his cellar; they created a stir when found twenty years ago, and can now be seen in the Musée Cluny; the present kings are re-creations by Viollet-le-Duc.

Below the kings are the three portals, interspersed with four framed sculptural groups: *St Stephen* on the left; the *Church and Synagogue* on the two centre piers, representing the 'true and false revelations'; and on the right pier, *St Denis*.

The **left portal** is dedicated to the Virgin Mary, a lovely composition *c.* 1210:

The tympanum is on three levels: the Coronation of the Virgin (on top), her Resurrection, and some of the kings and prophets who were her ancestors, with the Ark of the Covenant. Above are figures of angels, kings and prophets; below, the large statues of (unidentifiable) saints were replaced after designs by Viollet-le-Duc. Flanking the doors is a charming set of the *zodiacal signs* with the *labours of the months* corresponding to them. This is very common on medieval church doors, and one of the few secular subjects allowed in French Gothic works. In the Middle Ages, the New Year commonly began with the spring equinox; here though, that date is marked by Pisces instead of Aries. Someone in medieval Paris knew enough astronomy to correct the obsolete works of Ptolemy and the other ancients. The sculptors here got it right; most other cathedrals (and all modern astrologers) have it wrong.

The **right portal**, dedicated to St Anne:

This is the earliest of the portals (mostly *c.* 1170), and much of the sculpture may have come from an earlier church of Notre-Dame that stood where the apse of the cathedral is now. Why St Anne, the mother of Mary? Everything about the sculptural theme of Notre-Dame pertains to the Virgin, and the scenes here recount the earlier part of the story finished on the left portal. On the tympanum, scenes from the life of St Anne and Mary, below the *Virgin in Majesty*, flanked by figures once (erroneously) believed to be King Louis VII and Bishop Sully, the cathedral's founders; below, you'll recognize the *Annunciation*, the *Nativity* and the *Adoration of the Magi*. On the trumeau (the pillar between the doors) is a strange sculpture (redone) of St Marcel trampling a dragon.

The **central portal**, of the Last Judgement:

The largest and most impressive of the three, this was finished *c.* 1220. Even though everything else in the cathedral proclaims the glory of the Virgin, centre stage is nevertheless held by Christ, overseeing the distribution of saved and sinners. The surrounding angels bear symbols of the Passion, to remind us he saw some trouble too. From the bottom of the tympanum, the dead rise up and separate into upper and lower destinies. Note St Michael weighing souls, next to the Devil at the centre; this is an ancient motif that can be traced back through Venetian and Byzantine art to its roots in ancient Egypt. A statue of Christ occupies the trumeau; this, like the bottom levels of the tympanum, is a replacement since Soufflot (architect of the Panthéon) knocked out the original in 1771. This is painful, the thought of the hack of all hacks in the smug 18th century laying hands on Notre-Dame; he did it to make room for a processional cart to pass through. Viollet-le-Duc again designed the replacements. The saints that flank the door stand above small medallions picturing *virtues and vices*.

But besides all these biblical figures, save some of your attention for the floral fantasies that provide the trim around them. Both inside and out, there is much excellent work in this vein, closely modelled from nature in springtime; scholars have noticed a preference for plantain, cress and celandine in this church, while Sainte-Chapelle is full of the leaves of *ranunculus*, or buttercup.

Such fine portals deserve doors to match. The hardware and hinges for those on the left and right, still in good nick today, were made by an ironsmith named Biscornet. They are quite artistically done, and a little mysterious; to this day no one has figured out how he forged them. Biscornet never let anyone watch while he worked, and a legend grew up that he sold his soul to the Devil for help with this important commission. Once installed, the doors refused to open until holy water was splashed on them; the mortified smith fled Paris and died soon after. Biscornet's central door, replaced long ago, witnessed the curious marriage of Henri IV and Marguerite de Valois in 1572; not yet in the good graces of the Church, Henri stood just outside the door, Marguerite just within.

## Inside Notre-Dame

We can only guess what the interior furnishings looked like in the days before the Revolution. In the Middle Ages, when cathedrals were the great public living rooms of the cities and always open, there would have been no chairs, of course, just rushes strewn on the floor to soak up the mud from the hordes of people who passed through daily, gabbing, gambling, making business deals, eating their lunch, waiting for the rain to stop or listening to the choir practice—throughout the Middle Ages Notre-Dame was the musical centre of Europe, where much of the new polyphonic method was invented.

Despite the usually grim demeanour of the Parisian Church, people managed to have fun in Notre-Dame, especially at the Feast of Fools, when the hosts of clerics and lay people attached to the cathedral, including even the boys in the choir, would elect a mock bishop, make half-naked processions through the Cité (satirizing the parades of flagellants and other kinky penitents) and then celebrate a mock Mass, burning manure in the censers, before a night on the town with the rowdies and whores. After a few days of this, they would top it off by putting on utterly tasteless theatricals for the people of Paris, often a sort of bacchanal starring people dressed as monks and nuns. Originally this was an annual affair, but everyone liked it so much that by the 1500s they were doing it four times a year.

The decorations of the altar and chapels were certainly more colourful and artistic than anything there now. Besides the gifts of kings and nobles, the city guilds competed ardently to embellish the cathedral for centuries. A late survivor of this tradition was the *may* of the goldsmiths, originally a live tree brought each year at May Day, later a tree of gold, and finally, up to 1709, a painting for one of the chapels. The guild went broke in that year, thanks to Louis XIV and his war taxes; some of the *mays* can still be seen; there are two in the two chapels nearest the entrance in the right aisle.

Not all the decor was entirely religious. From an ancient custom, French generals victorious in battle were known as the *tapissiers* (drapers) *de Notre-Dame* for their habit of hanging captured flags and banners high in the nave. One of Notre-Dame's greatest marvels, a colossal Gothic statue of St Christopher, was removed by the clergy in 1785. It was considered good luck for travellers to see Christopher before a journey, so he was always made larger than life, but Notre-Dame's statue was exceptional—the congregation entered beneath his legs, heads brushing against his testicles for even more good luck.

Today, we must be content with the architecture and the remnants of the stained glass, but it's more than enough. And it's big enough: 430ft long, with room for some 9000 people, acccording to Viollet-le-Duc's calculations. The plan set the pattern for the other cathedrals of the Ile-de-France: a wide nave with four side aisles, which curve and meet around the back of the altar. The side chapels were not original, but added in the 13th century to hold all the gifts pouring in from the confraternities and guilds. Today, sadly, there is not a single noteworthy painting or statue in any of them.

Most of the chapels were remodelled to suit the tastes of the 17th and 18th centuries, or wrecked in the Revolution. But this is nothing compared to the two incredible acts of vandalism committed in the age of the Big Louies. In the 18th century, nearly all of the stained glass was simply removed, to let in more light. And in 1708, the scoundrels began wrecking the high altar and choir. Louis XIII, slow in the sack and without an heir after 23 years of marriage, had vowed to dedicate all of France to the Virgin if she would do something about the problem. Louis should have wished for a watermelon, since the best Mary could come up with was the unspeakable Louis XIV. To thank the Virgin for being born, the Sun King ordered the florid, carved-wood choir stalls, and a complete rebuilding of the choir, including a new altar, flanked by statues of His Majesty himself and his father. What could be more fitting for a Christian altar? It's interesting that no bishop since has had the nerve to remove them.

Thank God at least he spared the original choir enclosure, lined with a series of 23 beautiful **reliefs of the life of Christ**, done *c.* 1350 by Jean Ravy and his nephew

Jean le Bouteiller; recently these have been repainted to approximate their original appearance. Another rare survivor stands at the entrance to the choir, a fine 14th-century statue of Mary and child.

We can be even more thankful they didn't take out the three great **rose windows**. The one in the west front, heavily restored by Viollet-le-Duc, expresses the message of this cathedral's art even better than the portals: the Virgin sits in majesty at the centre, surrounded by the virtues and vices, the signs of the zodiac and the works of the months—all the things of this world. In the left transept rose, Mary is again at the centre, in the company of Old Testament prophets, judges and kings. In the right transept rose, a truly remarkable composition, she dominates the New Testament, amid the Apostles (in the square frames) and saints. As for the rest of the windows, much of the dull grey glass of the 18th century has been replaced, since 1965, by stained glass in abstract patterns, done with genuine medieval colours and techniques—but in a building where art is so meticulously organized, they still look a bit out of place. The fabulous organ (1867), back on line after an 11-million franc restoration and computerization, thunders like no other instrument in France (concerts on Sunday afternoons).

To the right of the choir is the entrance to the **Trésor de Notre-Dame** (*open Mon–Sat 10–6, Sun 2–6; adm*); with excruciating 19th-century reliquaries and chalices, mostly donated by Napoleon III. Other exhibits include St Louis's linen tunic, cameos of all the popes up to Pius X, items related to the three archbishops assassinated by the Parisians and choir books. The Crown of Thorns and all the other relics moved here from Sainte-Chapelle are displayed only during Lent and Holy Week by the Knights of the Order of Saint Sépulcre, founded in 1099.

> *Leaving the cathedral, turn right and right again, following the northern side of the cathedral along Rue du Cloître-Notre-Dame. Originally all of the island east of Rue d'Arcole was occupied by Notre-Dame's cloister, a veritable city within the city, enclosing 46 canons' houses, a round baptistry, a dozen small churches, as well as an episcopal school where Peter Abelard, St Dominic and St Bonaventure taught—hallowed land now occupied by police garages.*

> *At the beginning of Rue du Cloître signs beckon you to ascend the **Tours de Notre-Dame** for the Quasimodo's-eye view over Paris and a chance to eyeball the gargoyles at close quarters. (open 9.30–12.45 and 2.30–4.30, summer 10–5.30; adm 30F).*

> > *L'insatiable Vampire, l'eternelle Luxure,*
> > *Sur la Grande Cité convoite sa pâture.*

Over the great city, the insatiable vampire—eternal Luxury—longs for his pasture.

These lines appear under an engraving of one of the Notre-Dame monsters by Charles Méryon; you'll see it down the street in the Notre-Dame museum. Méryon was one of the great French artists of the early 19th century, a visionary who laid bare the darker side of the Parisian psyche in his scores of weird prints, showing the city's rooftops amid clouds of sinister black birds. Of course the French have forgotten him completely, and few of his works are displayed anywhere in Paris.

One of Méryon's favourite subjects was the incomparable gallery of spooks that inhabit the upper regions of Notre-Dame (they are *not* gargoyles). The one in the engraving is an intelligent-looking winged demon called the *Stryge*. Like the others, he is the work of Viollet-le-Duc, a brilliant re-creation of the original monster eroded to a smooth lump by centuries of wind. No one has ever come up with a satisfactory explanation for the hordes of fanciful beasts that inhabit medieval churches. They have no didactic religious meaning, and probably no esoteric meaning. They seem mere flights of fancy, though if you can pick these out from ground level, they are disconcerting enough. A Gothic cathedral is the microcosm of the Christian cosmos, and on its fringes lurk these wise, rather serene-looking creatures of the air: perhaps evil, perhaps only hinting of things undreamt of in the Christian philosophy.

To see them, you'll have to climb 238 steps. But it's worth it, not only for the monsters, but a great view over the city. There are also the bells. In the south tower hangs a big-bellied one named the Bourdon, its 13,000 kilos packing a mighty F sharp heard only on holidays; in the north tower, the largest weighs over 2 tons, made from melted-down Russian cannon captured at Sebastopol in the Crimean war. Her name is Angélique-Françoise, and she rings a C sharp. On the way up, there is a video presentation about the cathedral.

> *Rue du Cloître continues to the little* **Musée de Notre-Dame** *at no. 10 (open Wed, Sat and Sun 2.30–6; adm).*

This isn't a state museum, which explains its unusual opening hours. It is run by a society of friends of Notre-Dame, charming people who like to explain things to visitors and tell stories. The exhibits, mostly old prints, views, photos and plans, are quite fascinating, offering a wealth of detail on the history of the building and the quarter. There are drawings by Viollet-le-Duc (and a photo of him standing next to the *Stryge*), pictures of the old streets before Baron Haussmann demolished them, along with disappeared churches such as St-Landry and La-Madeleine-en-la-Cité. There are exhibits on the goldsmiths' *mays*, and scenes from the many royal funerals Notre-Dame has witnessed, when the cathedral was literally filled with candles and hung with sombre draperies.

*Almost directly across from the museum is Notre-Dame's **northern portal** (c. 1250), or Portail du Cloître, since it led to the cathedral cloister.*

The tympanum shows scenes from the childhood of Christ and illustrates the unusual legend of Deacon Théodore, who sold his soul to Old Nick but was saved by the grace of Mary; beneath, a figure of the Virgin is the only complete statue that survived the wrath of the Revolutionary mobs. Just to the left is another door, the **Porte Rouge**, from about the same date, with another Coronation of the Virgin on the tympanum, and various reliefs of the early 13th century to the left.

*If you're pressed for time, continue to Square Jean XXIII and Notre-Dame's apse; otherwise, take a dip into what's left of the old Cité by turning left on to **Rue Chanoinesse**, with the last two canons' houses to escape demolition (nos. 22 and 24), while the building where the police park their motorcycles replaces the shops of a pair of 14th-century Sweeney Todds, a barber and a pastry cook.*

The barber slit the throats of foreign students lodging in the canons' houses, while the pastry cook pounded and seasoned their flesh into a pâté reputed throughout Paris for its quality. Their diabolical little enterprise was given away by a German student's faithful dog, who witnessed his master's fate and barked night and day in front of the barber's shop, until residents became suspicious and questioned the barber closely. The story eventually leaked out and the partners in cannibalism were burned alive at the stake.

*From Rue Chanoinesse, turn right into ancient Rue de la Colombe.*

Its name (see the old plaque) dates back to the 1220s and a story of devotion that touched the heart of all Paris. A Breton stonemason who lived here while building Notre-Dame kept a pair of doves by his window. The Seine flooded and wrecked his house, and although the male dove managed to escape from the cage, the female was stranded in the debris, out of reach and doomed to starvation. But her mate refused to abandon her, and brought seeds for her, and even a hollow hay straw filled with water so she could drink. When the female was finally rescued, all the birds on the isle celebrated, according to the chronicles, 'like a dance in the sky'. You can trace Lutetia's Gallo-Roman wall along the top of no. 6, while the romantic little La Colombe restaurant conserves the doors and barrel vault of the Taverne Saint-Nicolas, founded in 1250.

*Turn right down Rue des Ursins, with a number of old houses, to **Quai aux Fleurs**, where at no. 9 a plaque and a pair of busts mark the site of the house of Canon Fulbert, the spiteful uncle of Héloïse.*

In 1118, in the golden age of troubadours, Héloïse was 18, and beautiful and intelligent enough to attract the attention of Notre-Dame's most brilliant scholar, Peter Abelard, then 38 years old, with such a reputation for continence and learning that when he approached Fulbert for lodgings, the old man quickly agreed, and asked in lieu of rent that the scholar tutor his bright young niece, 'authorizing me', wrote Abelard, 'to see her any hour of the day or night and punish her when necessary. I marvelled with what simplicity he confided a tender lamb to a hungry wolf ... well, what need to say more: we were united first by the one roof above us, and then by our hearts'. Abelard was a talented harper, and soon his love songs to Héloïse were being sung all over Paris, beautiful songs 'that would have drawn the soul of any woman', as Héloïse herself described them.

The trouble began when Héloïse became pregnant; Abelard took her off to his sister's in Brittany, where she gave birth to a son whom, trendy young couple that they were, they named Astrolabe. Abelard asked Héloïse to marry him, a proposal she strongly resisted, believing such a great philosopher should not tie himself down to one woman, and warned that even marriage would not appease her uncle Fulbert's anger. But Abelard insisted, and a few months later, sure enough, the canon sent his heavies to 'punish me where I had most sinned' as Abelard admitted later. He took orders as a monk at St-Denis and Héloïse obeyed his command to become a nun, but was never reconciled to her vows and never stopped loving Abelard. After ten years in the convent, she sent him a letter, asking why he no longer even wrote to her, and ending: 'I can expect no reward from God, as I have done nothing from love of Him. God knows, at your command I would have followed or preceded you to fiery places. For my heart is not with me, but with thee.' In response to her confession of rapturous love, Abelard cowered back into his sacraments, and composed a prayer for her, asking God to save both of them from a hell she cared nothing for.

> *Follow Quai aux Fleurs around to Quai de l'Archevêché and the eastern tip of the island. Until it was burned during the 'Three Glorious Days' of 1830, the archbishop's palace stood in **Square Jean XXIII**, concealing much of the magnificent soaring apse of Notre-Dame.*

When Viollet-le-Duc built the archbishop a medievalish house south of the cathedral, the Square was left clear, embellished with a 19th-century fountain of the Virgin and a bust of the Venetian playwright Goldoni, who died in Paris in 1791. Have a look at the apse; this is one of the few churches anywhere with a back end as beautiful as the front. The slender, delicate 312ft **spire** at the crossing, the highest part of the cathedral, can only be seen clearly from a distance. You'll never see the little figures at its base, but one of them bears the features of Viollet-le-Duc, who rebuilt it. Even more astounding than this—as their proud architects no doubt meant them to be—are the **flying buttresses** that support the walls of the nave, 50ft arches of stone seemingly hanging in the air.

> *Tour bus whales beach in rows on the east side; beyond them, on the tip of the island, vigilant mallards guard the stark **Mémorial des Martyrs de la Déportation** (open daily 10–12 and 2–5, till 7 in the summer).*

Dedicated in 1962 by General de Gaulle, this is a solemn, moving memorial to the 200,000 French residents sent by the Vichy government to the death camps. Each deportee is symbolized by a point; the prison-like interior of the monument, with its cold stone and iron bars, has inscriptions and a flame burns by the tomb of the Unknown Deportee.

But while the government can build memorials, after almost 50 years it still cannot tell the truth about the willing complicity of thousands of French officials and police in the deportations. War criminals such as those who led the Vel d'Hiv raid in 1942, in which 13,000 Parisian Jews were sent off to death, escaped prosecution for decades, protected by both right and left-wing governments. If anything, this hypocritical memorial should be a reminder of how the French political class knows how to look after its own.

> *From the Mémorial to the Quai de l'Archevêché extends the Square de l'Ile-de-France.*

Until 1914, when it was moved to the Quai de la Rapée, this site was occupied by the Morgue. Morgues are one of Paris' many gifts to the world, first set up in the 17th century. The word comes from *morguer*, 'to observe', for the whole point was to view (and identify) the corpses. By the 19th century it was one of Paris' biggest attractions: Méryon and his friend Baudelaire haunted it, and Dickens confessed that whenever in Paris, 'I am dragged by an invisible force into the Morgue'. People grumbled when there were only a few bodies to see, and all were surprised when Théodore Ribot's study of Paris' suicides concluded that the tramps and down-and-outs rarely put an end to their hard existence, 'but men gifted with happiness, or who have everything to be happy, are those who clasp the least tightly to life'.

> *Just to the north, a pedestrian-only bridge leads over to the flat barge towed by the ship of the Cité, **Ile St-Louis**.*

For 1900 years, Ile St-Louis was as neglected as the Cité was popular. Every now and then a medieval king would cross over to dub a knight or two (an old custom), but that was all. Under Charles V a defensive canal was dug (along modern Rue Poulletier) to split the island in two and a tower was built at the site of Pont de la Tournelle, while the islets, Ile aux Vaches and Ile Notre-Dame, both property of the canons of Notre-Dame, became the resort of milk cows, wild ducks, fishermen, bathers and laundresses. That this land, in the heart of one of Europe's most crowded cities, could have some practical value was only noticed in the wake of the Marais property boom. In 1614, bridge-builder and engineer Christophe Marie persuaded the king to let him bind the islets into one island, and tie it with bridges to the Right and Left Banks. In exchange for the work, Marie and his speculator-associates Lugles Poulletier and François Le Regrattier were given several concessions, building and running a *jeu de paume*, a real tennis court, and a *bateau-lavoir*, a picturesque wooden platform-boat floating beside the quay, where women paid a small fee to use the tubs for washing and rinsing and the roof for drying clothes (it remained a fixture of St-Louis's Quai de Bourbon until 1942). Most importantly, Marie and Co. could sell plots of the former cow pasture to developers. The simple grid of streets made subdivision easy, and aristocrats were more than welcome; their snob value increased land values and attracted the wealthiest members of the bourgeoisie—especially magistrates and financiers. The speculators, who didn't miss any trick, gave the quays a certain cachet by naming them after the royal houses of France. Its success was assured when the young, popular architect Louis Le Vau moved here in the late 1630s and became the chief speculator himself, designing and selling his elegant *hôtels particuliers*. In 1726 the island was given the name of its newly consecrated church.

Nearly all the houses on Ile St-Louis went up between 1627 and 1667, bestowing on the island an architectural homogeneity rare in Paris. Although it charmed the Parisians of the *Grand Siècle*, it fell out of fashion in the 18th century, and in the 19th enjoyed a Romantic revival among bohemians such as Cézanne, Daumier, Gautier and Baudelaire, who were drawn by its poetic solitude. Since the last war property prices have rocketed to the stars. The fine *hôtels* have nearly all been restored or divided into flats; bijou restaurants sprout at every corner, and during Paris' big tourist invasions its famous village atmosphere decays into the gaudy air of an ice-cream-spattered 17th-century funfair.

> *Although the inner streets and the island's dorsal Rue St-Louis-en-l'Ile are too narrow for trees, the quays of Ile St-Louis have some of the prettiest plane trees and poplars in Paris, casting dappled shadows across the façades of the* hôtels. *They were the first to make river-views fashionable; one of the finest, complete with a shady garden, is enjoyed by the lucky residents of the* **Maison de Centaure** *(turn left at the bridge to Quai de Bourbon, no. 45) a house built by Le Vau's brother and named after its pair of medallions showing* Hercules *fighting* Nessus*). If you continue along Quai de Bourbon to Rue Le Regrattier, note the headless statue of St Nicholas, patron saint of sailors but better known as the 'best woman in Paris' or the* Femme-sans-tête.

*Turn down Rue Le Regrattier and left into Rue St-Louis-en-l'Ile.*

This has always been the island's main commercial street, with enough little village shops to keep an islander from ever really having to cross over to the mainland. But there is one striking building as well, fat no. 51, the **Hôtel de Chenizot** (1730). A bearded faun's head and pot-bellied chimeras enliven its doorway, one of Paris' rare Rococo works; countless others lost similar playful façades to the severe neoclassical fashion that came with the Revolution. Further up, at no. 31, is one of the island's chief attractions: **Berthillon**, Paris' favourite ice cream, witnessed by the long queues for a cone—all the better to give you time to decide between the absurd number of flavours.

> *Backtrack slightly and turn north (right) up Rue des Deux-Ponts, a street widened in the early 1900s at the expense of all the houses on the odd-numbered side of the street and endangering the neighbourhood's fragile ecosystem. Rue des Deux-Ponts ends at* **Pont Marie,** *named after the master engineer who built it with his own money.*

Originally lined with houses, like most Paris bridges, it collapsed the day it opened in 1634, drowning 20 people. Since then it has continued to be one of Paris' more troublesome spans, and has often been rebuilt—since the 1790s, without the houses. Just to your left, the old cabaret **Au Franc Pinot**, with its decorative grille of grapes and vines, was until 1794 the home of the Renault family, whose daughter Cécile, inspired by Charlotte Corday, attempted to murder the tyrant Robespierre. She failed, and the whole family was sent to the guillotine.

> *Continue east along Quai d'Anjou to no. 17, the* **Hôtel de Lauzun,** *the only private 17th-century mansion in Paris open to the public. (But not often: mid-April to mid-Sept, Sat and Sun, 10–5.40; adm on same ticket as the Musée Carnavalet, see p.127, free Sun.)*

Sometimes attributed to Le Vau, this *hôtel* was built in 1656 and sold a few years later to the Duc de Lauzun, a favourite of Louis XIV and the man forced to wed Louis's cousin, the Grande Mademoiselle. In 1842 the *hôtel* was purchased by Jérôme Pichon, a bibliophile, who rented the extra rooms out to Baudelaire and Théophile Gautier, and to the Club des Haschischins, or 'hashish eaters'. The **interior**, after a cold, chaste façade dignified only with a wrought-iron balcony and gold trim, surprises with the exuberance of its original painted ceilings and woodwork; you can't help imagining what the hash-heads must have dreamt, staring up at ceilings such as *Time Discovering Truth* or the *Triumph of Venus.* Among the portraits inside is one by Mignard purporting to be the Grande Mademoiselle herself, but historians insist she was hardly as pretty.

*Continue east along Quai d'Anjou; on the next corner (facing 2 Rue St-Louis-en-l'Ile) stands the* **Hôtel Lambert.**

Designed in 1641 by Le Vau for Jean-Baptiste Lambert, secretary to Louis XIII, it was given lavish interiors painted by the top decorators of the day—Lebrun and Le Sueur; most of these decorations are still in place, minus a few squirreled away in the Louvre. In 1831 it was saved from ruin by the exiled Polish leader, Prince Adam Czartoryski; it became the headquarters of the Polish government-in-exile, and a cultural rendez-vous for émigrés such as Chopin, who taught piano to Polish princesses before running off to Majorca with George Sand. Today Hôtel Lambert belongs to the Rothschilds, and sometimes on weekdays they magnanimously leave the gate open so you can sneak a peek at the *cour d'honneur.*

*At this point you may want to wander across Boulevard Henri-IV; steps lead down to Square Barye, a park where pretty boys sprawl in the sun and there are more fun views of the barges and boats chugging up the Seine. When you're ready, turn west up Rue St-Louis-en-l'Ile, where a big clock over the street marks no. 19, the church of* **St-Louis-en-l'Ile***.*

The first tiny chapel on the island, dedicated to the Virgin, was quickly deemed too dinky and common by the new islanders, and in 1664 Le Vau designed a new parish church, which remained unfinished until 1725. Although the clock is the only distinguishing feature of the boxy exterior, inside this is the perfect Baroque society church, a cream-and-gilt pastry for the spiritually untroubled.

*Backtrack from the church to Rue Poulletier, turn right then right again into Quai de Béthune, originally called Quai des Balcons, for the balconies that grace the* hôtels *here, designed by Le Vau. On the other side of the bridge is Quai d'Orléans, so Parisian with its trees and views across to the Left Bank. But there is an exotic touch as well: at no. 6 is the 200,000-volume Polish Library of Paris founded in 1838, and the* **Musée Mickiewicz** *(open 3–6 Thurs only; July, Aug, Tues and Thurs).*

The first floor, devoted to Chopin, has original scores and the composer's death mask, while upstairs are ephemera on the life and times of poet and patriot Adam Mickiewicz (1798–1855), founder of Polish Romanticism. From 1841–44 he held the chair of Slavic literature at the Collège de France and was the leading voice of Paris' many Polish émigrés.

*There are more grand views of Notre-Dame if you cross to the Left Bank via* **Pont de la Tournelle** *(just east of the Polish library) with its rocket-to-Mars statue of Saint Geneviève, patroness of Paris and one of the leading ladies of Walk VIII—the Latin Quarter (see p.229).*

# II: Le Marais: *Le Grand Siècle*

**Start:** Ⓜ *Bastille*

**Walking time:** *this is one of the more serious journeys; give it 3 hours without the museums, of which there are quite a few.*

This is a long, but actually relaxing trek through one of the less frantic corners of old Paris. The Marais is the aristocratic quarter *par excellence*, its streets and old palaces a bit more jolly than the cadaverous hulks of the Faubourg

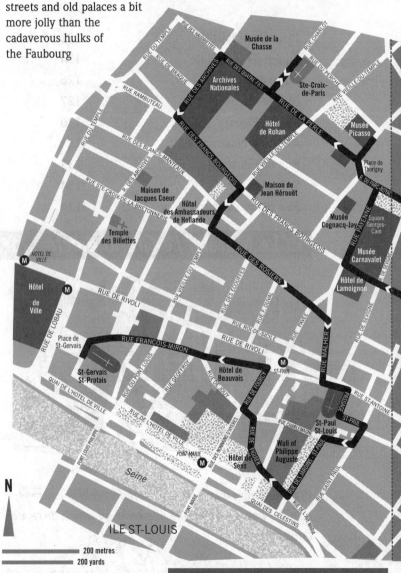

Musée de la Chasse

Archives Nationales

Ste-Croix-de-Paris

RUE DES QUATRE-FILS

RUE CHARLOT

RUE DU PERCHE

RUE DE BRAQUE

RUE DES HAUDRIETTES

RUE DU TEMPLE

RUE DE LA PERLE

Hôtel de Rohan

Musée Picasso

RUE VIEILLE-DU-TEMPLE

Place de Thorigny

RUE RAMBUTEAU

RUE DU TEMPLE

RUE DES BLANCS-MANTEAUX

RUE DES FRANCS BOURGEOIS

Maison de Jacques Coeur

Maison de Jean Hérouët

R. DU PARC-ROYAL

RUE DES ARCHIVES

R. DES ARCHIVES

RUE STE-CROIX-DE-LA-BRETONNERIE

Hôtel des Ambassadeurs de Hollande

RUE DES FRANCS BOURGEOIS

Musée Cognacq-Jay

Square Georges-Cain

RUE PAYENNE

Temple des Billettes

RUE DES ROSIERS

Musée Carnavalet

RUE DE SÉVIGNÉ

*HÔTEL DE VILLE* Ⓜ

Hôtel de Lamoignon

Hôtel de Ville

Ⓜ

RUE DE RIVOLI

RUE VIEILLE-DU-TEMPLE

RUE DES ÉCOUFFES

RUE DE LOBAU

Place de St-Gervais

RUE FRANÇOIS-MIRON

RUE DE RIVOLI

RUE ROI-DE-SICILE

RUE PAVÉE

RUE MALHER

RUE DE SÉVIGNÉ

St-Gervais St-Protais

QUAI DE L'HÔTEL DE VILLE

RUE DU PONT LOUIS

RUE GEOFFROY

Hôtel de Beauvais

RUE DE JOUY

Ⓜ ST-PAUL

RUE ST-ANTOINE

PASSAGE ST-PAUL

RUE DE L'HÔTEL DE VILLE

RUE DE FOURCY

RUE CHARLEMAGNE

St-Paul St-Louis

PONT LOUIS PHILIPPE

RUE DES NONNAINS D'HYÈRES

Ⓜ

RUE DE FIGUIER

Hôtel de Sens

Wall of Philippe Auguste

RUE DES JARDINS-ST-PAUL

Seine

PONT MARIE

QUAI DES CELESTINS

RUE DE L'AVE MARIA

**N**

200 metres
200 yards

# II: Le Marais: *Le Grand Siècle*

118

St-Germain. Being out of fashion for two centuries has done it no harm, and the most ambitious restoration effort of any quarter in Paris has it spruced up and ready for your inspection. The main attractions here are the grand *hôtels particuliers* of the 16th–18th centuries, and the museums they contain: museums of Paris, Picasso, locks and keys, hunting and fishing, historical documents, Victor Hugo, oriental puppets, Paris again and so on. Don't hurry this walk (you'll notice nobody who lives here ever seems to be in much of a hurry). In the area that has perhaps changed the least over the last 300 years, take time to look at details, like the 17th-century street signs carved into many old buildings, or the subtle sculptural decoration on the scores of old *hôtels*.

Some of the museums are closed on Mondays, some on Tuesdays. Rue des Rosiers, the small but intense Jewish quarter in the heart of the Marais, is shut up tight on Saturdays, and on Sundays the area can seem a bit sleepy—unless it's full of tourists and no one else. That leaves Wednesdays, Thursdays and Fridays as the perfect days.

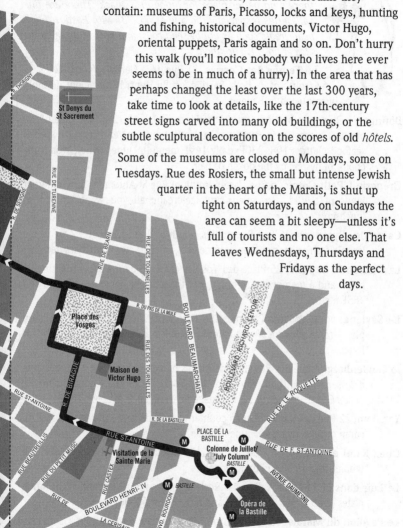

119

About halfway through this walk you'll be in **Rue des Rosiers**, where the food is guaranteed kosher and guaranteed tasty; there's no better place for lunch or a snack. There are fine pâtisseries (especially the one at no. 33) with Eastern European treats such as poppy-seed rolls, and kosher pizza by the slice at no. 11. For lunch:

**Le Temps des Cerises**, 31 Rue de la Cerisaie, ℂ 01 42 72 08 63 (south of Pl. de la Bastille, off Bd Henri IV). Ancient, friendly bistrot; good 60F menu.

**Bofinger**, 5 Rue de la Bastille, just off the Place, ℂ 01 42 72 87 82. One of the prettiest brasseries in Paris, and an institution for over a century; special seafood platters 198–230F; daily 169F menu (includes wine); wondrous choice of oysters by the dozen or half.

**Crêperie L'Petit Comic**, 6 Rue Castex, south of Rue St-Antoine. Thirty different kinds of crêpes, also salads and ice-cream; all you want for 65F at lunchtime.

**Caves des Pyrénées**, 25 Rue Beautreillis (south of Rue St-Antoine). One of the last old-fashioned, non-trendy wine bars; of character, and characters.

**La Guirlande de Julie**, 25 Place des Vosges, ℂ 01 48 87 94 07. A memorable lunch and a memorable setting under the arcades; generous 90, 140 and 185F menus.

**Le Sévigné**, corner of Rue Payenne and Parc Royal. Here the emphasis is on pies—*tarte provençale*, quiches, pies with aubergines; about 90F for lunch.

**Jo Goldenberg**, 7 Rue des Rosiers. The Marais branch of Paris' most famous delicatessen. You'll think you're in New York (the ultimate compliment for delis). Classic noshes to eat in or take out; full lunch at about 180F.

**Yahalom**, 22 Rue des Rosiers. Lunch counter with falafel and kafte sandwiches, to eat in or take away; 40F lunch special.

**Chez Rami et Hanna**, 50 Rue des Rosiers. Falafel, herring, chopped liver, the whole shtick; 70F and up for lunch.

**Le Loir dans la Théière**, 3 Rue des Rosiers. Tea room/restaurant. Light lunch plates (crab with sorrel, or figs and melons) for 60–80F.

**Le Pavillon du Marais,** 15 Rue François-Miron. A new restaurant in a 14th-century half-timbered building ; speciality of the house is famous Salers beef, which usually appears on the 115F menu and the 55F *plat du jour.*

**Miraville**, 72 Quai de l'Hôtel-de-Ville, ℰ 01 42 74 72 22. One of the finest restaurants in the Marais; *haute cuisine* with a Provençal slant—murderously expensive, except for the 150-F weekday lunch menu.

---

The Seine is a meandering river. Long before there were Parisians or even Parisii, it liked to change its bed every now and again. Thousands of years ago, it followed a course roughly following the route of the Grands Boulevards. When the Seine chose its present course, the old bed remained as low, marshy ground, especially in its eastern edge, the Marais of today. Left mostly outside Paris' original wall, the Marais was home to several monasteries; other parts of it were little more than a dump for garbage and dead animals. The religious orders owned most of the land, and they undertook the slow work of reclaiming it—particularly the Templars, whose fortified compound on the northern edge became a city in itself.

Charles V enclosed the Marais within his new wall in the 1370s, and set the tone for its development by moving in himself, taking residence for a period at the Hôtel St-Pol near the Seine (now vanished, and recalled only by the name of Rue des Lions-Saint-Paul—site of the royal menagerie). Nobles and important clerics followed, and the old swamplands began to sprout imposing *hôtels particuliers*. Both royalty and fashion deserted the Marais for a while, after Henri II was killed in a recreational joust in the courtyard of his residence in Rue de Tournelles (also vanished), but in the 1500s a few sumptuous *hôtels* in the Italian style were still going up, such as the Hôtel de Sens and the Hôtel Carnavalet.

What really made the Marais's fortune was Henri IV's construction of the Place des Vosges in 1605. For the rest of the century, even after Louis XIV moved the big show out of Paris to Versailles, the Marais was the place to be. Grand *hôtels* were still being built in the time of Louis XVI, although by then the area had clearly lost out in popularity to the Faubourg St-Germain. But whatever lingering spark of glamour there might have been was definitively extinguished by the Revolution. Most of the great *hôtels* were confiscated and divided up, starting them on a career as homes for clothing makers, warehouses and other small businesses.

They were still serving the same purpose in the 1950s and '60s, falling ever more into decay as Parisians finally rediscovered what had become a lost world. Owners of the palaces had been blithely demolishing them, without too much public outcry, but then the 'Malraux Law' of 1962 allowed the city to create preservation districts and plan for their renovation. Since then, scores of private individuals and cultural associations have helped in the effort, and today almost all of the *hôtels* have been restored, and good uses found for them. Changes in the neighbourhood have kept pace. The old population of workers and immigrants is long gone, and the Marais is settling quite comfortably into its new role as the centre of Paris' gay community. The young, well-off newcomers don't do much for neighbourhood colour—but there's still the lively old Jewish quarter around Rue des Rosiers, which with the help of new immigrants from North Africa and the Middle East has so far been quite successful at holding on to its character.

> *The walk begins in **Place de la Bastille**. There's nothing to see of the famous fortress, of course—unless you arrive on the no. 5 métro, coming from the Gare d'Austerlitz, where some of the foundations survive around the platform. The square has been redesigned, and you can follow the outline of the fortress along the pavement.*

This is the only square in town created not by kings or planners but by the people of Paris. Since they cleared the space back in 1789, the Place has been the symbolic centre of leftist politics, the setting for monster celebrations like the one that followed Mitterrand's election in 1981. Paris' *motards* (bikers) couldn't care less, but they come every Friday night for their traditional beery bike-in.

## Bastille: Castle

Every gate in the walls of Paris had some sort of castle to defend it. This one (the Porte St-Antoine) lay on the main road to the east, and was situated very close to the royal residences of St-Pol or the Tournelles; consequently it was the best defended of all. Begun in 1370, the Bastille's original purpose was keeping the English out. It was a proper castle, a tall, grim rectangle with eight round towers and very few windows; its outworks covered an area as big as the Place today. But well built as it was, militarily the Bastille never had any luck; seven times it was besieged during rebellions or civil wars, and six times it was quickly taken.

## Bastille: Prison

Under the English occupation, the Bastille garrison was commanded by Sir John Fastolf, sometimes claimed as a model for Shakespeare's Falstaff (but Fastolf, a tough and capable frog-basher over many campaigns, gets a bit role himself in the first part of *Henry IV*). It was Richelieu who determined the Bastille's role as a prison, and it soon became the most important calaboose in the realm, hosting such celebrities as the Man in the Iron Mask. More than anywhere else, it was a place where delicate cases could be held at the king's pleasure, under the notorious *lettres de cachet*—'letters of introduction' to the governor, asking him to simply hold the fellow until further orders. Accommodation in the Bastille was not all that awful, at least for the wealthy, who might bring in their servants, and could afford the choicer dishes on the governor's bill of fare (no one in those times ever considered it a state duty to feed prisoners gratis; at the Bastille, governors were constantly accused of exploiting the prisoners by their control over the kitchen). The poorer ones did get a bare minimum, along with a candle and five logs a day to burn in winter. Privileges—walking along the ramparts, using the library, being able to order dinner from outside—were at the discretion of the Lieutenant of Police, an arbitrary regime but not always unkind. Some prisoners are recorded as having invited in their friends for dinner parties.

In the 18th century the Bastille held a mixed bag of common criminals and prominent folk who had fallen into royal disfavour—Voltaire himself made two visits, one for over a year. By the 1780s there were very few prisoners at all kept under *lettres de cachet* (abolished in 1784), and the government had already appropriated the funds to demolish the Bastille when the Revolution hit. Two weeks before the first Bastille Day, one of the last few prisoners got himself in trouble, shouting out of his window, through a sort of bullhorn made from a drainpipe, that he and the rest of the inmates were about to be massacred, and pleading for the people to come and save him. This was, of all people, the Marquis de Sade, in since 1784 for the usual offences against public propriety and servant girls. The governor had him shipped to the madhouse at Charenton on 4 July 1789.

## The Storming of the Bastille

On the 11th, the king dismissed his minister Necker, and the people of Paris, losing all hope of mere reform, began to arm themselves. On the morning of the 14th, after a rousing speech by Camille Desmoulins in the Palais Royal (*see* p.174) some 600 people, including women and children, advanced across Paris to the grim fortress that had become a symbol of royal despotism. They went at it all afternoon with the small garrison of Swiss Guards and retired veterans; at about 5pm, the arrival of a detachment of revolutionary militia decided the issue. The gates were forced, the governor and many of the defenders massacred, and the last seven inmates of the Bastille were acclaimed as heroes among the crowd: the prisoners comprised four swindlers who were about to be transferred to another prison, an English idiot named Whyte, a gentleman whose family had petitioned the king to lock him up for incest and one genuine political prisoner—who had been in the Bastille since some obscure conspiracy in 1759, and who didn't want to leave.

The demolition commenced the day after. Popular enthusiasm started it, but very soon a clever rascal named Palloy took charge of the work, intending to make a profit from the Bastille in any way possible. Besides organizing patriotic dance parties on the site, 'Citizen Palloy' sold off the stones to build the Pont de la Concorde, and to repave the Pont Neuf and a few score Paris streets. His greatest coup was having stones carved into models of the fortress, and sending off one each to the 83 *départements* into which France had just been divided—accompanied by his salesmen, peddling smaller souvenirs to all and sundry. You'll see two of these models on this walk, in the Carnavalet and in the National Archives. When the revolutionary commissioners got a look at his books, Palloy himself ended up in the slammer for a while.

> *Today, the centrepiece of the Place de la Bastille is the 153ft* **Colonne de Juillet,** *commemorating the Revolution of 1830 (open daily except Tues, 10–6; adm).*

Napoleon had planned to decorate the spot with a gigantic elephant, surmounted by a tower (along with golden bees, elephants with towers or obelisks were one of Napoleon's personal symbols, representing little more than the Emperor's whimsy, and possibly inspired by the emblem of Catania, Sicily, or a Bernini sculpture in Piazza Minerva, Rome). The 50ft bronze mammoth was actually built, with its trunk designed to spout water into a fountain; Napoleon took a great interest in the work. After 1815 the beast sat in its workshop (where the Bastille Opéra is now) for 31 years, until the government sold it off for scrap. All that time it was guarded by an old soldier who slept in one of its legs, and who frequently got into trouble with the police for his Bonapartist sympathies.

The 'July column', recently restored for the bicentennial of the Revolution, was erected over the unfortunate elephant's pedestal in honour of those who died in the 1830 revolt. Ironically, it became a shrine to the overthrow of the regime that built it; in 1848 a new crop of revolutionaries burned Louis-Philippe's throne next to the column. On top is a figure of the 'Genius of Liberty'—familiar from the obverse of the new 10-franc pieces, possibly the ugliest coins ever minted on this planet. You may climb the 238 steps for a view over the East End, but the crypt where the bodies of the revolt's victims are buried is usually closed.

If, a thousand years from now, some archaeologist ever digs them up, he is going to get a surprise. The bodies, for some reason, were originally interred in the courtyard of the National Library, just as the Library's director had an unusual problem on his hands. Napoleon's expedition to Egypt had brought him back several mummies. The Parisian climate was causing them to decompose, resulting in aromas that did not go unnoticed among the readers. Bureaucratic considerations made it difficult to dispose of these national treasures, and so they were buried secretly in the Library's gardens—next to the spot where the revolutionaries had been planted. The princes of the Nile secretly accompanied them on their solemn progress to the crypt here, and they have rested in peace ever since.

> *As part of Mitterrand's notions of 'bringing culture to the people', he has conjured up the startling façade of the* **Opéra de la Bastille.**

There used to be a small railway station here, the Gare de la Bastille. Its buildings included a large métro pavilion that was one of the finest works of Hector Guimard; the government planners typically levelled it without a second thought when they began clearing ground for this dubious undertaking in 1985.

Uruguayan-Canadian architect Carlos Ott, whose career was made when he won the competition for this building in 1983, probably wishes he had never heard of Paris, so harsh and ignorant has been the criticism laid against him. People have their unconscious ideas about what an opera house should be, ideas derived from the likes of Charles Garnier, who wrote the book on the subject with Paris' old Opéra. Ott has different ideas, which cannot be proved or disproved overnight. He did everything you could ask of an architect: the sight lines and acoustics are excellent, and the façade makes an elegant and memorable image. The little squares of the glass skin, a motif cleverly repeated in small details throughout the building, are reminiscent of a French school notebook, and maybe that's the problem. They recall *dictées*, the more-than-perfect tense and everything else in French culture's chronic anal retentiveness. It's hard to imagine any classic Italian (or French) opera being performed in this cool geometric house.

But perhaps the future will bring operas that feel at home here. For the real objection to this building, ask any French taxpayer. *Three billion francs down the toilet*, that's what he'll say. The idea was preposterous that Paris, already having one of the world's most famous opera houses, should build another one. The bureaucracy's master chefs even cooked up a report proving that it would save money. Mitterrand's idea, the pretence of bringing culture closer to the people, has proved a joke, and the results have been a profound embarrassment for the government. Despite unlimited funds and hype, culturally the building seems already doomed. Former director Pierre Bergé (head of Yves St-Laurent and one of Mitterrand's corporate cronies, currently under investigation) has presided over a débâcle of infighting that the *Wall Street Journal* called: 'more tearful than *La Bohème*, more breathless than *Aïda*, and next to which the Ring Cycle would look simplistic'. In 1992 they got Pavarotti in for *Un Ballo in Maschera*, beamed out into the square on wide screens to lure the common man; stay tuned, as the government trys to find new ways to save the place.

> From the western edge of Place de la Bastille, start down lively Rue St-Antoine, the main street of the Marais, following the course of a Roman road. It's wide now, and in the Middle Ages it was the city's widest street because it was used for so many popular festivals and processions. You'll pass a statue of ex-Marais resident Beaumarchais on the right, and then on the left the domed Baroque church of the **Visitation-de-la-Sainte-Marie** (1634), the first work of François Mansart. Much more

*edifying, architecturally, is the '30s Art Deco **Post Office** around the corner on Rue Castex.*

*From Rue St-Antoine, turn right at Rue de Biragne, the street with an uncommonly graceful brick mansion closing its view; pass through its archways and meet the loveliest surprise the Marais has to offer, the **Place des Vosges.***

This spot's association with royalty began long before the Place ever appeared. The Hôtel des Tournelles, a turreted mansion built here in the 1330s, had belonged to a chancellor of France, a bishop of Paris and a pair of dukes before Charles VI purchased it in 1407. The Duke of Bedford lived here during the English occupation, and later kings such as François I occasionally used it for councils and state ceremonies. One such event was the going-away party for Henri II's daughter Catherine de France, who was off to marry Philip II of Spain. The celebrations included an old-fashioned joust, in which the king participated (in the grim and reactionary 16th century, nobles revived this archaic custom—like tycoons and bankers riding to hounds in our time). Wearing the colours of his celebrated mistress, Diane de Poitiers, the unfortunate Henri took a shot right through the visor from Montgomery, the captain of his Scots Guard. He died ten days later. The king forgave Montgomery, who soon left France, but Henri's widow, Catherine de' Medici, waited quietly for 15 years until she could catch Montgomery daring to set foot in France again—she had him executed in the Place de Grève, after some pretty thorough torturing.

Catherine had the cursed palace demolished, and she also seems to have had the original inspiration to replace it with Paris' first proper square (and possibly the first in northern Europe; London's first attempt, Inigo Jones' original Covent Garden, appeared in 1630). The idea was probably a memory of the fashionable, arcaded Piazza SS. Annunziata back home in Florence. Nothing came of it until the reign of Henri IV, and the space saw use for a time as a horse market and the site of a silk factory. In 1605, Henri finally began the building of what would be known as the 'Place Royale', a centrepiece that the sprawling Marais badly needed. Its architects are unknown; though the square is Italian in concept, the adaptation became something a 17th-century Frenchman could love—elegant, hierarchical and rigorously symmetrical.

In a way this square is the predecessor of Versailles. Behind the uniform façades were 36 noble palaces; the only buildings that stood out were the pavilions of the king and queen, at the northern and southern entrances to the square—a public place in an aristocratic setting, mirroring in its design the subjection of the nobility to the king. At first, the centre of the square was completely open, the perfect stage for the decorous promenading and public life of the era. The Place Royale was

Henri's pet project, and he visited the works almost every day. It was not completed, however, until after his assassination, in 1612.

The opening ceremonies ironically included another joust, a perfect prelude for the scenes witnessed in the Place's first decades. Besides stately promenading, the nobles of the age were fondest of duels. Despite Richelieu's attempts to outlaw them (he once lived on the square, at no. 21) the reign of Louis XIII was the golden age of the sport. Rapier in one hand, torch in the other, the hotbloods put on regular midnight shows for the neighbours who might still be awake. The contests were occasionally a difference of politics or religion, though usually it was over a woman. What finally put an end to the custom was not Richelieu's police, but the decision of the property owners in 1685 to enclose the centre of the square with an iron fence and make it a garden—this time imitating the new fashion from London.

During the Revolution, when all the names of *ancien régime* streets were changed, the Place Royale must have been one of the last; the revolutionaries could find nothing better to call it than the awkward Place de l'Indivisibilité. Napoleon handled it even worse, giving it its present moniker, Place des Vosges, in honour of the first department of France to pay completely its share of the new war taxes.

Today the Place is a thumping favourite with tourists, Parisians, groups of schoolchildren and everyone else. It's utterly pleasant under the clipped linden trees, and the statue of Louis XIII (an 1825 replacement for the original melted down in the Revolution) looks fondly foolish with his pencil moustache and Roman toga. The architecture, totally French, and refreshingly free of any Renaissance imitation, invites contemplation. If you do so, you'll notice a lot of the 'brick' is really painted plaster; even aristocrats can cut corners. Under the arcades are restaurants and antique shops—and always a few drunks and unfortunates crashed in the doorways.

*At no. 6 you can visit the* **Maison de Victor Hugo** *(open daily except Mon 10–5.45; adm).*

The master lived here between 1832 and 1848, and the place has been turned into a somewhat lugubrious shrine. Of interest, besides Hugo's charming mock-Chinese dining room, are original illustrations from his books, and a good number of Hugo's own peculiar drawings.

*Head left down Rue des Francs-Bourgeois, along the northern edge of the square, and at the second street on your right you'll come to Paris' city museum, the* **Musée Carnavalet** *(open daily except Mon 10–5.40; adm).*

It is only fitting that this museum should be housed in the grandest of all the Marais' *hôtels*. Begun in 1548 for a president of the *Parlement de Paris*, the Hôtel Carnavalet was rebuilt thoroughly in the *grand-siècle* style by François Mansart in

1660. The original may have been more interesting; from it survive most of the ground floor and loggia (court off Rue des Francs-Bourgeois), and some reliefs around the windows by Jean Goujon or his followers, representing the Four Seasons (court off Rue de Sévigné). In this court is a statue of Louis XIV by Coysevox that once stood in the courtyard of the Hôtel de Ville. The City of Paris purchased the mansion in 1866 with the intention of making it a museum, and the collections have grown steadily ever since—everything from Napoleon's toothbrush to a Boucher painting of 'Mademoiselle O'Murphy's foot'. Count on at least two hours for getting through it all.

*Carnavalet*, besides being the name of a former owner, also means a carnival mask; you'll notice one of these carved in stone over the entrance. It is a reminder of how the streets of old Paris, or any other city, were an empire of symbols and pictorial allusions in the days before everyone could read. The first room of the museum is entirely devoted to the charming **shop signs** of this Paris: a big Persian king carved in wood for a dealer in cashmere, St Anthony and his pig for a butcher, an inn at the sign of the Three Rats. These were the landmarks of the city before the 1800s and few are without artistic value. When you go back out into the Marais, imagine them still in place, and the blank, grey streets of the neighbourhood will come alive again.

The rooms that follow, devoted to ancient and medieval Paris, are rather scanty, but there are plans and models of ancient Lutetia and Merovingian Paris. The medieval section—Paris' most creative and influential age—is especially disappointing; the best they can manage is a few shoes and wooden spoons, miraculously preserved over the centuries. There is a fascinating, mad **model of Paris in 1527**, made by a monk in the early 1900s. It must have been the passion of a lifetime: every last building is present, made of paper, with the details painstakingly drawn in and painted.

On the first floor, room after room of prints, portraits, views and plans detail the growth of Paris from the Renaissance to the present. The 17th and 18th centuries are more than well represented, with the emphasis, unfortunately, on interior decorating and furniture; entire suites of rooms have been fitted out in styles from Louis XIII to the First Empire. From here there's an abrupt jump to modern times, with such exhibits as the faithfully reproduced **bedchamber of Marcel Proust**, where he would accept his morning *madeleine* (always on the same plate) and muse on fate and memory. Everything is cosy and tasteful, with a Chinese screen and a chaise longue, a sort of psychiatrist's couch, very in vogue at the time.

If you're nodding off after too much bourgeois plushness, the **ballroom of the Hôtel Wendel** will startle you back awake. This hotel, formerly on Avenue de New-York, gave Spanish artist José-María Sert carte blanche in 1924 to create a venue that would draw the avant-garde. Done in subdued monochrome paint over gold leaf, in a style faintly reminiscent of Tintoretto's chiaroscuros, the scenes of the ballroom walls portray the Queen of Sheba leaving to meet Solomon, with dwarfs, Mongols, ostriches, tumblers, elephants, potted palms and astrologers in attendance, all ephemeral in their flowing draperies and conspiring towards an informed parody of the *grand siècle*.

The ambition of moving this entire ensemble to a museum is impressive enough, but there is more to come: first, an earlier monument of abstruse modernism, the entire **Fouquet jewellery shop** from Rue Royale, *c.* 1901. Alfons Mucha, famous for his posters for bicycles, cigarette papers and Sarah Bernhardt, designed this Art Nouveau monument to conspicuous consumption, with peacocks and stained glass, rich wood carvings, fountains and mosaic floors.

Fouquet's baubles would have been displayed to advantage in the next tableau, a **private room** from the **Café de Paris** (formerly 41 Avenue de l'Opéra), showing Art Nouveau at its sweetest and most unaffected. The next section is devoted to paintings. Those of Jean Béraud (1849–1936) stand out, faithful recordings of Parisian life of photographic quality. The comings and goings of the boulevards are defined with clinical precision, along with scenes ranging from smoky gambling dens to the city police chemical laboratory.

From here, you'll digress in time to the Revolution (as in most museums in Paris, the numbered order of the rooms is impossible to follow). This section begins starkly, with naive **allegorical paintings** by a contemporary named Dubois. The first, from 1791, celebrates Louis XIV, the 'father of a free people'; another is a mystic work from the same year, declaring the 'hope of a golden age'. Dubois also paints the taking of the Bastille, with a much greater realism. Keys to the Bastille are on display, along with a model of the fortress, and original copies of the Declaration of the Rights of Man and the first Constitution—opposite a glass case with young Louis XVII's toys and his dad's shaving dish. French prisoners of war in Britain contribute model guillotines, painstakingly whittled from bone.

The revolution of 1830 is well documented, with paintings of the fights around the Louvre and Porte St-Denis, and a mad diorama of Louis-Philippe addressing a crowd at the Hôtel de Ville. The paintings go on and on—in 19th-century Paris there were so many events and so many painters to chronicle them. For the events of 1870, the best artists are the duo of Didier and Guiaud, with a heroic scene of *Gambetta's balloon escape from Paris* (almost life size), and fascinating views of bread queues and enlargements of the messages brought in by pigeons. Other artefacts fill out the atmosphere of Paris under siege, including ration cards, carrier-pigeon feathers, bits of ersatz bread later mounted on cards and sold as souvenirs, and a careful portrait of a rat that went to make some Parisian's dinner.

> *Leaving the Carnavalet, turn right and continue down Rue des Francs-Bourgeois. At the next corner, you'll see another Renaissance palace, the* **Hôtel de Lamoignon** *(entrance around the corner on Rue Pavée).*

Now housing the Historical Library of the City of Paris, this one was begun in 1580 for Diane de France, an illegitimate daughter of Henri II (notice the allusions to the mythological huntress Diana in the decorative reliefs). Everything is original except for the main portal closing the courtyard, added in 1718. The architecture shows how the French Renaissance could be affected by the spirit of the Italian, without merely copying its forms; the heavy pilasters that rise to the cornice, the fenestration and the eccentric pediments are all essentially Gallic.

> *Turn right again on Rue Payenne and walk north, passing the back of the Carnavalet and its back garden, to the* **Square Georges-Cain**. *Decorated with sculpted fragments from some of the Marais's lost hôtels, this is a pleasant place to rest your sore dogs after the big museum.*
>
> *From here, you can also contemplate three more façades along Rue Payenne. No. 5 was the house François Mansart designed for himself in 1666. In 1903 it became the 'Temple of Humanity' for the positivist religion founded by followers of Auguste Comte and the front was altered, apparently to match the sect's original temple in Rio de Janeiro. To the right, facing the Square, is the late 15th-century* **Hôtel de Marle**, *now the Swedish Cultural Centre; and to the right of that, the* **Hôtel de Chatillon**, *with a pretty ivy-covered courtyard.*
>
> *From the end of Rue Payenne, continue left on Rue du Parc-Royal, passing through the little triangular Place de Thorigny. If you were Louis XVI, who enjoyed his hobby of locksmithing much more than any affairs of state, you would certainly stop here for the* **Musée de la Serrurie** *(open Mon, 2–5pm, Tues—Fri 10–12 and 2–5; adm).*

The museum is housed in the 1685 Hôtel Libéral-Bruant, built by the architect of the Invalides for himself. The Bricard company, which makes (can you guess?) locks, has assembled a small collection of door and window hardware from Roman times to the present. Highlights include some fancy Renaissance door-knockers from Venice, and a reproduction of an old Parisian locksmith's shop.

> *Bear right, into Rue de Thorigny, for the 1656 Hôtel Salé, recently restored for the* **Musée Picasso** *(open daily except Tues, 9:30–5.30, in summer until 6; adm).*

The 'Salted Palace' takes its name from its original occupant, Jean Bouiller, a collector of the hated *gabelle* (salt tax) for Louis XIV. And modern France's taxmen have supplied the collections inside—Picasso's heirs donated most of the works here to the state in the 1970s in lieu of inheritance taxes. Few really important works are here, but all the diverse styles of Picasso's career are represented, from a 'blue-period' *self-portrait* of 1901 through the Cubist *Man with a guitar* (1912) and beyond. Works from the early 1920s, such as the *Pan's flute*, show a classicizing tendency, while those from the later '20s and '30s are the most abstract of all. This is Picasso at the top of his art, exquisite draughtsmanship and the most skilful use of colour, especially in the series of *corridas* and *minotauromachies*, employing mythological elements later seen in *Guernica*.

The last of Picasso, from his closing years at Mougins on the Côte d'Azur, is as interesting as any of the great periods: women with fat toes and Goya faces—effortless creation with a decidedly Spanish touch. One room of the museum contains paintings from Picasso's personal collection, including works by Corot, Matisse and Cézanne. There is also a covered sculpture garden of Picasso works from many periods, and an audiovisual room with slide shows and films.

> *Return to Place de Thorigny, making a right into Rue de la Perle. The next corner on the left, Rue Vieille-du-Temple, shows you one of the last and most ambitious of all the Marais mansions, the Hôtel de Rohan.*

The Rohan family, magnificent chiselers even by the standards of 18th-century French nobility, made their living off the Church. Four family members in succession were cardinals and bishops of Strasbourg—though they preferred to stay here in Paris, living off the income from Strasbourg and scores of other absentee clerical holdings around France. One of the last Cardinals de Rohan got caught up in the 1785 'Affair of the Diamond Necklace' with Marie Antoinette and Cagliostro. The first of them, Armand de Rohan-Soubise, had this *hôtel* built in 1705.

In the courtyard, over the door to the Rohans' stables, is a masterpiece of Rococo sculpture, Robert le Lorrain's theatrical **Horses of Apollo** (entrance on Rue Vieille-du-Temple; once inside go through the arch to the right). These high-relief beasts, ready to spring right off the calm sandstone wall of the court, make an unforgettable contrast with the restrained, neoclassical architecture of the palace.

The Hôtel de Rohan is part of the National Archives (*see* below), but during occasional special exhibitions it is open to the public. The interior is one of the best preserved in Paris, and it's worth keeping an eye out for such an occasion to gain an instructive insight into the world of the Rohans, in such decadent-but-cute fantasies as Boucher's *Chinese suite* or the grinning monkeys of the *Cabinet des Singes*.

> *Continue straight ahead on Rue de la Perle, which changes its name to Rue des Quatre-Fils.*

> At the right-hand corner of Rue des Archives, François Mansart designed
> the **Hôtel de Guénégaud** c. 1650. This is one of the few you can visit, if
> only because the passion and money of a big-game hunter named Sommer
> have turned it into the **Musée de la Chasse et de la Nature** (open daily
> except Tues; 10–12.30 and 1.30–5.30; adm). Along with Sommer's tro-
> phies there are antique weapons, elephant tusks and a surprising
> collection of art—hunting and wildlife scenes from Rembrandt to Monet.
>
> Turn left on Rue des Archives. Already you will have noticed the huge
> neoclassical bulk of the **Archives Nationales** on your left; you'll have to
> circumnavigate it, passing on Rue des Archives the oldest part of the
> complex, a turreted gateway built in the 1370s; this was the entrance to
> the home of a Constable of France named Clisson, and later the head-
> quarters of the Guises, evil protagonists of the Wars of Religion.
> Continue on, towards the entrance on Rue des Francs-Bourgeois (open
> daily, 1.45–5.45 pm; adm).

The truly grand horseshoe-shaped courtyard facing the street belongs to the main
part of the Archives, the **Hôtel de Soubise**. This is another work of the Rohan
family, built at the same time as the Hôtel de Rohan; originally the two palaces
were connected through their gardens. Seized during the Revolution, it has held
the National Archives since 1808. The part you can visit is called the **Musée de
l'Histoire de France**. It isn't for everyone, but with a little knowledge of French
and an interest in history, this collection of documents can be utterly fascinating.
Each is accompanied by a concise commentary and a copy of the text in modern
French (Latin written in Merovingian cursive can be a bit of a strain).

The earliest document is about (naturally) real estate, a decree of Dagobert I,
c. 630, written on papyrus; parchment wasn't widely used until the Middle Ages,
and the Egyptians were still selling a lot of papyrus to Europe even after the Arab
conquest. The heavy seals of the Merovingian and Carolingian kings add the proper
feudal touch, along with the weird pictographs that Charlemagne and others used
for a signature. The first document in French, fittingly, is a tax schedule for mer-
chandise from 1223—the ancestor of VAT. There's the Papal Bull of 1302,
justifying the confiscation of the estates of the Templars, and a letter from Joan of
Arc to the people of Rheims, encouraging them to resist the English.

Louis XIV's revocation of the Edict of Nantes is here, and the first copy of the Declaration of the Rights of Man (1789), along with curiosities such as the maps of
Louisiana colony, showing Natchez and Mobile and pictures of 'very dangerous
serpents', a poem written by Louise Michel in prison after the crushing of the Commune, and some of the requisition slips for the taxis that saved Paris in the Battle of
the Marne. Even so, the best thing in the museum is a painting on the far wall: a

gigantic, hysterically funny 16th-century allegory of the *Ship of Faith*, piloted by the Jesuits (from whom it was seized in the 1760s, when they were expelled from France), and rowed by priests and nuns, smiling beatifically down at the drowning sinners who missed the boat.

In the Soubise courtyard, the Archives run an unusual boutique, where besides books and prints you can get a copy of the personal seal of any French king.

> *Turn left at the exit, and continue down Rue des Francs-Bourgeois. This stretch has a formidable row of 17th–18th-century hôtels, incorporated into the Archives complex. Across the street, the **Crédit Municipal** is a city-owned bank in what was once the Mont de Piété, the city-owned pawnshop—a worthy institution known to almost every Parisian in the dark days before the invention of the overdraft. Gracing the corner of Rue Vieille-du-Temple is the pretty, leaning turret of one of the oldest buildings in the Marais, the 1510 **House of Jean Hérouët**.*

> *Turn right (south) at Rue Vieille-du-Temple. Or else, if you like, make a short detour straight down Francs-Bourgeois to see the **Musée Cognacq-Jay** , just around the corner at 8 Rue Elzévir (open daily except Mon, 10–5.40; adm).*

It's somewhat ironic that Ernest Cognacq, the thoroughly modern department store magnate who founded the Samaritaine, should have devoted his free time to accumulating bric-à-brac from that quaintest of centuries, the eighteenth. The collection of ladies' cosmetic boxes will leave you speechless. There is also ornate furniture and a good collection of painting: Chardin, Boucher, de La Tour, Rembrandt, Tiepolo (a ripe *Cleopatra's Feast*), Guardi and Canaletto are represented, among others.

> *Back on the main route (south on Rue Vieille-du-Temple), to your right will be the **Hôtel des Ambassadeurs de Hollande** (1655), one of the finest in the Marais.*

The name is a mystery; it doesn't seem that any Dutch diplomats ever stayed here. Beaumarchais did, in 1776, while he was writing *The Marriage of Figaro* and founding a fake trading company, headquartered here, which was really in the business of smuggling arms to the American revolutionaries. It's private today—no visits—but if the gate happens to be open, have a look into the lovely courtyard, decorated with big sundials and a relief of Romulus and Remus.

> *Now turn left again into **Rue des Rosiers**.*

Centre of a small Jewish community since the 1700s, a wave of immigration from Eastern Europe in the 1880s and '90s made it what it is today—one of the liveliest, most picturesque little streets in Paris. Recently, a number of Sephardic Jews from North Africa have moved in, adding to a scene that includes bearded Hasidim, old-fashioned *casher* (kosher) grocery shops, snack stands and famous delicatessen restaurants such as Jo Goldenberg.

> *There are several **synagogues**, including one around the corner at 10 Rue Pavée, designed with a stunning curvilinear façade by Hector Guimard.*
>
> *At the end of the Rue des Rosiers, turn right into Rue Malher, which takes you past Rue du Roi-de-Sicile (the 'King of Sicily' was St Louis's nasty brother, Charles of Anjou, who conquered the island for himself in the 1260s and provoked the Sicilian Vespers; he had a house here), and finally back to Rue St-Antoine, right in front of the gloomy façade of **St-Paul-St-Louis**.*

In the late 16th century, there developed in Italy the architectural fashion that art historians used to call the 'Jesuit Style'. Combining the confident classicism of the decaying Renaissance with a sweeping bravura that would soon be perfected in the dawning Baroque, this architecture was a key part of the Jesuits' plan to forge a swank, modern image for the Counter-Reformation Church. It took some 70 years for the style to find its way to Paris; Jesuit architects began construction of St-Louis in 1627, and Cardinal Richelieu himself celebrated the first Mass in 1641. Originally its name was simply St-Louis, flattering the Jesuits' benefactor Louis XIII; St Paul took refuge here when his church, nearby, was demolished in 1797. From its opening, this church was the showcase of the new Catholicism in Paris: the most sumptuous interior decoration, the Jesuits' best orators delivering vague but sonorous sermons, music supplied by great composers such as Lully and Charpentier (both organists here), and all the lights of Parisian society present among the congregation.

From their base here, the intelligent, determined Jesuits quickly became a power in France, the confessors of kings and educators of the élite (Voltaire, for one). As agents of the papacy, and stalwart upholders of orthodoxy in politics as well as religion, they made plenty of enemies; their slipperiness and sophistry often made even their friends doubt. Their expulsion from France in 1761 brought an abrupt end to St-Louis's glory days, but greater indignities were still to come. Thoroughly trashed in 1792, the church lost almost all of its treasures—even the statues on the façade are later additions—and it became a temple in the Revolution's cockamamie 'cult of Reason'. No longer a favourite of society, the church at least retained its popularity among revolutionaries—they came back to pillage it again in 1830, and once more in 1871.

Consequently, there's little to detain you inside. The design follows that of the Gesù in Rome closely, including the discreet dome—one of Paris' first, inspiring the Italianate domes of the Invalides and many others. The sculptural decoration around the dome and crossing by Martellange, the church's original architect, is fine, intricate work and very *grand siècle*. There is a statue of the Virgin sculpted by Germain Pilon (1586) in the chapel to the left of the choir, where the hearts of Louis XIII and XIV were kept (until they were ground up for paint: *see* Val-de-Grâce, p.370).

*Leaving the church by the door in the left transept takes you straight into the **Passage St-Paul**. (The street opposite the arcade's end, Rue Neuve-St-Pierre, was formerly the cemetery of St-Paul; it was never excavated, merely divided up into building lots. Plenty of bodies are still under the pavement, among them many who died as prisoners in the Bastille—including, in all probability, the Man in the Iron Mask). Turn right at the end of the arcade into Rue St-Paul, and right again into Rue Charlemagne. Here you're passing the **Village St-Paul**, a modern housing development that includes small courtyards filled with antique shops and art dealers (open daily except Tues 11–7).*

*Across Rue des Jardins-St-Paul from the complex, the small park of that name is bounded by the Right Bank's only remaining stretch of the 12th-century **Wall of Philippe-Auguste**. At the end of the park, turn right on Rue de l'Ave Maria; no. 15, a modern building, marks the spot where stood the stage entrance of Molière's Illustre Théâtre, which faced the Seine. At the end of this street, you'll be in the quiet Square de l'Ave Maria, facing the one real charmer among the Marais hôtels, the **Hôtel de Sens.***

Strangely enough, Paris did not become an archepiscopal see until 1623; for over a thousand years, its bishops were subject to the archbishops of the little town of Sens. In the Middle Ages these influential clerics spent most of their time in the capital. One of them, *c.* 1475, built this medieval confection overlooking the Seine (today it's two streets away). Later occupants included some genuine characters: one archbishop who drank so much he was known as the 'Cardinal des Bouteilles', and another saintly cleric who grew so angry when he heard the church bells announcing Henri IV's entry into Paris that he burst a blood vessel and died. The next archbishop, Rénaud de Béarn, a fellow renowned for eating dinner every four hours of the day, didn't care for the place and rented it to the king. Henri used it to park the amazing Queen Margot (Marguerite de

Valois) who was becoming too much of an embarrassment at court. Margot, 'la Reine Venus' of contemporary poets, has been described as 'the first modern Parisienne'; within a few years she had apparently had her way with every male in Paris—excepting possibly Henri, of whom she was quite fond in a platonic sort of way. At one point, she was being trailed by 20 incurably smitten former lovers. Henri eventually abjured her (no children), but they remained friends.

For the last three centuries, the archbishops were renting out the old palace to increasingly less elegant tenants; by 1916, when the city purchased it, it was half in ruins and being used as a laundry. But if these old stones could speak, about two-thirds would be bashfully silent; the restoration that began in 1936 was almost a complete reconstruction. Still, it is one of the loveliest buildings in Paris, an impertinently asymmetrical fantasy of gables, turrets and pinnacles that makes the *hôtels* of the *grand siècle* look staid and dull. Currently the palace houses the Bibliothèque Forney, a remarkable institution dedicated to the old crafts and industries of France; besides books it contains everything from advertising posters to wallpaper patterns. They often put on exhibitions, and you can have a look inside.

> *Turn right into Rue du Figuier; at the end head left, then immediately right again, into Rue de Fourcy. At the beginning of this street is a rare 18th-century **shop sign**, a carved relief of a cobbler at his job; Rue de Fourcy will take you into **Rue François-Miron**, a venerable street of much character that began as a Roman road. Turn left; at no. 68 is the **Hôtel de Beauvais** (1657).*

This sadly dilapidated *hôtel* was built by Catau la Borgnesse ('One-eyed Kate'), a knitting-girl from Les Halles who was the daughter of a dealer in old clothes. How'd she manage it? The year 1652 found Catau metamorphosed into Catherine Bellier, a lady of the chamber to the court who had a lucrative talent for administering a cure then fashionable among the fancy ladies, the social enema—a ceremony wreathed in polite conversation and giggles, backsides discreetly directed towards the fireplace. Contemporaries swore that Kate was as plain as a post, but perhaps skilled at winking with her good eye; she managed somehow to catch the fancy of 14-year-old Louis XIV, and accepted the duty of giving the king what the French gracefully call the *éducation sentimentale*.

By 1763 the *hôtel* was the home of the Bavarian ambassador. Leopold Mozart came to visit in that year, bringing his little prodigy, Wolfgang, to show off to the French. Long abandoned, the palace is being restored as the home of the city's office for the protection of historic buildings. All that survives of its former splendours, though, is an eccentric elliptical courtyard (usually closed), decorated with rams' heads, a pun on Mme Bellier's name.

*Further down the street, you can see some of the oldest houses in Paris, at nos. 44 and 46, where the neighbourhood restoration society has an **information office**; you may visit the medieval cellars underneath. Even older are the tall, half-timbered pair at **nos. 11 and 13**, typical examples of Paris buildings in the 1400s. Rue Miron ends behind the Hôtel de Ville, at the church of **St-Gervais-St-Protais**.*

The blank façade, currently under restoration, may not seem impressive nowadays, but it is a minor landmark of an architectural revolution, one of the first in Paris to attempt a classically inspired style instead of the good old tradition of French Gothic. Louis XIII laid the first stone for the façade in 1616. The rest of the building, begun in 1494, is the latest incarnation of a church that has been on this site since the 6th century. In March 1918, when the Germans were trying a last-ditch effort to terrorize France out of the war, a shell from Big Bertha came through the roof, while the choir was singing a hymn from Lamentations. Over a hundred people were killed.

After the usual Revolutionary depredations, the City of Paris spent huge sums to redecorate the church in the 1830s and '40s. But in truth there is not a single thing inside worth climbing the steps for, although the church does have some good stained glass in the Lady Chapel behind the altar, heavily restored in the 19th century, and Paris' oldest organ (1601), where eight members of the Couperin family, including the famous composer, held the post of organist until 1856.

*That's the end of the walk, but the Marais is one of the biggest quarters of Paris, and there are plenty of less significant sights we haven't dragged you blocks out of the way to see. Roughly from south to north:*

**The Arsenal**, *Rue de Sully, off Boulevard Henri-IV:*

In 1512 the state commandeered the old Celestine monastery here for the manufacture of munitions. After an explosion in 1563 took part of the neighbourhood with it, the arsenal moved across the Seine to La Salpêtrière, leaving only the name behind. Under Richelieu the complex became a court and a prison. Nicolas Fouquet, Louis XIV's importunate finance minister, who made the mistake of being ostentatiously richer than the king, endured his famous trial here (*see* Vaux-le-Vicomte, p.479). Since 1797 the buildings have housed branches of the Bibliothèque Nationale, including many of the libraries confiscated from nobles and monasteries during the Revolution. Tours are offered (*daily except Sun at 2.30,* © *01 42 77 44 21*), including some lavish 18th-century apartments.

*Behind the Arsenal, across Boulevard Morland, are Paris' municipal offices, and to the left of them the barracks of the **Garde Républicaine**. Of more interest than all these however, is the **Pavillon de l'Arsenal**, at*

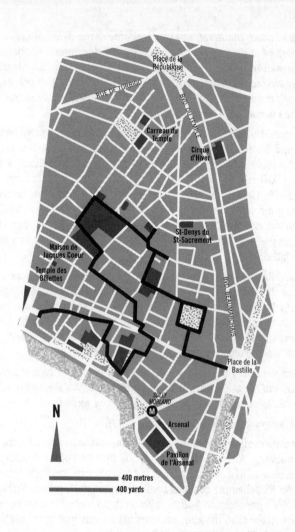

*21 Boulevard Morland a few steps from Boulevard Henri-IV. Since 1988 this has been a special exhibition dedicated to Paris, its history and the planning currently under way for its future (open daily except Mon 10.30–6.30; Sun 11–7).*

The exhibits, beginning with a 540-sq-ft model of the entire city that lights up to point out sites and stages in the city's development, is as high-tech and glitzy as the *grands projets* themselves; the whole thing is relentlessly educational, and does a good job of presenting the planners' doubtful case.

> **Lower Rue des Archives:** *There are two buildings worth a look on this street. The* **Temple des Billettes,** *an 18th-century monastic church at no. 22, has belonged to the Lutherans since 1812. Its cloister, simple and refined, is amazingly the only Gothic cloister left in Paris, after the other 30 or so were demolished by speculators after the Revolution. At no. 40, the 15th-century* **Maison de Jacques Coeur** *slept under a coat of stucco for centuries, until a chance restoration brought its brick-patterned façade to light in 1971.*

Coeur, a merchant of Bourges, was a fascinating man ahead of his time, a proto-capitalist who, like Nicolas Fouquet, got a little too big for the tastes of his king. Falsely accused of poisoning the royal favourite, Agnès Sorel, Coeur escaped prison and ended up in Rhodes, fighting the Turks.

> **Carreau du Temple:** *In any medieval view of Paris, you'll notice what seem to be little walled cities just outside Paris' own walls. This isn't just the medieval imagination at work; they really existed. Two of the largest were on what is now the fringes of the Marais: the Abbey of St-Martin des Champs (see Walk III, p.161) and especially the 'Quarter of the Templars'.*

The Knights Templars, an order of the noble élite originally founded in 1119 to protect pilgrims and defend the newly conquered Holy Land, attracted so much talent, land and money that it soon found itself to be a European power in its own right. Vows and piety went by the board; learning to move money around Europe and the Middle East to finance their activities, the Templars stumbled on the idea and methods of banking—and made the most of it, especially in France. By the 12th century they kept the royal treasury, and pretty much managed the economy of the nation. They owned most of the Marais; about the turn of the century they began building their extramural complex, partly for greater security, and partly to make even more money by sheltering merchants and artisans shut out by the monopolistic guilds of Paris.

Some estimates put the population of the Templars' new city as high as 4000. After the lightning seizure of the order and its property by Philippe le Bel in 1307, their enclave (given to the Knights of Malta) gradually dwindled as it was swallowed up by the expanding city. By the Revolution, little was left but the main tower of the Templars' headquarters. Confiscated by the Commune of Paris, it became the prison of Louis XVI and Marie Antoinette. Napoleon had it demolished in 1808 to keep Bourbon loyalists from turning it into a shrine.

Today there is not a single stone left of the Templars' city. The centre of the site is now occupied by the **Square du Temple**, a small park built by Haussmann with an iron bandstand. Across Rue Perrée, the lively cheap **clothes market** of the **Carreau du Temple** has been going strong since 1809, despite occasional attempts by the city to close it. The surrounding streets are the one part of the Marais that have not been totally gentrified. Much of the city's jewellery manufacturing is done here: many of the workers are immigrants from Asia or Yugoslavia.

### *Cirque d'Hiver,* Boulevard du Temple:

Probably the most famous circus venue in the world, originally this delightful round building was the *Cirque Napoléon.* Hittorff, Napoleon III's favourite architect, designed it in 1852, at the beginning of the golden age of the circus. Today, besides concerts and various other events, it still hosts the well-known Bouglione company for a regular circus season from November through April. Part of Fellini's *The Clowns* was filmed here.

> **Place de la République:** *It isn't pretty, but this is understandable, for the square was less an urban embellishment than a military installation, the key strongpoint in the never-ending job of defending Paris from its inhabitants.*

République took its present form under Napoleon III; the big barracks he built along its northern face are still occupied. The boulevards that radiate in all directions gave the troops easy access to all points in radical, working-class east Paris. To expand the square to its present dimensions, Baron Haussmann demolished the greater part of the Boulevard du Temple, the legendary theatre district that Parisians of the 19th century knew as the 'Boulevard du Crime' from the cops-and-robbers melodramas the public loved. Among the theatres knocked down was the Funambules, home of the great actor Frédérick Lemaître. All this will be familiar to anyone who has seen Marcel Carné's *Les Enfants du Paradis* (1943). In the memorable opening scene of this film the whole boulevard is displayed, with its teeming crowds, its jugglers and mountebanks. It was all reconstructed, the most expensive film set ever made in France, in a studio in Nice—and in the middle of the German occupation.

**Start:** Ⓜ *Hôtel de Ville. If you come in on Line 1, along the platform you'll see a display of old prints and maps, giving an overview of the Town Hall's history.*

# III: Les Halles and Beaubourg

**Walking time:** *3½ hours, not counting time spent in the Conservatoire and Pompidou Centre.*

This is the old Paris of merchants and markets, the only walk on the Right Bank that contains neither a royal palace nor a royal square; its history is entirely lacking in powdered noblemen, subtle philosophers, grand dames of the salon, soldiers or clerics. It was—at least until lately—the Paris of the Parisians, the place you would go to buy your turnips, pick up a strumpet or start a revolution. The streets are medieval, or older, and their names betray the gritty workaday spirit of the place: Street of the Knifesmiths, of the Goldsmiths, Goose Street.

Only 30 years ago, there were indeed knifesmiths, goldsmiths and geese, and these streets were crowded with handcarts and barrels night and day. No part of Paris has seen greater changes in those 30 years, and not always for the better. The megaprojects of the Fifth Republic—the Halles shopping mall and the Pompidou Centre—squat amidst the scant remnants of medieval conviviality like conquerors from space. Once *les Forts*, the porters' guild of the Halles, ruled the streets, shouldering real sides of beef through narrow alleys, and eating three-course dinners for breakfast to give them strength; today effete, black-clad young wraiths clamour for chemical hamburgers at the American chain outlets. But even the most mercilessly efficient city government in the world could not totally destroy such an urban heart. Compared to the City of London or Wall Street, Paris' old business centre got off lightly: old streets and buildings intact, a human scale, a good mix of people. The streets are fun for ambling and observing; there's a smattering of credible art, a wealth of history—and, strangely enough, all throughout this walk, a collection of clocks, automata and technical gadgets perhaps unequalled anywhere.

Do this walk in the afternoon: the Pompidou Centre doesn't open till noon (10am at weekends) and closes tight on Tuesdays, as does the Conservatoire.

### lunch/cafés

*With all the people and all the action here, you might expect that it is a hotbed of switched-on entertainment and good, authentic restaurants. It isn't. Trendy spots and chains are rife between the Halles and Centre Pompidou; around the Fontaine des Innocents you can walk into almost any door and get something to eat—don't expect anything transcendent.*

# III: Les Halles and Beaubourg

**N**

200 metres
200 yards

BVD. POISSONNIERE

BONNE NOUVELLE

Passage Brady

BOULEVARD DE BONNE-NOUVELLE

RUE DE LA LUNE

Porte St-Denis

BOULEVARD ST-DENIS

Porte St-Martin

STRASBOURG ST. DENIS R. STE. APOLLINE

BOULEVARD ST-MARTIN

BVD. DE STRASBOURG

RUE CLERY

RUE MESLAY

RUE D'ABOUKIR

RUE NOTRE DAME

RUE DU VERTBOIS

124 Rue Réaumur

Passage du Caire

RUE DU CAIRE

RUE ST-DENIS

Musée National des Techniques (Conservatoire)

100 Rue Réaumur

SENTIER

RUE REAUMUR

BOULEVARD DE SEBASTOPOL

RUE ST-MARTIN

St-Martin-des-Champs

REAUMUR SEBASTOPOL

Arts et Metiers

RUE BACHAUMONT

Rue Montorgueil Market

RUE GRENETA

St-Nicolas-des-Champs

RUE MANDAR

AVE. GRENETA

RUE ÉTIENNE

Hôtel de Poste

RUE TIQUETONNE

RUE DE TURBIGO

Caisse d'Epargne de Paris

RUE MONTMARTRE

MARCEL

R. MONTORGUEIL

R. DE MONTMORENCY

RUE COQUILLERE

RUE DU LOUVRE

St. Eustache

ÉTIENNE MARCEL

LES HALLES

RUE DU CYGNE

Maison de Nicolas Flamel

R. AUX OURS

R. QUINCAMPOIX

R. BRANTOME

RUE BEAUBOURG

RUE DE WARMES

Bourse de Commerce

RUE RAMBUTEAU

Quartier de l'Horloge Défenseur des Temps

RUE BEAUBOURG

Musée de la Musique Mécanique

Jardin des Halles Colonne Médicis

Forum des Halles

R. BERNARD DE CLAIRVAUX

RUE BERTHAUD

RAMBUTEAU

RUE BERGER

Square des Innocents

BOULEVARD DE

RUE ST-DENIS

RUE ST-MARTIN

Centre Pompidou

RUE ST. HONORE

Place Marguerite-de-Navarre

Fontaine des Innocents

LES HALLES

Place Georges-Pompidou

RUE DU RENARD

RUE DE RIVOLI

RUE DE LA FERRONERIE

Stravinsky Fountain

CHATELET LES HALLES

RUE DES LOMBARDS

R. DU CLOITRE ST-MERRI

St-Merri

RUE DU PONT NEUF

RUE DES HALLES

Tour St-Jacques

RUE DE RIVOLI

RUE DU TEMPLE

QUAI DE LA MEGISSERIE

CHATELET

AVENUE VICTORIA

HOTEL DE VILLE

Seine

Place du Châtelet

CHATELET

QUAI DE GESVRES

Place de l'Hôtel de Ville

Hôtel de Ville

R. DE LOBAU

PONT AU CHANGE

PONT NOTRE DAME

**Le Béarn**, 2 Place Ste-Opportune, ✆ 01 42 36 93 35. This area's budget champ—a lunch for 55F.

**Fuji**, 8 Rue Courtalon (just off Rue des Halles). Adequate, cheap and Japanese; 50–75F lunch menu includes, soup, starters, green tea and seafood. From 7–8pm, all the sushi you can eat for 120F

**Le Sous Bock**, 49 Rue St-Honoré. Complicated cocktails and the best imported beers; snacks of mussels and *frites* at all hours. Includes a booze boutique that is a tippler's dream—180 varieties of whisky. There is also a simple 58F lunch *formule*.

**Gambrinus**, 62 Rue des Lombards. Trendy bar with some 30 varieties of beer on tap; 60F lunch menu, or else *moules/frites*, sauerkraut and sausage, chili, goulash.

**La Cloche des Halles**, 28 Rue Coquillière. Wine bar of renown; excellent choices to go with snacks of cheese and *charcuterie*.

**L'Escargot Montorgueil**, 38 Rue Montorgueil, ✆ 01 42 36 83 51. Most of the decor is from the 1830s, and the big snail over the door proclaims the speciality of the house; another favourite is duck *à l'orange*. 140 and 180F lunch menus; reserve.

**Pharamond**, 24 Rue de la Grande-Truanderie, ✆ 01 42 33 06 72. Another ancient establishment, *belle-époque* décor and tripe *à la Caen* for a stalwart old clientele (but plenty of alternatives for the tripe-shy); 300F à la carte on average.

**La Table des Gourmands**, 14 Rue des Lombards. In an old vaulted cellar, light dishes for delicate souls: shrimp salad, cream of asparagus soup and such; lunch menu at 56, 68 or 128F.

**Au Petit Ramoneur**, 74 Rue St-Denis. Very convivial, crowded, tables out in the street; *petit salé* with lentils is the people's choice; 68F.

**Auberge Nicolas Flamel**, 51 Rue de Montmorency, ✆ 01 42 71 77 78. In one of the oldest houses in Paris (*see* below), refined cooking from *maigrets* cooked with cider to seafood raviolis; 69 and 98F lunch menus.

---

*To begin this walk through the Paris of the Parisians, it's only fitting to start in the* **Place de l'Hôtel-de-Ville***, in front of Paris' town hall.*

Medieval Paris never gave too much thought to urban amenities. If any Right Bank burgher wanted to stretch his legs, about the only place to do it was this square, the only large open space in the city. Back then it was called *Place de Grève* (of the strand). Laid out as a merchants' yard in 1141, when the docks of the Cité had become too crowded to handle the city's booming trade, the square quickly evolved as Paris' business centre and key to the growth of the Right Bank. It never was the most tranquil place for the burghers to promenade; its expanse would have been swarming with a cosmopolitan crowd of merchants and boatmen, along with their stacks of bundles and barrels—salt fish from the North Sea for Friday, wines from the Champagne (but no sparkling champagne yet, not for another 400 years!), iron nails and tools from Germany, novelties and luxuries from Byzantium via Venice (many of these were bound for England).

But there was room enough in the Place de Grève for all sorts of other activities. Executions were commonly held there, it being the only space large enough to accommodate the crowds. In 1793, at the beginning of the Terror, the guillotine was installed; the stench of blood was so overwhelming that cattle being herded to their own slaughter at Les Halles refused to cross the square. From medieval times, on any weekday men looking for work would mill about in one corner, and prospective employers knew they could find help there. To 'do the *Grève*' became a synonym for being out of work. Gradually, *grève* came to mean a strike, and a new word was thus added to the French language. As *grèves* had become common and threatening to the established order by the 19th century, the name was changed to the innocuous 'Town Hall Square' when Haussmann redesigned it.

As the city government developed out of the ancient establishment of the boatmen's guild, it was only natural that the first organization of the commune should have its headquarters here. A medieval landmark facing the Place was the small Maison des Piliers, the 'columned house', fronted by a portico built in an attempt to re-create the architectural grandeur of Roman times. Etienne Marcel commandeered it for his new city commune in the 1350s, and a Hôtel de Ville in one form or another has been on the site ever since. It has witnessed many events in the city's history: here Louis XVI was forced to accept a tricolour cockade from the mob in 1789; here Robespierre was arrested, five years later, ending the Reign of Terror. Crowds besieged the building in 1830 and again in 1848, when they were cowed by the insults of the poet Lamartine. Behind, on Rue de Lobau, Napoleon constructed an army barracks still in use today. A tunnel underneath Rue de Lobau permits soldiers to occupy the Hôtel de Ville in minutes—as they've had to do on at least a dozen occasions since 1800. In peaceful times the Hôtel de Ville was the traditional setting for state parties, celebrating everything from Napoleon's wedding to the reception of Queen Victoria in 1854.

The current incarnation isn't as old as it looks. After the Prussian victories of 1870, the Hôtel de Ville was seized by the provisional government and fortified. Its fall to the mob on 18 March 1871 marked the beginning of the Paris Commune;

throughout the fighting it served as the nerve centre of the Communards, and was burned to the ground in the last days. The new building, begun in 1874, generally follows the design of its predecessor, covered with over a hundred statues of famous Frenchmen. There are guided tours of the interior (*Mon mornings at 10.30; entrance on Rue Lobau*), of which the highlights are the big, colourful paintings in almost every room, all done in the most florid late 19th-century manner: a series of scenes from Paris history by J.-P. Laurens, and the *Four Seasons* by the Pre-Raphaelite Puvis de Chavannes.

> *From here, take the Quai des Gesvres west, with a pretty view over the Seine and the Ile de la Cité. Facing the Pont au Change, the quay opens into* **Place du Châtelet**, *with another memorial column to Napoleonic glories. The Place is named after a little medieval castle, demolished under Napoleon, that once guarded the approaches to the bridge.*

The Châtelet's last few centuries found it a notoriously unhealthy prison, where the police stowed the worst of the Parisian riff-raff; the worst of the worst were kept in great subterranean caves, before being shipped off to the galleys.

> *Now two theatres swathed in glass-fronted cafés flank the Place: on the west side the* **Théâtre Musical de Paris** *(1862), a typically lavish work of the Second Empire, and on the east, the* **Théâtre de la Ville**.

This one used to be called the Sarah Bernhardt. The great actress was flush enough in 1899 to buy it and name it after herself, and she spent the rest of her career here, bumping about histrionically on her wooden leg in ripe productions like *La Dame aux Camélias*.

> *If you like, you can digress a bit further down the Seine;* **Quai de la Mégisserie**, *west of the Place, is one of the major strongholds of the* bouquinistes—*mostly books and such, but there are still a few traders in the quay's traditional specialities: seeds, bulbs and birds.*

> *The opposite side of the Place faces a small, green square, laid out around the Gothic spire called the* **Tour St-Jacques**.

The butchers of medieval Paris always had one of the wealthiest and most powerful of the city guilds. This was their quarter, where names like Slaughter Street and Skinners' Street were changed to something less piquant in the prissy Victorian Paris of the Second Empire. St-Jacques-de-la-Boucherie was the butchers' church, one of the grandest in Paris, and a famous meeting place for French pilgrims on their way to Santiago de Compostela. That did not stop the Revolutionary government from levelling it in 1797 and renting out the land to a manufacturer of cheap clothes. Only the 170ft tower survives (1523), not for being one of the last and most glorious works of the Flamboyant Gothic in the city but because another industrialist of the 1790s found it useful as a shot tower, where spoonfuls of hot lead flung from the top formed into balls before hitting the water below. The platform at the top is eccentric enough, graced with a huge statue of St James as well as a bull, a lion and an eagle (symbols of the Evangelists, with James doing service as the man, the fourth symbol). These beasts are 19th-century reproductions; the lumpy, eroded originals are displayed below in the square. The windy tower has been the city's meteorological station since 1891; at its base is an equally eccentric statue of Pascal, with a broken nose and a big thermometer, reminding us that the great mathematician and Christian mystic, author of the *Pensées*, also did some pioneering scientific work on the weather in the 1640s. Baron Haussmann, who erected the statue, had mistakenly thought that Pascal did his experiments here.

> *Walk west on Rue de Rivoli and turn right at the next corner into slanting* **Rue des Halles.** *This is the part of old Paris where the medieval street plan has been least changed. Though sleepy enough today, it was one of busiest areas of the city even a century ago. A few blocks up Rue des Halles is Rue de la Ferronnerie.*

Henri IV was murdered on this street in 1610 (near no. 11), in front of an inn sign showing a crowned heart pierced by an arrow. The assassin, a Catholic fanatic named Ravaillac, was able to do the job because the king's carriage got stuck in a traffic jam. 'What is it, sire?' asked the Duke de Montbazon, taking him in his arms. 'It is nothing, nothing,' Henri murmured, and died.

> *On the right side of Rue des Halles, just before the triangular Place Marguerite-de-Navarre, have a look at the little exterminator's shop marked* **Destruction des Animaux Nuisibles.** *Its lovingly arranged window displays have been a Paris landmark, with a few score of the proprietor's furry victims strung up in neat rows. Along with the stuffed weasels, they've been there since 1925. Continue to the end of the street, and bear left into Rue St-Honoré; at the next corner turn right, where a lovely green iron pavilion welcomes you to what used to be* **Les Halles.**

The great market, the 'Belly of Paris' as Emile Zola called it, was an 800-year-old institution when it was sacrificed to the speculators in 1969. It began in the reign of Louis VI, a simple open place in Les Champeaux ('little fields') on the edge of the Right Bank. About 1183, Philippe-Auguste laid out a proper market, roughly on the site of today's Forum, with central buildings for clothes, furs and luxury goods, a vast open space around it for food called the *Carreau* and a surrounding wall—the better for the king to collect his taxes as the farmers and merchants brought in their goods.

The people of the market, organized in their various corporations, soon began to feel themselves representative of Paris as a whole, and they often played a hand in political affairs. It became the custom for the ladies to call on the king with a basket of lilies-of-the-valley every first of May, at which occasions they might politely mention some popular grievance that they felt had not come to the royal attention (this custom is still maintained today, with presidents instead of kings). Politeness wasn't always the rule. During the Hundred Years' War the market people favoured the Burgundians and the English. In 1418, when these allies captured the city from the Armagnacs, the market people revenged themselves on this unpopular faction—they dragged the Armagnacs out of the prisons and massacred the lot.

## Les Halles: Names and Trades

According to some, the name of the market comes not from market halls, but rather *les 'alles*, from the verb *aller*—because *tout le monde s'y allait* (went there). Every good Parisian could be counted on to turn up here, to purchase or simply to loaf and gab and enjoy the comings and goings of the metropolis' leafy, glistening link with the distant world of Mother Nature. The Halles was a world in itself, engulfing all the streets around the market proper. Each was dedicated to a particular trade. Some of these are remembered in the names, encompassing every possible business from Rue de la Ferronnerie (of the smiths) to Rue aux Ours (originally not 'bears' but *oies*, 'geese'). Rue des Lombards was home to the Italian moneychangers and bankers, like Lombard Street in London, and the seamier side of the market area is frankly remembered in Rue de la Grande Truanderie and Rue de la Petite Truanderie—dedicated respectively, it seems, to felonies and misdemeanours.

## Les Halles: The Covered Market

Napoleon reacted just as you'd expect he would. After a brief tour in 1810, he said, 'I don't like this mess … There is no discipline here. This market isn't worthy of the capital of an empire.' His architects made the first plans for a covered market but it was not until the reign of Napoleon III that anything was done. Architect Victor Baltard designed the the famous, graceful green pavilions in 1851. His first effort had been a typical stone building, but the emperor, who took a great interest in the market plan, ordered it to be demolished and insisted the architect realize his idea of 'iron umbrellas'. Baltard came up with a great success, both aesthetically and practically, the model for new markets all over Europe. Others continued to be built here until 1936, by which time the complex covered some nine acres.

This Halles, destined to obliteration by the technocrats, was in its way as much fun as its medieval predecessor. It lived by night, when the loads of meat and produce came rolling in from across France. Bars and *bistrots* thrived on its fringes; they stayed up all night too, giving the poets and prostitutes and insomniacs a place to refresh themselves while they relaxed in the company of the market people. In the 1920s, Parisian toffs and English and American swells liked to end up here after a night of carousing, for a glass of wine or the traditional bowl of onion soup and a stroll through the flower market.

## Les Halles: Demolition and the *Trou*

Although there had been talk of closing Les Halles since the 1920s, a serious effort had to wait for de Gaulle's new regime in the late 1950s. The general's favourite technocrats groaned about the market's 'inefficiency', and especially about the way it tied up traffic on surrounding streets. The hidden agenda behind their gripes was an infernal marriage of two forces. First, suiting the mood of the times and the inclination of the politicians, was the desire to sanitize and homogenize. Convivial and informal as they are, markets make such types nervous; not only do markets seem disorderly, as they did to Napoleon, but they make it harder to collect taxes (the new market at Rungis has lots of computers, and records are kept of everything). Second, a perverse conspiracy grew up between the government, developers and property interests. Here was an opportunity—the only one possible—to redevelop a vast space in the very heart of Paris, replacing small businesses with large ones and promising fat profits for anyone who got in early.

Although the vast majority of Parisians were shocked by the scheme, little organized opposition ever appeared. The myth of progress in those days was still too strong—and decisions about Paris are made so undemocratically that Parisians had become apathetically resigned to any atrocity visited upon them. Even the radical leftists of the 1960s found little time for the issue. Though the demolition of Les Halles was decided in 1962, work did not begin until 1969. It was a big job; the last of Baltard's pavilions did not disappear until 1977—the same year that London closed down Covent Garden. Two were bought by wealthy friends of the Halles and reconstructed: at Nogent-sur Marne, and Yokohama, Japan.

Confusion reigned over what would replace the markets; all that was certain was the construction of a vast new underground RER station. Consequently, there appeared the weird gargantuan 'Hole', the *Trou des Halles*, a fitting symbol of the void that had been created in the centre of the city's life. Parisians would bring their children down on Sundays to look at it. Finally, inevitably, the technocrats decided what the area really needed—a shopping mall. The *Forum des Halles* opened in 1979.

And what was the result of the planning geniuses' efforts? The boom in property values and development that was supposed to accompany the Halles's demise never happened. The *Trou* has hardly been filled by the bunker that replaced it.

The market people work in supposedly efficient new metal sheds out in the suburbs, in Rungis—though a third of the merchants, the smaller ones of course, were driven out of business by the transition. Every restaurateur who remembers the old days will tell you that the food isn't nearly as good or as fresh as it used to be, and any Parisian shopper has noticed that it is much more expensive. The displacement created a new class of middlemen whose job is to get the food into Paris; they take their cut, and their vehicles help create new traffic jams on the roads leading into the city to replace the old ones.

Probably no greater crime has been committed against a modern city in the name of progress. The joke is that it was unnecessary. If Les Halles had been left alone, it would have naturally declined quite a bit by now; modern chain supermarkets, which had just begun to appear in the France of the 1960s, take care of themselves and have little need for old-style wholesale markets. A smaller Halles would have become much less offensive to the motorists. It would still be there to give Paris a heart, purchasers a choice, and night owls a place to wander.

*About three-quarters of the new Forum is underground, and most of the old marketplace is now the **Jardin des Halles**.*

It isn't a very inviting park; habitués come with a bottle of beer, and sit quietly with looks of dismal resignation on their faces—the buskers, the crowds and the break dancers, anything that's alive, shun it like the plague and stick to the old streets to the east. The one fortunate inspiration of the entire Halles project is the green iron pavilions at the entrances, recalling the style of the Baltard market houses. The theme is carried further in the park's green trellises; copies of these are sprouting up all over town now—congratulations to Paris for being the first city to find an attractive way of hiding reinforced concrete. Inside, there is a delightful and innovative **playground**—no adults allowed, but you can watch the kids slide down slides and bounce in pits full of ping-pong balls. On the eastern edge of the park, you'll pass sculptor Henri de Miller's **fibreoptic sundial**, a clever combination of technology and art, and a tribute to Paris' modern obsession with time, measurement and precision. Graphs etched in the stone would allow you to correct the sundial time to the second—unfortunately, this expensive gizmo hardly ever works.

Behind the sundial, the circular **Bourse de Commerce** (the Merchants' Exchange, 1889) closes the park's western end. In medieval times an important palace, the Hôtel de Nesle, stood on the site; later there was a convent and then the exquisite 'Hôtel de la Reine' built by Philibert Delorme for Catherine de' Medici. The next occupant was an extension of the Halles, the *Halle aux Blés* from which the current building takes its circular shape.

One curious fragment of Catherine's palace remains: the tall column called the **Colonne de Médicis**, now standing at the southeastern corner of the building on Rue de Viarmes. Inside, a spiral staircase leads to a platform where Catherine and her astrologers (including, briefly, Nostradamus) would contemplate the destinies of the dynasty and of France. In the sophisticated courts of the Renaissance, nearly everyone wore magic talismans and consulted learned sorcerers, but Cathy was an extreme case. The Jesuits circulated pamphlets suggesting she was a devil-worshipper; other sources detail how she tried to deal with Coligny and the Prince de Condé, the leaders of the French Protestants. First she sent them poisoned apples, like Snow White's evil stepmother. Foiled in that (Coligny prudently gave the apple to his dog), she had a German magician make bronze voodoo dolls of the pair, covered with little screws that she could move in and out, according to the recommendations of the astrologers, to control her opponents' actions. It's a shame it didn't work; the queen might have spared France the St Bartholemew's Day Massacre.

> *One small redeeming feature of the Halles project was that it opened up the view of the market's own parish church, **St-Eustache**, behind Henri de Miller's huge stone egg-head, listening to the secret currents in Paris' bowels.*

The entrance is on Place du Jour; if it's warm, you may see Oscar, the pet boar at the Pied du Cochon restaurant across the street, bemusedly watching the Parisians stare at him as they pass by on the pavement. Next door, an Irish pub operates under a portrait of James Joyce. Wearing a fedora and sipping a Guinness, Joyce squints ruefully at what may be the most pathetic church façade in France. This neoclassical pudding was added in the 1750s to 'improve' one of Paris' last and finest Gothic buildings. The other three sides remain unmolested, revealing an exotic late bloom of medieval architecture, Flamboyant Gothic in design although a bit Baroque in spirit; note how the typical pointed arch over the windows has turned into a heart shape. Once there was a glorious spire over the crossing, like that of Notre-Dame. The French took it down in the 1800s because it was in the way of some telegraph wires.

The original St-Eustache, like the market, began in the time of Philippe-Auguste. Jean Alais, a rich burgher who was also chief of the mystery players, had loaned money to the king and gained a tax concession in the fish market in return. He grew so wealthy from it, and felt so guilty collecting all the dosh without work, that he decided to finance a chapel for the Halles. St-Eustache soon became one of the most important churches in the city, second only to Notre-Dame. Richelieu, Molière and Madame de Pompadour were baptized here, and Louis XIV had his first communion. Among the notables buried inside was Colbert, whose tomb can be seen in one of the ambulatory chapels. It isn't surprising that the present building should have a Baroque air about it. Begun in 1532, it was not completed until the 1630s, when the Baroque in Italy was well under way; here, remarkably, the Gothic style and building methods were faithfully carried through to this late date, including even some stained glass.

The interior shows the plan typical of great Parisian churches since Notre-Dame: five aisles, leading into ambulatories around the broad apse, and with a transept built into rather than projecting from the church. The forest of pillars and pointed arches is grand and impressive—though it's a little disconcerting to see Corinthian columns in a supposedly Gothic building. The art inside, meticulously detailed on the displays posted at the entrance, is disappointing: a slim collection of second-rate works, mostly by Italian painters, half-hidden among the gloomy furnishings and clutter. St-Eustache offers its parishioners one really novel service: in the right aisle you'll see a small wooden box marked 'Messages for Souls in Purgatory'.

Whatever you do, do not miss the forlorn chapel in the left aisle, near the entrance, entirely filled with Raymond Mason's 1969 work, **The Departure of the Fruits and Vegetables from the Heart of Paris**, a funny, very moving diorama of solemn, dignified market people, carrying their leeks and tomatoes and turnips in a sort of funeral procession, away from the Baltard pavilions and into suburban exile. A placard to the left carries Mason's commentary; Les Halles was 'much more than a question of commerce; it was a place of happiness …'.

> *Now you have a significant choice: conviviality or modernity? For a detour, go behind the apse of St-Eustache and look for **Rue Montorgueil**, with its lively street market, the last vestige of the old Halles district (begins north of Rue Etienne-Marcel; every day except Mon). Or save the market for later, and take one of the escalators by the side of St-Eustache down into the belly of the beast, the underground of the **Forum des Halles**.*

The pigeons are already making themselves at home here, swooping over your head down the escalator shafts and gleaning the concourses for crumbs of pizza and *croque-monsieur*. It isn't likely the planners considered them, though they did go to great lengths to make this something more than just another shopping mall. Besides the ice-cream and chain stores, there is plenty of modern art to study (note the big mural along Rue des Piliers, a strange panorama of human progress from the Stone Age up to Louis Armstrong), as well as questionable cultural amenities like the 'Pavillon des Arts' and the 'Maison de la Poésie'; you can shoot a game of inscrutable French billiards (no pockets) or watch the young at the indoor swimming pool, next to a tropical garden where orchids and a banana tree grow behind a glass wall. At the **Vidéothèque de Paris**, you can while away an afternoon watching old French television shows, movies or newsreels (*daily 12.30–9pm*); there are booths for individual viewing and also an auditorium with continuous showings, usually about Paris.

At its eastern end, the Forum rises up above ground into a row of pavilions, sheathed in glass and shaped like *girolle* mushrooms. There are more attractions here: a lending library of recorded music, and the **Musée Grévin/Les Halles,** a branch of the famous wax museum (*see* Walk IV, p.179) that specializes in Paris' *belle époque*—re-creating Les Halles and Montmartre of the 1890s (*open daily 10.30–6.45, Sun 1–6.30; adm expensive*).

> *Leaving the Forum by the southern end, cross Rue Berger and follow the crowds and street performers into the **Square des Innocents**.*

The crowds of young people, who have made this square their main centre-city rendezvous, can be seen literally dancing on the graves of their ancestors. There's one thing we didn't mention about the atmosphere of the old Halles—the aroma. For until 1786, the entire neighbourhood was perfumed by a ripe stench of decaying corpses from the Halles's neighbour, the Cimetière des Innocents.

There was a cemetery on this spot from Merovingian times. In the Middle Ages it acquired its name from the adjacent church of the Holy Innocents. Renowned for its soil, reputed to 'rot out a body in nine days', it became by the 1100s the main depot for the carcasses of Parisian paupers and other folk who had made no prior arrangements. The methods were refreshingly simple. Bodies were dumped into huge trenches; when they filled up, earth was piled on top and a new trench begun. When the corpses had entirely decomposed, they would be dug up and carted out of town—if the beggars from the nearby Cour des Miracles (*see* below) didn't steal them first; apparently after a few weeks in the ground the bones burned rather well and were prized as firewood.

Considering the open and understanding medieval attitude towards death, the souls down below would probably enjoy the thought of electric guitars and African dancers above. Philippe-Auguste built a wall around the Innocents, but by no means was it cut off from the life of the city. Even fashionable Parisians liked to make their evening promenades here. Prostitutes frequented it at night, along with lovers making their midnight trysts among the heaps of corpses, and in the day it was the home of the public scribes, gents with little tables who would crank out anything from a petition to the king to a *billet-doux* for the illiterate. The embellishment of the cemetery was entirely appropriate. A marble statue of a skeleton held pride of place in the centre of the courtyard, and in the early 15th century the Duc de Berry had his court painters do the outside walls with a *danse macabre* of grinning skeletons carrying off the Pope, the King, the Knight and everyone down to the Workman and the Child. This might have been one of the best of all Paris' innumerable lost artworks—the painters would most likely have been the same fellows who did the greatest of all late medieval illustrated manuscripts, the *Très Riches Heures du Duc de Berry*.

The Innocents' function, and its social scene, changed little from medieval times to the reign of Louis XVI. The decision to get rid of it was only made when the corpses, and their attendant hordes of crazed, flesh-eating rats started pushing through the walls of the neighbours' cellars; two miners who tunnelled in to explore were asphyxiated by poisonous gases emitted by the bodies. In 1786 the cemetery was demolished, the bodies were moved off to the catacombs (though there must still be lots of forgotten ones lurking under here) and the cleared site was converted into a market. Later it was remodelled into the present square, and the **Fontaine des Innocents**, which had previously stood outside the cemetery, was installed at its centre. The only surviving Renaissance fountain in Paris (1549) is a work of Pierre Lescot, though the lovely decorative reliefs are from the hand of Jean Goujon—mostly copies; the originals were hustled off to the Louvre.

*From the square, take* **Rue St-Denis** *south (right).*

If you're not in a hurry, however, take some time to explore this street in either direction. Once the main thoroughfare of the Right Bank, Rue St-Denis was the 'street of joy and sorrow'; the kings of France would follow it on their way into Paris, after their coronations, and their bodies would eventually retrace the route to join their ancestors in St-Denis's crypt. Since the building of Boulevard de Sébastopol, this narrow street has lost much of its importance. This part of it is now closed to traffic, and one of the most animated streets in Paris, with its *bistrots*, street characters, and pathetic sex shops—the real sleaze is a bit further north. As you pass Rue de la Ferronnerie, notice the **arcade** lining its northern side: this recalls the arcades of the Innocents' outer wall, where the *danse macabre* was painted. And, for a final ghoulish touch, the cemetery's wall was lined with windowless cells, for ladies who felt themselves (or were judged to be) so sinful that the only fitting penance would be complete withdrawal from the world. They were bricked up inside, and each day a plate of gruel would be pushed through a crack; when the plate didn't come back, the cell was ready for a new occupant.

*Two streets south of the square, on St-Denis, turn left at the Morriss column into Rue des Lombards. You'll cross the long, die-straight* **Boulevard de Sébastopol***, Baron Haussmann's contribution to the neighbourhood, built to replace Rue St-Denis and named after one of Napoleon III's few victories (in the Crimean War). The next street, narrow Rue Quincampoix, had an interesting mix of tenants in the old days— whores and bankers.*

*This too is a street worth exploring if you have the time, with a number of pretty iron balconies and carved portals on the old* hôtels. *At what is now no. 54 stood the headquarters of the most infamous banker of them all, John Law.*

A Scotsman, of course, Law was a man ahead of his time. Failing to interest Britain or any other state in his advanced ideas about credit and stock schemes, he brought them to nearly-bankrupt France in 1716 and soon gained the favour of the Regent. His first venture was the Mississippi Company, a state-backed monopoly of trade and development in the Louisiana Territory. Two years later, his success allowed him to combine the company with what was meant to be the first proper national bank, which could drive the economy by holding state funds and making loans off them. In his own life, Law had learned how rolling over paper could make real wealth, and he sincerely believed it could work for everyone. It was an instant success. Law had invented speculation, or rather speculation had invented itself. Shares in the company seemed a magic passage to instant wealth, and Law helped the boom along by ingenious advertising methods, such as parading gilded Indians through the streets and publishing prints showing mountains of solid silver in Louisiana. Even Paris' poor scraped together their *sous* to buy in. Rue Quincampoix turned into a rowdy outdoor stock market where everyone jostled for paper bargains and bid up the prices, while the usual ladies lounged in the doorways, waiting to get the winners in their clutches.

Law was on top of the world (an aristocrat wrote: 'A duchess has kissed his hand in public ... Where not, then, must other women kiss him?'). By 1720 over a million Frenchmen had a piece of the company, which had grown into a system controlling France's tax system and financing its national debt. It was no swindle. Law was utterly honest, and invested his own fortune in the company. Consequently, when the inevitable bust came in the autumn of 1720, he was completely ruined. Left alone, he might well have been able to save his system and learn from the experience, but by October 1720 his enemies had him banished from France. Law ended up in Venice, making a miserable living at cards, while in Paris the wealthiest aristocrats, many of whom had been burned, carved up the company and divided its assets among themselves. The small fry didn't get a penny back.

*Return to Rue des Lombards, turn left and you'll come to Rue St-Martin (note one of Paris' original street signs, from the 17th century); this is another ancient thoroughfare—it started as the Roman road to the north. The church to your left is* **St-Merri.**

Saint Merri, or Medericus, was an abbot of Autun buried here in the early 8th century. A chapel was built over his relics, on a site then on the outskirts of the city; in the Middle Ages, with all the bankers and cloth merchants in this area, it became one of the richest parish churches of Paris. The present building was begun *c.* 1500, in somewhat the same late Flamboyant Gothic style as St-Eustache, and not completed until 1612. The last part to be finished was the bell tower, which contains a 14th-century bell called the Merri, the oldest in the city. Only a century and a half later, Paris found St-Merri looking impossibly old-fashioned; Michelangelo Slodtz was commissioned to prettify the interior, with the help of his brothers (don't laugh; Slodtz, who spent 20 years in Rome and whose work can be seen in St Peter's, was actually one of the more accomplished sculptors of his time. But then, probably all 18th-century French sculptors should have been named Michelangelo Slodtz).

During the Revolution, St-Merri served the nation as a saltpetre factory. The mobs had done a fairly thorough job of trashing its façade, so what you see on it today is largely replacements from the 1840s, including the statues of saints and the little winged, supposedly **hermaphroditic demon** that leers over the main portal. French occultists have had some fun explaining this one; it is claimed that secret cults used to meet in St-Merri's crypt. Inside, the Slodtz brothers didn't do too much mischief; the body of the church survives as it was, with delicate traceries on the vaulting and an especially nice crossing. The major Slodtz contribution is the neoclassical remodelling of the choir and altar; several of their carved saints can be seen around the church. From the original church, there remains some 16th-century stained glass (along both sides of the nave), and a majestic organ ensemble carved in wood by Germain Pilon in the 1640s. There are frequent concerts on Sunday afternoons; after these, you can have a free guided tour (first and third Sunday of each month).

> *Leaving St-Merri, circle around it to your right, down Rue du Cloître-St-Merri; after admiring its flamboyant buttresses and gargoyles, you'll be startled back into the 20th century by the* **Stravinsky Fountain**.

Built at the same time as the Centre Pompidou behind it, this broad sheet of water serves as a play pool for a collection of monsters created by that delightful sculptress from Mars, Niki de Saint-Phalle. Her colourful gadgets are each dedicated to one of Stravinsky's works (it isn't always easy to guess which); at any moment, they are likely to start spinning around and spraying you with water. The black metal mobiles between them are the work of Jean Tinguely.

> *And there it stands, the* **Centre National d'Art et de Culture Georges Pompidou**. *Nearly everyone calls it simply 'Beaubourg'. The big tilted open space in front is the Place Georges-Pompidou, known to one and all as the 'Plateau de Beaubourg' (Centre open daily except Tues, 12–10 pm; Sat and Sun 10–10 pm; separate adm for all exhibits). All tickets are sold at the windows on the ground floor only. For information about what's on, ring 01 42*

The 'Beau Bourg' was a village, swallowed up by Paris
in the Middle Ages, that has lent its name to the neighbourhood ever since. By the 1920s it had become a grey,
unloved place; the government cleared a large section, meaning to relocate the
flower market from the overcrowded Halles. Nothing happened, and the empty
space remained a tantalizing challenge to Paris planners until the 1970s. It was the
grey, unloved president, Georges Pompidou, who came up with the idea of a
'department store for culture', a centre that could break with the traditional
museum concept and make art and ideas more accessible to more people.

For such an idea, it was obvious to all that the building would have to be an attraction in itself, and the design finally chosen was the most radical of all those
submitted. The architects, Richard Rogers and Renzo Piano, were committed to a
brand of modernism that meant to turn traditional ideas of building upside down—
or rather, inside out. To allow larger, more open spaces on the inside, and to
expose frankly what a modern structure really is, they came up with a big rectangle
of girders, from which the insides are hung, a kind of invertebrate architecture,
with an insect's shell instead of a skeleton. Much more provocative was the idea of
putting the technological guts of the building on the outside—celebrating the
essentials instead of hiding them, and painting them in bright colours keyed to help
the observer understand how it all works: electrics in yellow, air conditioning in
blue, white for ventilation ducts, etc. These are best seen on the back of the
building, along Rue Beaubourg.

It was more controversial than anything since the Eiffel Tower. Critics grumbled
about connections with the Martian war machines from *War of the Worlds*, and
complained about the lack of respect for the 'historic architecture' of the quarter
(you'll have noticed by now, however, that Beaubourg has hardly any). After the
Centre opened in 1977, Parisians and tourists voiced their opinion by making it
overnight the most visited sight in the city, surpassing even the Eiffel Tower. The
'Plateau' in front, redesigned by Piano into an austere, sloping rectangle decorated
only by surreal ventilation shafts from the car park below, became an instant hap-
pening that even Georges Pompidou might have enjoyed (from a safe distance),
where Paris' old coterie of repulsive oral tricksters—sword swallowers, cigarette
munchers and bicycle eaters—performed amid buskers, tramps, backpackers and
portrait sketchers.

As its shiny surfaces have weathered and grown dull, the ballyhoo has died down a
bit and the centre seems to fit right in among the drab buildings of Beaubourg.
Rogers' and Piano's high-tech architecture, although eventually accepted by the

city and the critics, has become a post-modernist cul-de-sac with few followers. The crowds now are not quite so large, and there have been complaints about the management of the Centre and the lack of imagination in its exhibits. But the centre is still far from exhausting its potential. It stands as a perfect symbol for both the strengths and the failings in the French approach. It represents, on the one hand, boldness and vision, and a genuine desire to make something democratic out of this vague business called 'culture'. On the other hand it embodies the rather outlandish assumption that planning, subsidies and government direction can make creativity magically sprout up, like any other strategic industry, according to the rules Pompidou's generation learned in the *Grandes Ecoles*.

But give them credit. No one can say yet that the architecture won't go down in the books as a brilliant precursor of the next century, or that the Centre will not find its role as a cultural clearing house for some future Renaissance. They're already planning for the future. To the right of the entrance, the **Clock of the Millennium** counts down the seconds left before 1 Jan 2000, making the Centre the unofficial headquarters of the new age. Inscriptions promise big surprises when the digital display reaches zero, to encourage all Paris to be here on that fateful New Year's Eve; meanwhile, you can put in a coin and get a postcard stamped with the exact time of your visit in relation to the big event—at the time of writing, there are still some 140,174,000 seconds to go.

You'll still probably have to wade through musicians, portraitists and dancing Brazilian warriors with complete rhythm sections to get in (two original performance artists were spotted recently: one selling vegetable choppers, and another who comes in the morning with a case of beer and spends the day sitting on the pavement, emptying the bottles and arranging them in patterns). Inside, the first thing to do is look at the ticket booths on the ground floor, with placards for everything going on along with schedules and prices. You won't need a ticket for the **escalator** to the top, by far the Centre's most popular attraction. Like everything else mechanical, it runs along the outside, providing a spectacular view over Paris that changes dramatically as you ascend; for a special treat, come back and do it at twilight, when the monuments of the city are illuminated.

> *The major permanent feature of the Centre is the **Musée National d'Art Moderne** on the fourth floor.*

This superlative collection of 20th-century art takes up where the Musée d'Orsay leaves off: at the turning point of modernity in 1904, when the Fauves (Derain, Vlaminck, Matisse, Marquet) liberated colour from its age-old function of representing nature. Van Gogh had blazed a trail by using colour to express emotions. The Fauves went a step beyond, applying colour and line on a two-dimensional surface as an intellectual expression, the way a poet uses words on a piece of paper (see the work of Matisse, the most lyrical and profound of the Fauves, especially his *Bocal des Poissons Rouges* (1914) and *Nu sur Fond Ornamental*).

Fauvism flickered out after only four years, but set off an immense burst of creative energy. Picasso formulated the creed of modern art when he wrote: 'I don't work after nature, but before nature—and with her.' New developments happened at a dizzying pace. 'We were like alpinists, all linked to one another,' said Braque, and one of the first examples of this linkage is his own *Viaduc à L'Estaque* (1908), hanging in the room of Fauves but painted in homage to Cézanne. As Van Gogh was a prophet for the Fauves, Cézanne's experiments in rendering volume with nuances of colour inspired Cubism. In the next rooms the Cubist works of Picasso, Braque, Juan Gris, and Duchamp analyze form by depicting it simultaneously from a hundred points of view on a flat surface; note, too, Léger's *La Noce*, a rare Cubist work depicting movement instead of a still life. A prism of aftershocks fills the next rooms, especially the first abstract works, born of Wassily Kandinsky's imaginative expressionism and the geometric fundamentals of Mondrian and his de Stijl followers.

There are important works from most of the big-name artists who continued modernism's sometimes amusing and delightful, sometimes distressing and painful inquiry into art, expression and its meaning: stylized figurative painters Chagall, Soutine and Rouault; the dadaists Picabia and Man Ray; the surrealists Dalí (his funny *Six Images of Lenin on a Piano*), Magritte, Tanguy, Masson and Ernst; Jean Dubuffet who in 1948 founded the Compagnie de l'Art Brut to sell the work of mental patients and questioned the very meaning of culture (he came out against it). Then there are two rooms by the abstract Ecole de Paris (de Staël, Bazaine, Bran van Velde); wire portraits and mobiles by Calder, a room of Giacometti's sculptures, drips from Jackson Pollock, works by Miró, Francis Bacon, Balthus, Hartung, Warhol, Rauschenberg, Oldenburg and Rothko. The terraces have monumental works by Calder and Tinguely. Your ticket also includes the third floor, with changing exhibits from Beaubourg's contemporary art collection, along with two permanent works: the *Magasin* by Ben and Dubuffet's *Jardin d'Hiver*.

Also in the Centre:

**Grandes Galeries**, (fifth floor), where the Centre's exhibitions are held.

**Galeries Contemporaines**, (ground floor), with smaller exhibits of contemporary artists.

**IRCAM**, the *Institut de Recherche et de Coordination Acoustique/Musique*, founded by Pierre Boulez; this is a working school and studio, now housed in the building across the square from the Centre; there are often concerts of avant-garde sonic disturbances.

**BPI**, the *Bibliothèque Publique d'Information*, an excellent library, and a real innovation in France—open to everyone, without restriction, always crowded.

**CCI**, the *Centre de Création Industrielle*, on the ground floor—an institution central to Pompidou's original concept, dedicated to the interrelationships between art and everyday life, in architecture, planning, design and the communications media; small temporary exhibitions.

**Salle Garance**, named after the heroine, played by Arletty, in *Les Enfants du Paradis*; shows cinema classics several times daily.

**Atelier de Brancusi**, outside, on the Plateau; a reconstruction of the Paris studio where the Romanian sculptor lived from 1925 to 1957.

**Atelier des Enfants**, an art workshop for children 6 to 12 years old.

> *From the Plateau, cross Rue Rambuteau. Ossip Zadkine's sculpture of Prometheus, stealing the heavenly fire, points the way down Rue Brantôme, into the **Quartier de l'Horloge**.*

It has become customary to malign this large project of the 1970s—but look again at one of the modest but meaningful successes of Paris' redevelopment. Intimate, protected from cars and built on a human scale, the design avoids brash architectural pretensions in favour of a comfortable community for people to live and work in. Halfway down Rue Brantôme is the project's centrepiece, the **Défenseur des Temps**. This golden mechanical clock, the work of Jacques Monestier (1979), portrays a curious fancy, the 'defender of time' battling with his sword each hour against a monster of the earth (a dragon), of the air (an eagle) or of the sea (a crab). At noon, 6pm and 10pm he must take on all three.

> *Leave the Quartier de l'Horloge by the short Rue Bernard-de-Clairvaux, leading into Rue St-Martin. Here, turn right. At Rue de Montmorency, around the corner at no. 51 (right of St-Martin) is one of the oldest houses in Paris, the much-restored 1407 **Maison de Nicolas Flamel**.*

Flamel was a famous character of his time, an official of the university reputed to be an alchemist. People thought he had got the gold to buy this mansion from finding the philosophers' stone—but really he married a rich widow.

> *Continue on Rue St-Martin to the church of **St-Nicolas-des-Champs**.*

In the 12th century, the monastery of St-Martin (*see* below) had become such a large and wealthy concern that it could build this substantial church just for its servants. The present building was begun in the 15th century, a fine flamboyant work with a bit of playful asymmetry on the window over the main portal. The 16th-century south portal is just as good, carved with nervous, wiry Renaissance grotesques after a design by Philibert Delorme. Don't expect anything particularly edifying inside; as at St-Merri, much of the interior, and all of the stained glass, succumbed to the tastemakers of the 18th century. Now St-Nicolas is a simple parish church, its busiest altar the one dedicated to St Rita, patroness of unappreciated housewives, where there are always a few candles burning.

> *Across Rue Réaumur stands the former monastery of St-Martin, later the Conservatoire des Arts et Métiers and now the world's original museum of technology, the **Musée National des Techniques** (the museum is closed for restorations until some time in 1997; a few sections are still open, daily except Mon 10–5.30).*

Along with St-Germain on the Left Bank, St-Martin-des-Champs was one of medieval Paris' two great monasteries. Today no more rural than London's 'St-Martin-in-the-Fields', it was well outside town in Merovingian times, when an oratory is recorded here, dedicated to France's original patron saint; according to legend, Martin cured a leper on this site. The first monastery was destroyed by the Normans in the 1060s and rebuilt almost immediately, growing over the next century into a walled complex that ruled over scores of other monasteries, and wielded great influence in political affairs. St-Martin owned much of the Right Bank, and had the right of administering justice in 'fifty streets' of the city.

Consequently, the monks ran a rather large prison. The kings had taken this over by 1718, when John Law had a bright idea to make use of the inmates—he talked the authorities into marrying 190 of them to 190 jailed prostitutes, and shipped them over the ocean to populate just-founded New Orleans. During the Revolution, the monastery served as an arms factory until the Conservatoire, a scientific laboratory and technical school, was established in 1798. Some important work was done here. The first balloon ascent for scientific purposes left from the courtyard in August 1804; the researchers went up to 13,000ft and learned, among other useful things, that it was damned chilly up there.

Jacques Vaucanson, a maker of machines and automata, contributed his own collection to start the Musée des Techniques in 1802. In the years since it has grown into an enormous, odd and dusty hoard of gadgets and models, scientific breakthroughs and techno-dinosaurs, with more junk than any junkyard and more mad-scientist gear than the Universal Studios properties department.

But before going in, have a look at the monastery from the outside. The **church**, visible from Rue Réaumur, is (again, along with St-Germain) one of the only two important Romanesque works left in Paris. The façade and nave are later rebuildings, but the truncated **bell tower** and the lovely **choir and apse**, with its radiating chapels, survive from the 1130s. The narrow arches and intricately carved floral capitals show a Byzantine influence; the rows of tiny human and monster heads under the cornice are an essentially French feature, seen on half the Romanesque churches in France (and traceable back to the ancient Gauls, who liked to decorate their sanctuaries with the real heads of their enemies). Around the back of the complex, on Rue du Vertbois, part of the abbey's medieval walls can be seen.

The main buildings, facing Rue St-Martin, were rebuilt from 1712 in a surprisingly graceful style—more like a Marais *hôtel* than a monastery. Off the main courtyard the fine Gothic **refectory** was spared, but it's almost always closed to the public. The entrance to the museum is here, guarded by statues of French inventors Nicolas Leblanc (who thought up a method for extracting sea salt) and Denis Papin (who made a sort of steam engine a century before Watt). Start on the ground floor, where an old painting of an 'Allegory of Science'—as a voluptuous woman, naturally—welcomes you. This hall is a trick echo chamber; whisper into one corner, and someone else will be able to hear you clearly in the corner opposite.

First comes a room with the quaint instruments of the great chemist Lavoisier (a key figure in the birth of modern chemistry, Lavoisier was guillotined in 1794 for having been one of the profiteers who grew fat from the Farmers-General tax wall before the Revolution). Next comes a mercilessly didactic exhibit on weights and measures through the ages, and another on railways, including some wonderful **model trains** built in the SNCF's own workshops. There are **mathematical instruments**—among them the first calculating machine, designed by Blaise Pascal—and **astronomical instruments**, with some fascinating old astrolabes and orreries.

Absolutely, positively do not miss the magnificent collection of **18th-century clocks**. These are some of the finest creations of the type on earth; a combination of rich materials and exquisite jewellers' work producing mythological conceits for musing poetically on time. Less poetic is a ten-hour clock, the brainchild of some manic rationalizer during the Revolution and eerily reminiscent of the film *Metropolis*. Don't miss the room of **automata** hidden in the far corner: charming old barrel organs and hurdy-gurdies, clockwork dolls and a mechanical dulcimer player that belonged to Marie Antoinette.

For readers of Umberto Eco's *Foucault's Pendulum*, the highlight of the museum will be the interior of St-Martin's church, now stuffed full of cars, aircraft engines, pumps and some heavy bits that defy all identification, incongruously sprawling under the medieval vaulting. One of Stephenson's early locomotives is here, along with the very first automobile, Joseph Cugnot's 1771 steam-powered *fardier*. Designed to pull cannons, the thing never did work right; a later version's first and only voyage ended at a stone wall. Amadée Bollée's 1873 *L'Obéissante* was one of the first steam coaches; it ran from Paris to Le Mans at 12mph, and looks to have been almost comfortable.

The mystic **pendulum** (1855) hangs from the vaulting. Léon Foucault, who also first measured the speed of light, thought up this toy, which proves the rotation of the earth by tracing a daily circle in its oscillations (the earth turns underneath it). The original experiment, conducted in 1851 under the dome of the Panthéon, had a swing wide enough to keep it going a full day. This one doesn't, but there's nothing magic about it; timed electronic magnets, hidden in the base, keep the pendulum moving. Of course nobody in 1851 doubted that the earth rotated, but this bagatelle did find some scientific importance—as a precursor of relativity, when it led later scientists such as Mach to reconsider Newton's false idea of a possible 'absolute motion'. Eco fans might be disappointed; not only are the church and its exhibits far less weird and sinister than he portrayed them, but the pendulum itself is a small, trifling thing, its wire too thin to hang a literary editor.

Nothing upstairs, on the **first floor** of the museum, is equally compelling: prototypical vacuum cleaners from 1906, a 19th-century vegetable slicer based on the guillotine, and displays that explain nuclear power and how your fridge works. There are tons more scientific instruments, including the apparatus of Foucault's light experiment. Other sections cover optics, meteorology, glassworking and ships (a tremendous 1812 model of the ship of the line *Roi de Rome*). The section on **communications** is good, with detailed exhibits on two French specialities: photography and cinema, including early equipment and works by Niepce, Daguerre and the Lumière brothers.

> *Continue north on Rue St-Martin, and in three blocks you'll be at the Grands Boulevards, slightly obstructed at this point by the two* **Triumphal Arches of Louis XIV***.*

When the course of the Boulevards was still Paris' city wall, the two grandest and most important of the gates stood here, at Rues St-Denis and St-Martin; both were castles in themselves, crowned with sculpted turrets and pinnacles. Something had to replace those venerable landmarks, and what better than another tribute to the glories of His Solar Majesty? Both these precursors of the Arc de Triomphe and the Grande Arche celebrate military victories in Holland and along the Rhine. The **Porte St-Martin**, built in 1674, is unusually austere, more like an 18th-century neoclassical work than something from the *grand siècle*. The **Porte St-Denis** (1672), two streets west, is much more in keeping with the spirit of the age, a veritable cascade of flowery sculptural allegories and trophies, and a bit phoney. Like everything else in this quarter, both could use a good wash.

## Rue St-Denis, the Sentier District and the Cour des Miracles

*We wouldn't want to add all this territory on to the walk; it's been long enough already, and what follows won't necessarily be to everyone's taste. There aren't any real sights either, but you still might find a stroll through this breezy, sleazy paragon of urban depravity a breath of fresh air in such a cute and tidy town. We'll start with **upper Rue St-Denis**, a place where police and prostitutes have reached a civilized truce.*

They managed it in a way only the French could, without any of the Puritan stupidity and violence of American cities, or the capitalist sex-kitsch of Hamburg or Amsterdam. The ladies stand in doorways, dressed for the role but conservative about the make-up; they chat in a matter-of-fact way while waiting for clients, like suburban matrons gossiping over the back fence. They share St-Denis with Turkish restaurants and lingerie shops with names like the 'Mae West' and the 'Flying Skirt'. Somehow it all seems so wholesome and normal; if you're looking for exoticism, romance, danger or anything besides a pleasant and polite business transaction, this may not be the right city. No matter how familiar this street and its business may be, it remains an eternal surprise to all of us who aren't French. Watch the ladies who are *not* prostitutes—they will stand in a doorway, to check the weather or wait for a friend, without feeling self-conscious in the least.

*North of the Grands Boulevards, the street becomes Rue du Faubourg-St-Denis.*

There are still plenty of whores, and they get scraggier the further north you go, amidst a raucous bazaar of gentlemen with earrings, doner kebabs, unintelligible languages, fluorescent orange pastries, large menacing dogs, half-plucked chickens, and a lingering scent of cumin.

*The centre of the action is the incredible **Passage Brady**, running two blocks from St-Denis to St-Martin.*

This is the unofficial capital of the Indian and Pakistani communities in Paris. The arcade, one of Paris' oldest, was the headquarters of the avant-garde Nabi painters of the 1890s; they fuelled up and issued their manifestos from a long-gone bar in the arcade. Today, the Brady boasts a Muslim barber, Bengali fast food and shops selling everything from linoleum to blue polyester lingerie and giant aluminium pots. Lakes appear on the pavement whenever it rains.

*South of the Boulevards it's a different picture altogether. From the Porte St-Denis, you can look over into what seems a vision of medieval Paris: tall, leaning tenements, shoehorned into narrow streets that slice weird angles across the prevailing grid. This is the back door of the **Sentier**.*

First impressions deceive; this is no picturesque backwater, as you'll notice the farther in you go, but the quarter of Paris that perhaps works the hardest for its living. The Sentier stitches together France's clothes, everything from the heights of designer glitz to T-shirts with 'Naf Naf' printed on them. Anyone from New York will recognize the place immediately. It's a Parisian double of the Garment District: huge shops that sell nothing but buttons or zippers or silk ribbons, frantic lunch counters brimming with weird, coded conversation, overdressed, languid shopgirls, slow, serene Hasidim, and young men in sweatshirts bowling you over with their speeding clothes trolleys along Rue d'Aboukir.

*The exotic street names of the Sentier—Aboukir, Alexandrie and Caire, come from enthusiasm over Napoleon's victories in Egypt. Today, the* **Passage du Caire**, *two streets north of Réaumur off Rue St-Denis, is a dingy but respectable showcase for the Sentier's manufactures; until 1667, though, this was the most notorious quarter of all Paris, the ghetto of thieves and beggars called the* **Cour des Miracles***.*

An old aristocratic property like the Palais Royal, where the police could not go, the Cour des Miracles in the 1600s became the centre of Paris' huge population of predatory beggars. The 'miracles' occurred every evening when the scoundrels came home—the blind regained their sight, the lame were healed, and crutches and wooden legs were packed away for the night. When not begging, the Cour's inhabitants cleaned the pockets of the Parisian crowds. La Reynie, Louis XIV's famous police chief, finally got the royal authority to clear out the Cour in 1667, and he managed it with panache. One night his men surrounded the area and announced that the last nine men leaving it would be hanged. The Cour was empty within ten minutes.

*The Sentier has a remarkable main street,* **Rue Réaumur***.*

For two decades after 1897, when it was cut through the old neighbourhood, Réaumur bade fair to become the commercial centre of Paris. Publishing and fashion businesses rushed to buy in, while developers threw up ostentatious, ultra-modern buildings of iron and glass to accommodate them. The boom was cut off by the First World War, and Réaumur never achieved its early promise. Small-time fashion houses rent most of the space now.

Rue Réaumur makes a fascinating architectural museum of early 20th-century passions and folly. Many of the buildings were winners in the city's annual *concours* (competition) for new façades, and on almost all of them the architects have proudly signed their names. Beginning at Boulevard de Sébastopol, there's the florid and silly **Rotonde Félix Potin** (1910), headquarters of Paris' ancient, recently liquidated grocery chain. **No. 100**, the magnificent monster on the north side of the street, looks like a department store but really was the home of the newspapers *L'Intransigeant* and *Paris-Soir* (1924). **No. 116** was a *concours* winner (1897), as was its neighbour, **no. 118**; this 1900 work of Guiral de Montarnal is a seminal piece of Parisian Art Nouveau, with a front all curves and nearly all glass. Georges Chedanne's **no. 124**, another one built for a now deceased newspaper, is stunning and uncompromisingly modern, boldly showing off its girders and rivets in a way that the Parisians of 1903 must have found profoundly shocking. Finally, another work of de Montarnal is at **no. 130** (1898), with a well-preserved original lobby and grand stair.

BOURSE DE COMMERCE

# IV: Palais Royal and Grands Boulevards

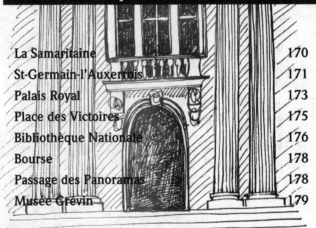

**Start:** Ⓜ *Pont Neuf*

**Walking time:** *a leisurely 2½ hours, with time for the Musée Grévin and some window shopping in the arcades.*

Welcome to the most unabashedly retro area of Paris. Dusty, dignified, quiet and thoroughly obsolete in a number of unimportant ways, it hasn't really been popular with Parisians or tourists or anybody else since the 1830s. But you may find it one of the most unexpected delights Paris has to offer. This walk is about old books, pretty things and good architecture; in other words, the elements of civilization. The only thing you'll encounter on it from the 20th century is an ambitious modern sculpture (that will confirm all your worst suspicions about the current dark age).

Any day would be good for this walk, even a rainy day, since for about half the trip you'll be sheltered under the glass roofs of the *passages*.

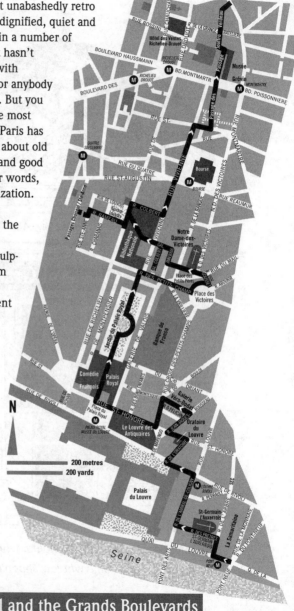

# IV: Palais Royal and the Grands Boulevards

**Terrasse de la Samaritaine**, Quai du Louvre. 80–105F menus—a pleasant lunch on the department store's roof terrace; view over the best of Paris.

**Chez La Vieille**, 37 Rue de l'Arbre-Sec, ✆ 01 42 60 15 78. *La Vieille* may have recently retired, but the food is still first-rate; a classic French repast for about 250F à la carte.

**Au Dauphin**, 167 Rue St-Honoré, ✆ 01 42 60 40 11. Another place that hasn't changed since the '20s, with a regular clientele from the Palais Royale offices; classic dishes on a 79F menu.

**La Gaudriole**, 47 Palais-Royale under the arcades. Elegant surroundings, and a good 160F menu for all of us who can't afford the nearby Grand Véfour.

**Aux Bons Crus**, 7 Rue des Petits-Champs. A gracious, long-established wine bar where you can also get a satisfying lunch for less than 70F.

**Au Pied de Biche**, 6 Rue La Vrillière, ✆ 01 42 61 43 78. An old-fashioned *bistrot* with dishes from the Midi, about 150–200F.

**Le Grand Colbert**, in the Galerie Colbert, Rue des Petits-Champs. Meticulously re-creates the arcade's 19th-century opulence; lunch seems dear (160F and up), but you may enjoy its incarnation as a tea room/oyster bar, 4–7pm.

**A Priori Thé**, Galerie Vivienne, no. 33. Come in for tea and scones, or a simple 85F lunch menu; tables 'outside' under the arcade's glass roof.

**Les Noces de Jeannette**, 14 Rue Favart (south of Blvd des Italiens), ✆ 01 42 96 36 89. A reopened classic restaurant with some wonderful dishes, such as the chicken with wild mushrooms, and a good wine list; menus 88 and 160F.

**Chartier**, 7 Rue du Faubourg-Montmartre, ✆ 01 47 70 86 29. A landmark that hasn't changed much since 1892. Simple food at low prices; 80F lunch.

---

Hang around the gardens of the Palais Royal long enough, and you may see a dignified, well-dressed gentleman with the face of a Pierrot and pockets full of birdseed, who comes nearly every day. In an instant, the numerous sparrows of the gardens line up on a fence before him to do their tricks. With the panache and flourish of an orchestra conductor, he makes them sit on his fingers or spring in the air after the seed. Every few minutes, he will pull out a notebook and jot something down. 'There are a few of them I still do not know yet,' he explains.

Such friends of the birds have always been common in this city, but in the lovely Palais Royal it is a spectacle to restore your faith in human nature and Western civilization. And it's a good introduction to this short, somewhat eccentric, tatterdemalion walk through the most serene and neglected parts of the metropolitan centre. Though not a well-defined quarter like the Marais, it has assumed and thrown off various identities over the centuries: it was an area of court servants, artists and hangers-on when kings lived at the Louvre or Tuileries, and briefly Paris' tenderloin when the Palais Royal was full of bordellos. Though containing the Bourse and the Banque de France, it has miraculously been spared the fate of becoming a soulless business centre. Just how is not easy to explain—doubtless some good angel of cities is keeping watch over it.

The first three sights on the tour are a department store, an ancient church and a royal palace—on three successive streets, giving you an idea of the diversity of this area. What really ties it together is the *passages*, of which there are 13 on or near the walk. The precursors of the modern department store, these glass-roofed arcades became the craze in the 1820s. Now well out of the mainstream of commerce, their charm is perfected. In any city where there are arcades, it's the same; they attract old-book dealers, stamp and coin shops, men who carve pipes by hand, doll hospitals and specialists in music boxes—all the fond foolishness that an angel fond of cities would find worthy of her protection.

> *Start at the Right Bank side of the Pont Neuf. The bridge itself, with the twin façades of the Place Dauphine across the Seine (see p.97), make an exceptionally graceful cityscape. It's a hint of what is to come—as much as are the* bouquinistes *with their old books and postcards just to your left on the Quai de la Mégisserie. A few steps to the north, on Rue de la Monnaie, is Paris' greatest Art Nouveau monument: not a palace or a public building but the department store* **La Samaritaine***.*

The name comes from a statue atop the old pumping station, built on the Pont Neuf under Henri III and long a city landmark. Ernest Cognacq started his business nearby in 1869, about the same time as Boucicaut's Au Bon Marché, but he was not able to build his great palace of consumption until 14 years after his Left Bank competitor. Architect Frantz Jourdain designed the building in 1900, with a façade that is a remarkable marriage of technology and blooming whimsy. The exposed ironwork, painted with colourful floral motifs, was a revolutionary feature; it both defines the structure brilliantly and permits huge areas of glass, including at the street level Paris' first big shop windows (an innovation created the year before in the building that provided some of the inspiration for this one, Louis Sullivan's Carson-Pirie-Scott store in Chicago). In spite of the present management's attempts to make the Samaritaine look like every other department store in the world, the most important features of the original interior survive: a flowing grand staircase under a glass skylight and more Art Nouveau fantasy decoration—peacocks and passionflowers the predominant theme.

The main part of the building, facing the Seine, was unfortunately altered in 1927. Three years later, the still-growing business built an addition across the street in a sadly subdued brand of Art Deco; there's a restaurant under the roof.

> Walk behind the old building, to Rue de l'Arbre-Sec (the 'dry tree' was a gibbet; executions were often held near the fountain still surviving at the northern end of the street). Here, standing near the old lamppost that has been determined to be the exact geographical centre of Paris, you are looking at the Renaissance apse of *St-Germain-l'Auxerrois*.

This Saint Germain was a 5th-century bishop of Auxerre who died in Paris after distinguishing himself fighting heretics up in England. There has been a church in his honour on this site since Merovingian times, and the version you see today contains a bit of everything from the 12th century onwards; the oldest part is the Romanesque **bell tower**, visible from the rear of the church (next to the south transept). On the night of 24 August 1572, the bells in this tower gave the signal for the St Bartholomew's Day Massacre; the Protestant leader, Admiral de Coligny, was staying just around the corner on what is now Rue de Rivoli where he was surprised and murdered.

From the 14th century on, whenever kings chose to live in the Louvre, St-Germain was the royal parish church. The rich decoration it received in this period largely succumbed to the pathetic taste of the 18th century; as at Notre-Dame, much good sculpture was destroyed, and even most of the stained glass was removed. Things got worse; the Revolution turned the church into a public granary, and it was only saved from demolition in the 1830s through the efforts of the writer Chateaubriand. Since the days when the scores of painters and sculptors working on the Louvre came here for Mass, St-Germain has been the artists' church in Paris; many are buried here and pious artists (there must be a few) still turn up, following an old tradition, for Mass on Ash Wednesday.

St-Germain's best feature is a charming **porch**, built in the late 1430s. In the Middle Ages most of the churches in Paris were preceded by such works, but this one and the much less elaborate porch of the Sainte-Chapelle are the only examples that remain. Look closely to see the imaginative medieval bestiary discreetly included in the carved decoration: a monkey playing bagpipes, a hippo gobbling up a grimacing savage, cats chasing rats. Some of the gargoyles are winged monks with asses' ears. All the large statues on the porch are 19th-century restorations.

For all the troubles this church has suffered, a few noteworthy works of art can still be seen inside. In the left aisle there is a remarkable Flemish altarpiece (*c.* 1530), Italian Renaissance tinged with the naïve, in scenes of the Passion of Christ and the life of the Virgin. In the right aisle the *Chapelle Paroissiale* contains the original statue of the expressive, long-haired *Ste-Marie-l'Egyptienne* depicted on the porch

(Marie, a 4th-century prostitute who became a holy hermit, was popular in France and often confused with Mary Magdalene). In the centre aisle, the royal family attended Mass in the 17th-century *banc d'oeuvre*, designed by Charles Lebrun; further on, near the entrance to the enclosed choir are 15th-century statues of St Germain and St Vincent. What is left of the original *stained glass* (16th century) survives in the transept windows on both sides.

*Next to St-Germain, a complementary neo-Gothic façade was built in 1859 for the mairie of the 1ᵉʳ arrondissement; its tower has a mechanical carillon that plays tunes by Rameau and other 18th-century composers. They wind it up for concerts most Wednesdays at 1.30.*

*From the front of the church, head right on Rue de l'Amiral-de-Coligny, from which you can admire Claude Perrault's grand colonnades on the oldest part of the* **Louvre***, the seminal work of grand-siècle classicism (see p.321). Continue on, crossing* **Rue de Rivoli**—*and while you're waiting for the lights to change, take a glance down this long, busy street, lined on both sides with imposing, if not beautiful, buildings.*

The part to the west was begun by Napoleon, who conceived it as a personal monument, a 'triumphal way' perfect for military parades, to be bordered by arcades—the forerunner of the *Grand Axe* along the Champs-Elysées. The eastern end was only completed after 1848, passing the Hôtel de Ville into the Marais.

*Once across, turn left; just after the corner of Rue de l'Oratoire is the melodramatic* **Monument to Amiral Coligny** *(1889), roughly on the spot where the Protestant leader was murdered. The monument is attached to the rear of the* **Oratoire du Louvre***; to see the front, head up Rue de l'Oratoire and turn left on Rue St-Honoré.*

This sober neoclassical building (1616, façade mid-18th-century) was the Louvre's unofficial chapel, where Bourbon kings and their entourage would often come to hear famous sermonizers such as Bishop Bossuet, while avoiding the commoners at St-Germain. Napoleon gave it to the Protestants, who have used it ever since; now it's hardly ever open.

*A right on the next street, Rue J-J. Rousseau takes you to one of the oldest and prettiest of Paris' passages at no. 17, the* **Galerie Véro-Dodat***.*

Built in 1826, the Galerie wowed the Paris crowds with its mahogany, marble and bronze decoration, as well as its use of a new technological marvel—gas lighting. Véro and Dodat were two butchers who made it big; riding the crest of the new fad for arcades, they went out of their way to impress. Today, the ornate columns and *putti* (cherubs) still glister, though it could all use a coat or two of varnish. There are some interesting shops, a smattering of galleries dedicated to warmed-over abstract art, and one of Paris' eternal wonders: Robert Capia's curiosity shop at no. 26. Paris' leading antique-doll expert, Capia likes everything else that is old and unusual; the stuff in the windows is fascinating, and inside it's jammed up to the ceilings.

> *Once through the Galerie, turn left, and then right on Rue St-Honoré. The big building on the left houses the* **Louvre des Antiquaires** *(open daily except Mon, 7–11pm).*

Don't expect any of the charm of the arcade shops or the flea markets out in the suburbs. Built into a converted department store, this is literally a shopping mall for antiques. And an enormous one, packed with sumptuous shops and tiny booths where a bored dealer with one Louis Quinze clock and table will muse over his crossword puzzle all day (apparently if he sells either, he can retire).

> *Across from the entrance, Rue St-Honoré opens up into a small square facing the* **Palais Royal.**

Originally it was the *Palais du Cardinal.* Cardinal Richelieu built it for himself, beginning in 1629; perhaps he was fed up with being kept awake at night by duellists under his window in Place des Vosges (*see* p.126). Naturally he willed it to the king, whose money he was playing with, long before his death in 1642. Anne of Austria and four-year-old Louis XIV moved in soon after, but left for the more defensible Louvre when the wars of the Fronde got hot. Louis' childhood memory of the threats to himself made him hate the place, and he gave it to his brother Philippe, Duke of Orléans (usually known simply as 'Monsieur'); the palace stayed in his family until the Revolution. Much rebuilt since Richelieu's time, the Palais Royal is of little architectural interest; it currently houses the *Conseil d'Etat*, which advises on proposed laws and serves as an appeal court for administrative decisions.

On its left, the **Théâtre Français** was attached to the Palais-Royal complex in 1786. Ever since, it has been the home of the Comédie Française, the company founded by Louis XIV out of Molière's old troupe and some others. Louis' motives were predictably dishonourable; the king was much less interested in supporting the theatre than having it under his thumb. All French rulers until the 1970s upheld the tradition, keeping the Comédie not merely state-funded but state-controlled. In the lobby, Houdon's famous statue of Voltaire is displayed along with the chair on which Molière died—after collapsing on stage, ironically playing the lead in his *Le Malade Imaginaire* in the Palais Royal's original theatre.

> *But the real attraction is not these mournful buildings, but the sweet surprise behind them. Pass under the arch between the theatre and the palace into the* **Jardin du Palais Royal.**

Before the gardens, though, comes the **Cour d'Honneur**. In 1986 a sculptor named Daniel Buren was permitted to transform this space into an abstract ensemble of grey, striped columns, making it look somewhat like a factory roof. Considerable controversy has been aroused by these concrete stumps and the equally incongruous big steel balls on the court's two fountains. The state realized its folly and tried to stop the Frankenstein they had commissioned—but too late. Buren was nobody's fool, and his lawyers got the courts to affirm 'the artist's right to finish his work'. Still, they must go, the sooner the better. To the right you see the last remaining bit of Richelieu's original palace, decorated with prows of ships, reminding us that the cardinal was, among other things, Minister of the Navy.

The gardens lie just beyond this. The last descendant of 'Monsieur' to be Duke of Orléans, the notorious 'Philippe Egalité' of Revolutionary fame (*see* p.36), had in 1781 hit on the idea of cutting down his enormous debts by selling off part of the gardens for building lots. His architects chopped the greenery down by a third, and enclosed it with an arcaded quadrangle of terraced houses, *à la* Place des Vosges.

The new development was an immediate success, if not entirely as respectable as its predecessor in the Marais. Under the arcades, several cafés soon opened (Caribbean rum, a novelty in Paris, was the trendy poison); gambling houses and bordellos thrived. The latter were quite refined establishments, fronting as hat shops or even furniture shops (one madam had brochures, showing the latest styles in beds, along with the 'rental prices' for each). Napoleon, arriving in Paris in 1787, got his first tumble here, like many another lad from the provinces. The police couldn't do a thing about it. They could not, in fact, even enter the Palais grounds without the duke's permission—such were the privileges of princely families before 1789.

Ironically enough, this privilege helped make the Palais-Royal gardens, and the cafés that proliferated around its arcades, one of the birthplaces of the Revolution. Like the Tuileries, this was one of the bastions of the *nouvellistes*, or newsmongers. But in the Tuileries, as every Parisian knew, one talked about fashions and court gossip. You came here, among the 'unorganized and invisible empire' of free thought, the only opposition possible under *ancien régime* despotism, if you wanted to argue politics. The famous salons of powdered ladies are still overestimated in our history books, but ultimately this was the one that mattered—the salon of public opinion. Typically, the attack on the Bastille was spontaneously conceived here, when Camille Desmoulins jumped onto a café table and started talking, on the morning of 14 July. (And four years later, minus a day, Charlotte Corday stopped here to purchase a knife at no. 177 on her way to see Marat.)

Under Napoleon, and for a long time after him, the Palais gardens continued to be Paris' public forum for vices, if no longer for political ideas. In 1814, under the occupation, the allied commanders (all except for the virtuous Duke of Wellington) actually took up lodgings here. Parisians claim the amount fleeced from them at gambling was greater than the entire amount of war reparations levied against France; Prussian Field Marshal von Blücher, co-victor of Waterloo, lost a million francs in one night at the bézique table. Fashion and vice both moved to the Grands Boulevards after 1838, when Louis-Philippe closed the gambling houses; ironically enough, as Orléans heir the king owned the place. Later, because the Dukes of Orléans were pretenders to his throne, Louis-Napoleon confiscated both the gardens and the palace, which had to be partially rebuilt after the Communards torched it in 1871.

Ever since, the garden has kept well out of the mainstream of popularity. The arcades that were once packed day and night now hold only a few quietly fascinating shops, selling antiques or recycled designer clothing from the 1950s, or music boxes (no. 95); there are also a few restaurants, including one you must take a look at it: the celebrated **Grand Véfour** at no. 79, around since 1784 and still appointed with most of its original decor and furnishings. The gardens themselves are well clipped and neat, a peaceful retreat for the birdman and a few other habitués.

> *Leave from the far end, walk a block up Rue Vivienne, and turn right on Rue des Petits-Champs. Passing no. 22, say a prayer for Stendhal, that delicate soul, who had an attack of apoplexy on the pavement here and died in 1842. At the corner of Rue La Vrillière stands the rear end of the Palais Royal's monolithic neighbour, the* **Banque de France,** *where the national sou-pinchers work amidst gilt-edged 18th-century splendour; the blank façade, added after 1870, hides a palace that was built by François Mansart for La Vrillière, Louis XIII's secretary of state (no visits). Continue straight ahead, to the circular* **Place des Victoires***.*

The second of Paris' 'royal' squares (after Place des Vosges), it was laid out by Hardouin-Mansart in 1685 to commemorate the rather trivial French victories against the Dutch and the annexation of the Franche-Comté. Like its predecessor, it was planned as an intimate, enclosed public space. Hardouin-Mansart designed both the Place and the uniform circle of buildings around it with no little skill; the proportions were related to each other and to the centrepiece, a bronze Louis (melted down in the Revolution; the present statue dates from 1822).

Over the last century, the Parisians have done their best to spoil the effect. Façades were altered, and in 1883 Rue Etienne-Marcel was cut through the Place, entirely wrecking its dignified and enclosed atmosphere. By the 1950s it had reached a nadir of tackiness, jammed with zipper wholesalers, news offices and advertising signs. Lately there has been a clean-up; the place now attracts high-fashion shops— the sort that paint the mannequins silver or black—and the Place is gradually making its way back.

*One problem with a circular square is finding your way out of it. Look for little Rue Vide-Gousset ('street of the cut-purses'), on the northern side, which will take you to the church of **Notre-Dame des Victoires**.*

Begun in 1629 for the monastery of the Petits-Pères, now demolished, several well-known architects (Libéral Bruant among them) got their oar in before the last roof tile was laid in 1740, resulting in a blasé work with the air of a mortuary chapel; the thousands of *ex-voto* plaques add to the effect—the church is the centre of a pilgrimage to the Virgin Mary (but this may be ending; the shop across the street that sold the plaques has been bought out by a British clothes designer). Somehow, somewhere there might be a reader impassioned enough about 18th-century religious painting to appreciate Carle van Loo's seven scenes of the *Life of St Augustine* in the choir. The French think very highly of them.

*Leaving the church, turn right, and in less than a minute you'll be under the glass ceiling of the **Galerie Vivienne**.*

Together with the adjacent **Galerie Colbert**, it makes up an elegant *passage* complex. Both were built in the 1820s, and along with the Véro-Dodat they are the most luxurious survivors of the genre in Paris. Light and airy, with neoclassical reliefs and mosaic floors, these arcades make a dreamy setting for their little shops and cafés. Both arcades have recently been well restored, though sad to say the Colbert has had most of the life squeezed out of it by the Bibliothèque Nationale, which has taken over most of the space for its bookshop and a deathly art gallery.

*Leave the Galeries by the far exit, into Rue Vivienne. Across the street stands the **Bibliothèque Nationale**; Cabinet des Médailles et des Antiques (open daily 1–5, Sun 12–6; adm).*

The first inventory of a royal library comes from the 1370s; in those troubled times, the king only had a choice of some 900 books to toddle off to bed with. But they did let them pile up over the years. A decree of 1537 inaugurated the *dépôt légal*, the requirement that anyone publishing a book must send a copy to the king—they were less concerned with building the library than with making sure they had a look at anything that might be seditious. Louis XIV's minister, Colbert, put the library on a sound footing when he consolidated all the king's holdings in two adjacent *hôtels* he owned on Rue Vivienne. Now, after various additions and remodellings, the library occupies the entire block.

With some 12 million books (not to mention 12 million engravings, and a few million miscellaneous manuscripts, pamphlets, maps and sound recordings, plus 24 shelf-miles of periodicals in a building out in Versailles), the Bibliothèque claims to be the largest library in the world. It's crowded and obsolete—but looming on the horizon in the far eastern stretches of Paris is the monster that is replacing it; the biggest, the most expensive, the most controversial, and by far the most hideous of all the *grands projets* of the Mitterrand era, out at Tolbiac near the Gare d'Austerlitz (*see* p.368).

You can't consult the books without a reader's card, but by all means do have a look inside at the old building. Through a big glass door, you can see one of the architectural masterpieces of Paris, the **main reading room**. Henri Labrouste had already pioneered the use of iron for a library hall at Ste-Geneviève; here, in 1863, he took the structural freedom that iron afforded to make an incredible flight of fancy. A few spindly columns with gilded capitals support the entire hall; nine intersecting domes soar high over the readers' heads, each with a glass oculus at its centre. This is architecture a century ahead of its time. Blending strangely well with the anachronistic décor—blue-green landscape murals, gilt trim and endless shelves of dusty leather-bound books—the total effect is unforgettable.

The **Cabinet des Médailles et des Antiques**, occupying its own wing of the Bibliothèque complex, is an amazing little museum that not one visitor to Paris in a thousand has heard of, let alone seen. The collection, really the treasure-trove of the kings of France, goes back at least to Philippe-Auguste in the 12th century. Nationalized during the Revolution and combined with the confiscated church treasures of St-Denis and Sainte-Chapelle, it contains the 1st-century AD *Camée de Sainte-Chapelle*, the biggest cameo ever made, showing Emperor Tiberius and his son Germanicus; the *Treasure of Berthouville*, an impressive hoard of Gallo-Roman jewellery; good collections of Greek, Roman and Etruscan jewellery; decadent masterpieces from the Hellenistic age such as the 'Cup of the Ptolemies', carved out of sardonyx. Just as surprising are the oriental items in the next room: a rock crystal cup *c.* AD 700 decorated with scenes of the legendary King Khusrau, and the exquisite Moorish sword of Boabdil, the last King of Granada.

There's more that glitters, including the splendidly barbaric *Treasure of Childeric*, with state-of-the-art Merovingian goldsmiths' work from the 5th century, as well as King Dagobert's throne. Coins, medals and commemorative medallions follow, in which the show is stolen by a fine collection from the undisputed, all-time greatest in this medium, the Renaissance Italian Pisanello.

> *If you can find the exit on the opposite side of the Bibliothèque, you'll be on Rue de Richelieu, facing the little park called the **Square Louvois**, with a pretty fountain (1844) allegorizing the 'Four Rivers of France': the Seine, Loire, Garonne and Saône—the last is an unusual choice, replacing the usual Rhône. Determined arcade fans can make a detour to seek out another one, the lively **Passage Choiseul/Passage Ste-Anne**, a block west (follow Rue Rameau from the southern side of the square). If not, take Rue de Richelieu north a few steps to Rue Colbert, then right,*

*and a left on Rue Vivienne, which will bring you to the* **Bourse** *(guided tour, Mon–Fri 11 and 12.30; summer 11.30 and 12).*

You may have already noticed the denizens of Paris' stock exchange ducking out for a coffee; they try hard to dress like people in automobile ads, exactly like their counterparts in New York. Neither New York nor any other financial centre, though, can offer its jobbers and yellers such elegant digs. After John Law (*see* Walk III, p.155) modern capitalism had a bad name in France, and open stock trading was not organized until the opportunist free-for-all of Napoleon's time. The Bourse is the masterpiece of neoclassicist Alexandre-Théodore Brongniart (1808). The finely-sculpted Corinthian colonnade, similar to that of the Madeleine, defines the structure; the building was carefully extended with two short, identical wings in 1907 to give it its cruciform shape. Also like the Madeleine, it gives a good idea of how Napoleon would have transformed Paris, had he won.

*Continue north on Rue Vivienne; a right on Rue St-Marc will take you to Paris' largest arcade complex, the* **Passage des Panoramas**.

Robert Fulton, the American pioneer of submarines and steamboats, also invented the popular entertainment called the 'panorama', in 1796. This was a huge circular painting, illuminated from behind and plotted in exact perspective to give spectators inside the circle the impression of being in the middle of a scene from ancient history, or a famous battle. Though such static spectacles were a passing fad, big theatres were built for them in major cities, including the one here (demolished long ago), built in conjunction with one of the first of Paris' arcades (1800).

Five distinct arcades intersect here (Galeries Feydeau, St-Marc, des Variétés, Montmartre and the Passage des Panoramas), to make a little self-contained city of a hundred shops. Mostly they're utilitarian establishments, with a few stamp and coin shops, printers and even a Turkish bath. Have a look in the windows of *Graveur Stern*, a print shop in business here since 1840, which loves to put its best work, along with some curiosities, on display.

*Follow the Panoramas to its end, and you'll be on Boulevard Montmartre. The* **Théâtre des Variétés**, *a few doors to the right on the boulevard, has changed little since it was built in 1807. In the heyday of the Grands Boulevards this was a famous venue, one where Offenbach put on many of his operettas. Cross the boulevard (easier said than done), and continue the arcade tour opposite, in the* **Passage Jouffroy**.

If you still haven't come to love the peculiar little world of the *passages*, this one might do the trick. A pretty play of dappled shadows lights up the faded grandeur of this busy 1846 arcade, which boasts its own hotel, and a wax museum. There are antique toys, oriental rugs, *Cinédoc*, a great shop for cinema books, posters and

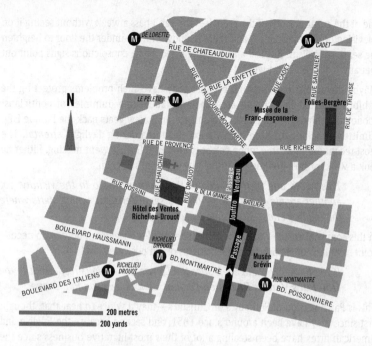

memorabilia, and an outlandish selection of antique walking sticks and canes at *Segas*, no. 36, under the stuffed moose.

> *Just outside the entrance, on Boulevard Montmartre, is something you might find eminently missable, or perhaps the highlight of the walk, the* **Musée Grévin** *(open daily 1–8pm; adm expensive).*

After surrendering an outrageous sum to get in, you notice there are no labels near any of the figures—on cue, a little man comes up and sells you a programme for another 5F. But no matter; this is a blatant tourist attraction, and fun, and maybe even worth it. The Grévin is built inside an old theatre lobby, and the delicious 19th-century brass-and-upholstery setting quite upstages the wax dummies, which aren't that lifelike anyhow. But it's done with some wit: Woody Allen taking a spacewalk (where he belongs, they seem to think), fake museum guards giving you a real glass eye, or the lady in a corner, adjusting her stocking.

On the top floor, current celebrities are portrayed doing things celebrities do: eating dinner, or staring blankly at the walls. Downstairs in the dungeon-like *galeries souterraines* are a series of tableaux from the history of France. In the inevitable cinema section, the star attraction is a soulful, white-clad Marilyn Monroe, a foot away from you, emoting on her subway grating from *The Seven Year Itch*. This is one of the cultural icons of the French—you can't pass a week without seeing it on television or in a magazine—and there is a powerful fan under the floor to heighten the sense of realism. But lest anyone get carried away, conspicuous signs point out that any indiscreet hand will set off loud alarms.

Maybe the admission is so high because they have such problems protecting the exhibits. Excited Frenchmen are constantly molesting dummies of politicians; voodoo worshippers stick pins in pop singers, and a few years back the Basque ETA admitted knocking off King Juan Carlos' head in a daring daylight *attentat*. The most recent outrage came when celebrity chef Paul Bocuse went missing. Either he took a walk, or he's holding the dishcloths in a rival's kitchen.

*This is the end of the walk but there's more to do in the vicinity: yet another arcade, for starters—the **Passage Verdeau**, which starts where the Jouffroy ends, across Rue de la Grange-Batelière.*

In this convivial arcade you can visit a Chinese self-service, learn how to do needle-point samplers, or shop for antique cameras or old postcards.

*If you have any change left after the Louvre des Antiquaires, take it to the **Hôtel des Ventes Richelieu-Drouot**, a block away on Rue Drouot.*

This is Paris' version of Sotheby's or Christie's—they'd wince to hear that, though: first since they have been around since 1851, and second because the English and American firms have been stealing a lot of their most lucrative business since the war.

*The area around it, Rue Drouot and Rue de Provence, is full of antique dealers and restorers. The latter street leads into Rue Richer and the **Folies-Bergère**, which closed in January 1993, though you can admire the Art Deco trim on the façade. And finally, there's the spooky, modern, aluminium-clad building just around the corner on Rue Cadet which houses the **Musée de la Franc-maçonnerie** (open daily except Sun, 2–6 pm; adm).*

France's oldest masonic organization, an offshoot of Britain's in the 18th century, tells its story in documents, pictures and memorabilia. The role played by Freemasonry in the Revolution, and much that has happened since, has been significant (and beneficial); come here and you'll see which politicians belonged.

*After the drowsy archaism of this walk, you may be surprised to find yourself in one of the liveliest areas in Paris. The **Faubourg Montmartre** is hardly beautiful, and boasts no greater attractions than those listed above. But it is cosmopolitan, full of hotels, small shops, cinemas, Turkish, Jewish, Greek and Lebanese restaurants and sandwich stands.*

# V: Opéra and Faubourg St-Honoré

**Start:** Ⓜ *Gare St-Lazare*
**Walking time:** *a 2-hour cakewalk with few museums to slow you down; more if you continue to Parc de Monceau and its museums (route 84 bus from the end of the walk at Place de la Madeleine).*

This area was to the Paris of the early 1800s what the Champs-Elysées would be later in the century: the city's showcase and playground of the élite. It's still the home of all luxury, the main source of what the French call *articles de Paris*; here you'll find the gilded fashion houses and the jewellers whose names are known around the galaxy and beyond. Close to the Louvre and the *Grand Axe*, this corner of town attracted monumental projects from three of France's most unpleasant despots: Louis XIV's Place Vendôme, Napoleon's self-memorial that became the Madeleine, and Little Napoleon's incomparable Opéra, a popular subject for wallpaper patterns on both sides of the Atlantic. These men, and the style of the buildings they left behind, set the tone for the area, which is a little stuffy, a little faded, more than a little over the top and eternally, unashamedly Parisian. If you're looking forward to window-shopping at places such as Pierre Cardin or Cartier, this walk may be the highlight of your stay.

Go in the afternoon (except Tuesday) if you want to top off the walk with a visit to the excellent Musée Jacquemart-André.

## lunch/cafés

**Brasserie Mollard**, 113 Rue St-Lazare, across from the station, ✆ 01 43 87 50 22. Spectacular decoration of 1895: mirrors, terracotta, rare marble and ceiling mosaics of everything that could conceivably be eaten or drunk in a brasserie. Lots of oysters and other seafood; menus 130 and 192F.

**Café Terminus**, 108 Rue St-Lazare, ✆ 01 42 94 22 22. Another trip to the gay 1890s, excellent cuisine on a bargain 128F menu (also 195F).

**Chez Léon**, 5 Rue de l'Isly, ✆ 01 43 87 42 77. The only *Routier* listed restaurant in Paris is a longtime neighbourhood favourite; genuine truck stop cooking, with *plats du jour* at 40 and 60F.

**Higuna**, 32 Rue Ste-Anne. A classic Japanese noodle bar on the Japanese strip; ramen noodles with a wide choice of dishes for about 60F.

**Le Souris Vert**, 50 Rue Ste-Anne, ✆ 0140 20 03 70. Good cooking, and three courses of it for 61F; also big salads for 40F or a serious 139F menu.

**Lescure**, 7 Rue Mondovi, ✆ 01 42 60 18 91. Run by the same family since 1919, with a classic menu featuring warming stews and game dishes; 100F menu.

**Manoir Normand**, 77 Boulevard de Courcelles, ✆ 01 42 27 38 97. Near Parc de Monceau; unpretentious place with lovely food; 120 and 160F menus.

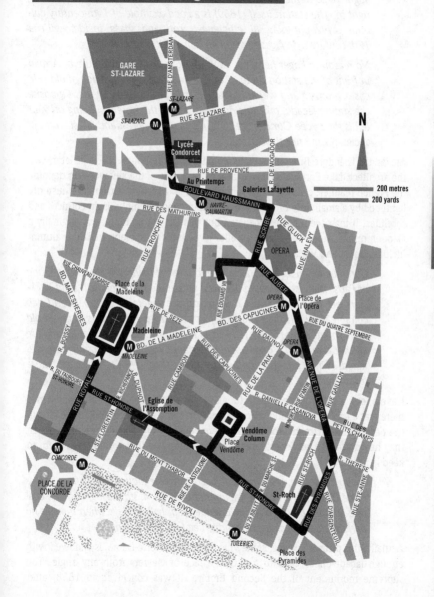

*The **Gare St-Lazare** isn't the most promising place to start a walk, but it might be convenient—you can get off the train, check your bags and start right in. The station itself (1889) is a good example of 19th-century cultural schizophrenia: all efficiency, iron and glass inside, with a 17th-century-style façade pasted on to make it respectable.*

*No reason to linger here, but have a look at the witty sculpture by Arman in front of the station (in the Cour de Rome), a column made of old suitcases bronzed and welded together, called 'Consigné a Vie'. Opposite the station façade, take Rue du Havre south; the stately building on your left is the **Lycée Condorcet** (1783), one of the purest and finest works of ancien régime neoclassicism.*

Alexandre-Théodore Brongniart, who would design the Bourse 25 years later, was the architect. Like Perrault's Louvre façade, this is one of the key works in defining the French manner: classical forms reinterpreted in original arrangements, austerity lightened by a small dose of sculptural ornament, and an emphasis on cornices and rooflines. It may seem hard to believe, but this elegant building was originally a Capuchin monastery. It became an élite lycée under Napoleon in 1804; alumni include Proust and Verlaine.

*Continue down Rue du Havre, and turn left at Boulevard Haussmann, one of Paris' liveliest shopping districts, where the managers still send hucksters out on to the street to demonstrate vegetable choppers and dab cologne on the ladies. You have just passed **Au Printemps**, a grand old department store (1889–1911); the lovely cupolas, a Paris landmark, are all that remain of a once-spectacular building now thoroughly homogenized. The **Galeries Lafayette** next door (1900) has been more fortunate.*

Have a look inside for the wonderful glass dome and Art Nouveau details. Once there was a spectacular grand staircase from the same era. According to the girls in the perfume department, the management ripped it out almost overnight when they heard the city was considering a preservation law that would force them to keep it.

*Facing this store, the **Opéra** displays its tremendous derrière from across Place Diaghilev. (Tours of the interior daily 10–4.30; museum 10–5; separate adm for both. Tours include the main hall on days when there is no performance; check beforehand to see Chagall's ceiling.)*

Actually, this pleasure palace, somewhat larger than Notre-Dame, is endowed with enough façade-cheesecake to toss in the face of viewers from any angle. The supreme monument of the Second Empire, it was conceived in 1858, after

Napoleon III was leaving a slightly more intimate theatre and one of the rabble got close enough to try and assassinate him. A competition was organized for a new Opéra, and the plan chosen was the largest, submitted by a fashionable young architect named Charles Garnier. The work took 14 years, partly because of the massive foundations that were necessary—the first excavations revealed a subterranean lake on the site. Also, work was interrupted by the Prussian siege and the Commune. After the unfinished building was taken by the Versailles troops, some dozens of Communards were massacred among the foundations and covered up; bodies are still occasionally found during repair work.

Finally open in 1875, three years after Napoleon's death, the biggest and most sumptuous theatre in the world soon passed into legend. Most of this was due to Gaston Leroux's novel *Fantôme de l'Opéra*, about a mad engineer named Erik who worked on the foundations for Garnier and sneaked off to build himself an underground palace across the lake. There were controversies, such as the one over Carpeaux's flagrant statuary outside. The artist's rivals pretended to be shocked (naked women, in Paris!) and threw bottles of ink at them. Anarchists plotted to blow the place up, and everyone whispered about the famous Opéra masked balls ('great festivals of pederasty', one writer called them). In 1896 one of the giant chandeliers fell on the audience during the climax of *Faust*; miraculously only one woman was killed, and the morning headlines screamed '200,000 Kilos on the Head of a Concierge!'

Envied and copied throughout the world, this building contributed much to the transformation of opera into the grand spectacle and social ritual it became in the *belle époque*, that world of top hats and lorgnettes designed for Groucho to tease Margaret Dumont, and for Harpo to drop sandbags on pompous oily tenors. It may have seemed that way to François Mitterrand, when in the 1980s he decided on the overtly political gesture of sentencing opera to the proletarian Bastille. Today the behemoth sits a bit forlorn, home only to its dance company, controversially run until a few years ago by the late Rudolf Nureyev. Major foreign ballets also call here, and occasionally there's even an opera.

But as a monument, the Opéra still plays a leading role in the Paris mystique. And its architecture still raises comment, on a spectrum from those who call it a Mecca of kitsch to those who find it a welcome antidote to the deathly concrete and glass of our own time. After winning the competition, Garnier still had to convince a sceptical Napoleon and Eugénie. Asked what style his work was meant to be, the architect replied: 'It is no style. Not Greek or Roman; it is the style of Napoleon III'. That brought the Emperor over immediately (and he reportedly added: 'Don't worry about my wife; she doesn't understand anything').

Circumnavigating its vast bulk is an experience. It *is* a little Greek and a little Roman, with some Baroque and Rococo and Renaissance and God knows what else mixed in. Asked how one should consider his building, Garnier recommended 'silent awe'. Its very size prevents us from noticing its height—224ft to the silly golden Apollo on top of the dome, enough height for a 17-storey building. On the western side, notice the double ramp for carriages up to the Imperial Box, meant to protect Napoleon III from those pesky assassins. Of the exterior embellishments, only Jean-Baptiste Carpeaux's allegory *La Danse* stands out, the second group from the right on the lower level of the façade. The French make much of it; the languorously draped bodies and vapid smiles remind them of the art of Louis XIV. This is a copy (by Jean-Paul Belmondo's dad, like many others in Paris); the original, eroded by traffic fumes and still with some traces of ink on it, was retired in 1960 and can be seen in the Musée d'Orsay.

The inside is just as impressive, awash with gold leaf, frescoes, mosaics and scores of different varieties of precious stone, from Swedish marble to Algerian onyx. Amazingly, the 'world's biggest theatre' seats only some 2100 people; the rest of the space is given over to grand lobbies and marble staircases dripping with more mythological statuary, along with the rooms of the French national dance academy (where Degas painted many of his pretty ballerinas). The highlight of the tour may be the hall itself, with its **ceiling** (1964) painted by Marc Chagall; the nine scenes, lovely if perhaps incongruous in this setting, are inspired by some of the artist's favourite operas and ballets.

The **Musée de l'Opéra** is in the Imperial Pavilion (enter from main entrance); it has a collection of memorabilia and art, including a portrait of Wagner by Renoir.

> *From the western side of the Opéra, you might cross the street and take a peek through the Impasse Sandrié, leading to an interesting street called Rue Edouard-VII, sneaking under arcades and archways of the surrounding buildings. Along it are two theatres and two tiny squares, one with a statue of the British monarch (who certainly deserves one; before his reign he spent more money in Paris than anyone ever before).*

> *The **Place de l'Opéra**, in front, naturally became one of the status addresses in Paris, including the original **Grand Hôtel**, opened for the World Fair of 1867. To your left and right stretch the western **Grands Boulevards**: Boulevard des Italiens, Boulevard des Capucines and Boulevard de la Madeleine.*

A century ago these were the brightest promenades of Paris, home of all the famous cafés and restaurants. Today the glamour is gone but the streets are popular and crowded just the same; they're a good place to take in a movie—and have been since the world's first public film show was put on by the Lumière brothers at no. 14, Boulevard des Capucines, on 28 December 1895. (Of the 22 punters who attended, only five thought that moving pictures had any future; one of the five was to become the first great French director, Georges Méliès).

> *But after these digressions, follow **Avenue de l'Opéra** a while as it slopes down to the Louvre.*

Baron Haussmann cut it through the neighbourhood in the 1860s to give the Opéra a proper setting; originally it was called *Avenue Napoléon*. There are no trees, thanks to Garnier, who insisted they would spoil the view of his masterpiece, but its drabness has not prevented it from becoming one of the major tourist strips of Paris. Americans predominate: there's Brentano's fine bookshop and Harry's New York Bar, which never lets anyone forget it is the Birthplace of the Bloody Mary, or that Hemingway frequently got stewed here; the grandpa of all the world's 'Harry's Bars' has been just around the corner on Rue Daunou since 1911. Lately the Japanese have been moving in; another side street, **Rue Ste-Anne**, is lined with their restaurants, shops and private clubs.

> *Turn right onto Rue des Pyramides, named after Napoleon's victory in Egypt. At the end of the street you can see the golden statue of Joan of Arc in the **Place des Pyramides**—but you don't want to walk out of your way to go there; it's a traditional meeting place for the far right—Jean-Marie Le Pen's crowd, young fascist hoodlums, monarchists and such. Instead turn right again into Rue St-Honoré. And another right, through the portal of **St-Roch**.*

There were outbreaks of plague in France as late as the 17th century; to be on the safe side, Parisians finally decided to build a church to St Roch, the medieval plague saint from Montpellier. Louis XIV helped lay the cornerstone in 1653, but with increasing financial problems work on this low priority project ground to a halt. Finished in the 18th century, thanks to funds from a lottery and a big gift from banker John Law (*see* Walk III, p.155), St-Roch became one of the society churches of Paris. Famous folk buried here include Diderot, Le Nôtre and Corneille.

The church had the misfortune to be in the way of the final act of the French Revolution. On the 13th of Vendémiaire, l'An 6 (5 Oct 1795), the Royalists of Paris rose in revolt against the new constitution of the Directory. A column of rebels was marching down Rue St-Honoré on its way to the Tuileries, when it was intercepted by a loyal force commanded by General Napoleon Bonaparte. Napoleon, who always believed in massed artillery, had had the presence of mind to bring some along. Firing point-blank into the rebels, he won the day and made a name for himself in Paris (he had already negotiated his price for saving the Republic—the command of the Army of Italy that was to be his stepping-stone to power). The results of his work on that day can still be read, just barely, in St Roch's pock-marked façade.

Inside, it's just another overblown and insincere church of the Age of Louies. Like the goods in the designer shops that infest the quarter, the church displays its 'SR' monogram everywhere, as if it were a trademark. The best part is the frothy **Lady Chapel** behind the altar, a large circular work with a pleasing unity of equally dubious 18th-century painting, sculpture and glass. On the right, note the plaque for the tomb of Admiral de Grasse, who helped make American independence possible by trapping the British at Yorktown.

*Continue down Rue St-Honoré, which hasn't always been so posh. Roughly on this part of the street stood the Porte St-Honoré in the Middle Ages; Joan of Arc besieged this gate in 1429 while trying unsuccessfully to retake Paris from the English. During the Revolution it was the radical hot spot of Paris. On the corner of Rue du Marché-St-Honoré stood the confiscated Jacobin convent that became the chief nest of ultramontanist intriguers—the Jacobin Club. Robespierre lived just down the street at no. 398. If you look north up Rue du Marché-St-Honoré, you will see a big new shopping mall, designed by Ricardo Bofill, on the spot where the market used to be.*

*Turn right at Rue de Castiglione, which leads into* **Place Vendôme**.

The second of Louis XIV's 'royal squares', after Place des Victoires, was laid out in 1699 by the same architect, Jules Hardouin-Mansart. The king's sycophants were at first divided between calling it 'Place Louis le Grand' or 'Place des Conquêtes', but posterity settled the issue by giving it the familiar name of a *hôtel* that had previously occupied the site, that of the Duc de Vendôme (one of Henri IV's bastards). The most satisfactory of all 17th-century French attempts at urban design, the square seems the utter antithesis of a building like the Opéra—but both were built to impress. Here, however, Mansart does it with absolute decorum. Only two streets lead into the square, which was conceived as a sort of enclosed urban parlour for the nobility. Balls were sometimes held in it, but cafés or anything else that would encourage street life or spontaneity were strictly forbidden.

Originally, the square was to house embassies and academies, but the final plan proposed the present octagon of eight mansions, with uniform façades, and an equestrian statue of—guess who—in the centre. From the start, the buildings were occupied by the wealthiest bankers; a joke of the time had it: 'Henri IV on the Pont Neuf with his people, Louis XIII in the Place Royale (Place des Vosges) with his nobles, Louis XIV in Place Vendôme with his financiers'. Later residents included

John Law and Chopin (who died at no. 12). Today the square still has a not-too-discreet aroma of money about it, home to the Ritz Hotel, Cartier, Van Cleef & Arpels and a fleet of other carriage-trade jewellers who never put prices in the window displays. Shed a tear at no. 12 when you pass by, not only for Chopin but for the 200-year-old jewellery house of Chaumet—if it's still there. In a wonderful moral tale of the 1980s this family firm went spectacularly bust, partly from the Chaumet brothers' 18th-century approach to book-keeping, but mostly from a clientele of jet-set deadbeats that included Arab princesses and third-world dictators. The brothers, pious Catholics both, trusted until the end, then tried some charmingly inept financial prestidigitation to cover up the losses. When the end came, they assumed personal responsibility and went off to the calaboose in majestic silence. A New York conglomerate owns the place now.

*In the centre, where Louis' statue presided before the revolutionaries melted it down to make cannons, is the **Vendôme Column**.*

Nothing could speak more eloquently on the philistine emptiness of the first Napoleon's reign than this rather elegant bronze abomination. The Louis XIV statue here had been dressed as a Roman emperor, but Napoleon's men came up with something even better, a precise copy of Trajan's Column in Rome. Napoleon himself can be seen in several places on the spiralling reliefs, beating everyone's armies, dedicating bridges and bestowing on grateful conquered helots the benefits of French civilization and the metric system. The statue of the Emperor at the top, throughout the 19th century, was a weather-clock marking changes in French politics. The original, with Napoleon in a toga like Louis, was replaced during the restoration with a Bourbon lily. Louis-Philippe put up a new Napoleon in a more modest military uniform; you can see it today in the Invalides. Napoleon III put his uncle back in Roman gear; a copy of that is what you see today.

The entire column, in fact, is a copy of a copy, thanks to the Communards of 1871 and in particular Gustave Courbet. As artistic director of the Commune, the painter led the campaign to destroy this symbol of blind militarism—he also complained that it 'offended him aesthetically'. The demolition was made into a public festival, on 16 May, and the crowds and soldiers fought over the bronze scraps for souvenirs. A year later, as one of the final ironies of the Communal comedy, a republican government ordered it rebuilt and made an example of Courbet by sentencing him to prison for six months, and billing him 250,000 francs for the reconstruction; the painter chose exile in Switzerland.

Rue de la Paix, leading north from the Place, has been a swank shopping street since it was laid out in 1806. The first of the great *couturiers*, Englishman Charles Worth, opened his house at no. 7 in 1858, just in time for the conspicuous consumption orgy of the Second Empire. Fashion houses have favoured this area ever since; Coco Chanel, creator of the little black dress in the 1920s (and later a wartime collaborator), had hers two streets to the west, at 31 Rue Cambon.

> *But return to Rue St-Honoré and turn right. At the corner of Rue Cambon, the domed **Eglise de l'Assomption** was a convent church built in 1676; since 1850 it has been the Polish church in Paris. Continue on, and turn right on Rue Royale. If there's time, you might detour left instead for the Place de la Concorde, the monumental centre of this end of Paris (see Walk VI, p.200). Rue Royale was a part of architect Gabriel's plan for the Place. To close its view, he provided for a building at the end of the street, which eventually became the **Madeleine**.*

Construction was begun in 1764, but this church was fated to see many changes before its completion. The death of the architect in 1777 occasioned a complete rethinking; the new man opted for a neoclassical Greek cross plan, imitating Soufflot's Panthéon. Only a quarter finished by 1792, the revolutionary government pondered over a new use for the project—perhaps the seat of the National Assembly, the Banque de France or the National Library. But Napoleon knew what was best—a Temple of Glory, dedicated to himself and his Grand Army.

The plans were scrapped, the foundations razed, and in 1806 architect Barthélemy Vignon came up with an imitation Greek temple. Napoleonic efficiency got the colonnades up in nine years, but once more, political change intervened; after 1815 the restored Bourbons decided to make it a church after all. The exterior was kept as Vignon planned it, not a proper Greek temple, more the Romantic souvenir of one. The arrangement of the columns, about which the ancients were very particular, follows no accepted pattern; an ancient Greek would shake his head, perhaps call it 'pseudo-dipteral', then admit it's a fine building just the same. It is: the reliefs on the pediments, and the Corinthian capitals are carved with a grace and precision that the French had been working towards for two centuries.

After the chilly perfection of the Madeleine's exterior, the inside comes as a surprise: windowless and overdecorated, creamy and gloomy, more like a late Baroque Italian church—or ballroom. The rustic cane chairs contrast strangely with the gilded Corinthian columns and walls covered with a dozen varieties of expensive marble, in imitation of the Pantheon in Rome. Over the altar is a series of frescoes on 'Heroes of Christianity', from Constantine to Joan of Arc, and including that most cynical of agnostics and kidnapper of popes, Napoleon himself. One expects church interiors in Paris to be either saccharine or dilapidated or both, but this one is downright surreal. The combined efforts of so many 19th-century artists will never convince you that this building, the scene of Paris' high-society marriages and funerals, could possibly have anything whatsoever to do with the

Christian religion. The crowning touch, near the entrance, is an intrusive glass booth with a sign reading 'Priest on Duty' in five languages. There he sits, at a desk with a telephone, reading the newspaper.

*The Place de la Madeleine, which surrounds the church, is one of Paris' gourmet paradises, with famous restaurants such as Lucas Carton, and many of the city's finest food shops, all on the north side: small places specializing in caviar (no. 17) or truffles (no. 19), the Confiserie Tanrade, Hédiard and the incredible Magasins Fauchon with just about anything you could imagine from any corner of the globe. The upper crust trusts them to cater for their fancier affairs, and businessmen come to buy their mistresses strawberries in December. The window displays of the* traiteur *(caterer) department are entirely over the top: delicacies that go for over a thousand francs a kilo, and all-too-beautiful plates in gelatine that have the appearance of embalmed food.*

*The Place also has a small but cheerful **flower market** (daily except Mon), the poshest **public restrooms** in Paris, well worth a visit, and the **kiosque-théâtre**, where you can get cheap tickets for most of the plays in town.*

*That's the end of this short walk but, lest you feel cheated, you can continue on towards the Parc Monceau for a few minor sights:*

**Rue du Faubourg-St-Honoré**: *a continuation of Rue St-Honoré that is another big-name shopping street, and also has the greatest concentration of cops per square metre in France.*

Besides the British Embassy at no. 39 (built for Napoleon's tart of a sister, Pauline Borghese), there are the Americans, the Japanese, and the President of France, who resides under the hundred chandeliers of the **Palais de l'Elysée** (1718). Napoleon signed his abdication here in 1815, and Napoleon III lived here from his election in 1849 until he decided to make himself Emperor two years later. The *hôtel* has been the official residence of the head of state since 1873. Opportunities for a visit are very rare, but you might see important guests arriving at the main courtyard.

**Chapelle Expiatoire**: *Boulevard Haussmann north of the Madeleine.*

During the restoration, Louis XVIII had this dolorous temple built to the memory of his brother martyred in the Revolution. Previously, the site had been the cemetery of the Madeleine, where the royal family and some 3000 other victims of the Terror had been buried in unmarked graves. Most are still somewhere under the grass, including Charlotte Corday and Philippe-Egalité, to whom there are small memorials, as well as Danton, Hébert, the Desmoulins and Madame du Barry. The royal family was exhumed, and rested for a short time in the chapel before being removed to St-Denis. If it really was them, that is. They were sure about Marie Antoinette (they recognized her knickers) but the body they claimed as Louis XVI was just a guess; many believed it was really a vile toady of Robespierre's named Henriot—one of the men most responsible for Louis' execution.

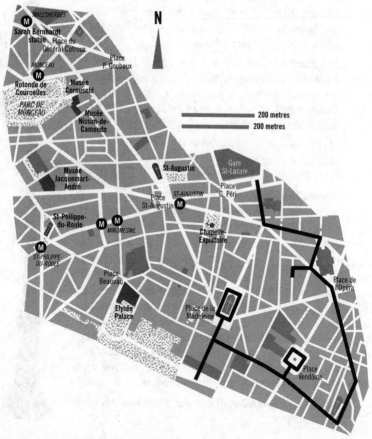

**St-Augustin:** *Boulevard Malesherbes at Boulevard Haussmann.*

This church (1871) is by Victor Baltard, and like his lost market buildings at Les Halles is made mostly of iron, though disguised in pseudo-Renaissance frippery.

> **Musée Jacquemart-André:** *158 Boulevard Haussmann (open daily except Tues, 1.30–5.30; adm). If one day you want to look at some beautiful pictures, but don't care to tackle the terrible Louvre, there's probably no better choice than this museum, assembled by Edouard André and his wife Nélie Jacquemart at the turn of the century.*

Nélie was a painter herself, and had a sharp eye. The works from the Italian Renaissance rival the Louvre's own collection, beginning with Paolo Uccello's dream-like *St George Slaying the Dragon* and Carpaccio's exquisite and fanciful *Embassy of the Amazon Queen*. Other greats represented include Mantegna, Pontormo, Cima da Conegliano, Alessandro Baldovinetti and Carlo Crivelli, as well as a Donatello relief and a set of *cassoni*, painted wedding chests from Florence. And don't miss Tiepolo's fresco on the stairway, the *Reception of King Henri III in Venice*, commemorating one of the most spectacular parties of all time (1573). French painters of the 17th and 18th centuries are also well represented, as are the Dutch, including two works of Rembrandt.

> **Parc de Monceau:** *on Boulevard de Courcelles, north of Boulevard Haussmann.*

As with the Palais Royal, Paris owes this rare oasis to Philippe d'Orléans (Philippe-Egalité) who had it landscaped in the 1770s—and redone a decade later, shocking Parisians by hiring a Scotsman named Blakie to turn the grounds into the city's first large English garden. History was made here in 1797, when a man named Garnerin made the world's first parachute jump: 1000ft from one of the Montgolfiers' balloons, and he lived to tell about it. The park is lovely and immaculately kept; it includes a large pond called the *Naumachie* near a colonnade believed to have originally stood at St-Denis, from a failed project of Catherine de' Medici to build a mausoleum for the Bourbons.

> *Boulevard de Courcelles, the northern boundary of the park, follows the course of the Farmers-General wall. One of Ledoux's less ambitious **barrières**, called the **Rotonde**, marks the park's main entrance. Near the eastern entrance are two more museums: **Musée Cernuschi**, 7 Avenue Velasquez (open daily except Mon 10–5.30; adm).*

A small and seldom visited museum, bequeathed (along with the house) by another turn-of-the-century collector, this one is entirely devoted to Chinese art, from a serene 5th-century seated Buddha to a T'ang dynasty spittoon. The rooms upstairs are given to exhibitions of contemporary Chinese painting.

**Musée Nissim de Camondo:** *63 Rue de Monceau (open daily except Mon, Tues, 10–5 and 2–5; adm).*

Nowhere more than here does one get the sense of French culture contemplating its navel. In a building modelled on the Petit Trianon are two floors quite full of 18th-century furniture, tapestries, ceramics, silverware, snuffboxes, soup tureens, carpets, candelabras, knick-knacks, gimcracks and gilded geegaws.

For something more edifying, walk up Boulevard Malesherbes two blocks, to Place du Général-Catroux, where you can see a **statue of Sarah Bernhardt**, in the role of Racine's Phèdre.

**Rue Daru:** *Just south of Boulevard de Courcelles, two blocks west of Parc de Monceau, this small street has been the focus of Paris' Russian community for over a century. At its centre is the onion-domed **Cathédrale Alexandre-Nevsky,** built in 1861. Nearby are the Russian library and a flurry of tea-rooms and restaurants.*

**Start:** *in the Louvre courtyard;* Ⓜ *Palais Royal-Musée du Louvre or Tuileries.*

# VI: Up the *Grand Axe*

**Walking time:** *2 hours at the least—if you take the bus up the Champs-Elysées—but even less if you skip La Défense.*

There's little chance of getting lost on this walk, or even fatigued—it's a perfectly straight line of about 8km (5 miles), and you can cover most of it on the bus. Frankly, the charms of this trip are few, and—as a glance at the map will demonstrate—far between. But this is a part of Paris that every first-time visitor feels obliged to see. From the Louvre to La Défense, the monuments line up like pearls on a string—some natural, some cultured, and some fake. Paris' main drag recalls destiny and de Gaulle; its breadth and majesty still proclaim to the world that this is the place to be. It has been an irresistible magnet for parades ever since it was built: Napoleon's Grande Armée did it, and Bismarck made a Champs-Elysées promenade part of the armistice terms in 1870—even though the Prussians couldn't capture Paris. And on both sides of the Atlantic, there are still plenty of stout fellows around who will never forget the day they did this walk in uniform, on 26 August 1944.

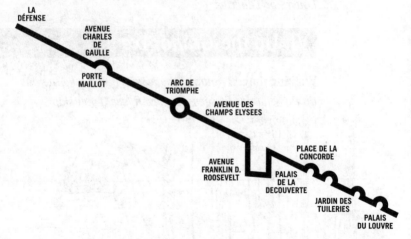

## lunch/cafés

*You won't necessarily starve on this linear trek, but abstinence might be a reasonable alternative to the chain restaurants of La Défense, the overpriced cafés on the Champs-Elysées, and the polythene crêpes and hot dogs served in the snack stands of the lower Champs-Elysées and Tuileries.*

**Les Ambassadeurs**, Place de la Concorde, in the Hotel Crillon, ✆ 01 44 71 16 16. If you've got 340F to burn, you could do worse than this lunch menu, which is a relative bargain; one of Paris' most sumptuous settings and a highly rated cuisine of Byzantine complexity. Book way ahead.

**La Fermette Marbeuf 1900**, 5 Rue Marbeuf, ✆ 01 47 23 31 31 (off Ave George-V). Lovingly restored Art Nouveau décor; almost over the top in its way, but redeemed by an honest 169F menu.

**Virgin Café**, 52 Avenue des Champs-Elysées, ✆ 01 46 74 06 48 (in the Virgin Megastore). A trendy favourite, and a big surprise; delightful, innovative cooking at reasonable rates; everything from gazpacho to salmon on toast to hamburgers to *saltimbocca alla romana* (80–160F).

**La Boutique des Sandwiches**, 12 Rue du Colisée, north of the Champs-Elysées. Better than you would guess from the name: seriously good sandwiches made Alsatian style; also onion soup and other treats on an 80F menu.

**Roi du Pot au Feu**, 40 Rue de Ponthieu, just north of the Champs-Elysées, ✆ 01 43 59 41 62. As the name implies, this place specializes in that old French standby—wonderful on a cold day; 75F lunch menu.

**Le Fouquet's**, 99 Avenue des Champs-Elysées. A wood-panelled, century-old bar, perhaps the last remnant of the Champs-Elysées' glory days, still frequented by the arty-political set; also an expensive restaurant.

**Bistrot de l'Etoile**. 13 Rue Troyon, ✆ 01 42 67 25 95. Near the Etoile, a spin-off of celebrity chef Guy Savoy's famous restaurant; classic 'bistro' food for about 200F; closed Sun.

> *Don't put lunch off until you get to La Défense; if you're looking for an inexpensive decent meal, you won't find one. The alternatives are sorrowful (the only restaurant facing the Parvis is a McDonald's) and/or expensive; this is strictly expense account country.*

---

Like so much else in Paris, the *Grand Axe* began with those Medici girls from Florence. Catherine fixed the eastern point, with her Louvre extensions and Tuileries gardens in the 1560s. Fifty years later Marie started the landscaping of a park around what would later become the Champs-Elysées. No one, probably not even Le Nôtre, who actually laid out the famous avenue for Louis XIV, suspected that a unique work of long-range planning was under way.

Since then, the logic of the *Grand Axe* has always unrolled in mysterious ways. In 1768, a year before Napoleon was born, the decision was made to clear and level the circular *place* that would one day hold the Arc de Triomphe. An Egyptian pasha gave the French a tall obelisk just when they were desperate for something

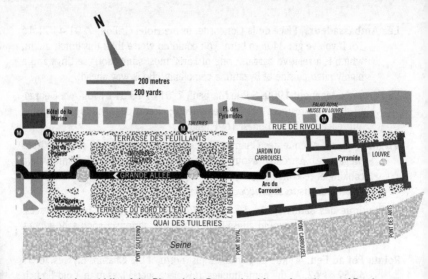

to plant in the middle of the Place de la Concorde. After a few glasses of Bordeaux, French poets and statesmen start talking about the way holy Paris 'radiates culture through the world'. For that, and for a large part of the Paris mystique, this long radian makes a perfect symbol.

> *The beginning of the* Grand Axe*, properly punctuated by the new Pyramid and the old Arc du Carrousel, is in the courtyard of the Louvre (see p.322). Beyond these it continues up the* Grande Allée *of the* **Jardin des Tuileries***.*

For the last few years, the gardens have been full of fences and pits; at time of writing the redesigning of the Tuileries, part of the Grand Louvre project, is nearly completed. There is now a sloping terrace down from the Place du Carrousel, leading to dense alleys and enclosed gardens, a subdued post-modernist reinterpretation of Le Nôtre's 17th-century plan.

The first gardens on this site were built at the same time as the Tuileries palace, in the 1560s. It was Catherine de' Medici's idea, following the latest fashions in landscaping from Renaissance Italy; she purchased a large tract of land behind the palace, part of which had been a rubbish dump and part a tile works—hence the name *tuileries*. Her new pleasure park, designed by Philibert de l'Orme and others, was soon the wonder of Paris; symmetrical and neat, it became the model for Le Nôtre's work and all the classical French landscaping that followed. Contemporary accounts suggest it must have been much more beautiful, and more fun, than the present incarnation, with such features as a hedge maze, elaborate sundials and other astronomical devices, a 'grotto' lined with Sèvres porcelain and statuary (another innovation brought by Catherine's people from Tuscany, where such things can still be seen) and a semicircle of trees cleverly planted to create an echo effect.

André Le Nôtre, who had been born across the street from the park, and who had worked his way up to become one of the chief gardeners, was given the task of redesigning the Tuileries in 1664. His elegantly classical reworking of the original plan, capturing perfectly the mood of the *grand siècle*, made his reputation. A story has it that Charles Perrault, Louis XIV's controller-general of public works and author of the famous fairy stories (and brother of Claude, the Louvre's architect), convinced the king to open the park to the public. Louis, who never spent much time in Paris anyhow, was amenable, and the new Tuileries became Paris' most fashionable promenade; it continued as such through the 18th century, featuring such novelties as Paris' first public toilets and first newspaper kiosk. The first gas airship took off from a spot near the octagonal pond in 1783, the same year as the Montgolfiers' pioneer hot-air balloon.

Although Le Nôtre's basic plan remains unchanged, there have been many minor alterations over the last two centuries. The biggest change, of course, was the disappearance of the Tuileries Palace, burned during the fighting in 1871. Visitors who haven't been to Versailles may wonder what all the fuss is about; without the meticulously kept flowerbeds and other decorations it once had, Le Nôtre's design seems unexceptional—just a park like the ones back home. It does have plenty of statuary, beginning, as you enter from Avenue du Général-Lemonnier, with four works by Rodin flanking the Grande Allée (*Méditation*, the *Grand Ombre* and two portrait statues).

The centre of the park is shaded by avenues of chestnut trees, the *Quinconces des Marroniers*. Further up the Grande Allée comes the **octagonal basin**, surrounded by some statues that have survived from the days when the Tuileries was a royal park: allegories of the *seasons*, and of *French rivers*, also the *Nile* and the *Tiber*. The two on winged horses, the **Chevaux Ailés** at the gates facing Place de la Concorde are by Louis XIV's chief sculptural propagandist, Coysevox: *Mercury* and *Fame* (both copies).

Le Nôtre's plan included narrow raised terraces at the northern and southern ends, the *Terrasse des Feuillants* and the *Terrasse du Bord de l'Eau*; regrettably the latter has had its Seine-front view spoiled by Pompidou's Right Bank motorway, but both remain favourite tracks for Parisian joggers. At the Concorde end, the terraces expand into broader plateaus supporting buildings from the time of Napoleon III.

> On the right, the **Jeu de Paume,** was built for real tennis, the crazy medieval game where the ball bounces off walls, roofs and turrets. This sport was the rage in the 17th–18th centuries, and enjoyed a brief fad in

> *the Second Empire. Once the Impressionists' museum in Paris, it has seen its collections shipped off to the Musée d'Orsay, and now sits a bit forlorn, hosting exhibitions of contemporary art (open Wed, Thurs, Fri 12–7, Sat, Sun 10–7, Tues 12–9,30; adm).*

> *But its museum counterpart in the southwest corner of the Tuileries, the* **Orangerie** *(Orangery), still has a small permanent collection (open daily except Tues, 9.45–5.15; adm).*

The paintings, from the Impressionists to the 1930s, come courtesy of Domenica Guillaume-Walter, who willed the collections of her two husbands to the nation in 1977. *Don't* come here before you've seen the Musée d'Orsay and the Musée National d'Art Moderne in the Pompidou Centre. In the Orangerie, many of the big-name artists of the 20th century are represented, but the works are seldom among their best: dissolving landscapes of Chaim Soutine, Cézanne still lifes and portraits of his wife and son, rosy Renoir *fillettes* bathing or at the piano, Paris scenes by Utrillo, a trio of Modigliani weird sisters.

Picasso contributes some formidable primeval women, in the *Femmes à la Fontaine* and the *Grande Baigneuse*, both from 1921, and Matisse counters with a series of *Odalisques*; these, and the several paintings by Derain, are later works, with little of the verve of the artists' Fauve days. For most people, the high point will probably be the luminous canvases of Monet, including one of the famous *Nymphéas* (Water Lilies), and two wonderful pictures by the Douanier Rousseau, looking as out of place among the sophisticated moderns as his rustic subjects would among the Orangerie's visitors today: a nasty-looking *Little Girl with a Doll* (1907), and the pinched-faced provincial family on *Père Junier's Cart* (1910), a painting much beloved by the Surrealists.

> *Leave the Tuileries between Coysevox's winged horses, and you're up against the boiling traffic of the* **Place de la Concorde.**

Without the cars, it would be a treat, the most spacious square and the finest architectural ensemble in Paris. The fourth in the series of Bourbon *Places Royales* was decreed by Louis XIV, just outside what was then Paris' western wall. An unusual location—but Louis owned most of the land around it, and no French king was ever averse to a bit of property speculation on his own behalf. Jacques-Ange Gabriel, a hitherto undistinguished architect (Ecole Militaire, Petit Trianon), won the competition over Soufflot, among others, by coming up with something utterly, unaccountably brilliant and original. Breaking completely with the enclosed, aristocratic ethos of the other royal squares, Gabriel laid out an enormous rectangle, built up on one side only, with the Seine facing opposite and the two ends entirely open, towards the parklands of the Tuileries and the Champs-Elysées. It was clear that

Paris was growing rapidly, especially towards the west, and Gabriel consciously intended his new square to be a colossal focal point for the city as a whole.

Later generations perfected the Place. The Pont de la Concorde over the Seine opened in 1790; under Napoleon, the Madeleine (*see* Walk V, p.190) and Palais Bourbon (*see* Walk XI, p.294) were added to close the views and brilliantly complete the architectural ensemble. A new exclamation mark along the *Grand Axe*, the Egyptian obelisk, appeared in 1836. But in the meantime, the Place had changed its name six times, and seen more trouble than any square deserves. There was a bad omen in 1770, only six years after its inauguration, when a festival was being held to celebrate the marriage of the future Louis XVI with Marie Antoinette; some fireworks misfired, and caused a panic in which over a hundred people were crushed to death. Twelve years later the name had been changed to Place de la Révolution, and Louis XV's statue, where the obelisk stands today, had already been melted down for munitions. That same spot now held a guillotine, the venue for all the most important executions under the terror; Louis and Marie were the most famous victims, but neither the first nor the last—Danton, Desmoulins, Charlotte Corday and finally Robespierre himself held centre stage here while Madame Defarge knitted.

When the chopping stopped, the Convention chose the new name *Concorde* as a gesture of national reconciliation. The restored Bourbons would have none of that, but couldn't decide whether to give it its original name or call it after the martyred Louis XVI. In 1830 the revolutionaries proclaimed it Place de la Charte, after the charter they had obtained; only a few years later the authoritarian Louis-Philippe decided Concorde wasn't such a bad name after all.

This is a square made for strollers and carriages. The fumes and menace of six lanes of traffic, zooming around the obelisk as fast as they can, has made its enjoyment nearly impossible—come at dawn on Sunday morning, or right after a rare big snowfall if you want some idea of the original effect. The centre island is an octagon, as Gabriel designed it, with allegorical statues of eight **French cities** at the corners (clockwise from the bridge: Bordeaux, Nantes, Brest, Rouen, Lille—modelled on the Lille police prefect's daughter—Strasbourg, Lyon, and Marseille). Baron Haussmann's architect, Jacques Hittorff, added the ornate lampposts and two incredible bronze **fountains**, with rows of perplexed marine deities sitting on benches and cradling fishes, all looking as if they're waiting for the tram home from the market.

The **obelisk** comes from Luxor on the Nile, *c.* 1250 BC in the time of Ramses II. It was a gift from France's ally Muhammad Ali, semi-independent Ottoman viceroy of Egypt in the 1830s, and this spot was chosen for it because any political monument would have been a sure source of controversy in the future. Accepting an obelisk is one thing; floating the 221-tonne (225-ton) block to Paris and getting it upright again a different matter. Look at the inscriptions on the base: scenes of the erection carved in intricate detail, with thanks in big gold letters to M. LEBAS, INGENIEUR, for managing the trick, 'to the applause of an immense crowd'. A battalion of artillerymen helped him raise it; you can see the machinery Lebas built for the job in the Marine Museum (*see* Walk XI, p.308).

Gabriel's impressive pair of buildings on the north side of the Place were meant as government offices. The one on the right, the *Hôtel de la Marine*, still is; it has housed the navy department since 1792. The one on the left saw the signing of the United States' first foreign alliance, the treaty of 1778 that brought diplomatic recognition and material aid to the new nation, and made all the difference in the War of Independence. Today it is the luxury Hotel Crillon—we've all seen magazine adverts photographed on its colonnaded terrace a dozen times or more. Fittingly just around the corner, on Rue Boissy-d'Anglas, is the southern part of the **US Embassy** complex, on the site of an 18th-century *hôtel* that formerly held the embassies of Russia and Turkey. Gabriel also laid out **Rue Royale** between his buildings, and planned for the future Madeleine to close its view. The architect built his own house at no. 8; across the street no. 3 is the famous **Maxim's**.

> *On the western edge of the Place, another pair of winged horses complements those on the Tuileries side. These familiar landmarks are the **Marly horses**, sculpted by Coysevox's nephew, Guillaume Coustou, in the 1740s. Like their conterparts across the Place they originally came from Louis XIV's château at Marly, destroyed in the Revolution. Thanks to the exhaust fumes all these horses are copies; their eroded originals have been let out to pasture in the Louvre. The Marly horses mark the entrance to the **Avenue des Champs-Elysées**.*

This was the second step in the creation of the *Grand Axe*. In 1616 everything west of the Louvre was royal meadows and hunting preserves; in that year Marie de' Medici ordered the first improvement, a tree-lined drive along the Seine called the *Course la Reine* (now part of the Right Bank motorway). In 1667 Louis XIV had Le Nôtre lay out a long straight promenade through the area, continuing the perspective of the Tuileries' Grande Allée. For almost two centuries, nothing more happened. Cows and sheep grazed the fields; gentlefolk took their Sunday drives, and a few bought land and built villas along the route. Their friends thought them eccentric, living so far from Paris. In 1709 the pleasure promenade took its present name, the 'Elysian Fields'.

British and Prussian troops found the open land convenient in 1814, when they camped here after the defeat of Napoleon and cut down most of the trees. For the next few decades, the Champs-Elysées was a less aristocratic promenade; all Paris

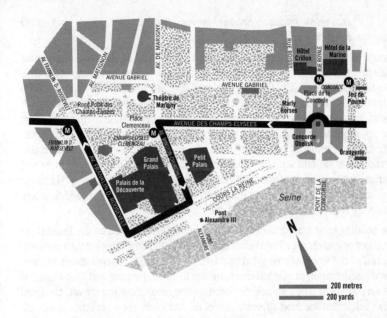

came on Sundays for a bit of fresh air. The upper part of the avenue, already partly built-up, saw a speculative boom in the reign of Napoleon III. The lower part, below the Rond-Point, was saved only because it served as a pleasure ground for all the late 19th-century exhibitions, an almost too delightful bower of groves and avenues, elaborate flower beds, Chinese lanterns, brightly-painted pavilions, ice-cream and lemonade. There was a glassed-in Winter Garden with banana trees and camellias; dances were held there at night. Outside there was more dancing and café-concerts under the trees, *Guignol* and toy stalls for the children, buskers and jugglers, balloon ascents and Louis Daguerre's new-fangled photographic panoramas. The Champs-Elysées became Paris' greatest tourist attraction; Parisians and visitors agreed that it was the pleasantest place in the world.

It isn't nearly so extravagant now, but pleasant enough for a stroll. The only buildings on the right-hand side are a small pavilion renamed after Pierre Cardin and used for fashion exhibits, and the circular **Théâtre de Marigny**, replacing an earlier theatre where the operettas of Offenbach had their first successes in the 1850s. The iron fence across Avenue Gabriel marks the rear of the Palais de l'Elysée—President Chirac's back garden.

> *Across the Champs-Elysées is Place Clemenceau, with a statue of the 'Tiger' in a billowing mac that makes him look more like a cod fisherman*

*than a prime minister. Behind him you have probably already noticed the elephantine but cute **Grand Palais.***

It's one of the biggest surprises in Paris, and beyond any doubt the capital's most neglected and unloved monument (the main hall is currently undergoing a long-overdue restoration). The Grand Palais was completed just in time for the 1900 Exhibition. There's nothing modest or shy about this little 1100ft pavilion; it astounds the eye like an Egyptian pyramid or the Empire State Building. And there was not much shyness about the architects or the fair promoters either. They built their folly in a pompous eclectic style already obsolete, and adorned it with an allegorical jungle of florid scupture and sententious hogwash. The colossal horses and chariots at the corners represent 'Immortality Vanquishing Time' and 'Harmony Routing Discord'; mighty sculptural reliefs bear titles like 'The Arts and Sciences Rendering Homage to the New Century'.

The building itself was an allegory: 'A Monument Consecrated by the Republic to the Glory of French Art'. The French got half the exhibition space for their painters; the rest of the world shared what was left. The Grand Palais itself shows the aesthetic sophistication of official French culture in 1900. Painting was little better; at the very moment when French modernists were revolutionizing the art, the Exhibition celebrated the most tiresome sort of academicism. For a novelty, though, 22 works of the major Impressionists—already a bit dated—were included in a separate room, something that would have been unthinkable in 1878 or 1889. When President Emile Loubet came to see the show, he thought he might take a look at the work of such notorious, anti-social radicals as Pissarro, Renoir and Degas. A fashionable academician named Gérôme was showing him around; when they came to the Impressionists' room, Gérôme flung himself in front of the doorway, crying: 'Go no further, Monsieur le Président; here France is dishonoured!' It was but straw in the wind. The 1900 show in fact proved a turning point, where modern art made its first big breakthrough to a wider public.

Special exhibitions are still held in the northern end of the Grand Palais—some of them blockbusters, like the recent shows of Gauguin and Celtic treasure (*open daily except Tues 10–8, 10–10 on Wed; adm*). The southern third of the building houses a branch of Paris University. But walk around to the **main entrance**, on Avenue Winston-Churchill. The doors will probably be locked, but you can peek through to the grandest interior space in Paris, if not all Europe. That 1100ft length is a single glass arcade with a glass dome at the centre, flanked by several levels of balconies, and with a magnificent grand stair. It hosts an annual book show, a motor show and little else; the rest of the year this glorious arcade stands forlorn and deserted, filled with ugly remnants of partitions and exhibition stands. As much as the Eiffel Tower, the Grand Palais is a symbol of an age, of both France and Europe at the height of their power and confidence. It reflects, more than any building except the lost Crystal Palace in London, the exuberance of an architecture that had just realized its technological capabilities.

> *Avenue Winston-Churchill was originally named after the reactionary Tsar Alexander III, from an era (1891–4) when France was desperately courting a Russian alliance. They changed it after the Second World War, trying cleverly to please the Brits and Stalin at the same time. This was the central boulevard of the 1900 Exhibition, aligned for a view of the* **Pont Alexandre III** *(see Walk XI, p.293) and the dome of the Invalides on the Left Bank. Across from the Grand Palais, what would you expect but the* **Petit Palais**? *(open daily except Mon 10–5.40; adm).*

'Petit' is relative, for a building the size of the Opéra. Like its big sister, this Palais served the Cult of Art at the 1900 Exhibition, holding a retrospective of 19th-century French painting and sculpture. The sculpture is just as flagrant, with the *Four Seasons*, the *Seine and its Tributaries* and, dominating the façade, the **City of Paris Protecting the Arts**. There is a 'permanent collection' inside, but not quite a 'museum'—restorations and rearrangements have been going on for years.

There is a large collection of 18th-century art and furniture (busts of Voltaire and Franklin by Houdon), and a smattering of works from as far back as the Renaissance, including Italian majolica and Venetian glass. The main attraction is 19th-century French painting and sculpture, though special exhibitions are frequently mounted, including some from the Petit Palais' vast collection of prints and engravings.

> *Circumnavigate the Grand Palais (not the Petit Palais) in either direction, just so you end up on Avenue Franklin-D.-Roosevelt). The rear of the behemoth has been declared a palace in itself, the science museum of the* **Palais de la Découverte** *(Palace of Discovery) (open daily exc Mon 9.30–6, Sun 10–7; adm. Separate charge for planetarium shows, Mon–Sat 11, 2, 3.15 and 4.30, Sun these times and also 5.45). Before you go in, look at one of the glories of the Grand Palais' original decoration, a colourful frieze of Sèvres terracotta designed by Joseph Blanc. It represents* The Triumph of Art, *beginning in earliest times and passing through Greece, Rome, Charlemagne's Empire, Renaissance Florence, Rome and Venice, and ultimately, of course, Paris.*

Paris must be the only city in the world with *three* important science museums: the dusty Conservatoire, space-age La Villette and this one, which opened in 1937 and still has a quaint flavour—especially in the astronomy section, reminiscent of old Flash Gordon serials on the planet Mongo.

Neither you nor the children will be bored, even if you can't read much French; there are lasers to play with, ant colonies, computers to make simple programmes on and white rats for whom you can design your own experiment. For all of you, the best part may be the **Eureka** rooms, up the left staircase from the entrance: hands-on games and tricks to learn about colours, optics and elementary physics. The scary stuff is kept at the back of the ground floor and mezzanine: big Van de Graaff generators that crank out a million and a half volts (but hardly any amperage; you can touch it, making your hair stand on end), and a nuclear exhibit where the kids can make various objects radioactive.

> *When you leave, turn right on Franklin-D.-Roosevelt, which will take you to the **Rond-Point des Champs-Elysées**, the boundary between the garden and the built-up halves of the famous avenue. Over the last few decades, the upper Champs-Elysées decayed into a well-tended reservation for all the dreariest things a Parisian shop window could possibly shelter: car dealers, hamburger stands, banks, tourist perfume shops and obscure airline offices. You could see a film; all Paris still comes to the fancy first-run palaces such as the Gaumont Colisée or the Paramount Mercury. Tourists come to see tits and feathers at the Lido (no. 110), or to buy 'duty-free' perfume at prevailing retail prices.*

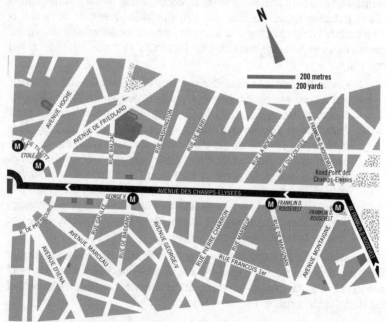

*In 1994, Paris completed an ambitious two-year $45 million project to reclaim the avenue from ennui: the pedestrian pavements have been widened, and another row of trees planted. It seems to be working; the great avenue is always packed, and it's a considerably more lively and interesting place than ten years ago. You can walk it if you like, or see it from the window of the 73 bus; get on at the stop just before the Rond-Point and off at the **Arc de Triomphe** (open daily 9.30am–10.30pm, Sun and Mon 9.30–6.30; adm). Don't try to cross the frenetic Etoile—officially Place Charles-de-Gaulle—there is a pedestrian tunnel at the right-hand side of the Champs-Elysées.*

This is *not* a tribute to Napoleon, although it certainly would have been if the Emperor had been around to finish it. The arch commemorates the armies of the Revolution: the heroic, improvised citizen levy that not only kept the rest of Europe at bay, but actually conquered new territories. It's a bit saddening that the French include Napoleon's brutal wars of conquest, as a mere continuation of what was originally a fight for freedom.

In the 18th century, the Etoile was a rustic *rond-point* on the boundaries of the city; one of the *barrières* of the Farmers-General wall stood where the arch is today. Napoleon did have the idea for the arch, after his smashing victories of 1805–6; originally he wanted it in Place de la Bastille, but his sycophants convinced him that this prominent spot in the fashionable west end would be much more fitting. A life-size model was erected in 1810, during the celebrations for Napoleon's marriage to Marie-Louise of Austria.

Not surprisingly, work stopped cold in 1815. Eight years later, Louis XVIII had the really contemptible idea of finishing it as a monument to his own 'triumph'—sending an army to put down a democratic revolt in Spain. But by the reign of Louis-Philippe, the 'myth of Napoleon' had already begun its strange progress. Times were dull; Frenchmen had forgotten the 2,000,000 of their countrymen Napoleon had sent to die for his glory, and the 18 years of misery and tyranny suffered by those left at home. The myth was helped along by the ex-Emperor's own lying memoirs, and his romantic exile on St Helena. A massive effort to complete the arch was mounted in 1832, and they had it finished four years later.

And four years after that, Napoleon's remains rolled under the arch, on a grey November day where the silence of the crowds was broken only by a few old veterans croaking 'Vive l'Empereur!' Napoleon III had Baron Haussmann make the Etoile into Paris' showcase. Then, only five streets met at the circle; Haussmann added seven more (including Avenue Foch, originally named after Empress

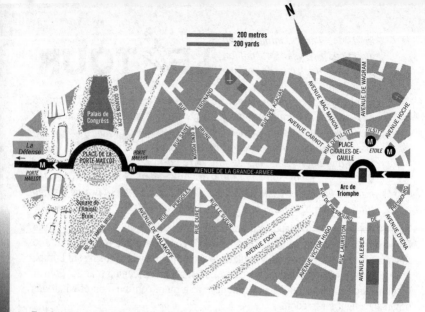

Eugénie and still the broadest street in Paris), and sent his architects to build a set of matching façades around the circle.

It isn't just its location and historical connotations that make this such an important landmark. It's also a rather splendid arch, one of the finest examples of the dignified brand of classicism that came in with the Revolution and went out with Napoleon III. Much of the sculptural work is first-rate. Any Frenchman would recognize the group on the right side, facing the Champs-Elysées: the dramatic *Departure of the Volunteers in 1792*, also known as the *Marseillaise*—it truly is the Marseillaise in stone. None of the other works of the sculptor, François Rude, are well known, but the French think so much of this one that they put Rude on a commemorative 10-franc coin.

Inside is a small museum of the arch; from there you can climb up to the roof for a remarkable view of the *Grand Axe* and the pie-slice blocks around the Etoile.

> *After the Arc, the Champs-Elysées becomes Avenue de la Grande Armée, and later Avenue Charles-de-Gaulle; there's nothing at all to see along either of these broad boulevards, so, if you dare, take the 73 bus towards that looming presence on the western horizon (punch two tickets on the bus) and follow the Grand Axe to its logical conclusion, the spooky, high-tech corporate ghetto of* **La Défense**.

Thirty-four years ago, when the first plans were made, this was a dismal suburban industrial area; its only feature was a *rond-point*, laid out by Madame de

Pompadour's brother, back in 1765 when the area was still a noble park and hunting preserve. After the siege of 1870, a statue commemorating the defence of Paris was set up in it; 'La Défense' gradually gave its name to the whole area. In 1955 the national (not Paris) government decided to make a modern, American-style business district here, and set up a development corporation called EPAD to do the job.

The biggest construction project in France since the Maginot Line started digging three years later. They weren't fooling. Over 25,000 people were relocated from the 3-sq-mile site, along with some 700 factories and businesses. By 1960, glass skyscrapers were sprouting like toadstools, a surreal scene for older Parisians. French directors were not slow to seize on La Défense's cinematic potential. Jacques Tati's poor bewildered Monsieur Hulot was baffled by glass doors and accosted by Germans demonstrating appliances in the sweet '60s film *Playtime*. In the *Little Theatre of Jean Renoir*, one of that director's last films, there is a vignette of a modern woman who has fallen hopelessly in love with her electric floor pol-isher; the tidy corporate people of La Défense provide a sort of Greek chorus, singing her tragic fate as they march up and down the métro entrances.

With bad times in the 1970s, building slowed and EPAD almost went bust. Prime Minister Raymond Barre intervened in 1978 with another infusion of money; the government induced 14 of the top 20 French corporations to move in, with a little bribery and a good deal of discreet arm-twisting, and La Défense really took off. Today, the concrete is hardly dry, but already about 100,000 people work here ('two-thirds of them executives or managerial class', EPAD's literature brags; they must be sharing secretaries). There are about 35,000 residents.

In the pharaonic atmosphere of the Mitterrand decade, EPAD went entirely out of control. The latest stage of the plan includes such projects as the Colline de la Défense (originally called the Colline de l'Automobile), a vast complex dedicated to man's best friend, with a motor museum, car company offices, space for motor exhibitions and plenty of parking. Everywhere you go in La Défense, in fact, you may feel the internal-combustion shibboleth's hot breath on your shoulder. Other plans include a gay garland of new motorway connections, and a new headquarters for Esso—the oil company's old building, the first to be completed in La Défense, will also be the first to be demolished. EPAD believes in modern art, and they have commissioned a '40ft thumb' from the sculptor César at the Colline de l'Automo-bile to show motorists the way out. But the most ambitious project of all is something still in the planning stage, at a place called the 'Triangle of Madness' (*Triangle de la Folie*), just across a motorway from the Grande Arche; this will include what may become the tallest building in the world, the cylindrical *Tour Sans Fin* proposed by architect Jean Nouvel.

Much like the Pompidou Centre, La Défense exposes for all to see the best and the worst of French ideas about planning and architecture. On the good side is the audacity and can-do spirit of the enterprise. It got built, it worked, and if the public expenditure was large, it was not wasted or gobbled up in corruption. The extension of the *Grand Axe* was a brilliant *tour de force* of cultural continuity, connecting the Paris of the centuries to the Paris of the future. And the segregation of modern business in a new quarter undoubtedly saved central Paris from some real horrors of speculative building. Even aesthetically there are some good points. La Défense is full of pedestrian spaces, and its public transport connections are as good as any place in Paris.

On the other hand, basic planning and design are primitive. Cars and people may be laudably kept separate, but the formless labyrinth of pedestrian spaces is chilly and anomic, inevitably lined with blank walls; almost everything is inside or underground, as if this were a base on the moon. You'll notice people scurrying nervously between the buildings like bugs, afraid of getting squashed. Most of the architecture is beneath contempt—pure corporate American, but far below the level of any American city centre. Buildings of the 1960s and '70s exploit the austerity of the International Style to mask a total lack of inspiration and skill; later works, like the huge Elf Tower, tend to be lukewarm rehashes of reflecting-glass postmodernism from across the Atlantic. The worst atrocities include a grim new Japan Tower on the western fringes, and especially the **Quartier du Parc**, La Défense' main residential area. You can catch a glimpse of it from the Grande Arche (to the south), a nest of amoeba-shaped towers with round windows, painted in camouflage patterns of brown, white and blue.

> Climb the stairs from the bus stop, and find your way through the maze to the **Parvis**, also called the Podium or the Dalle, the long pedestrian mall aligned with the Grand Axe. Wander at your leisure among these sorry structures, dubbed with classically French acronyms such as GAN, Coface, PFA and SCREG, and interspersed with a wealth of abstract sculptures and mosaics. At the eastern end of the Parvis, with a broad view over Paris, is the **Takis Fountain**, illuminated in the evenings with coloured lights. In the centre, near the **Agam Fountain**, is the original sculpture of the 'Défense'. And at the end, the 'biggest shopping centre in Europe', **les Quatre Temps**, faces one of the project's original buildings (1958), a vast hall for conventions and trade exhibitions called **CNIT**; triangular in shape, the entire weight of the structure rests on its three points. Outside is a 50ft red 'stabile', the last work of Alexander Calder. The colourful giants scattered about this part of the Parvis are from works by Joan Miró.

*But, since its opening in 1989, the star of the show has unquestionably been François Mitterrand's personal monument, the* **Grande Arche**.

The first two proposals for filling this space were backed by Presidents Pompidou and Giscard d'Estaing—Giscard threw out Pompidou's, and Mitterrand cancelled Giscard's, both for 'reasons of economy'. But money proved to be no object when Mitterrand started to take a personal interest in it. Here was a chance to plant a monument on the most conspicuous spot available in Paris, and the president wasn't about to leave it to his successor—and, unlike his predecessors, Mitterrand won a second term. One big problem was finding a purpose for whatever would eventually be built; the original proposal was for an 'International Communications Centre', but no one was found who could explain just what such a centre might be. Another plan was to make it the seat of the 'Foundation for the Rights of Man'. No such foundation existed, unfortunately—but now that they've got a building, one has been created.

By 1983 the government stopped worrying about such trivial matters and decided to build. A competition was proclaimed; the winner, selected by Mitterrand himself, was an obscure architect named Otto von Spreckelsen, who previously had built only a few churches in his native Denmark. In the late 1980s work went on at a furious pace, in an attempt to get the monster ready for the Revolutionary Bicentennial; on one memorable day the girders went up for eight entire storeys. Von Spreckelsen never lived to see the climax of his career finished; he died in 1987 and the last details were sorted out by other hands. The appointment with the Bicentennial was made, and the Arche opened in grand style on 14 July 1989, with the president hosting a meeting of the G-7 heads of state at the top. Filling it up still proved a problem. The government was able to sell most of the space at bargain-basement prices, but interestingly enough the deal included having them rent half of it back; the left side of the Arche now houses the entire Ministry of Transport and Public Works.

Criticism of the Arche has come from all angles. Inevitably, as in any big project, the architecture has taken some blows. David Gentleman called it a 'television with a blank screen'; also, architects have noticed that about half the space inside is wasted, unusable for offices. Right-wing papers decry the 'democratic Caesarism' of Mitterrand's plans, and above all the mismanagement that resulted in a 1.3 billion franc project ending up running over budget by more than 100 per cent—luxuries such as 350ft of Carrara marble don't come cheap. But the great gleaming cube may be a triumph just the same. Some facts and figures would be appropriate: the Arche's official name, which never caught on, is the *Arche de la Fraternité*; it weighs some 300,000 tons, and its publicists never fail to remind us that Notre-Dame, or the broad Champs-Elysées could fit easily through the hole in the middle (we think both are untrue—but no two sets of published dimensions for the thing are the same; intentional obfuscation is suspected). You'll notice it isn't exactly aligned to the *Grand Axe*; subsurface conditions made this impossible, but Von Spreckelsen managed to tilt it at an angle of 6° 33', exactly the same as the deviation of the Louvre courtyard. There are other subtleties for archaeologists to puzzle over in some distant future age: the Arc du Carrousel measures 25m (82ft), the Arc de Triomphe 50m (164ft), and Von Spreckelsen continued the ratio, making his exactly 100m (328ft) (this statistic too may not be accurate; nobody knows). And it isn't quite a perfect cube, but about 20ft wider than it is high—just enough to create the optical illusion, from most viewpoints, that it really is perfect.

But unlike most of the other grand projects of the 1980s, the Arche has had a warm reception from both critics and the public. If you don't like it, consider that modern steel-frame buildings can last a millennium or two without necessarily suffering any structural deterioration. The president chose his monument well; you, and Paris, will have to live with it for a while. Visiting it is a surreal experience; while speakers hidden in the trees regale you with Serge Gainsbourg tunes, climb the monumental stair and stop to catch your breath at the top. There's a lift, running up a glass tube through the hole; buy a ticket (expensive) and take it through the air to the top for a view of the city slightly better than the one you have from the base. An audiovisual presentation is thrown in free.

> *Just to the south of the Grand Arche, on the Colline de la Défense, is the* **Musée de l'Automobile** *(open daily 12–7, Sat until 9; adm expensive). This is a part of the planners' efforts to make La Défense a little more fun, with over a hundred antique cars, mostly French. Next door is another new attraction, the* **Dôme Imax**. *The '90s' answer to Cinerama seems to be these hyper-dramatic shows on a circular screen; the one here is claimed to be the biggest in the world, taking you to natural experiences such as the Grand Canyon or Niagara Falls—some big sharks too, of course. (Shows daily at 12, 1.30, 3, 4.30 and 6; ring © 01 36 67 06 06 for information; adm expensive.)*

# VII: Montmartre

Start: Ⓜ *Abbesses*.

Walking time: *3 hours. Save this walk for a day you're feeling fine; it's almost all up and down hill. If you're feeling lazy, take the funicular to Sacré-Coeur (two blocks north from* Ⓜ *Anvers), from where you can do much of this walk backwards. The pint-sized city bus, Montmartrobus, departs from Place Pigalle and ascends Rue Lepic to Sacré-Coeur.*

From the Eiffel Tower or the top of the Pompidou Centre, Montmartre resembles an Italian hill town from Mars, gleaming white under the beehive domes of the palace of Emperor Ming the Merciless. A closer inspection reveals honky-tonk tourist Paris at its ripest, churning francs from the fantasy-nostalgia mill for the good old days of Toulouse-Lautrec, cancan girls, Renoir and Picasso. On

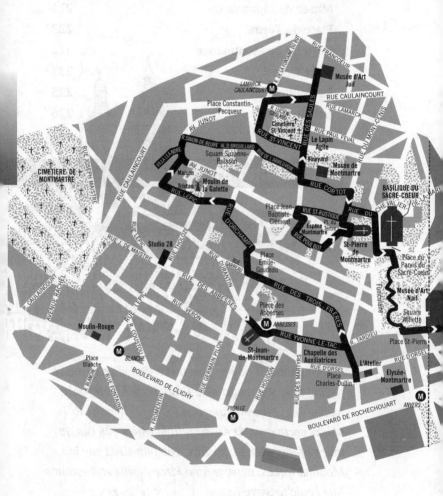

the other hand, the Butte has some of Paris' last secret alleys and picturesque streets, just as pretty as they were when Utrillo painted them. Needless to say, this walk has its ups and downs, and ends up leaving you with a sudden thump in a completely different world, now endangered as too bohemian for Paris' tastes: the Goutte d'Or quarter, grotty, cosmopolitan and alive, home to many immigrants and Paris' cheapest shops; it's an agreeably urbane and funky place, if a little bit dangerous at night.

# VII: Montmartre and the Moulin Rouge

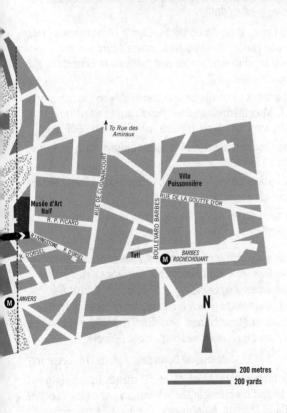

**Chez Claude et Claudine**, 99 Rue des Martyrs (a block east of Place des Abbesses). A cosy neighbourhood place, firm stronghold of onion soup-and-bourgignon traditional cooking; 69F lunch.

**Le Restaurant**, 32 Rue Véron (south of Rue des Abbesses), ✆ 01 42 23 06 22. Imaginative new restaurant with an exotic touch, by a chef from Cameroon; good-value lunch menu at 70F (closed Sun and Mon).

**La Montagnard**, 162 Rue Lepic, ✆ 01 42 64 28 42. Highlights are *fondue pyrénéenne* and other mountain specialities; 58F lunch menu.

**Le Relais de la Butte**, 12 Rue Ravignan, ✆ 01 42 23 94 64 (by Place Emile-Goudeau). An inn since 1672, and a good place for an old-fashioned simple lunch at simple prices (around 90F).

**La Pomponnette**, 42 Rue Lepic, ✆ 01 46 06 08 36. Classic Montmartre *bistrot*, lively atmosphere and chock full of posters, watercolours and other souvenirs; delicious mackerel in white wine and homemade desserts (200F and up, closed Mon).

**A. Beauvilliers**, 52 Rue Lamarck (near the intersection with Rue Caulaincourt), ✆ 01 42 54 54 42. Montmartre's gourmet restaurant in a lavish Second-Empire time capsule; most affordable at lunch, with 185 and 300F menus.

**La Poulbot**, 3 Rue Poulbot. One of the less touristy places around Place du Tertre; menus 55, 62 95 and 159F

**L'Eté en Pente Douce**, 23 Rue Muller. Tea and rich patisserie on a lovely terrace with a view, just east of Sacré-Coeur.

**Chez Aida**, 48 Rue Polenceau, ✆ 01 42 58 26 20. A block north of the Goutte d'Or, authentic Senegalese cooking on a 79F lunch menu.

---

> *Here on the summit of the mountain where St Denis and his companions were put to death still flourishes a village that took it name from the martyrs, the friends of Christ. Here stone is quarried to which is added plaster, so useful in the construction of our houses, whose brilliant whiteness transforms Paris into a town wearing a cloak of snow.*

Rodolphe Boutenais, *Lutetia* (16th-century)

The Romans called this 423ft 'mountain' Mons Mercurii, after its hilltop shrine to the god of commerce, but he lost his billing in the 9th century, when the abbot of St-Denis renamed it the Hill of Martyrs, Montmartre, the *Butte Sacrée*. Foremost among the saints was Paris' patron, Denis, although he didn't care for the place; after the Romans gave him the chop in the 3rd century he picked up his head and walked to the northern suburbs (*see* p.355). In 1133, Louis the Fat and Adélaïde of Savoy founded the Benedictine Royal Abbey of Montmartre on the site of the first Merovingian church to St Denis, leaving the rest of Montmartre covered with vineyards, windmills, gypsum (plaster of Paris) quarries and a modest hamlet. Only Henri IV briefly interrupted its tranquillity in 1589, when he lugged his cannons up the Butte to besiege Paris.

Montmartre became a commune (pop. 638) during the Revolution, when it was renamed Mont Marat. Napoleon wanted to build a temple of peace on the Butte, but the Russian occupation in 1814 precluded such flagrant hypocrisy. The population of the commune soared as workers took refuge from Baron Haussmann's demolitions, but Paris came after them and gobbled up Montmartre itself in 1860.

In February 1871, after the fall of Paris, members of the National Guard made off with 170 cannons that were meant to be surrendered to the Prussians; the money for the cannons had been raised by public subscription, so the Guardsmen reasoned they were rightfully theirs, and dragged them to the summit of the Butte. On 8 March before dawn the regular Army was sent up to seize the guns but forgot the horses to pull them, causing a fatal delay; by morning schoolteacher Louise Michel, the Red Virgin, had sounded the alarm, bringing out a sea of angry, tense and neurotic Guards and civilians. They captured two generals, Thomas and Lecomte, and summarily executed them. Montmartre's 29-year-old mayor, none other than Georges Clemenceau, arrived after the fact, crying *'Pas de sang, mes amis!'* and burst into tears when he saw that he was too late. Meanwhile Thiers and the national government fled to Versailles and Paris' revolutionary leaders, caught by surprise, scrambled to improvise the ill-fated Commune.

The first artists, poets and composers had already moved into Montmartre with the workers, drawn by cheap rents and the quality of its air and light. The police knew the village rather as the resort of *apaches*, gangs of Parisian toughs distinguished by their wide berets and corduroy trousers; when Eric Satie began his career playing piano in a Montmartre cabaret, he came to work armed with a hammer. After the First World War the bohemians moved off to the lower rents of Montparnasse, leaving their reputation to the sideshow artists who obligingly provide the tourist busloads something to spend their money on. Off the main stampedes, however, exists a Montmartre that evokes better than any other quarter what Parisian streets looked like before the Second Empire; although the Wallace fountains in the rest of Paris are mostly dry, in Montmartre they still flow, luxuriantly sending little rivulets down the steps. The whole is a rare ensemble, part gentrified and part neglected, now menaced by new buildings entirely out of proportion with the area.

*The walk begins halfway up the slope of the Butte, in **Place des Abbesses**. Part of this little square's delight is Guimard's métro entrance, the only one (along with Porte-Dauphine) to survive with its glass roof intact. The outlandish church decorated with turquoise mosaics is one of Paris' architectural milestones, the neo-Gothic **St-Jean l'Evangéliste**, the first important building in reinforced concrete (the bricks are sham), built in 1894–1904 by Anatole de Baudot, a pupil of Viollet-le-Duc; step inside to see Baudot's innovative play of interlaced arches.*

*From here, continue east down Rue Yvonne-Le-Tac (left of the post office) to no. 11, the **Chapelle des Auxiliatrices** (open Sat and Sun 9–7).*

Although Roman Prefect Sisinius Fescennius ordered Paris' first bishop, Denis, to be executed on the summit of the *Mons Mercurii*, the executioner was far too lazy to walk up, and Denis was separated from his head roughly here. Although Denis posthumously walked off in search of a holier burial ground, the Christians of Montmartre thought the plot of land sufficently sanctified and had themselves buried in what became known as the Martyrium. On 15 August 1534, the former Basque soldier and Paris University student Ignatius of Loyola led his fellow Basque St Francis Xavier and five other companions to the Martyrium to recite the initial vows that led to founding the Company of Jesus, better known as the Jesuits.

But Christ's propagandists moved on to Rome and the Martyrium fell into decay. In 1611 the Abbess of Montmartre ordered its restoration, and all Paris buzzed with the news when workers came upon an ancient catacomb, revealing what appeared to be traces of the martyrdom of St Denis, especially the graffiti MAR CLEMIN and DIO, conveniently interpreted as Martyr, Pope St Clement (who had sent Denis to Gaul) and Denis (Dionysos). It became a pilgrimage destination until the Revolution, when a plaster merchant purchased it for its gypsum, and tore out all traces of 'superstition'. This present chapel was erected in 1887; it has a 7th-century altar, and a 13th-century bas-relief of Denis' martyrdom.

*Continue up Rue Yvonne-Le-Tac, turn left up Rue des Trois-Frères to the third right, the set of steps leading up to **Place Emile-Goudeau**.*

This leafy, asymmetrical square with its Wallace fountain, steps and benches is the antithesis of the classic Paris square down on the 'plain'; note the curious perspective down Rue Berthe, which seems to lead to the end of the world. This square was the site of the famous **Bateau Lavoir** (no. 13) a leaky, creaking wooden warehouse that Max Jacob named after the floating laundry concessions on the Seine. Among the 'passengers' who rented studio space in the Bateau were Braque, Gris, Van Dongen, Apollinaire, Francis Carco and Picasso; in winter the tea in the communal pot froze every night and had to be melted for breakfast. In 1907 Picasso painted his *Demoiselles d'Avignon* (not Avignon girls, but some prostitutes he knew in Barcelona's Carrer de Avinyó) and set Cubism on its path. In 1908 Picasso held his famous banquet in honour of Henri (Le Douanier) Rousseau in the Bateau Lavoir, hung with flags and Venetian lamps; unkind critics claimed he did it as a joke, although the young Picasso, one of the first to recognize the Douanier's talent, meant it from the bottom of his heart.

One critic of the Bateau-Lavoir artists was Montmartre prankster Roland Dorgelès, who thought to fool their spokesman, Apollinaire, by tying a paintbrush to the tail of an ass and calling the result *Et le Soleil se coucha sur l'Adriatique*, by a certain Boronali. It was a great success at the Salon des Indépendents, sold for 400F and fooled all the snobs—except Apollinaire. The rest of Montmartre laughed itself silly. In 1970, just as the Bateau Lavoir was to be converted into a museum, it burned down and has been replaced by 25 more comfortable if less picturesque studios; there's a small display on its predecessor in the window.

> From here, turn left up Rue d'Orchampt; among the wooden houses reminiscent of the Bateau Lavoir is no. 5, said to be Paris' first prefab house, brought here from the 1889 World Fair. A big plaque at whimsical no. 11 marks the last residence of the 1970s pop singer Dalida, who since her death has become something of a cult figure among the romantic middle classes. Rue d'Orchampt returns you to winding Rue Lepic and the last two of Montmartre's 30 windmills, **Moulin du Radet** (now an Italian restaurant) and to the left, **Moulin de la Galette**, built in 1640 and currently being restored.

In the 1814 occupation (according to local legend) the miller of the Galette, his three brothers and eldest son defended their property against the Cossacks; all but one were killed, and one of the brothers was crucified on the sails of the windmill as an example. Only the eldest son miraculously survived, and although he lived on nothing but milk for the rest of his life, he still loved to dance and converted the windmill into a popular *guinguette* painted by Renoir (in the Musée d'Orsay).

> Continue west down Rue Lepic and turn right up the first stairway passage, which climbs up to **Avenue Junot**; this 'Champs-Elysées of Montmartre' was laid out in 1910 in Montmartre's long empty maquis, now a rare street of peaceful Art Deco houses with gardens. Anouk Aimée lives here; no. 13 is decorated with mosaics designed by Francisque Poulbot (d. 1946), the artist otherwise guilty of those cloying postcards of Montmartre urchins; at no. 15 is the **house of Tristan Tzara** (1926) designed by Viennese architect Adolf Loos.

Tristan Tzara read the first Dadaist manifesto in a Zurich café on 8 February 1916, with Hans Arp sitting in with a brioche hanging from his nose. After the war, Tzara joined Picabia in bringing Dada to Paris, causing riots with his 'poetry readings' chosen at random from the newspaper or telephone directory, and announcing to Paris' artists 'Cubism is a cathedral of *merde* (shit)'. For his own pad, however, Tzara wasn't having any nuttiness; the austere Loos was the author of the manifesto of functionalism, *Ornament and Crime*.

> *Have a look at peaceful cul-de-sac Villa Léandre (at no. 25), one of the most desirable addresses in Paris, then continue up Avenue Junot and turn right up Rue Simon-Dereure. To your right is the entrance to the little* **Square Suzanne-Buisson,** *where children play and old men toss their boules under the strange watchful gaze of a statue of St Denis, head in hands (the story goes that he stopped at a fountain here to wash the blood off). Back in Rue Dereure, the street narrows into the romantic, ivy-covered Allée des Brouillards (up the stairs), named after a lost 18th-century folly, the white* **Château des Brouillards** *(castle of mists).*

> *Continue straight on along Rue de l'Abreuvoir to Rue des Saules (the Maison Rose on the corner was often painted by Utrillo) and turn left to see Montmartre's* **vineyard***.*

It was planted by the Montmartrois in 1886 in memory of the vines that once covered the Butte. If nothing else the harvest is an excuse for a colourful neighbourhood wine crush, which results in some 400 bottles of weedy gamay called *Clos de Montmartre*, the perfect accompaniment, perhaps, for a roast Paris pigeon fed on cigarette butts; it is sold to raise money for the Butte's old folks.

> *Further down Rue des Saules is the famous* **Le Lapin Agile***.*

It opened in 1860 as the Cabaret des Assassins, but in 1880 a painter named Gil painted the mural of a nimble rabbit avoiding the pot, a play on his name: the *lapin à Gil* or, as the cabaret became known, the *lapin agile*. In the early days, when it was a favourite of Verlaine, Renoir and Clemenceau, customers would set the table themselves and join in singsongs, originating an informal style the French call *à la bonne franquette*. In 1903 Aristide Bruant purchased the place to save it from demolition, and thanks to the good humour of his friend Frédé, it enjoyed a second period of success. Artists could pay for their meals with paintings—as Picasso did with one of his *Harlequins*, now worth millions. Now, every evening, *animateurs* attempt to recapture that first peerless rapture, trying to get befuddled Japanese tourists to join in the chorus.

*Just above the Lapin Agile, turn left down Rue St-Vincent, passing on the left Place Constantin-Pecqueur; under the statue of an embracing couple is buried the artist Théophile Steinlen (d. 1923) famous for his cats and satirical cartoons of Paris. He was originally buried in the tiny **Cimetière St-Vincent** (entrance is a sharp right turn in Rue Lucien-Gaulard).*

Buried here are Swiss composer Arthur Honegger, film actor Harry Baur (d. 1943, after being tortured by the Gestapo), proto-Impressionist Boudin, *belle époque* poster artist Jules Chéret, and Maurice Utrillo (1883–1955), son of artist Suzanne Valadon, who taught him to paint as therapy for adolescent alcoholism. The result was his haunting, empty street scenes of Montmartre. Their feeling of solitude was no accident. Utrillo, like Sartre, thought hell was other people; he reacted so violently whenever a woman appeared in the street (he was prone to exposing himself and shouting: 'This is what I paint with!') that he was only allowed out with a chaperone.

Note the tomb, of a certain Platon and Papuoe Argyriades; built in the form of a little house with roof tiles and front garden, it has a curtained window with a painting of Platon and Papuoe looking out. After all the grieving angels, urns and usual funerary crustations it is sweetness itself, reminiscent of the pagan tombs under St Peter's in Rome shaped like little sitting rooms, with frescoes of their inhabitants.

*From the end of Rue Lucien-Gaulard, turn right into Rue Caulaincourt; on the left, steps lead down to the extension of Rue des Saules and at no. 42, the **Musée d'Art Juif** (Museum of Jewish Art) (open Sun–Thurs 3–6; adm; closed Aug).*

Here are works by Soutine, Benn, Max Libermann and Chagall (an illustrated Bible), ritual items, casts of tombstones from Prague and a fascinating collection of models of fortified synagogues in Lithuania and Poland. The museum will move to the Marais at some time (✆ 01 42 57 84 15 to find out the current status).

*Backtrack up Rue des Saules past the vines and turn left into Rue Cortot, where no. 12, the oldest house on the Butte, is now the **Musée de Montmartre** (open daily exc Mon 11–6; adm).*

Especially if you've already been to the tourist inferno of Place du Tertre, you might think this is a contrived attraction; in fact it is a genuine neighbourhood museum, set up and run by the people of Montmartre. Behind a pretty courtyard full of fuchsias, so healthy they are turning into trees, you'll see prints, pictures and souvenirs that tell the real Montmartre story: the old gypsum quarries that made most of the hill unbuildable until the 19th century, pictures of soldiers chasing revolutionaries through the quarries in 1848 and the old Montmartre skyline of windmills. There are plenty of old photos and maps of the area, some of Toulouse-Lautrec's posters and even the original sign from the *Lapin Agile*. One little exhibit is absolutely chilling—an overview of a 1933 city plan to partially level the hill, eradicate all of old Montmartre and create a new gridiron street plan for the developers.

> *Continue along Rue Cortot to Rue du Mont-Cenis and turn right, passing the water tower that pokes its way into all the views of Sacré-Coeur. The sudden increase in trinket shops and fast food warns you that the monster basilica itself is nigh, but first, duck to the right down cobblestoned Rue St-Rustique, the oldest street in Montmartre; Van Gogh painted* La Guinguette *(in the Musée d'Orsay) at* A la Bonne Franquette. *At the end of the lane, veer down the curve to the left, to Place Jean-Baptiste-Clément, named after the composer of the song* Au Temps des Cerises *(hence the cherry tree in the square), the cherries symbolizing the Red Flag of the Commune and the hope that it would one day fly again. (The other smash hit born of the Commune was* The Internationale, *words by a worker named Pottier, music by Degeyter.) Here, too, is Montmartre's original water tower, an octagon with a quaint Renaissance-style fountain from 1835.*

> *Return towards Rue St-Rustique, but turn right into Rue Poulbot; no. 11, the former wax museum, is now the* **Espace Montmartre** *with exhibitions mostly on Salvador Dalí. A bit further on is Place du Calvaire, the dinkiest square in Paris but one affording one of the most tremendous views over the capital, and the best possible viewpoint for the Bastille Day fireworks. Continue around and you are smack in* **Place du Tertre**, *once the main square of Montmartre village.*

It's hard to imagine a more blatant parody of the Butte's hallowed artistic traditions: unless you come bright and early, you can scarcely see this pretty square for the easels of 200 artists (the law permits two per square metre) waiting to immortalize you in one form or another. A plaque on no. 6, the restaurant Chez la Mère Catherine, marks the invention of the word *bistrot*, when in 1814 the occupying Cossacks, who were forbidden alcohol by their captains, demanded their drinks on the sly and quickly (*bistro* in Russian). The current owner led the successful fight against the deforestation of Place du Tertre proposed by municipal technocrats, who regard beautiful old trees as a menace to society.

> *At the east end of Place du Tertre is the Butte's oldest church,* **St-Pierre de Montmartre**, *disguised with a 19th-century façade.*

This is the last relic of the Royal Abbey of Montmartre, which disappeared in the Revolution when the elderly, blind and deaf Mother Superior was condemned to death by Fouquier-Tinville for 'blindly and deafly plotting against the Revolution'. Begun at the same time as the basilica of St-Denis, in 1133 a new church was built with the foundation of the abbey. Consecrated in 1147 by Pope Eugenius III, the tunnels and quarries underneath have so undermined it that the columns of the nave bend inwards like a German Expressionist film set. Otherwise there is little to see—two 7th-century Merovingian columns near the entrance, 1950s stained glass resembling African textiles and the ghostly tombstone of Adélaïde of Savoy (d. 1134), wife of Louis VI the Fat, who spent her last years at the abbey. St-Pierre has a romantic little cemetery, but it's only open on 1 November.

> *Just north of St-Pierre de Montmartre, in Rue du Chevalier-de-la-Barre, stood temples to Mercury and Mars.*

The last traces of them vanished in the 19th century, but enough of Mars' temple remained intact for Henri IV to use it for a platform to bombard Paris. Indeed, the violent spirit of the war god has dominated this area. The street itself is named after the 18-year-old Chevalier de la Barre, who failed to raise his hat before a religious procession in Amiens. His sentence, confirmed by the Paris *Parlement*, was to have his hand cut off and his tongue torn out, followed by decapitation. This did not happen during the Counter-Reformation witch hunt but in 1766; the case was taken up most notably by Voltaire who wrote about it with a mix of blistering satire and eloquent pleas for mercy and humanity.

> *Looming overhead, and over all of Paris, is the puffed-up excrescence of lard called the **Basilique du Sacré-Coeur** (open daily 11–7. Dome and crypt open 10–5, summer 9–7; adm).*

The story goes that between 1673 and 1689 Jesus Christ appeared to a nun from the Royal Abbey of Montmartre, demanding a church to the glory of his Divine Heart 'to serve France and repair the bitterness and outrages that have wasted her'. The project was put to every regime that followed, but nothing happened until the Commune and the fall of Rome (Napoleon III had been protecting the pope from the Italians, who captured Rome in 1870). These events brought a new urgency to the task. An influential band of fervent Catholics made 'a national vow' to build Sacré-Coeur to 'expiate the sins' of France—in particular, those of the Communards.

Many Parisians regard the result with some embarrassment, not only for its preposterous neo-Byzantine architecture, but for the fact that Sacré-Coeur postcards sell better than any other subject in town. The national vow was imposed on the city by a vote in the National Assembly in 1873, despite opposition by radicals and many Montmartrois, who claimed it would ruin the character of the Butte (as indeed it has, drawing 5 million visitors a year). In the design competition the most pompous entry, by Paul Abadie, was chosen. It drove Adolphe Willette (the designer of the Moulin-Rouge) crazy: 'It isn't possible that God, if he exists, would consent to live there,' he declared. On the day the first bit, the crypt chapel, opened, he ran in and shouted: '*Vive le diable!*' The Montmartrois have honoured him with a square at the foot of Sacré-Coeur's stairs. But other locals were completely in favour of the basilica, especially the ultra-Catholic critic Léon Bloy, who celebrated the sinking of the *Titanic* (and the demise of so many Protestants at one swoop) by announcing in Montmartre's bars: '*Je suis le iceberg!*'

Every hour around the clock since 1 August 1885, even in 1944 as bombs shattered the windows, there has been someone on duty praying in Sacré-Coeur for the sins of the Commune. Shuffling with the crowds through its numbing, gloomy vastness, watched over by an enormous apse mosaic of Jesus in the jet-plane position, with Joan of Arc and a host of others kneeling at his feet, you may well sense that there is something fundamentally wrong about the whole enterprise, that the rota of prayers are for the wrong side: if muddle-headed, the Commune's aims were idealistic—their real sin was losing, allowing Paris to be devastated, and some 20,000 Parisians slaughtered, at the hands of the self-righteous government that built this basilica.

For a real descent into the abyss, visit the clammy **crypt**, with its neglected chapels, broken chairs, dingy cases of relics salvaged from the Royal Abbey of Montmartre, overgrown statues of praying cardinals, and a slide show on the building of Sacré-Coeur. The view from the dome isn't that much more spectacular than the view from the parvis, but you can look vertiginously down into the interior of the basilica.

> From the basilica, take the panoramic stairs or the funicular down to Place St-Pierre and turn left. The old glass-and-iron market of St-Pierre, built by a student of Baltard in 1868, has been converted into a children's **Musée en Herbe**, with changing exhibits, and a **Musée d'Art Naïf Max-Fourny**, with some 500 works by naif painters from around the world (both open daily except Mon 10–6).

> The walk ends here, but if your feet aren't too sore, you might wish to explore the **'Plain of Montmartre'**, stretching along Boulevard de Clichy. From here, head east along Rue Livingstone and abruptly into an entirely different world from the touristy, artsy hill.

The east end of the 18$^e$ is the lively capital of North African Paris, during the day a veritable souk full of bargains that draws shoppers from all over Paris. In 1991, when the National Front's high poll ratings made racism fashionable, Mayor Jacques Chirac embarrassed nearly everybody when he walked down the area's main Boulevard Barbès proclaiming that real French people didn't like the smell of foreigners' cooking and complaining about 'polygamists who bring over three or four wives and a dozen kids to live off the state' (the Gallic version of Ronald Reagan's 'welfare queens'). In reality, many of the men are on their own, living in squalid dormitories; the second reality is that this neighbourhood doesn't at all square with the monumental shopping-mall Paris the politicians are trying to create, and hence it is in the process of being destroyed. Meanwhile, the souk isn't going down without a fight; Rue Livingstone and environs offer the cheapest textiles in all France, attracting women from every background, as colourful as the fabrics on display.

The souk's main drag is manic Boulevard de Rochechouart, where the pink-plaid plastic bags sprouting from every hand, like crocuses in spring, all hail from the massive kinetic vortex of **Tati** (4 Boulevard de Rochechouart), where prices are so low that shoppers from the posher arrondissements come for a prowl (although they are careful to transfer their loot into more expensive designer bags).

If you're at all interested in architecture, consider a 10-minute detour north up Rue de Clignancourt to Rue des Amiraux to see no. 13, the white-tiled **Immeuble à gradins** (1922), a low-income housing project by Henri Sauvage—his masterpiece, with stepped gardens and swimming pool.

*Adjacent Boulevard Barbès is the border of the **Goutte d'Or** quarter.*

The name 'golden drop' comes from a white wine produced here in the misty past, but it is a name that has evoked a certain piquancy ever since Zola made it the street where the courtesan *femme fatale* of his **Nana** grew up in poverty. Now immigrants from some three dozen different countries live together, the luckiest in the Villa Poissonnière at no. 42 Rue de la Goutte d'Or (the first street north of Boulevard de Rochechouart). Stands spilling into the sidewalks offer kebabs and spicy snacks, and North African music sends its fatalistic laments from the cafés, where the habitués look pretty fatalistic themselves, waiting for Chirac's bulldozers.

*To the west, along Boulevard de Rochechouart, is **Place Pigalle:***

Jean-Baptiste Pigalle was a neoclassical sculptor, and he would be pained if he knew his name conjured up live sex shows instead of his graceful 'Mercury tying his Sandal' in the Louvre. But times are hard in the seedy sex industry: a good half of Pigalle's businesses are boarded up, and the fear of AIDS and the new 33% luxury tax on the porn trade have taken their toll. During the day desultory balls of fast-food litter roll about like tumbleweed.

The first taverns and *guinguettes* appeared here in the 18th century, just beyond the Farmers-General wall where booze was cheaper. The **Café de la Nouvelle Athènes**, once at no. 9, was a favourite of Manet and the Impressionists, who had a permanently reserved table. East of Place Pigalle stood two famous nightspots: the 1807 *guinguette* **Elysée-Montmartre** (72 Boulevard de Rochechouart, crowned by a pretty if crumbling bas-relief now familiar to alternative rock fans) and the much later **Le Chat Noir**, founded in 1881 at no. 84, featuring arty, satirical songs in Parisian slang, accompanied by shadow puppets. It owed part of its tremendous success to the fringe literary clubs that camped out here—the *Hydropathes*, the *Hirsuites* and the 'Epileptic Pickled Herrings'. The *chansonnier* Aristide Bruant (1833–1925) got his start here, always dressed in the same red shirt, black scarf and hat that Toulouse-Lautrec made famous. Bruant later took over the premises and opened his own club, Le Mirliton, which drew the slumming bourgeoisie who in their thousands paid to be insulted and provoked by this new François Villon of the 'other Paris' and its underworld (*see* Topics, p.59).

> *Just to the west on Boulevard de Clichy is Place Blanche, embellished with the red wooden sails of a Paris landmark as familiar as the Eiffel Tower, the **Moulin Rouge**.*

The Moulin Rouge was founded by an ex-butcher named Zidler, who was the first to understand the immense business potential in Paris' congenital vulgarity. Zidler's inspiration was the Elysée-Montmartre (*see* above) where people came to dance the *chahut* (meaning 'noise, mayhem, high spirits'), as well as its more difficult offspring, a Second Empire quadrille called the *cancan*, performed by women only—thumping and sweating, the most extrovert and erotic dance of the day, with its knicker-revealing high kicks, cartwheels, *grands écarts* (splits), *port d'armes* (holding a foot as high as possible over one's head), and saucy displays of one's bottom, all to the lilting tunes of Offenbach's popular operetta tunes.

The *cancan* became orgasmic when danced by the Elysée's La Goulue, whose name 'the glutton' came from her habit of greedily sucking up the dregs of every possible pleasure ('her nose sniffing after love, nostrils dilating with the male odour of chestnut trees and the enervating bouquet of brandy glasses' according to one journalist). Her partners included the gaunt, rubbery Valentin-le-Désossé ('the boneless one', the original of John Travolta in *Saturday Night Fever*), by day a mild-mannered wine merchant, at night in his top hat a dancing fool, and a dignified girl known as *Grille-d'Egout* ('sewer grating') because of the spaces between her teeth. All were immortalized by Toulouse-Lautrec, that insatiable moth who haunted Montmartre's cabarets with his sketchbook.

Zidler bought an old dance hall, and left its decoration to a painter named Willette who stuck a mock windmill on the façade and purchased a plaster elephant with a tiny stage in its gut from the 1889 World Fair, just the thing for hoochie-coochie dancers. From the day it opened on 6 October 1889, the Moulin Rouge was a roaring success: not only did Zidler lure away La Goulue, Valentin-le-Désossé, and Grille-d'Egout from the Elysée, but his PR techniques made it respectable for *tout Paris* to attend the show. Perhaps Zidler's greatest theatrical coup was in 1892, when he starred Joseph Pujol of Marseille, 'Le Pétomane', who played all the popular songs of the day with his specially-gifted aspirating anus; the king of the Belgians made a special trip to Paris just to hear him. Other regulars of the Moulin Rouge were the *chanteuse* (singer) Yvette Guilbert of the long black gloves, the Edith Piaf of her day, and Jane Avril, or Jane la Folle, who came to dance for her own pleasure with a sinuous rapture that personified decadence to the connoisseurs; an admiring Arthur Symons called her 'a creature of incarnate degradation.' In 1894 Zidler left the Moulin Rouge, and if it didn't decline, it lost its innovative spark (and Jane Avril) to its competitors. Meanwhile, the Moulin Rouge has lurched into the 1990s with stars the calibre of Michael Jackson's sister, performing Las Vegas kitsch extravaganzas.

> *Continue west on Boulevard de Clichy. Poet Jacques Prévert lived and died in Cité Véron (the first right); across the boulevard, note the little chapel of Ste-Rita, the patroness of unhappy women and for decades the special church of Pigalle's prostitutes. Take the second turn right, Avenue Rachel, to* **Cimetière de Montmartre***.*

Despite the viaduct overhead, this is one of Paris' most romantic graveyards, a favourite last pasture for composers, painters, actors and writers. Actor Sacha Guitry and his actor father lie near the entrance; there's Berlioz, one of Montmartre's first arty residents, and further up Avenue Berlioz, the great German poet Heinrich Heine (who spent long agonizing years dying in Paris, threatening to report God to the Humane Society), film director François Truffaut, painter Fragonard, poet and critic Théophile Gautier, to whom Baudelaire dedicated *Les Fleurs du Mal*; Alexandre Dumas *fils*, Henri Mûrger, author of *Scènes de la Vie de Bohème*, written from bitter experience, Edgar Degas (De Gas on the family tomb), Foucault of pendulum fame, Offenbach (in the northwest corner), Nijinsky, the Goncourt brothers, Stendhal (whose potty epitaph reads: 'To live, to love, to be a Milanese'), Frédérick Lemaître, the great actor portrayed in *Les Enfants du Paradis*, the celebrated beauty Juliette Récamier, who is said to have died a virgin, and, back near the entrance and exit, the beautiful courtesan Alphonsine Plessis (1824–47) better known as Marguerite Gautier, *La Dame aux Camélias*, who really did die of consumption in the arms of Alexandre Dumas *fils*, who made her the literary saint of unrequited love.

> *If you want to backtrack to Place des Abbesses, walk to Place Blanche and up Rue Lepic, trail-blazed by gypsum wagons, which would trundle down*

to Place Blanche, coating the buildings with white powder (hence its name). Up at the curve is one of Montmartre's last authentic bistrots *Au Virage Lepic, worth keeping in mind (dinner only)*, but for the moment turn right into *Rue des Abbesses*. On the first street on your left, at 10 *Rue Tholozé*, was the Right Bank's first art cinema, named **Studio 28** after the year it was founded. When Buñuel and Dalí's *l'Age d'Or was premiered in 1930, Catholic conservatives ripped the screen to shreds*.

# VIII: The Latin Quarter

**Start:** Ⓜ *Maubert Mutualité*
**Walking time:** *2 hours, but add another 2 for the Musée de Cluny, and another couple for the Panthéon and other museums.*

The Latin Quarter is one of Paris' great clichés, where Abelard taught, Villon fought, Erasmus thought and Mimi coughed. Its name was bestowed by a student named Rabelais, for Latin (with an excruciating nasal twang) was the only language permitted in the university precincts, spoken by the blackhearted judges of the Sorbonne down to their sooty kitchen scullions, until Napoleon said *non*. Napoleon's 19th-century successors tended to regard the Latin Quarter itself as an anachronism, and rubbed most of its medieval abbeys, colleges and slums off the map; since 1968 even most of the students have been dispersed throughout Paris and its suburbs. But once you too have dispersed any lingering romantic or operatic notions that the Latin Quarter evokes, it can be good fun, especially at night when it becomes the headquarters for an informal United Nations of goodwill. There's plenty to see during the day as well: Gothic churches, the Panthéon, two generally ignored museums full of Paris trivia—that of the police (closed Sun) and public assistance (closed Mon and Tues)—and, best of all, the Musée de Cluny with its sensational collection of medieval art (closed Tues).

## lunch/cafés

*Dodgy fast food, Greek sandwich stands, Chinese restaurants, Tunisian pastry shops and such line busy Rue de la Huchette and surrounding streets, where half the Left Bank seems to go for lunch and dinner. This is the easiest place to find sustenance but other choices are not lacking:*

**Al-Dar**, 8 Rue Frédéric-Sauton, ✆ 01 43 25 17 15. Flashy but crowded for its delicious Middle Eastern dishes (menu 90F).

**Le Grenier de Notre Dame**, 18 Rue de la Bûcherie, ✆ 01 43 29 98 29. Has simple vegetarian and macrobiotic dishes (75–105F menus, also childrens' menu).

**La Bûcherie**, 41 Rue de la Bûcherie, ✆ 01 43 54 78 06. A classic serving delicious classics (*coquilles St-Jacques* and wild duck) with views over Notre-Dame; fine woodwork inside, and an open fire in winter (230F menu, with wine).

**La Petite Hostellerie**, 35 Rue de la Harpe, ✆ 01 43 54 47 12. Amidst the bustle in the cheap lunch heaven around Rue de la Huchette is one excellent inexpensive restaurant—nothing fancy but the cooking is fine; 69F lunch menu.

**The Tea Caddy**, 14 Rue St-Julien-le-Pauvre. Soft-lit tea room from the 1920s, bestowed by the Rothschilds on a favourite English governess.

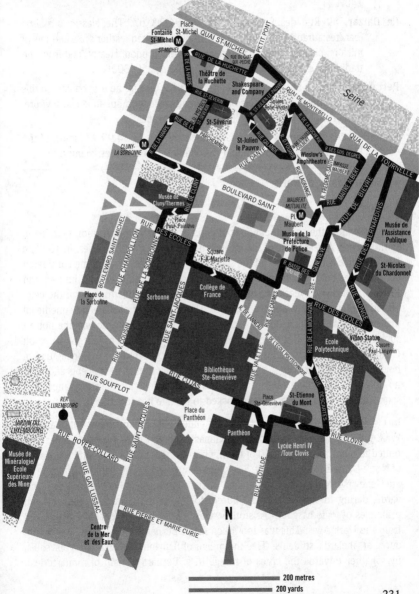

# VIII: The Latin Quarter

Place St-Michel
Fontaine St-Michel
ST-MICHEL
QUAI ST-MICHEL
PETIT PONT
RUE DE LA HUCHETTE
RUE DU CHAT-QUI-PÊCHE
RUE DE LA HARPE
Théâtre de la Huchette
RUE ST-SÉVERIN
Shakespeare and Company
Seine
QUAI DE MONTEBELLO
St-Séverin
PARCHEMINERIE
RUE DE LA
CLUNY-LA-SORBONNE
RUE DE LA HARPE
RUE DES PRÊTRES-ST-SÉVERIN
St-Julien le Pauvre
RUE GALANDE
R. D'YDOURG
Winslow's Amphitheatre
R. DES GDS DEGRES
IMPASSE MAUBERT
RUE FRÉDÉRIC SAUTON
QUAI DE LA TOURNELLE
RUE DE BIÈVRE
Musée de l'Assistance Publique
Musée de Cluny/Thermes
RUE DE CLUNY
BOULEVARD SAINT
MAUBERT MUTUALITÉ
Pl. Maubert
RUE MAÎTRE ALBERT
RUE DES BERNARDINS
Place Paul-Painlevé
RUE DES ÉCOLES
Musée de la Préfecture de Police
St-Nicolas du Chardonnet
BOULEVARD SAINT MICHEL
RUE CHAMPOLLION
RUE DE LA SORBONNE
Square F-A-Mariette
R. BASSE DES CARMES
STE-GENEVIÈVE
RUE MONGE
Sorbonne
Collège de France
RUE DE LANNEAU
RUE DES CARMES
RUE DE LA MONTAGNE
RUE DES ÉCOLES
Villon Statue
Square Paul-Langevin
Place de la Sorbonne
RUE SAINT-JACQUES
R. DE L'ÉCOLE POLYTECHNIQUE
Ecole Polytechnique
RUE COUSIN
Bibliothèque Ste-Geneviève
RUE VALETTE
RUE DESCARTES
RUE SOUFFLOT
RUE CUJAS
RER LUXEMBOURG
Place Ste-Geneviève
St-Etienne du Mont
JARDIN DU LUXEMBOURG
RUE ROYER-COLLARD
RUE SAINT-JACQUES
Place du Panthéon
Panthéon
RUE CLOVIS
Lycée Henri IV/Tour Clovis
Musée de Minéralogie/Ecole Supérieure des Mines
RUE GAY LUSSAC
RUE CLOTILDE
RUE PIERRE ET MARIE CURIE
Centre de la Mer et des Eaux
N

200 metres
200 yards

231

**Auberge des Deux Signes**, 46 Rue Galande, © 01 43 25 46 56. One of the Latin Quarter's gourmet addresses with a medieval atmosphere; lunch menu 140F.

**Le Balzar**, 49 Rue des Ecoles, © 01 43 54 13 67. The classic *brasserie* (bar/restaurant) of the Quarter, with old-fashioned leather seats and lots of mirrors, packed with academics and editors at noon. Hearty food from the traditional choucroute to *raie au beurre noir*; 250–300F.

**Perraudin**, 157 Rue St-Jacques, © 01 46 33 15 75. One of the best choices in this part of Paris, a comfortable old-fashioned place with fine food and few pretensions. The 63F lunch menu is a great bargain.

**La Vallée des Bambous**, 35 Rue Gay-Lussac, © 01 43 54 99 47 (south of the Panthéon). Good dim-sum and reasonable Chinese dishes; menu 60F.

---

## The University of Paris

### Abelard

This walk tours the ancient confines of Paris University, an institution founded in spirit by Peter Abelard, one of the greatest thinkers of the Middle Ages. In 1099 he left his native Brittany to attend the school of Notre-Dame, at that time considered second rate, behind the far more rigorous episcopal schools at Chartres and Rheims. But the 20-year old Abelard chose Paris just to hear one man: the celebrated Guillaume de Champeaux, Notre-Dame's master of dialectic—medieval dialectic that is, or the art of reasoning through debate. Dialectic was the hottest subject of the day, and it didn't take the gifted Abelard long to talk the pants off Champeaux and formulate his own doctine, called 'conceptualism'. Conceptualism holds that abstract concepts, or universals, exist only as mental concepts and have no objective existence. Abelard's lectures were famous for their brilliance, and soon students from all over Europe flocked to Paris to hear them.

In 1118, when his love affair with Héloïse ended with the unkindest cut of all (*see* Walk I, p.112), Abelard retired to the monastery of St-Denis. Yet his disciples continued to pour into Paris, 3000 of them, clamouring for his return until the bishop of Notre-Dame booted them out. They took refuge on the Left Bank's Montagne de Ste-Geneviève and by popular demand Abelard joined them, lecturing in the vineyards, daring to subject sacred Church dogma to the rigours of dialectic and principles of logic based on Aristotle, whose books had just recently resurfaced from the Dark Ages. This was too much for St Bernard of Clairvaux, who thundered at Abelard's students: 'Flee the milieu of Babylon, flee and save your souls, fly together towards the cities of refuge' (i.e. Bernard's chain of monasteries).

When they failed to heed, Bernard manoeuvred to have the teachings of Abelard and his inspired student, Arnold of Brescia, condemned as heresy at the 1140 Council of Sens. Abelard appealed to the pope, only to be told: 'Shut your mouth and burn your books.' In 1142 Abelard started for Rome to defend himself in person and died on route.

## A Paradise of Pleasure

But the cat was out of the bag. Arnold of Brescia led a genuinely democratic revolution in Rome—though eventually he was betrayed to the pope and burned at the stake. In Paris the high standards of inquiry and scholarship set by Abelard made the Left Bank a 'paradise of pleasure' for intellectuals and students from across Europe. Private citizens and religious orders built college-hostels to house the scholars, usually divided by nationality. In 1180 Philippe-Auguste enclosed the whole area in his enceinte, walls that until the 18th century defined the University Quarter. Not everyone was pleased by the student invasion. Left Bank residents fought them tooth and nail, and in a riot in 1200 they murdered five German students. Scholars demanded justice from Philippe-Auguste, who obliged by tossing some of the townies in the dungeon and officially recognizing the Left Bank masters and students as a corporation called the *Universitas Magistrorum et Scolarium Parisiensium.* In 1215 the pope confirmed its charter and, most importantly, freed it from the bishop's tutelage, making it accountable only to ecclesiastical courts. The university rector held the same rank as a prince, with the stupendous postmortem benefit of being buried with the noble stiffs at St-Denis.

## The Intellectual Bread of Humanity

The heady freedom of thought that made Paris University great in the 13th century drew the greatest thinkers of the day: Albertus Magnus from Germany, Thomas Aquinas from Naples and Roger Bacon from England. In 1255 it took the revolutionary step of making all the known works of Aristotle mandatory in its syllabus. 'France is the oven where the intellectual bread of humanity is baked,' marvelled a visiting papal legate. High spirits came in the yeast, and boys will be boys. Scholars interpreted the privileges granted by the king and the pope as a licence to rob, murder and rape. In 1223 another town-and-gown battle ended with 320 dead scholars pitched into the Seine. This time the king was less sympathetic, and the university began a great Paris tradition by going on strike for several years. Subsequent high jinks were more subdued, although during the Renaissance theology students had to be chastized for attending church in drag, wolfing down roast chicken during Communion, satirizing the Mass responses and playing dice in the chapels.

Sadly, 'the intellectual bread of humanity' had already begun to grow mould by the late 1200s. Aristotelian logic coagulated into the blind scholastic formulae mocked by Villon and Rabelais, a stilted conformism that drove serious scholars to Oxford, Cambridge, Padua and Cologne. When Philippe le Bel convinced the theological judges at the Sorbonne that they should condemn the Knights Templars in 1312, he cursed the university with a political role that compromises its independence to this day. The Hundred Years' War came close to compromising its very existence. The university supported the English and Burgundian claims, and at the trial of Joan of Arc the Sorbonne supplied the prosecutor, Pierre Cauchon, who sent the Maid to the stake.

## Reaction and Revolution

In 1470 three Germans were invited to the Sorbonne to start the first printing press in France, beginning a renaissance of intellectual life on the Left Bank. Unfortunately, the Sorbonne was too reactionary to satisfy the new thirst for knowledge ('A drink! A drink! A drink!' bellowed Gargantua as he was born) and in 1530 an alternative, the humanist Collège de France, was founded to teach Greek, Hebrew and forbidden classical authors. The Counter-Reformation soon cut off the taps, however: after giving its approval to the St Bartholomew's Day massacre, the Sorbonne concentrated not on printing books but on repressing them. Richelieu, appointed chancellor in 1622, tried to revive the Sorbonne's flagging status with an extensive rebuilding of the college. Nothing he could do, however, halted the Latin Quarter's decline into a volatile slum. The Revolution had no qualms about closing the whole university down as the gangrened rubber stamp of King and Church, and deconsecrated its beautiful Gothic abbeys, churches and colleges. Left empty, they fell easy prey to speculators in the 1820s and '30s—a 'methodical and thought-out vandalism' as one of the very few protesters called it. More frequent were demands to have the whole Latin Quarter razed.

## Resuscitation and Rebellion

Napoleon resuscitated the university, but there was no going back to the old ways—if the Sorbonne was political, so were the post-Revolutionary students, who played important roles in the upheavals of the 19th century, who battled the Nazis in Place St-Michel, protested against the war in Algeria and in May 1968 shocked the government by rising up against the mandarin structure and archaic teaching methods of the university itself. The protests on 2 May in the faculty at Nanterre spread the next day to the Sorbonne, which immediately closed. The nervous government overreacted and sent police into the university's sacred precincts, provoking demonstrations in the streets and further repressions, until in true Parisian tradition up went the barricades on 10 May. What had begun as a protest against the state of the university had spread to a rebellion against the boredom and apathy of the de Gaulle era, with a succinct motto: 'It is forbidden to forbid.' The result: one student killed, hundreds wounded and arrested, and a debate over university reforms that continues to this day. But the government has accomplished its agenda: the rebellious Sorbonne has been blasted into a centreless prism of thirteen blandly numbered campuses scattered throughout Paris.

> *Begin in **Place Maubert**, the Platea Mauberti of 1202 and medieval centre of the Latin Quarter.*

Maubert is said to be an elision of Maître Albertus—the philospher Albertus Magnus, who gave alfresco lectures on dialectic in this square. Albertus had as his assistant a magic, know-it-all brass head until one of his students, St Thomas Aquinus, smashed it to smithereens, beginning the sorrowful tale of Place Maubert's next 700 years. Lectures gave way to low taverns, and Sorbonne theologians made it a barbecue pit for the three Hs: humanists, heretics and Huguenots, staging so many *auto-da-fés* that Place Maubert was for centuries a pilgrimage site for Protestants. The most famous victim was Etienne Dolet, who published unauthorized, unexpurgated versions of *Gargantua* and *Pantagruel* (much to the dismay of Rabelais, who spent most of his own life ducking and dodging Sorbonne diehards). Dolet was burned with all his books in 1546, and although a bronze statue was erected to him in the 19th century even that was melted by the Nazis, leaving only the pedestal (now a planter). Another casualty was the Gothic cloister of the Grands-Carmes, the most beautiful in Paris until it was demolished in the 1820s to make way for a market. In its shadow the poorest of the poor ran an alternative market in stale bread and cigarette butts collected from the gutters, dried and sold as economy *cigarettes à la main*. When Haussmann enlarged the square, he impatiently obliterated the lot. These days a civilized street market takes place on Tuesdays, Thursdays and Saturdays, amid the useful Vietnamese and Thai grocers.

> *From here walk down Rue Maître-Albert, once the notorious Rue Perdue and resort of scoffers of the law, who made good use of the subterranean passages that to this day link the houses. Turn left in Rue des Grands-Degrés, then into Rue Frédéric-Sauton, then sharply left into dead-end **Impasse Maubert**, where the first Greek college in Paris was founded by the Patriarch of Constantinople in 1206, in the days when a reconciliation between the Eastern and Western Churches still seemed possible. Its neighbour, no. 4, was a poison laboratory in the 1700s, discovered only when the fumes accidentally asphyxiated the three weird sisters who brewed the stuff. Note, too, no. 8 with its rare gable roof, a once popular style banned in the 1600s because of dampness problems.*

*Backtrack to Rue de la Bûcherie and continue on to the elegant 17th-century Rue de l'Hôtel-Colbert, where an old street sign still gives its old name—Rue des Rats. The circular structure on the corner here was Paris' **first School of Medicine.***

The buildings date from 1472, except for the triple-tiered, circular amphitheatre inaugurated by the Danish anatomist Winslow in 1745. In between those two dates were long years when only a handful of students gathered to discuss questions that still seem pertinent today: does debauchery make men bald? Can a woman turn herself into a man? Dissections, banned by the Church, could only take place in the winter, when the weather preserved the corpses swiped from the nearby graveyard of St-Séverin. One body-snatching story, however, had a happy ending: a young girl, buried too hastily in the morning, revived by the time the students had her on their table. She had no idea what had happened, and afraid of frightening her back to death, the future doctors told her she had been confided to their care. They put her to bed, gave her a warm broth and sent a servant around to fetch her astonished parents while they discreetly beat a hasty retreat.

Much of what we know about stolen bodies in Paris has come down in the writings of Restif de la Bretonne (1734–1806), literary police informer, self-proclaimed *espion de vice* and pervert, who lived at no. 16. Restif's masterpiece, a series of fragmented sketches called *Les Nuits de Paris* (1789), has inspired urban writers from Baudelaire to Henry Miller. But paper could hardly contain all of Restif's thoughts, and he took to carving notes in Latin on the bridges to Ile St-Louis. Passers-by could follow his separation from his wife (*Abiit hodie monstrum*, 'the monster left today'), his liaison with Sara Devée in 1776 (*Data tota—felix*, 'she gave herself completely—happy'), and even his meals (*Coena ad belved*, 'had supper on the boulevard'). Although he died in poverty amid well-founded suspicions of incest with his daughters, a cortège of 2000 admirers, from whores to duchesses, buried him in style.

*At the end of Rue de la Bucherie is **Square René-Viviani,** a spot of green that replaces a fetid sick ward attached in 1602 to the Hôtel-Dieu on the Ile de la Cité.*

To link the two, the hospital built the **Pont au Double**, named after the double toll it charged—one to get on and another to get off (its modern reincarnation is right across the busy Quai de Montebello). Until 1835 the bridge was also lined with sickrooms, and the whole hospital-bridge-annexe ensemble formed a fascinating U-shaped ensemble that positively reeked. Square Viviani's Gothic odds and ends, melted by wind and rain, were found near Notre-Dame; the tree on concrete crutches is the oldest in Paris. It's a false acacia, called a *robinier*, after Robin the botanist who planted it in 1602.

*This is one of the rare corners of Paris to preserve the pre-Haussmann higgledy-piggledy of a Charles Méryon drawing. To see it all turn briefly south in Rue Lagrange, and right into **Rue du Fouarre**, a mere stump of a street that in the 12th century was the very embryo of the University, named after the straw bales (fouarre in Old French) that served as benches for the first students. Tradition has it that Dante attended classes here in 1304. Turn right at **Rue Galande**, once the start of the bustling Roman road to Lyon.*

These days the action happens on weekends at the Studio Galande, local perpetuator of *The Rocky Horror Picture Show*. Incongruously over its door is a 14th-century bas-relief from the nearby church of St-Julien le Pauvre. It depicts a scene from the legend of St Julian the Hospitaller, who came home one day to find a couple in his bed. Thinking his wife had a lover, he slew the pair, only to learn they were his own parents. In despair he and his wife sailed up the Seine and founded a hostel to serve the poor. One day a leper asked Julian and his wife to ferry him across the river, and revealed himself to be the forgiving Christ.

Other houses on Rue Galande are medieval, but have been much restored. No. 65 has another rare gable roof, while the Auberge des Deux Signes (no. 46) contains Gothic fragments from St Julian's chapel of St-Blaise and, more appropriately, the monks' old refectory. At the end of Rue Galande, the **Caveau des Oubliettes** supper and song club is believed to stand over the grimmest dungeons (*oubliettes*, or forgotten places) of the Petit Châtelet, the mini-fortress that guarded the southern approaches of the Petit Pont.

*On a happier note, turn right at the corner for the diminutive transitional Gothic church of **St-Julien le Pauvre**, originally built to provide hospitality for pilgrims to Santiago de Compostela (open 9–1 and 2.30–6.30; singing Mass Sun at 11am).*

Dating back to 587, St-Julien is one of the oldest churches in Paris, a last token of a score of chapels founded at the same time as Notre-Dame. Enlarged in 1208, it became the university's assembly hall, an association that went sour when a student riot in 1524 left the church half-ruined. All members of the university were henceforth banned, and migrated up the hill to St-Etienne du Mont (*see* below), while poor St-Julien was practically abandoned. In 1651 it was on the verge of collapse when the roof was lowered and the nave lopped off (the ruins on the left show the original size) and it became a chapel for the Hôtel-Dieu. The fine Gothic vaulting in the right aisle is original, and although the arches in the chancel (1180) are pointed, the builders went back to the Romanesque for the arcade in the nave. Two Romanesque capitals survive in the chancel, the one on the left portraying not angels, but harpies from Greek mythology. Perhaps they have felt more at home since 1889, when St Julian was given to the Greek Catholic rite.

> *Continue towards the river on Rue St-Julien, turning left at Rue de la Bûcherie for what must be the most famous English-language second-hand bookshop on the continent, **Shakespeare and Company** (open daily noon to midnight).*

This is the namesake of Sylvia Beach's English bookshop that stood in Rue de l'Odéon between the wars. Beach's kindness and free lending library made her a den mother for many expat writers, but none owed her as much as James Joyce. After the *Ulysses* obscenity trial in 1921 precluded the publication of the book in Britain or the US, Beach volunteered to publish it herself. Joyce returned the favour by handing back galley proofs with 10,000 smudgy corrections. The gracious George Whitman, great-grandson of Walt Whitman, has continued the tradition, performing many kindnesses to impoverished writers.

> *Just to the west, the **Petit Pont** (1853) spans the same stretch of river as Paris' first bridge, built in the time of Julius Caesar at the narrowest point of the Seine. It linked the Ile de la Cité to Lutetia's main street, named Rue St-Jacques after the thousands of cockleshelled pilgrims who walked along it to Santiago de Compostela. Those with a few sous jangling in their pouch will have taken the first right (as you should) for a slab of roast ox in **Rue de la Huchette**.*

The 13th-century 'street of the little trough' is a suitable name for a vocation the lane holds to this very day, except that the fat *rôtisseurs* (meat roasters) described in awe by so many medieval visitors have been replaced by greasy spoons serving souvlakia or kebabs. On weekend evenings the aroma draws half of the students in the world. If Rue de la Huchette seems a squeeze, take a look down the first right, **Rue du Chat-qui-Pêche** (named after a long-ago inn sign of a fishing cat). At 6ft it's the narrowest street in Paris, and the last really medieval one, which gives you an idea of what Haussmann demolished. Unlike modern thoroughfares, Rue du Chat-qui-Pêche did not divide two rows of houses as much as it served as a communal parlour for residents. Originally it was named Rue des Etuves after a public steam bath: there were 29 such baths in Paris in the 1300s, nearly all run by the Jews, who were in the avant-garde of cleanliness and fun. When its mixed naked clientele started having too much of the latter, the baths were forced to close.

The jazz cellar of the **Caveau de la Huchette** at 5 Rue de la Huchette is even more retro than its music; some historians believe it was a secret Templar meeting place linked to the Petit Châtelet dungeons. No. 10 was a hotel in 1795, where a certain Brigadier-General Bonaparte lived while he schemed his way to the top. The little **Théâtre de la Huchette** at no. 23 produces Paris' equivalent of London's eternal *Mousetrap*: Ionesco's *La Cantatrice Chauve* and *La Leçon* premiered here in 1957 and are still going strong.

> *Rue de la Huchette peters out in **Place St-Michel**, a traffic vortex laid out under Napoleon III and decorated with a striking fountain by Davioud of **St-Michel slaying the Dragon**. It marks the beginning of the Latin Quarter's main drag, **Boulevard St-Michel**, or simply Boul' Mich, laid out in 1859.*

What you can't see any longer are its paving stones, which proved too convenient for slinging at the police in May 1968 and now lie under a thick coat of asphalt. If you come after dark the traffic, both in the street and along the pavements, creeps along at a snail's pace, even if (or perhaps, because) most of the cafés have been replaced with up-to-date fast food infernos.

> *Escape to the left up Rue de la Harpe, which follows a street of Roman Paris. Rue de la Harpe, currently named after a 16th-century sign over a harp-makers' shop (now lost), wins the prize for having had the most recorded names (14) of any street in Paris. Turn left into Rue St-Séverin, where over a two-bit cabaret at no. 12 the Abbé Prévost d'Exiles wrote* Manon Lescaut, *the only one of his hundred-plus novels remembered today. Further up, a row of sinister serpentine gargoyles jut three feet out over the street, threatening to puke rainwater or worse on your cranium. But not to worry; they're held on a tight lead by **St-Séverin** (open Mon–Sat 11–7.30).*

Séverin was a 6th-century hermit who lived on this spot when it was a swamp, and whose most notable feat was talking Clovis' grandson Cleodald into taking religious orders. Cleodald took them so seriously he was canonized as St Cloud, and in gratitude his uncle Childebert I dedicated a chapel to his old mentor, Séverin. It grew into such an important church (several Merovingian sarcophagi were found in the area) that in 1031 Henri I replaced it with a Romanesque church. This took the next 450 years to complete and gradually evolved into Flamboyant Gothic. Still, it failed to suit the fickle taste of Louis XIV's cousin, the ornery Grande Mademoiselle, who no sooner joined the parish than she paid Lebrun to redecorate the interior. Lebrun's mischief can never be competely undone—columns remain ridiculously fluted; pointed arches were rounded off.

The carved 13th-century portal in Rue des Prêtres-St-Séverin was brought over from St-Pierre-aux-Boeufs, a church on the Ile de la Cité demolished in 1837. It has a fine rose window, but is obscured inside by the Rococo organ (1745), an otherwise fine instrument whose ivories Saint-Saëns and Fauré would come to tickle on Sunday afternoons. Lacking space to expand lengthwise, the 14th and 15th-century builders of St-Séverin added a whole extra set of aisles and chapels, creating a rare visual breadth that culminates in St-Séverin's most remarkable feature: a palm-ribbed **double ambulatory** that seems to unwind organically from the twisted spirals of the centre column. Even the smeared, dirty watercolour stained glass added in 1966 can't spoil the effect. Other details are concentrated in the first three bays of the nave, the only part of the church to survive a 15th-century fire: exquisite flamboyant tracery in the vaults and the Romanesque capitals, as well as 15th and 16th-century stained glass in the clerestory. St-Séverin's peaceful garden, enclosed by arcades, is actually the last charnel house in Paris. When the graveyard became too crowded, bones were dug up and embedded in the arches, half of which still stand. In 1474, the first known operation for gallstones took place here. The patient, a condemned man, was offered his freedom if he survived. Using a cemetery as a surgical theatre hardly suggests optimism, but the patient was on his feet in two weeks. The techniques went on to become one of the very few operations offered by the Hôtel-Dieu that the patient had even odds of surviving.

> *Leaving the church, turn left into Rue des Prêtres-St-Séverin and right into Rue de la Parcheminerie.*

The latter is named after parchment makers, who manufactured Paris' first 'paper' from degreased lambskins; a complete folio would require a whole flock of sheep. Along with the illuminators the parchment makers moved here from the Petit Pont in the 1200s to be nearer the university. It was the beginning of the Left Bank's leading role in French publishing, a status confirmed in 1666 when Colbert corralled all of Paris' printers into the Latin Quarter to keep a close eye on them.

> *A left turn into Rue de la Harpe brings you to the busy crossroads of Boulevards St-Michel and St-Germain. Aim for the **Hôtel and Thermes de Cluny** on the southeast corner; follow its garden (going left) around Boulevard St-Germain to Rue de Cluny.*

Facing Boulevard St-Germain are the baths (*c.* 215), the most impressive Roman relic in Paris. They survived because people lived in them until the 1330s, when the Benedictine abbey of Cluny bought the land and converted the baths into a hanging garden. Their adjacent *hôtel* is one of only two Gothic/early Renaissance residences to survive in Paris. In its day it was sufficiently magnificent to house papal nuncios and royal guests, most famously the frisky 17-year-old Mary of England, sister of Henry VIII. Married to Louis XII, she so overwhelmed the elderly monarch that he died three months after the wedding, and was succeeded by his cousin François d'Angoulême (François I), whose overriding concern was the possibility that Mary might bear Louis a posthumous heir. François's close surveillance paid off when he found the young widow in bed with an Englishman; before you could say Jack Robinson he whisked the couple into Cluny's chapel for instant marriage and shipped them home. Note the exterior design of the chapel from Rue de Cluny, set gracefully over a pair of ogival doors.

*Turn right at Place Paul-Painlevé, with its* **statue of Montaigne**, *a 1988 copy of the original that nearly had its feet rubbed off by students hoping for luck on their exams. The beautiful Gothic porch at no. 6 leads into the* **Musée de Cluny** *and one of the world's greatest collections of medieval art (open daily except Mon 9.30–5.45; adm (half-price Sun).*

As in many later *hôtels*, a screening wall separates the street from the Hôtel de Cluny's *cour d'honneur*, a lovely late Gothic/early Renaissance work in its own right. The warm cinammon walls peak in a balustrade and openwork gables; in the middle of the façade a narrow hexagonal tower, carved with the cockleshells of Santiago, encloses a spiral stair. The colonnade on the left probably held the house kitchens, while its water was supplied by the charming 15th-century wellhead.

In 1832 Alexandre du Sommerard rented the first floor of the mansion to hold his private museum of medieval art. Although du Sommerard was considered a junk-collecting oddball at first, interest in his museum quickly grew as the writings of Ruskin and Hugo brought the Middle Ages back into fashion. In 1844 the state purchased the collection, baths and *hôtel* for a museum. Unfortunately for you, there are no boring bits to skip, but a continuous trove of the rare and the beautiful in exquisite detail to linger over all afternoon. Among the highlights: in **Salle II**, the *Offrande du coeur* from the early 1400s (the oldest tapestry in the tapestry-rich Cluny), showing the miracle of St Quentin saving the horse thief; in **Salle III**, a gorgeous English leopard embroidery believed to have been the saddlecloth of Edward III; in **Salle IV**, a delightful series of six tapestries called *La Vie seigneuriale* on the good life 500 years ago, contemporary with the Hôtel de Cluny itself; in **Salle V**, 15th-century alabasters from Nottingham.

Beyond, in the Roman section of the Museum, **Salle VIII** contains the museum's newest exhibit: 21 sad, solemn, erosion-scarred heads of the Kings of Judea from the façade of Notre-Dame, commissioned by Philippe-Auguste in 1220. Revolutionaries, mistaking them for French kings, had beheaded the statues in 1793; a Catholic Royalist carefully buried them face down in a courtyard in Rue de la Chaussée-d'Antin, where they lay until their rediscovery in 1977. In **Salle IX** are lively, ornate 11th- and 12th-century Romanesque capitals from St-Germain-des-Prés and Ste-Geneviève, and in **Salle X** four magnificent statues of apostles made in the 1240s for Ste-Chapelle.

## The Thermes

Lofty, vast **Salle XII** is the *frigidarium* of the Roman baths. Wide-arched openings admit light; there are niches in the walls for statues and remains of drains in the floor. It is the only Roman bath in France to keep its roof—three barrel vaults linked by a groin vault in the centre, ending at the corners with capitals carved with ships' prows that suggest the baths were built by or for the powerful *nautae Parisiaci*, the boatmen's guild of the Parisii. In the centre are five large blocks from an altar to Jupiter, erected during the reign of Tiberius and discovered under the choir of Notre-Dame: among the Roman figures are the Celtic gods Tavros Trigarnus (the bull with three cranes perched on his back), Cernunnos (the god sprouting antlers), and more reliefs of the *nautae Parisiaci*. There's also a 4th-century statue of Julian the Apostate, who, before becoming Emperor, may have bathed here—or in the larger *hammam* in Rue St-Jacques.

## The Lady and the Unicorn

Upstairs, **Salle XIII** is a rotunda containing Cluny's greatest treasure: the six Aubusson tapestries of *La Dame à la Licorne*, dating from the late 15th century. Woven for Le Viste, a Lyonese noble family (whose arms are incorporated into each scene) the tapestries were only rediscovered in the 19th century, rolled up and mouldering away in an obscure château in the middle of France. The lady, unicorn and lion appear in each scene, on a blue foreground and red background called *millefleurs*, strewn with a thousand flowers, birds and animals in the early Renaissance's fresh delight in nature. The first scenes appear to be allegories of the five senses, but the meaning of the sixth, where the legend on the tent reads *A mon seul désir* and the lady is either taking or returning a necklace from a coffer of jewels, will always remain a charming mystery.

**Salle XIV**, a long gallery of retables, painting and sculpture, contains two masterpieces: the *Pietà de Tarascon* (1450s) influenced by Italian and Flemish artists who painted in the papal entourage of Avignon, and a moving figure of *Marie Madeleine*, sculpted in Brussels *c.* 1500. **Salle XV** contains ivories (diptychs, chess pieces, etc.) from the 4th to 12th centuries, while all that glitters really is gold in **Salle XVI**: barbarically splendid 7th-century Visigothic crowns; a rare golden rose, of the type distributed by medieval popes to their friends and allies; reliquaries (including a 15th-century container for Jesus's umbilical cord); 4th-century lion heads in rock crystal, and exquisite works in gold and enamel. In **Salle XVIII**, where you can leaf through a 15th-century Book of Hours, the walls are hung with the first of 23 tapestries on the *Life of St Stephen* (1490) from the cathedral of Auxerre—one in the series, in **Salle XIX**, has a delightful porcupine, the symbol of the dukes of Orléans. The same room holds a sumptuous golden altar front (1020) donated to the cathedral of Basel by Emperor Henry II, and the retable of Stavelot (1160). The chapel (**Salle XX**) is a flamboyant gem, its rib vaulting supported by a central palm-tree pillar, while a little spiral stair descends from the ornate doorway in the corner. **Salle XXI** features a late 15th-century tapestry series on the *Life of the Virgin* from the cathedral of Bayeux. If your eyes can still focus, cast a glance at **Salle XXIII**'s curious lead tokens dredged up from the bottom of the Seine, some impressed with the symbols of Paris' guilds, others with religious themes, perhaps fallen off the hats and staves of passing pilgrims.

> *Cross Place Paul-Painlevé, at the rear of the museum, and take Rue des Ecoles left (east), passing the grim fortress of the **Sorbonne**.*

Paris' first college, supplying room and board to poor students, was founded in 1180 by a Londoner named Josse, and among the scores that followed was this one, founded in 1257 by Robert de Sorbon, chaplain to St Louis. It differed from its predecessors by offering teaching in the 'sacred studies', and eventually it evolved as the headquarters of Paris' dread Faculty of Scholastic Theology.

In the 1630s the college was rebuilt on an ambitious scale by its titular chancellor, Cardinal Richelieu, but even that was judged too small and replaced in the 19th century by the current ponderous buildings. These have been reduced from their once glorious status as the seat of the university to merely housing Paris branches III and IV. Enter the *cour d'honneur* at 17 Rue de la Sorbonne, to see what survives from Richelieu's day: the domed **Chapelle de Ste-Ursule de la Sorbonne** (1630), open only (and rarely) for temporary exhibitions. Modelled after the Gesù church in Rome, it was the first in Paris in the new Roman 'Jesuit' or Baroque style. The interior decoration was destroyed when the sans-culottes converted it into a Temple of Reason, except for paintings in the spandrels by Philippe de Champaigne and the white marble *tomb of Richelieu* (designed by Lebrun and completed in 1693). The latter only escaped by the hair of the Cardinal's chinny-chin-chin, when monument-monger Alexandre Lenoir (*see* Walk X, p.276) threw himself bodily between the revolutionary smashers and the tomb, only to receive a bayonet in the leg for his trouble. If you come between lectures (or can manage to sit through one—they're free), take a look in the **Grand Amphithéâtre** to see the celebrated fresco in lollipop colours of *Le Bois Sacré* by Puvis de Chavannes.

> *Continuing down Rue des Ecoles, right after the Sorbonne come Place Marcelin-Berthelot and the prestigious **Collège de France**.*

As the Sorbonne became mired in reactionary scholasticism and arguments over angels dancing on the head of a pin, humanists led by Guillaume Budé petitioned François I for an alternative, a 'republic of scholars' where they could study

Hebrew and 'pagan' Greek and Latin texts banned at the Sorbonne. In 1530 the king complied, and to this day it maintains its scholastic independence, although the state provides all its funds. The older buildings around the courtyard date from 1778, decorated with statues of its famous scholars—Champollion, who cracked Egyptian hieroglyphs with the Rosetta stone (by Bartholdi, 1875), Budé, the historian Michelet, and the physiologist Claude Bernard (d. 1878), a pioneer in research on diabetes and the pancreas gland. Paul Valéry, Roland Barthes and Michel Foucault gave lectures here; these days the lectern is held by the likes of Pierre Boulez and Emmanuel Le Roy Ladurie. Altogether, the intellectual bread served up here has proved no more nutritious than the Sorbonne's; this college was the source of much of the cynical, pointless psychobabble that infects universities today, especially in America.

> Carry on eastwards along Rue des Ecoles and turn left into Rue des Carmes; in the modern police station here is the **Musée de la Préfecture de Police**, with a fascinating collection of archive material on the second floor of the modern police station (open Mon–Fri 9–5, Sat 10–5).

The Parisians, for all their fine manners, can be a rascally herd of cusses. The Fronde uprising in Louis XIV's minority revealed how many weapons were loose in the streets; although only gentlemen and soldiers on active duty were allowed to carry swords, in practice the whole city was armed to the teeth. People were openly robbed and swindled, even on the Pont Neuf, and no one disagreed when the satirist Boileau wrote in 1660: 'The darkest forest is a safe haven after Paris'.

Louis XIV reacted to this crime wave by founding the ancestor of the modern Paris police in 1667. His lieutenant was the tough but fair-minded Nicolas-Gabriel de La Reynie, who personally did much to temper the king's more inhumane commands. It was just as well, for La Reynie and his successors, with their teams of sergeants and informers (*mouches*) not only policed but governed Paris, responsible for the city's security, equipment and modernization, and also its morals, religious affairs and public health. Louis himself didn't give a fig for Paris, but he would summon his lieutenants to Versailles to hear the latest gossip of dukes caught singing rude ditties or pissing out of windows, which always made Louis chuckle before he sent stern notes threatening them with the Bastille. Original documents in the museum range from his *lettres de cachet* to the criminal report on Verlaine and Rimbaud; there are police uniforms, a guillotine blade, a model of Fieschi's assassination machine (which failed to blow up Louis-Philippe), anarchist bombs, documents on the ex-convict Vidocq (who, like Ahmed the Moth in *The Arabian Nights*, was appointed chief over a unit of reformed crooks in the 1830s), Grandville's hilarious engraving of conspiring umbrellas called the *Cauchemar du Préfet de Police*, documents on the Venus of Milo (who survived the ravages of the Commune concealed under a mound of files in the cellar of the Préfecture de Police) and others relating to the rosy-cheeked Marquise de Brinvilliers (1630–76), who was much praised for bringing bonbons to hospital patients, although no one seemed to notice that her presence sent them into mortal convulsions. It was only when a cabinet of venom and a list of victims (including the Marquise's father and brothers) was discovered after the death of her lover—who *wasn't* poisoned—that La Reynie's police put two and two together. La Brinvilliers was hanged and burned; when the smoke cleared, not a few Parisian perverts poked about the ashes for relics, believing she was a saint. The biggest exhibit covers *anthropométrie*—the method invented by commissioner Alphonse Bertillon to identify crooks by photographing and measuring their noses, ears and eyes. In 1903 Bertillon obtained the first conviction in Europe using fingerprints as evidence, a mere 1400 years after Chinese detectives did it.

> Continue east along Rue Basse des Carmes and turn left into Rue de la Montagne-Ste-Geneviève, crossing Boulevard St-Germain and the milling gendarmes for **Rue de Bièvre** (pedestrians only). François Mitterrand's private residence was at no. 22. At **Quai de la Tournelle** there's a delicious prospect of Notre-Dame pinioned by its flying buttresses, a view that would have been much more cluttered in 1691, when the Filles de Ste-Geneviève (women devoted to visiting the ill) were installed by their benefactress, Madame de Miramion, at no. 47, in a handsome 17th-century hôtel, now the **Musée de l'Assistance Publique** (open 10–5, closed Sun and Mon; adm).

Although most cities would prefer that visitors judge them by their public monuments, Paris' hospitals have gamely created this museum to chronicle the treatment of the down-and-out. Their fate has varied with society's attitudes, from the medieval view that poverty was a Christ-like virtue to be graced by works of charity, to the ungenerous 16th-century position (sadly familiar today) that the poor are a menace to society. In 1656, in the wake of the Fronde uprisings, Cardinal Mazarin and Louis XIV solved the poverty 'problem' by creating the infamous Hôpital Général. The scheme kicked off with a *Grande Renfermement*, in which archers at the crossroads rounded up Paris' 40,000 misfits—the blind, paupers, madmen, orphans, prostitutes, alchemists, homosexuals, idlers, unemployed soldiers, heretics, blasphemers, witches and thieves—and forcibly confined them in workhouses. Naturally it was 'for their own good'. Grimmest of all was the fate of abandoned infants. In 1638 a priest named Vincent de Paul discovered that foundlings were being sold off for a few coins to beggars, who broke their arms and legs to excite the pity of passers-by. Appalled, Vincent founded the foundling hospital by the Parvis de Notre-Dame, although this was quickly overwhelmed as poverty increased: the 438 foundlings who showed up in 1660 rose to 7676 in 1772, or roughly 21 abandoned children a day. Only the fittest survived (one grew up to become the brilliant mathematician and Encyclopaedist, D'Alembert). Five whose fate is unknown were fathered by J.-J. Rousseau, who forced his mistress to abandon them.

The Church's opposition to dissection and to doctors attending births limited medical progress until the end of the 18th century. In 1776 the Hôpital Necker became Paris' first institution founded exclusively for treating the ill. By the early 1800s nearly all the hospitals had followed suit, releasing Paris' prostitutes and poor to fend for themselves. The museum contains a wide assortment of memorabilia: early medical instruments, pharmaceutical jars, bead bracelets that parents would leave with a foundling in case they ever had the means to retrieve the child, and works of art from the hospitals, from the richly illuminated *Livre de vie active* (1482) by Jean Henry, Proviseur of the Hôtel-Dieu, to the stupefying *Louis XIV admired by the Universe*, which used to hang in the Salpêtrière.

> *Backtrack along the quay to Rue des Bernardins, with the only 16th-century arcade to survive in Paris. Cross Boulevard St-Germain again; the church on your right with a strict neoclassical façade of 1930 and sleepy angels is* **St Nicolas-du-Chardonnet** *(1656–1709).*

This is the Left Bank's heart of the *intégriste* movement of the late bishop Lefèbvre, the site of the famous anti-Vatican II sit-in in 1977, and your chance to hear a Mass in Latin from the 1560s. The church marks the site of a medieval chapel in the thistle fields (*chardons*) belonging to the abbey of St-Victor, which counted St Bernard and Thomas à Becket among its alumni; the chapel survived when the abbey was fecklessly destroyed in the 1820s. The highlight inside is the tomb that Charles Le Brun designed for his mum (her effigy popping out as an angel sounds the trump of doom) in the left ambulatory; Le Brun himself, a parishioner, gets a mere obelisk.

> *Continue south along Rue Monge to the corner of Rue des Ecoles, where the Square Paul-Langevin has a* **statue of François Villon** *(1431–?), the virile if rather sooty archangel of the Latin Quarter—student, murderer, thief and the greatest lyrical poet of his day.*

Although a master of the highly-structured verse forms bequeathed by the troubadors, Villon wrote with a remarkable directness on subjects from his own wayward life, using an idiomatic language rich in Parisian slang. He excelled in complicated, 13-line, double-rhyme stanzas called *rondeaux*, the form of his exquisite 'Ballade des dames du temps jadis' with its bittersweet refrain *Mais où sont les neiges d'antan? (Where are the snows of yesteryear?)*. His last known masterpiece, the poignant 'Ballade des pendus' was composed while sitting on death row in Paris in 1462. Villon's sentence was lightened to exile from the capital for ten years, whereupon he vanished from history.

> *Turn right in Rue des Ecoles, then left for Rue de la Montagne-Ste-Geneviève.*

In a Vietnamese restaurant along this street Ho Chi Minh began his career as a dishwasher, before moving up to Boston's Parker House hotel; anyone who has read Orwell's dishwasher adventures in *Down and Out in Paris and London* will understand how the experience could galvanize anyone to start a revolution.

> *On your left, the building with a vine-bearded stair used to be the **Ecole Polytechnique**, founded by the Convention in 1794 and one of France's most elite Grandes Ecoles, whose graduates are known simply as 'les Xs' from the crossed swords on their badges. One X, Valéry Giscard d'Estaing, was President of France in 1977 when the Polytechnique was decentralized to the suburbs at Palaiseau, leaving its old headquarters to become the Ministry of Research and Technology. Keep left at the next crossroads onto Rue Descartes, then turn right at Rue Clovis, the summit of the Gallo-Roman Mont Leucotitius (Mont Lutèce), known since the Middle Ages as **Montagne Ste-Geneviève**, after Paris' patron saint.*

In 451, fresh from pillaging and deflowering 11,000 virgins in Cologne, Attila and the Huns marched towards Lutèce looking for more fun. Paris' Romans fled in terror, but the Parisii stuck around when Geneviève, a holy virgin living on this hill, assured them that God would spare the city. And indeed, at the last minute, the Huns veered off and sacked Orléans instead—precisely where Paris' Romans had fled. Scoffers have long claimed that Geneviève's intervention was less decisive than Attila's discovery that Paris was no place to look for virgins. But Attila was something of a sucker to begin with—he had earlier spared Rome itself when Pope Leo I threatened him with an eternal nosebleed.

When Clovis converted to Christianity ('Oh, if only my Franks had been there!' he sighed, when first learning about the Crucifixion), he built on Montagne Ste-Geneviève a basilica dedicated to SS Peter and Paul. In 512 he was buried there, next to his wife Clotilde and Geneviève. Such a cult grew around the miracle-working tomb of Geneviève (*see below*) that the church was expanded and renamed after the thwarter of Attila; an abbey was erected and the Montagne covered with vineyards, providing an open-air classroom for the rebellious Abelard.

> *In 1220 Philippe-Auguste's wall around the Latin Quarter was finished—at no. 3 Rue Clovis you can see a stretch of it, minus its original*

*crenellations. By the next year, so many students had moved into the quarter that a new chapel, St-Etienne, was built next to Ste-Geneviève to accommodate them. In 1802 old Ste-Geneviève was demolished to make way for Rue Clovis, leaving only its tall Romanesque tower, the **Tour Clovis** a captive within the walls of the élite Lycée Henri IV.*

*Fortunately, **St-Etienne du Mont** remains charming, asymmetrical and intact on Place Ste-Geneviève (open 7.30–12 and 3–7).*

This St-Etienne was begun in 1492, to squeeze in the great press of students; accounts of the university's four annual processions from St-Etienne to St-Denis claim that the rectors in front would enter St-Denis *before* the last students had left St-Etienne, a feat that would require at least 30,000 students, teachers and support staff.

Charles VII's invasion of Italy in 1494 gave the French their first toe-dip in the Renaissance. They made St-Etienne their sampler; although it had been begun in Flamboyant Gothic in the choir, they made the façade their own, stacking up three different pediments like building blocks. Inside, the Renaissance nave is closed off by a very fetching arched *jubé*, or rood screen—the only one surviving in Paris—flanked by two openwork spiral stairs, galleries and balustrades, Gothic in structure but entirely coated in Corinthian frosting. A few other details managed to survive the Revolution, when St-Etienne became the Temple of Filial Piety: the great organ of 1630, a carved pulpit of 1650 with a baldachin, and Renaissance stained-glass windows.

In the ambulatory are the graves and epitaphs of one of France's greatest thinkers, Blaise Pascal (d. 1662), and one of her greatest playwrights, Racine (d. 1699), both of whom lived among the fleshpots and died pious and austere Jansenists. Just beyond them, surrounded by *ex-voto* plaques and paintings, is the **Chapel of Ste-Geneviève**, still one of the busiest pilgrimage sites in Paris. Whenever the city needed some really big juju, especially against inclement weather or invasions, her reliquary, so big that it required 10 men just to lift it, would go on procession through the city, joined by a host of other saintly relics before ending up at Notre-Dame. Although Geneviève rarely let Paris down, in 1793 anti-clerical revolutionaries melted down her reliquary, burned her bones and tossed the ashes into the Seine. A replacement reliquary holds a stone from her original sarcophagus, but Geneviève has shown that she can still occasionally hold the Huns at bay: as one *ex voto* reads, a three-day prayer vigil here in September 1914 preceded the Battle of the Marne.

Before leaving, take a look at the deep-coloured, 17th-century enamelled glass windows in the **Galerie des Charniers**, all that remains of the old charnel-house cloister where the bodies of Mirabeau and Marat lay after their ejection from the Panthéon (Mirabeau's remains are now in the catacombs, while Marat's were lost after he was tossed into a gutter). The iconography of the windows contrasts Old and New Testament scenes: one, the bizarre 'Mystic Winepress' (1618), has the patriarchs of Israel digging in a vineyard, while the crucified Christ spurts blood into a wine trough, which the doctors of the Church, assisted by Pope Paul III and Emperor Charles V, store in barrels in a church.

*Old Ste-Geneviève was demolished because Louis XV, after a close call with the grim reaper in 1744, had vowed to construct a new basilica to hold the relics of Paris' patroness. Unfortunately the crown was flat broke, and only after 10 years of lotteries did construction begin, in 1755. It had just been completed in 1790 when the Revolution kicked off its muddled history by co-opting it as a **Panthéon** to honour its Great Men (open daily 10–12 and 2–4.45; adm).*

The trials and tribulations of this 'dunce cap on a hill' really began when Louis XV commissioned Jacques-Germain Soufflot (otherwise best known for demolishing Notre-Dame's magnificent central portal) as architect. Soufflot's stated aim, that he would synthesize the perfect harmonies of the Greek temple and the central basilica with the audacity of the Gothic cathedral hint at mental delusion on a grand scale—367ft by 274ft to be precise. Some French critics trumpet the result as 'the first example of perfect architecture', when in fact the Panthéon is a textbook case of how *not* to build, an impoverished bastard of design that has always had difficulties fulfilling even the most basic tenet of architecture: standing up. In 1985, when stones came plummeting from the vaults, it had to be closed. Repairs have been under way for a decade now, and most of the building is open again for visits.

The project was ridden with difficulties from the start. The subsoil, pocked with Roman quarry shafts, presented the usual problems, and Soufflot's design took far too many technical risks. Although the building was supported by flying buttresses hidden in the walls and iron staples secreted in the masonry, Soufflot made the interior columns too slender to support the structure and, in his neoclassical daydreams, forgot he was in cold, humid Paris instead of dry, sunny Athens: the roof terraces and vast unprotected stone surfaces let the rain sink in and rust the aforementioned iron staples, rot the murals, and warp and bend the windows out of shape. Cracks developed in the walls even before the building was finished, and Soufflot, as stressed out as his structure, died of anxiety in 1780. The dome, copied from London's St Paul's, was meant to have been supported by columns, but subsidence was so great that Soufflot's successor, Rondelet, had to opt for 10,000 tons of solid walls and pilasters. And like St

Paul's, it's a trick—there are actually three domes fitted like Chinese boxes one inside the other—so that from the inside the dome would seem to float over the planned baldachin that would have sheltered Geneviève's relics. It never did, but in 1851 the dome came in handy, when Foucault hung his pendulum from the top to prove the rotation of the earth.

To be fair, had the whole worked out according to Soufflot's plans, the interior would have been filled with a refined play of light and shadow. The sun was to have filtered between the columns coming not only through the openings in the dome but also through the original 42 enormous windows walled up by the Assembly in 1791 when the church was converted into the Temple of Glory and Immortality. Even this didn't start on the right foot, when two of the first pan-theonized corpses, those of Mirabeau and Marat, were given the bum's rush in the changing political climate. Napoleon reconverted the Panthéon to a church, and the remains of two other inmates, Rousseau and Voltaire (who disdained each other in life), were shunted off into an unmarked closet. Louis-Philippe thought the church was better as a Panthéon, and had David d'Angers replace the temple pediment (this was in 1837, and the fourth pediment in 50 years) with a frieze of Liberty handing palms to *La Patrie* who doles them out to France's civilian and military heroes, beginning with Napoleon. His presence per-haps ensured the frieze's survival in 1851, when monks persuaded Napoleon III to reconvert the building to a church. In 1871 the cross was turned into a pole for the red flag when the Panthéon became the Left-Bank headquarters of the Commune. It went back to a church again until 1885, when Victor Hugo died. Hugo was so inflated that no ordinary tomb would hold him, and his funeral inaugurated the building's current status as the Panthéon of France's Great Men. The best thing inside is Puvis de Chavannes's mural on the *Life of Ste-Geneviève*, in the right aisle.

The **crypt**, intended for the monks of Ste-Geneviève, is certainly grand and gloomy enough for Great Men—Voltaire, Rousseau and Soufflot himself in the first section; then Hugo and Zola, Louis Braille, Jean Jaurès, Resistance leader Jean Moulin, Jean Monnet (a founder of the EC), René Cassin (author of the UN Declaration of Human Rights), 40 dignitaries from the First Empire, Gambetta (although only his heart is here), and the newest stiff of all, André Malraux, pantheonized in 1996. And there's one woman: the wife of chemist Marcelin Berthelot, but only because she was buried in the same casket as her husband.

> *Soufflot is also responsible for the cold stone field called the **Place du Panthéon**, and designed its twin curved buildings, now the Faculté de Droit and the mairie of the 5th arrondissement. On the north side, the*

*building covered with the names of writers is the **Bibliothèque Ste-Geneviève**, containing the only monastic library to survive the Revolution. Just try to get in, though.*

Originally this site was occupied by the Collège de Montaigu, notorious for its harsh treatment of scholars at a time when beatings and reciting long verses in Latin while kneeling in salt were common punishments. At the Collège de Montaigu students bedded down on the cold floor with swarms of bugs and ate so many beans that the school was called 'Hôtel des Haricots'. Not surprisingly, Montaigu's alumni turned out to be either proto-hippies or proto-fascists: they included Rabelais and Erasmus, and Calvin and Ignatius de Loyola. The Bibliothèque, built on the site in 1843–50 by Henri Labrouste, may be a mild-mannered neo-Renaissance building from the street, but hides a magnificent reading room, crowned by a twin-naved, barrel-vaulted iron roof. It was the first time that iron was used in a 'serious' work of architecture, and its success encouraged Labrouste to create the incredible reading room at the Bibliothèque Nationale (*see* Walk IV, p.177). Among the works in the Salles de la Réserve are Baudelaire's manuscripts and St Augustine's *City of God*, beautifully illustrated by the 15th-century school of Jean Fouquet.

*That's all, but there are a few more sights in the area if you have the time. The Panthéon stands close to the centre of Roman Paris' gridiron plan. Rue Cujas, one street to the north, was its* decumanus *(the main east–west street) while Rue St-Jacques was the* cardo*, or main north–south street. At this crossroads stood the Forum of Lutetia. Only fragments (now in the Musée Carnavalet) were uncovered when Rue Soufflot was laid out in 1847. Even less remains of the famous monastery founded here in 1218 by St Dominic himself, whose Parisian followers became known as Jacobins from their Rue St-Jacques address. One alumnus was the fanatical monk Jacques Clément, who in 1589 murdered Henri III while the king was sitting on the toilet.*

*Although the Luxembourg gardens beckon to the west, the stout of heart and sturdy of sole will stump up Rue St-Jacques to visit no. 195, the **Centre de la Mer et des Eaux** (open 10–12.30 and 1.15–5.30, closed Mon; adm).*

The aquariums and interactive exhibits (good fun for small fry) are part of the Institut Océanographique. This was founded by Jacques Cousteau's great merman predecessor, Albert I of Monaco, who used the profits from his casino to finance the scientific exploration and study of the sea.

Lastly, anyone in the least dazzled by rare or precious stones should head for Boulevard St-Michel and the **Musée de Minéralogie** of the Ecole Supérieure des Mines, housed in the ex-Hôtel de Vendôme (no. 60) (open Tues and Sat 10–12.30 and 2–5; Wed–Fri 2–5). This scintillating dragon's lair of precious stones in their natural state is so valuable that you have to ring the staff to get in, and ring them again to escape.

# IX: Jardin des Plantes and Mouffetard

Start: Ⓜ *St-Marcel*
Walking time: *2 hours to walk, 2 for dallying in the Jardin des Plantes, and 2 for the Gobelins tour.*

This walk, east of the medieval walls that cradled the Latin Quarter for most of its history, offers an unusual cocktail of sights and smells that hardly seems to belong to the same city as the Eiffel Tower and Champs-Elysees—gossipy village streets, a tropical garden, an Hispano-Moorish mosque, old geezers playing *boules* in a Roman arena and, as a chaser, one of the world's most famous tapestry factories. Thursday is the ideal day to visit, when everything is open; otherwise the museums in the Jardin des Plantes are closed on Tuesdays, and the Arab Institute and St-Médard are closed on Mondays. Gobelins factory tours are run on Tuesday, Wednesday and Thursday afternoons. Note that Rue Mouffetard comes into its own at weekends, but closes down on Mondays.

### *lunch/cafés*

**Café of the Grande Mosquée**, 39 Rue Geoffrey-St-Hilaire. A delightful café where you can sip mint tea in a garden patio built in the style of the Alhambra.

**Restaurant de l'Institut du Monde Arabe**, Quai St-Bernard, ✆ 01 46 33 47 70. French and North African fare served on the terrace overlooking the Seine, but a bit dear (around 200F); delicious mint tea in the afternoon.

**Le Petite Navire**, 14 Rue des Fossés St-Bernard, ✆ 01 43 54 22 52. A popular neighbourhood spot with good seafood; the 150F menu is well worth the expense.

**Moissonnier**, 28 Rue des Fossés-St-Bernard, ✆ 01 43 29 87 65. Long-established *bistrot* serving unadulterated Lyonnais *cuisine de terroir* (150F lunch menu).

**Le Baptiste**, 11 Rue des Boulangers. Popular for its generous portions of French basics and its prices—fill up, wine included for 71F.

**Le Bateau Ivre**, 40 Rue Descartes. A lively bar, especially during the very extended Happy Hour, when beers are half-price.

**Chez Léna et Mimille**, 35 Rue Tournefort, ✆ 01 47 07 72 47 (parallel to Rue Mouffetard). A pretty terrace, solid cooking—98F lunch menu.

**Cave la Bourgogne**, 142 Rue Mouffetard. Good wine and everything else to drink, plus excellent sandwiches.

**Gelati**, 45 Rue Mouffetard. For delicious Italian ice cream.

**La Verre à Pied**, 118bis Rue Mouffetard, ✆ 01 43 31 15 72. Authentic old Parisian watering hole, a favourite with locals, students and journalists.

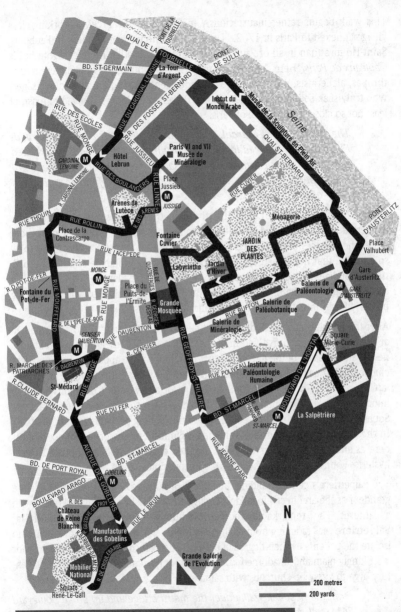

IX: Jardin des Plantes and Mouffetard

This walk begins rather inauspiciously in Faubourg St-Marcel, a working-class village annexed to Paris in 1702. 'There's more money in one house in Faubourg Saint-Honoré than in all of Faubourg St-Marcel,' Sebastien Mercier wrote in his *Tableaux de Paris*. 'Here, far from the traffic in the centre, hide ruined men, misanthropes, alchemists, maniacs, narrow-minded rentiers, and a few studious sages, who truly seek solitude.' Needless to say, these are no longer allowed to exist, at least not so close to the centre of Paris.

> The church of **St-Marcel**, just south of the métro in Boulevard de l'Hôpital was replaced in 1966, unfortunately in the middle of architecture's most recent dark age. On the same street, just north of the métro, the **Salpêtrière**, is Paris' largest hospital and a relic from an earlier dark age—of public morality.

Originally the arsenal of Louis XIII, the Salpêtrière (the saltpetre works) was converted by Louis XIV in 1654 into a prison-workhouse for orphans and the poor under the auspices of the Hôpital Général. Locking up *les misérables* proved to be so effective that the Salpêtrière was expanded to take in female criminals, prostitutes, repudiated wives and the insane. By number of 'patients' it was the world's largest hospital by the time of the Revolution, although it had only begun to care properly for its inmates when the first infirmary was installed in 1783.

After the Revolution abolished the workhouses, the 'Pavilion of the Mad' remained at the Salpêtrière, and evolved into a leading centre of research into mental illnesses and diseases of the nerves. At first conditions were appalling. Patients were chained or left naked in filthy rooms. If it was a slow day at the Morgue (*see* Ile de la Cité, p.113), visitors could come and stare for a few *sous*. Conditions began to improve in the 1790s when Dr Pinel (whose statue is to the left of the entrance in Square Marie-Curie) took the radical step of unchaining his patients from the wall. In the 1880s a young neurologist named Sigmund Freud worked for six months here as an intern; his observations of the then current use of hypnotism to treat hysterics contributed to his theory of the unconscious.

The Salpêtrière's central building, by Libéral Bruant (1677), has the same austere grandeur as the architect's Invalides, crowned this time by an octagonal dome with a lantern. The remarkable geometric church it protects, **St-Louis-de-la-Salpêtrière**, has radiating from its high altar four large naves divided by chapels, to isolate the patients by their degree of physical or social contagiousness. The interior is strikingly plain and unadorned, somehow having been forgotten in the 19th-century urge to gussy up churches with salon art.

> From the hospital, walk under the métro bridge and up broad Boulevard St-Marcel. At the corner of Rue René-Panhard, a curious frieze of cavemen at work dignifies the **Institut de Paléontologie Humaine** (1912), built

*by Prince Albert I of Monaco. When you reach Rue Geoffroy-St-Hilaire, turn right. The sleepy residential streets around here scarcely remember when this was Paris' boisterous, odoriferous and cacophonous horse, pig and dog market; the only memories of this are a few old signs, like the horse's head over no. 11. In the old days, further up the street, the corner of Rue Buffon reverberated with the croaks from the weekly* marché aux crapauds, *or toad market. The buyers? British, and later French, gardeners plagued by slugs and other pests, and young ladies who would have soothsayers read their fortunes in the toads' entrails. Now you can buy books about toads at the corner's Natural History Bookshop, or model dinosaurs or even baobab seeds, if, unlike the Little Prince, your asteroid is big enough to handle them. The next block belongs to yet another world—the exotic white and green Hispano-Moorish* **Grande Mosquée de Paris.** *From Rue Daubenton proceed to the entrance in Place du Puits-de-l'Ermite (open for visits daily except Fri, 9–12 and 2–6; adm).*

Built in 1922 in remembrance of the Muslim dead in the First World War, this is the main mosque for France's 3 million-plus faithful as well as a cultural institute and business centre. A delicious interior patio modelled on the Alhambra gives on to the sumptuous prayer room, where the domes were decorated by rival teams of artisans competing in geometric ingenuity. The *muezzin* has not chanted the call to prayer from the minaret for years, in a move to mollify the neighbours. Even so, politics still intrude in this quiet oasis: since its founding, the mosque has been under the religious control of the Algerians, a state of affairs non-Algerian Muslims have found unsavoury since the advent of the Islamic Salvation Front and its crackdown. Behind the mosque, at nos. 39 and 41 Rue Geoffroy-St-Hilaire there's a Turkish *hammam* (*men Fri and Sun, women on the other days exc Tues, 11–8*), a quiet café serving mint tea and gooey oriental pastries, a couscous restaurant and an arts and crafts shop.

*Rue Geoffroy-St-Hilaire ends at a crossroads embellished by the* **Fontaine Cuvier,** *honouring Georges Cuvier, father of comparative anatomy. It quaintly depicts Mother Nature musing among her lieutenants—a lion, a contortionist crocodile, a walrus, an eagle and a veritable seafood platter. There is something disconcerting about it, a lost 19th-century exploitative, pedantic but slightly contemptuous attitude towards the natural world that haunts all of the neglected, unloved buildings in the* **Jardin des Plantes** *beyond the gate.*

In 1626 doctors Jean Hérouard and Guy de La Brosse convinced their best-known patient, Louis XIII, to establish a botanical garden of medicinal plants in the capital, similar to the one Henri IV founded at the university of Montpellier in 1593. Some of France's most famous botanists—the three Jussieu brothers, Daubenton and especially the Comte de Buffon (1707–88), the great 18th-century curator—travelled around the world to collect 2500 species of medicinal plants and exotic trees. In 1793 the Convention created the School and Museum of Natural History, and galleries and research laboratories went up along the flanks of the gardens. In one pavilion along Rue Cuvier, radioactivity was discovered in 1896 by Henri Becquerel, who shared the Nobel Prize with the Curies.

The most endearing feature of the Jardin des Plantes is a 17th-century dump that Buffon converted into a garden **labyrinthe** (up on the little hill just to the right), topped by a little bronze temple with a sundial called the **Gloriette de Buffon** (1786). Near the maze towers a cedar of Lebanon, a seedling from Kew Gardens brought to Paris in 1734 by Bernard de Jussieu, who made all Paris laugh by appearing with the baby tree in his top hat (the pot broke on the way). South of the Grand Amphitheatre (really a small neoclassical building near the entrance), look for one of the oddest trees, the ironbark from Iran, while near the sea-lion pool don't miss the *statue of Henri Bernardin de Saint-Pierre* (d. 1818), student of Rousseau, founder of the Ménagerie and author of the romantic idyll to love in its natural state, *Paul et Virginie*, evoked by the lovers smooching on the pedestal.

The tropical forest of the **Serre Tropicale** (Winter Garden) just to the south (*open 1–5.30, closed Tues; adm*) is sheltered in one of the world's first iron and glass pavilions (1830, by Rohault de Fleury). The contents seem to have been lifted directly from the works of another Rousseau—Henri the Douanier, complete with mini-waterfall, stream and turtles; a second hothouse at the back bristles with cacti. In front of the pavilions, a fence encloses the 2600 labelled plants of the **Botanical School gardens** (*open 8–11 and 1.30–5, closed Sat, Sun and hols*).

> At the far west end of the formal parterres looms the impressive Zoology Building, now the centre of the Jardin des Plantes' ensemble of museums, the **Musée National d'Histoire Naturelle**. The new centrepiece of this recently expanded and modernized collection is the **Grande Galerie de l'Evolution** (entrance Rue Censier; open daily exc Tues 10–6, Thurs until 10; adm, reduced adm 10–1).

After being closed for thirty years, the former zoology section is back with a vengeance—full of every sort of 'interactive exhibit', and audio-visual trick, all on the theme of evolution and the diversity of life (pull-out English translations are slotted in the benches). Of course the old stuffed critters are still present, including hundreds of butterflies, a blue whale and rhinoceros that once belonged to Louis XV. It's a good place to bring the kids; the environmental message is relentless in exhibits from the dodo to modern man.

The long building beyond it houses the **Galerie de Minéralogie** (*open 10–5, closed Tues; adm*), displaying giant crystals from Brazil that imprison rainbows in hundreds of kilos of quartz, as well as meteorites, and the museum treasure—two rooms of precious gems on their own and in schmaltzy *objets d'art* that belonged to Louis XIV. A cross-section of a 2000-year-old sequoia on the porch was donated to the soldiery of France by the same of California, although it was barely a twinkle in Ma Nature's eye compared to the other tree displayed here—a petrified stump from the marshes that covered the Paris basin 33,000,000 years ago. To learn more about the evolution of plants through fossils, pop into the **Galerie de Paléobotanique** next door.

> *Opposite the formal parterres, and east beyond the rose gardens, Allée de Jussieu leads to the **Ménagerie** (open 9–5, closed holidays; adm).*

In 1793 the Commune ordered all the wild beasts in circuses and travelling zoos be sent to the Jardin des Plantes to form a public Ménagerie. The tattered horde was richly augmented two years later during the Flanders campaign, which bagged the entire zoo of the Stadtholder of Holland. Some animals became celebrities—the giraffe given by the Pasha of Egypt to Charles X in 1829 was the first ever seen in France, and set a veritable giraffe fashion mania. There was Jacqueline the chimp, who wore gloves and slept in a bed with sheets with her pet dog and cat; and then there was a singularly homicidal brown bear, who permanently k.o.'d an Englishman on a bender who had only wanted to box, and later devoured one of Napoleon's impoverished veterans, who had jumped into his pit believing that the gold-coloured button the bear played with was really a *louis d'or*. The black-humoured Parisians named the bear Martin after the soldier. And to this day every bear in the Ménagerie is named Martin.

Humanity had its revenge during the siege of Paris in 1870, when the zoo appeared on the famous Christmas menu at Voisin's: stuffed head of ass (the hors d'oeuvre), *consommé d'éléphant*, roast camel *à l'anglaise*, *civet de kangourou*, bear ribs *sauce poivrade*, leg of wolf *sauce chevreuil*, roast cat with a side dish of rats, *terrine d'antilope aux truffes*, all washed down with a Mouton-Rothschild 1846 (wine was one item the Parisians never had to ration out during the siege). Nowadays larger zoo creatures are kept at Vincennes, while the Ménagerie has smaller animals, to be viewed up close—reptiles, birds of prey, fetus-like albino axolotls, insects (in the Micro-zoo) deer, monkeys—and a pair of Martins.

> *Last and most surreal is the massive and eclectic brick **Galerie de Paléontologie**, overlooking Place Valhubert and the Gare d'Austerlitz (open daily exc Tues 1–5, Sat and Sun 10–6; adm).*

The bas-reliefs of bugs, scorpions and violent battles (man v. bear, man v. crocs) that decorate the exterior reach a climax just inside the door, with a huge statue of an orang-utan strangling a man. The displays, with their little Latin (only) tags, haven't been touched for decades—skeletons of mammoths, mammals and giant birds burdened with names like Mégaptère Boops march in frozen ranks down the centre of the galleries. Along the walls, glass cases contain a nightmarish collection of disembodied, greyish organs in bottles—a tiger's liver; a giraffe's uterus; camel, elephant and rhino willies; a two-headed baby named Marie et Christine; and a plaster model of ostrich guts. The first floor has the dinosaur bones, the second floor breathtakingly boring exhibits on the palaeontology of the Ile-de-France.

> *As you escape through Place Valhubert gate, give at least a passing nod to the **statue of Lamarck** (1744–1829), the great biologist whose theory of evolution held that what we do and learn in our lifetime can be passed on to our offspring—an idea mocked by biologists for over a century, but one that seems to be making a comeback today. Turn left in Place Valhubert and walk along Quai St-Bernard, where a **Musée de la Sculpture en Plein Air** was set up in 1980, modelled after one in Tokyo; along with all the usual river activities to see are sculptures by Brancusi, César and Zadkine, among others. Just before the Pont de Sully a ramp leads up to the **Institut du Monde Arabe**, built in 1987 (open 10–6, closed Mon).*

This coolly elegant riverside tower is nearly everyone's favourite contemporary building in Paris. The competition for the institute's design was won in 1981 by Jean Nouvel (a Frenchman, for once), who came up with a pair of long, thin buildings, one gracefully curved to follow the line of the quay. Their walls are covered with window panels inspired by ancient Islamic geometric patterns, but equipped with photo-electric cells that activate their dilation or contraction according to the amount of sunlight—with a gentle high-tech whoosh that takes you by surprise the first time you experience it. The institute is financed by the French government and 22 Arab countries, with the goal of introducing Islamic civilization to the public and facilitating cultural exchanges. Besides an extensive library (on the third floor, around a great spiral ramp) there are special exhibitions, a shop of books and crafts, and recordings and films to see in the Espace Son et Image. The **museum** (*adm*), spread out on several floors, displays examples of the art and exquisite craftsmanship of the Arab world beginning with pre-Islamic times (2nd- and 3rd-century stone and alabaster carvings from Yemen, Hellenistic art from north Arabia and funeral busts from Palmyra) and continuing to intricate ceramics, tiles, textiles, brass, carpets and astrolabes from the Middle Ages to our day, accompanied by explanatory mini-videos, some even in English.

> *Continue west along the quay. The next bridge, **Pont de la Tournelle** (1656, enlarged in 1851) is named after a pair of medieval towers (tourelles) that stood on either bank, linked by a chain ready to barricade*

*the river at a moment's notice. The tower on the Left Bank was converted in 1582 to an inn known as* **La Tour d'Argent***.*

In the earliest days the *patron* would get up at the crack of dawn to shoot the day's menu in the marshlands of what is now Ile St-Louis. Henri III knighted him for his heron pie, and according to tradition the king learned how to use a fork here (although it was more likely that Henri III, who had spent an extraordinary week being entertained in Venice where forks had been commonplace since Byzantine times, introduced the utensil to the Parisians). The pressed duck remains the stuff of legend, and France's gourmet bibles continue to lavish stars on this grand old restaurant, with the longest gastronomic tradition of any in the capital of cuisine. Although the original tower was demolished in the Revolution, a new Tour d'Argent was resurrected on the same site. Clients can visit a little museum, with famous menus, autographs, china and the 'table of three emperors', set as it was in June 1867 for the future Kaiser Wilhelm I, Bismarck, Tsar Alexander II and the future Tsar Alexander III, all in town for the Exhibition.

> *Turn left into Rue du Cardinal-Lemoine. If you only have a few score francs jingling in your pocket, you can take some comfort in munching an Alsatian pretzel or a* kugelhopf *nearby at* **Pâtisserie Lerch** *(no. 4). The most lavish mansion in the quarter is no. 49, the* **Hôtel Lebrun** *(1700), built according to the proportions of the golden number, its door decorated with a figure of Bacchus. Watteau spent the last years of his life here; now it is the national public housing (HLM) office.*

> *Turn left into* **Rue des Boulangers***, a remarkably quaint village street of 17th- and 18th-century houses and wee gardens, which curves down gently to Place Jussieu. The city and the developers are currently scheming to obliterate it, perhaps hoping to replace it with something more like what lies at the end of the street—the sinister steel, glass and concrete vortex of* **Paris VI and VII***, the university's chief science faculty.*

Originally this was the site of the famous abbey of St-Victor, founded in 1108 when Guillaume de Champeaux, master of dialectics at the Ecole de Notre-Dame, retreated here with his disciples after being upstaged by his pupil, Peter Abelard. Made a royal abbey in 1113, St-Victor was destroyed in the Revolution, replaced by a *halle des vins* that was in turn swept away in the 1960s for this malignant fairy ring of bleak, wind-whipped towers on stilts. It was scarcely finished when students scaled the glacial cliffs of its entrance to cover it with Maoist slogans. Rather than paint over them, the authorities connected the letters to form evil alien messages, which blend in perfectly with the massive, harrowing tile-mural of a primal scream. The ordinary *frissons* offered by the fight-to-the-death decorations of the Galerie de Paléontologie (*see* above) seem naive before this relic of the know-it-all world of 1960s science nerds. The joke's on them; the entire complex is laced with asbestos, and at time of writing the authorities haven't decided whether to gut it and renovate, or simply knock it down and try again.

Meanwhile, fittingly, the only thing to see is a small **Musée des Minéraux** in Tower 25 (*open Wed and Sat 2–6*) and its rare specimens of lapis lazuli, malachites, quartz and uranium in its pre-nuke state. You may find yourself unconsciously looking for anti-radiation iodine tablets in the University vending machines.

> *From Place Jussieu take Rue Limé south and turn right into Rue des Arènes for the **Arènes de Lutèce**.*

'Passerby, dream before the oldest momument in Paris,' reads the plaque of 1951, commemorating the city's second millennium. 'May the city of Paris also be the city of the future and of your hopes.' The slight remains of Lutetia's Roman amphitheatre (now a garden, football pitch and *boules* court) date from the 2nd century. Originally it could seat 10,000—half the entire population of Lutetia, which if nothing else proves that Parisians have always been inveterate theatre-goers. A unique feature was the stage at the east end, adaptable for gladiator shows or less brutal theatrics. The amphitheatre was too convenient a quarry to survive the Dark Ages, when its stone went into fortifying the Ile de la Cité. What remained was forgotten until rediscovered in 1869, restored in 1917 and, incredibly, almost demolished in 1980 for a housing project. In the gardens that encompass the arena, don't miss the knotty beech, famous as the crookedest tree growing in Paris.

> *At the end of Rue des Arènes, cross Rue Monge and walk up the stair to Rue Rollin, a treeless street of blonde houses more Mediterranean than Parisian. A plaque at no. 14 marks Descartes' address in Paris.*

A good Catholic, he nevertheless preferred the Protestant Netherlands, and sniffed that while in France 'what most disgusted me was that no one seemed to want to know anything about me except what I looked like, so I began to believe that they wanted me in France the way they might want an elephant or a panther, because it is rare, and not because it is useful'.

> *At Rue Cardinal-Lemoine, you'll see a plaque for another famous resident: Ernest Hemingway. Turn left here for **Place de la Contrescarpe**.*

Picturesque and piquant, the square dates only from 1852, when the 14th-century Porte Bourdelle was demolished. For the next hundred years Paris' tramps flocked here, and now, even though most of the houses have been restored (the one with the painted sign *Au Nègre Joyeux* used to be a tea room) it still has a bohemian atmosphere, especially at weekends. Rabelais, Ronsard and du Bellay and the other

Renaissance poets of the Pléiade would come to make merry at the famous Cabaret de la Pomme de Pin, at the corner of Rue Blainville (plaque at no. 1). Just off the Contrescarpe, at 50 Rue Descartes a relief shows the original appearance of Porte Bourdelle with its drawbridge; further along, there's another Hemingway-was-here plaque, and one at no. 39 (now a restaurant) commemorating Paul Verlaine, who died in 1896 in a squalid hotel. In his last years, after his fiery love affair with Rimbaud ended with pistol shots and a prison term, the poet had become Paris' most famous anti-hero, a wasted, pathetic figure, haunting Left Bank cafés to extinguish his brain cells in absinthe, often in the company of his 'secretary', a drink-cadging charlatan named Bibi-la-Purée.

> *Cross Place de la Contrescarpe and continue down lively, narrow **Rue Mouffetard**, named after the* mofette *or stench that rose from the tanners and dyers along the Bièvre. This once bucolic tributary of the Seine that rolled through woodlands and meadows became an open sewer over the centuries and was eventually covered over.*

Rue Mouffetard itself is one of the most ancient streets in Paris, following the path of the Roman road to Lyon. Ever since then it has been lined with inns and taverns for the wayfarer; while strolling down the 'Mouff' and poking in its capillary lanes and courtyards you can pick out a number of old signs, such as the carved oak at no. 69 for the Vieux Chêne, which began as a Revolutionary club (*see* lunch, above). Rue du Pot-de-Fer owes its name to the Fontaine du Pot-de-Fer, one of 14 fountains donated by Marie de' Medici when she renovated a Roman aqueduct to feed the fountains in the Jardin de Luxembourg. In 1928, 25-year-old George Orwell moved into a seedy hotel at 6 Rue du Pot-de-Fer to live off his meagre savings while he learned the craft of writing; when he was robbed, he was reduced to washing dishes in a big hotel in the Rue de Rivoli—the source for his first published book *Down and Out in Paris and London.*

Further south, beyond Rue de l'Epée-de-Bois begins Rue Mouffetard's market, where shops spill out to join pavement stalls, cascading with fruit and vegetables, cheeses, seafood, pâtés, sausages, bread and more, with an occasional exotic touch such as the African market in Rue de l'Arbalète. Note the old painted sign 'A la Bonne eau' at no. 122 Rue Mouffetard, and at no. 134, the Italian *charcuterie* Facchetti's covered with pseudo-sgraffito hunting scenes.

> *Opposite stands the the old village church of **St-Médard**, founded in the 9th century where Rue Mouffetard once crossed the Bièvre.*

The present church was rebuilt from the 15th century, and is a pleasant, if unremarkable, building with a few windows from the 1620s. But in the 18th century its cemetery (now replaced by a garden) was the scene of a peculiar hullabaloo: François

Pâris, son of a city councillor, had renounced a prosperous legal career and a rich inheritance to help the needy of Faubourg St-Marcel in the most direct fashion possible, even learning to knit so he could make them socks. Too humble to aspire to the priesthood, he served merely as a deacon at St-Médard, and when he died in 1727 at the age of 37, he was buried here. The good deacon's mourners were many; his simple goodness greatly appealed to those austere fundamentalists, the Jansenists, who regarded him as a saint at a time when they were being persecuted by the Jesuits. At his graveside a few teenage girls became so emotional that they were siezed with convulsions. The fits were contagious: within two years the *convulsionnaires* numbered over 800 young women, jumping and spinning in the cemetery, barking like dogs or mewing like cats, eating soil from the deacon's grave and drawing huge numbers of curious onlookers. Miracle cures and prophecies followed in quick succession. In 1731 St-Médard's pious carnival took an ugly turn, as the *convulsionnaires* began to whip and beat themselves in a frenzy of voluptuous pain. The most extreme asked to have their hands and feet nailed to planks. On 27 January 1732 Louis XV ordered the cemetery closed, and on the gate posted the notice:

> *De par le roi, défense à Dieu*
> *De faire miracle en ce lieu.*

Not only was God forbidden to perform any more miracles, but the *convulsionnaires* were faced with imprisonment and went underground, where they continued to convulse until 1761—the same year that the Jesuits were expelled from France.

> *From St-Médard turn right in Rue Mouffetard, and right again into the narrow alley of Rue Daubenton, where shops occupy part of the old cemetery wall. It takes you into **Place Marché-des-Patriarches**. Until 1953 this was the site of the famous market, apparently named after a hapless band of ecclesiastical cannibals.*

In the 1340s prelates of Notre-Dame who had dined on the *pâté d'étudiant étranger* sold in Rue Chanoinesse (*see* Walk I, p.111) were excommunicated for their unwitting sin, and in their misery decided to walk barefoot to Avignon to beg forgiveness of Pope Clement VI. They got as far as the modern Gobelins factory before they gave up and turned to begging. Then one day Jean de Meulan, Paris' bishop, was accosted here by brigands and was saved when the beggared priests joined in the fisticuffs. In gratitude he granted them absolution and the concession to open a flea market here.

> *Rue Mouffetard is the perfect place to end this trek and have lunch, but anyone fond of tapestries and tradition might want to carry on, south along Rue Monge to **Avenue des Gobelins**, the continuation of the*

*Roman road to Lyon, but lined with more recent buldings, most ornately the apartment house (1902) at no. 4.*

Up until the 19th century, the little river Bièvre still flowed openly through here, its banks lined by tanners and dyers. The most famous of the latter was a family named Gobelin, who owed their great fame and fortune to the discovery of a prized scarlet dye.

*In 1520, with all the pretentions of the nouveaux riches, the Gobelins built themselves a castle (turn right at Rue des Gobelins, and left into Rue Gustave-Geffroy, then follow the dusty courtyard of workshops back at no. 4bis). This is a strange, grey-towered relic called the **Château de Reine Blanche**, after a 14th-century castle on the site, built for either Blanche de Provence or Blanche de Bourgogne, wife of Charles IV.*

*Ironically, the Gobelins have gone down in history for tapestries, an art they themselves never touched but still on display (at least for the time being) at the **Manufacture Nationale des Gobelins**, 42 Avenue des Gobelins (guided 1½-hour tours in French only; Tues, Wed, Thurs at 2 and 3; adm).*

Since 1940 the three state weaving factories—the Gobelins, Beauvais and the Savonnerie—have been located here at the old Gobelins site, producing as they have for the past 300 years all the tapestries, rugs and furniture covers required by the French state. Then Jack Lang, former Minister of Culture, dropped his bombshell. First, the Beauvais section is to be moved back to Beauvais (bomb damage in the war had forced its removal to Paris), and second, all the other remaining state manufactures are to be eventually sold off. The weavers are up in arms; in 1992 only two apprentices were accepted for the seven-year training course, and they may well be the last, their ancient, meticulous art threatened by changing times and the *classe politique*, which would rather subsidize private than national industries. A final decision has yet to be made.

Although Henri IV was the first to have the idea of a royal tapestry works, the plan was only put into action in 1663, after Fouquet's extraordinary fête at Vaux-le-Vicomte made Louis XIV green with envy (*see* Day Trips, p.479). Colbert bought the Gobelins' property, built factories and housing for 250 tapestry-makers (three-quarters of them Flemish) and put them under the insufferable Charles Lebrun. The goal was to furnish the royal residences and especially Versailles with items of the highest quality—made in France. Artistic squabbles began immediately. Lebrun replaced the traditional cartoons used by the weavers (which allowed for considerable artistic interpretation) with oil paintings they were to copy strictly. This mixing of media became ridiculous after 1748, when under new supervisor Jean-Baptiste

Oudry the Gobelins insisted on 36,000 different colours, the better to imitate the subtleties of paintings by Mignard, Watteau and Poussin.

After the Revolution, governments kept the Gobelins around to crank out servile copies of paintings that flattered their egos. Only when half of the factory was burned during the Commune in 1871 did the authorities consider renewing the true, decorative art of weaving. After the Second World War all 18th-century models were dropped for good (except when replacing or repairing worn-out items in the Elysée palace, for instance) and now all three factories rely on designs by living artists. With very few exceptions their works are still for the state, which stores them in the adjacent Mobilier National and distributes them to offices and ministries as it sees fit. A weaver can spend seven years on a large project and never discover its eventual destination. Prices are just as secret, although it is estimated that the few private commissions permitted average 80,000F per square metre.

The Gobelins remains a village enclave remote from Paris and the 20th century. It has pretty cobbled courtyards with statues of Colbert and Lebrun, its own chapel and shady gardens. The serene 17th-century workers' housing is decorated with medallions on the tapestry craft, and of the hundred Gobelins weavers (mostly women since the war) half still live there. Neither has the technology changed, although chromatic science has reduced the number of colours to a more manageable 14,000 or so. The tall vertical looms of the Gobelins are identical to the ones set up by Colbert. Similar looms, used for making carpets, are over in the newer buildings of the **Savonnerie** (it was originally founded in a soap factory) although the weaving technique is the reverse of tapestry. In the adjacent **Beauvais** section, if it's still there when you arrive, weavers use a horizontal warp which must, if anything, be more of a strain on the eyes, spine and mind than the Gobelins. The Beauvais factory was created by Colbert in 1664 to weave tapestries for individuals after Louis XIV banned private purchases of Flemish goods. In the 19th century it began to specialize in upholstery for all those big Louis chairs that fill the halls of the upper-crust French officialdom, although now, as at the Gobelins, the main emphasis is work based on cartoons by contemporary artists.

> *The tour leaves you next to the vast **Mobilier National**, built in the 1920s over the Gobelins' orchards (free fruit used to be one of the tapestry-workers' perks) and where all the state tapestries and furnishings are stored. Two stone mastiffs lazily guard the entrance, while a line of old poplars growing in the adjacent **Square René-le-Gall** marks the site of an islet in the Bièvre known as the Ile des Singes—where organ-grinders and boatmen could let their monkeys frolic in freedom. This is still a tranquil corner of Paris, where you can have a rest before catching the métro to your next destination—there's a station in front of the Gobelins.*

# X: St-Germain

Start: Ⓜ *Odéon*
Walking time: *4 hours including the churches and museums.*

France is one country where brainy philosophers get respect, and St-Germain is their citadel; in the postwar decades there were enough eggheads here to make omelettes, sizzling and puffing away with the latest fashionable philosophy. Since the 1960s it has cooled considerably; and in the inevitably urban cycles the haunts of the avant-garde have now been gentrified and artsy-fied. But despite the absurd rents and surplus posers, St-Germain's essential conviviality remains intact. Its narrow streets, scarcely violated by the planners of the last two centuries, its cafés and bookshops, and the Luxembourg gardens cluttered with chairs all invite you to gas the day away in the spirit of those first eggheads, Voltaire and Diderot, if not Camus, Sartre, Simone de Beauvoir, Foucault and the more recent *germanopratine* sages—yes, this quarter even has its own adjective.

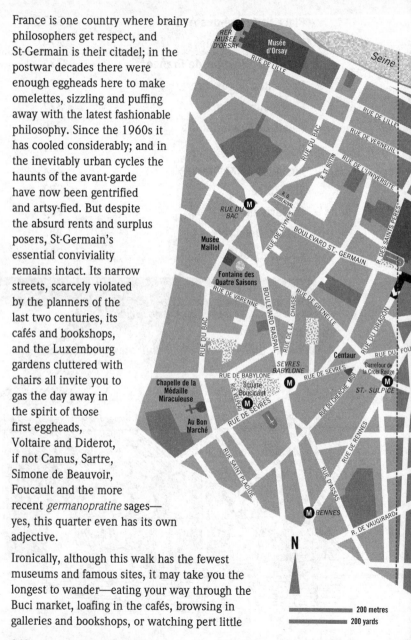

Ironically, although this walk has the fewest museums and famous sites, it may take you the longest to wander—eating your way through the Buci market, loafing in the cafés, browsing in galleries and bookshops, or watching pert little

Parisians captain ships in the Luxembourg's basin. Note that on Mondays the Musée de la Monnaie is closed, and on Tuesday and Thursday afternoons there are tours of the Mint's workshop; the Delacroix museum is closed on Tuesdays.

X: St-Germain

Seine

QUAI MALAQUAIS

Palais de l'Institut de France

QUAI DE CONTI

PONT NEUF

RUE BONAPARTE

Ecole des Beaux-Arts

RUE DES BEAUX ARTS

Hôtel des Monnaies

RUE VISCONTI

RUE GUENEGAUD

RUE DE NEVERS

QUAI DES

Faculté de Médecine

R. JAQUES-CAILLOT

RUE JACOB

Les Deux Magots

Sq. Laurent-Prache

Musée Delacroix

RUE MAZARINE

R. DE NESLE

R. DU PONT-DE-LODI

RUE DAUPHINE

AUGUSTINS

GRANDS-

Le Flore

RUE DE L'ABBAYE

St-Germain-des-Prés

Carrefour de Buci

Le Tabou

Lapérouse

RUE SEGUIER

LE

AUGUSTIN

Place St.-Germain-des-Prés

Palais de l'Abbaye

RUE DE BUCI

RUE DE SEINE

RUE DES GRANDS-

ST-

GERMAIN-DES-PRÉS

R. DES OISEAUX

Sq. F. Desruelles

R. DE L'ECHAUDE

R. DE L'ANCIENNE

RUE ST. ANDRE DES ARTS

R. DE L'HIRONDELLE

ST-MICHEL (R.E.R)

Cour de Rohan

Place St. Andre des Arts

ST.- MICHEL

RUE MABILLON

M

BVD

MABILLON

Former Comédie-Française

COUR DU COMMERCE

Place Henri Mondor

Danton Statue

R.DE HAUTEFEUILLE

DU

FOUR

RUE DE BONAPARTE

RUE

RUE GUISARDE

RUE

RUE GRÉGOIRE

ST.-

ODÉON

M

Carrefour de l'Odéon

GERMAIN

Musée de l'Histoire de Médecine

Place St.- Sulpice

RUE ST.- SULPICE

Maison Auguste Comte

R. DE L'ODEON

RUE ANTOINE

R. DE L'ECOLE DE MEDECINE

DUBOIS

Paris VI Cordeliers

St.- Sulpice

RUE GARANCIER

RUE DE TOURNON

RUE DE CONDE

RUE DE SEINE

RUE MONSIEUR-LE-PRINCE

BOULEVARD SAINT- MICHEL

RUE FEROU

Place de l'Odéon

Odéon

Palais du Luxembourg

RUE DE VAUGIRARD

RUE DE MEDICIS

RUE DE VAUGIRARD

M

Fontaine de Médicis

LUXEMBOURG (R.E.R.)

M

JARDIN DU LUXEMBOURG

**Osteria del Passe Partout**, 20 Rue de l'Hirondelle, ✆ 01 46 34 14 54. Salmon *carpaccio,* wide choice of pasta and other Italian treats (lunch menus 65 and 70F, along with many more expensive ones); closed weekends.

**Polidor**, 41 Rue Monsieur-le-Prince, ✆ 01 43 26 95 34. A favourite of Joyce and Verlaine, and one of the few places they could still afford; good brasserie cooking and lots of it for around 85F (also a 55F lunch menu).

**Jacques Cagna**, 14 Rue des Grands-Augustins, ✆ 01 43 26 49 39. One of Paris' most gracious institutions, offering an unforgettable lunch menu for 270F (without wine).

**Mariage Frères**, 19 Rue de Savoie, on the corner of Grands-Augustins. Paris' premier purveyors of fine tea since 1854 (400 varieties) and a *salon de thé.*

**Le Datcha des Arts**, 56 Rue St-André-des-Arts, ✆ 01 46 33 29 25. Tea, blinis and cakes, or delicious Russian dishes from borscht to sprats for *c.* 160F.

**Allard**, 41 Rue St-André-des-Arts, ✆ 01 43 26 48 23. A *bistrot* unchanged (except for the prices) in 40 years; try the duck with olives; menus 150 and 200F.

**La Pallette**, 43 Rue de Seine, ✆ 01 43 26 68 15. A charming café and terrace, but brace yourself for some of that legendary Parisian snootiness.

**Des Beaux Arts**, 11 Rue Bonaparte, ✆ 01 43 26 92 64. Arrive early to get a table at one of St-Germain's nicest and cheapest restaurants; 55 and 75F menus.

**A la Cour de Rohan**, in the arcade at 59–61 Rue St-André-des-Arts, ✆ 01 43 25 79 67. A tranquil *salon de thé* to recharge your batteries.

**Café Procope**, 13 Rue de l'Ancienne-Comédie, ✆ 01 43 26 99 20. Paris' oldest, restored for the Revolution's Bicentennial; lunch menus from 70F.

**Lipp**, 151 Boulevard St-Germain, ✆ 01 45 48 53 91. The most famous brasserie in Paris, and a favourite of several presidents, little changed since the 1920s, including the menu, now 210F.

**Le Petit Zinc**, 11 Rue St-Benoît, ✆ 01 46 33 51 66. When their lease in Rue de Buci ran out, the brothers Layrac opened this brasserie with a 1900 décor, with the same menu (168F). They also run the ornate **Le Muniche**, around the corner at 22 Rue Guillaume-Apollinaire, ✆ 01 46 33 62 09, with similar food; slightly less expensive (148F menu).

**Le Petit St-Benoît**, 4 Rue St-Benoît, ✆ 01 42 60 27 92. Cosy and friendly, basic but tasty French classics for around 100F.

If urbanity is St-Germain's middle name, it owes much to its parent, the Benedictine abbey of St-Germain-des-Prés. Like the Temple and the Latin Quarter, it was a walled fiefdom for hundreds of years, a law unto itself but ruled by abbots (one was a retired king of Poland) with a certain cosmopolitan flair. The scholarly monks, specialists in ancient manuscripts, set the intellectual tone of the quarter; art, food and fashion from the rest of Europe and the East were introduced into Paris through the abbey's month-long fair. Theatres prospered; the first coffee houses opened here; and actors, Protestants, foreign artists and workers outside the pale of Paris' monopolistic guilds could live in independent St-Germain, so that by 1697 the population included 16,000 foreigners, far more than in any other quarter of Paris. Ideas circulated more freely as well; if Rousseau and Voltaire got short shrift at the Sorbonne, they were published and discussed in St-Germain. Local clubs and cafés later became hotbeds of Revolutionary activity.

The two wives of Henri IV, Marguerite de Valois and Marie de' Medici, started the fashion for building hôtels and palaces in St-Germain and its more illustrious Faubourg. Aristocratic presence helped to preserve the area from 19th-century modernizers, and even from the worst of the Occupation. In its cafés (the coffee was ersatz, but the stove fires were irresistible) Paris' intellectuals kept the spark alive in a circle around Jean-Paul Sartre and Simone de Beauvoir, the notebook-scribbling high priest and priestess of St-Germain. After the war the spark spread into smoky jazz cellars, private clubs, galleries spilling over with abstract works of the *Ecole de Paris*. Everyone was tremendously cool, which meant being tremendously bored; jaded youth stewed in existential ennui, divesting its unwanted consciousness on pinball machines, *le drugstore* and the latest Godard film.

Today jaded youth can hardly afford a coffee in Boulevard St-Germain, and switched-on couples go deep into debt to buy a former maid's rooms tucked under the steep slope of a mansard roof. The contemporary Parisian art world has flown over the river to the Marais, Beaubourg and Bastille quarters, while the arteries of St-Germain's galleries harden around well-established artists and plain old antiques. But St-Germain has always been too rarefied for many tastes. Jacques Prévert, perhaps the quintessential Parisian, got fed up with it and moved to Montmartre. 'St-Germain has never been a real neighbourhood,' he griped. 'You can't find any whores or peanut vendors there.'

> *This walk begins just to the west of Odeón métro in Place Henri-Mondor, where an unflatteringly corpulent but helpful* **Statue of Danton** *shows motorists the way down Boulevard St-Germain.*

Before Haussmann got his mitts on it, this was the site of Danton's house, where Robespierre's toadies arrested 'the tribune of the people' in April 1794. 'I would rather be guillotined, than a guillotiner,' Danton declared. 'Besides, my life is not worth the trouble, and I am sick of the world.' When Danton and his neighbour, Camille Desmoulins, went to the scaffold on the same day, the Revolution lost its last advocates of humanity and moderation and Paris sank into the Terror.

*Behind Danton, cross the Carrefour de l'Odéon, proceeding left up Rue Monsieur-le-Prince, a street that follows Philippe-Auguste's medieval moat. Among the elegant town houses that replaced the sewer is no. 4, the **Hôtel de Bacq** (1750); note the lively proto-Art Nouveau portal incongruously decorated with globes, geographical instruments, swans and a leering face. Nearby at no. 10, you can pop into Paris' murkiest museum, the **Maison Auguste Comte**, maintained as a shrine to the 'Father of Sociology' (on the second floor, open Mon–Fri 2.30–5).*

Born in 1798 with a photographic memory, Comte was an apostate disciple of social reformer Saint-Simon before he cooked up his six-volume *Cours de Philosophie Positive* (1830–41), based on the loopy theory that everything could be known through pure science—taking mathematics as the base of knowledge, wisdom rose in a strict hierarchy through physics, chemistry and biology to reach the ultimate science: sociology. This pyramid of wisdom gained a sentimental side in 1844, when Comte (already married to an ex-prostitute) met his ideal woman, Clotilde de Vaux. She died two years later, and Comte devoted the rest of his life to her cult, which he called the 'Religion of Humanity', a mix of science, social improvement and mumbo-jumbo that fascinated Brazilians (*see* Walk II, p.130); this house-museum here was founded in the 1920s by the Brazilian ambassador, who repurchased all the furnishings Comte's disgruntled widow had sold.

*Descend the steps on the left to Rue Antoine-Dubois and Rue de l'Ecole-de-Médecine. On 13 July 1793, in a house that stood at this crossroad, the putrefying Marat was soaking as usual in the tub (with a fine sense of historical irony, the old regicide had caught scrofula, 'the king's disease') when Charlotte Corday knifed him. The doctors opposite, in the **Faculté de Médecine** (now Université René Descartes) came only to declare him a goner. The Faculté, a fine-proportioned neoclassical number built in 1776, makes the most of its available space with an upper floor that runs over the traditional screening wall. Within (ask or you'll never find it) the **Musée de l'Histoire de Médecine** has recently reopened (open 2–5.30, closed Thurs, Sun and hols; adm).*

After a major restoration the museum reopened on 7 January 1992. That very night a fire brought down the roof. Fortunately its prizes have survived: the very first stethoscope (invented by Laënnec in 1817, just in time to hear the dying heartbeats of Madame de Staël); a 3000-piece wooden skeleton commissioned by Napoleon; a 17th-century Japanese mannequin showing acupuncture points; and the lancet used on Louis XIV's anal fistula in 1687, an operation of momentous posterity because it was the first time a surgeon performed the actual cutting instead of talking a barber through it. There was one casualty. In beating out the time of a Te Deum celebrating the king's recovery, the opera composer Lully struck himself in the foot with his cane and died from the infected wound.

> *Opposite, from nos. 15 to 21 stretches the **Université Paris VI** (courtyard open on schooldays 10–6).*

Originally this was Paris' most important Franciscan convent, known as the *Cordeliers* after the ropes the friars wore instead of belts. The Franciscans were chucked out in the Revolution, and within their walls Danton founded his club, the rival to Robespierre's hard-hearted Jacobins on the Right Bank. The convent was demolished in the 19th century for the medical school, but in the courtyard, the Flamboyant Gothic refectory and dormitory (1370) stand apart from the bustle, a sweet forget-me-not from the past.

> *Rue de l'Ecole de Médecine narrows here—continue to no. 5, where a linguistic institute occupies the **amphithéâtre de St-Côme**, built in 1695 for the College of Surgeons and crowned with a tall tea-cup dome and lantern. Sarah Bernhardt was born here in 1844.*

> *Backtrack to Rue Hautefeuille, turn right, and follow it across Boulevard St-Germain to the corner of whiffy Impasse Hautefeuille, like many cul-de-sacs proof that not all Parisians are willing to pay to pee in their spaceship toilets.*

The curious 16th-century turret on the corner, with its conical roof, is a lone survivor of a town house built by the abbots of Fécamp—like the abbots of Cluny every major religious house in France longed to have a cosy residence in Paris.

> *Rue Hautefeuille gives into bustling **Place St-André-des-Arts**, the convergence point of a web of narrow lanes. Take one of the most picturesque, Rue de l'Hirondelle (under the arches across from the fountain), keeping an eye peeled for no. 20, with the relief of François I's fiery salamander emblem, and turn left into **Rue Gît-le-Coeur**.*

The street's romantic name is said to be a quote from another king, Henri IV, who confided to a friend: *'Ici gît mon coeur'* referring to a mistress who lived here. The street sign irritably insists that it's named instead after a cook, Gilles-le-Qurux. Scholars who disagree can cross swords at no. 6, the **Salle d'Armes**, a wonderfully atmospheric 19th-century fencing arena.

*When you reach lively Rue St-André-des-Arts, turn right, then right again into Rue Séguier, one of St-Germain's oldest streets (1179), leading to Paris' oldest quay, the **Quai des Grands-Augustins** (1313). Veer left. The 'big' Augustines who used to live in a convent here would have been shocked to know that their old wine shop at no. 51 would in the 1860s become the restaurant **Lapérouse**.*

Those watery pictures of game and oysters enclose a sumptuous interior that was famous not for its food but for upper-crust hanky-panky: the intimate alcoves on the first floor were especially booked by lawyers and politicians, who, according to a convenient French law, could not be arrested for adultery in what was technically a public place. The cooking has since improved, but the waiters still knock before entering your little bower of bliss.

*Turn left at Rue des Grands-Augustins.*

The stately *hôtel* at no. 7 was from 1936–55 Picasso's last and most luxurious address in Paris, as well as the setting for Balzac's *The Unknown Masterpiece* (a much better story than Jacques Rivette's tedious film adaptation, *La Belle Noiseuse*). Picasso painted a masterpiece here that is hardly unknown— *Guernica*—and remained here during the Occupation, far too monumental for even the Nazis to harass, as much as Hitler despised his politics and art.

*A right at Rue du Pont de Lodi will plunge you on to frenetic Rue Dauphine (turn left), laid out in 1607 as the southern extension to Pont Neuf and so fashionable that it was chosen for Paris' first street lamps in 1763, so brilliant that Paris earned the name City of Lights. The hôtel at no. 31 has beautiful 18th-century ironwork, while next door at no. 33 was **Le Tabou**, the most renowned of the postwar existentialist jazz cellars, where Juliette Greco and Boris Vian sang to slouching young Parisiennes in black turtlenecks, black nails and black lipstick.*

*Backtrack to Rue de Nesle and follow it around to 13th-century **Rue de Nevers** (turn right), a tight squeeze for cars and a favourite graffiti canvas for the less-existentialist thoughts of today's teenagers. It traces Philippe-Auguste's wall, the original boundary between the university quarter and St-Germain. Walk through the arch (look back to see its heroic bas-relief of Paris as a naked woman with a paddle), and turn left along the Quai de Conti for the mastodontic **Hôtel des Monnaies**, which until recently minted all the francs in France (entrance in Rue Guénégaud; open daily except Mon 1–6; Wed until 9; adm, free Sun; free tours of the medal workshops Tues and Fri at 2 and 2.45).*

Jean-Denis Antoine, charged by Louis XV to design the Mint, bucked every lingering Rococo urge of the day in favour of clean lines and minimal decoration. The interior offers decidedly more: a fine double-curving stair by the main entrance, handsome courtyards, one with marker indicating the Paris meridian, and the **Musée de la Monnaie**—not dusty cases of coins and medals, but a vivid, historical display that makes money indecently engrossing. Although a new mint has been built near Bordeaux, the Hôtel des Monnaies still produces commemorative medals, a Renaissance art inspired by ancient Roman coins (see Pisanello's medal of Lionel d'Este). No one familiar with the taste of Napoleon III will be surprised to find his railways commemorated with medals of naked ladies stroking big locomotives; more recent medals, designed by Dalí and Dufresne, are on sale in the mint's shop.

> *Just up the Quai de Conti stood the baleful Tour de Nesle, marking the west end of Philippe-Auguste's 1188 wall. It is most famous as the retreat of the widow of Philippe V, Jeanne de Bourgogne (d. 1329) who, when tired of her lovers, stuffed them into sacks and chucked them out of the window. Legend has it that one of her victims was the brilliant university rector Jean Buridan ('Où est la reine/Qui commanda que Buridan/Fût jeté en un sac en Seine?' wrote Villon, not knowing that Buridan survived the queen by 20 years). In 1662 the tower was toppled for the Collège des Quatre Nations, now called the **Palais de l'Institut de France**, the seat of the Académie Française. Its distinctive dome and curved wings form a handsome Baroque set piece complementing the Cour Carrée of the Louvre, just across the Pont des Arts. (Guided lecture tours Sat and Sun at 3 pm; adm expensive; Bibliothèque Mazarine open Mon–Fri 10–6, closed 1–15 Aug; leave your ID at the gate.)*

On his deathbed, France's ace grafter, Cardinal Mazarin, willed 2 million *livres* to construct a college to educate 60 students from Alsace, Artois, Piedmont and Roussillon, the four provinces incorporated into France during his regime. To honour his wishes Louis XIV plumped for a new quay, and commissioned Le Vau as architect. As a nod towards Mazarin's Roman origins, Le Vau gave the college a strong Italian flavour, complete with a bundle of *fasces* over the door and an oval dome à la Bernini. If you're game for the dull, expensive, pedantic tour, the highlight is **Mazarin's tomb** by Hardouin-Mansart, a masterpiece of 17th-century French sculpture. Otherwise, pop in to see the **Bibliothèque Mazarine**, which in 1643 (in another location) was Paris' first public library. It has since been restored to its original ochre and green appearance. Travellers used to visit the library to ogle a statue of skinny old Voltaire in the nude, but the Academicians have since tucked him into their private study for their own delectation.

In 1805 Napoleon made the College the seat of the Institut de France, a body created in 1795 to unite the academies of Sciences, Inscriptions et Belles Lettres and, the granddaddy of them all, the Académie Française. The last was born in 1635, when the preciosity of salon hostesses (one lady would greet guests with: 'Do satisfy the desire that this chair has to embrace you') drove a handful of literary men to meet informally on their own. Richelieu got wind of their meetings and, ever suspicious, offered them his 'protection', which they could hardly refuse. It solved the eternal problem of what to do with potentially disaffected intellectuals: recruit them into an *Académie* to serve the state. This they do by 'defending' the French language, especially from the hundred-headed Hydra, franglais; they even have swords to match their bottle-green uniforms. Every Thursday afternoon they meet to compile their official dictionary; they're closing in on the letter I.

'If to enter here, glory, genius and creativity were required, the seats would often be empty,' confessed one 'Immortel' in his acceptance speech. Although everyone knows that the writers *not* admitted into its ranks (Diderot, Flaubert, Balzac, Proust, Camus, etc.) make a far more distinguished list, membership of the Académie is still a plum to campaign for. In 1980 novelist Marguerite Yourcenar broke the sex barrier to become the first *Immortelle*. Now there are two.

> *Continue along the Quai past the Institut, turning left into Rue Bonaparte, built over the canal that fed the moat under the walls of St-Germain abbey. It is the sole street in Paris named after Boney—but only for his services to France as a general, as the street sign states. On your right is the gate into the* **Ecole des Beaux-Arts**. *Courtyards open 8–8pm, other admission only during exhibitions held in the oldest buildings on this site: Queen Marguerite de Valois' Chapelle des Louanges (1606; the first dome in Paris) and a chapel (1619, with elegant doors by Goujon) built for an Augustine monastery after Marguerite's death.*

During the Revolution, the painter Alexandre Lenoir hijacked the monastery as a depot for 'worthy' religious art (especially the kings' tombs from St-Denis) that he salvaged from the sledge-hammers of the sans-culottes. From 1795–1814 Lenoir put his collections on display as a museum of French monuments, where the hitherto despised Romanesque and Gothic art—displayed in a shadowy, mysterious, 'medieval' atmosphere—made a great impression on visitors and nurtured a Romantic revival of the Middle Ages. In 1816 the convent became the school of fine arts. The main courtyard contains a collage of architectural fragments, most notably the central façade of Henri II's Château d'Anet (1548), with another fine door by Goujon. Other bits were wrecked in May 1968 by art students, an insolence the authorities continue to punish by banning the annual Beaux Arts ball.

> *Opposite, continue (left) along* **Rue des Beaux-Arts**, *one of the main axes of the slowly churning St-Germain art world.*

The original galleries opened in the 1920s and shocked the public by being the first to show modern and abstract works. It's hard to be shocked any more, although you may fall into a trance as you stroll past the rows of big picture windows, inadvertently juxtaposing works of rare enchantment with brain-dead dog meat. On Rue des Beaux-Arts you'll find Di Meo and Patrice Trigano, both specializing in the abstract *Ecole de Paris*, and Claude Bernard, who specializes in figurative works by Hockney, Bacon, Botero and others. In 1900 Oscar Wilde, aged 46 but broken by his prison term, came to die 'beyond his means' in the former Hôtel d'Allemagne (no. 13). At least he kept his good taste to the very end. 'Either this wallpaper goes, or I do,' he grumbled and, never failing a cue, kicked the bucket. Anyone who has spent much time in older French hotels knows just how he felt. In the 1840s the poet Gérard de Nerval lived at no. 5 in the company of a pet lobster that he took for walks, with a blue ribbon around its neck.

*When you reach Rue de Seine, turn right.*

After Queen Marguerite split with Henri IV, she haughtily expropriated a goodly stretch of St-Germain's meadow, especially the part the abbots had ceded to the university known as the Pré-aux-Clercs—a favourite ground for duels and romps. Marguerite's château faced Rue de Seine, the gardens extending to the present Musée d'Orsay; all the houses from where you stand to the river belonged to her entourage.

> *George Sand lived at no. 31, scandalizing the quarter with her male attire and smelly cigars. Turn right into Rue Jacques-Callot, graced with its bronze sculpture of the Muse of art and a building called the* **Grande Masse des Beaux-Arts**, *where many students have studios. At the corner of Rue Mazarine, just to the left (no. 41), the first opera in French was presented in 1671, in the* **Théâtre Guénégaud**.

Like all of Paris' first theatres, this was really a *jeu de paume*, an enclosure for real tennis. The opera was *Pomone*, by Perrin and Cambert and featured a ballet of men in drag. It had an eight-month run, long enough for the nobles to learn the songs and sing along with the cast—which the singers acknowledged as a great honour—before the jealous tyrant Lully, who had purchased the opera concession in Paris, forced it to close. When Molière died in 1673, his company was expelled from the Palais-Royal by the same Lully, and it performed here until the Sorbonne profs at the new Collège des Quatre Nations kicked the actors out again, citing the danger to the morals of their charges.

> *Continue south up Rue Mazarine to the* **Carrefour de Buci**, *in the 18th century one of the most fashionable crossroads of the Left Bank, and now the city's most fashionable market. At weekends it goes into high gear, when friends gather in the cafés after choosing the fattest melons or crispest frisée lettuce for the one day of the week when they actually have the time to prepare a proper meal. When you can pull yourself away from the meticulous displays of smoked salmon and* **pâtés en croûte**, *take a*

*few giant steps east on Rue St-André-des-Arts for a look at the cobble-stoned* **Cour du Commerce St-André,** *opened in 1776 on the site of a* jeu de paume *that skirted Philippe-Auguste's wall.*

This is Paris' oldest *passage*, built before new iron and glass engineering techniques were to make them the marvel of the Right Bank. It now holds a Russian tea room, Café Procope's backside and the Relais Odéon brasserie with colourful *belle-époque* mosaics. Midway, to your left, extend three minute courtyards known collectively as the **Cour de Rohan**. In the first courtyard, the gentle Dr Joseph-Ignace Guillotin and a carpenter named Schmidt used sheep to test their decapitation machine, a design improvement on the 15th-century *mannaja* used in Italy, Provence and Edinburgh. Guillotin claimed that the victim felt only a cool 'puff of air on the neck', but to the end of his life (he died peacefully, in bed) protested against the use of his name for the device. Unfortunately for him ballad singers could rhyme *guillotine* with *machine* but *schmidt* didn't rhyme with anything. A few years later, a few yards away in the Cour du Commerce, a less kindly doctor, Marat, printed his *Ami du Peuple*, proposing they try Guillotin's 'puff of air' on 200,000 aristocrats. There's a pretty Renaissance house covered with vines in the second courtyard, part of the *hôtel* of Diane de Poitiers; the iron tripod in the corner is a once common urban sight, a *pas de mule* (horse mount).

*Near the far end of the Cour du Commerce, take the archway to your left into* **Rue de l'Ancienne-Comédie,** *named after the old Comédie Française. The company performed at no. 14, where a figure of Minerva by Le Hongre uncharacteristically (for a goddess of wisdom) reclines across the façade.*

In 1680, the better to control the content of Paris' theatres, Louis XIV ordered Molière's troupe at the Théâtre Guénégaud to merge with a company at the Hôtel de Bourgogne to form the Comédie Française (to distinguish it from Comédie Italienne). The combined company moved to a *jeu de paume* here and converted it into the first Italian-style hemicycle theatre in France, with seating for 1500 arranged in three tiers. It reopened in grand style in 1689 with Racine's *Phèdre* and Molière's *Le médecin malgré lui* and prospered, although by contemporary accounts the audience behaved like cowboys on a spree. The royal darlings—the musketeers and the Swiss Guard—forced their way in without paying and often interrupted the performance with whistling or pistol shots, or even duels; dandies subscribed to seats on the stage and when bored they upstaged the hapless actors. In 1770 the Comédie lost its lease. Theatre-loving Louis XV let them perform in the Tuileries palace while constructing the Odéon.

*Across the street is Paris' oldest coffee house,* **Café Procope,** *which relocated here from Rue de Tournon to be near the theatre.*

Coffee came to France by way of Turkey and was first sold by street vendors at the St-Germain fair. In spite of warnings that it caused impotence, the new beverage swept Paris by storm; women abandoned their breakfast wine for pots of *café au lait* so fervently that for a hundred years it was impossible to buy milk in Paris after 9am. Armenians opened the first cafés, but it was an enterprising Sicilian street vendor named Procopio dei Coltelli who in 1686 hit on the right formula, serving coffee, chocolate, alcohol and food, while encouraging customers to smoke and gamble. It was so successful that France's greatest historian, Jules Michelet, wrote that coffee was in part responsible for the Revolution because it made people talk more than ever. The Procope certainly supplied a caffeine buzz to some champion jawers—Voltaire, Ben Franklin, Danton, Napoleon, Victor Hugo and Oscar Wilde—and among its many claims to fame boasts that its customers were the first to don the red Phrygian caps of the Revolution.

> When you find yourself back at the Carrefour de Buci, turn left up Rue de Buci, and immediately left again into Rue Grégoire-de-Tours, a street famous until the First World War for its 'brasserie de femmes' *(the sort of joint popular at the time, where the waitresses were prostitutes). This brasserie was for lesbians, who would bet on razor fights among the girls. Follow the street across Boulevard St-Germain, and at the end, turn right, then left, into Rue de la Seine, which soon changes its name to* **Rue de Tournon**, *a street of distinguished 18th-century* hôtels particuliers *and bookshops.*

You could fill a wax museum with the luminaries who once graced this street, many remembered with plaques: Balzac, de Musset and André Gide (at various times) lived at no 2; the American Revolutionary admiral John Paul Jones died at no. 19, after serving in the navy of Catherine the Great; Casanova lived at no. 27; the Concini conspirators, and later Louis XIII, lived at no. 10, the **Hôtel des Ambassadeurs** during the 'Day of the Dupes' (*see* below). At no. 6 the **Institut Français d'Architecture** (*open daily 12.30–7*) offers imaginative exhibits and displays on architectural projects going up around the world.

Most adventurous was the first of St-Germain's 'amazons', Théroigne de Méricourt, who lived next door at no. 8. Few women had better Revolutionary credentials: she was awarded a sabre of honour for her role in the taking of the Bastille, and in October 1790, painted red, dressed in feathers and armed with the aforementioned sabre, pistols and smelling salts (against the stench of the unwashed Parisian mob), she led the march of women and children on Versailles, where she boldly gave Marie-Antoinette a piece of her mind. Later, she would lead a column of women on the assault of the Tuileries (20 June 1791).

Théroigne de Méricourt's boudoir in this *hôtel* was as famous for its decorations—prints of the executions, weapons and copies of the Declaration of the Rights of

Man—as for its visitors: Danton, Camille Desmoulins and the 'Archangel' Saint-Just. On Revolutionary playing cards her likeness replaced the queen of spades. Her flamboyant speech and dress (she wore nothing but tricolour costumes and face-paint) and countless lovers infuriated Robespierre's prudish Madame Lafarges, who ambushed, stripped and whipped her one day as she went to the Assemblée Nationale. This display of fury from her fellow women deranged her, and she ended up in the madhouse at the Salpêtrière, last seen before she died in 1817 crawling about on all fours, naked, and howling like a beast.

> At the top of Rue de Tournon squats the cyclops-gateway to the **Palais du Luxembourg,** where every French schoolchild learns that the history of France was changed, in a 24-hour soap opera called 'The Day of the Dupes'. Since 1958 the palace has been the seat of the French Senate, but terrorist bombings in 1986 have made it touchy about visitors. If it's in session, you can watch France's 322 senators grumble away in the Salle des Séances (passports required). Otherwise the interior is open Sunday only for guided tours; call © 01 42 34 20 00 for hours.

'Twas a dark and stormy night when the newly-widowed Marie de' Medici, Regent of France, ordered her coachman to drive her to the Bastille, where she brazenly pinched all the money her husband, Henri IV, had set aside in case of war. Marie used it to buy land south of Rue Vaugirard to be near her favourite Italian intriguers: Concini (whom she made a *maréchal* of France) and his wife, Leonora Galigaï. And in 1612, on the death of the Duke of Luxembourg, Marie added his *hôtel* (now the Petit Luxembourg) to her estate. But the regent's ambitions were hardly petite; in fact, she dreamed of a replica of her girlhood home, Florence's enormous Pitti Palace. Architect Salomon De Brosse managed to dissuade her in favour of a more traditional French mansion, but decorated it with Florentine touches—especially the rusticated bands of stone that give it a corrugated look, and its 'ringed' Tuscan columns. For the interior, the regent with typical Medicean modesty commissioned Rubens to paint 24 heroic paintings on her life that today offer the Louvre's best comic relief.

For of all the queens of France, Marie most resembled *Alice in Wonderland*'s Queen of Hearts: stout, arrogant, stupid and a ghastly mother. Even when he reached his majority and was crowned king, the highly strung Louis XIII despised her, and showed it by ordering the assassination of Concini and the trial of Galigaï, who was found guilty of witchcraft and burned at the stake. Marie herself was torn between ingratiating herself into Louis' favour, and hoping he would drop dead and leave the throne to her favourite son, Gaston d'Orléans. Another divided soul was Cardinal Richelieu, who owed Marie a favour (she gave him his start at her court at Blois) but knew that his own future depended on becoming indispensable to her son. Increasingly Marie found Richelieu not only ungrateful, but in the way of her own schemes.

Similar feuds within the royal family had undermined France's political unity for centuries. Richelieu knew that Gaston d'Orléans had already conspired once to bump him off, and he smelled a rat on 10 November 1630 when he learned that the queen mother was closeted with the king in the Luxembourg palace and not receiving visitors. Alarmed, Richelieu acted boldly and burst through a secret passage into the queen's apartments. The triumphant look in Marie's eye said all; she launched into such a vicious attack on his policies and character that Richelieu fell on his knees and burst into tears. Louis, at first sheepish, was disgusted to hear his mother shout like a fishwife, and said as much. Marie then turned on him for preferring a 'servant'—Richelieu—to her, and burst into tears herself.

His nerves shattered by the scene, Louis slumped off to Versailles, while Marie's party, certain of victory, took control. Richelieu was about to flee Paris for his life, when he received a summons to Versailles. After another tearful scene, Louis put his trust in the cardinal, and eventually made him a duke. Marie and her fellow dupes became the laughing stock of Paris, and the queen spent her last 10 years in impoverished exile in Cologne. The net result of all the boo-hoos: family feuds never again challenged the authority of the king or his ministers, paving the way toward the autocracy of Louis XIV.

During the Revolution the Palais de Luxembourg served as a prison for the likes of Danton, Desmoulins, Thomas Paine, Jacques David and Joséphine de Beauharnais before becoming a seat for the assembly. Delacroix painted the library with the scenes of *Dante and Virgil in Limbo* and *Alexander placing Homer's Poems in Darius' Golden Casket* that provide the lukewarm artistic highlight inside.

> *At the west end of the big Palace, at Rue de Vaugirard, the delightful **Petit Luxembourg** was Paris' first public art gallery, and still offers temporary exhibits in its **Musée de Luxembourg** (open daily exc Mon 1–7, adm). Opposite, under the portico at 17bis, the wall is marked with a metre, a rare survivor of the Revolution's campaign to familiarize the population with its newfangled measure. Follow Rue de Vaugirard east two blocks for the **Théâtre de l'Odéon**.*

Built by Louis XV in 1782, the neoclassical Théâtre de l'Odéon was the first public theatre in Paris designed exclusively for drama. Its austere Doric temple façade is attractively set in the semicircular Place de l'Odéon, while porticoes on either flank integrate the building into the square itself. After fires in 1807 and 1818, the theatre was faithfully reconstructed to the original design.

For decades, however, the Odéon was a commercial flop. During the Revolution its troupe split, the pro-Republican actors going off to the Comédie Française and the Royalists sticking it out here until they were carted off to the slammer. In the next century the theatre had a few successes (Bizet's *L'Arlésienne*, in 1872), but it only became popular after the Second World War, when Jean-Louis Barrault and Madeleine Renaud quickened its pulse with contemporary drama. In May 1968 Barrault and Renaud even took their enthusiasm to the streets, distributing Roman helmets from the wardrobe to protect student skulls from billy clubs. They were immediately sacked. Contemporary performances are still staged in the Petit Odéon around the back, while the main Odéon Théâtre d'Europe, under a ceiling painted by André Masson in 1965, features visiting European companies.

> Behind the Odéon, a gate leads into the **Jardin du Luxembourg**, nick-named 'Luco', from Lucotitius, the name of a military encampment from the time of Julian the Apostate.

Near the gate, this very welcome Left Bank oasis of greenery remembers its foundress with the long pool of the **Fontaine de Médicis** (just east of the Palais du Luxembourg), a romantic rendez-vous under the plane trees, dating from 1624 and adorned with 19th-century statuary of the lovers Acis and Galatea about to be ambushed by the jealous cyclops Polyphemus. They are only the first of the Luxembourg's numerous marble men and women, a cast big enough for a Cecil B. De Mille costumier. Big Marie de' Medici herself figures among the Great Women of France posing around the central basin (southwest, next to Henri IV's first wife, Marguerite); in the trees towards Rue Guynemer, there's a midget *Statue of Liberty* by Bertholdi, who modelled her on his monolithic mom and gradually made her bigger (as on the Ile des Cygnes) and bigger (as in New York). Metal chairs scattered under the trees desire you to receive their embrace, although the scarce lawns are out of bounds, unless you're in the company of a toddler. But the kids have all the fun, on an opulent carrousel designed by Charles Garnier, riding pony carts and mini-cars, sailing boats in the Grand Bassin, or watching performances of Guignol in the **Théâtre des Marionettes** (*open Wed at 2.45 and 3.45, Sat and Sun at 3 and 4.15; adm*).

> Leave the gardens on Rue de Vaugirard (the longest street in Paris), walking north on Rue Férou for **Place St-Sulpice**. Its centrepiece, the **Fontaine des Quatre Evêques** (1844), is punningly known as the Fontaine des Quatre Points Cardinales—each bishop faces a cardinal point, but none were ever (point) made cardinals. Behind rises **St-Sulpice**, a church with the charm of a train station.

In the 12th century the abbots of St-Germain founded a church to St Sulpicius (a 6th-century archbishop of Bourges) for the peasants of their domain, who were not allowed in the monastic church. St-Sulpice's present incarnation dates from 1646; by the time the builders reached the façade in 1732, the original Baroque plan seemed old-fashioned, resulting in a competition, won by an even more antique design by a Florentine named Servandoni. Other architects stripped Servandoni's plans down to a double-decker Doric and Ionic loggia bookended by a pair of factory chimney bell towers, never crowned with the soaring pinnacles Servandoni intended. One wonders how many Parisians mumble Raoul Ponchon's lines whenever they pass by: 'I hate the towers of Saint-Sulpice!/ Every time I chance upon them/I piss upon them.'

Inside the grey, cavernous nave, railway clocks tick down the minutes to the next TGV to heaven. The organ is one of the most seriously overwrought in Paris; the holy water stoups are two enormous clam shells, gifts from Venice to François I. In such a setting, the lush, romantic murals by Delacroix in the first chapel on the right radiate warmth: *Jacob wrestling with the angel* and *Heliodorus in the temple* (1858–61). The last chapel before the right transept contains the Hallowe'en *tomb of Curé Languet de Gergy* (1750) by Michelangelo Slodtz. The copper strip across the transept traces the Paris meridian, and if you come at the winter solstice you'll see a sunray strike the centre of the obelisk. Lastly, the fourth chapel on the left has no art, but is worth a mention for its dedication to St Vincent de Paul and his *Filles de la charité*, lay sisters in St-Sulpice parish who cared for the poor too frightened to enter the pestilent Hôtel-Dieu. The sisters also cared for abandoned children, a special interest in the parish continued in 1734 when the curé founded the *Maison de l'Enfant Jésus* clinic and a new discipline: paediatrics.

> From Place St-Sulpice turn down **Rue des Canettes**, 'Duckling Street', named after the happy quackers carved over no. 18. Almost opposite the ducks, take Rue Guisarde over to **Rue Mabillon** (turn left), once the centre of the famous fair of St-Germain.

The main source of funding for the abbey of St-Germain, this was the biggest fair in Paris from 1482 until the Revolution. It began on 3 February and lasted until Palm Sunday, and sold everything except weapons or books: fabrics the first week, crockery and porcelain the second, and luxuries the third (dressing gowns from Marseille, Siamese bonnets, Milan cheeses, gold necklaces, cement to fill smallpox scars) which drew the greatest crowds—commoners during the day, and the gentry, including the king himself, at night, when the fair was illuminated like fairyland. The distractions were non-stop: acrobats, operas, comedies, fortune-tellers, games of chance and cabarets offering the finest wines. The white Marché de St-Germain was built over the fair pavilion, while the buildings on the left mark the ground level of the street in the fair's heyday.

> The seven entrances into the fairgrounds were along Rue du Four (turn left), a street named after one of the abbey's most important monopolies—bread ovens. Cross this busy street and head down narrow Rue des Ciseaux (named after the old Golden Scissors inn) to Boulevard St-Germain, where a **statue of Diderot**, quill in hand, seems to be studying the church of **St-Germain-des-Prés** for an article in his Encylopédie.

Perhaps it would read like this: when Childebert I, son of Clovis, returned from the siege of Saragossa in 543, his booty included a piece of the True Cross and the tunic of St Vincent. Germanus, bishop of Paris, convinced Childebert that he should found an abbey to house the relics, and the king endowed it with land stretching from the Petit Pont to the suburb of Meudon. When Germanus himself was canonized, the church changed its name to St-Germain—St-Germain the Golden, people called it, for all its shimmering treasures and mosaics. It was one of the most important Benedictine monasteries in France, and until Dagobert (d. 639) it was the burial place of the Merovingian kings. After the Norman pillage of 866, St-Germain was rebuilt on its Merovingian foundations, and protected by high walls and turrets. Of this early Romanesque church, little has survived: capitals now mostly in the Musée de Cluny and the base of the massive tower on the west front. The nave, choir, east and west towers were rebuilt in 1193. Architect Peter de Montreuil added a Lady Chapel, as beautiful as his Sainte-Chapelle.

It became the custom for the king to appoint abbots, or the abbots to become kings: the grandfather and father of Hugues Capet were abbots, as was Hugues himself before becoming king in 987. Its royal patrons enabled St-Germain's scholars to do as they pleased, and in 1530 they were the first to translate the Bible into French, in face of violent opposition from the Sorbonne and Parlement.

In 1789 St-Germain's precious tombs and reliquaries were destroyed, the famous library confiscated (to become the core of the Bibliothèque Nationale), while the church was converted into a saltpetre factory. The damage had only just begun: in 1840 Victor Hugo led a campaign for St-Germain's restoration, and for the next 20 years much of what the Revolutionaries missed fell victim to the hacks hired to save it. To create Rue de l'Abbaye, the beautiful Lady Chapel, cloister and refectory were sacrificed. Two of the church's three towers were truncated, fine details were bashed up or replaced by cheap copies, and the walls botched by Ingres' most mal-adroit pupil, Hippolyte Flandrin (1854–63)—murals so excruciating that a score of petitions have been circulated to have them painted over.

The front porch of St-Germain underwent an earlier act of vandalism; only a dam-aged carved lintel survives from the original entrance, redone in the 17th century. Squint past Flandrin's colours to appreciate the proportions of the church—the choir, with its mix of ogival and rounded arches and five radiating chapels for an especially lovely example of the transition from Romanesque to Gothic. The marble shafts in the short columns above the arcade are from the 6th century, the only Merovingian work *in situ* in Paris. The wall on the right was rebuilt in 1646, when the right transept was extended to create a chapel of Ste-Marguerite. This was necessitated by the crowds of pregnant women who came to pray by the girdle that Marguerite used to harness a fierce dragon, centuries before latex.

The first chapel in the choir contains the mausoleum of Scotsman James Douglas, who died serving Louis XIII. The next contains the remaining bits of René Descartes (1596–1650), who died in Stockholm, his frail health a victim to Queen Christina's insistence on having her philosophy lesson at 5am, even in the middle of a Swedish winter. When Descartes' writings began to attract attention, France demanded his body. After extracting a few souvenir teeth and fingers, the Swedes transported Descartes by land to avoid English relic pirates. His skull is in the Musée de l'Homme. In the north transept lies John Casimir (d. 1672), king of Poland, who preferred to spend his last years as abbot of St-Germain.

*Leaving the church, turn right; in **Square Laurent-Prache,** at the corner of Place St-Germain-des-Prés and Rue de l'Abbaye are fragments of Pierre de Montreuil's Lady Chapel, chapter house (against the wall) and refectory (ruined window). Here, too, is a bronze Head of a Woman by Picasso (1959), a memorial to his friend, poet Guillaume Apollinaire.*

Apollinaire died of influenza in the 1918 epidemic (Gertrude Stein wrote that in his delirium he overheard crowds outside shouting 'A bas Guillaume!' and became sad, unaware that they were really referring to Kaiser Wilhelm).

*Head down Rue de l'Abbaye, where at no. 5 stands the austere **Palais Abbatial** (1586).*

One of the few Renaissance buildings to survive the storms of Paris, it was built by the Cardinal-Abbot Charles of Bourbon, who in 1589 let himself be proclaimed King Charles X by the Catholic League in place of the rightful heir, his nephew Henri IV. When Henri captured Paris, he bagged his presumptuous uncle as well, who died a year later of chagrin.

*Take Rue de Furstemberg (named after the cardinal who laid it out) left to serendipitous **Place Furstemberg** and its delicate pawlownia trees, a dainty gem of urban design that traces the ancient cloister-courtyard of the abbots' palace. In the old abbey stable (no. 6) is the **Musée Delacroix** (open 9.45–12.30 and 2–5.15, closed Tues; adm).*

This was the last home of Eugène Delacroix, who moved here in 1857 to be close to St-Sulpice. Sketches, etchings and a dozen minor paintings hang in his lodgings and atelier, and there's a quiet garden that suited the old bachelor to a T. For despite the romantic, exotic pre-Impressionistic fervour of his paintings, Delacroix liked his peace and quiet. Soon after painting his most famous work, *Liberty leading the people*, he wrote to his mistress: 'Those people (the republicans) nauseate me. I wish I were an Austrian.'

*Winding Rue Cardinale (off to the right), nearly solid with interior-design boutiques, traces the limits of the monks' tennis courts (did they wear their cowls while they played? The historians don't say). At the next cross-roads, veer slightly left for Rue de l'Echaudé which deposits you back on Boulevard St-Germain. Turn right: St-Germain's flying buttresses (among the first in France) form a handsome backdrop to* **Square F. Desruelles**.

The now-dingy glazed portico on the wall was made for the Sèvres factory pavilion in the 1900 Exposition. Two hundred years ago this was the abbey's cemetery, near the abbey prison; in September 1792, a mob of thugs, fresh from hacking up 116 Carmelites in Rue Vaugirard, took over the prison and held mock trials before butchering 318 more monks in their own graveyard.

*Continue west along Haussmann's Boulevard St-Germain, a street slashed through the heart of the Left Bank in 1880. Across the boulevard in Place du Québec, concrete Canadian ice floes of a fountain called* **Embâcle** *(by Charles Daudelin) crack and rise up from the pavement in chaotic abandon. This corner is best known for four germanopratine institutions: firstly,* **Les Deux Magots** *in Place St-Germain-des-Prés.*

Whether it's '*le Rendez-vous de l'élite intellectuelle*', according to its own menu, or the 'Two Maggots' of American teenagers, the café does offer grandstand views of St-Germain and a hot chocolate that hits the spot on wet winter days. Inside, the two statues of Chinese mandarins or *magots* date from the shop's original vocation—selling silks. The name was retained when it became a café in 1875; the present décor dates from 1914. Mallarmé, Verlaine and Rimbaud gave it its literary seal of approval in the 1880s, and the café has distributed its own literary prize since 1933. A few doors down, its rival **Le Flore** opened in 1890 with its banquettes built for two. It too attracted a brainy clientele; Picasso and Apollinaire would edit art magazines in the back, Sartre and Camus were regulars, only to ignore stalwartly each other's presence. On the south side of the boulevard 'Le Drugstore', a groovy hangout in the 1960s, has recently succumbed to changing tastes, although its neighbour, **Brasserie Lipp**, still packs Paris' Who's Who in with a *choucroute* unchanged since 1920.

*Continue west on Blvd Saint-Germain; here you are entering the 7e.*

This is a genuine border, between regular old St-Germain and its blue-blooded *Faubourg*. Cross it, and enter into a realm as steeped in privilege as Proust' *madeleine* in his cup of tea. High heels crack like rifles in hushed streets, hemmed in by aristocratic mansions where, by communal consent, nothing ever happens. Bigwigs began migrating here in the 17th and 18th centuries from the Marais, often by way of Versailles where they had been bored to tears. The descendents of those lucky enough to keep their heads still live in the same apartments, although ministries, institutes and embassies now occupy the grandest *hôtels particuliers*. Others around Rue des Saints-Pères have become antique shops, site of an antiquarians' fair in May.

*For a bittersweet detour, you might have a look up Rue des Saints-Pères on the right: no. 30 is Paris' oldest chocolate shop, **Debauve et Gallais**, founded by an apothecary in 1800, although its delicious chocolates are no longer spiked with medicinal drugs. At no. 54 the **Musée de l'Histoire du Protestantisme Français** displays items relating to France's Huguenots, who often lived underground, or in the 'wilderness' in the Cévennes region near Nîmes (open Sun, Mon and Tues by appointment, ☎ 01 45 48 62 07).*

*If you turn left at this corner, you'll be on **Rue du Dragon**.*

Paintings were a popular buy at the St-Germain fair, especially those by the colony of foreign (often Protestant) artists who did not belong to the official artists' guild, the Maîtrise. Many of these 'pirates' had their ateliers in Rue du Dragon (most notably no. 37). To transport their works to the fair they had to cross 200 feet of land belonging to the city of Paris—where guild members lay in ambush to seize and destroy their 'illegal' paintings. The Rue du Dragon artists retorted by hiding their canvases in loaves of bread, up ladies' skirts, and outrunning guildsmen in the middle of the night.

*You can end your St-Germain travels here—the Faubourg isn't the most inviting place for tramping about unless you mean to do some serious window shopping. But if you want to carry on, here are some of the 7e's major sights, beginning down Rue du Dragon to the **Carrefour de la Croix Rouge**.*

In the 16th century a ruined temple of Isis still survived, attracting a few infidels on the sly until priests exorcised the bogeys with a giant crucifix painted red. Paganism has made a comeback, however, in the form of a saucy *Centaur* contrived of metal bits and bobs by César in 1985. The tail resembles the contents of a gardener's shed, and it comes equipped, unlike classical centaurs, with male pokers at the front and back. The virile ensemble is in homage to Picasso.

The curved Rue du Cherche Midi runs south from here. At no. 8, **Poilâne** is the home of the famous round, vaguely sourdough *miche Poilâne*, introduced in the 1950s by the father of the current master baker, Lionel Poilâne. The curious name Cherche Midi ('seeking midday') is apparently derived from the bas-relief of the astronomer consulting his sundial at no. 19.

Further on, down Rue de Sévres **Square Boucicaut** has as its muse a white marshmallow statue of the plump but caring Madame Boucicaut as an allegory of charity. Her husband Aristide was the founder of **Au Bon Marché**, across Rue Velpeau.

The world's first department store, Au Bon Marché caused a revolution in retailing and consumer attitudes when it opened its doors in 1852. Boucicaut's innovations were in essence three: prices fixed and clearly marked on each item (compared to the old bazaar-like haggling), low price mark-ups to encourage volume sales (thanks to the new Industrial Age glut of machine-made goods), and the concept of browsing through *entrée libre*—free entrance to anyone, whether or not they wanted to buy (previously, merely to enter a shop implied a purchase). What made the department store a booming success from the start (turnover rose from 450,000 francs in 1852 to 7 million francs in 1863) was the phenomenon Marx called 'commodity fetishism': Boucicaut's ingenious displays, juxtaposing the most incongruous items in exotic settings, gave consumer goods a magical mystique and a status far removed from their use. Objects became desirable in themselves, so instead of saving money in department stores, people spent more.

To accommodate the masses of entranced shoppers, Louis-Charles Boileu and Eiffel designed a new Au Bon Marché in 1878. Based on the iron and glass *passages* of the Right Bank, the store features a central glass-roofed well, surrounded by hanging iron galleries. The basic structure survives behind a 1920 façade, minus the grand staircase that was once its glory. On the other side of Rue du Bac a second building, (1900) offers an equal array of gastronomic fetishism.

Between the two Bon Marchés stretches Rue de Bac (named, not for the exam, but the old ferry over the Seine), where you'll notice most of the traffic pulls up in front of no. 140; what from a distance appears to be a common Parisian garage entrance is in fact the bizarre **Chapelle de la Médaille Miraculeuse**, where in 1830 the Virgin made the very first of a string of appearances in France. She asked a young Fille de Charité named Catherine Labouré to mint a holy medal with her image on it, promising that 'all who wear it around their necks will receive great rewards'. Since then, 500 million have been sold (5F in the vending machine by the door). The Virgin also recommended an armchair (now in the sacristy) for cases where extra-powerful juju was required.

A few streets to the north lies one of the important streets of the 7e, **Rue de Grenelle**. At no. 59, the **Musée Maillol/Fondation Dina Vierny** (*daily exc Tues 11—7 pm; adm expensive* ) is dedicated to the French-Catalan sculptor whose other works can be seen around the Arc du Carroussel by the Louvre (and in scores of First World War memorials across France); there is also a collection of modern and naive paintings. Next to the museum, in the 1730s, the merchants' provost Etienne Turgot thought to supply the area with much-needed water and panache by commissioning the fine theatrical Rococo **Fontaine des Quatre Saisons** (1739), from the sculptor Bouchardon. 'Plenty of stone for a little bit of water,' snorted Voltaire. The allegory represents the city of Paris, enthroned between the Seine and the Marne, while bas-reliefs of the four seasons pose on the curved wings. At no. 51, **Barthélemy** provides the presidential table with the best-ripened cheeses in Paris.

Start: Ⓜ *Invalides*

# XI: Exhibition Paris

**Walking time:** *Vanity demands her due. Count on at least 4 hours for a sprint, but make it a whole day to take in two or three of the museums.*

Frankly, visitors seeking the Paris of quaint *bistrots* will find this a death march of urban megalomania. Distances and buildings are naturally vast at this crossroads of the planet, on a scale first set by the Roi Soleil himself with the Invalides and its Esplanade, then continued through the many world fairs that took place here. Anyone familiar with the history of Paris will read Giraudoux's prayer (*see* p.292) with no little astonishment (except for the bit about Paris talking the most) and realize that

Giraudoux got it backwards: you can feel some of those lofty sentiments looking *at* the Eiffel Tower, not *down* from it; it reminds you of the good Paris of light and magic, the city that could first imagine and then weave iron in the air—as opposed to the Paris of control and power, of the Louvre squatting up-river waiting to pounce and squash. The Eiffel Tower could only dance.

RUE BOISSIÈRE

AV GEORGES V

AVENUE PIERRE-1ER-DE-SERBIE

Palais Galliera /
Musée de la Mode
et Costume

ALMA
MARCEAU

Musée
Guimet

AVENUE DE IENA

AV DE IENA

PRESIDENT-WILSON

DU
Place
d'Iéna

AVENUE

RUE
BRIGNOLE

Place
l'Alma

IENA

AVENUE KLEBER

AV GEORGES
MANDEL

TROCADERO

Place du
Trocadéro

Cimetière
de Passy

M

Palais de
Chaillot

Musée du
Cinéma /
Musée des
Monuments
Français

Palais de Tokyo /
Musée d'Art Moderne
de la Ville de Paris

PONT DE
L'ALMA

AVENUE DE NEW YORK

Seine

M

Jardins du
Trocadéro

Musée de
l'Homme /
Musée de
la Marine

Place de
Varsovie

RUE BENJAMIN-FRANKLIN

AVENUE DELESSERT

AVENUE DE NEW YORK

PONT D'IENA

QUAI BRANLY

Square
Rapp

Liceo
Italiano

AVENUE DE LA BOURDONNAIS

RUE SEDILLOT

AVENUE RAPP

Eiffel
Tower

CHAMP-DE-MARS
TOUR EIFFEL

M

PARC DU CHAMP
DE MARS

N

PARC DU CHAMP
DE MARS

AVENUE DE SUFFREN

200 metres

200 yards

Village
Suisse

RUE DU LAOS

This walk covers not only the Invalides and relics from the busiest of World Fair grounds, but a slice of the best of Faubourg St-Germain, Art Nouveau extravagances, a whiff of Paris' sewers, a Japanese garden and a topped-up grabbag of museums (including the lovely Musée Rodin and the oriental art in the Musée Guimet). All close on either Mondays or Tuesdays; the Eiffel Tower, Army Museum and Napoleon's tomb in the Invalides are open daily.

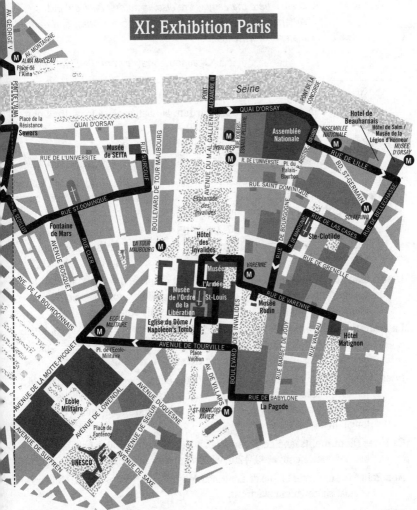

# XI: Exhibition Paris

*I have under my eyes the five thousand hectares of the world where the most has been thought, the most spoken, the most written. The crossroads of the planet which has been the most free, the most elegant, the least hypocritical. In this light air, this void below me, are so many accumulated stratifications of l'esprit, of reason, of taste. And so with all the belittlings and mutilations men undergo, there is a better chance here than anywhere else, including Babylon and Athens, to make the fight against ugliness, tyranny and the material worthwhile.*

Jean Giraudoux, *Prayer from the Eiffel Tower*

## lunch/cafés

**Café in the Musée Rodin garden**. No better place for a drink or a simple lunch on a lovely day (60–90F).

**La Pagode**, 57 Rue du Babylone. Unique café, set in a fantasy-Chinese folly of 1868; tea and cakes for 50F (*see* below, p.301)

**Chez Germaine**, 30 Rue Pierre-Leroux, ✆ 01 42 73 28 34. A bit out of the way (south of Rue de Babylone, parallel to Rue Vaneau) but worth it for a delicious lunch for 65F; get there early (closed Sun).

**Thoumieux**, 79 Rue St-Dominique, ✆ 01 47 05 49 75 (west of Blvd de La-Tour-Maubourg). Lively family-run brasserie crowded with civil servants, cuisine from the southwest: *cassoulet, confit de canard*; 72 and 150F menus.

**L'Ami Jean**, 27 Rue Malar, ✆ 01 47 05 86 89 (west of the Invalides, around the corner from St-Pierre du Gros Caillou). Owned by a former *pelote* champion, who serves good Basque dishes in a friendly atmosphere (160F).

**La Fontaine de Mars**, 129 Rue St-Dominique, ✆ 01 47 05 46 44. Traditional *bonne femme* cooking, with checked tablecloths outside in a bijou square near the Eiffel Tower; 85F *formule*; closed Sun and Aug.

**Jules Verne**, private lift to the 2nd platform of the Eiffel Tower, ✆ 01 45 55 61 44 (reserve). *Haute cuisine* as highly rated as its position, 400ft above Paris; succulent *poulet de Bresse* with mushrooms and much more (weekday lunch menu 290F).

**Café des Monuments**, and **Le Totem** both in the Palais de Chaillot; both have popular set price menus (100/120F with wine) and views of the Eiffel Tower.

**Aux Pain Perdu**, corner of Rue de Longchamps and Kléber (by the Musée Guimet); popular sit down sandwich bar.

When the Revolution undermined Paris' royal pageantry and annual fairs, it left the city restless, without an outlet to strut what the French call their 'world-record-breaking spirit'. In 1851, the solution came like a revelation from over the Channel: the Great Exhibition in London, with its dazzling display of industrial prowess in the awesome Crystal Palace that drew 6 million visitors from around the globe.

Paris put on its first *Exposition Universelle* in 1867 in the muddy old military parade grounds, the Champs de Mars. Fifteen million visitors came to try out the first *bateaux-mouches* and make balloon ascents with the irrepressible photographer Nadar, to gape at strange substances called petroleum and aluminium—'the wonder metal' (so precious that Napoleon III ordered himself an aluminium dinner service). There was a reconstruction of Rome's catacombs; prostitutes and cabarets featuring the latest Second Empire dance, *le chahut* or can-can, did a roaring trade. When critics complained that the Exposition showed Paris as the capital of orgies rather than a competitor in industry, the Comte de Fleury shrugged: 'In any case, we had a devilish good time', a spirit that summed up the real reason why Paris became an addict, putting on fairs in 1878, 1889, 1900, 1925, 1931 and 1937.

> *The next two fairs were remarkable for their architecture and technological innovations: although only the Swedish Pavilion (now in Courbevoie) survives from 1878, the 1889 Exposition saw the construction of the Eiffel Tower. The 1900 edition, although generally noted for its vertiginous clutter and gaudy neo-Baroque pastiches, has left Paris the most souvenirs in situ: the Gare d'Orsay and the mastodons, the* **Grand and Petit Palais** *(see Walk VI, pp.204 and 205) where brave souls may want to begin this walk to relive the complete world-record-breaking, feet-aching experience. From there cross* **Pont Alexandre III**; *if you're starting at* **Ⓜ** *Invalides, walk to the bridge along Rue Robert-Esnault-Pelterie.*

The decision to hold a fair to celebrate the new century was announced only two years after 32 million visitors made the 1889 Exposition a roaring triumph; mainly because the French wanted to squelch any attempts by hated Berlin to upstage Paris with a fair of its own. 'France owes it to herself as the Queen of Civilization to hold a great exhibition that will become one of her many claims to glory,' announced Deputy Ernest Roche. In 1899 the Queen of Civilization's fair was threatened by an international boycott after Dreyfus' scandalous retrial and reconviction, a real enough threat that convinced the President to pardon him.

One legacy of the Exposition was the new *petit axe*, opening a view from the Champs-Elysées down Avenue Winston-Churchill (between the Grand and Petit Palais) to the golden dome of the Invalides. For such a view, the Parisians borrowed a bridge from an opera: the **Pont Alexandre III**, named after the Tsar at the height of Republican France's love affair with Imperialist Russia and larded with sumptuous doodads that almost obscure its graceful 320ft steel arch. The 50 million visitors who crossed in 1900 gaped at horseless buggies, X-rays, wireless telegraphs, Loie Fuller's Art Nouveau scarf dances, a film (synchronized to a phonograph) of Sarah Bernhardt playing Hamlet in the duel scene, and the prototype of Cinemascope (a balloon ascent on eight screens); they rode a mock Trans-Siberian railway, a Ferris wheel 330ft in diameter with 1600 seats, and took the brand new métro to the Bois de Boulogne. An anarchist tried to spoil the show by tossing a bomb at the Shah of Persia, but he missed.

> *Turn east down the **Quai d'Orsay**, synonymous with the first building you pass, the Ministry of Foreign Affairs. Beyond is the Palais Bourbon, the seat of the 577 members of the **Assemblée Nationale** (admission to sessions by prior application, © 01 42 97 64 08; Sat guided tours of the interior at 10.30, 2 and 3).*

The Bourbon in question was the daughter of Louis XIV and Mme de Montespan, who in 1728 completed the palace. Louis XV purchased it in order to change its façade to harmonize with his Place de la Concorde, a plan that had to wait until 1807, when Napoleon required a matching temple bookend for his Madeleine. In 1827 it became the seat of the National Assembly. Inside, the best bits are concentrated in the Library, its domes and pendentives decorated with Delacroix's grand murals on the *History of Civilization* (1838–45), its collection including illuminated manuscripts, the original records of Joan of Arc's trial, Rousseau's manuscripts, and more. But don't count on seeing any of it during the tour.

> *Take Rue Aristide-Briand south, along the eastern side of the building, to see the more modest charms of the original Palais Bourbon hiding behind its neoclassical facelift. Neoclassical is not the most rousing of styles, but a pair of gems in handsome Rue de Lille merit a detour: **Hôtel de Beauharnais** (no. 78), residence of Josephine's son Eugène Beauharnais, who gave it a neo-Egyptian portico and delicate Empire furnishings—visitable if you have business with the German embassy which has occupied it since the Prussian siege in 1871. The second, bijou **Hôtel Salm** (1783), is at the corner of Rue de Bellechasse (by the Musée d'Orsay, see p.337) and houses the **Musée de la Légion d'Honneur** (open Tues–Sun 2–5; adm).*

'Crushed between tall apartment houses and an overwhelming railway terminal, it smiles on, refined, undismayed, as the noblity knew how to smile on the steps of the guillotine,' as Albert Guérard put it. The Hôtel Salm is French neoclassicism at its most graceful, small in scale, with a miniature triumphal arch and Ionic colonnade around its forecourt. This is a replica (the original was burned in the Commune); there's another copy in San Francisco.

The museum, however, is a reminder that one of the first tasks of any French regime was to create a system of Brownie points for good eggs; the Revolution no sooner abolished the monarchy's orders of merit than it created a 'Victor of the Bastille' pin for those who participated in the riot. Then on 4 May 1802 Napoleon proposed the creation of the much grander Legion of Honour at a meeting of the Conseil d'Etat. Members protested: weren't medals 'the baubles of monarchy'? '*Eh bien*,' replied the little cynic. 'It is with baubles that men are led ... Sacrifices must by made to vanity and the joy of possession ... I do not believe the French people love liberty and equality. The French are not changed by ten years of revolution. They are what the Gauls were, proud and frivolous. They believe in one thing: Honour! These feelings must be nourished and channelled. France can expect great results from this creation, if my successors have the good sense not to spoil it.' None of his successors has dared to touch it. Besides medals, the museum contains Napoleana and historical odds and ends.

> *From the Hôtel Salm, take Rue de Bellechasse south to Rue Las Cases; if you haven't taken the detour, continue south to Place du Palais Bourbon and Rue de Bourgogne; turn right into Rue Las Cases, where* **Basilique Sainte-Clotilde** *confronts the Defence Ministry across the square.*

Ste-Clotilde is a perfect 13th-century Gothic church—designed in 1840 by F. C. Grau. Its innovative use of iron upset conservatives, and construction was delayed until after Grau's death in 1853. There's a surplus of academic painting to see but nothing else, although readers of *Tropic of Cancer* may find a brief visit irresistible after Henry Miller's description of his first and last Catholic Mass, when he and a friend wandered into Ste-Clotilde at dawn after a night's revels: 'A weird, unearthly noise assailed my ears ... No music except this undefinable dirge manufactured in the subcellar—like a million heads of cauliflower wailing in the dark ... That this sort of thing existed I knew, but then one also knows that there are slaughter-houses and morgues and dissecting rooms.'

> *Behind Ste-Clotilde, take Rue de Martignac and turn right into Rue de Grenelle, then make a quick left back into Rue de Bourgogne. There's something Florentine about Faubourg St-Germain's lack of trees and the heavy blank faces that its* hôtels *turn to the streets; this was the first purely residential area in Paris, and shops or cafés remain scarce. The increasing police presence hints that you are nearing the* **Hôtel Matignon** *(to the left in Rue de Varenne), the second-most expensive hotel in Paris—residence of the Prime Minister. But the big treat is to the right at 77 Rue de Varenne: the* **Musée Rodin**, *in the beautiful Hôtel Biron. Open daily*

*except Mon, 9.30–5.45, Oct–Mar, 9.30–4.45; adm; half-price Sun; small fee to visit the gardens only.*

The Hôtel Biron (1731) was built after a plan by Jacques-Ange Gabriel for Peyrenc de Moras, who made a fortune by getting out of John Law's 'Mississippi Bubble' scheme before it popped. It is one of the most charming and best-preserved mansions in Paris from the period (several rooms have their original woodwork), fitted with distinguished façades overlooking both the front courtyard and back gardens, the latter rivalling the Prime Minister's as the largest in Faubourg St-Germain. When Auguste Rodin moved here in 1908, he was 68; his reputation as France's greatest sculptor was in the bag, and it was agreed that he would leave the state his works after he died (in 1917, ten days after marrying his mistress of over 50 years).

Rodin was the last of the great Romantics. He sculpted the literary subjects of the day, but with a personal vision, intensity and integrity that liberated sculpture from its stagnant rut as mere portraiture, public decoration or patriotic propaganda. He studied Michelangelo in Italy and came back to cause his first sensation in 1876 with *The Age of Bronze* (*L'Age d'Airain*, Room 3), so realistic that he was accused of casting a live man in bronze. In 1880 Rodin was commissioned to make a bronze door for a museum of decorative arts, resulting in the *Gates of Hell* (in the garden). Although never completed, the Gates fired the sculptor's creative imagination, and many of the 200 figures he planned for their decoration became sculptures in themselves. Studies are scattered throughout the museum: the *Three Shadows*, Paolo Malatesta and Francesca da Rimini in *The Kiss* (Room 5) and *The Thinker* (outside), in a pose reminiscent of the Lost Soul in Michelangelo's *Last Judgement*. The famous *La Main de Dieu* (1898) in Room 4 inaugurated Rodin's departure from academic tradition in a composition purely from his imagination. Room 6 is dedicated to sculptor Camille Claudel, sister of poet Paul and Rodin's model for his *La France* and *L'Aurore*; here too are examples of her work before she went mad, a portrait of Rodin and her masterful *L'Age Mûr*. Room 7 has portraits of society ladies Mrs Potter Palmer, Lady Sackville-West and the poignant *Mother and her dying daughter*, the faces and hands almost engulfed, overwhelmed by the raw marble, an emotional device Rodin often employed, inspired by Michelangelo's *nonfiniti*.

Upstairs, studies and models trace the evolution of Rodin's two great public monuments, *Balzac* and *The Burghers of Calais*. Here, too, are paintings that Rodin owned and left to the state, most notably Van Gogh's *Les Moissonneurs* and *Père Tanguy* (a portrait of the kind-hearted colour dealer) and Monet's *Paysage de Belle-Isle*. Outside, amid the roses of the *Cour d'Honneur* are Rodin's *Thinker* and other masterpieces, a delightful garden filled with studies for the *Burghers*, and a serene duck pond containing the most harrowing sculpture of all, *Ugolin and his sons*. As you leave, note the plaque by the gate commemorating Rainer Maria Rilke (1875–1926) who worked as Rodin's secretary from 1908–11.

*The dome of the **Hôtel des Invalides** glows like a second sun over the Rodin gardens. Reach the front entrance by turning right into Boulevard des Invalides. Stretching down to the Seine is the 550yd long **Esplanade des Invalides** (laid out in 1720), recently spruced up but still too formal and crisscrossed by traffic to be very inviting.*

This was the Plain of Grenelles in 1670, when Louis XIV's under-minister of war, Louvois, persuaded his warmongering king to provide a military hospital for old soldiers (most of whom lived in disgraceful penury), which could just incidentally double as a monument to the military glory and triumphs of Louis himself. The latter consideration called for nothing less than the grandest Paris project of the *Roi Soleil*'s reign, financed by taxing monasteries, markets and docking the miserable pay of active soldiers. The competition for the design was won by Libéral Bruant: a rhythmic 650ft façade with pavilions at either end, a crown of dormer windows shaped like armoured torsos and a central doorway in a magnificent built-in arch rising to the roofline. This frames an equestrian relief of Louis XIV, flanked by Justice and Prudence, two virtues somehow hoodwinked to bear the tyrant company. These are copies; the originals by Coustou were smashed in the Revolution, which began here the morning of 14 July 1789, when the mob clambered over the now-dry moats and broke into the subterranean armouries, pillaging 28,000 rifles to capture the Bastille.

*Even if you don't visit the museums, do step under the arch into Bruant's majestic cobblestoned **Cour d'Honneur** (open daily 7–6, until 7 in the summer). Bristling with cannon, its double-decker arcades were inspired by the cloister of El Escorial in Spain, although Bruant's corners project inwards and his arcades playfully resemble rows of windows. More sculpted trophies adorn the round dormer windows; the fifth on the left, along the central arcade, is encircled by wolf paws as if it were the eye of a wolf (le loup voit), a mason's pun on Louvois' name. The façade of **St-Louis des Invalides** (open 10–6) closes the south end, guarded by the statue of Napoleon, 'the Little Corporal', in his old grey coat and hat. This held pride of place on the Vendôme column from 1833 until 1863, when Napoleon III replaced it with a silly statue of his uncle modelling the latest in togas.*

The Invalides has Siamese-twin churches, back to back, originally sharing the same altar and chancel: St-Louis for the old soldiers and staff, and the Eglise-du-Dôme for royals (*see* below). St-Louis was designed by Bruant, but built by his rival, Jules

Hardouin-Mansart when Louvois fired Bruant for insubordination. It was obviously felt that French veterans were tough enough to take their religion straight without painted saints or pomp, and even today St-Louis is striking for its austerity. The strictness was relaxed for a sumptuous 17th-century organ that played in the world premiere of Berlioz's *Requiem* in 1837, a memorable performance accompanied by artillery booming away in the Esplanade.

A few dozen flags, including swastikas, hang like forgotten laundry above the gallery; during the Revolution, St-Louis was converted into a 'Temple of Mars' and the captured enemy banners that had hung for centuries in Notre-Dame's nave were moved here, but briefly; in 1814, when the allies entered Paris, the governor of the Invalides threw 1417 of them into a bonfire. Among Leclerc and the other generals buried in the crypt is the heart of Madamoiselle de Sombreuil, daughter of an earlier governor of the Invalides, who during the September Massacre, 1792, threw herself between the thugs and her father. Touched by her youth and beauty, the murderers offered to spare her father—only if she drank a goblet of human blood from the victims they had already slaughtered. Afterwards, she could never bear to look upon a glass of red wine.

> *As you leave the church, the arcade to your left enshrines one of the 700 Paris taxicabs requisitioned during the night of 6 September 1914 to transport 7000 soldiers 35km to the front and save Paris at the Battle of the Marne. It's a preview for the vast collections of the **Musée de l'Armée** (open daily 10–6, 10—5 Oct through Mar; adm; tickets, sold under the right arcade, are good for two consecutive days).*

*Bête comme la paix* ('as stupid as peace') is an old Parisian expression, one that seems to sum up the spirit of this unmatched horde of military paraphernalia. The sections in the east arcade cover the 17th–19th centuries, the period of France's obsession with military *gloire*. On the ground floor huge wall paintings of Louis XIV's Flanders campaign of 1672 decorate the veterans' refectory, now hung with French battle banners and Ingres' portrait of *Napoleon I on the Imperial Throne*, while a second gallery holds a remarkable collection of silly cavalry uniforms and not so silly rifles.

The first floor displays 100,000 more uniforms and at least as many rooms, interspersed with a few gems: rooms devoted to Lafayette and French involvement in the War of American Independence, a model of the Bastille and items from the Revolution (when the army became identified with nation; every fit man was a potential soldier, and 'carried a marshal's baton in his knapsack' as Napoleon put it). A large section is devoted to Boney himself, with his coat and hat, his stuffed dog and white horse, paintings of his retreat from Moscow and *Napoleon at Fontainebleau*, the Emperor like a little boy slouching in his chair with a sulky look on his face as he abdicates for the first time; further on are locks of his hair, his death mask and a reconstruction of the room where he died on St Helena.

Napoleon's military genius was intuitive and, unlike the strategies of subsequent French generals, completely void of dogma. His only theory was to rally his *grognards*, or grumblers, to strike unexpectedly and deliver a decisive blow in one big battle, a style of battle that perfectly fitted the French tradition of personal, gallant bravery and (often futile) gestures. In the displays on the second floor, you begin to note how after Napoleon French military tacticians were always one battle behind—as de Gaulle warned in the 1930s, while the French were building their First World War-style Maginot line. The most interesting exhibits relate to the siege of Paris and the Commune—ration tickets and petrified bread made from sawdust (*brioche dynatique, 300g par jour*), photographs of the barricades and balloons, machine guns (Paris' secret weapon of 1870, but not used until it was too late), and a rare survival of a *Panorama* (a 360° painting that spectators would view from the middle to relive an event, in this case the 1870 Battle of Rezonville).

The exhibits continue across the courtyard, in the ground-floor refectory of the west arcade, where murals of Louis XIV's Dutch campaigns of 1672–8 look down on ancient Greek, Merovingian, medieval and Renaissance weapons and armour; there's a suit worn at the battle of Crécy in 1346, François I's 'Lion armour' and just to the left of the entrance of Salle Henri IV a curious visor with what looks like an armoured cigarette in its mouth. Adjacent galleries hold swashbuckling Turkish, Chinese and Japanese weapons. On the first floor landing, a case of Gulf War exhibits is already in place, while the first floor is jammed with material relating to the First and Second World Wars—paintings, models of a trench and the battlefield at Verdun, and one of Krupp's three Big Berthas for the First, for the Second an electric map of the allies' invasion campaign, items from Vichy, the Free French and the Resistance, an original copy of *Mein Kampf* and harrowing photos from the concentration camps. The horrors of war must have seemed depressing to the staff, for this floor is enlivened with piped-in music so inappropriate that the exhibits take on a surreal quality: Sousa marches, Offenbach's *Gaieté Parisienne* and, most incredibly, Wagner's *Flight of the Valkyries*.

The recently rearranged top floor, under the massive joists of the roof of the Invalides, houses the **Musée des Plans-Reliefs** (*same ticket*). Louis XIV began to collect these huge scale relief models of France's fortified cities and towns upon Louvois' advice in 1686—some, such as those of Perpignan and Strasbourg, fill entire rooms. The last models were made in 1870; until 1927 they were considered a military secret.

> *Save your ticket for the **Eglise-du-Dôme**, which requires a trek all the way around to the south; there's an overpriced snack bar west of the church if you desperately need sustenance (same hours as the Musée de l'Armée).*

Designed by Hardouin-Mansart and completed in 1706, the pointy dome is so impressive that the church itself is named after it, and so prominent on the Paris skyline that it was freshly gilded with 27½ lb of gold for the bicentennial of the Revolution (necessary after arch-thief Fantômas 'The Master of Fright' stripped it of its last gold, in Souvestre and Allain's popular romances). What most books on the Invalides omit is how closely the architect copied the dome of Ste-Anne-la-Royale, a Paris church begun in 1662 by Guarino Guarini, the master Baroque architect from Turin, but demolished in 1823.

Beneath his dome, Hardouin-Mansart designed a Greek cross plan, with radiating circular chapels, while the altar is yet another copy of St-Peter's baldachin. Although unusual, the interior leaves so cold an impression that in 1800 Napoleon made it a military pantheon, when he installed the remains of Louis XIV's Marshal Turenne (whom he admired for his strategy of surprise attacks). Perhaps Napoleon had an inkling that one day he himself would be the top-of-the-bill stiff in the pit.

'The future will tell whether it would not have been better if neither I nor Rousseau had ever lived,' Napoleon mused, although he himself had no doubt and compared his martyrdom on St Helena to that of Jesus Christ. The greatest main-chancer in history, responsible on his own estimate for the death of 1,700,000 Frenchmen, died on 21 May 1821, vomiting from stomach ulcers (caused either by the poisonous 'Paris green' in the plaster of his room or the fact that his French chef on St Helena retired, abandoning him to English cuisine. The question he asked on his deathbed, over and over again, was 'What is my son's name?'

Napoleon's wish, inscribed over the bronze doors to the crypt ('I wish to be buried on the banks of the Seine, in the midst of the people of France, whom I have loved so dearly') was imprudently granted by Louis-Philippe in 1840 as a bid to gain popularity (all it gained was unfavourable comparisons between the heady days of the Grande Armée and his own stolid bourgeois regime). Napoleon's body was fetched from St Helena by a committee headed by Louis-Philippe's son, the Prince of Joinville; before loading the coffin aboard ship the committee took a peek inside and were amazed to see old Boney 'perfectly intact' (although his toenails had grown through his boots). The official record omits the fact that somewhere along the way a souvenir-hound lopped off the imperial organ and pickled it—a shrivelled, inch-long curiosity that occasionally appears in London auctions. Still, the aura of Napoleon was so uncanny that, once the authorities had him back in Paris, they packaged him up as tight as possible in six coffins of mahogany, tin and lead, all fitted like Chinese boxes within an enormous 43ft by 21ft porphyry sarcophagus the colour of dried blood. The design of the tomb in the circular crypt is by Louis Visconti—by far the most restrained proposal submitted in the tomb competition.

Napoleon's last resting place exacerbates the ambiguity of his memory; 12 winged statues of Napoleonic Victories, who at their height should be playing basketball, guard his tomb, while the passage around the crypt displays a series of bas-reliefs of the dead man apotheosized as Caesar or Jupiter sententiously bragging of his accomplishments (the quotes are taken from the Las Cases memoirs written on St Helena), enough to make you want to spit on the holy of holies or burst out laughing. Politically, the French are grateful that Bonaparte's hatred of liberalism, contempt for democracy and obsession with patriotism and *la gloire* have survived only in France's far right wing. As a myth, however, he has a frightening resilience. Every successful dictator owes a debt to his innovations in self-serving propaganda and mass psychology, the better to manipulate, exploit and control millions of people. As a tribute from the 20th-century's master of the art, the remains of the King of Rome, or Napoleon II—the son whose name Napoleon couldn't remember—were transferred in 1940 from Vienna to the crypt, next to a marble and gold statue of his dad.

There are two other Bonapartes buried here; the chapel just to the right of the door holds Napoleon's big brother Joseph (1768–1844), the unhappy King of Naples and later of Spain, who after his abdication in 1813 spent the rest of his life in Bordentown, New Jersey. In the chapel to the left lies Napoleon's youngest and favourite brother Jérôme (1784–1860) who had American connections as well—he married Baltimore beauty Elizabeth Patterson, a marriage annulled by his imperial brother, who made him marry into royalty and become the King of Westphalia, where he was popularly known as the 'Merry Monarch'. In the far right-hand chapel, Marshal Foch (1851–1929), hero of the Battle of the Marne, has an impressive monument supported by eight soldiers.

*The park in front of the church is the one place where you might meet some of the 70 current residents, compared to the 6000 accommodated when the Invalides opened in 1674. And there's yet another museum to the west, facing Boulevard de La-Tour-Maubourg: the* **Musée de l'Ordre de la Libération** *(open 2–5, closed Mon and Aug; adm).*

Housed in an elegant residence built for officers, the museum houses items relating to the Ordre de la Libération, created by de Gaulle in 1940 to reward all who joined him. Other exhibits cover the Resistance and deportation.

*If you need an antidote to the Invalides, turn left in Avenue de Tourville just south, and then right into Boulevard des Invalides; cross it and turn left at Rue de Babylone, where at 57bis you can have a drink in the garden of* **La Pagode** *(open 4–10, Sun 2–8).*

This is last vestige of the craze that swept Paris after 1868, when Japan opened its ports to the West and exported the prints that fascinated Van Gogh, Degas and nearly every other artist working in Paris. This pagoda was built in 1896 as a *petite folie* by Mme Boucicaut, wife of the owner of Au Bon Marché; her receptions were so much in vogue that people would rent the balconies of adjacent flats to watch them through binoculars. Saved from destruction by film-director Louis Malle, the building now doubles as a cinema and a delightful tearoom.

> *The main walk continues to the right on Avenue de Tourville. If you're pressed for time carry straight on to Place de l'Ecole-Militaire—avoiding the half-mile walk around the **Ecole Militaire**, the second important classical complex on the Left Bank (take a left on Avenue de Lowendal).*

Although Louis XV took no interest whatsoever in the idea of a royal military academy, the real king of France, Mme de Pompadour, approved the idea in 1751. Beaumarchais contributed the idea of raising funds by taxing playing cards, and the plans for the school were confided to Jacques-Ange Gabriel, who created one of the most palatial barracks of all time; the Place de Fontenoy façade, with its colonnaded wings, its pediment, four massive Corinthian columns and steep roof fits squarely into the tradition begun by Perrault's Louvre. The star pupil was the Corsican in the porphyry box in the Invalides, who left in 1780, as an 18-year-old lieutenant of the artillery.

> *On warm afternoons, Paris' cabbies gather in Place de Fontenoy to play boules, waiting for fares from the surrounding ministeries or the headquarters of **UNESCO** (1958), the squabbling UN cultural agency.*

Designed by the Italian Nervi, Frenchman Zehrfuss and American Breuer, UNESCO is a big Y perched on stilts. Usually no one cares if you want to poke around in the lobbies to see the works by Picasso, Arp, Le Corbusier and Giacometti among others. At the east end there's a quiet Japanese garden by Noguchi; at the west, along Avenue de Suffren, there's a curious trapezoidal Assembly Hall, pleated like a concrete accordion, as well as a clanking mobile by Alexander Calder, a monumental *Figure en repos* by Henry Moore and a wall by Miró. If you tramp north up Avenue de Suffren, past the 19th-century annexes of the Ecole Militaire, you'll find on your left another relic from the 1900 Exhibition, the **Village Suisse**, now a village of antique dealers (*closed Tues and Wed*).

> *From either the Village Suisse or from Place de l'Ecole-Militaire, take Avenue de La Motte-Picquet to the north façade of the Ecole Militaire, facing the **Parc du Champ de Mars**.*

This front is more austere, but has the better view down the formal gardens of the Champ de Mars to the Seine and Eiffel Tower. Gabriel converted the space, originally market gardens, into a parade ground for the cadets. In 1780 it was open to the public, providing space for essential Parisian events such as balloon ascents and horse racing. On the first anniversary of Bastille Day in 1790, the Festival of Federation was held here, featuring Talleyrand and 300 priests chanting Mass while Lafayette and Louis XVI led the crowd in oaths of allegiance to France and its constitution. Four years later Robespierre staged his massive Festival of the Supreme Being, inaugurating the new state cult. In 1889, much of the Champ de Mars went under the roof of the extraordinary Galerie des Machines, the horizontal counterpart to the Eiffel Tower, a pavilion in iron measuring 1390ft by 380ft (demolished in 1910, an act Walter Benjamin labelled 'artistic sadism'). At this point your feet may be wishing that another marvel from the 1900 Exhibition was still in place: a rolling walkway that crossed the entire Champ de Mars.

> *Again, if you're in a hurry, walk straight on for Mr Eiffel's folly (see below); if not, spend some time exploring the 'goose foot' of streets between the Esplanade des Invalides and the Champ de Mars known as the Quartier Gros Caillou. Unlike the Faubourg St-Germain east of the Invalides, this didn't become a residential area until the mid-19th century; it has trees, shops and even a dollop of street life. Backtrack east up Avenue de La Motte-Picquet and take the second street on the left, pedestrian-only **Rue Cler**, the centre of Paris' most exclusive food market. From Rue Cler turn right in the quarter's other main shopping street, Rue St-Dominique; at no. 64 the Boulangerie Excelsior has kept its 1900 Art Nouveau décor by Benoist and a ceramic floral ceiling.*

> *From here Rue Surcouf leads to the **Musée de la SEITA** (open Mon–Fri 11–7; adm).*

Although Jean Nicot gave his name to nicotine in 1560, the first French cigarettes weren't made until the 19th century at the Tabacs de Gros Caillou, in a huge factory built over a farm once belonging to Beaumarchais. When the area became residential in 1905, only the administration building remained; the museum first opened for the 1937 Exposition. Exhibits cover the history of tobacco, smoking paraphernalia and the evolution of its social acceptance (Sir Walter Raleigh was once enjoying a pipe when his servant, thinking he was on fire, put him out with a bucket of water). There are frequent, excellent temporary exhibitions on subjects other than tobacco, often in conjunction with the Bibliothèque Nationale.

> *Return to Rue St-Dominique and head west; at no. 110 there's another ornate bakery (1896), this time in the Louis XV style. Further along is the **Fontaine de Mars** (1806), a charming neoclassical fountain, showing the Greek health goddess Hygeia in the form of a circus snake woman caring for Mars, an allusion to the military hospital that once stood here.*

*Almost opposite the fountain turn right in Rue Sédillot to see the exuberant* **Liceo Italiano** *with its circular door (no. 12), one of three buildings in the neighbourhood by Jules Lavriotte (1864–1928), Paris' craziest Art Nouveau architect. Follow Rue Sédillot down to Avenue Rapp and turn left for the even greater Lavriotte confection,* **no. 29,** *an apartment house built in 1903 that visually ambushes the unwary passer-by with its luxuriant, fluid stone, ceramics, and extraordinary detail (especially the nymph and dead poodle and the lizard-shaped door handle). After ravishing your eyes, you can ravish your tastebuds at the adjacent no. 27, the Chocolatier* **Puyricard,** *before continuing south to* **Square Rapp,** *with its lattice-work trompe l'oeil wall.*

Here Lavriotte shows himself to be the slightly indigestible precursor of Dr Seuss, his building sporting the quirkiest, crookedest tower in Paris, his asymmetrical balconies stretching over rows of children's faces all holding their breath. Opposite is the dusty Société Théosophique, founded in 1875 by Madame Blavatsky, the widow of a Russian general, and dedicated to studying the mysterious forces inside humankind and creating a universal fraternity guided by benevolent spirits. In 1908 the society's leader, Annie Besant, announced the reincarnation of Christ in a 13-year-old Hindu lad named Krishnamurti at the society's headquarters in Adyar, India. Krishnamurti eventually broke with the Theosophists; Yeats dallied with the sect and Rudolf Steiner joined, only to found a dissident group, Anthroposophy, in 1913. Theosophy still claims over a million members; its current leader claims to come from Venus.

*From here it's a short walk back up Avenue Rapp to the Seine and Place de la Résistance; at the corner of Quai d'Orsay is the entrance to Paris'* **Egouts,** *or sewers (open 11–6; Nov–Apr, 11–5, closed Thurs and Fri; adm).*

Although Baron Haussmann is best known for Paris' boulevards, he was personally more interested in the sewers, which he entrusted to an engineer named Belgrande; Paris, Haussmann realized, would never be a modern city as long as its inhabitants risked being washed away in open sewers on rainy days. Victor Hugo, in his long digression on Paris' intestines in *Les Misérables*, gave these drains a peculiar romance to match their aroma, and ever since the World Fair of 1867 visitors have descended to the sewers (1274 miles), originally to be pulled along in little torchlit wagons. These were replaced by boats, which since 1972 have been replaced by a silly film, a museum and a stroll along the edge of a smelly sewer. It's reassuring to learn that this humid underworld has its own street signs corresponding to the ones above, in case you ever fall down one of the 26,000 manholes.

*Place de la Résistance gives onto the **Pont de l'Alma**, built in 1856 to commemo-*

*rate Napoleon III's victory in the Crimea. Its flamboyant Zouave, the only survivor of the original four stone soldiers who guarded the span, is Paris' flood gauge; in January 1910 the worst overflowing of the Seine in memory tickled his beard.*

*From here head west along Quai Branly. The pile across the river is the 1937 Fair's Palais de Tokyo (see below), while stretching up unavoidably in your path is the incomparable souvenir of the 1889 Fair, the **Eiffel Tower**, built to celebrate the Revolution's centenary and the resurrection of France after her defeat in 1870. It has also been the scene of 370 suicides and one birth (in a lift). (Open daily 9am–11pm for the first two platforms, until 8pm for the 3rd, adm exp.) Count on a good hour's wait for the lift to the first (20F), second (40F) and third platforms (56F). The tower draws nearly 5 million visitors a year, but think twice about the ascent if it's hazy. You even have to pay 12F to walk up as far as the second platform.*

Derided over the last hundred years as 'a suppository', 'a giraffe', 'a criminal, sinister pencil-sharpener', the Eiffel Tower is 300m (1000ft) of graceful iron filigree; belly-up between its four spidery paws, its 9700 tons may look menacing, but they sit with extraordinary lightness on the soft clay of Paris, exerting as much pressure as that of a man sitting in a chair (4kg per sq cm, or 57lb per sq in). It was erected in two years, for less than the estimated 8 million francs, welded together with 2,500,000 rivets and built without a single fatal work accident. Until surpassed in 1930 by the Chrysler Building in New York, it was the highest structure in the world. Originally the tower was painted several tints, lightening to yellow-gold at the top, so its appearance dissolved and changed according to the time of day and weather; now every five or six years, forty painters cover it with 7700lb of a sombre maroon colour called *ferrubrou*. On a very clear day, about an hour before sunset, the view from the third level (899ft) extends 50 miles into the environs of Paris. Sometimes the Parisians hold races up the 1652 vertiginous steps to the top.

In its day, such engineering daredevilry bent quite a few Parisians out of shape. Residents around the Champ de Mars feared it would fall on their heads (Eiffel took personal responsibility that it wouldn't). The artistic élite, led by Charles Gounod, Charles Garnier and Alexandre Dumas, signed a vitriolic petition against the profanation and dishonour of the capital; one signer, Guy de Maupassant, left Paris for good so as never to look upon its 'metallic carcass' again, insulted in his soul that the best his generation could produce resembled 'a factory chimney'.

The competition for the design of a 1000ft tower resulted in 700 proposals, including a giant lighthouse, a sprinkler to cool Paris off in August and a guillotine in memory of victims of the Terror. In the end a 'functionless' entry from the workshop of Gustave Eiffel was given the nod. Eiffel was already famous for his daring bridges and viaducts; in 1886 he had designed the structural frame of the Statue of Liberty, defying all the nay-sayers who said her arm would surely blow off. In return for building his '300-metre flagpole' as he called it, Eiffel was granted a 20-year concession (it paid for itself within a year) and a cosy office by the top platform that you can peek into through the window. When the tower reverted to the state in 1909, it was about to be destroyed when at last it found a practical use, as a meteorological station and wireless antenna. The latter played an important role in the First World War, especially after the Germans' code was broken in 1915; a series of mysterious messages about a certain 'H 21' led to the arrest and execution of Mata Hari, who only a few years back had performed her pseudo-Javanese dances in the first platform's restaurant. For the 1925 Exposition des Arts Décoratifs, André Citroën paid to make the Eiffel Tower the world's largest advertising sign. In 1986 sodium lamps were installed in the structure; it's usually lit up until midnight, but if you want to impress somebody you can keep it on all night by footing the electric bill (for information, ℂ 01 44 11 23 23).

The Eiffel Tower has proved a litmus test of modernity. Georges Seurat painted it soon after it was built, anarchists tried to blow it up, Hitler saw it and sniffed 'Is that all?' In a city as self-contemplative as Paris, it has been the subject of volumes of poetry and speculation; Roland Barthes was fascinated by it as a structure that was nothing but metaphor, a symbol 'in the grand itineraries of dream' of nothing and everything at the same time, of communication, science, the 19th century, a rocket, a phallus, a lightning conductor, an insect. In 1924, René Clair may have had the last word in his film *Paris qui Dort*, in which an evil spell puts the whole world to sleep—except for a handful of people visiting the top of the Eiffel Tower.

> *From here, continue at your pleasure—there's nothing more on this walk but museums. From the tower, cross the* **Pont d'Iéna**, *commissioned by Napoleon I after his victory at Jena in Prussia and decked out with proud Imperial eagles; in 1815, Blücher, in charge of the Prussian allies in Paris, found it so irritating that he ordered it blown to bits. 'If you do,' retorted Louis XVIII, 'I will have my sedan chair carried to the middle of it, and be blown up with it.' During the World Fair, the bridge groaned with crowds going between the Champ de Mars and the* **Jardins du Trocadéro**.

A medieval village named Chaillot once stood on this hill, around a Palais de Chaillot that plunged its toes into the Seine. In the mid-16th century Catherine de' Medici replaced it with a summer retreat; this was purchased by a companion in arms of Henri IV, the Maréchal de Bassompierre, a famous gambler and Don Juan. In 1631 Bassompierre got on the wrong side of Richelieu and was ordered off to the Bastille, although he made his arresters wait as he gallantly burned 6000 love letters. The building was later acquired by Queen Henrietta Maria of England, who made it a convent, although the reputation of the philandering *maréchal* was such that the nuns were known as les Soeurs Bassompierre. Two of Louis XIV's flames, Maria Mancini (Mazarin's niece) and Mlle de la Vallière, took refuge here from the hot but unwanted attention of the Sun King—so unwanted in the case of the latter that she became a nun to avoid him.

Upon the birth of his son, Napoleon cleared everything off the hill and ordered his top Empire architects to create for the baby 'the largest and most extraordinary palace in the world' stretching to the Bois de Boulogne. The project collapsed with Napoleon, but inspired others as grandiose for the empty site—a life-size copy of Castel Sant'Angelo for Napoleon's tomb (the very idea is enough to make you appreciate the Invalides), a triumphal arch in honour of Napoleon III's victories in Italy, a war monument by visionary architect Tony Garnier in 1920. No government stayed in power long enough to accomplish anything, until a Palais de Chaillot curved like a Colosseum with minarets was built for the 1878 World Fair.

The name Trocadéro is derived from the French capture of the fort of Trocadéro near Cádiz in 1823, a battle that helped restore a diehard reactionary government in democratic Spain. The gardens stretching down to the Seine were laid out for the 1878 fair and restored in 1937; today they are home to a 1900s carrousel and the fattest, most complacent colony of stray cats in all Paris. In the central pool are **fountains** that dance in vertical columns. On the Bastille Day the gardens blaze with fireworks.

*Unlike the 1867 **Palais de Chaillot**, its 1937 replacement has a terrace in its middle, offering a superb view across the Champ de Mars.*

In 1937 the Palais was one of the World Fair's chief works in *Art Moderne*, the clean but often dull successor of Art Deco, influenced in Europe by Italian fascist neoclassicism but made sublime in the New York World Fair in 1939. The giant sententious epigrams in gold letters wrapped around the building were composed by Paul Valéry. Underneath the terrace is the **Théâtre National de Chaillot**, where France's great postwar director, Jean Vilar, formed the first Théâtre National with actors such as Jeanne Moreau and Gérard Philippe, before setting up the Avignon Festival. Vilar's enthusiasm motivated an entire generation of French theatre-lovers, but his spartan sets and costumes stand in direct contrast with the later director, the late Antoine Vitez, a founding father of the Parisian school of virtuoso designer-drama spectaculars.

*Across the terrace on Place du Trocadéro are the entrances to the Palais de Chaillot's four museums. The oldest, in the east wing, is the **Musée des Monuments Français**, perhaps the most undervisited museum in Paris (open 10–6, closed Tues; adm).*

Viollet-le-Duc had the idea of creating a central collection of exact, lifesize copies of France's finest architectural features, sculptures and mural paintings from the early Romanesque period to the 19th century. The result was first exhibited at the 1889 World Fair; over the years the collection has grown to 2000 replicas, all arranged to help you study the evolution of French art and architecture.

*Walk through the vast lobby and the middle of the monuments museum to reach the **Musée du Cinéma** downstairs (open daily except Tues, 2-hour guided tours in French at 10, 11, 2, 3, 4 and 5; adm). At the end of 1997 it has to move—perhaps to the Palais de Tokyo.*

Dedicated to Henri Langlois, founder of the Cinémathèque, the museum only has room to display 3000 items—a mere 10 per cent of its material. The collection was the inspiration for London's Museum of the Moving Image, although it isn't half as much fun for dilettantes because nothing here actually, well, moves. But cineastes will love the archive material dating back to the Lumière brothers and Georges Méliès, who in his studios in Meudon cranked out 500 films and pioneered special effects; exhibits include his moonman from the 1902 *Voyage dans la Lune*, a reproduction of the German Expressionist set of *The Cabinet of Dr Caligari*, Olivia de Havilland's gown from *Gone with the Wind*, posters, models, sets, cameras and projectors. Although the tour is compulsory, the guides are fairly liberal about letting you wander about. The tour leaves you at the end of the east wing, near the **Cinémathèque** film library, which, like its counterpart at Beaubourg, screens several vintage flicks daily except Monday.

*In the west wing, you will find the **Musée de l'Homme** (open daily except Tues 9.45–5.15; adm). This, too, is slated for big changes; part of the collection is going into the Louvre, and part may be sold by late '97.*

This excellent anthropology museum, opened the year after the 1937 World Fair, offers lots of dusty display cases and long explanations in French of things you never dreamed existed. The temporary exhibitions can be fun (like the recent one demonstrating how we are all at least sixteenth cousins to everybody else on Earth) but the best part is the gallery of **African cultural anthropology**, with fascinating exhibits on the life and architecture of the rather mysterious Dogon of the Sahel (who told anthropologist Marcel Griaule lots of things he didn't know about astronomy), a facsimile of the 1858 Royal Palace façade of King Gleté of Dahomey, and brilliant art from all over the continent. Other galleries contain excellent artefacts from Australian and New Zealand aborigines, Eskimo ivories, jewellery from Yemen, kites from Malaysia, bagpipes from Scotland ...

*You'll also find the **Musée de la Marine** (open daily ex Tues 10–6; adm).*

Haughty Brits may sneer, but France has its own proud tradition on the sea, and you'll get an extra helping of it here. As you might expect, gloriously detailed ship models make up the bulk of the exhibits: Cousteau's *Calypso*, the carrier *Clemenceau*, pride of the modern French fleet, a room-sized 120-gun *L'Océan* from Napoleon's time, and on and on. Historical reconstructions enable you to see how an ancient Roman galley or a Renaissance galeass looked and worked. There are carved wooden figureheads, entire ships, such as Napoleon's gilded state barge of 1810, Joseph Vernet's 18th-century series of paintings on the ports of France, and another series Louis XVIII had commissioned on the naval battles of the War of American Independence. Don't miss the collection of old navigational instruments, and numerous compasses, all pointing in different directions.

*Take your life into your hands and manoeuvre through the traffic to the west side of Place du Trocadéro for the **Cimetière de Passy**.*

Like other Parisian cemeteries it has its celebrities—Edouard Manet and Berthe Morisot, the horse-faced Fernandel, Debussy, Gabriel Fauré and Jean Giraudoux, who probably enjoys his posthumous view of the Eiffel Tower. But as usual it's the unknowns who have the most memorable memorials: a copy of Michelangelo's *Pietà* encased in plexiglass; the powerful sculpture on the tomb of a painter named Cierplikowski.

*Opposite Place du Trocadéro, walk up Avenue du Président-Wilson to Place d'Iéna, with an equestrian statue of George Washington for a centrepiece, a gift to Paris from the Daughters of the American Revolution. On the corner of Rue Boissière, at no. 6 is the **Musée Guimet**, which will regrettably be closed for restorations until the end of 1998.*

Founded in 1879 by an industrialist from Lyon, Emile Guimet, this is one of the world's richest collections of art from India, China, Japan, Indochina, Indonesia and central Asia. The collection of Khmer art from the 8th century to the mid-12th (the period of Angkor Wat and meditative smiles) is the best outside Cambodia. There are magnificent bronzes and shadow puppets from Java, paintings from Nepal and Tibet, Chinese ivories from as far back as the 17th century BC and a superb collection of lacquer ware; masterpieces from India include the torso of the King Serpent of Mathoura (2nd century AD) and a Cosmic Dance of Shiva. The fascinating **Salle Hackin** proves ancient commercial and artistic links between East and West in Hellenistic times, producing some charming, sensual works—(*Préparatifs du Grand Départ*). On the top floor are works from Japan (a

17th-century screen showing the arrival of the Portuguese), a 3rd-century Korean crown, and a collection of Chinese ceramics from the Han dynasty to the Ming.

> *Until it reopens you can visit the annexe, the **Panthéon Bouddique**, in a town house at 19 Avenue d'Iéna (open daily exc Tues 9.45–6, adm).*

The Panthéon hold Guimet's unique collection of Buddhas and figures of the Six Hierarchies from Japan and China, dating back to the 6th century. Afterwards, you can put your feet up in the peaceful Japanese garden in the back.

> *From Place d'Iéna, walk up Avenue Pierre-1er-de-Serbie for the pseudo-Italian-Renaissance **Palais Galliera** (1894), built to house the 17th-century Italian art that the Duchess of Galliera meant to donate to Paris, until she changed her mind and gave it to Genoa instead. Paris did get the palace, however, and since 1977 uses it for the **Musée de la Mode et Costume** (open except Mon 10–5.45; adm).*

Because of space and the fragility of its 16,000 piece collection, the museum devotes its entirety to two exhibitions a year, either by designer, period or theme.

> *From here, backtrack to Rue Brignole and cross Avenue du Président-Wilson for the last stop on this marathon walk, the **Palais de Tokyo**, housing the **Musée d'Art Moderne de la Ville de Paris** (entrance at the east end; open except Mon 10–5.30, until 7 Sat and Sun; adm).*

The palace was built for the 1937 World Fair on the site of the old Savonnerie carpet factory (now at the Gobelins, *see* Walk IX, p.265), and in the manner of the Palais de Chaillot it is split into two for the view, linked by a portico of white stone; terraces descend to the Seine, decorated with a reflecting pool and mega-bronzes by Bourdelle, dominated by his towering *Allegory of France* (1948).

At the entrance is nothing short of 'the largest picture in the world', made for the Light Pavilion of the 1937 fair: Raoul Dufy's *La Fée Electricité*, 250 panels covering 6,095 sq ft, depicting all the great philosophers and scientists who studied it, and all the magic the electric fairy has performed for humanity. Beyond, nearly all the artistic movements of the 20th century get their say, although in quality rarely soaring to the level of the Pompidou Centre—but don't miss the Fauves and Matisse's enormous *La Danse* (1932), a preliminary work for his masterpiece in Meryon, Pennsylvania; the colourful abstract *Rhythms* of Robert and Sonia Delaunay; Rouault's prostitutes from the turn of the century; Bonnard's lovely *Nu dans le bain* (1937); and, among the Surrealists, the curious enlaced bodies of the white plaster *Conglomeros* (1944) by Victor Brauner, a Romanian who lived in Paris.

> *The Paris of the World Fairs and endless museums ends here. Stagger three blocks east to the nearest cafés and the métro station, in Place de l'Alma.*

# Museums

Paris is a museum junkie's dream city with something for all tastes, from the mega Louvre to the micro Edith Piaf collection of shoes and memorabilia in a room in someone's flat. The following list should help you find what you crave, and where it's located in the text. Opening hours often change with the season: longer summer hours usually begin in May or June and last through September. Admission charges range from 10–40F. Note, however, that many museums offer reduced admissions on Sundays and after 3.30 and sliding fees for other days—one price (often free) for under 18 years, another for 18–25-year-olds, another for EU citizens over 60 and a heftier charge for everyone else. If you have to pay the full whack and mean to average more than two museums or monuments a day, consider a *Carte Musées et Monuments*, valid for one day (70F), three days (140F), or five consecutive days (200F), which can save both money and time waiting in queues. Purchase your pass at the museums, tourist offices or in the larger métro stations. Participating museums are marked with an asterisk in the listing below. One of these, the **Musée du Louvre**, defies all categorization: look for it on p.318.

## Painting and Sculpture

**Espace Montmartre Salvador Dalí** (*open daily*), see p.222.  *Abbesses* Ⓜ

*****Musée d'Art Moderne de la Ville de Paris**, 20th-century art (*closed Mon and holidays*), see p.310.  *Alma-Marceau* Ⓜ

**Musée d'Art Juif**, works by Jewish artists (*closed Fri and Sat and Aug*), see p.221.  *Lamarck-Caulaincourt* Ⓜ

**Musée d'Art Naïf Max Fourny**, naïf paintings (*open daily*), see p.224.
*Anvers* Ⓜ

*****Musée Antoine Bourdelle**, sculptures by Bourdelle (*closed Mon*), see p.376.
*Montparnasse-Bienvenüe* Ⓜ

*****Musée Delacroix**, works by Delacroix in his home and studio, *see* p.285.
*St-Germain-des-Prés* Ⓜ

**Musée Jacquemart-André**, Italian Renaissance and French painting, by appointment only (*closed Mon*), see p.192.  *Saint-Philippe-du-Roule* Ⓜ

*****Musée Départmental Maurice Denis-La Prieuré**, Symbolist and Nabis paintings (*closed Mon and Tues*), see p.352.  *St-Germain-en-Laye* RER A

**Musée Gustave Moreau,** Symbolist femme fatales, *see* p.352.  *St-Georges* Ⓜ

**Musée Maillol-Fondation Dina-Vierny,** sculptures by Maillol (*closed Tues and hols*), *see* p.288. *Rue du Bac* Ⓜ

**Musée Marmottan,** 19th-century art, especially Monet (*closed Mon*), *see* p.347. *La Muette* Ⓜ

\***Musée National d'Art Moderne,** 20th-century art in the Pompidou Centre (*closed Tues*), *see* p.158. *Châtelet-les-Halles* Ⓜ

\***Musée National des Monuments Français,** casts of French scupture and architecture (*closed Tues*), *see* p.307. *Trocadéro* Ⓜ

\***Musée National de l'Orangerie des Tuileries,** Impressionist paintings (*closed Tues*), *see* p.200. *Concorde* Ⓜ

\***Musée d'Orsay,** all aspects of late 19th-century art (*closed Mon*), *see* p.335. *Solférino* Ⓜ

\***Musée du Petit Palais,** hodgepodge of mostly 19th-century art that the Orsay didn't want (*closed Mon and hols*), *see* p.205.
*Champs-Elysées-Clemenceau* Ⓜ

\***Musée Picasso,** Picasso in a 17th-century mansion (*closed Tues*), *see* p.130. *St-Sébastien-Froissart* Ⓜ

\***Musée Rodin,** Rodin's sculptures (*closed Mon*), *see* p.295. *Varenne* Ⓜ

**Musée de la Sculpture en plein air,** outdoor sculpture (*always open*), *see* p.260. *Austerlitz* Ⓜ

\***Musée Zadkine,** Zadkine's sculptures (*closed Mon*) *see* p.378. *Notre-Dame-des-Champs* Ⓜ

## Historical

**Cabinet des Médailles et des Antiques,** treasures of the kings of France (*open daily*), *see* p.177. *Bourse* Ⓜ

\***Musée des Antiquités Nationales,** palaeolithic to Merovingian France (*closed Tues*), *see* p.352. *St-Germain-en-Laye* RER A

\***Musée Carnavalet,** history of Paris (*closed Mon*), *see* p.127. *St-Paul* Ⓜ

**Musée de l'Histoire de France,** in the National Archives, documents on French history (*closed Tues and holidays*), *see* p.132. *Rambuteau* Ⓜ

\***Musée National du Moyen Age–Thermes de Cluny,** medieval art starring the Lady and the Unicorn tapestries (*closed Tues*), *see* p.241. *Cluny-La Sorbonne* Ⓜ

**\*Musée de la Vie Romantique**, George Sand and Romanticism
(*closed Mon and holidays*), *see* p.352. St-Georges Ⓜ

**Musée de Montmartre**, neighbourhood memorabilia
(*closed Mon*), *see* p.221. Lamarck-Caulaincourt Ⓜ

## Military

**\*Musée de l'Armée**, military collections and Napoleon's tomb in the Invalides
(*open daily*), *see* p.298. Varenne Ⓜ

**\*Mémorial du Maréchal Leclerc et de la Libération de Paris–Musée Jean
Moulin**, the history of the resistance and liberation (*closed Mon*),
*see* p.375. Gaîté Ⓜ

**\*Musée de la Marine**, history of French navy, ship models
(*closed Tues*), *see* p.309. Trocadéro Ⓜ

**Musée de l'Ordre de la Libération**, the liberation of France in the Second
World War, *see* p.301. Latour-Maubourg Ⓜ

**\*Musée de la Légion d'Honneur**, medals and awards from around the world
(*closed Mon*), *see* p.294. Solférino Ⓜ

**\*Musée des Plans-Reliefs** in the Invalides, 19th-century fortress models
(*open daily*), *see* p.299. Varenne Ⓜ

## Monuments and Subterranean Paris

**\*Arc de Triomphe**, the monument and its history
(*open daily*), *see* p.207. Charles de Gaulle Ⓜ

**\*Basilique St-Denis**, the first Gothic church anywhere and last resting place of
the kings of France (*open daily*), *see* p.355. St Denis-Basilique Ⓜ

**Catacombes**, 5 million dead Parisians
(*closed Mon*), *see* p.372. Denfert-Rochereau Ⓜ

**\*Château de Vincennes**, former royal residence and prison
(*open daily*), *see* p.365. Château de Vincennes Ⓜ

**\*Conciergerie**, prison of the Revolution (*open daily*), *see* p.98. Cité Ⓜ

**\*Crypte de Notre-Dame**, Roman and medieval finds
(*open daily*), *see* p.110. Cité Ⓜ

**Grande Arche de La Défense**, immense views
(*open daily*), *see* p.211. La Défense Ⓜ

\***Musée des Egouts de Paris**, Paris' sewers
(*closed Thurs and Fri*), *see* p.304.  *Alma-Marceau* Ⓜ

\***Panthéon**, (*open daily*), *see* p.249.  *Cardinal Lemoine* Ⓜ

\***Sainte Chapelle** (*open daily*), *see* p.99.  *Cité* Ⓜ

\***Tours Notre-Dame**, towers of Notre-Dame, *see* p.109.  *Cité* Ⓜ

## Science, Medecine and Technology

\***Cité des Sciences et de l'Industrie– La Villette**, science and technology
(*closed Mon*), *see* p.357.  *Porte-de-la-Villette* Ⓜ

\***Conservatoire des Arts et Métiers**, machines and inventions
(*closed Mon*), Rue St-Martin, 3ᵉ  *Réaumur-Sébastopol* Ⓜ

**Musée de l'Histoire de la Médecine**, evolution of medicine
(*closed Thurs and Sun*), *see* p.272.  *Odéon* Ⓜ

**Musée d'Histoire Naturelle**, several branches in the Jardin des Plantes include
Paleontology, Evolution, Anatomy, Mineralogy, Geology, Botany
(*all closed Tues*), *see* p. 258.  *Austerlitz* Ⓜ

**Musée de l'Assistance Publique**, history of hospitals and social welfare
(*closed Mon, Sun and Aug*), *see* p.245.  *Maubert-Mutualité* Ⓜ

**Musée de Minéralogie**, gems and minerals
(*closed Mon and Sun*), *see* p.252.  *Cluny-La Sorbonne* Ⓜ

**Musée Minéralogique de l'Université Pierre et Marie Curie**, gems and
minerals (*open Wed and Sat only*), *see* p.252  *Jussieu* Ⓜ

**Palais de la Découverte**, hands on science
(*closed Mon*), *see* p.205.  *Champs-Elysées-Clemenceau* Ⓜ

## Temporary Exhibitions

**Fondation Cartier pour l'Art Contemporain,** 261 Blvd Raspail, international
contemporary art exhibits (*open 12–8pm, adm, closed Mon*)  *Raspail* Ⓜ

**Fondation Dapper**, temporary exhibits of African art, *see* p.351. *Victor-Hugo* Ⓜ

**Galerie Nationale du Jeu de Paume**, changing exhibitions
(*closed Mon*), *see* p.199.  *Concorde* Ⓜ

**Grand Palais**, blockbuster shows (*closed Tues*), *see* p. 204.  *Champs-Elysées* Ⓜ

**Musée de Luxembourg,** state sponsored exhibits in the Senate
(*closed Mon*), *see* p.281.  *Luxembourg* RER

## Design and Decorative Arts

**Manufacture Nationale des Gobelins**, tapestry factory
(*open Tues, Wed, and Thurs afternoons*), *see* p.265. *Gobelins* Ⓜ

**Fondation Le Corbusier**, two houses by the architect
(*closed Sat and Sun*), *see* p.349. *Jasmin* Ⓜ

*****Musée Cognacq-Jay**, 18th-century decorative arts
(*closed Mon*), *see* p.133. *St-Paul* Ⓜ

*****Musée des Arts Décoratifs**, medieval to 20th-century furnishings, etc.
(*closed Mon and Tues*), *see* p.334. *Palais-Royal* Ⓜ

**Musée des Arts de la Mode et du Textile**, 16th–20th-century fashions
(*closed Mon and Tues*), *see* p.335. *Tuileries* Ⓜ

**Musée Baccarat**, crystal glass and chandeliers
(*closed Sun*), *see* p.353. *Poissonière* Ⓜ

**Musée de la Mode et du Costume**, French fashion
(*closed Mon*), *see* p.310. *Alma-Marceau* Ⓜ

*****Musée National de la Céramique**, Sèvres St Cloud, porcelain and ceramics
from around the world (*closed Tues*) *Pont-de-Sèvres* Ⓜ

*****Musée Nissim de Camondo**, 18th-century decorative arts
(*closed Mon and Tues*), *see* p.193. *Villiers* Ⓜ

## Famous People

*****Maison de Balzac**, Balzac ephemera (*closed Mon*), *see* p.347 *La Muette* Ⓜ

**Musée Georges Clemenceau**, all about Clemenceau
(*closed Mon, Wed, Fri and Aug*), *see* p.347. *Passy* Ⓜ

**Musée Edith Piaf**, on the Little Sparrow
(*closed Fri, Sat, Sun and hols*). *see* p.361. *Ménilmontant* Ⓜ

**Musée Lénine**, on Lenin's Paris years
(*by appointment only*), *see* p.369. *Alésia* Ⓜ

**Musée Pasteur**, Pasteur's life, work and tomb
(*closed Sat, Sun, hols and Aug*), *see* p.379. *Pasteur* Ⓜ

*****Maison de Victor Hugo**, all about you-know-who
(*closed Mon and holidays*), *see* p.127 *Chemin-Vert* Ⓜ

## World Art and Ethnographic Collections

\***Musée Cernuschi**, Chinese art (*closed Mon*), *see* p.193.  *Monceau* Ⓜ

\***Musée d'Ennery**, Far Eastern art
(*open Thurs and Sun only, closed Aug*), *see* p.351.  *Porte Dauphine* Ⓜ

\***Musée Guimet des Arts Asiatiques**, major oriental art
(*closed Tues*), *see* p.309.  *Trocadéro* Ⓜ

**Musée de l'Homme**, world wide ethnographic exhibits
(*closed Tues*), *see* p.308.  *Trocadéro* Ⓜ

\***Musée de l'Institut du Monde Arabe**, Arab and Muslim art
(*closed Mon*), *see* p.260.  *Jussieu* Ⓜ

\***Musée National des Arts d'Afrique et d'Océanie**, art from Africa, the
Maghreb, Oceania and a tropical aquarium (*closed Tues*), *see* p.364.
*Porte Dorée* Ⓜ

\***Musée National des Arts et Traditions Populaires**, ethnographic collections
on old France (*closed Tues*), *see* p.350.  *Sablons* Ⓜ

## One-offs

**Musée des Arts Forains,** 50 Rue de l'Eglise, reconstruction of a fun fair
*c.* 1890 (*open Sat and Sun 2–7pm*), *see* p.380.  *Félix Faure* Ⓜ

**Musée de l'Automobile,** 1 Place du Dôme, Colline de La Défense, historic collection of mostly French cars and auto memorabilia (*open daily 12–7,
until 9pm Sat*), *see* p.212.  *Grande Arche de La Défense* Ⓜ

**Musée de la Contrefaçon,** counterfeiting (*open Mon, Wed and Fri*),
*see* p.351.  *Porte Dauphine* Ⓜ

**Musée de la Curiosité et de la Magie,** 11 Rue Saint-Paul, historical items
related to magic, games and demonstrations of conjuring tricks (*open Wed,
Sat and Sun 2–4*), *see* p.317.  *St-Paul* Ⓜ

**Musée de la Franc-Maçonnerie,** French freemasonry
(*closed Sun and hols*), *see* p.180.  *Cadet* Ⓜ

**Musée Grévin,** wax museum (*open daily*), *see* p.179.  *Rue Montmartre* Ⓜ

**Le Grévin Forum,** wax museum evoking Paris' *belle époque*
(*open daily*), *see* p.153.  *Les Halles* Ⓜ

**Musée de la Chasse et da la Nature,** hunting
(*closed Tues and Sun*), *see* p.132.  *Hôtel-de-Ville* Ⓜ

**Musée de l'Histoire du Protestantisme Français**, French Protestantism
(*closed Sat and Mon*), *see* p.287.                           *St-Germain-des-Prés* Ⓜ

**Musée Fragonard de la Parfumerie**, 9 Rue Scribe, old and famous perfumes
and bottles (*open 9.30–2.30*), *see* p.318.                              *Opéra* Ⓜ

**Musée des Lunettes et des Lorgnettes de Jadis**, spectacles
(*closed Sun, Mon and holidays*), *see* p.347.                       *La Muette* Ⓜ

*****Musée du Cinéma Henri Langlois**, history of cinema
(*closed Mon, Tues and holidays*), *see* p.308.                     *Trocadéro* Ⓜ

**Musée Galerie de la Seita**, tobacco history and artefacts
(*closed Sun and Mon*), *see* p.303.                                 *Invalides* Ⓜ

**Musée d'Histoire de la Préfecture de Police**, crime and punishment
in Paris (*closed Sun*), *see* p.244–5.                    *Maubert-Mutualité* Ⓜ

**Musée Mickiewicz**, Polish émigrés (*open Thurs*), *see* p.116.    *Pont Marie* Ⓜ

*****Musée de la Monnaie**, history of money (*closed Mon*), *see* p.274.  *St-Michel* Ⓜ

*****Musée de la Musique**, musical instruments, at the Cité de Musique at
La Villette (*closed Mon*), *see* p.359.                       *Porte de Pantin* Ⓜ

**Musée de l'Opéra**, opera memorabilia (*open daily*), *see* p.186.     *Opéra* Ⓜ

*****Musée de la Poste**, postal museum
(*closed Tues and holidays*), *see* p.376.        *Montparnasse-Bienvenüe* Ⓜ

**Musée de Radio France**, history of French radio and TV
(*closed Sun and holidays*), *see* p.347.                         *Ranelagh* Ⓜ

**Musée de la Serrure** (or Musée Bricard), antique locks, keys, knockers
(*closed Sat, Sun and holidays*), *see* p.130.                       *St-Paul* Ⓜ

**Musée du Vin**, wine (*open daily*), *see* p.347.                      *Passy* Ⓜ

**Pavillon de l'Arsenal**, Paris plans and projects
(*closed Mon and holidays*), *see* p.318.                     *Sully-Morland* Ⓜ

## Musée du Louvre

Here it is, the delicious, often indigestible 99-course feast that sooner or later all visitors to Paris must swallow. 'Biggest Museum in the World' they call it, certain they have surpassed the Vatican, the Smithsonian, the British Museum and the other monsters. It isn't even as big as it used to be, for all post-1848 art has been moved to the Musée d'Orsay. Risking total exhaustion, it can be done in a day if you concentrate on the highlights and do not follow your fancy too far. For a good look at everything, expect two full days or a lifetime.

*Open daily except Tues, 9–6; Mon and Wed evenings until 9.45 (Wed evenings everything is open; Mon evenings Richelieu wing only). Admission is half-price on Sundays and after 3pm; under 18, free adm. At weekends or on any day in summer, come early to avoid the long queues. For details on which rooms are closed on any given day © 01 40 20 51 51.*

---

## A Palace by the Seine

'Louvre' was the name of the area long before any palaces were dreamt of. The best guess anyone has to the origin of the name is 'leper colony', though historical evidence is lacking. The original castle was built some time after 1190 by Philippe-Auguste, perfecting his new city fortifications by protecting against attacks from up-river. Charles V rebuilt and extended it in the 1360s, after the revolt of Etienne Marcel taught him the value of having a well-fortified residence in turbulent Paris. During the worst of the Hundred Years' War, 1400–1430, the kings abandoned the Louvre and Paris, spending their time in the Marais or among the châteaux of the Loire valley. The first to return was François I, in 1527; he demolished the old castle and began what is known today as the *Vieux Louvre*, the easternmost part of the complex, in 1546. François, a great patron of the arts, contributed more than anyone to building the Louvre's picture collection, the 'Cabinet du Roi'. Two works by his friend Leonardo da Vinci, the *Mona Lisa* and *Virgin of the Rocks*, originally hung in the royal bathroom.

After Henri II was accidently killed in a tournament at his residence in the Marais (*see* Walk II, p.126), his widow Catherine de' Medici decided to forsake east Paris; not caring for the half-completed Louvre, however, she commissioned Philibert de l'Orme, the greatest French Renaissance architect, to start yet another palace just to the west—the great *Tuileries* (1563; named after a tile works on the site). Catherine also began a long, stately gallery on the banks of the Seine, the present south wing, to connect the Tuileries with the Vieux Louvre. Unfortunately an old sorceress friend of Catherine's told her she would die in the Tuileries, and the most superstitious of all queens abandoned the works in 1572.

Henri IV, Louis XIII and Louis XIV all contributed in turn to the palace. Henri began the custom of housing artists in the Louvre, which continued until Napoleon booted the last of them out in 1806; among those enjoying room and board at the kings' expense were Boucher, Fragonard and David. When Louis XIV abandoned the Louvre for Versailles in 1682, however, the palace fell on hard times. Louis rented out the rooms to just anyone, and the place was in such bad shape by the 1750s that there was talk of tearing it down.

The next royal resident, however unwilling, was Louis XVI, brought here by force from Versailles in October 1789 and installed in the Tuileries, where the National

Assembly could keep a close eye on him. From here the royal family began its ill-fated flight to Varennes in June 1791. In June 1792 the Paris mob attacked the Tuileries and put a liberty cap on the frightened king's head, making him drink to the Revolution. Two months later, when it became clear that Louis was plotting with the *émigrés* to overthrow the Revolution, the mob came back in earnest, besieging and finally taking the Tuileries, massacring hundreds of the king's Swiss Guards after they surrendered.

Republican governments kept their offices in the Tuileries after 1795; they consolidated the art collections and made them into a public museum in 1793. Napoleon moved in in 1800, and started work on the northern wing. During the next 15 years, his men looted the captive nations of Europe for their finest paintings and statues, most of which ended up here. The picture of Napoleon as a sensitive art connoisseur is one of the sillier by-products of the Napoleonic myth. Like Hitler, Napoleon was a philistine, obsessed with art for the sake of status, and determined to make the Louvre—now the 'Musée Napoléon'—the greatest, perhaps the only, museum in the world. The allies made the French give most of the art back in 1815—though in a hundred towns, especially in Italy and Spain, people remember the stolen masterpieces that never found their way home.

The crowned heads of France chose to reside in the Tuileries from then on, though it brought them bad luck; out of five, only one (Louis XVIII) was allowed to finish his reign in peace. The last of them, Napoleon III, built more of the present Louvre than anyone else, including almost all the façades around the huge courtyards, the Cour Napoléon and Jardin du Carrousel. After his capture by the Prussians in the war of 1870, the people from the Paris provisional government inspecting the Tuileries were shocked, finding the Emperor's pleasure-palace 'more like a brothel than a royal residence'. Public indignation over the exposés of life at the Tuileries contributed much to the onset of the Commune—and to the failure of monarchists to interest anyone in finding a new king after 1871. During the 'Bloody Week' of the repression of the Commune, the Tuileries was burned to the ground by a Communard officer; the rest of the Louvre nearly went with it.

It's been a quiet palace since. In 1981, his first year in office, President Mitterrand decided to shake it a up a bit with the *Projet du Grand Louvre*, a total refurbishing of the palace, museum and the adjacent Tuileries gardens. First the cars were chased out of the courtyards, which had become shabby parking lots. Then the Pyramid and the new museum lobby beneath it were begun. The entire north wing, which had housed the Ministry of Finance, was cleared to expand the museum space, and a giant underground car park and plush shopping mall was burrowed under the Jardin du Carrousel; the excavations uncovered remains of what was a very busy quarter in the 1500s, and also a stretch of Philippe-Auguste's city wall, which will be retained.

# A Tour of the Exterior

The Louvre was 350 years in the building, a veritable museum of French architecture. The best parts are the oldest. Start on the eastern end, on Rue de l'Amiral de Coligny. If you're fortunate enough to possess a 200F note (designed in the 1960s), take it out of your pocket and take a close look at it, and at the majestic **colonnade** (begun 1668) in front of you. These two artefacts mark the parameters of the French classical style. The key is in the decorative line, the graceful, precise line that you'll see in all the best work from the Renaissance up to the time of Napoleon, a line that draws familiar classical motifs in such a way as to make them forever French.

The architect was Claude Perrault, brother of Charles, the famous writer of fairy tales. After the Bernini fiasco, in which the most fashionable architect of the age was called from Italy and failed three times to create a design that satisfied the king or Colbert, the job was entrusted to a committee that included Lebrun, Le Vau, Perrault and others; the plan of Perrault, an amateur, won out, and no one ever regretted it. His ineffable colonnade has been slightly tampered with since; the relief on the pediment is from Napoleon's time, and the windows on the ground level replace Perrault's simple niches, perhaps intended for statues. The dry moat, part of the original design, was filled in the 1700s, a time when every sort of shack crowded around the walls of the abandoned Louvre. André Malraux, de Gaulle's Culture Minister, dug it up again for history's sake.

Walk under the central portal into the **Cour Carrée** (usually open when there's not a fashion show inside; otherwise try the side portals facing the Seine or Rue de Rivoli) and you will see a work as revolutionary in its time as the colonnade out front. The western side, the first to be completed, was a collaboration between architect Pierre Lescot and sculptor Jean Goujon (1546–70). Goujon's sculptural trim, anticipating the classical style, highlights a nervous, ultra-refined architectural composition well in tune with, and in some ways ahead of, the new Italian Mannerist architecture of the day. The architects of Louis XIV's time, who respected little of anything, at least respected this precocious work; Le Vau and Le Mercier completed the other three sides of the Cour Carrée in the 1640s to match it. Goujon's work can be seen framing the three round windows (west side): allegorical figures of 'abundance', 'war' and 'science'. On all four sides you can play the game of puzzling out the royal monograms built into the façades, from H, C and D on the original side for Henri II, Catherine de' Medici and Diane de Poitiers, the king's mistress; to LMT for Louis XIV and Marie-Thérèse.

The outer façades of the **north wing**, facing Rue de Rivoli, are contributions of Napoleon (right half, viewed from the street) and Napoleon III (left half); both lend much to the imperial dreariness of that street. As for the **south wing**, facing the

Seine, the left half is the beginning of Catherine de' Medici's long extension; its completion (right half) was done under Henri IV.

The Napoleons, with their symmetrical brains, naturally had to make the Louvre symmetrical too; between them they more than doubled the size of the palace, expanding the south wing and building the northern one to mirror it, levelling an entire quarter in the process. Before the Communards burned down the Tuileries, which connected the two long wings, the Louvre must have been the only place in the world where a king could take a walk around the block without leaving his house—a walk of over a mile. The Louvre's great courtyard, including the Place du Carrousel and the Cour Napoléon, could easily fit twelve Notre-Dame cathedrals inside. What else could fit inside this courtyard fit for an Emperor? The Empire State Building, on its side, or the Gare du Nord *and* the Gare de l'Est. You might hear the echo of Nero, after he had cleared a quarter of Rome for his Golden House: 'At last I am lodged like a man!'

## Arc du Carrousel

The burning of the Tuileries in 1871 made the Louvre's interior court a public affair—unfortunately, since it exposed to everyone's view one of the capital's greatest architectural embarrassments. Napoleon III's architects, Beaux-Arts sycophants to a man, were ordered to surpass the work of the Renaissance, and they replied with pastiche façades dripping with pointless statuary—all in cheap stone; the government is currently spending millions of francs to clean and restore it.

There was a Place du Carrousel, though much smaller, long before the Arc appeared; before a *carrousel* became a merry-go-round, the word meant a knightly tournament, involving races, jousts and even singing. In the Place's centre, the **Arc du Carrousel**, like the other monument Napoleon built to himself, the Vendôme column, is a mere copy, in this case of the Arch of Septimius Severus in the Roman Forum. The reliefs of Napoleon's army on its campaigns are done with remarkable verisimilitude, down to the buttons on the uniforms. On top, the Emperor placed the greatest prize of his career, the *quadriga* of four bronze horses he stole from St Mark's in Venice in 1805 (the Venetians nicked them from the Hippodrome in Constantinople in 1204; Constantine, who had placed them there, had stolen them either from Chios or Rome). In 1815 the allies made France give the famous ponies back. The current ones are copies; after 1815 an allegorical figure of the 'Restoration' was made for the chariot. A sculptural ensemble in bronze in the Jardin du Carrousel appears to represent a crack ladies' rugby team at practice. In fact these are a collection of separate **works by Aristide Maillol**, a wonderful turn-of-the-century, Catalan-French sculptor who started his career at age 40 and believed that any conceivable subject could be most effectively represented by female nudes of heroic proportions (he specialized in memorials of the First World War); the damsels represent 'the Night', 'Action in Chains' and 'Ile-de-France', among others.

## The Pyramid

For a simple geometric bagatelle, it has certainly generated a lot of talk. Ever since I. M. Pei's new entrance to the Louvre opened in 1988, the windier sort of Frenchmen have been on about it. *Le Figaro* calls the controversy a revival of the famous 17th-century literary battle, the 'Quarrel of the Ancients and Moderns'. For some traditionalists, it was the crowning atrocity of a period when Paris has been transformed out of recognition by metal and concrete monsters straight from science fiction. To others, it was a chilly, inhuman blast of rude geometry in the sacred precincts of art. Occultists, never lacking in Paris, point out with a smile that the Grand Axe that points from here to La Défense can be followed in the opposite direction back to the Great Pyramid of Giza; they also claim it is a secret solar temple, noting (correctly) that the Pyramid is made of exactly 666 panes of glass, the sum of the numbers in the Sun's magic square.

The Pyramid and the Hall Napoléon beneath it are *open until 9.45pm (except Tues)*, and that is the best time to come and see for yourself. Illuminated from inside it is undeniably beautiful, almost inspiring. Behind the glass, the supporting metal struts and cables make an intricate and delicate pattern, a marvel of intelligence and grace. An architecture that can be so provocative and so simple seems an advance of light years over the surrounding Second Empire buildings.

A lot of the ink that has been spilled deals with the architectural cliché of 'relating the building to the site', but Pei's problem was hardly one of respecting buildings around it. Pei himself was very discreet on the subject, but the most striking feature of his Pyramid is what seems to be an intentional contrast with the Louvre wings. Instead of the ponderous, pretentious Beaux-Arts, something light, almost immaterial. The most sophisticated technology available was employed (after four years of studies and calculations!) to let the aluminium mullions be as thin as possible—the entire Pyramid weighs only 88.5 tonnes (90 tons).

It cost Mitterrand some 90 million francs, which works out at 1100F a kilo—almost as much as some of the seafood platters at Fauchon's. But compared with some of the other budget-busters among the *grands projets*, that was a pittance. Some minor problems have occurred since the opening. Cleaning the glass, for one; no machine could manage it, and the Louvre has consulted alpine guides to devise a system of hooks and cables for the intrepid window-washers to do the job. And one thing every visitor is sure to notice—the Pyramid may be Art, but the world's largest museum now has only one entrance door, allowing us to enjoy waiting in *two* queues instead of just one.

# The Collections

Once through the door and down the long curving stairway, you are in the **Hall Napoléon**, where you can buy your ticket (*40F in change for the ticket machines will allow you to avoid the second queue*); there are also cafés and restaurants, an auditorium, a bookshop and space for temporary exhibitions. From here you have a choice of three entrances into the labyrinth, up escalators cryptically marked **Denon**, **Sully** and **Richelieu**, the three sections into which the Louvre has been divided under the new organization scheme.

This needs some explanation. First of all, this scheme is somewhat irrational, not corresponding at all to the nature of the exhibits (Sully is the old Louvre, Denon the south wing, Richelieu the north wing, but that will do you little good when you're trying to find your way around inside). A free, colour-coded **orientation guide** is available at the front desk; as long as they keep it up to date, it will allow you to find the sections you're most interested in. And the museum is divided not by rooms, but vaguely defined areas, numbered from one on each floor. So if you want to see Goya's *La Solana*, for example, you'll find her in Denon 10 (red), at the far end of the first-floor, south wing.

## History of the Louvre Exhibit

If you take the Sully escalator, you can begin your visit with the story of the Louvre itself. From this exhibit, walk down to the crypt under the Cour Carrée to see the foundations of the **wall and keep** of Charles V's Louvre, unearthed in recent excavations and completely intact, as well as a detailed model of the castle.

## Egyptian Art

This may be the finest and most complete collection outside Egypt itself. Thanks to Napoleon, of course, the French got a head start. His 1798 expedition to the land of the pharaohs took along a fair-sized platoon of scientists and scholars interested in Egyptian antiquities. Among them was an artist named Denon, a later museum director after whom a wing of the Louvre is coincidentally named; he and his fellows eventually turned out a 24-volume study that became the foundation of Egyptology. The army carted tons of art and mummies back to Paris, where Champollion, the director of the Louvre's new Egyptian department, first deciphered the hieroglyphics.

A great granite **sphinx** from the 4th dynasty (*c.* 2500 BC) welcomes you in at the entrance, *Sully 7 (entresol, or pyramid level)*. For most people, the greatest revelations here will be the earliest works. Under the first dynasties, in the third millennium BC, Egyptian artists were creating amazingly naturalistic painted statues, showing serene, likeable-looking folk like the *Majordomo Koki*,

*Ambassador Kanefer and his wife Neferiret* and the Buddha-like *Seated Scribe*; see also the strange *stele of the Serpent King* from about 3000 BC, the very beginning of the Old Kingdom. Another very distinctive chapter in Egyptian art is the 'Amarna period', presided over by the original Sun King—*Amenophis IV Akhenaton* (1372–54 BC), represented here by a striking statue. Pharaoh and prophet, Akhenaton moved the capital to his new city of Heliopolis, or Amarna, and created a short-lived religious revolution based on a transcendent sun god—as Freud wrote, the beginning of monotheism; art of the period employs new symbols and motifs, and reflects a preoccupation with the spiritual side of life.

Sarcophagi there are in plenty, but keep an eye out for the surprises that make the subtle Egyptians come to life—like the dog with a bell around his neck, a sort of Alsatian, with a quizzical look. Or the *pyramidal stone* from the 30th dynasty with the 36 decan demons carved on it (three for each sign of the zodiac), representing an important theme in the later Egyptians' deep astrological mumbo-jumbo. Don't miss the **Mastaba of Akhetep**, a complete small funeral chapel (*c*. 2300 BC) from Saqqara. The interior walls are completely covered with a wealth of magnificently detailed reliefs: fish, birds, trees, oxen and donkeys, along with scenes of Akhetep's funeral feast and the preparing of his tomb.

The collection doesn't end with ancient Egypt, but carries on through exceptional exhibits of **Coptic Art** up to the Middle Ages. Building on a Greek-Hellenistic-Byzantine heritage, Egypt's Christians produced some remarkable work, especially in bronzes and embroidery; note the Roman-era **sarcophagus of a girl**, made of fabric strips woven in a wonderfully intricate pattern. There's an entire Coptic church here—the **Monastic Church of Baouit** (begun in the 6th century AD), with fine decoration that combines classically-inspired reliefs, geometric motifs that seem to anticipate Islamic art and a very Byzantine icon.

## Middle Eastern Art

Like the Egyptian collection, it is extremely rich and it goes on forever. The various civilizations of **Mesopotamia** (*Richelieu 3, 4, ground floor*) are well represented. As always, this necessarily means a preponderance of grim, arrogant works celebrating viciousness and raw power, bragging over the murders and conquests of Saddam Hussein's spiritual ancestors. It starts with what may be the oldest known historical monument, the Sumerian *stele of the Vultures*, with inscriptions of 2450 BC. Early Akkadian steles show kings trampling the bodies of their enemies.

You may have never heard of **Mani**, a great civilization centred on the Euphrates, now in Syria, that reached its height *c*. 1800 BC, but its people were some of the Middle East's most talented artists, represented here by statues and a rare surviving *fresco*. From **Babylon**, which destroyed Mani, there is a black monument carved with the **Code of Hammurabi**, the oldest known body of laws. For a fitting climax, there's the work of those sweethearts of antiquity, the **Assyrians**. A distinctly chilling touch permeates the weird, winged bulls of their palace façades, and especially the reliefs of those ever-victorious generals with those curly beards that must have taken their hairdressers hours to do.

Cultures on the fringe of the Fertile Crescent are also present. From **Persia**, and in particular from the 6000-year-old city of Susa, come large collections of ceramics and jewellery. The Elamite kingdom contributes a memorable two-ton statue of *Queen Napir-Asu* (*c.* 2000 BC), and from classical times, King Darius's palace at Susa (500 BC) surrenders imposing, Mesopotamian-influenced reliefs like the *Frieze of the Archers* sculpted in beautifully coloured terracotta. From the ancient Levant, there are Phoenician ivory inlaid work, sarcophagi and idols of Baal and Tanit; other works come from Cyprus, Palestine and Syria. Finally, a room of **medieval Islamic** ceramics and metalwork (*Richelieu entresol*) includes the *Font of St Louis*, used to baptize future kings of France. Louis picked it up in Aleppo while crusading.

## Classical Antiquity

*This section is spread out on the ground floor (Sully 7, Denon 8) and on the first floor (Sully 7). The exhibits are not always in order but we'll try to account for them all, if not always chronologically.*

Begin at the top of the 'Denon' escalator up from the Pyramid, with the Atlantes from the Theatre of Dionysos in Athens. Their presence in this conspicuous spot—four colossal, satyr-like creatures, each bemusedly contemplating his corkscrew-twisted John Thomas—proves that not only the Greeks but even the Louvre curators have a sense of humour.

From here you are in Denon 8, with stylized Archaic Greek works such as the Egyptian-influenced *Lady of Auxerre* (late 7th century) and the headless *Hera of Samos* (really a *kore*, maiden). Some exceptional works are displayed in the round hall to Sully 7; note the transitional-style, early 5th-century Pharsalian relief the French call the *Exaltation de la Fleur* (Robert Graves, who put the relief on the cover of his *Greek Myths* thought it not a flower, but the hallucinatory fly agaric mushroom, and that the ladies pictured were about to use it in a Dionysian ritual). Nearby are a number of fine reliefs from Olympia, including part of a series on the *Labours of Herakles*, and some from the Parthenon in Athens; these are a tease, with only a few beautiful fragments surviving.

Along with Mona Lisa, the reigning sex symbol of the Louvre has always been the *Venus de Milo (Sully 7)* for whom neither date nor provenance is known, only that the villagers of Milos sold her to the French in 1820 to keep the Turks from getting her. Venus has led a charmed life; during the Commune she was hidden under a mountain of files in the Préfecture de Police, because officials were afraid that the Commune's art director, Gustave Courbet, meant to do her some harm (he was already partly responsible for blowing up the Place Vendôme column). During the *Semaine Sanglante* she survived a fire there only because a water pipe miraculously burst over her head.

Several large rooms are filled with **Roman-era copies** of Greek works—the main stock of any museum of antiquity. Though of uneven quality, as always, in the Louvre they are very well documented, giving many insights into the art of their originals—and how the copies were made. After these, continue by backtracking into Denon 8 for **Etruscan art**. The talented Etruscans put on a good show: happy, sophisticated-looking folk like the smiling couple reclining on a 6th- century BC *sarcophagus from Caere* (modern Cerveteri). They liked to build in wood, with architectural decoration in painted terracotta, which accounts for many of the exhibits here, as in the exquisite scene of a *religious procession*, also from Caere. They were also good at fashioning jewellery (many engraved bronze mirrors) and ceramics; the black-figure ware from Caere and elsewhere shown here is better than you'll see in most museums in Tuscany.

The Etruscans' grim nemesis, **Rome**, comes next. Romans didn't show much interest in art until Augustus' time, and then their best work was in penetrating, naturalistic portrait busts: a good selection here includes *Caligula, Nero, Hadrian, Marcus Aurelius,* the *Priestess Melitina* and a cute little boy, *Caracalla.* Note here a fine, classical relief of the *preparation for a sacrifice, c.* AD 150. The collection of carved sarcophagi and mosaics are among the best anywhere. Much of the good mosaic work comes from North Africa or around Antioch (the *Judgement of Paris,* and the spectacular *Qabr Hiram mosaic* from Lebanon, with intricate scenes of hunts and workers in the vineyard).

As an ironic juxtaposition there's a statue of Paris' own emperor, *Julian the Apostate* (360–3), dressed as a priest or philosopher (he was both); nearby is a large floor mosaic showing a *phoenix,* from the famous pleasure-dome of Daphne, at Antioch. Julian, who loved Daphne, probably walked over it many times; now it's here, while the Emperor's body was buried back near Antioch after he died on a campaign in Syria. Some of the best antique works from all periods are assembled in the big room called the **Cour du Sphinx**: the *mosaic of the Four Seasons,* another lovely work from Antioch, Hellenistic *friezes of the Battles of Greeks and Amazons* from Magnesia in Ionia and a huge anthropomorphized *River Tiber,* from the Isis temple in Rome.

After Julian, classical antiquity hasn't long to run; the section closes with a bang, in 5th–7th-century **early Christian art**, mostly from Syria. Suddenly the most artistically talented corner of the Western world is producing barbarically rough work with motifs of birds and snakes. Interesting reliefs show rare views of *early churches* (Syrian Greeks fleeing the Muslims probably contributed more than a bit to the beginnings of Romanesque); there is also *St Simeon Stylites*, the spookiest spiritual athlete of his day, squatting atop his pillar outside Antioch and preaching the word of the Lord.

*But there's still more upstairs on the first floor in Sully 7.*

You'll pass the Hellenistic *Winged Victory of Samothrace* (2nd century BC) on the stairs, impressive for her dynamic sense of movement and skilfully carved flowing draperies—even if important bits are missing (a hand turned up in 1950; it's in a glass case to the right). There is a room of *objets d'art* from **Crete and Cycladic Greece**, and then a large but somewhat disappointing collection of **Greek vases**, including works from southern Italy and other parts of the classical Greek world, and finally ancient bronzes and jewellery.

## Sculpture

*This means sculpture from the Middle Ages onwards, and can be seen in entresol and ground floor of Denon and Richelieu. Since medieval times, the French have probably taken sculpture more seriously than other nations; they still do, and this section (Richelieu ground floor 2 and 3)shows predominantly French work.*

The medieval section is not one of the Louvre's richer collections, even though it was an age when French sculpture led Europe. When the Louvre became a museum, medieval art was still disparaged by most people, and work saved from all the demolished churches and cloisters is more likely to have ended up at the Musée de Cluny. Still, there are some good capitals and reliefs, including one capital of *Daniel in the Lions' Den*, that shows how skilfully Parisians could sculpt in the 800s. There are excellent 12th-century statue columns of *Solomon and Sheba* from a church at Corbeil, and a lovely *jubé* (altar screen) from Bourges Cathedral with scenes of the Passion. There are some imposing Gothic tombs, including the *gisant of Charles V* and the uncanny *tomb of Philippe Pot* from the Abbey of Citeaux, a *gisant* held in the air by black-hooded monks (late 15th century).

The collection of **French Renaissance sculpture** is a must, not only for the quality of the work but also because there's hardly any of it in the rest of Paris. Sixteenth-century artists like Michel Colombe (*St George and the Dragon*) and Jean Goujon (mythological *reliefs from the Fontaine des Innocents*) recapture the brilliant, precise draughtsmanship of the Italian quattrocento, while giving it a flowing grace that is essentially French. Germain Pilon's creamy marble *Three Graces* (1560) was another work that helped determine the national aesthetic; it was made to hold the heart of Henri II.

After these triumphs French sculpture retained its high polish while growing more naturalistic. In the 1600s, like much of French culture, it renounced thought altogether; works in Richelieu's glass-roofed courtyards such as Guillaume Costou's *Marly horses* (*c.* 1740, the originals of the ones in the Place de la Concorde) are virtuoso productions as intellectually challenging as a chocolate éclair. In the same vein is the work of Provençal Pierre Puget (*Perseus and Andromeda*) and Antoine Coysevox, a sculptor whose career consisted largely of flattering studies of Louis XIV (here, groups of water allegories from Marly, among others). Empty mythological pastiches make up the bulk of French work through the 1800s, including the works of Napoleonic-era favourites Jean-Antoine Houdon and Antonio Canova.

Other nations are also represented, notably Italy (*Denon 9, entresol and ground floor*): starting with a 13th-century wood polychrome *Deposition* from Umbria, and a *Virgin and child* said to have once graced Dante's tomb in Ravenna. From the Renaissance, compare a group of other *Madonnas* from the quattrocento's greatest: Donatello, Luca della Robbia, Desiderio da Settignano, Jacopo della Quercia and Agostino di Duccio. On the ground floor the highlight is Michelangelo's so-called *Slaves*, sensuous, tormented, *nonfinito* figures 'in love with their own death' as Sir Kenneth Clark wrote, that were meant for the unfinished tomb of Pope Julius II in Rome.

## French Painting

*French painting is arranged chronologically, starting on the second floor in Richelieu 3 then followed by Sully 4–7.*

The section begins with the earliest known French easel painting, a 1350 portrait of *King Jean le Bon.* Stricken by war and other troubles, the French missed out on the beginning of the Early Renaissance, but recovered *c.* 1450 with fine artists such as Jean Fouquet (*Portrait of Charles VII*) and Enguerrand Quarton (*Pietà d'Avignon*). The introduction of unfamiliar mythological subjects by the Fontainebleau painters, patronized by François I, brought a certain strangeness to French compositions, as in the lovely uncanny *Eva Prima Pandora* by Jean Cousin.

In the **17th-century rooms**, pearls are mixed with the dross—acres of tedious religious painting and Louis XIV fluff pieces like the giant *battle scenes* of Charles Lebrun, chief decorator of Versailles. But France at this time had good many painters who rowed against the flow: Georges de la Tour, greatest of the French followers of Caravaggio, with startling contrasts of light and shadow (*St Joseph*, the *Adoration of the Shepherds*); or Louis le Nain (*Repas des Paysans*) who with his brothers Mathieu and Antoine was among the first to portray the everyday lives of simple folk. After these come two rooms of landscapes, including some by Lorrain and Poussin—the mysterious *Shepherds in Arcadia* that has caused no little comment in our time.

## 18th–19th-Century French Painting

Some of these are works of genius, among them Watteau's *Gilles*, the clown who now shares his secret sorrows amongst the merely amusing or downright awful—plenty of dogs, flabby mythological creatures and missal-picture madonnas. The exceptions are mostly portraits, bright-eyed Age of Enlightenment souls you'd like to invite to dinner, like Jean-Baptiste Perronneau's *Madame de Sorquinville* or Nattier's *Portrait d'une Jeune Fille*. Chardin's *Boy with a Top* fairly casts a spell with its simplicity and quietude. In portraits after 1789 the bright eyes are gone and people tend to dress in black; mythological paintings have turned into cigar-box nudes (plenty of examples from David and Ingres).The section ends with delightful landscapes by Corot and the Barbizon school, forerunners of Impressionism.

The age of kitsch painting inaugurated by Napoleon bursts into full bloom downstairs on the first floor, in Denon 8 and 9. Not surprisingly, the Louvre has the best collection of its kind. Just as the Revolution had used classical motifs to equate an imagined Roman political virtue with the new age they wished to inaugurate, so Napoleon could use art to compare his own deeds with the great stories of antiquity. Mytho-kitsch (David's *Oath of the Horatii*) shades into military kitsch (David's *Leonidas at Thermopylae* or the many scenes of Napoleon's campaigns by Jean-Antoine Gros), and political kitsch (David again, with the *Sacre de Napoléon*, a colossal, Hollywood-pageant view of his self-coronation). And of course there is sex kitsch, where mushy proto-porn masquerades as art: here Picot's *Cupid and Psyche* is an early classic.

On the other hand, look at David's unfinished *portrait of Madame Récamier*, the famous Paris beauty, for a glimpse at everything that was best about the era, a breath of fresh air and simplicity, and a hint at the modern world that was dawning out of the wreck of Napoleon's Empire. Nearby are two other famous works: Delacroix's *Liberty Leading the People*, the Revolutionary icon painted for the revolt of 1830, where the bourgeois and workers fight side by side; and Géricault's dramatic *Radeau de la Méduse*, painted after a shipwreck that was very much in the news at the time.

## Flemish, Dutch and German Painting

There are well over a thousand Flemish and Dutch paintings in the Louvre, *(second floor in Richelieu 1, 2 and 3)* thanks in large part to the acquisitiveness of Louis XIV and Louis XVI. Many of these paintings are choice: fine 15th-century altarpieces by van Eyck, van der Weyden and Memling, Hieronymous Bosch's delightful *Ship of Fools*, an allegory of worldly folly (flying the Turkish flag), Joachim Patinir's gloomy *St Jerome in the Desert*, and some beautiful, meticulous works of Quentin Metsys (*The Moneylender and his Wife*). From the height of the

Renaissance, from Duke Federico's Palace at Urbino, come 14 remarkable *Portraits of Philosophers*, a collaboration of Juste de Gand and the Spaniard Pedro Berruguete, a student of Michelangelo. There are two masterpieces of light and depth by Jan Vermeer, the *Astronomer* and the *Lacemaker*, both from the 1660s (both painted with the aid of a camera obscura). Also present are joyous scenes of peasant life by David Teniers and others, some odd allegories from Jan Brueghel (*Air, or Optics, Earth, or the Terrestrial Paradise; Wind* and *Fire* are in Milan) and 15 Rembrandts (*Bathsheba* and a touching *self-portrait* in his old age).

Forget art for a minute. The real reason we've come to the Louvre is to see the over 1000 sq metres of unchained Peter Paul Rubens, recently installed up here in Richelieu 2. The edifying subject is the *life of Marie de' Medici*. Besides Henry IV and her servants, Marie has cupids, sea-nymphs, angels, archangels, *amoretti*, spirits of the air, minor Olympian deities and satyrs to help her through the little crises of life. Rubensian buttocks fly every which way, in colours that Cecil B. De Mille would have died for. Among the best of the 21 queen-sized pictures are the *Presentation of the Portrait*, where Henri sees Marie's mug and says 'That's the girl for me!', and the *Apotheosis of Henri IV*, one of the most preposterous paintings ever attempted.

The Germans weigh in with a young Dürer *self-portrait* and Lucas Cranach's unsettling *Effects of Jealousy*, as well as Holbein's celebrated and moving *portrait of Erasmus*. **English painting** isn't the Louvre's forte, but there are fine works of Reynolds and Gainsborough, an unfinished landscape by Turner and Henry Fuseli's outrageous sleepwalking *Lady Macbeth*.

## Italian Painting: The Grande Galerie

In Denon 8 (first floor) is the entrance to the Grande Galerie. For all the great works in it, the star attraction is undeniably the room itself, running the length of the Louvre's south wing, flooded with light and full of pictures as far as the horizon. This is the room that gave the world its idea of what a picture gallery should look like. Somewhere in it you might chance upon Hubert Robert's 1796 scene of this very gallery, with quaintly-attired folk strolling up and down or sketching, initiating themselves in the modern cult of Art. Clothes may change, but the democratic hordes that flood the place today seem little different.

Until recently, artists and periods were jumbled, much as they were when the Gallery first opened, but the new dispensation has given the floor to the Italians. At the far end is the oldest of these, what some critics, amazingly, still call 'primitives'—Italian art from the late Middle Ages: madonnas by Cimabue and Lorenzo Veneziano, Giotto's *St Francis Receiving the Stigmata*. Early Renaissance Florentines are here in force (a very representative work is Bernardo Daddi's *Annunciation*); the Sienese get a small glass case on the left (Sano di Pietro's

*St Jerome* predella, Sassetta's *Damnation of the Miser's Soul*, and north Italians one on the right (Pisanello's very stylized portrait of an *Este princess*).

One work familiar to many is the third (and least well preserved) part of the three-piece *Battle of San Romano* by Paolo Uccello, greatest and strangest of the Early Renaissance's slaves of perspective (the other two parts are in Florence's Uffizi and London's National Gallery). Further on come some fine late altarpieces by Botticelli (but he was never the same after he burned out and got religion), an eerie *Crucifixion* by Mantegna, and good works by da Messina, Baldovinetti, Piero della Francesca (a *portrait of Sigismundo Malatesta*, Renaissance bad boy and builder of the famous 'Temple' in Rimini), Carpaccio and Perugino. Raphael's dreamlike *St Michael and the Dragon* and his portrait of the perfect Renaissance courtier, *Baldassare Castiglione* are near the end, along with Leonardo da Vinci's haunting *Virgin of the Rocks* and *Virgin and Child with St Anne*

## More Renaissance—the Salle des Etats

The rooms off the Grande Galerie (Denon 8 and 9) have all been given over to Italian painting. In the Salle des Etats awaits the Louvre's undisputed superstar, **Mona Lisa**, 'the most famous artwork in the world', as a local guide trumpets her. She smiles from behind the glass (installed after she was slashed a few years back), as the tourists with their flash machines close in like paparazzi. Someone once claimed the paintings in great museums tend to grow uglier over the centuries from 'too many ugly people looking at them'; La Gioconda, at worst, seems a little tired just now. Most of her devotees have no time for the other great works in this room: Titian's smiling portrait of François I and works by Correggio, Pontormo, del Sarto and others. All are rather upstaged by Paolo Veronese's room-sized *Wedding at Cana* (a bit of Napoleonic plunder that never went back to Venice), which besides Jesus and Mary includes nearly all the political and artistic celebrities of the day: Emperor Charles V, François I and Suleiman the Magnificent sit at the table, while Titian, Tintoretto and other artists play in the band—Veronese himself is on viola.

## Late Italian and Spanish Painting

Continuing is a long stretch of 17th–18th-century Italian art, the sort of paintings most prized by old French collectors (so naturally they often frenchify their names: Zampieri or Domeniquin = Domenichino; Carrache = Annibale Carracci). There are some good works by Guido Reni and Caravaggio, but the Venetian Francesco Guardi's colourful series of 12 works on *Venetian Festivals* (1763) steals the show, a sweet document of the *Serenissima* near the end of its career.

On the grand staircase (by Denon 8, next to the *Winged Victory of Samothrace*) is one of the Louvre's treasures, a detatched Botticelli fresco called **Venus and the Graces**: five perfect Botticelli maidens maintaining their poise and calm in the midst of the crowds. If this seems like a magic picture, that is because it was intended as one. No one ever knows for certain what this artist's pictures are about—the title given is an educated guess—but this one, like his famous works in Florence, is a secret allegory, expressing some unrecoverable idea from the Neo-Platonic planetary mysticism current in the Florence of his day. We may expect that nothing in it is left to chance; the composition, proportions and colours would somehow mirror the symbolic concept behind the work.

The **Spanish painting** is neatly consolidated on the first floor in Denon 10. The collection is small but representative. From the 16th century, there is one El Greco *Crucifixion*; from the golden age of Spanish painting in the 1600s, at least one of each of the masters: Velázquez (*Infanta Margarita*), Ribera, and two Zurbaráns from the cycle of *St Bonaventure*; these come from Seville—among Napoleon's thefts that never were returned. Some of the several Murillos are stolen goods too; note the wonderful fantasy of the *Kitchen of the Angels*. There are several Goyas, the comically weird *Les Vielles* and the famous portrait of *La Marquesa de la Solana*, as Spanish as *churros* and chocolate.

## Objets d'Art

This is a trip to Citizen Kane's Xanadu—except that instead of a mere newspaper tycoon the mad collector had the resources of all the kings of France. The sumptuous clutter is stupefying: blinding jewels and heavy gold gimcracks, tapestries, delicate porcelain knick-knacks, watches, Renaissance bronzes, Merovingian treasure, chinoiserie, sardonyx vases . . . They've squirrelled away everything from George III's silverware to Marie-Antoinette's make-up case.

The greatest treasures are in the extravagantly decorated **Salle d'Apollon** (Denon 8, first floor): Louis XIV's crown jewels (three cases full), Henri II's rock crystal chess set, Napoleon's crown and Josephine's earrings, the sword of the Grand Master of the Knights of Malta, Charles V's gold sceptre, Charlemagne's dagger, St Louis' ring, the jewellery of Arnegonde, wife of Clotaire I (*c.* 570), Louis XV's crown, and a 107.88 carat ruby in the shape of a dragon called *La Côte de Bretagne*.

> *The rest of the collection is separate, on the first floor in Sully 4–5 and Richelieu 1, 2 and 3. Don't miss it.*

Look for the small bronze *equestrian statue of Charlemagne*, a rare and skilful work from the Dark Ages, and another relic from that time, the *eagle of Abbot Suger*, a porphyry vase enclosed in a golden eagle (*c.* 700) that once was the pride of the treasure of St-Denis, the richest in France (*Richelieu 2*). There is a small but rich collection of medieval and Byzantine reliquaries and trinkets, Renaissance bronzes from the master of the art, Andrea Riccio, beautiful majolicas from Moorish Spain and Renaissance Italy, and rooms of furniture from Louis XIV through Louis XVI.

# Musée des Arts Décoratifs

*And if the 99-course cultural feast hasn't filled you up, the Louvre has two museums to offer for dessert; both entrances on Rue de Rivoli. Open daily except Mon and Tues, 12.30–6; adm.*

The biggest, the Musée des Arts Décoratifs (*under renovation at the time of writing; ℗ 01 44 55 57 50 for information*) was founded in 1877, initiated by an organization now called the *Union Centrale des Arts Décoratifs*, dedicated to maintaining artistic standards in industrially made items. The museum's purpose was to show the public beautiful things so that people would be more demanding about what they bought for themselves.

Although it means confusing the chronology, the easiest way to visit is to take the lift to the **fourth floor** and work your way down. This floor offers a long expanse of *Louis XV and Louis XVI furnishings and trinkets*: porcelain from Sèvres and other places in the Paris region, figurines, jewellery, snuffboxes with painted miniatures, an entire room of silverware. Madame de Pompadour's sauce dishes are on prominent display. In the opposite corridor are *19th-century decorative arts*, beginning with the coldly elegant neoclassicism of the Empire style through to the Restoration, which was also partly a restoration of pre-1789 lightness and frivolity as well as the age when flowered wallpaper began to dominate the national consciousness. Eccentricity gathers momentum into the Second Empire, France's first great age of popular conspicuous consumption: enamelled plates with ferns, snakes and lizards for decoration; florid interiors, captured in paintings, showing more gold, more colour, more exotica—more everything.

The excruciating **third floor** covers the *age of Louis XIV*, with the bastard Renaissance hand-me-downs that passed for design in the 'Grand Siècle'. It was a great age for *faïence*, however, mostly in provincial centres such as Moustiers, Marseille, Nevers and Strasbourg, all represented here. The opposite corridor covers France's timid flirtation with Rococo, in the *age of Louis XV*.

On the **second floor** are works from the *Middle Ages to the 16th century*. Of course not much has survived of medieval decorative arts besides luxury goods like the lovely 15th-century *Venetian ivories*, or church paraphernalia and reliquaries. Much of the space is filled with paintings: a lot of Flemish works, and some good retables (a *Last Judgement* made in the 1420s for the Duke of Bedford, occupation governor of Paris). Among the most important furnishings, for those who could afford them, were *tapestries*, providing insulation and a lot of pretty greenery for houses with few windows; there's a good set here, with scenes from the all-time most popular medieval romance, the *Romance of the Rose*. Among the *15th–16th-century ceramics*, the work from Italy and Moorish Andalucía stand out, as well as France's own enamelled work from Limoges, with its distinctive dark, glistening colours.

**Art Nouveau and the 20th century** occupies the ground floor, by far the most popular part of the museum. The Art Nouveau hall is an attraction in itself: the glorious *Salon de Bois* saved from the 1900 Exposition (from a pavilion sponsored by the Union des Arts Décoratifs) and reconstructed here. It houses an exceptional collection of *glasswork*, showing the surprising breadth and imagination of the movement. The rooms that follow contain Art Nouveau furniture, including a bedroom suite by Hector Guimard; there is also a delightful exhibit of *jewellery*, from the 1900s through to Art Deco.

The collection goes right up to the present, though mostly concerned with those unexpected icons of modernity—chairs. From early experiments like Gerrit Rietvelt's 1934 do-it-yourself model and Marcel Breuer's famous 1932 design, the parade of chairs continues through the Scandinavians, to things you didn't know were Art (the *stackable plastic chair*, a triumph of British design invented by Robin Day in 1963). American architect Frank Gehry (who is incidentally doing a new American Center building in Bercy) contributes a practical cardboard rocker. And finally, an unforgettable parlour suite by Niki de Saint-Phalle.

## Musée des Arts de la Mode

> *Entrance just down the street at 109 Rue de Rivoli. Same opening hours as for Arts Décoratifs; adm.*

France has a fashion industry managed by an enormously influential cabal of the top luxury-goods makers called the Comité Colbert. Governments have always supported the industry—since Colbert's time—but it was only during the rule of Socialist Culture Minister Jack Lang that the state's cultural machinery was enrolled in the effort. The Louvre is centre stage, with frequent fashion shows in the Cour Carrée, exhibitions of jewellery in the Musée des Arts Décoratifs, and above all this museum, opened in 1986 under the premise that women's clothing, if sufficiently expensive, is an art that enriches all our lives. The museum has a large permanent wardrobe of duds going back to the 16th century, as well as the collections of successful early 20th-century designers such as Poiret and Schiaparelli, though only a small part is on display, in changing temporary exhibitions.

## Musée d'Orsay

> *Entrance 1 Rue Bellechasse Ⓜ: Solferino or RER C: Musée d'Orsay. Open 10–6 daily except Mon, Sun 9–6, Thurs 10– 9.45pm, adm 35F, half-price Sun; free under 18.*

At peak times count on waiting half an hour or so to get inside this former train station, where the engines have been replaced with a dynamo collection of the art that hauled painting and sculpture into the modern era. Moreover, it is specifically the art of Paris, born in the last half of the 19th century, when the city was both mother and battleground of modernity; here under one huge roof are gathered all its combative schools of painting and sculpture from 1848–1910, rounded out with a magnificent array of furniture, decorative arts, architectural exhibits and photography. You could easily spend a day here, and neither thirst nor starve, thanks to the museum's restaurant and rooftop café.

The Gare d'Orsay is itself a monument born on the cusp of the 19th century: a daring work of iron weighing more than the Eiffel Tower, with a nave taller than Notre-Dame, thrown up in two years for the 1900 World Fair to serve trains from the southwest. The architect, Victor Laloux, professor of architecture at the Ecole des Beaux-Arts, was hired to make the façade a dignified foil for the Louvre across the river. The net result is pure Napoleon III rococola—so lavish for a train station that a luxury hotel was added next door to take advantage of its cream-puffery (the hotel ballroom survives, fit for a Prince Charming. And in 1958 the hotel did provide the setting for France's own Prince Charming, Charles de Gaulle, to announce his return to power, rescuing his 'fairy-tale maiden' as he called France from the political chaos brought about by Algeria's war of independence).

Soon after that, the Gare d'Orsay, its platforms being too short for modern trains, was abandoned. Orson Welles made use of the huge space left behind to film his seldom-seen tribute to Kafka, *The Trial* (1962), and for a few years it served as a theatre-circus for the Renaud-Barrault Company, after Malraux booted them out of the Odéon for supporting the students in 1968. In 1970 the government decided to level the station for a huge hotel. But the Parisians, after fatalistically letting Les Halles perish, would have none of it, and in 1973 Pompidou caved in and declared the station a historical monument. In 1977 a competition for converting the innards was won by the Italian Gae Aulenti, who came up with the idea of five levels of exhibition space set back along the sides, tucked full of little visual surprises, illuminated by as much natural light as possible. The undertaking foundered in financial and technological problems until 1981, when Mitterrand was elected and simply tripled its budget (he wasn't called *Dieu* for nothing). Inaugurated in December 1986, the Musée d'Orsay's core exhibits came from the former Jeu-de-Paume Museum and the 19th-century rooms of the Louvre.

## First Level

### The Entrance and Nave: Sculpture

**Sculptures** command the entrance: Rude's piece of Romantic hyperbole, *Le Génie de la Patrie*, from the Arc de Triomphe, followed inside the main door by a *Lion* by Barye (d. 1875), animal sculptor extraordinaire, and Rude's *Napoleon awaking to Immortality* commissioned by the little egomaniac's Grenadiers. Below, the nave of the museum is dominated by the originals of large public works by Napoleon III's favourite sculptor, Jean-Baptiste Carpeaux (1827–75): the figures of the fountain of the Observatoire and a finger-biting *Ugolin*, which makes an interesting contrast with Rodin's plaster upstairs. Keeping them company is a selection revealing the official taste of mid-century, a chorus of suffering, semi-erotic figures, either bound or twisted into some salon-approved position, and given classical names for respectability's sake. The Hollywood flabbergaster on the wall, ***Les Romaines de la Décadence*** by Thomas Couture (Manet's teacher), won a top medal in the salon of 1849, fulfilling all the prerequisites for success: a titillating pseudo-classical subject with a story, painted in the beautiful Grand Manner that flattered the supremely philistine salon public.

## Classicism, Romanticism, Decorative Arts, Precursors of Symbolism

In the rooms behind the Decadent Romans, the last gasp of **classicism** is represented by some late Ingres (*La Source*, 1856), while its intense rival, **Romanticism**, checks in with Delacroix's *La Chasse au Lion*; note his inventive use of broken colour and 'drunken brush' strokes that presage the Impressionists. Beyond are gems from the Académie, including Cabanel's *La Naissance de Vénus*, a tasty tomato that tickled the salon of 1863 and Henri Regnault's startling *L'Exécution sans Jugement sous les Rois Maures de Grenade*, with an extra helping of blood and guts. The next rooms (behind Couture's decadent Romans) offer **Decorative Arts from 1850–1880**: exquisitely crafted, pompous and overwrought dust-magnets from Paris' World Fairs (a pseudo-Merovingian medals cabinet and hyper-eclectic *La Toilette de la Duchesse de Parme*). The last set of rooms on the right is dedicated to the **Precursors of Symbolism**: the still, melancholy pastels of Puvis de Chavannes (*Le Pauvre Pêcheur*) and the Byzantine, mythological fantasies of Gustave Moreau (1826–98), who helped to invent one of the *fin de siècle*'s favourite motifs, the *femme fatale* (*Jason* and *Orphée*). Here too are rather unpleasant pre-1870 works by Degas (1834–1917), when he was besotted with Ingres (*La Famille Bellelli*).

## Salle de l'Opéra

At the far end of the ground floor is the **Salle de l'Opéra**, dedicated to Garnier's extraordinary folly, with Carpeaux's original *La Danse* pixies from the façade. A model of the Opéra (from the 1900 World Fair) is cross-sectioned so you can see all the machinery behind the scenes; embedded in the floor under glass is a 1:100 scale relief map of the Opéra Quarter *c.* 1914, detailing the unlikely setting of its moonstruck bulk. The room to the left bares the structure of the Gare d'Orsay as an introduction to the **Architecture of 1850–1900**; the several floors of a tower called the *Pavillon Amont* offer a compendium of Second Empire and Third

Republic Paris façades and architecture from Viollet-le-Duc to Frank Lloyd Wright. Best of all is a massive 1855 **View of Paris** painted by Victor Navlet from a balloon floating over the Observatoire, when the outer Left Bank still had virginal meadows and farms, unstraddled by the Eiffel Tower.

### Caricatures, Barbizon Landscapes, Courbet, Precursors of the Impressionists

Backtrack now towards the entrance and follow the rooms and galleries along the left side. The first room (closest to the entrance) contains what may come as a surprise: the works of the political satirist **Honoré Daumier** (1808–1879), whose 36 terracotta caricatures of Louis-Philippe's political cronies, each representing a vice, prefigure *Spitting Image*. In painting he experimented with reducing detail to a minimum (*Crispin et Scapin*, also the mother and daughter of *La Blanchisseuse*). Following are several landscapes from the **Barbizon School**, a movement inspired by photography and a longing to return to nature. Look for works by its theorist, Théodore Rousseau, and the lyrical, dissolving landscapes and figures (*La Dame en Bleu*) from the last half of Corot's (1796–1875) career. A third member, peasant-born Jean-François Millet (1814–75) worked making signs for taverns before he got a break at the age of 60. Here are his rainbow-lit *Printemps*, *L'Angélus*, and *Les Glaneuses*, which scandalized the 1857 salon for showing rural poverty and hard work instead of the frolicking shepherds and shepherdesses preferred by the bourgeoisie.

The next room is dedicated to the greatest works of **Gustave Courbet** (1819–77), the formulator of **Realism** and the first artist to completely buck the salon system—'I have no master; my master is myself. There is not, and never has been, any painter other than myself.' He horrified the salon in 1850 with his *L'Enterrement à Ornans*, a picture of an unsentimental, muddy country funeral in his home town. His huge *Atelier* (1855), an 'allegory of my last seven years as a painter', shows the artist painting amid a motley crowd, including his naked muse, Realism, his patrons and friends (among them Baudelaire with his nose in a book). In 1869 Courbet went to the Mediterranean, and was mesmerized by the light (*Falaises d'Etretat après l'Orage*), before his career was cut short by his political activities in the Commune. In the adjacent gallery hang less threatening Realist painters of animals and landscapes: Rosa Bonheur, Daubigny and Troyon.

The next rooms house a superb collection by artists generally lumped all together as **precursors of the Impressionists**: for example, landscape painter Eugène Boudin (1824–98), who in 1848 was the first to paint out of doors, so intent on capturing the atmosphere that he wrote in the margins of his paintings the date, the hour and direction of the wind (*La Plage de Trouville*, 1864). Others declared themselves followers of Delacroix, as seen in Fantin-Latour's *Hommage à Delacroix* (1864), a group portrait of the first rebels in the arts—including

Whistler, Baudelaire again and **Manet** (1832–83). Manet was the direct, if reluctant, father of the Impressionists, although he never showed his work at their exhibitions, never understanding why the official salon and critics lashed out so violently against him. *Olympia* (1865), his most famous work here, made them spit venom when shown in the Salon des Refusés: not so much because of the nude (although Manet outraged many by giving her an erotic black cat instead of the usual dog, symbol of fidelity) but especially because Manet merely sketched in the bouquet of flowers—a photograph-inspired blur of movement that damned it in the eyes of critics like Paul de Saint-Victor who wrote: 'The crowd presses, as at the Morgue, before *Olympia*, reeking and horrible. Art descended so low doesn't even merit censure … Look, and pass on.'

Here too are Manet's *Le Fifre* (also refused by the salon), *Portrait of Zola* (painted in gratitude for the writer's support), *Claire de la Lune sur le Pont de Boulogne* and *Le Balcon* (one of the ladies is Berthe Morisot, Manet's sister-in-law). Adjacent rooms contain **Impressionist paintings before 1870**, when Monet, Renoir and Bazille (who died in the Franco-Prussian War) first took their easels out of doors: there's Bazille's sun-dappled *Réunion de Famille* and a baker's dozen by Monet (1840–1926), filled with the freshness of new discoveries: *Coquelicots*, *La Pie*, *Pont du Chemin de Fer* and *Femmes au Jardin*.

Next, tucked in a room of murky **realists**, are paintings by Monticelli, a native of Marseille who applied thick, unmixed paint with short feverish strokes and inspired Van Gogh's technique and his move to Provence. The last room, **Orientalism**, displays sundrenched canvases of exotic settings, a popular fad in the Second Empire, inspired by Delacroix's Algerian paintings.

## Top Level—Impressionism and Postimpressionism

*From here, signs for the 'Deuxième partie de la visite' direct you up the escalators to the topmost floor.*

The reason for this unusual arrangement is the presence of overhead natural light, for light is the heart and soul of the treasures the museum has tucked under its roof: one of the world's most luminous collections of **Impressionist** paintings. In the mid-19th century, new optical theories on the derivation of colour from light inspired a group of young artists working in Paris (especially Monet, Renoir, Sisley and Pissarro) to subordinate all academic notions of line and architecture of composition to catching 'objectively' the effects of light and atmosphere. Their theories may have (theoretically, at least) reduced the artist to a mechanical seeing and painting machine, but their results are among the most radiant and joyous works ever committed to canvas; the everyday scenes they favoured comprise a delightful chronicle of Paris on either side of the Franco-Prussian War and the Commune.

Starring in the first room is Manet's delicious *Déjeuner sur l'Herbe* (1863), an updated version of Giorgione's *Concert Champêtre* in the Louvre and the key inspiration for the Impressionists with its masterly, experimental handling of paint. Nearby is a portrait by an American friend of Manet and Baudelaire, who in his delight for arty names called it *Arrangement in grey and black no. 1*, although everyone knows it as *Whistler's Mother*.

## Impressionism 1870–80

Key works follow: Monet's *Régates à Argenteuil*, Pissarro's *Les Toits Rouges* and *L'Inondation à Port-Marly*, considered the masterpiece of Albert Sisley (1839–99), who was born in Paris of English parents and concentrated on the nuances of the changing colours and sensations of water, sky and mists. Of Paris, there's Monet's steam-filled *Gare Saint-Lazare* and his *Rue Montorgueil*, and by Renoir (1841–1919) an irresistible evocation of Paris' *bal-dansants*, the *Moulin de la Galette* (1876). This and *La Balançoire* nearby are not only masterful studies of light and shadow on the human figure, but an updating of the tradition of Watteau's *scènes galantes*. Renoir's *Chemin montant dans les Hautes Herbes* shows a charming if rarely used talent for landscape.

The next room contains paintings from the same decade by Manet, who after inspiring the Impressionists was himself in turn inspired by their techniques in capturing outdoor light (*Sur la Plage*), as well as depicting everyday Paris scenes (*La Serveuse de Bocks*). His interests in turn influenced Berthe Morisot (1841–95), the *grande dame* of Impressionism, whose subjects from her life and that of her friends form a woman's diary in paint (*Le Berceau*). The same room also contains works by Degas, whose unusual compositions were inspired in part by the spontaneity of photography and Japanese prints, although unlike the other Impressionists he never painted out of doors, but from memory (*A la Bourse*, *L'Absinthe*, *Les Repasseuses*). The ballet and race track became special interests of Degas after 1874, affording opportunities for unusual compositions and also for the study of movement. When his failing eyesight precluded further painting, he modelled ballerinas in wax; a glass case holds the bronzes cast after his death.

## Impressionism after 1880

Beyond are **Impressionist works after 1880**: Monet for his part continued to paint 'as the birds sing', ever surrendering himself to light and atmosphere, especially in his series that portrays the same subject at different times of day: the museum has *Les Meules*, five of *Les Cathédrales de Rouen* and two versions of the waterlilies (*Nymphéas*) painted at Giverny, where representation of form is so minimal as to verge on abstract constructions of pure colour. Renoir took a trip to Algeria (*Paysage Algérien*, *Fête Arabe à Alger*) and Italy, where he become disillusioned and convinced that the light touch he had cultivated (which was just becoming popular) was a cheat. After concentrating on line (*Danse à la Ville*, *Danse à la Campagne*) he developed his own pearly synthesis of line and colour, epitomized in *Les Grandes Baigneuses*, an extraordinary work from a man paralysed by rheumatism, who had to have his brushes strapped to his wrists.

The next room contains a large selection of Pissarro's landscapes, works by Morisot and the American Mary Cassatt (*Femme Cousant*). The paintings collected by Van Gogh's art-loving friend Dr Gachet (Monet's *Chrysanthèmes* and Renoir's *Margot*) lead into a room of painting by **Van Gogh** (1853–90). Contact in Paris with the Impressionists (*La Guinguette*) lightened his palette before he journeyed to Arles and discovered colour as the only medium powerful enough to express his emotions: *L'Arlésienne*, *La Chambre de Van Gogh à Arles* and the merciless *Autoportrait*, painted during his first fit of madness in Arles. The most uncanny work of the collection, *L'Eglise d'Auvers-sur-Oise* (1890), is full of dark forebodings of his suicide; it was painted while Van Gogh was living with Dr Gachet.

Beyond are the works of the most pivotal figure in the museum, **Paul Cézanne** (1839–1906), who himself began with a heavy murky style (*Portrait d'Achille Emperaire*) before 1872, when he moved from his native Provence to the same Auvers-sur-Oise, where Dr Gachet was the first person to buy one of his pictures. Contact with Pissarro considerably lightened his colours: *La Maison du Pendu*, which he showed in the first Impressionist exhibition in 1873 and *Une Moderne Olympia*, inspired by Manet. The other Impressionists were not very impressed by him or vice versa, and after 1877 Cézanne spent most of his time in Aix, becoming a legend towards the end of his life, the old grouch who thumbed his nose at Paris (French critics even up to the 1920s labelled his work 'drunken scavenger's paintings'). Cézanne's goal was to give ephemeral Impressionism an intellectual, architectural underpinning of geometry, structure and composition, ever seeking new solutions for 'an art parallel to nature'; he was a superb colourist but never permitted himself any tricks or false bravura. The Musée d'Orsay has masterpieces of his three favourite subjects: a landscape (*L'Estaque*), figures (*Femme à la Cafetière*, *Les Joueurs de Cartes* and *Baigneurs*) and still lifes (*Pommes et Oranges* and *La Nature Morte aux Oignons*).

The next room is dimly lit to protect the subtle, refined colours of the **pastels by Degas**, whose experiments in the medium, especially his complex crosshatchings (*Danseuse au Bouquet saluant sur la Scène*), sparked a fresh interest in pastels in other artists, especially Toulouse-Lautrec. Adjacent, you can refuel for more art in the museum's **Café des Hauteurs** next to the enormous station clock, with a terrace overlooking the Seine.

## Post-Impressionism

The next rooms, devoted to the **Post-Impressionists**, offer another barrage of masterpieces, beginning with the last, great, unfinished painting by Georges Seurat, *La Cirque*. The most scientific of painters, Seurat (1859–1891), set out to rescue Impressionism from the charges of frivolity by developing his distinctive pointillist style, based on the colour theories of physicists Chevreal and N. O. Rood on the optic mixing of tones and the action of colour; when viewed from a distance, each dot of colour takes on the proper relationship with the dots around it, although remaining visible as an optic vibration. In *La Cirque* Seurat was dealing with the problem of using linear rhythms to express movement and gaiety while preserving the serene, classical proportions of the Golden Section. Nearby are the gaudy efforts of his followers, Signac and Cross.

## Pastels: Redon and Toulouse-Lautrec

Beyond, the **Salle Redon** is devoted to the works of the elusive Odilon Redon (1840–1916), master colourist and pre-Freudian painter of dreams, who belonged to no school but greatly inspired the Symbolists, Surrealists and Metaphysical painters who followed (*Portrait de Gauguin*). There are several other rooms of pastels, culminating in the **Salle Toulouse-Lautrec**. Lautrec (1864–1901), a descendant of the counts of Toulouse, broke both legs as a child, which seriously impeded his growth. His physical afflictions may have contributed to his empathy in the penetrating portraits of 'occupationally-distorted souls', especially of prostitutes, whom he drew while living amongst them. Lautrec strove to 'paint the truth, not the ideal' and he took the portrayals of the contemporary entertainment world by Degas to a unique level of individual portraiture, the most sincere of the *belle époque* (*La Goulue, Jane Avril dansant, La Clownesse Cha-U-Kao*).

## Galerie Bellechasse: Rousseau, Gauguin

The long **Galerie Bellechasse** kicks off with another unique painter, Henri Rousseau (1844–1910), known as 'Le Douanier' from his job in a customs bureau. Rousseau generally is classed as a naif, which distracts from his intuitive mastery of the same architectural problems that Seurat wearied himself into an early grave trying to solve (*La Guerre* and the magical *La Charmeuse des Serpents*). Then come the painters of Pont-Aven, a fishing village in Brittany where Gauguin (1848–1903) first fled in his search for a simpler life. Younger painters followed, especially Emile Bernard (1868–1941), who with Gauguin formulated **Synthetism** (although the egocentric Gauguin never acknowledged Bernard's work, perhaps because it preceded his own). Another reaction against the 'mindlessness' of Impressionism, Synthetism was based on the subordination of objects in a picture to one overall rhythm, 'synthesizing' them to bring out the meaning the whole evoked in the artist. Admirers of primitive art for its power and simplicity, the

Synthetists similarly ignored perspective to simplify forms into large, expressive, coloured patterns with dark outlines (a style sometimes called cloisonnism for its resemblance to medieval cloisonné enamels: note Gauguin's *Les Lavandières à Pont-Aven* (painted during his first stay) and *Les Meules Jaunes*, painted after Gauguin's 1888 period with Van Gogh in Arles. Hanging nearby are works by other Pont-Aven painters, Sérusier and Emile Bernard (his masterpiece, the haunting *Madeleine au Bois d'Amour*, modelled on his sister).

After cold, wet Brittany comes the sensuous tropical breeze of Gauguin's lush paintings from the South Seas, where he fled to escape 'diseased' civilization to rejeuvenate art by becoming 'one with nature': *Femmes de Tahiti, Le Repas, Cheval Blanc, Et l'Or de leur Corps*. There are examples of his sculptures, *Oviri* and the carved lintel from his door in the Marquesas Islands, where he died in 1903, ill, broke, depressed, at odds with the colonial authorities whom he accused of exploiting the natives. Gauguin's work, fanatical attitude and long slow suicide have had a powerful influence on subsequent artists, both as a guide and a warning.

### The Nabis and Fauvism

Following are the works of another school that developed out of Pont-Aven, the **Nabis** (Hebrew for 'prophet'), born in 1889 when Gauguin showed Sérusier how to paint a forest scene on a wooden cigar-box lid (*Le Talisman*). Sérusier (1864–1927) took it back to his young comrades of the progressive Académie Jullien who decided that they, too, would rejeuvenate art. In 1890 their precocious spokesman, Maurice Denis (1870–1943), wrote the essential dictum of all modern art: '... a painting, before being a warhorse, a naked woman, some anecdote or whatnot, is essentially a flat surface covered with colours arranged in a certain order' (see his *Tâches de Soleil sur la Terrasse* and *Les Muses*). Edouard Vuillard (1868–1940) was the decorative Nabi of intimate bourgeoisie interiors and gardens, perhaps becaused he lived with his mother until well into his 50s (*Au Lit*); Bonnard (1867–1947), the most inspired by Japanese prints (*Les Femmes au Jardin, Le Peignoir*); Félix Vallotton (1865–1925), whose compositions are the most innovative (*Le Ballon*); and Aristide Maillol (1861– 1944), the Nabi who went on to sculpt monumental women (*La Femme à l'Ombrelle*).The logical conclusion of Maurice Denis's dictum was Fauvism, represented by André Derain's *Le Pont de Charing Cross* (1902) in the Kaganovitch collection in the last room on this floor (along with more by Van Gogh and Gaugin); the Pompidou Centre's Musée d'Art Moderne chronologically continues from here.

## Middle Level

After all these Top Level fireworks, the Middle Level starts out by showing you the art that people actually bought at the time, to the extent that the artists lived like princes: after Toulouse-Lautrec, Bourguereau's *Birth of Venus* in the gaudy old hotel **Ballroom** seems little more than a hussy painted for bar-room winks. Then come six rooms from the official salons from 1870–1914, huge trumpeting white elephants—pseudo-prehistoric subjects such as Cormon's *Le Fils de Caïn*, or patriotic pieces (the plaster *Le Forgeron* by Dalou, cast in bronze for the monument honouring the republic in Place de la Nation), or picturesque everyday life (*The Docks of Cardiff*, by Lionel Waldem), or violence from battle of the Commune (André Devanbez's *La Charge*). One room has a marble *bust of Sarah Bernhardt* and works by the Divine Sarah herself, and a *bronze of Robert de Montesquieu*, dandy and critic synonymous with *fin-de-siècle* decadence.

Beyond is a hotchpotch selection of artists classed as **Symbolists**: *The Wheel of Fortune* by Burne-Jones, who made the Pre-Raphaelites popular in France, *Summer Night* by Winslow Homer, the famous *Portrait of Proust* by Jacques-Emile Blanches, *Le Rêve* by Puvis de Chavannes, *Nuit d'Eté* by Munch and the extraordinary, pastel-coloured *Ecole de Platon* by Jean Delville, where naked youths with Gibson girl hairdos languidly listen to philosophy under the wisteria.

Along the museum's central nave is a second terrace of **Sculpture**: Frémiet's model for the St Michael and the dragon from Mont St-Michel; *L'Age Mûr* and other works by Camille Claudel (1864–1943), Rodin's ill-starred student, model and mistress. There are original plasters by Rodin (1840–1917), of his works displayed in the Musée Rodin and in Meudon: *Ugolin*, *Balzac*, *La Muse* (from the monument to Whistler) and the great *La Porte de l'Enfer*.

Off the terrace is a series of rooms devoted to the extraordinary renewal of fine workmanship and design known as **Art Nouveau**: dragonfly jewellery by Lalique, furniture by Guimard (*Banquette avec Vitrine*), a desk by Henry Van de Velde, glass by Tiffany (his *Au Nouveau Cirque*, after a drawing by Lautrec) and Emile Gallé (*Plat d'Ornement*). Don't miss Robert Carabin's *Library*, with its Symbolist allegories on the Triumph of l'Esprit over Ignorance and a *Dining Room* with woodwork by Charpentier. Near Rodin's sculpture, the **Tour Guimard** displays **furniture designed by architects**: beautiful chairs by Guimard, Gaudí, Bugatti, Mackintosh and Frank Lloyd Wright; others are in three small rooms along the south (Rue de Lille) galleries. The **sculptures** on the terrace here are by Rodin's contemporaries (Bartholomé and Bourdelle) and his successors, Maillol (*Méditerranée*) and Joseph Bernard.

The last set of rooms along this sculpture terrace is devoted to **Paintings after 1900**, following the careers of the artists who began as Nabis: more interiors by Vuillard, who worked with egg tempera for its fresh fresco colours (*Coolus*, and the large *Bibliothèque*); Maurice Denis, who remained closest to the original ideals (*Jeu de Volant*) and Bonnard, who moved to Cannes and found a more Impressionist aesthetic (*En Barque*).

# Peripheral Attractions

These are mostly what planners poetically call 'urban grey areas', where not even Haussmann's boulevards can dispel the prevailing anomie. It is *cinéma verité* country, and if you spend enough time here you'll begin to understand the nihilism that pervades the life of Parisian intellectuals and informs the *Nouvelle-Vague* (New-Wave) films of the 1960s. But you should have seen it back in the old days. Perhaps the reason why Parisians are traditionally so introspective is that, before the railways, any trip outside the holy city meant traversing a desert of refuse heaps and open graves, haunted by vicious robbers and hungry vermin.

By at least the 1300s, the approach to every city gate was embellished with mountains of human faeces. Farmers would cart it away to flavour the vineyards of Argenteuil and Champagne, but they could never keep up with the supply. Beyond these came even larger dumps of dead animals and offal. Wolves feasted on abandoned babies, as well as the escaped thieves and social misfits who made up the nomadic population of this pre-industrial twilight zone. The one landmark on the northern side was the Gibbet of Monfaucon, a huge scaffolding of 5-ft-thick tree trunks, built in 1233 near what is now the St-Louis hospital. The kings or the city provosts could hang 60 men at a time on it when necessary. It was dismantled in 1790 as a humanitarian measure; the French had invented a much kinder way to do the job—the guillotine.

Now that you're in the mood, let's begin on the Seine, at the west end of the Right Bank, and continue around Paris more or less clockwise, ending on the far west of the Left Bank.

## The 16e: Passy and Auteuil

Most major cities have a neighbourhood of moneyed sterility like Paris' 16e: Belgravia and Mayfair, or Park Avenue in New York. This may be the champ of them all. Everything is as neat and pretty as can be, along the broad avenues lined with elegant *belle-époque* blocks of flats where there are more ambassadors than children. It's probably a nice place to live, but it's murder to visit for more than an hour at a time. Fortunately there's little reason to: only a few museums, ranging from the eccentric to the unnecessary, and a sprinkling of good architecture—including most of the life's work of Art Nouveau master Hector Guimard.

The terrain of the 16e used to be the farmland of two villages: Auteuil, to the south, and **Passy**. The centre of this one, still with a trace of its village origins, lies around

Place de Passy and Rue de l'Annonciation. Among the museums you'll find the atmospheric **Musée Georges Clemenceau**, 8 Rue Franklin (*open 2–5 except Mon, Wed, Fri and Aug, Ⓜ Passy*), in the apartment where the 'Tiger' spent his last 37 years, and the **Musée du Vin**, of all possible addresses—Rue des Eaux! (*open daily 10–6 pm; adm, Ⓜ Passy*), with didactic exhibits and wax dummies set in old quarries that were converted into wine cellars by monks in the 1400s. Ticket price includes a *dégustation* at the end. From here, walk down Rue Raynouard to no. 47 and the **Maison de Balzac** (*open daily except Mon and hols 10–5.40; adm, Ⓜ Passy or La Muette*). The great novelist had a dozen Paris addresses in his lifetime, but he spent seven years here working like a slave to pay off his creditors. Rue Berton, behind the house, is one of the few streets unchanged from the times when Passy was a rustic village.

Further west is the **Musée des Lunettes et Lorgnettes**, 2 Avenue Mozart (*open daily except Sun and Mon 10–7; adm, Ⓜ La Muette*). The French are fond of everyday life's little precisions: they write with fountain pens, wear old-fashioned watches with diamonds in them, and take little bits of glass seriously. So a museum of glasses is a natural; gathered by an enterprising optician are examples from the Middle Ages (magnifying lenses were an Arab invention, first put to practical use by the Italians) up to a ruby-studded pair that belonged to Sarah Bernhardt.

From here Avenue du Ranelagh leads into the **Jardin du Ranelagh**, a pretty park laid out as a private dancing-ground by Lord Ranelagh in 1774—a time when such fancies (like the Vauxhall Gardens) were the mode in London; Marie-Antoinette herself enjoyed a *tour* here. At the edge of the park, at 2 Rue Louis-Boilly, are some of Monet's best works at the **Musée Marmottan** (*open daily except Mon 10–5.30; adm, Ⓜ La Muette*). The Marmottan family also collected medieval miniatures, tapestries, and Napoleonic art and furniture, but the Monet works are the highlight: some of the *Nymphéas* (Water Lilies), a view of the *Pont de l'Europe* behind Gare St-Lazare, one of the *Cathédrales de Rouen* and a view of the British Houses of Parliament. In 1985 the Marmottan's most famous painting, Monet's *Impression: Soleil Levant* (1874) for which Impressionism itself was derisively named, was brazenly heisted during opening hours, but after a six-year leave of absence in Corsica it's back on duty on the wall.

Every Parisian knows the 16e's most imposing landmark, the **Maison de Radio-France** on the Seine. A round aluminium-and-glass complex begun in 1953, it is the perfect symbol of postwar Paris—a weird, inhuman tribute to unchained technology, housing a weary, state-controlled media bureaucracy. Some of its own employees call the place 'Alphaville' after the spooky 1960s science-fiction film by Godard. Numbers are everywhere, and every room has its Cartesian identification plaque: the 32nd room on the 4th floor in the 5th sector is, with relentless logic, no. 4532; in the basement, the employees enjoy the reassurance of having their own nuclear shelter. The architect, Henry Bernard, had been a winner of the academics' Holy Grail, the *Prix de Rome*. The tour of the **Musée de Radio-France** (*open daily except Sun, 10.30, 11.30, 2.30, 3.30; and 4.30, adm; ring © 01 42 30 21 80 for times of tours in English;* RER: *Ave du Président Kennedy-Maison de Radio-France*) offers exhibits on the beginnings of French TV, going back to the first broadcast in 1931 (America didn't manage one until '39). Before privatization, this building was also the home of ORTF, the television monopoly that acted as a shameless propaganda organ for the government in the de Gaulle years.

From here, you can see the Seine divided by the thin **Ile des Cygnes**, which according to legend is made of the bones of horses. The Protestants murdered in the 1572 St Bartholemew's Day Massacre are said to have been buried here; folks claimed that made the grass grow thicker and sweeter than anywhere else in Paris. The swans (*cygnes*) were a gift from Denmark in the 1600s, which Louis XIV installed here. The island is only wide enough for a narrow promenade, the Allée des Cygnes, though that did not stop duellists from making it a favourite night-time rendezvous in the 17th century; by day, the housewives of Paris came to wash their tripes. The familiar lady at the southwestern end is Paris' largest model of the **Statue of Liberty**, an 1885 gift from the American colony of Paris.

---

## Auteuil: Guimard's Houses

From the rear of the Maison de Radio-France, follow Rue La Fontaine southwards. This street, a poor area not even paved in the 1880s, was destined to become the showcase of France's greatest Art Nouveau architect. The first building, at no. 14, is Guimard's most famous work, the **Castel Béranger** (1894). Don't expect a transcendent masterpiece; Guimard was no Gaudí, though like Gaudí he personally designed every facet of his buildings down to the very furniture inside. Castel Béranger was built as a simple and typical middle-income apartment block of the 1890s; the details, including the wrought-iron decorative work and the doors and windows, are wonderful, and they are all you'll get to see of this private apartment building. For it, Guimard suffered the insults of his contemporaries that were a badge of honour for any Art Nouveau architect. Parisian critics called Castel Béranger 'Castel Dérangé'.

The Guimard tour continues down Rue La Fontaine: more fine buildings at nos. 17 (the Bar Guimard) 19, 21 and 60, and also around the corner on Rue François-Millet, no. 11. No. 65 Rue La Fontaine, the **Studio Building**, is a work of the interesting early 20th-century architect Henri Sauvage. There's more Guimard all around, on 34 Rue Boileau, and on Avenue Mozart, nos. 120 (his own house, built in 1909) and 122; scholars are uncertain whether the last design was really by

Guimard or his wife, who was a painter. For Guimard's later works, already experimenting with Art Deco, see no. 10 Rue Jasmin, and no. 18 Rue Henri-Heine (1922), where the architect lived before moving to New York in 1938, fearing for the safety of his Jewish wife. For a building that at least equals the Castel Béranger, walk a few blocks south to the extraordinary block of flats at **142 Avenue de Versailles**; don't miss the stair.

For the next generation of French architects, you need only walk a few steps to Square du Docteur-Blanche and the **Fondation Le Corbusier** (*open Mon–Fri 10–12.30 and 1.30–6; adm,* Ⓜ *Jasmin*). The home of the foundation, which puts on exhibitions about Le Corbusier and his contemporaries, is the Swiss architect's best Parisian work, the adjacent La Roche and Jeanneret houses. Both look like modern additions to small art museums, but that is only because Le Corbusier has had so many followers in our day. These are good buildings, and it isn't hard to imagine how revolutionary they must have looked in 1927 when they were built. They would be fun to live in now. For another variation on this theme, visit **Rue Mallet-Stevens** (three streets north of the Le Corbusier houses, on Rue du Docteur-Blanche). Robert Mallet-Stevens, a Belgian avant-garde stage and film set designer, fancied himself a 'cubist' architect, and got a chance to express himself in an entire short street.

## Bois de Boulogne

> *I could feel that the Bois was not really a wood, that it existed for a purpose alien to the life of its trees; my sense of exaltation was due not only to the admiration of the autumn tints but to a bodily desire.*

> Marcel Proust, *Du côté de chez Swann*

Not so long ago plenty of people who have never heard of Proust have felt exactly the same way; after the Eiffel Tower, the Bois de Boulogne was the most visited place in Paris—'the world capital of prostitution' no less, where every day over a million francs changed hands, and not a *sou* going towards the 6 million francs it cost to make the Bois respectable for daytime visitors. Now all the access roads are blocked off at night, things are considerably more staid.

Perhaps it was something in the air. The first story about the Bois de Boulogne concerns the Countess of Provence's troubadour, Arnaud Catelan, whose reputation was such that Philippe le Bel begged the countess to send him to Paris for a season. The countess obliged, and sent sweet herbs and wine with Catelan; when Philippe le Bel's guards came to escort the troubadour through the perilous forest, they thought his baggage contained treasure, and murdered him in the central meadow (still known as the Pré Catelan). King Philippe found the murderers out, when he noted they smelled of lavender.

The bandits and *routiers* (unemployed English mercenaries in the Hundred Years' War) continued the reign of terror until Louis XI gave the forest to his barber-surgeon as a game reserve, and sent in squads of police to protect the stags. François I had Girolamo della Robbia build him the Château de Boulogne here, where he installed his mistress, La Ferronnière, for whom, it is said, he died of loving too fervently. Other kings installed their own loves—Diane de Poitiers and Gabrielle d'Estrées lived here; even after the Revolution, when the château was razed, the Bois kept its reputation for love. In the 17th century its bowers were full of impetuous couples, as one Parisian wrote at the time: 'There are two types of public gardens in Paris. In the first, one goes to see and be seen, and in the second, one goes not to see nor be seen by anyone'.

The Bois owes its current appearance to Napoleon III, who spent his early years in London and gave the Bois to the city as its own Hyde Park. Roads, riding and walking paths crisscross it, and during the day at least it remains a high-fashion rendezvous, with its two race courses—**Longchamp** and **Auteuil** (for steeplechasing)—one of Paris' haughtiest clubs, the Cercle du Bois de Boulogne, **Stade Roland Garros** (tennis stadium, site of the Paris Open), Paris' polo grounds, private riding clubs and restaurants, mostly of the pricey variety.

For anyone with crumbsnatchers in tow, the biggest attraction is on the Neuilly side, to the north (Ⓜ *Les Sablons*) where the **Jardin d'Acclimatation** has nearly every possible activity for kids—camel and canal-boat rides, playgrounds, a small zoo, a doll's house with antique toys, a *guignol* (puppet show), children's theatre, bumper cars, crafts and games (*open 10–6, special activities at weekends and during school holidays; adm to the park; separate adm to some activities and rides*). Another good bet for older crumbsnatchers (and especially for adults) is the nearby **Musée National des Arts et Traditions Populaires**, 6 Avenue du Mahatma-Gandhi (*open daily except Tues 9.45–5.15; adm*), a 1969 functionalist building housing beautiful displays of pre-industrial art and cultural artefacts from France's provinces, arranged according to the dictum of Claude Lévi-Strauss: 'All human civilization, no matter how humble, presents two major aspects: on one hand, it is in the universe, on the other, it is a universe itself.' Top it off with a few strikes at the **bowling** alley, a few steps away near the Mare St-James.

The most scenic spots in the Bois include the **Lac Inférieur**, with its islets and emperor's kiosk (near RER: *Ave Henri-Martin* or Ⓜ *Ranelagh*); the **Shakespeare garden** by the open-air theatre in the **Pré Catelan**; the **Grande Cascade**, an artificial Swiss Alps waterfall, just east of Longchamp; and for garden and rose lovers, the sumptuous **Parc de la Bagatelle** (*a 15-min walk from* ⓜ *Pont de Neuilly or take bus 244 from* ⓜ *Porte Maillot or RER Reuil-Malmaison, adm 10F*).

The original Château of Bagatelle was built for Gabrielle d'Estrées's nephew; in 1777 it was purchased by the Comte d'Artois (the future Charles X), who bet Marie-Antoinette that he could knock down the old palace and erect a new folly in 64 days. He succeeded—although at the cost of 1,200,000 livres, double the building's original estimate. After the Revolution one owner made it into a paying attraction called 'Mohammed's Paradise' before the 4th Marquis of Hertford purchased it for less than a quarter of what the Comte d'Artois had spent. The 3rd Marquis had served as Thackeray's model for Lord Steyne in *Vanity Fair*, and his tight son was little better, the man who let his Irish tenants starve during the potato famine and who boasted on his deathbed: 'When I die I shall at least have the consolation of knowing that I have never rendered anyone a service.' When his illegitimate son, Richard Wallace, inherited Bagatelle, he made up for his father's stinginess by becoming the most generous man in Paris, funding field hospitals and keeping the poor Parisians and the British community from starving during the siege in 1870. He was given the Légion d'Honneur for his good deeds, but was so disgusted by the Thiers government that he left Paris for good, taking to London the paintings that were to form the Wallace Collection, but leaving masses of money behind for the 80 public fountains that bear his name.

## Quartier Dauphine

At the east end of the Bois de Boulougne, near ⓜ **Porte Dauphine**—the most beautiful of the original Art Nouveau stations built by Guimard—there are three small museums that may pique your curiosity: **Musée de la Contrefaçon**, 16 Rue de la Faisanderie (*open Mon and Thurs 2–5 and Fri 9.30–12; adm*), is run by Paris' Manufacturers' Union to display the thing they hate most: counterfeits. Cartier watches, rum labels, Lacoste shirts, some pretty good and some ludicrous; but as long as the name is spelled differently (Channel No. 5, Contreau Triple-Sec) and there's a slight variation in the wording of the label, it's legal in France, so *caveat emptor*. To the east, up Avenue Foch at no. 59, the **Musée d'Ennery** (*open Thurs, Sun and hols from 2–6*) housing Far Eastern art, puppets, masks and especially *netsukes*—fantastically carved Japanese buttons. To the south, in Place Victor-Hugo, the church of **St-Honoré d'Eylau** has a good Tintoretto (*Adoration of the Shepherds*); walk up Avenue Victor-Hugo to no. 50 for the 1902 masterpiece of Art Nouveau architect Charles Plumet (1861–1928), more popular than Guimard for his references to French classical styles. At the end of its courtyard is the entrance to the **Fondation Dapper**, which puts on first-rate exhibitions of pre-colonial African art (*during exhibitions, daily 11–7*).

## Saint-Germain-en-Laye

West of La Défense, the old town of Saint-Germain-en-Laye (RER:A) grew up around a priory founded by Robert the Pious in 1050. The priory became a château lavishly rebuilt in brick by François I, and it saw the dawn of the Sun King, who spent most of his first 40 pre-Versailles years here and hired Le Nôtre to lay out the long gardens. There are regular tours of the château, and the excellent **Musée des Antiquités Nationales** (*open daily 9–5.15, closed Tues, adm*), an archaeological collection ranging from Lower Paleolithic to Merovingian France. The Marquise de Montespan's old digs in Saint-Germain-en-Laye house the **Musée Départmental Maurice Denis-La Prieuré**, 2bis Rue Maurice Denis (*open Wed–Fri 10–5.30, Sat, Sun and hols 10–6.30, adm*), containing Symbolist and Nabis paintings by Denis, Bonnard, Vuillard, and company.

## North Paris: Museums of the 9e and 10e

Scattered in some of the sleepiest areas of Paris are a few corners you may want to explore. The area south of Montmartre is grandly known as **Nouvelle Athènes**, apparently because of its neoclassical architecture, mostly neo-boring and now filled with insurance companies. The most attractive parts are **Rue de la Tour-des-Dames** east of Ste-Trinité church and the **Square d'Orléans** (entrance 80 Rue Taitbout), where George Sand and Chopin lived opposite one another. Their time is documented in **Musée de la Vie Romantique** (Maison Renan-Scheffer), at 16 Rue Chaptal (*open daily except Mon, 10–5.45; adm, ⓜ St-Georges*). Exhibits concentrate on George Sand: her jewels, ties, drawings and bric-à-brac—typical of the Romantics, the ambience is more important than the ephemeral exhibits.

The *quartier*'s second museum is a different kettle of fish, the **Musée Gustave-Moreau**, 14 Rue de La Rochefoucauld (*open 10–12.45 and 2–5.15, Mon and Wed 11–5.15, closed Tues; adm, ⓜ St-Georges*). The introspective Symbolist Moreau lived here with his Mom and Dad, painting his strange mythologies and mystical exotica from dead civilizations with lush jewel-like encrustations of paint which personify *fin-de-siècle* decadence, especially his *femmes fatales*, some of whom obviously eat men for breakfast. Most of his students, among them Matisse, Marquet and Rouault, found more benign muses.

From the late 1830s, the neighbourhood was famous for its *lorettes*, young women who upset the good bourgeoisie as much as Moreau's Salomés. Building specula-tors along Rue Notre-Dame-de-Lorette had rented their unwanted houses cheaply to the women, hoping to create a respectable street by making it look occupied. Lorettes were neither interested in working or becoming anyone's mistress, but wanted to enjoy themselves, drifting from lover to lover.

In the 10ᵉ, Rue du Paradis (⓪ *Poissonnière* or *Château d'Eau*) fits its name if you're shopping for crystal and porcelain. On no. 30bis, the sparkle reaches a rainbow flashing apogee in the **Musée des Cristalleries de Baccarat** (*open Mon–Fri 9–6.30, Sat 10–5.30; adm*), next to Baccarat's showroom. Producing wine services and chandeliers since 1764, Baccarat began making duplicates of major commissions in 1824; here they glitter in the least aristocratic of quarters.

## Les Puces

Paris has in fact three permanent flea markets, but the biggest and most famous is just outside the city at **St-Ouen** (*open more or less all day Sat, Sun and Mon*; ⓪ *Porte de Clignancourt*—**not** ⓪ *Porte de St-Ouen*; then walk down Avenue de la Porte de Clignancourt and under the Périphérique motorway). All around Paris, the cleared space outside Adolphe Thiers' city wall of 1841 became the *Zone*, a weird desolation inhabited by the most unfortunate of Paris' poor. Many of them went into the junk and old-clothes trades, and by the 1880s it became a custom to visit the *Zone* to buy such things. Around 1920, when the walls were demolished, the dealers coalesced into regular markets—just in time to be discovered by André Breton, looking for bizarre and incongruous items of refuse with which to haunt the dreams of respectable folk.

Les Puces (literally, 'the fleas') has been upscaling ever since. Today it harbours every sort of flea, from posh antiques merchants to desperate rag-pickers. If the market had been a few hundred yards south, in Paris proper, it would have been gentrified or destroyed by the government long ago. As it is, in the tatty suburb of St-Ouen, it has troubles enough, between an unsympathetic Communist government and the Paris developers who have bought up some of the buildings; they say they'll retain the character of the place, but no one believes them.

We include Les Puces here, instead of in the shopping section of this book, because while you may not have room in your grip for a Louis Quinze chair, a visit can still be one of the most entertaining things to do in Paris. Breton was right, because Les Puces is Surrealism itself, where all the disembodied things of a city's past are whirled in the modern mixmaster. Buying a gilt-framed picture of somebody else's grandmother is the essential Surrealist experience.

It starts, in the empty fields south of the doleful Périphérique, with a vast expanse of cheap clothes stands, typical of those you'll see in any French market. Beyond the motorway, if you continue straight on Avenue Michelet you'll find the entrance to the first and perhaps poshest of the covered markets, the **Marché Biron**: lots of fancy gilt atrocities from the Second Empire, and choice Art Nouveau and Deco pieces. There's less ambitious stuff in the back alley; a good shop for posters and reproductions at no 140, beautiful nautical and scientific instruments at nos. 173

and 181. Beyond the Biron on Avenue Michelet is the domain of the leather stands, along with stands that sell hardware and ten-a-penny nails.

The far end of the Biron opens onto **Rue des Rosiers**, the main drag of Les Puces, where the entrances to most of the other covered markets are. There are more antiques in the **Marché Dauphine**, a modern metal barn with palm trees and a fountain in the centre, and a delightful **mural** of market life at the entrance. The **Marché Paul-Bert**, currently fashionable, was begun in 1945, its spaces reserved for dealers who had their businesses confiscated during the German occupation. The **Marché Serpette** is newer, with mostly 20th-century serious antiques and kitsch items, while the **Marché Vernaison** is the biggest and the most like London's Camden Lock; the trendiest and most popular of all is the **Marché Malik**, with clothes and bric-à-brac from the 1960s and Americana.

For ambience no place in France can match, visit the Funky Broadway of the Puces, **Rue Jean-Henri-Fabre**, parallel to the Périphérique. Everyone has music playing; the current favourites seem to be Peruvian pipe bands and Barry White. The metal buildings and concrete pylons are decorated with posters for Kurdish Communist groups and the latest offerings of the local cinema, films like the *Two Twat Tango*. The pavements are lined with stands selling old postcards, Rastafarian paraphernalia, wigs and books (lots of used Tintins with crayon marks); behind are sheds where you can buy ladders by the dozen or bulk lots of toilet paper. Between the stands, three-card monte artists prey on chumps (the game's called *bonneteau* in Parisian slang). Saddest are the areas at the end under the overpasses of the Périphérique. Buyers and sellers alike are dressed in grey; goods displayed on cloths include tampons, dead televisions and grimy rubber ducks.

The back streets, such as Rue Paul-Bert and Rue Lecuyer, offer more surreal treats: barbers' chairs, bugles, bronze flamingos or a 20ft home-made model of a French aircraft carrier. Bet it's still there when you pass by—with a lower price .

**The other Puces:** there are two, both also just outside the Paris boundaries. On the Left Bank, the trendy **Puces de Vanves** (*open Sat and Sun,* Ⓜ *Porte de Vanves*) is nothing at all like the big show at St-Ouen; just stands out on the pavements along Avenue Georges-Lafenestre with a wide selection of just about everything, but with lots of competition from sharp-eyed Parisiennes for anything decent and cheap. Shabbiest of all, but still fun, is the **Puces de Montreuil**, in a degraded area just outside the Porte de Montreuil (*open Sat, Sun, Mon,* Ⓜ *Porte de Montreuil*). Running this long desperate gauntlet of rubbish, you might well find something interesting—it's the best of the three *puces* for old records, and there will be finds in books and old clothes. ('I've been looking for this book for five years,' I said. 'But where have you been? It's been *here* five years,' they told me.) Dealers selling new clothes and household items show up on Sundays.

The métro is the only way to go to this close-in northern suburb. It's the last stop on the number 13 line (*direction* St-Denis-Basilique). Climbing out of the tube stop—and especially if you arrive on market days—it will seem as if the métro has magically transported you to an especially lively village. Paris is a world away, and you are surrounded by crowds of Frenchmen doing what Frenchmen were born to do—haggle good-naturedly over oysters, geese and asparagus.

St-Denis, with its great abbey that was the necropolis of the kings of France, is today one of the classic *banlieues défavorisées*. Communist-run, gritty and poor, it saw its transformation from rural idyll to industrial inferno in the 19th century, when some 60 factories making everything from cars to pianos moved in. Today the old village is only the centre of a suburban agglomeration of over 100,000 people. It's well run, and still has a noticeable sense of civic pride, as you'll learn talking with the folks at the **city tourist office**, 2 Rue de la Légion d'Honneur, across the street from the abbey. One of these charming ladies is probably responsible for St-Denis's new slogan: 'The city of dead kings and a living people'.

## The Abbey Basilica

St Denis, who shambled up here from Montmartre with his head tucked underneath his arm (*see* Walk VII, p.217) to begin his career as patron of France, is a truly shadowy character. All the stories connected with his name are so utterly facetious, it's hard to credit any of it. Like so many other French saints—St Pol (Apollo) or St Saturnin (Saturn)—he may be a half-conscious fabrication, papering over survivals of paganism that early missionaries had assimilated into the new faith. And what would be more natural than retaining Denis—really *Dionysus*—as guardian deity of the wine-quaffing Gauls?

In any case, there was a cemetery here from Roman times, and an abbey from perhaps the 5th century, favored by Dagobert and other Merovingian kings, who began the tradition of making it the site for royal burials. St-Denis's present glory is entirely due to its rebuilding under the remarkable Abbot Suger (1081–1151). Diplomat, counsellor to Louis VI and Louis VII, and ruler of France while the latter was away on the Crusades, Suger also found time, according to his own accounts, to invent Gothic architecture single-handedly. Perhaps his architects had something to do with it too, but the good abbot, constantly cajoling, suggesting, kibitzing over the sculptor's shoulder and even helping hoist the stones, must get a fair share of the credit; his ideas may well have been decisive in the use of pointed-arch vaulting and rose windows in the new architecture.

To promote his beloved abbey, Suger wrote influential works on history and government, practically creating by himself the mythology of the sacred kings of France, while emphasizing the importance of the abbey and the role of St-Denis as protector of all the kings since Clovis. After his death, St-Denis seems to have become a regular forgery factory, as monks cranked out false chronicles, charters and bequests dating from as early as Charlemagne's time to prove certain rights of the abbey and its royal patrons. Wealth, influence and royal cadavers accumulated over the centuries, and not surprisingly St-Denis and its 'frightful reminders of our former tyrants' became one of the chief targets of the revolutionaries of 1793. Twelve hundred years' worth of anointed bones was tossed into a pit; the revolutionaries trashed the tombs and carted off France's richest church treasure (much of which finally found its way to the Cabinet des Médailles in the Bibliothèque Nationale). Under the restoration, Louis XVIII started fixing the place up, and Viollet-le-Duc came to finish the job in 1859.

The basilica's **façade** is one of the triumphs of Suger and his architects, a marvel of clarity and order that pointed the way to all the Gothic cathedrals that followed; the sculptural trim on the upper levels and the three carved portals became a Gothic commonplace; thanks to the revolutionaries almost all the reliefs and statues are copies. Inside, notice that the nave and transepts are in a different style, a confident mature Gothic—they weren't completed until the mid-13th century under the masterful eye of Pierre de Montreuil. The unassuming **choir** is the real Gothic revolution, with its ribbed vaulting. From the west portals you can see how the walls now tilt backwards a bit. The lovely **rose window**, with seasons and signs of the zodiac, is one of the few remaining bits of medieval glass, as are the *Tree of Jesse* and *Life of the Virgin* in the apse behind the main altar.

From the right aisle, you begin the tour of the **royal tombs**, laid out haphazardly since the 1820s restoration (*open daily 10–7, Sun 12–7; adm*). These too have been heavily restored after the desecrations of 1793 and few are of artistic interest, even though they go as far back as Dagobert, who died in 639 (for all the early kings, *gisants*—horizontal effigies atop the sarcophagi—were remade during the Middle Ages). Some that stand out: near the entrance to the tombs, **François I**, praying with his wife Claude de France, on an elaborate Renaissance tomb, designed by Philibert de l'Orme; beyond these, **Charles V**, with his faithful Constable of France **Bertrand du Guesclin**, who helped keep the English out in the Hundred Years' War; on the left side of the choir, **Louis XII and Anne de Bretagne**, another Renaissance spectacular, largely the work of Germain Pilon. In the right ambulatory hangs the **oriflamme**, flame-covered battle standard of the French kings, a 15th-century copy of the medieval original, lost in the Hundred Years' War. In the **crypt**, Louis XVIII reinterred the jumbled bones of his ancestors. A marble tablet calls the royal roll, referring to Capetians, Valois and Bourbons as numbered Dynasties.

## Musée de l'Art et de l'Histoire de la Ville de Saint-Denis

St-Denis has a delightful modern museum, housed in an old Carmelite convent (*open daily except Tues, 10–5.30, Sun 2–6.30; adm*) on Rue Gabriel-Péri (take Rue de la Légion d'Honneur south from the basilica). St-Denis's reclusive Carmelites were refugees from the 18th-century Austrian Emperor Joseph II, the enlightened despot who thought such things were archaic and silly. From nun portraits and memorabilia, and an exhibit on medieval daily life, the scene changes to 20th-century, industrial St-Denis: paintings by local artists of the canals, gas works, old shop fronts and the *roulottes* (caravans) many workers lived in. The biggest exhibit is devoted to the **1871 Commune**; a floor of paintings, posters, cartoons and newspapers relate the story more thoroughly than you'll ever see it in Paris.

## Parc de la Villette

From 1867 until just a few years ago, this corner of northeastern Paris was the city's stockyards, a vast complex of market halls, slaughterhouses and marshalling yards—a place where tired male Parisians would go to get a hot glass of bull's blood from the butchers to pep them up (or else, like Marcel Proust, they'd go just to ogle the butcher-boys). In the 1960s the government began a new complex—a juicy political pork-barrel scandal just when old-fashioned stockyards were disappearing everywhere thanks to refrigerated transport. The huge building—the biggest slaughterhouse in the world—stood abandoned until Giscard d'Estaing's government picked it up for one of their *grands projets* in 1974.

## Cité des Sciences et de l'Industrie

> **Ⓜ** *Porte de la Villette. For a different way to start a day's excursion, sail to La Villette in a catamaran from the Musée d'Orsay (see below). The Cité des Sciences is open daily except Mon; Tues, Thurs and Fri 10–8, Wed 12–9 pm, Sat, Sun and holidays 10–6; adm 45F, 25F after 4, under age 7 free— the Cité des enfants, Techno city, expositions, Music City, the Argonaute, Cinaxe and the Géode require separate admission.*

Now the slaughterhouse has metamorphosed into the Cité des Sciences et de l'Industrie, a rectangle of glass and exposed girders reminiscent of the Pompidou Centre, Mitterrand's critics have had their fun with this project too. As a science museum, it duplicates the fine Palais de la Découverte off the Champs-Elysées, only it's a little flashier and more up to date.

A *little* flashier? With its own internal television station, its staff of smartly costumed *animateurs* speaking 15 different languages, its computerized magneto-sensitized tickets, its 'infra-red headphones', giving a running commentary of what you're seeing, and its lasers, buzzing gimcracks and whirling gizmos that may for all we know be threatening us with total obliteration at any moment. Bring the children to help you get through alive.

The main part is called **Explora**, three floors of hyperactive exhibits, video shows and gadgets to fiddle with, including some 60,000 video screens. On **level 1**: space, with a model of the Ariane rocket with a simulated space voyage; a working model of the new French bathyscape, the *Nautilus*; ecological exhibits where you can manipulate the environment and foul it up all by yourself; a high-tech greenhouse; a pseudo-nuclear reactor; experiments with sound, sight and photography you can do—the most fun part of the museum.

Upstairs on **level 2**, one is constantly pestered by talking robots. There are some captivating astronomical exhibits; a biology section where you can test your own body; a transportation section that includes a simulated ride on the Airbus 310. There are **Planétarium** shows (with English translations) and 3-D films in the **Louis Lumière cinema**. On the ground floor, the **Cité des Enfants**, is a brilliant place for children to experiment with plants, animals and computers, with expert attendants to help. There are two sections: one for ages 3–5, one for 5–12; **Techno Cité** is designed for children from age 11 up (*but open only on Wed and Sat during the school year*).

## The Géode and Music City

All around Science City stretches the **Parc de la Villette**, the 'Park of the 21st century' designed by American Bernard Tschumi, who won Mitterrand's competition. The grass has taken hold, and the little trees are getting on gamely, but the place still has something of a stockyards air to it. The **Canal de l'Ourcq** runs right through the middle, and scattered around are a dozen bright red **follies**. These interesting constructions, each a variation on a single high-tech architectural theme inspired by Le Corbusier, house various activities: video and plastic arts workshops for kids (*come Sat or Sun at 2.30*), an **information centre**, a café, and a chain hamburger stand. Some of the follies are just for fun, and one is the entrance to the **Argonaute**, a 1957 submarine open for your exploration. Also for the children, there are three delightfully innovative **playgrounds**, the Jardin des Vents for toddlers, the Jardin des Voltiges and the Jardin du Dragon.

The park is full of surprises; there's a witty Claes Oldenburg 'monumental sculpture', the **Buried Bicycle**, a **Garden of Mirrors**, a **Bamboo Garden** with a strange sort of stone cylinder in the middle 'for meditation' and **Le Cinaxe**, a moving, vibrating film theatre set on hydraulic jacks that simulates space flight and other moving, vibrating scientific experiences. No doubt you've been wondering about the giant steel marble, sitting in its pond next to the Cité. Already a familiar landmark of Paris, this is the geodesic sphere, or **Géode**, housing yet another theatre (*a show every hour Tues–Sun 10am–9pm, book in advance, © 01 36 68 29 30, or try to get a ticket as soon as you arrive at the park*). Outside, 6433 stainless-steel geodesic triangles provide the mirror effect; inside is a 180°, 4000 sq-ft screen showing overwhelming 70mm science films.

Across the Canal de l'Ourcq from the Cité and the Marble, the southern half of the park is occupied by the two new white asymmetrical buildings of the **Cité de la Musique,** designed by French architect Christian de Portzamparc: concert halls (one with hyper-acoustics designed by Pierre Boulez), the Conservatoire of dance and music, and a **Museé de la Musique** with 4500 instruments, including Stradivarius and Guarnieri violins, and Beethoven's clavichord, all cosily gathered together in one place (*open Tues–Sat, 12–6; Thurs until 9.30, Sun 10–6; adm*). The **Zénith** concert hall is already a popular rock and schlock venue. In a rare fit of soft-heartedness, the government passed up a chance to demolish another fine old building. Instead they turned the market house of the old stockyards, the **Grande Halle**, into a place for jazz concerts (Salle Boris-Vian). The magnificent 780ft glass and iron hall, built in 1867 by Jules de Merindol, is perhaps the least known of 19th-century Paris' architectural wonders. A no-nonsense, utilitarian building, yet one inspired by the Crystal Palace and at the ends strangely reminiscent of Pisa cathedral.

## Rotonde de la Villette

From the Parc, the **Bassin de la Villette** stretches southwest towards Place Stalingrad, connecting the Canal de l'Ourcq and the Canal St-Martin. This wide spot in the canal system was intended as a place of recreation when it was built under Napoleon I, the 'Champs-Elysées of the East'; it isn't much to look at now, and still won't be when the city finishes its plans to surround it with skyscrapers. At its Stalingrad end stands the largest of Claude-Nicolas Ledoux's four surviving *barrières* from the Farmers-General wall. The sandstone Rotonde (1784) looks too grand to have been a customs house; it has been beautifully restored, but the city hasn't found a better use for it yet than to house a small library.

## Canal St-Martin

Finished in 1825 to bring freight into the centre of the city, this relic of the Industrial Revolution once was lined with factories, warehouses and crowded dwellings. In the 1970s, when commercial traffic was declining rapidly, the Pompidou government proposed to fill it in and build a motorway, the key to the planners' dream of making Paris an American-style automobile city. For once Parisians reacted; the plan fell through under the weight of its own ridiculousness. But the last 15 years have been hog heaven for the building speculators; the neighbourhoods along the canal have very little character left, and the entire area will be unbroken concrete within another decade.

Which is sad, because the canal itself is still a charming place for a promenade: lined with big trees, and graced with high, Venetian-style bridges, and its original, hand-operated locks still in use. For two km (one mile) north of the Bastille, the canal flows underground, under great stone vaults beneath Boulevard Richard-Lenoir. You can travel the whole thing between April and mid-November in a catamaran *Le Canotier* or *La Patache* from the Quai Anatole-France (i.e. the Piscine Deligny parking lot, by the Musée d'Orsay), departing at 9.30; or from the Information 'folie' in the Parc de la Villette at 2.30. Book, © 01 42 40 96 97.

One landmark along the canal is the **Hôtel du Nord**, from the famous Marcel Carné film of the same name (1938), starring Arletty and Louis Jouvet. Anyone who saw the film may regret the contrast between the lively canal-side neighbourhood of '38 and the present reality; the hotel is closed, but for the moment it still hangs on at 102 Quai de Jemmapes, under imminent threat from developers.

## Belleville and the Parc des Buttes-Chaumont

Once upon a time this was a pretty village where people went to get away from Paris. Belleville in particular was one of the major pleasure grounds of the city in the 18th and early 19th centuries, its main street, Rue de Belleville (then Rue de Paris!), lined with cabarets and *guinguettes*, unpretentious café-gardens for dancing; half of Paris would come up on any warm Sunday afternoon. They had to 'come up', because Belleville is the second-highest point in Paris, only a few metres shorter than Montmartre. They 'came down' on Ash Wednesday, in the *Déscente des Courtilles*; anyone who had a coach or wagon, or could afford to hire one, joined a delirious parade down from the *guinguettes* to Paris, singing and tossing candied almonds and flowers to the crowds.

In the 1850s Belleville started to fill up with working people as Paris expanded outwards. Haussmann annexed the district in 1860, and used it as a sort of overflow tank for the tens of thousands his new projects were dispossessing. Seemingly overnight, the area changed from a garden suburb to the worst slum Paris had ever seen: little water, no sanitation and no building controls. The *guinguettes* became dangerous dives, ruled by young thugs who had read Wild West stories and called themselves *apaches*. Belleville became the heart and soul of the Paris Commune, and the Communards' last stands were around the *mairie* and Père-Lachaise cemetery. The 1900s brought waves of immigration—at first everyone from Auvergnats to Russian Jews, and later, after the war, North Africans, Yugoslavs and Asians; lower Rue de Belleville has become the Right Bank's Chinatown. Belleville kept its reputation as Paris' proletarian capital until the 1970s, when the government began to liquidate the area systematically in favour of concrete housing estates. Not so long ago a rather charming quarter of old houses and neighbourhood character, it is currently being swamped by vast tracts of redevelopment hideous even by Parisian standards.

At least the area still has Paris' loveliest park—ironically also Haussmann's creation, the **Parc des Buttes-Chaumont** (Ⓜ *Buttes-Chaumont*). A rocky haunt of outlaws in the Middle Ages, well known to François Villon, the park was begun in 1867. In an age when the 'picturesque' was fully in vogue, the natural charms of the Buttes weren't quite good enough. Haussmann's designers brought in thousands of tons of rock and created the artificial cliffs that are its fame today. The centrepiece is a familiar landmark, a steep island in a lake, crowned by a small classical **temple**, modelled after the Temple of the Sybil in Tivoli. The climb rewards you with a seldom-seen view over Montmartre and the northern parts of Paris; before the Eiffel Tower was built this was the favourite spot for suicides. Other great views points are the old village green, **Place des Fêtes** (Ⓜ *Places des Fêtes*) with a market Tuesday and Friday, and the ultra-modern, terraced **Parc de Belleville** (Ⓜ *Pyrénées*), a great place to watch the sun set over Paris.

Edith Piaf was literally born on the streets below, under a streetlamp, shielded behind the cloak of a kindly gendarme (there's a plaque at 72 Rue de Belleville). Daughter of an itinerant singer and an Italian acrobat, Piaf and her half sister were raised in a provincial whorehouse before taking to the streets of Belleville to sing for their supper. Edith's voice soon attracted attention, and her career as Paris' most beloved singer and songwriter was launched. She eventually bought a grand *hôtel particulier* at Boulogne, but used her ornate marble bathtub with gold taps for her goldfish—she went through life with dirty feet. Very tiny, bird-like, dirty feet, judging by her shoes in the **Musée Edith Piaf** (south towards Père-Lachaise, in a flat at 5 Rue Crespin-du-Gast, *Mon–Thurs 1–6 by appointment only,* Ⓒ *01 43 55 52 72, closed July;* Ⓜ *Ménilmontant*). Here too are all her recordings, the gown she wore at Carnegie Hall, her large stuffed teddy bear, letters and more.

## Père-Lachaise Cemetery

> Ⓜ *Père-Lachaise or Philippe Auguste. Open daily 7.30–6, Sat 8.30–6, Sun 9–6; winter hours, 6 Nov–15 Mar, 8–5.30.*

Père-Lachaise (La Chaize, really) had the best job in France. As Louis XIV's confessor, he held the keys to heaven for a king who was both superstitious and rotten to the core. It isn't surprising that Lachaise got lots of presents, which he converted to real estate here in what would later be the centre of the 20$^e$. In 1804, under

Napoleon's orders, Prefect of Paris Nicholas Frochot bought the land for cemetery space, something Paris was in dire need of at the time. Frochot was a clever fellow; it's said he thoroughly fleeced the baron who owned the land, then later sold him back a plot at a ridiculously high price. To popularize the new development, the prefect invited in a couple of celebrity corpses—Molière's and La Fontaine's. They didn't mind a bit.

The 'most famous cemetery in the world', and the largest in Paris, Père-Lachaise has always been a favourite place for a stroll; Balzac said he liked to come here to 'cheer himself up'. In design, it is a cross between the traditional, urban sort of French cemetery, with ponderous family mausolea in straight rows, and the modern, suburban-style model. Brongniart, the architect of the Bourse, laid it out like an English garden (the original part, near the main entrance on Boulevard de Ménilmontant); its curving lanes and greenery influenced later cemetery designers, even in Britain.

At the main entrance, you can buy a good map to all the famous stiffs for 10F. There are few signs to help you find the graves you're looking for, except rock poet Jim Morrison's; his fans have thoughtfully decorated everybody else's tombs with directions in felt pen. From the entrance, the Avenue Principale will take you to Avenue du Puits, where you can pay your respects to **Colette**, then turn right for section 7 and the tombs of Père-Lachaise's senior residents, **Héloïse and Abelard**. Few of the cemetery's residents have known as many posthumous troubles. Héloïse died 20 years after her faint-hearted lover, in 1164, and according to her wish was laid in his tomb near Troyes. Legend says that when the sepulchre was opened to put in the body of Héloïse, Abelard held out his arms to receive her and embraced her. In the 17th century prudish abbesses would pry their remains apart and put them in separate tombs, and romantic abbesses would reunite them. In 1792 they were moved and placed in a double coffin, with a lead barrier 'for decency's sake'; in 1817 the coffin was brought here by Alexandre Lenoir.

The next left, onto Chemin Denon, will take you to **'Fred' Chopin** (sec 11) and **Adolphe Thiers** (sec 12); the man responsible for the massacres of the Commune felt no irony in choosing to be buried near the spot where the last of the shootings took place (*see below*), but Parisians don't forget; they have been desecrating his tomb regularly since 1877.

Across from Thiers is the cemetery **chapel**. In the sections to the left of it you can seek out **Michelet** (sec 52), Balzac (sec 48), poet **Gérard de Nerval** (sec 49), **Bizet** (sec 68), early socialist **Louis Blanc** (between 57 and 67) and **Delacroix** (sec 48); near the painter is a large phallic something, the strangest tomb in the whole cemetery. It immortalizes one Félix de Beaujour, and from the decoration it is impossible to tell if Félix was the high priest of a shadowy cult or if he simply wanted a tomb in the style archaeologists of the time thought was 'ancient Etruscan'.

To the right of the chapel is the oldest and loveliest part of Père-Lachaise, with florid statuary and dead politicians around the **Rond-Point Casimir-Perier**, along with philosopher and part-time crank **Auguste Comte** (sec 17). British Admiral Sidney Smith, who helped beat the French in the Napoleonic Wars, always loved Paris (sec 43); you'll find him near **Corot** (sec 24), **Hugo** (sec 27), and **Moliére** and **La Fontain**e (sec 25). A clique of Napoleon's marshals rests quietly in adjacent secs 28, 29 and 39: **Cambacérès, Murat, Masséna** and **Ney**, along with the painter **David** (sec 39). For **Jim Morrison**, follow the crowds to sec 6. The cops keep a constant eye on the place, and past sights—wild-looking Germans cooking sausages on a camp stove, naked trippers sprawled over other graves and chanting in tongues—are no longer common. Devotees today leave flowers, smokes and playing cards (face cards only), incense and small toys. There is no proof, incidentally, that Morrison is actually buried here; many people claim he isn't even dead.

The wide path called Avenue Transversale No. 1 (with Félix's monument closing the view at the northern end) neatly bisects the cemetery. Just beyond it, near the centre, you can visit **Simone Signoret** (sec 44), keeping company with fellow actress **Sarah Bernhardt** (just across a path in sec 91). Nearby are **Auguste Blanqui**, a leader of the 1848 revolt and the Commune (sec 91), **Proust** (sec 85) and **Apollinaire** (sec 86), and an unpleasant outsider in sec 85, **General Rafael Trujillo**, dictator of the Dominican Republic until 1961 and one of the champion nasties of this nasty century. The large structure in sec 87 is the **Columbarium**, in which are kept the ashes of dancers **Loïe Fuller** and **Isadora Duncan**.

Near the divine Sarah, in 44 is a small tomb that draws as many worshippers as Morrison's, that of **Allan Kardec**. Kardec, born Léon Rivail in 1804, was one of the fathers of 19th-century spiritualism. His followers are still numerous enough, in Paris, to keep up a near-permanent vigil around the flower-bedecked shrine. Don't fool with these people; they will come after you if you hang around too long, or if you try to photograph the tomb. But take time to read the incredible notice posted behind Kardec by the City of Paris, a calm and reasoned philosophical tract warning against the folly of adoring the remains of a mortal being.

Kardec's street leads straight to the eastern gate. Turn right before the exit, and you'll come to sec 89 and one of the grandest tombs of all, Sir Jacob Epstein's tribute to **Oscar Wilde**. As everyone knows, Oscar is here due to certain character flaws in the people and institutions of his native land. Epstein's memorial, a sort of looming Egyptian Art Deco deity, ensured that Wilde would find no peace even in the afterlife. The statue's prominent winkie became the talk of Paris. First a fig leaf was put on it, and then in 1922 an unidentified Englishwoman who apparently knew the deceased batted it off, fig leaf and all; the busted winkie was last seen serving as a paperweight on the cemetery keeper's desk.

Press on to the far southeastern corner of the cemetery; in sec 94, the fellow with the dynamo in his lap is **Théophile Gramme**, a Belgian who invented the thing in 1869. Near the wall in 94 are **Gertrude Stein** and **Alice B. Toklas**, and in 96, **Modigliani**. In the far corner is section 97; this was the last bit of free Paris in 1871, where the Versailles troops lined up the last 150 Communards against the wall (the *Mur des Fédérés*). The wall is a place of pilgrimage for French leftists, many of whom are buried nearby, including 1950s Communist chief **Maurice Thorez**, and there are memorials to the Parisians deported to the Nazi camps during the occupation. But the most famous resident of 95 is no doubt **Edith Piaf**. **Eugène Pottier**, who wrote the *Internationale*, is over in sec 95, and for one last political martyr, there's **Victor Noir** in sec 89. Noir was a brave journalist who criticized Napoleon III; a cousin of the Emperor shot him in cold blood in 1870, and got off in a fixed trial, causing big demonstrations. His *gisant* shows him exactly as he was when he died, with an apparent state of excitation that Parisian girls used to come and rub for good luck.

## Musée des Arts d'Afrique et d'Océanie

*239 Ave Daumesnil,* **Ⓜ** *Porte Dorée. Open daily except Tues, 10–12, 1.30–5.30; Sat, Sun 12.30–6; adm.*

In 1931 Paris felt compelled to put on another World Fair, the first in six long years. This one was a little different: the *Exposition Coloniale* was a government effort put on to show the French how wonderful it was to be imperialists, and how much money they were earning by it. The White Man's Burden was a commonplace in France up to the 1960s, not surprising in a country that has always felt it had a *mission civilisatrice*, even vis-à-vis its immediate neighbours. As a journal of 1931 expressed it: 'Colonialism isn't just building docks, factories and railroads, it also means winning over for the sweetness of humanity the ferocious hearts of the savannah and the desert.'

The fair, the first not to be held around the Champs-Elysées, took place in the Bois de Vincennes and surrounding areas; the star attraction was a life-size lath-and-plaster replica of the central temple of Cambodia's Angkor Wat. The one permanent building was the 'Museum of the Colonies' which became after the war the 'Museum of Overseas France'. Though necessity has made the name change again, at least it's still there—not just a relic of a silly pretension, but one of the best collections of African and Pacific Islands art anywhere in Europe.

But before the art, in the basement is an excellent **Tropical Aquarium**, with everything from electric eels to the crocodile from the Nile. On the main floor, the strangest ethnic artworks are the painted Art Deco celebrations of colonialism by the French themselves. **Oceanian art**, in two rooms on the main floor, includes everyday objects from Melanesia and some exceptional bark paintings from Australian aborigines. Upstairs, the first floor is devoted to artefacts from **Black Africa**—and not only from French colonies—such as the beautiful masks and figurines from the Ashanti and Akan of Ghana, and the Yoruba of Nigeria. The Dogon of Mali, with their complex, ancient culture and myths, have been much more of an influence on the French than the French have been on them, and their sculpture is well represented here. The **Maghreb**—Algeria, Morocco and Tunisia—gets the second floor to itself.

## Bois de Vincennes

*Ⓜ Porte Dorée for the zoo; Ⓜ Château de Vincennes for the castle.*

Like the Bois de Boulogne, its matching bookend at the other end of Paris, Vincennes owes its existence to the French kings' love of hunting. They set it aside for that purpose in the 1100s, and Philippe-Auguste even built a wall around it to keep out poachers. In the 14th century the Valois kings built its castle—a real fortified castle, not just a château, for this was the time of the Hundred Years' War. As long as the nearby Marais was fashionable, so was Vincennes, but when Louis XIV left Paris in the opposite direction, for Versailles, the neglected hunting ground was turned into a public park. During the Revolution most of it became a space for military training grounds and artillery practice, and it had to be almost completely reforested in the 1860s.

Besides the open spaces, the main attraction is the **Zoo**, one of the largest in Europe (*open daily 9–5, –6 in summer; adm*). It offers giant pandas and a 67m (220ft) artificial mountain (which has started to collapse). Adjacent is one of the prettier parts of the park, the **Lac Daumesnil** with its islands, one blessed with a fake romantic ruin like the one in Buttes-Chaumont. Further east (*Ⓜ Château de Vincennes, then bus no. 112*) is the **Parc Floral** (*open daily 9.30–8, adm 10F*): water lilies, orchids and dahlias, and a good place to bring the kids at weekends, with rides and special entertainments.

# The Castle

*At the northern edge of the park,* ⊕ *Château de Vincennes. Open daily 10–5, from April–Sept 9.30–5; guided tours on the hour; adm.*

The finest example of medieval secular architecture in Paris, this 'Versailles of the Middle Ages' shows what the French could build even in the sorrows of the 1300s. Begun under Philippe IV in 1337, it was completed in 1380 in the same half-fortress, half-residence style of the old royal palace on the Ile de la Cité, a walled enclosure with a keep built into the walls, and inside additional state buildings and a chapel—a Sainte-Chapelle just like the one on the island.

Under Cardinal Mazarin the complex was modernized, just in time for Louis XIV to go off to Versailles and forget about it. Louis was always short of prison cells—no king in French history locked up so many political prisoners—and Vincennes made a convenient calaboose; in the 1700s Mirabeau spent three years here on a *lettre de cachet*. In the 1730s a porcelain manufacture was started on the grounds that later became the famous Sèvres works.

Napoleon, another ruler who liked to keep his cells full, made it a prison again while rebuilding the fortifications just in case. Unwittingly he provided Vincennes with a chance for a short but brilliant military career—the only bit of Paris that never surrendered in the Napoleonic Wars. The hero of the story is General Daumesnil, who had lost his leg fighting the Austrians and was given the easy job of commandant here. When the Allies took Paris in 1814, peg-legged Daumesnil refused to submit; he sent them a message: 'The Austrians got my leg at Wagram; tell them to give it back or else come in and get the other one.' Daumesnil stood fast until the Hundred Days, but after Waterloo he was besieged again. And he held out again, until he could surrender Vincennes to a Frenchman, King Louis XVIII. He was still commandant during the Revolution of 1830. When an armed mob came for the hated ministers of Charles X, who had been imprisoned there, he kept them out too, saying he'd ignite the powder room if they tried to storm the place. During the First World War the trenches around the castle were used for shooting spies—Mata Hari was one of them.

The highlight of the tour is the **donjon**, the 14th-century keep (*closed for restoration until 2000*), strong and taciturn outside, but a beautiful residence within, containing stained glass and excellent sculptural work, especially in the Grande Salle. The Salle des Gens d'Armes, like the one in the Conciergerie, is a lovely Gothic vaulted space. In the bedroom on the second floor England's King Henry V died in 1422; they par-boiled him in the kitchen to keep him nice for the trip home to London.

Besides these, the tour inside takes you through the **Résidence Royale**, built by Le Vau for Louis XIV, and the **Sainte-Chapelle**, almost a copy of the famous one, though built in the flamboyant Gothic in fashion at the time (1400). Long neglected, the chapel was finished true to its original style by Renaissance architect Philibert de l'Orme in 1522. The stained glass inside is also from the 1500s.

On the back fringes of the Bois de Vincennes, you can seek out the last magnificent glass-and-iron **Baltard Pavilion** from Les Halles, reconstructed as a kind of mini-convention centre in **Nogent-sur-Marne** (from Paris take RER: *Nogent-sur-Marne*; the Pavilion is just left past the Syndicat d'Initiative (Tourist Office), in Avenue Victor-Hugo). Amongst the modern tower blocks it looks like a secret message from another star, but the Nogentois—many refugees from Paris among them—have done their best to make the old iron maiden feel at home, with a Wallace fountain, cobblestones and a Paris lamppost.

## Faubourg St-Antoine and Bercy

From the Place de la Bastille, the new Opéra seems to hide the entire quarter; walk around behind it, and you'll find one of the most attractive of Paris' old workingmen's areas, now becoming trendy and upscaling rapidly. The main street, Rue du Faubourg-St-Antoine, has been famous for its furniture makers, and there are still a few—most of them making ghastly 18th-century imitations. The old Faubourg still survives around picturesque and increasingly arty **Rue de Lappe** and the **Marché d'Aligre**, which got its start centuries ago, when a good-hearted abbot of St-Antoine, which owned the land, allowed traders to sell clothes to the area's poor, providing they kept the prices very low (Ⓜ *Ledru Rollin* or *Gare de Lyon*; *takes place every morning until 12.30 or so*). In Rue d'Aligre most of the stalls are North African, perfumed by fresh mint, coriander and the raw ingredients of a couscous; it's also a good place to pick up a bargain *tagine* (clay pot) to make your own. Just south, a mile long railway viaduct over of Avenue Daumesnil has been converted into the **Viaduc des Arts**, where the brick arches have been restored to house traditional crafts workers–lace, furniture, ceramics, glass, wrought iron, hunting horns and so on, while the walkway on top has been planted with a serpentine hanging garden. Further down Avenue Daumesnil, the *mairie* of the 12$^e$ is a wonderful idiosyncratic Art Deco building, supported by a bevy of caryatids.

Further east, along the Seine, the old village of **Bercy** used to make its living by unloading all the wine and grain that came down the river to Paris. By our times the area had filled up with a miasma of docks, warehouses and factories, and today it is the biggest redevelopment area in Paris. The *grands projets* already completed include the **Palais Omnisports de Paris-Bercy**, seating 17,000, used by sports events as well as the biggest pop concerts and shows. On the riverfront, the monolithic grey bunker **Finance Ministry** (1989) stretches away from the Seine as if it were a continuation of the adjacent Pont de Bercy. Elegant, in its way, it neverthe-less cannot escape having the look of a place where poor souls tot up numbers all day; Mitterrand picked the design of architects Huidobro and Chemetov himself, after a competition.

## The 13e

Sinister, desolate, surreal are this arrondissement's traditional adjectives. In its traditional poverty, its one claim to fame is having introduced horsemeat to France (the first butcher was in Place d'Italie in 1866). But despite all the dismal words that have been written about the old 13e, the soulless anomie left behind by the planning yoyos of the 1950s and '60s is worse. Its positive features are its nega-tives—no tourists, no Nouveau Parisian yuppies, no gentrification.

Even this may change by the big millennium. In this most woebegone corner of Paris, Mitterrand the First planted his last *grand projet*, the new **Bibliothèque Nationale** located on a 17-acre riverside site between Ponts de Bercy and Tolbiac. Parisians jokingly call it the TGB—*Très Grande Bibliothèque*. A hitherto unknown Frenchman, Dominique Perrault (no relation to the architect of the Louvre) won the design contest with four 280ft high towers with sunken gardens and subter-ranean reading rooms, a design blasted when someone finally noticed that glass-walled skyscrapers provide the worst possible conditions for keeping old books (dark metal screens were added to keep out the sunlight, for a few million more francs). The TGB is so breathtakingly ugly that no one seems in a rush to move in, although the folks in charge promise the move from the old Bibliothèque Nationale will be complete by the end of 1997.

There are two areas in the 13e that merit a detour: **Butte aux Cailles**, Quails' Hill, landing point of history's first manned balloon flight (*see* Topics, p.54) and an old quarter that had the gumption to unite against the cement mixers (*take* Ⓜ *Corvisart and walk south*). It is one of the few neighbourhoods in Paris with a strong sense of community; on Rue de la Butte-aux-Cailles you'll find a workers' cooperative restaurant (Le Temps des Cerises, *see* Food and Drink, p.401), a coop-erative jazz and raï bistrot (Le Merle Moqueur) and a library devoted to re-educating the unemployed and helping kids with their schoolwork. The local swimming pool (1924) is an neo-Gothic confection in brick, in Place Paul-Verlaine.

The second neighbourhood is Paris' **Chinatown**, the southeastern corner of the 13e roughly south of Rue de Tolbiac and east of Avenue de Choisy. The name Chi-natown encompasses a dozen nationalities, many of whom came to France as refugees from Cambodia, Vietnam and Laos and, by dint of the age-old immigrant recipe of hard work and sacrifice, have prospered even in this concrete twilight zone; the covered shopping centre Olympiades is a veritable Oriental shopping mall (Ⓜ *Porte d'Ivry*), but for the casual visitor the main interest is gastric, either as a voyeur in the supermarkets along Avenue d'Ivry or as a client in one of the scores of restaurants from noodle kitchens to the some of the best Vietnamese restaurants west of Hanoi.

## Parc Montsouris and the Cité Universitaire

Parc Montsouris or 'Mount Mouse' (**RER**: *Cité Universitaire*) with its lawns, old-fashioned merry-go-round and exotic trees, is the second largest park in Paris *intra muros*, after Buttes-Chaumont. The highest point of the park is occupied by the **Bardo**, an impressive replica of the palace of the beys of Tunis built for the World Fair of 1867, and reconstructed here by Ferdinand de Lesseps, builder of the Suez Canal; a weather station until 1974, it now serves as a Tunisian cultural centre.

South of Parc Montsouris stretches the **Cité Internationale Universitaire de Paris** (*main entrance at 1–6 Boulevard Jourdan*). Founded in the 1920s to offer students decent lodgings in the spirit of the Latin Quarter's medieval colleges, this vast campus was set aside for various nations to build pavilions for their Parisian scholars around the big communal manor house, the **Maison Internationale** (a gift from John D. Rockefeller). Go here to find out if there's anything going on (usually not; the 6000 bright young things from France and 122 other countries don't mingle as much as one might hope, and the only time the Cité makes the news is when the students have political dust-ups). But the 35 pavilions offer a curious architectural sampler: note the geometrical **Dutch Pavilion** (1928, by Dudok), the **Swiss Pavilion** (1932) by Le Corbusier, one of his first buildings set up on *piloti*, or stilts, and next door, the rougher-edged **Brazilian Pavilion** (1959), Le Corbusier's last Paris work, designed with Lúcio Costa, and the World Fairish **Fondation Avicenne** (1969, by Parent, Foroughi and Ghiai).

Lenin spent his last four years in Paris at 4 Rue Marie-Rose (between Rue du Père-Corentin and Rue Sarrette, Ⓜ *Alésia*) now a little **Maison-Musée Lenine**, with items relating to his Paris stay, including his dishes and chess set (donated by Gorbachev in 1986)—in the old days every official Soviet visitor made the pilgrimage (*open by appointment*, ✆ 0142 79 99 58). With the collapse of the Party in the USSR, reporters gathered on Rue Marie-Rose, probably hoping someone would soap Lenin's windows at least, only to be told by representatives of the left-wing 14ᵉ: 'Communism is dead. Long live Communism!' On Saturday and Sunday, untamed capitalism rears its head at the ungentrified fleamarket, the **Puces de Vanves** (Avenues Georges-Lafenestre and Marc-Sangnier, Ⓜ *Porte de Vanves*).

## Abbaye Royale du Val-de-Grâce

**Ⓜ** *Port-Royal. Open 10–12 and 2–5; Gregorian chant Sun 11am.*

Before the Revolution, vast areas of Paris were covered by wealthy monastic complexes; Val-de-Grace, on Rue St-Jacques at Bd Port-Royal, is the only one to survive intact. Anne of Austria, wife of Louis XIII, installed the first Benedictine nuns here in 1621 and built for herself a small pavilion—complete with a false floor—directly over the gypsum quarries, where she kept a nest of Spanish spies to abet her plots against Richelieu. The cardinal got wind of what was going on in 1637 and abruptly banned further religious retreats by the queen. Miffed, Anne vowed to build a magnificent church in exchange for a little Louis, and proved that God was on her side by giving birth the next year after 23 childless years (one story about Louis XIV's prisoner, the Man in the Iron Mask, says that he was the physician of Louis XIII, who had announced in the post-mortems that the old king was impotent). François Mansart drew the plans, and a seven-year-old Louis XIV (the little bastard) laid the foundation stone in 1645. Progress was slow, because of difficulties shoring up the gypsum galleries; Anne impatiently fired Mansart and hired Lemercier to complete the task. The galleries came in handy later when Anne had a point of access drilled from her quarters, famous as 'the hole in the service of Madame the Queen', a wondrous innovation in the days when French kings received visitors while unburdening themselves on a *chaise percée*.

The church itself is cold potatoes, but then few French architects ever got a handle on Baroque. Val-de-Grâce's plan is a copycat of Palladio's Redentore in Venice; over the altar rises a quasi-clone of Bernini's baldachin in St Peter's; in the lofty dome (also modelled on St Peter's) Pierre Mignard's fresco, the *Gloire des Bienheureux* has a cast as big as an old Broadway musical and figures three times life-size, all pap—just like St Peter's. In a niche under the chapel to the left the embalmed hearts of queens and kings were buried in canopic lead cases—until the Revolution, when Val-de-Grâce became the military hospital it is today. The lead cases were melted down into bullets destined for other royal tickers, while their contents were auctioned off to a pair of painters, St-Martin and Martin Droling, who ground up the hearts of Louis XIV and many others to make a much sought-after, brownish glaze for oil paintings.

A door from the St-Louis chapel leads out to the cloister and gardens, where you can take a look at Anne of Austria's pretty pavilion, supported in part by rusticated columns, and the monumental façade of the old convent with its mansard roof. A new hospital stands at the end of the gardens, where researchers are developing methods to zap brain tumours with lasers, computers and 3-D cameras.

Nearby, on Rue du Faubourg St-Jacques is the **Maternité Port-Royal**. In the aftermath of the Wars of Religion, many guilty consciences were appeased by founding convents and hospices in the *faubourgs* of the Left Bank. One was the Cistercian convent of Port Royal, founded in 1646, which became the centre of Jansenism in Paris. Louis XIV suppressed Jansenism in 1664 and converted the convent into a prison; in 1814 it became the first maternity hospital in Paris. Its cloister and chapel with paintings by Philippe de Champaigne are open Sun and Mon mornings.

## Denfert-Rochereau: Observatoire and the Catacombes

**Ⓜ** *Denfert-Rochereau. Write ahead (61 Ave de l'Observatoire, Paris 75014) to join the guided tours on the first Sat of each month at 2.30.*

As Sun King, Louis XIV was a natural patron of astronomers, and he commissioned Claude Perrault to build them an observatory. The result, a parcel of perfect symmetry, was begun on the day of the summer solstice in 1667, each corner orientated to a cardinal point, its centre pierced by the Paris meridian (2° 20' 17" east, a longitude that rivalled Greenwich as the base measure of the entire world until 1884, when Greenwich was universally adopted—except in France and Ireland, which held out until 1911). Besides its careful alignment, the Observatoire was constructed without wood or iron, to prevent fires and magnetic distortion of its instruments.

Nevertheless, when it was half completed, the Academy of Science's director, Giandomenico Cassini, complained to Louis that the building would be useless for observations unless Perrault redesigned the top floor. Perrault and the king categorically refused. The debate grew sharp, and Cassini, realizing that they were more interested in the observatory's appearance than its function, began like a good Italian to argue and gesticulate at the Sun King, who slowly eclipsed at such disrespect. Colbert saved Cassini from the Bastille by whispering to Louis: 'Sire, this babbler doesn't know what he's saying'. There was no saving the Observatory, however, which was completed to Perrault's plans (the white, ball-shaped dome is from a later date). French architectural know-how forced Cassini to erect his tubeless, cranelike 150ft long 'air telescope' on its lawn, where he was the first to see four of Saturn's moons. But the greatest contribution of Louis XIV's scientists was their measurements: the calculation of the earth's circumference, confirming the ancient Greek estimate; the distance between the earth and sun—20 times greater than what Ptolemy had believed (very gratifying to a Sun King, who wanted to be as far above humanity as possible); and the speed of light, which the Greeks had never thought of measuring.

The academy's zest for measurements continued in the Revolution. To replace a thousand higgledy-piggledy medieval measures used under the *ancien régime*, the academicians invented the metric system in 1791, as logical as pie; its metre was calculated as one ten-millioneth of a quarter of the distance from the North Pole to the Equator. Then there's the story of Urbain-Jean Leverrier (1811–77) whose statue graces the front of the Observatoire. Studying the hitherto mysterious perturbations in Uranus's orbit, Leverrier calculated the existence of another planet, its orbit, mass and distance from the earth, and in 1846 wrote to a colleague in Berlin, suggesting that if he pointed his telescope in a certain direction on a certain day, he would see a new planet. Leverrier was perfectly right. He modestly declined giving his name to what we know as Neptune, and when offered the chance to view his discovery through a telescope himself, refused. He had *known* in his mind that the planet was there; visual proof was unnecessary.

The Observatoire continues to measure away: under the monumental stair, a path leads 92ft down to a subterranean quarry, where the temperature never varies, the perfect atmosphere for the Coordinated Universal Clock that keeps France's official time, calculated to a millionth of a second.

Around the back of the Observatoire is **Place Denfert-Rochereau**, once known as the *Tombe d'Issoire*, after a giant Saracen who came to destroy Paris in the time of Charlemagne, but was cut down and buried on the spot. In 1774, 300 sq m of the square and surrounding lanes abruptly disappeared when the Roman quarries beneath gave way. Now it's one of the Left Bank's busiest traffic fandangos, guarded by the sphinx-like **Lion de Belfort**, a beast designed by Bartholdi to commemorate Colonel Rochereau's defence of Belfort in 1870, the sole 'victory' the French salvaged from the Prussian fiasco. Despite grabbing Alsace and Lorraine in the peace treaty, Bismarck let France keep Belfort in exchange for the humiliation of Paris: a Prussian triumphal march down the Champs-Elysées.

The two pavilions with carved friezes survive from the *Barrière d'Enfer*, or tollgate of hell, in the Farmers-General wall. An apt name, as one of the pavillons (no.1) serves as the entrance to the **Catacombes** (*open daily except Mon and holidays 9–11 and 2–6; adm*). Down, down the 90 steps of a spiral stair are pictures of the old gypsum quarries that make Paris a gruyère cheese under all her fine frippery. Next it's a tramp through damp and dreary tunnels to a toytown Fort of Port Mahon (Menorca), hollowed out of the wall by a bored caretaker once imprisoned there. Then there's a vicious blue puddle called the *source de Léthé*, inhabited by little pale-eyed creatures who dine on bone moss. Then the doorway inscribed: 'Halt! This is the empire of the dead.' But of course you don't halt at all, for beyond is the main attraction: the last earthly remains of Mirabeau, Rabelais, Madame de Pompadour and five to six million other Parisians removed here beginning in 1786 from the putrid, overflowing cemetery of the Innocents and nearly every other churchyard in Paris. Tibias are stacked as neatly as the tinned goods in a supermarket. Skulls, with a nice patina of age, are arranged decoratively in cross or heart shapes.

The ossuary was dubbed the catacombs in Paris' eternal effort to ape Rome, and like the morgue (*see* Walk I, p.113), it soon became a tourist attraction. The acoustics are so remarkable that in 1897 a midnight concert took place featuring the *Danse Macabre*; heavy-metal attempts to follow suit have been quashed by the authorities. During the war, the Nazis never suspected that the catacombs were the headquarters of Resistance leader Colonel Rol-Tanguy. Pinching souvenirs must be common, for bags are thoroughly checked at the gate.

## Cimetière du Montparnasse

The third-largest cemetery in Paris, Montparnasse (**M** *Edgar Quinet* or *Raspail*)saw its prestige grow along with fashion, as the quarter's habitués decided to spend eternity on the Left Bank, enjoying a view of the Tour Montparnasse rising behind the tombs. Even if cemeteries give you the heebie-jeebies, walk briefly down Rue Emile-Richard (the only municipal street in Paris with no living residents) and take the first path to the left to see the lighthearted Tomb of the Famille Charles Pigeon. M. Pigeon invented the non-exploding gas lamp, and is depicted here in the matrimonial bed next to his sleeping wife, reading by the light of his miraculous invention. Other famous folk buried east of Rue Emile-Richard include André Citroën, Bartholdi (sculptor of the Statue of Liberty), César Franck, Guy de Maupassant and Alfred Dreyfus who unwittingly had the most famous affair in the history of Paris. In the new, larger section to the west, there's a cenotaph to Baudelaire, with a bust of the poet overlooking a cocooned body near the corner of Rue Emile-Richard and Avenue Transversale (he is buried on the far side of the cemetery, under the name of Aupick, his mother's second husband); here too are Sartre, Simone de Beauvoir, Brancusi, Rude, Houdon, Bourdelle, Saint-Saëns, Serge Gainsbourg, Jean Seberg, Soutine, Zadkine and Vichy premier and German collaborator Pierre Laval, who committed suicide by swallowing arsenic the night before his execution was due, but was strapped to a chair and shot anyhow. In the southwest corner of the cemetery is the truncated 15th-century tower of Montparnasse's last windmill, which once stood in a farm where young Voltaire was wont to roam. Just north of the windmill, in Allée des Sergents-de-la-Rochelle take a look at the bittersweet statue exiled from the Luxembourg Gardens for offending public morality, called *La Séparation d'un Couple*, the woman sending a last kiss to her lover from beyond the grave.

There are a few good buildings in this neighbourhood: two Art Deco works on Rue Froidevaux near the south exit, and an Art Nouveau spectacular at 31 Rue Campagne-Première near the Raspail Métro, a magnificent confection (1911, by Arfvidson) with a ceramic façade by Bigot.

Paris' Mount Parnassus began its career as a weedy heap of tailings dug up from the many Roman quarries in the area, a mound where students came to frolic with bottles of wine and buxom muses—hence its tongue-in-cheek name taken from the holy mountain of Apollo, the god of art and poetry. In the Middle Ages, Montparnasse ground the flour for the Left Bank's baguettes; in 1780 there were still 18 working windmills. The first houses date from the 17th century, when Louis XIV built the Observatoire to create an *axe* or prospect, with the Palais de Luxembourg, and laid out the Grand Cours du Midi (now Boulevard du Montparnasse). Land was still cheap enough in the early 1800s for Montparnasse to experience a first flash of fashion with its dance halls, *guingettes* and cabarets. After the construction of the Gare Montparnasse (the terminus from Brittany), a piquant workers' quarter grew up south of the Boulevard du Montparnasse; even today the area boasts a strong Breton flavour.

In the 1870s Verlaine, Anatole France and Sully-Prudhomme called themselves 'The Parnassians', giving Montparnasse its first real association with the arts. Other Parnassians arrived in the early 1900s: Modigliani and Apollinaire in the lead, fleeing rising prices in Montmartre. Art connoisseurs Gertrude and Leo Stein moved in just behind them; Lenin, Trotsky and so many other revolutionaries lived in the area that the Tsarist police had a special Montparnasse unit to keep an eye on them.

After the First World War, these pioneer *Monparnos* were followed by artistic and literary pilgrims and refugees from all over the world, part of 'the great migration into new prairies of the mind', as Malcolm Crowley rhapsodized. Others, the Hemingways, Fitzgeralds and so on, came as refugees from Prohibition; made instantly rich thanks to the dollar exchange rate, they helped to create the frenzy of *les années folles* as the French call the 1920s, partying the night away in Montparnasse's cafés—very much playing the old gringo role of being 'overpaid, overfed, oversexed and over here'. Or as Sinclair Lewis described the Café Dôme: 'It is, in fact, the perfectly standardized place to which standardized rebels flee from the crushing standardization of America'.

After the Second World War, the scene changes again; the culture vultures retreat back to St-Germain and the north side of Boulevard du Montparnasse, while the neighbourhood where Americans drank themselves silly was singled out for Paris' first experiment in American-style property development, in a toadstool project called Maine-Montparnasse. Planned back in 1934, but begun only in 1961, this incorporated Paris' first skyscraper, a new railway station, a shopping mall and a concrete wasteland of urban anomie. Technocrats hoped to make Montparnasse La Défense of the Left Bank and, like cancer cells, development spread to the south in the old working-class neighbourhood of Plaisance. Promising to erect housing, the planners instead built huge new hotels and offices; 2000 families were moved off Rue Vercingétorix to create a radial motorway direct to the Périphérique ring road (a project aborted in 1977 thanks to a neighbourhood organization). This and similar displacements since 1975 have resulted in the 14ᵉ losing a fifth of its population, nearly all of them workers forced out into deathly suburbs.

## Tour Montparnasse

> Ⓜ *Montparnasse-Bienvenüe—they aren't really welcoming us; this station is named after Fugence Bienvenüe, the engineer who designed Paris' first métro line in 1896). Viewing platforms are open from 9.30am–11.30pm summer, 10am–10pm winter, last ascent 30min before closing; adm.*

Until the advent of London's Canary Wharf, this was the highest skyscraper in Europe, 656ft high and perched at the top of Rue de Rennes; visible for miles around, it sticks up like a sore tombstone, way out of proportion to the rest of the skyline. As a building, however, the Tour Montparnasse—an elegantly curved oval of smoked glass—isn't too bad compared to some of the looming warts at La Défense. The closed-in 56th floor offers not only views but a bar, *Ciel de Paris* ('the highest in Paris!') and a film of aerial views over Paris; the 59th floor is an open terrace. On a clear day you can see for 25 miles; for many people this has the added plus of *not* seeing the Tour Montparnasse.

The ungainly, submerged shopping mall in front overlooks Place du 18 Juin 1940, the date of de Gaulle's famous BBC speech encouraging the French to fight on. A plaque near the C & A door commemorates the surrender of unburnt Paris by General von Choltitz to the liberation forces of Leclerc a little over four years later on 25 August 1944. The nearby **Mémorial de Maréchal Leclerc de Hauteclocque et de la Libération de Paris et Musée Jean Moulin** *(Bâtiment Nord-Parc, open Tues–Sun, 10–5.40; adm)*, with exhibits and audio visuals on the wartime career of the general and the Resistance leader.

The surrender was signed in the **Gare Montparnasse**, first built in 1852. It had already entered Parisian mythology in 1898, when the brakes of a train speeding at 37 miles an hour failed just as it approached the station. The guard applied the Westinghouse brake and saved the passengers, but the engine went hurtling through the glass wall and came to a halt halfway across the square, crashing into a kiosk where it killed an old woman. A postcard showing the accident was so popular it had to be reprinted seven times. A repaired glass arch façade was stuck onto the latest incarnation of the station behind Tour Montparnasse, where you can still catch a train to

Brittany, or a GV to Toulouse. Nothing, however, remains to recall the famous restaurant La Grande Californie that stood nearby, on Rue du Départ. Until it closed in 1866 its enormous hall served the cheapest food in the city (including hundreds of free meals for the poor), and no one seemed offended that the plates and cutlery were chained fast to the tables; the owner was elected mayor of the arrondissement.

A block north, at 16 Rue Antoine-Bourdelle is the **Musée Bourdelle** (*open 10–5.45, closed Mon; adm*). Antoine Bourdelle (1861–1929) was a student of Rodin, whose admirable maxim was *L'art fait ressortir les grandes lignes de la nature*. Even more prolific than Rodin, he left some 900 statues and studies in this curious red-brick building. Bourdelle's great obsession was Beethoven, whom he carved 62 times, using his death mask as a model; here too are bas-reliefs from the Théâtre des Champs-Elysées (1912) inspired by Isadora Duncan and the violent *Héraklès archer* (1909). If you don't want to go in, look at the courtyard: a monumental petrified garden party gate-crashed by the Trojan horse.

Not far from here, just behind the Gare de Montparnasse at 32 Blvd de Vaugirard, a cream-coloured building decorated with concrete prisms holds the **Musée de la Poste** (*open Mon–Sat 10–6; adm*). Five floors offer an overview of postal history, from ancient letters on clay tablets to the modern PTT. There's a complete collection of French stamps (note the lovely, meticulous engravings on issues up to the 1960s), vehicles and uniforms; from the siege of 1870, a balloon and microfilm messages brought on the legs of carrier pigeons into the capital.

## Plaisance

This old working-class quarter to the south of the Montparnasse complex got its name from its many pleasant *guinguettes* in the 18th century. Though increasingly threatened by high rents, and by the concrete office blocks that are sprouting like toadstools all around the Montparnasse centre, it still lives up to its name—one of the few places anywhere in Paris with a genuine neighbourhood feel to it.

Facing the Gare and the Tour, though, the developers have had their way with a big piece of Plaisance, in what is now the **Place de Catalogne** (Ⓜ *Gaîté*). Designed by the neo-neoclassical Catalan architect Ricardo Bofill, this monumental colonnaded and pedimented amphitheatre (1974) may look like a Stalinist project of the '50s, but it has the advantage over the other bunker-mentality buildings in the area in that it replaces old working-class housing with affordable flats (425 subsidized units out of 574). It's a sorry sign of our times that Place de Catalogne doesn't even pretend to be a place where residents can meet and linger; traffic spins around a centre entirely hogged up by a pretentious fountain called *The Crucible of Time*, where water (sometimes) flows up and spills over the tilted disc, made of 500,000 blocks of Breton granite.

There are pedestrian zones and lawns to the south, however: Place de l'Amphithéâtre and, through a giant arch, grassy Place de Séoul, surrounded by angular reflective glass and closed off by three Doric columns the size of sequoias. The whole was only a practice run for Bofill's even bigger neo-neoclassical housing project, Montpellier's Antigone (1983).

Plaisance has a remarkable parish church: **Notre-Dame du Travail** *(open 8–12.30 and 2.30–7)*, just off Place de Catalogne at 36 Rue Guilleminot. This is a monument to its abbé Soulange-Bodin (1861–1925), who spent his career founding mutual-aid societies, food cooperatives and workingmen's clubs. His idea for 'Our Lady of Work' was to make a 'universal sanctuary' for workers, and as most of the funds for its building were raised by popular subscription it was built as economically as possible. The result is Paris' most striking and honest ironwork church, designed by Jules Astruc (1899–1901); his delicate use of girders in the nave and chapels has had few imitators. The basic style of the interior is Art Nouveau rather than the usual Gothic, and it has recently been restored, unfortunately to the detriment of its original frescoes in the apse, showing the patron saints of the trades dressed in workers' smocks of 1900.

To see the reheated remains of old Plaisance, wander around the neighbourhood's central streets to the south: Rue Pernety and Rue Raymond Losserand (**Ⓜ** *Pernety*). To the north, on the other side of Avenue du Maine, lies another street that helped to give Montparnasse its reputation in the old days: **Rue de la Gaîté**. This will be a sad trek for anyone who remembers the Montparnasse of even 15 years ago, especially since its last great music hall, Bobino's, was converted into a disco. Like its counterparts in Montmartre, this old 'street of gaiety' grew up outside the Farmers-General tax wall where the tax on drink was low. One old-timer, the **Théâtre de la Gaîté-Monparnasse** at no. 26, still has its stucco masks; at no. 17 the **Comédie Italienne** performs Goldoni and *commedia dell'arte*, just as in the days of Watteau. There's no plaque for the street's most famous resident, Trotsky, amid dilapidated sleazola capitalist sex shops. Further north, Gaiety Street changes its name to Rue du Montparnasse, famous for good Breton crêpes in a number of old-favourite crêperies.

## Boulevard du Montparnasse: Famous Cafés

Boulevard du Montparnasse has been devoted to pleasure ever since it was the summit of the knoll where the students sang and danced, until Louis XIV levelled it for the Cours du Midi. Before the First World War, La Rotonde (at no. 102, now prettified beyond recognition) was a favourite of Picasso, Apollinaire, Trotsky and Lenin. Trotsky often gave fiery speeches, while Lenin bided his time playing chess or enjoying the charms of his favourite prostitute, who after his rise to power complained to anyone who would listen that the cheapskate still owed her money. Le Sélect (no. 99), famous for its fights in the 1920s, is still the noisiest of the four and has kept its original décor intact. Le Dôme, with an interior designed by Slavik, is the quietest of the four and most touristy. In 1927 its owner made a near-fatal blunder when he fired his managers, who got their revenge by converting an old coal depot a few doors down into a rival, La Coupole, which was immediately, and remains today, one of the trendiest spots to be seen in Paris; recently restored as much as possible to its original appearance, its 24 pillars are decorated with paintings by Othon Friesz and 30 other artists. (Near here, at Rue Vavin 26, don't miss the '**Bathroom Building**' covered with blue and white tiles built in 1912 by Henri Sauvage, who wanted to create inexpensive 'hygienic' housing for the poor).

Further east, where Boulevard du Montparnasse crosses Avenue de l'Observatoire, the famous *guinguette* **La Closerie des Lilas** first opened its doors in 1847, in an immense grove of lilacs over the current RER Port Royal station. Baudelaire, Verlaine and Mallarmé were regulars of this first version; after the First World War it was reborn here as a bar and restaurant, a favourite rendezvous of the Surrealists, who during a feast in 1925 got into a heated argument with some other poets over patriotism. When the waiter served what André Breton called '*un assez triste colin sauce blanche*', it proved the Surrealist point that there was nothing to be patriotic about; the police arrived to find them swinging from the chandelier shouting '*A bas la France!*' ('Down with France!'). A plaque in the bar marks the spot where Hemingway stood (a victim of haemorrhoids) while writing *The Sun also Rises*.

La Closerie looks across to a statue of Napoleon's 'bravest of the brave', Marshal Ney, who was executed near here after refusing all chances to escape from prison after Waterloo, and the Fontaine de l'Observatoire (1875) by Carpeaux, where sassy tortoises spit in the eyes of rearing horses with seal tails and four nymphs balance the world as easily as a beach ball. Towards the Jardin du Luxembourg, you'll find Rue Michelet, guarded by a fantastical Assyrian-Egyptian brick **Institut d'Art et d'Archéologie**. Rue Michelet leads to Rue d'Assas, where at 100bis you can visit the delightful garden and sculptor's studio of the **Musée Zadkine** (*open daily except Mon, 10–5.30; adm*). Ukrainian Osip Zadkine purchased this charming house in 1928; among the works displayed here is a model of his masterpiece, The Destroyed City (1947), in Rotterdam.

## The 15ᵉ

The 15ᵉ is the largest and most populated arrondissement in Paris with some 200,000 souls, but for the visitor it has nothing very compelling to show for it, unless you count the thrills on the waterslides at the huge sport complex,

Aquaboulevard (*see* Sports, p.452). At weekends, visitors to the aforementioned Puces de Vanves may want to meander across the tracks to Rue Brancion, site of the excellent **weekend book market**. This skirts Paris' newest park, **Parc Georges-Brassens** (1985) named after the singer-songwriter who spent his last years nearby, in Rue Santos-Dumont. It replaces the old Vaugirard abattoir—hence the two bronze bulls at the entrance at Rue des Morillons (nearest ⓜ *Porte de Versailles*). The park has a good playground for kids, a pond and along Rue des Morillons a scent garden for the blind (and everyone else) and Paris' newest mini-vineyard, planted in 1985 and yielding a *clos de Morillons* that is said to be a notable improvement on Montmartre's *pipi de chat.*

At 2 Passage de Dantzig stands Paris' first *cité* for artists and its most singular historical monument, **La Ruche** (the 'hive'). Designed by Eiffel as the wine pavilion in the 1900 World Fair, the Ruche was scheduled for demolition in 1902 when a mediocre academic sculptor, Alfred Boucher, purchased it and several other cheap pavilions and relocated them to this site, then within ear-shot of the slaughterhouse. In all, *père* Boucher created 140 studios and flats (the 24 in the Ruche were triangular wedges so narrow they were nicknamed coffins), which he leased to his 'bees'—impoverished painters and sculptors—at a nominal or uncollected rent. Many of the first residents, Brancusi, Soutine, Chagall, Zadkine, were émigrés from Eastern Europe; the place reeked of tea, sausages and horseradish. During the First World War the Ruche was requisitioned to house refugees (Chagall returned to find all his paintings gone, except for a handful used to roof the concierge's rabbit hutch). To this day, some 80 'bees' still buzz in the hive.

The 15ᵉ is the address of the prestigious **Institut Pasteur**, 25 Rue du Dr-Roux (ⓜ *Pasteur*) recently in the news in the who-discovered-the-AIDS-virus controversy. It was founded by Louis Pasteur in 1888 and continues his research into vaccinations; his apartment, drawings, portraits, items relating to his career and to the Institute, are part of the **Musée Pasteur** (*open 2–5.30, closed Sat and Sun and Aug; adm*). After his death the government wanted to stick him in the Panthéon, but his family preferred him to lie where he had worked, in the crypt.

To see the 15ᵉ at its best, take a stroll down slightly dilapidated Rue du Commerce, the main artery of the old village of Grenelle, annexed to Paris in 1860; note no. 78, one of the oldest butcher's in Paris. A bit further south stands an enchanting Art Nouveau building full of vegetative florishes at no. 24 Place Etienne-Pernet. From here, walk down Avenue Félix-Faure to see other pretty buildings: no. 13 with a ceramic frieze, no. 31 with sculptures, and best of all no. 40, with a sculpture representing La Fontaine's fable of the crow and the fox.

To the north, Boulevard de Grenelle is the great divider between the chic (rubbing shoulders with the aristo 7ᵉ) and the unchic (i.e. Rue du Commerce). It has a rare overground métro line for a girdle, rather like the 'El' in Chicago which whisks over Pont de Bir-Hakeim in between the towers of Passy. The last stop, near the Eiffel Tower, passes over one of the saddest sights in Paris: the **Place des Martyrs Juifs du Vélodrome d'Hiver**, where in July 1942 the Paris police rounded up 13,152 Parisian Jews for Auschwitz. Only a handful survived. Downstream along the Seine, the **Quartier Javel** gave its name to *eau de javel* (bleach), when it was manufactured in the chemical plant of the Comte d'Artoise; André Citroën built cars here in 1915, a plant that closed in 1976 along with the rest of Javel's industries, opening up a vast area for a new park and hyper-modern, hyper-ugly buildings with a few poignant remains of the past wedged between. A new bright note just to the east, however, is the new **Musée des Arts Forains**, 50 Rue de l'Eglise ⓜ *Félix Faure* (*open Sat and Sun 2–7; adm*), a reconstruction of a funfair *c.* 1890 and a great place to take the children, with its old-fashioned booths, merry-go-rounds organ grinder and jesters.

# Food and Drink

History suggests that Paris has always known how to put on a fine feedbag. 'For the Greeks, eating lots is a sign of gluttony, but the Gauls do it naturally,' commented Emperor Septimius Severus at the beginning of the 3rd century AD, when the Parisians, like Obélix, tucked into whole roast boar smothered in fat and garlic. This good Lutetian soul food gradually fell victim to the overrefined influences of Roman epicureanism, at least among the elite, and accounts of feudal feasts can be quite alarming—in the 14th century, roast swans and peacocks, pies as big as dumpsters and fish sprinkled with sugar were all the rage. Smacking his lips over such fare, François Villon declared: *'Il n'est bon bec que de Paris'* (the only good grub's in Paris), an opinion seconded by many visitors.

Even the kings got into the act. Henry IV, whenever he wasn't tending to matters of state or trying to get a tumble from Queen Margot, liked nothing better than helping with the soups and salads. Louis XV loved to whip up omelettes for Madame du Barry. Louis XVI's favourite hobby was eating till he passed out (a habit that kept him from consummating his marriage to Marie-Antoinette for eight years). In 1791, when the royal family tried to flee the Revolutionaries, they were caught at the village of Varennes, a place famous for pigs' trotters; Louis had to stop and try some.

As a rule, 'good' really meant portions bordering on the obscene. The well-to-do maintained a *table ouverte*, a buffet constantly laid for whenever they felt like eating or entertaining; a typical evening meal for these trenchermen began with a first course of *potage* with boiled meats, four entrées and two hors d'oeuvres (sausages, pigeon or partridge pie or quails), a second course of one great and two small plates of roast meats, and two entremets—pigs' ears, game dishes, eggs, artichokes, *blanc-manger* or testicles—and dessert, a huge plate of fruits and four compotes. Leftovers from these groaning tables were sold in street stands at the *pavillons des bijoux*, so named because of the bright colours of the dishes.

As for etiquette, refer to the rules in the 1695 *New Treatise on Manners Practised in France among Honest People*: Don't look greedily at the meat platter as if you wanted to eat it all yourself. Never let more than half of what you're conveying to your mouth fall on your cravat. Lick your spoon clean before sticking it in the serving dishes. Don't put food in your pocket to eat later. Never put glasses on the table, but beckon to the lackey for a glass of wine and drink it all in one gulp.

The first great celebrity chef was a Parisian, Marie-Antoine Carême (1784–1833), who invented choux pastry and raised the status of the profession from domestic to artist with his elaborate Greek temples of cake and spun sugar. 'The arts are five in number,' declared Carême. 'Painting, sculpture, poetry, music and architecture, of which pastry is the principal branch' (take that, I. M. Pei!). His books did much to hoist Paris' reputation as the gastronomic capital of the world, initiated by the Revolution, when the unemployed chefs and sommeliers of the nobles opened the first restaurants (from *restaurer*, to restore, refresh). Restaurants were the new form of dining out that was already replacing cabarets (where food was incidental to the wine) and *tables d'hôte* (where customers sat at one huge table and only the ones at the top got enough to eat and drink). In 1791 the first menu, listing a hundred dishes, appeared at the Restaurant Méot, run by the ex-sommelier of the Duke of Orléans. People still stuffed themselves to bursting point—food historians reckon that the typical 19th-century Parisian gourmand consumed 20,000 calories per day, and no one raised an eyebrow at slurping ten dozen oysters at a sitting. One Paris restaurant weighed its clients when they arrived and when they departed, and would be disappointed if they hadn't gained a few pounds. Another, in Montparnasse, paraded every dish that came out of the kitchen around the dining room, then auctioned it off to the highest bidder.

Cooking styles, like everything else in Paris, go in and out of fashion. What some enthusiastic food writers call *haute cuisine* is really what the French call *cuisine bourgeoise*—elaborate dishes concocted as much to impress as to please in the pretentious food temples of the boulevard restaurants a century ago. Lots of places still cook this way, for tourists or for nostalgic Parisians—a caloric culinary period piece in any case. *Nouvelle cuisine* (expensive ingredients, new and strange combinations, minute portions artily presented on huge plates at indigestible prices) began as a reaction to bourgeois cooking; you won't see much of it now, but the fad did much to turn the French back to a more natural way of cooking. The current style, *cuisine de terroir*, is a reaction to *nouvelle cuisine*, favouring less exotic, but fresh, seasonal and 'authentic' ingredients from the market, prepared with a minumum of fuss and a minimum of fat. Some restaurants even have their own farms, supplying organic produce, free-range fowl and beef grazed in pastures. Although vegetarians will still have a hard time in restaurants, at home Parisians eat more seafood and vegetables now than ever before.

## A Few Tips for Eating Out

Nearly all the restaurants listed below offer set-price menus, sometimes including wine, and little adventures *à la carte* are liable to make prices double. As anywhere in France, inexpensive/moderate places usually expect that most of their guests will order one of the menus, especially at lunch, and they do their best to make it a good deal. The easiest way to tell a useless restaurant or a tourist exploiter without going inside is to look at the menus—any place that offers you *crudités* and a steak/frites for over 90F, for example. Some expensive restaurants put on an inferior, inexpensive lunch menu just to get people in the door. On the other hand, some of the most famous places offer excellent bargain lunch menus that even budget-balancers can treat themselves to perhaps once or twice.

For dinner, bookings are essential—weeks in advance (lunch too) for real gourmet citadels. For the average moderate/inexpensive range restaurant, you will probably get a table weekday nights without booking, but don't try it on weekends. *Brasseries* tend to have lots of tables, and spare ones aren't difficult to find except at the most famous of them.

What restaurants choose to call themselves means little, whether it's an *auberge*, a *relais* or, most fashionable these days, a *bistrot*. The original *bistrots* evolved from the old *bougnats bois-et-charbons* run by rough-edged Auvergnats, who sold wine and snacks along with wood and coal; real ones have a friendly, neighbourhood feel, where you wait for a table over a glass of wine at the bar (all zinc before the Nazis melted them down) and dine on hearty country classics like sausages and *andouillettes*, boeuf bourguignon and salt cod. A few examples of the big, working-class restaurants called *bouillons* still survive, like the famous Chartier. *Brasseries* were founded by refugees from Alsace-Lorraine in 1871, and specialized in beer and *choucroute* (sauerkraut), along with such Paris classics as *steak/frites*, *moules/frites*, *plâteau de fruits de mer* and *steak tartare* (the Tartars, at least, stuck it under their saddles for a few hours, but Parisians eat it barbarously raw). Brasseries usually serve meals around the clock until midnight, rather like American diners, and many offer breakfast. Other restaurants open more or less from 12–2 and 7 until 10.30 or 11; in Paris though, the trend is towards staying open later and later, and nightowls will have little trouble finding somewhere in the neighbourhood that's still cooking at midnight or later.

For lunch look for the *plat du jour* (the chef's special) or a *formule* (set-price little-choice menu); nearly any café will make you an omelette, steak and *frites*, a hot dog, a horseburger with egg or plastic cheese on toast called *croque-monsieur* or *croque-madame* (monsieur with an egg). At whatever price range, be firm with pushy waiters who try to make off with your plate before you've finished. Restaurants are usually good about serving children's portions if you ask; and as a last resort every possible fast-food chain is present, in almost every possible place frequented by students and tourists. If you need help decoding a menu, *see* p.484.

For the restaurants listed below, the price range for an average meal, with wine and service included is:

| *luxury* | over 600F | *inexpensive* | 100–200F |
|---|---|---|---|
| *expensive* | 350–600F | *cheap* | up to 100F |
| *moderate* | 200–350F | | |

## Ile de la Cité and Ile St-Louis                *Restaurants*

### moderate

**Au Monde des Chimères**, 69 Rue St-Louis-en-l'Ile, 4ᵉ, ✆ 01 43 54 45 27. A pretty *bistrot* with a *brandade de morue* just the way *maman* prepared it on a good day; around 350F, lunch menu 160F with wine (closed Sun and Mon).
*Pont Marie* Ⓜ

**L'Orangerie**, 28 Rue St-Louis-en-l'Ile, 4ᵉ, ✆ 01 46 33 93 98 (dinner only; book). One of the most elegant and romantic dining rooms in Paris, founded by actor Jean-Claude Brialy as an after-theatre rendezvous for his colleagues; refined *cuisine bourgeoise*; menu only at 380F, wine included.      *Pont Marie* Ⓜ

### inexpensive

**Au Gourmet en l'Ile**, 42 Rue St-Louis-en-l'Ile, 4ᵉ, ✆ 01 43 26 79 27. Well-prepared dishes from Corrèze, in the rural southwest; 130F menu.      *Pont Marie* Ⓜ

**Brasserie de l'Ile Saint-Louis**, 55 Quai de Bourbon, 4ᵉ, ✆ 01 43 54 02 59. One of the oldest restaurants on St-Louis, informal, noisy, a good place to make friends over a plate of *choucroute* (closed Thurs lunch and Wed); popular with rugby fans.
*Pont Marie* Ⓜ

**Au Pont Marie**, 7 Quai de Bourbon, 4ᵉ, ✆ 01 43 54 79 62. In this comfortable and welcoming *bistrot*, the emphasis is on the southwest: paté, charcuterie and hearty main courses from the Aveyron. 120F menu; closed Sun.      *Pont Marie* Ⓜ

### cheap

**Au Rendez-vous des Camionneurs**, 72 Quai des Orfèvres, 1ᵉʳ, ✆ 01 43 54 88 74 (reservations suggested). Good and inexpensive menu (69F); clientele of lawyers, gays, and everyone else on the island.      *Cité* Ⓜ

### *expensive*

**Benoît**, 20 Rue St-Martin, 4ᵉ, ℰ 01 42 72 25 76. Considered by many the most genuine Parisian *bistrot*, opened by current owner Michel Petit's grandfather, devoted to the most perfectly prepared dishes of the *grande cuisine bourgeoise française* with a wonderous *boeuf mode* (closed Sat and Sun). *Châtelet* ⓜ

### *moderate*

**Caveau François Villon**, 64 Rue de l'Arbre-Sec, 1ᵉʳ, ℰ 01 42 36 10 92. A *bistrot* in a 15th-century cellar, with a strumming guitar in the evening; delicious fresh salmon with orange butter (closed Sun and Mon). *Louvre Rivoli* ⓜ

**L'Escargot Montorgueil**, 38 Rue Montorgueil, 1ᵉʳ, ℰ 01 42 36 83 51. A giant snail marks *the* place in Paris to dine on the tasty little gastropods, prepared in a number of ways (try *colimaçon d'escargots aux trois parfums*). The interior has changed little since 1830; the ceiling frescoes of scullery boys belonged to Sarah Bernhardt (closed Mon and Aug). *Etienne Marcel* ⓜ

**Ambassade d'Auvergne**, 22 Rue du Grenier-St-Lazare, 3ᵉ, ℰ 01 42 72 31 22. Mouth-watering *cuisine de terroir* from the Auvergne (*soupe aux choux et au roquefort, Charlotte aux marrons*), near Beaubourg (closed two weeks in July only). *Rambuteau* ⓜ

**Pharamond**, 24 Rue de la Grande-Truanderie, 1ᵉʳ, ℰ 01 42 33 06 72, since 1832. Where the *belle-époque* interior is a national monument, and the recipes could be as well, especially the roast pheasant and rich *tripes à la mode de Caen* (closed Sun, Mon lunch, first half of Aug); 180F lunch menu.
*Etienne Marcel, Les Halles* ⓜ

**La Tour de Montlhéry**, 5 Rue des Prouvaires, 1ᵉʳ, ℰ 01 42 36 21 82. An old-fashioned *bistrot* with lots of character and excellent cooking; try the mutton with white beans. In the moderate/inexpensive range; open 24hrs but closed Sun.
*Les Halles, Louvre Rivoli* ⓜ

### *inexpensive*

**L'Alsace aux Halles**, 16 Rue Coquillère, 1ᵉʳ, ℰ 01 42 36 93 89. A brasserie that never closes, with plenty of shellfish to go along with the *choucroute* and Alsatian whites. Menus from 167F. *Les Halles* ⓜ

**La Taverne du Nil**, 9 Rue du Nil, 2ᵉ, ℰ 01 42 33 51 82. A Lebanese stalwart of the Sentier 'garment district': fine kebabs, grilled lamb and falafel; very inexpensive lunch menus from 51F (lunch) up. *Sentier* ⓜ

**Chez Nénesse**, 17 Rue de Santonge, 3ᵉ, ℰ 01 42 78 46 49. A popular neighbourhood *bistrot* with better-than-average cooking; 80F menu for lunch, more expensive in the evening (closed Sat and Sun). *Filles-du-Calvaire* ⓜ

### cheap

**Fuji**, 8 Rue Courtalon (off Rue des Halles), 1ᵉʳ, ✆ 01 45 08 40 25. Simple Japanese; menus under 80F. *Châtelet* Ⓜ

**Au Petit Ramoneur**, 74 Rue St-Denis, 1ᵉʳ. A lively neighbourhood favourite with tables out on the pavement. Cuisine honest if unexciting; the favourite is *petit salé* with lentils. *Etienne Marcel, Les Halles* Ⓜ

**Au P'tit Rémoleur**, 2 Rue de la Coutellerie, 4ᵉ, ✆ 01 48 04 79 24. Not to be confused with the above; another bargain spot with fine home cooking, plenty of seafood (closed Sun). *Hôtel-de-Ville* Ⓜ

**Chez Léon de Bruxelles**, 120 Rue Rambuteau, 3ᵉᵉ. A chain with the best of Belgian cuisine—meaning mussels, *pommes frites* and good beer. *Les Halles* Ⓜ

**La Tavola Calda**, 39 Rue des Bourdonnais, 1ᵉʳ, ✆ 01 45 08 94 66. One of the hardest things to find in Paris is a decent pizza; this is the place. *Chatelet* Ⓜ

---

## Right Bank: Marais — *Restaurants*

### luxury

**L'Ambroisie**, 9 Pl des Vosges, 4ᵉ, ✆ 01 42 78 51 45. Under the supreme fine touch and imagination of master chef Bernard Pacaud, one of the top gastronomic addresses in the capital, in the elegant hôtel de Luynes; a short *carte* but every dish a winner from the succulent *feuillantine de langoustines* with sesame to the bitter cocoa tart (closed Sun and Mon). *Bastille* Ⓜ

### expensive

**Miravile**, 72 Quai de l'Hôtel-de-Ville, 4ᵉ, ✆ 01 42 74 72 22. A favourite of the politicians from the town hall, with its fragrant, innovative dishes from Provence (closed Sat lunch, Sun; open in Aug). *Hôtel de Ville, Pont Marie* Ⓜ

### moderate

**Chez Janou**, 2 Rue Roger-Verlomme, 3ᵉ, ✆ 01 42 72 28 41 (just north of Pl des Vosges). Friendly tiled *bistrot* from 1900 with inventive dishes from chef Marie-Odile Chauvelot, down to the roast figs in honey (closed Sat and Sun); 200F menu. *Chemin Vert, Bastille* Ⓜ

**Bofinger**, 5 Rue de la Bastille, just off the Place, 4ᵉ, ✆ 01 42 72 87 82. A bit touristy, but worth a trip for the sumptuous *belle-époque* decor and the poshest bathrooms in Paris. Specializes in seafood, especially oysters; 169F set menu with wine.

*Bastille* Ⓜ

**Marais-Cage**, 8 Rue de Beauce, 3ᵉ, ✆ 01 48 87 49 19. Sun-filled, luscious Caribbean cuisine (*Colombo de porc*) that can perk up even the greyest Parisian days (closed Sat lunch and Sun); 130F lunch menu. *Filles du Calvaire* Ⓜ

**Chez Paul**, 13 Rue de Charonne, 11ᵉ, ✆ 01 47 00 34 57. Solid family cooking (*rillettes*, duckling with prunes, beef cooked in salt) in an old Paris setting straight out of a Doisneau photo, complete with a pretty terrace. *Bastille* Ⓜ

**Les Philosophes**, 28 Rue Vieille-du-Temple, 4ᵉ, ✆ 01 48 87 49 64. Forthright cuisine (*aiguillette de canard*, warm apple pie) amongst the stone walls or outside on the terrace (closed Sun). Menus 82—128F *St-Paul, Hôtel de Ville* Ⓜ

**Piccolo Teatro**, 6 Rue des Ecouffes, 4ᵉ, ✆ 01 42 72 17 79. Not an Italian restaurant, but the best vegetarian place in the area; imaginative dishes with pretentious titles; 45, 55F lunch menu. *St-Paul* Ⓜ

**Le P'tit Gavroche**, 15 Rue Ste-Croix-de-la-Bretonnerie, 4ᵉ, ✆ 01 48 87 74 26. An old *bistrot* that has remained popular by never changing; *confits* and *coq au vin*. *Hôtel de Ville* Ⓜ

**Le Ravaillac**, 10 Rue du Roi-de-Sicile, 4ᵉ, ✆ 01 42 72 85 85. An unusual establishment, a Polish restaurant with authentically heavy stuffed cabbage and *pirogi*; named after the assassin of Henri IV; good bargain. *St-Paul* Ⓜ

**Thalassa**, 56 Rue Amelot, 11ᵉ, ✆ 01 43 55 17 11. Local Greek Cypriot taverna, with a limited but authentic menu (closed Sun). *Chemin Vert* Ⓜ

**L'Aquarius**, 54 Rue St-Croix-de-la-Bretonnerie, 4ᵉ, ✆ 01 48 87 48 71. Vegetarian, non-smoking but non-ideological; good salads and desserts. Closed Sun. *Hôtel-de-Ville* Ⓜ

**Le Grand Appetit**, 9 Rue de la Cerisaie, 4ᵉ, ✆ 01 40 27 04 95. A rare macrobiotic restaurant in Paris. Friendly place; good (especially the desserts) and no doubt good for you; also a macrobiotic food store. *Bastille* Ⓜ

**Le Temps des Cerises**, 31 Rue de la Cerisaie (south of Place de la Bastille, off Blvd Henri-IV), 4ᵉ, ✆ 01 42 72 08 63. Ancient, friendly *bistrot* (lunch only) with a good 50F menu; always a crowd (closed Sat). *Bastille* Ⓜ

**Le Trumilou**, 84 Quai de l'Hôtel-de-Ville, 4ᵉ, ✆ 01 42 77 03 98. Another popular old Auvergnat *bistrot*, overlooking the Seine (though you can't see it); menus under 100F, with lamb chops or duck with prunes. *Hôtel de Ville* Ⓜ

## Right Bank: Palais Royal/Bourse *Restaurants*

**Le Grand Véfour**, 17 Rue de Beaujolais, 1ᵉʳ, ✆ 01 42 96 56 27. More a temple than a crass commercial enterprise, this grandest of grand old restaurants with one of the loveliest dining rooms in Paris has recently hired a promising new young chef, Guy Martin, to maintain a tradition in the Palais Royal now 200 years old; lunch menu 330F, dinner 700–950F (closed Sat and Sun).

*Palais Royal, Bourse* Ⓜ

**Pile ou Face**, 52 Rue Notre-Dame-des-Victoires, 2ᵉ, ℰ 01 42 33 64 33. A great restaurant, where many of the ingredients come from the proprietors' farm in Normandy. Innovative cooking, along with simple roast fowls and lots of wild mushrooms; good wine list (closed Sat and Sun). *Bourse* Ⓜ

*moderate*

**Gallopin**, 40 Rue Notre-Dame-des-Victoires, 2ᵉ, ℰ 01 42 36 45 38. Grill-and-seafood house, in business since 1876; good 150F menu (closed Sat and Sun).
*Bourse* Ⓜ

*inexpensive*

**La Gaudriole**, Jardin du Palais-Royal, 1ᵉʳ, ℰ 01 42 97 55 49. Delicious terrace dining in fair weather, offering a generous 160F menu with wine.
*Louvre Palais Royale* Ⓜ

**Le Gavroche**, 19 Rue St-Marc, 2ᵉ, ℰ 01 42 96 89 70. The archtypical family-run *bistrot à vins* of old; authentic without even trying. Hearty country cooking from *cassoulet* to *pot-au-feu*, and very good wines. *Bourse* Ⓜ

**Les Noces de Jeannette**, 14 Rue Favart, 2ᵉ, ℰ 01 42 96 36 89. In the old theatre district, this restaurant took its name in the 1850s from a popular operetta. Wonderfully friendly, wonderful *canard a l'orange confite*. *Richelieu-Drouot* Ⓜ

*cheap*

**Chartier**, 7 Rue du Faubourg-Montmartre, 9ᵉ, ℰ 01 47 63 33 37. A rare survivor of the big, popular restaurants that used to be called *bouillons*. A listed landmark where nothing has changed since 1892; simple food at rock-bottom prices—they grill 11 tonnes of beefsteaks a year. You can't be a waiter here unless you can race about with 15 full plates at a time. *Rue Montmartre* Ⓜ

**Drouot**, 103 Rue de Richelieu, 2ᵉ, ℰ 01 42 96 68 23. Same management as Chartier—same deal and same prices. *Richelieu Drouot* Ⓜ

**Jhelum**, 30 Rue St-Marc, 2ᵉ, ℰ 01 42 96 99 43. Indian–Pakistani; menus 78 and 105F.
*Richelieu Drouot* Ⓜ

**L'Incroyable**, 26 Rue de Richelieu, 2ᵉ, ℰ 01 42 96 24 64. Ridiculously cheap *bistrot* only stays open until 9pm (closed Sun, Sat lunch and Mon eve).
*Richelieu Drouot* Ⓜ

## Right Bank: Opéra/Madeleine/St-Honoré *Restaurants*

*luxury*

**Lucas Carton**, 9 Pl de la Madeleine, 8ᵉ, ℰ 01 42 65 22 90. The perfect marriage of tradition, beautiful surroundings and one of the top-rated modern chefs, Alain Senderens. Splurge on the lunch menu of 395F (closed Sat, Sun). *Madeleine* Ⓜ

**Maxim's**, 3 Rue Royale, 8ᵉ, ℗ 01 42 65 27 94. Still the most beautiful restaurant in the galaxy, with perfectly preserved *belle-époque* rooms, and the food isn't bad either—but it is the fate of any place so famous to become more of a tourist attraction than a mere restaurant. Overpriced (closed Sun). *Concorde* Ⓜ

**Drouant**, 18 Rue Gaillon, 2ᵉ, ℗ 01 42 65 15 16. Since 1914 the seat of the Académie Goncourt, where it bestows France's most sought-after literary prize. Sumptuous Art Deco interior, famous for its elegant sauces, wine cellar and its *grand dessert Drouant*; 600F and up; 195F lunch menu (open daily and in Aug).

*Opéra, Quatre Septembre* Ⓜ

**Les Ambassadeurs**, Hôtel de Crillon, 10 Pl. de la Concorde, 8ᵉ, ℗ 01 44 71 16 16. One of the most unabashedly monumental dining rooms in Paris, and serving some of the capital's most elegant, refined and pricey cuisine—*gratin dauphinois de homard* in sour cream with caviar and much more; weekday lunch menu at 340F, dinner 610F. *Concorde* Ⓜ

### expensive

**Goumard Prunier**, 9 Rue Duphot,1ᵉʳ, ℗ 01 42 60 36 07. A top-rated seafood restaurant since the 1890s near the Madeleine, recently completely renovated (though the original bathrooms are a listed monument; closed Mon; open Aug).

*Madeleine* Ⓜ

### moderate

**Androuët**, 41 Rue d'Amsterdam, 8ᵉ, ℗ 01 48 74 26 93. If, like gastronome Brillat-Savarin, you believe 'a meal without cheese is like a beauty with one eye', come to this mouse heaven, with its cheese platters, cheese dishes and cheese *dégustation* from over 200 varieties (closed Sun). *St-Lazare* Ⓜ

**Pierre à la Fontaine Gaillon**, Pl Gaillon, 2ᵉ, ℗ 01 47 42 63 22. Seasonal menus based on seafood in the mansion of the Duc de Lorgues, tables out on the terrace by the Fontaine d'Antin (closed Sat lunch and Sun). *Opéra, Quatre Septembre* Ⓜ

**Mollard**, 113 Rue St-Lazare, 8ᵉ, ℗ 01 43 87 50 22. The talk of Paris when it opened in 1895 for its incredible ceramic Art Nouveau decor; now a modest seafood brasserie; 170F menu including wine. *St-Lazare* Ⓜ

**Le Poquelin**, 17 Rue Molière, 1ᵉʳ, ℗ 01 42 96 22 19. Opposite Molière's birthplace and popular with actors from the Comédie Française who enjoy Michel Guillaumin's light, innovative cooking (salmon with cream of chives sauce and warm *tarte aux pommes*); menu 185F, *carte* 300–420F (closed Sat lunch and Sun).

*Pyramides* Ⓜ

### inexpensive

**Aux Lyonnais**, 32 Rue St-Marc, 2ᵉ, ℗ 01 42 96 65 04. Century-old neighbourhood *bistrot*; come starving hungry to fit in the like of *boeuf gros sel* with triple potatoes (closed Sat lunch and Sun); 87F lunch menu. *Quatre Septembre* Ⓜ

**Le Roi du Pot au Feu**, 34 Rue Vignon, 9 ᵉ, ✆ 01 43 59 41 62. A rather eccentric restaurant entirely devoted to the most humble and traditional of all French dishes. Closed Sun. *Madeleine* Ⓜ

**La Ferme St-Hubert**, 21 Rue Vignon, 8ᵉ, ✆ 01 47 42 79 20. The restaurant annexe to the famous *fromager*, serving a variety of cheese dishes based on country recipes; 160–200F (closed Sun; open Aug). *Madeleine* Ⓜ

## Right Bank: Champs-Elysées and Passy     *Restaurants*

### luxury

**Alain Ducasse**, 59 Ave Raymond-Poincaré, 16ᵉ, ✆ 01 47 27 12 27. Ever since the retirement of the one and only Joel Robuchon in 1995, the hob at the Relaid du Parc's gourmet citadel has been manned by Alain Ducasse, the bright young talent of Monte Carlo's famed Louis XV restaurant. Ducasse is determined to become the first chef to earn three Michelin stars two places. Book months in advance and take out a loan for the experience of a lifetime (closed Sat, Sun, July) 750F and up. *Iéna* Ⓜ

**Taillevent**, 15 Rue Lamennais, 8ᵉ, ✆ 01 45 61 12 90. Still at the top with brilliantly prepared classic dishes, in handsome hôtel of the Duc de Morny; from 700F.

*George V* Ⓜ

### expensive

**Copenhague**, 142 Ave des Champs-Elysées, 8ᵉ, ✆ 01 42 25 83 10. Sophisticated Scandinavian cuisine specializing in a wide variety of delicious salmon dishes—or try reindeer *en terrine*; 350–500F. Prices are about 100F lower downstairs at the **Flora Danica** (closed Sun and holidays). *George V* Ⓜ

**Don Juan**, Pont de Grenelle, 15ᵉ, ✆ 01 44 37 10 20. The Don Juan is a wood-panelled yacht of the 1930s, now refitted as a floating restaurant with a two-Michelin-star chef in the kitchen; evening dinner cruises down the Seine with menus of 490, 630 and 820F.

*Ave Président Kennedy–Maison de Radio France* Ⓜ

### moderate

**Bistrots de l'Etoile**, 16 Rue Lauriston,16ᵉ, ✆ 01 40 67 11 16; and 13 Rue Troyon, ✆ 01 42 67 25 95. Both are near the Arc de Triomphe, and are spinoffs of Guy Savoy's famous restaurant nearby. The idea is to make a modest version of *haute cuisine* available to more people. One of Savoy's assistant chefs runs each (closed Sun). *Etoile* Ⓜ

**La Fermette Marbeuf 1900**, 5 Rue Marbeuf, 8ᵉ, ✆ 01 53 23 08 00. It was a formica-lined, self-service restaurant when Jean Laurent purchased it in 1978 and set about redecorating. Behind the formica Laurent found a perfectly preserved wall of beautiful Art Nouveau ceramics, hidden for 30 years. In 1982 he heard of a similar salon by the same artists (Hurtré and Wielharski), bought it and created one of the most delightful restaurants in Paris. Specialities of the house (*feuilleté* de crabe, *gâteau fondant au chocolat amer)* choice of menus 169—480F; open daily, even in Aug. Book way ahead. *Iéna* Ⓜ

**Montecristo Café**, 68 Ave des Champs-Elysées, 8ᵉ, ℘ 01 45 62 30 86. Lip-smacking good margaritas and Cuban cuisine in a pseudo-Havana setting, near capitalist gringo dinosaurs Planet Hollywood and the Disney shop. Around 250F.

*George V* Ⓜ

### inexpensive

**Le Scheffer**, 22 Rue Scheffer, 16ᵉ, ℘ 01 47 27 81 11. Neighbourhood *bistrot* serving good *entrecôte bordelaise* and a diet-demolishing dark *mousse au chocolat* (closed Sun). A la carte, near the moderate range in price. *Trocadéro* Ⓜ

## Right Bank: Montmartre                  *Restaurants*

### luxury

**A. Beauvilliers**, 52 Rue Lamarck, 18ᵉ, ℘ 01 42 54 54 42. Montmartre's top gourmet restaurant and unofficial museum of the ripe days of Napoleon III; *langoustines* with pine nuts and knockout chocolate cake; lunch menus 185, 300F.

*Lamarck Caulaincourt* Ⓜ

### moderate

**Charlot Roi des Coquillages**, 12 Place de Clichy, 9ᵉ, ℘ 01 48 74 49 64. A 1930s brasserie serving the best *bouillabaisse* outside Marseille and delicious platters of seafood and oysters. *Place Clichy* Ⓜ

**La Pomponnette**, 42 Rue Lepic, 18ᵉ, ℘ 01 46 06 08 36. Classic Montmartre bistrot, zinc bar, the works—and delicious food; in the same family for over 80 years (closed Mon lunch, Sun and Aug). *Blanche* Ⓜ

**Le Restaurant**, 32 Rue Véron (south of Rue des Abbesses), 18ᵉ, ℘ 01 42 23 06 22. One of the newest and best in Montmartre with dishes such as *queue de boeuf en papillotes de chou et fromage blanc*; good-value lunch menu at 70F, diner 120F (closed Sat lunch, Sun and Mon). *Abbesses* Ⓜ

### inexpensive

**Chez Ginette**, 101 Rue Caulaincourt, near the métro, 18ᵉ, ℘ 01 46 55 62 48. Very reasonable, with plenty of fun around the piano player in the evening; a complete night out (closed Sun and Aug); 65F lunch menu; about 100F evenings.

*Lamarck Caulaincourt* Ⓜ

**La Moulin de la Galette/Da Graziano**, 83 Rue Lepic, 18ᵉ, ℘ 01 46 06 84 77. A fine Italian restaurant underneath one of the last of Montmartre's old windmills. 60F lunch menu, also 150 and 189F. *Abbesses* Ⓜ

### cheap

**L'Afghani,** 16 Rue Paul-Albert, 18ᵉ, ℘ 01 42 51 08 72. Just your average neighbourhood Afghani restaurant. Actually it might be the only one in France, which is a shame. Delicious starters and filling main courses: roast meats or *ashak* (Afghan raviolis) for 100F or less. *Chateau-Rouge* Ⓜ

**Au Rendez-vous des Chauffeurs**, 11 Rue des Portes-Blanches (at the northern end of Blvd Barbès), 18ᵉ, ✆ 01 42 64 04 17. Out of the way, perhaps, but a rare place in the 18ᵉ for good home cooking at very reasonable prices; 63F menu (closed Wed). *Marcadet-Poissoniers* Ⓜ

## Right Bank: 9ᵉ, 10ᵉ, 11ᵉ, 18ᵉ, 19ᵉ, Bois de Boulogne

### *luxury*

**La Grande Cascade**, Bois de Boulogne, by Longchamp, ✆ 01 45 27 33 51. Napoleon III's pavilion in the park, gloriously redecorated and turned into a restaurant for the 1900 World Fair; excruciatingly correct cuisine and service, with one of the biggest wine cellars in town. Overpriced 285F menu.

**Le Pré Catelan**, Rte de Suresnes, Bois de Boulogne, ✆ 01 45 24 55 58. Lovely *belle-époque* restaurant immersed in garden far from the hubbub, food fit for an emperor—pressed pigeon, succulent langoustines, heavenly chocolate deserts (closed Sun night).

### *expensive*

**Le Pavillon Puebla**, Parc des Buttes-Chaumont, 19ᵉ, ✆ 01 42 08 92 62. Sunny, unsubtle Catalan cuisine with wines to match, in a Napoleon-III pavilion in the park; slim menus at 180 and 230F; otherwise dear enough (closed Sun and Mon). *Buttes Chaumont* Ⓜ

**Le Train Bleu**, Gare de Lyon, first floor, 12ᵉ, ✆ 01 43 43 97 96. After Maxim's, perhaps the most spectacular decoration in Paris; frescoes and gilt everything from this showpiece, built for the 1900 World Fair. Cuisine not memorable but good enough; 250F lunch menu. *Gare de Lyon* Ⓜ

### *moderate*

**Au Cochon d'Or**, 192 Ave Jean-Jaurès, 19ᵉ, ✆ 01 42 45 46 46. The best of the old meat restaurants around La Villette, specializing in pig's trotters, *ris de veau aux girolles* and steaks; menu 240F. *Porte de Pantin* Ⓜ

**Chardenoux**, 1 Rue Jules-Vallès, 11ᵉ, ✆ 01 43 71 49 52. Auvergnat-run bistrot, with *confits* and *blanquette de veau* in authentic *belle-époque* surroundings (closed Sat lunch and Sun). *Charonne* Ⓜ

**Le Quercy**, 36 Rue Condorcet, 9ᵉ, ✆ 01 48 78 30 61. *Confits* and *maigrets*, *cassoulet*, *cabécou* and Vin de Cahors: all the delights of this part of southwest France famous for its *cuisine du terroir*; 152F menu. *Anvers* Ⓜ

### *inexpensive*

**Baalbek**, 16 Rue de Mazagran, 10ᵉ, ✆ 01 47 70 70 02. Superb Lebanese food and hors d'oeuvres, with belly dancers after 10pm (reservations essential; closed Sun). Ⓜ
*Bonne Nouvelle* Ⓜ

**Brasserie Flo**, 7 Cour des Petites-Ecuries, 10ᵉ, ✆ 01 47 70 13 59. Genuine Alsatian brasserie decor and solid dishes to match (now part of a chain); a good bet after midnight, at least until 1.30am. inexpensive menus at lunch and after 10pm.

*Château d'Eau* Ⓜ

**Haynes's**, 3 Rue Clauzel, 9ᵉ, ✆ 01 48 78 40 63. The oldest American restaurant in Paris (since 1947). Dixie cuisine includes proper barbecue, chili and pie à la mode; jazz some evenings. *St-Georges* Ⓜ

**Clown-Bar**, 114 Rue Amelot, 11ᵉ, ✆ 01 43 55 87 35. An old gathering place for circus folk near the Cirque d'Hiver. Fascinating decor of old circus memorabilia, and simple but gratifying dinners (closed Sun). Mostly a wine bar, with an inexpensive lunch menu. *Filles du Calvaire* Ⓜ

**La Galoche d'Aurillac**, 41 Rue de Lappe, 11ᵉ, ✆ 01 47 00 77 15. On a street once lined with *bal-musettes* (there are still a couple), this surly old Auvergnat *bistrot* hung with wooden clogs and hams is more popular than ever: try the *salade au foie gras de canard* and the morels in fresh cream, on Fridays the *potée de Cantal* (closed Sun and Mon). *Bastille* Ⓜ

**Terminus Nord**, 23 Rue de Dunkerque, 10ᵉ, ✆ 01 42 85 05 15. Lively brasserie vintage 1925, decorated with floral ceramics; on the menu three kinds of *choucroute* and other traditional brasserie fare, along with *fruits de mer* and fish soup. 119F lunch menu. *Gare du Nord* Ⓜ

### cheap

**Aux Arts et Sciences Réunis**, 161 Av. Jean-Jaurès, 19ᵉ, ✆ 01 42 40 53 18. Simple but good choice near La Villette. *Ourcq* Ⓜ

**Port de Pidjiguiti**, 28 Rue Etex, 18ᵉ, ✆ 01 42 26 71 77. Dishes from Guineau-Bissau, in a restaurant owned and run by a village, which as the photos show, puts the profits to good use; menus 88 (lunch) and 100F (closed Mon) *Guy Môquet* Ⓜ

## Left Bank: Latin Quarter                    *Restaurants*

### luxury

**La Tour d'Argent**, 15 Quai de la Tournelle, 5ᵉ, ✆ 01 43 54 23 31. Established here in the reign of Henri II in 1582 and recently brought back to splendour by a new chef, who has added his own innovations to the classic *canard au sang* (pressed duck). Add unforgettable, romantic views of Notre-Dame, unique atmosphere and a superlative wine cellar, all for 800F minimum; lunch menu 395F (closed Mon). *Maubert Mutualité* Ⓜ

### moderate

**Atelier de Maître Albert**, 1 Rue Maître-Albert, 5ᵉ, ✆ 01 46 33 13 78. Stone walls, exposed beams and an open fire create one of Paris' most medieval environments; try the rack of lamb with tarragon; around 250F. Open 24 hrs.

*Maubert Mutualité* Ⓜ

**Auberge des Deux Signes**, 46 Rue Galande, 5ᵉ, ✆ 01 43 25 46 56. Part of the medieval monastic complex of St-Julien le Pauvre, which seems to bring out the most traditional flavours of the *confits de foie gras* and dishes from Quercy and the Auvergne; expensive à la carte (closed Sat lunch and Sun). *St-Michel* Ⓜ

**Le Balzar**, 49 Rue des Ecoles, 5ᵉ, ✆ 01 43 54 13 67. The one brasserie in the Latin Quarter most likely to square with all your Paris fantasies; a favourite beanery of celebrities and the fashion crowd; book ahead. Delicious onion soup in the evening (only), and open until 1am (closed Aug). *Maubert Mutualité* Ⓜ

**La Bûcherie**, 41 Rue de la Bûcherie, 5ᵉ, ✆ 01 43 54 78 06. Extraordinarily pleasant on a winter's evening; delicious French favourites including game dishes, on a covered terrace with a log fire and a view. *St-Michel* Ⓜ

**Chez Maître Paul**, 12 Rue Monsieur-le-Prince, 6ᵉ, ✆ 01 43 54 74 59. Snug and handsome, with dishes from the Franche-Comté to match—*poulette à la crème gratinée* and delicious apple or walnut desserts, washed down with wines from the Jura; lunch menu with wine 155, 190F (closed Sat lunch and Sun).

*Odéon* Ⓜ

**Dodin-Bouffant**, 25 Rue Frédéric-Sauton, 5ᵉ, ✆ 01 43 25 25 14. Delicious seafood (especially oysters) and excellent wines; the terrace is a better option than the first floor with its low ceiling (closed Sun and Aug); good lunch menu at 180F.

*Maubert Mutualité* Ⓜ

**Au Pactole**, 44 Blvd St-Germain, 5ᵉ, ✆ 01 43 26 92 28. Fashionable and excellent restaurant with a terrace and a delectable *côte de boeuf*; good-value menus at 150F (lunch) and 280F (closed Sat lunch and Sun). *Maubert Mutualité* Ⓜ

### inexpensive

**Chieng-Mai**, 12 Rue Frédéric-Sauton (off Pl Maubert), 5ᵉ, ✆ 01 43 25 45 45. Paris' most authentic Thai restaurant; reserve; menus 130–180F. *Maubert Mutualité* Ⓜ

**Espace Hérault**, 8 Rue de la Harpe, 15ᵉ, ✆ 01 46 33 00 56. Features the Langdocienne specialities from the Hérault; fans of fish soup should try the *bourride de lotte*. A Hérault wine bar and exhibitions from the area are added attractions; menus 110 and 140F (closed Sun). *St-Michel* Ⓜ

**Le Grenier de Notre Dame**, 18 Rue de la Bûcherie, 5ᵉ, ✆ 01 43 29 98 29. One of the city's better macrobiotic choices, with a choice of organic wines.

*Maubert Mutualité*Ⓜ

**Le Vivario**, 6 Rue Cochin (south of Quai de la Tournelle), 5ᵉ, ✆ 01 43 25 08 19. Authentic Corsican–Sicilian cuisine, including pasta dishes and grilled fish, with dense sun-drenched flavours and high-octane wine; reserve a table outside (closed Sat and Mon lunch, Sun, and Sept). *Maubert Mutualité* Ⓜ

### cheap

**Al-Dar**, 8 Rue Frédéric-Sauton, 5ᵉ, ✆ 43 25 17 15. Paris' favourite Lebanese restaurant, superb starters and succulent kebabs; 80F menu. *Maubert Mutualité* Ⓜ

**Chez Hamadi**, 12 Rue Boutebrie, 5ᵉ, ✆ 01 43 54 03 30. Not much to look at but good North African cuisine for 85F with wine. *St-Michel* Ⓜ

**Le Petite Hostellerie**, 35 Rue de la Harpe, 15ᵉ, ✆ 01 43 54 47 12. A standout among the kebab stands and tourist places of this area; nice traditional cooking at bargain prices. *Cluny-Sorbonne* Ⓜ

## Left Bank: Panthéon, Rue Mouffetard    *Restaurants*

### expensive

**Le Petit Marguery**, 9 Blvd de Port-Royal, 13ᵉ, ✆ 01 43 31 58 59. Innovative brasserie run by the Cousin brothers, who perform an aromatic magic with seasonal ingredients; black truffles in the spring, game dishes and wild mushrooms in the autumn, and a heavenly *crème cassonade*. Lunch menu 165F; otherwise 300F and up (closed Sun and Mon). *Gobelins* Ⓜ

### moderate

**Chez Léna et Mimille**, 35 Rue Tournefort, 5ᵉ, ✆ 01 47 07 72 47 (parallel to Rue Mouffetard). One of the best in the area, convivial, reliable and unpretentious; closed Sat and (exc in summer) Sun. 98F lunch menu. *Monge* Ⓜ

**Les Délices d'Aphrodite**, 4 Rue de Candolle, 5ᵉ, ✆ 01 43 31 40 39 (opposite the church of St-Médard). The Mavromatis family serves some of the best Greek food in Paris, in one of the most serendipitous locations. Casual, lots of tables on the sidewalk (closed Mon). *Censier Daubenton* Ⓜ

**Moissonnier**, 28 Rue des Fossés-St-Bernard, 5ᵉ, ✆ 01 43 29 87 65. Intimate *bistrot* serving genuine Lyonnais *cuisine de terroir* since 1961 (closed Sun night, Mon and Aug). *Jussieu* Ⓜ

**Le Petit Navire**, 14 Rue Fossés-St-Bernard, 5ᵉ, ✆ 01 43 54 22 52. Simple and honestly priced seafood dishes; 150F menu; otherwise over 200 (closed Sun and Mon). *Jussieu* Ⓜ

### inexpensive

**L'Ecureuil, L'Oie et le Canard**, 3 Rue Linné, 5ᵉ, ✆ 01 01 43 31 61 18. *Maigrets* and *cassoulet* from the southwest, along with some Basque dishes; 89F lunch menu. *Jussieu* Ⓜ

**Macchu Pichu**, 9 Rue Royer-Collard, 5ᵉ, ✆ 01 43 26 13 13. Good, spicy Peruvian treats like fish marinated with green pepper; dinner only. *Luxembourg* (RER)

**Perraudin**, 157 Rue St-Jacques, 5ᵉ, ✆ 01 46 33 15 75. Lots of *bonhomie*, in a favourite for traditional cooking since 1913. You won't do better than their 63F lunch menu anywhere in the neighbourhood (dinner would be about 150F). Closed Sun. *Luxembourg* (RER)

**Tashi Delek**, 4 Rue des Fossés-St-Jacques, 5ᵉ, ✆ 01 43 26 55 55. Paris' first Tibetan restaurant, run by refugees, who offer dishes from the Himalayas (try the *langch-*

*momok*) and an optional cup of tea with salty butter (not quite authentic—it's cow butter, not yak); 105F menu. *Luxembourg* (RER)

### cheap

**Le Baptiste**, 11 Rue des Boulangers, 5ᵉ, ℰ 43 25 57 24. Popular with the students from the nearby Paris VI–VII complex, an unpretentious place where you might prefer splurging for seafood or a *maigret* than the prosaic but filling 71, 128 and 185F menus (lunch 61F). *Jussieu* Ⓜ

**Coup de Torchon**, 187 Rue St-Jacques, 5ᵉ, ℰ 01 46 33 22 93. A neighbourhood favourite; simple home cooking at the lowest prices in the 5ᵉ. Closed Sat lunch and Sun. *Luxembourg* (RER)

**La Vallée des Bambous**, 35 Rue Gay-Lussac (by the Jardin du Luxembourg), 5ᵉ, ℰ 01 43 54 99 47. Very popular, very good and reasonably priced Chinese packed (closed Tues). *Luxembourg* (RER)

## Left Bank: St-Germain                    *Restaurants*

### luxury

**Jacques Cagna**, 14 Rue des Grands-Augustins, 6ᵉ, ℰ 01 43 26 49 39. A favourite of Parisians as well as visitors from far and wide, located in one of the most tasteful and charming addresses on the Left Bank, decorated with 16th-century woodwork. But the main attraction is some of the expertly prepared food, imaginatively based on country recipes (*saint-pierre rôti citron confit*); great value lunch at 260F. Closed Sat lunch, Sun. *Odéon* Ⓜ

### expensive

**Lapérouse**, 51 Quai des Grands-Augustins, 6ᵉ, ℰ 01 43 26 68 04. Luscious Second Empire decor and private alcoves for a romantic rendezvous; some highly innovative dishes from the new Basque chef (closed Sat lunch, Sun). *St-Michel* Ⓜ

### moderate

**Lipp**, 151 Boulevard St-Germain, 6ᵉ, ℰ 01 45 48 53 91. A clubbish haunt of politicians and celebrities, perhaps the most celebrated choucroute-ladelling brasserie in Paris; little changed since the 1920s, including the food (195F).
*St-Germain-des-Prés* Ⓜ

**Le Petit Zinc**, 11 Rue St-Benoît, 6ᵉ, ℰ 01 42 61 20 60. No longer in the centre of the Buci market, but still good brasserie dishes and seafood; turn-of-the-century decor and sidewalk tables; modest 165F menu. Until 2am.
*St-Germain-des-Prés* Ⓜ

**Vagenende**, 142 Boulevard St-Germain, 6ᵉ, ℰ 01 43 26 68 18. Superb, listed Art Nouveau interior, but more a feast for the eyes than stomach; go for the 135F lunch menu. *St-Germain-des-Prés* Ⓜ

**Aux Charpentiers**, 10 Rue Mabillon, 6ᵉ, ✆ 01 43 26 30 05. Located in the former car-penters' guild hall (with a little museum about it), serving excellent *pot-au-feu*, *boudin* and other everyday French basics; economical *plats du jour*.

*Mabillon* Ⓜ

**Café Procope**, 13 Rue de l'Ancienne-Comédie, 6ᵉ, ✆ 01 43 26 99 20. Touristy place, founded on the site of Paris' oldest café, and done up in honour of the Revolu-tion's leaders, who used to meet here; lunch menus from 105F; à la carte can be moderate. *Odéon* Ⓜ

**Indonesia**, 12 Rue de Vaugirard, 6ᵉ, ✆ 01 43 25 70 22, a workers' cooperative and Paris' first Indonesian restaurant; try lots of small dishes with the *table de riz* or *sambel goreng* (seafood in coconut sauces); menus from 80F. *Odéon* Ⓜ

**Le Muniche**, 22 Rue Guillaume-Apollinaire, 6ᵉ, ✆ 01 42 61 12 70, similar to Le Petit Zinc; unexciting. Until 2am. *St-Germain-des-Prés* Ⓜ

**Le Petit St-Benoît**, 4 Rue St-Benoît, 6ᵉ, ✆ 01 42 60 27 92. Atmospheric neighbourhood joint at the centre of St-Germain nightlife; good French classics.

*St-Germain-des-Prés* Ⓜ

**Polidor**, 41 Rue Monsieur-le-Prince, 6ᵉ, ✆ 01 43 26 95 34. An institution from the late 1800s, where even poets can afford to eat; still good value and wonderful ambi-ence, lunch 55–100F; stays open till midnight too, except Sun. *Odéon* Ⓜ

**Orestias**, 4 Rue Grégoire-de-Tours, 6ᵉ, ✆ 01 43 54 62 01. Substantial good Greek starters and main dishes, served with Hellenic bonhomie (closed Sun); 44F menu *Odéon* Ⓜ

**Osteria del Passe Partout**, 20 Rue de l'Hirondelle, 6ᵉ, ✆ 01 46 34 14 54. Good Italian place in a picturesque alley just west of Place St-Michel; menus from 60F (closed Sat lunch and Sun). *St-Michel* Ⓜ

**Le Petit Vatel**, 5 Rue Lobineau, 6ᵉ, ✆ 01 43 54 28 49. When they say *petit* they mean minuscule but good *grand-mère* style meat and vegetable dishes that rarely hit 90F . *Mabillon* Ⓜ

## Left Bank: Eiffel Tower/Faubourg St-Germain  *Restaurants*

**Jules Verne**, Eiffel Tower (private lift to 2nd floor),15ᵉ, ✆ 01 45 55 61 44. Dining on the Eiffel Tower may sound like a corny tourist trap, but this is one of Paris' top (literally) gourmet havens, with a cuisine that is predominantly nouvelle; book weeks, even months in advance, esp. for dinner; weekday lunch menu 290F .

*Bir-Hakeim* Ⓜ

## expensive

**Morot-Gaudry**, 8 Rue de la Cavalerie, 15ᵉ, ✆ 01 45 67 06 85. An epicurean delight with a hanging terrace far from the tourist crowds; perfect food with a Mediterranean touch, excellent weekday lunch menu at 220F (closed Sat and Sun).
*La Motte Picquet* Ⓜ

**Le Récamier**, 4 Rue Récamier, 7ᵉ, ✆ 01 45 48 86 58. In a quiet cul-de-sac, a favourite of Left Bank publishers and journalists, who dawdle in the Empire dining room over a *boeuf bourguignon* or a perfect Chateaubriand, or linger over a lobster salad on the delightful terrace in summer (closed Sun). *Sèvres Babylone* Ⓜ

## moderate

**La Bourdonnais**, 113 Ave de la Bourdonnais, 7ᵉ, ✆ 01 47 05 47 96. Beautifully pre-pared dishes from the fragrant Midi: *croustillant de homard risotto safrané*, *turbot à la crème de citron confit* and delicious raspberry desserts; great-value menus at 240F (lunch, wine included), diner 320F and up. *Ecole Militaire* Ⓜ

**Tan Dinh**, 60 Rue de Verneuil, 7ᵉ, ✆ 01 45 44 04 84. Vietnamese cooking in a way Parisians like it—steamed crab pâté, lobster triangles with ginkgo nuts and much more (closed Sun). *Solférino* Ⓜ

## inexpensive

**Chez L'Ami Jean**, 27 Rue Malar, west of the Invalides, 7ᵉ, ✆ 01 47 05 86 89. Jovial and offering some of the best Basque cooking in Paris (closed Sun).
*La Tour Maubourg* Ⓜ

**Au Pied de Fouet**, 45 Rue de Babylone, 7ᵉ, ✆ 01 47 05 12 27. Le Corbusier's favourite restaurant, checked table clothes and long queues for its tasty and affordable meals that can even dip below the 100F line; closed Sat night, Sun and Aug.
*St-François-Xavier* Ⓜ

**La Fontaine de Mars**, 129 Rue St-Dominique, 7ᵉ, ✆ 01 47 05 46 44. Unpretentious and convivial restaurant near the Champ de Mars, with table outside in the summer—try the *fricassée de canard haricots blancs* (closed Sun).
*Ecole Militaire* Ⓜ

**L'Oeillade**, 10 Rue de St-Simon, 7ᵉ, ✆ 01 42 22 01 60. A pleasant old-fashioned *bistrot* packed with regulars; heartwarming *cassoulet* and warm cinnamon-scented apple tart; 148F menu (closed Sat lunch and Sun, first half Aug). *Rue du Bac* Ⓜ

**Thoumieux**, 79 Rue St-Dominique, 7ᵉ, ✆ 01 47 05 49 75. A lively, long established brasserie featuring the red wine and delicious duck and goose *confits*, *cassoulet*, and pâtés from the southwest of France that according to recent reports promote longevity; menu 72F (closed Sun lunch). *La Tour Maubourg* Ⓜ

## cheap

**Chez Germaine**, 30 Rue Pierre-Leroux, 7ᵉ, ✆ 01 42 73 28 34. Best bet for good cheap food in the area (for non-smokers, at least) and usually packed; closed Sat night, Sun. *Vaneau* Ⓜ

### moderate

**Le Bergamote**, 1 Rue Niepce, 14ᵉ, ✆ 01 43 22 79 47. Laid-back, tiny *bistrot* featuring Provençal dishes, with lunch menus under 100F (closed Mon and Sun).

*Pernety* ⓜ

**La Coupole**, 102 Blvd du Montparnasse, 14ᵉ, ✆ 01 43 20 14 20. The police had to control the crowds when it opened its doors in the 1920s, and it's still a brasserie to see and be seen in; recent restoration has spared some of the original Art Deco detail. Wide variety of dishes on the menu, and old-fashioned dancing in the afternoon can be fun. Open until 2am; 112F menu for lunch and after 10pm.

*Vavin* ⓜ

**Dominique**, 19 Rue Bréa, 6ᵉ, ✆ 01 43 27 08 80. A favourite of Paris' Russians since the 20's, with succulent chicken Kiev, *chachlick caucasien* and Russian cheesecake (*vatrouchka*); 98 and 150F lunch menus, 160F evening; closed Sun, Mon lunch.

*Vavin* ⓜ

### inexpensive

**L'Amuse Bouche**, 186 Rue du Château, 14ᵉ, ✆ 01 43 35 31 61. A minute place run by the former chef of Jacques Cagna, serving lovely ravioli filled with langoustines in a white leek sauce and much more to warm the cockles of your heart; lunch menu only 120F, 160F evenings (closed Sat lunch and Sun).

*Pernety* ⓜ

**Le Vin des Rues**, 21 Rue Boulard, 14ᵉ, ✆ 01 43 22 19 78. Idiosyncratic traditional *bistrot* with delicious food *à la Lyonnaise* (*jambon persillé*) and a lip-smacking Beaujolais (closed nights Sat–Tues). *Denfert Rochereau* ⓜ

### cheap

**Aux Artistes**, 63 Rue Falguière, 15ᵉ, ✆ 01 43 22 05 29. Named after Montparnasse's bohemians, and prices are still on the bohemian level; popular neighbourhood atmosphere and a good 75F menu, including wine (closed Sat and Sun lunch).

*Pasteur* ⓜ

## Left Bank: Periphery—13ᵉ, 14ᵉ, 15ᵉ  *Restaurants*

### moderate

**Le Clos Morillons**, 50 Rue des Morillons, 15ᵉ, ✆ 01 48 28 04 37. Very personal cuisine with exotic southern touch; closed Sat lunch and Sun. *Convention* ⓜ

**Pavillon Montsouris**, 20 Rue Gazan, 14ᵉ, ✆ 01 45 88 38 52. One of the most delightful and romantic restaurants in Paris, in a 1900 *belle-époque* glass pavilion with a terrace overlooking pretty Parc Montsouris; excellent 199 and 265F menus and exhaustive wine list. *Cité Universitaire* (RER)

**Les Vieux Métiers de France**, 13 Blvd Auguste-Blanqui, 13ᵉ, ℘ 01 45 88 90 03. You may have your doubts about the decor, but the *épaule d'agneau rôtie aux épices à la semoule d'orge* will make it look rosy; special 300F *dégustation* (closed Sun and Mon). *Place d'Italie* Ⓜ

### inexpensive

**Le Temps des Cerises**, 18 Rue de la Butte-aux-Cailles, 13ᵉ, ℘ 01 45 89 69 48. Worker's co-op restaurant, but this is Paris: dishes include *avocat* sorbet, smoked *magret de canard*, and rabbit in asperagus bisque. Closed Sat lunch and Sun; 56F lunch menu. *Corvisart* Ⓜ

### cheap

**Café du Commerce**, 51 Rue du Commerce, 15ᵉ, ℘ 01 45 75 03 27. 130 years old, vast and still bustling *bouillon*, serving some of the cheapest good meals in Paris—sit in the gallery if you can, to watch the pageant unfold below; good tarragon chicken. Open daily til midnight. *Emile Zola* Ⓜ

**Au Rendez-vous des Camionneurs**, 34 Rue des Plantes, 14ᵉ, ℘ 01 45 42 20 94. Tasty, substantial fare from the Auvergne for under 100F; lots of character, and neighbourhood characters; closed Sat and Sun. *Alésia* Ⓜ

**Hawaï**, 87 Ave d'Ivry, 13ᵉ, ℘ 01 45 86 91 90. Authentic Vietnamese, often packed with locals; delicious soups, barbecued chicken and grilled shrimp. *Porte d'Ivry* Ⓜ

# Wine Bars

Sometimes called *bistrots à vin* or like the English, *bars à vin*, this once common city institution is enjoying a revival as Parisians have begun to expand their wine consciousness. There are even chains like L'Ecluse that aim to recreate the old *bistrot à vin* environment as Parisians have begun to seek their roots. It isn't always clear where to draw the line between a wine bar and a restaurant; any old traditional *bistrot à vin* will serve something to go along with the wine: plates of sausages or paté, onion soup, cheese, sandwiches or even three-course meals.

## Right Bank                                                    *Wine Bars*

**A la Courtille**, 1 Rue Envierges, 20ᵉ. New wine bar near Parc Belleville, with a top selection of crus for wine lovers and superb views over Paris from the summer terrace; good 100F lunch menu too. *Pyrénées* Ⓜ

**Le Baratin**, 3 Rue Jouye-Rouve, 20ᵉ. Popular new *bistrot à vin*, with delicious, hearty snacks (till midnight). *Pyrénées* Ⓜ

**A La Cloche des Halles**, 28 Rue Coquillière, 1ᵉʳ. Wine bar of renown; excellent choices to go with solid country snacks of cheese and *charcuterie* (closed Sat night and Sun). *Châtelet* Ⓜ

**L'Entracte**, 47 Rue Montpensier, 1er. A favourite of Diderot when it was called La Pissotte, now specializing in wines from the Loire and plates of tasty *charcuterie*; reasonable prices (open daily till 2am or so). *Palais Royal* Ⓜ

**Café Mélac**, 42 Rue Léon Front, 11e. Jovial proprietor ages his Château Mélac plonk (from his drainpipe vine) in the fridge, and has even organized a cooperative of urban wine growers, the Vignerons de Paris (the firemen of the 9e, with their vine, belong too); also has a range of very drinkable wines not made in Paris, and Auvergnat snacks (closed Sat and Sun, Mon night). *Charonne* Ⓜ

**Aux Négociants**, 27 Rue Lambert, 18e. Very affordable and affable, and a good bet for lunch (closed Sat and Sun). *Château-Rouge* Ⓜ

**Le Rubis**, 10 Rue du Marché-St-Honoré, 1er. One of the oldest and best; range of delicious snacks and affordable wines by the glass (closed Sun). *Pyramides* Ⓜ

**La Tartine**, 24 Rue de Rivoli, 4e. Unchanged more or less for over 90 years, though newly fashionable (closed Tues). *St-Paul* Ⓜ

**Willi's Wine Bar**, 13 Rue des Petits-Champs, 1er. A well-regarded British wine bar in Paris, and one of the few to serve wines from around the world; good for lunch, with a 140F menu (till 11pm, closed Sun). *Pyramides* Ⓜ

Islands and Left Bank      *Wine Bars*

**Henri IV**, 13 Pl du Pont Neuf, 1er. Long established and good snacks with a southwest flavour; Beaujolais and Loire wines (closed Sat night and Sun). *Pont Neuf* Ⓜ

**Caves Solignac**, 9 Rue Decrès, 14e, ℰ 45 45 58 59. Wine bar with good rustic food (baked Saint-Marcellin cheese and bacon on toast) to accompany your special bottle (closed Sat and Sun); good 99F lunch menu. *Pernety* Ⓜ

**Millésimes**, 7 Rue Lobineau, 6e. Little *bistrot à vin* with an international list of wines to choose from, and cold snacks to keep them company; reasonable prices (daily til 1am). *Odéon* Ⓜ

**Le Rallye**, 6 Rue Daguerre, 14e. Owned by the same family for over 80 years, with the biggest variety of bottles to choose from (especially Beaujolais) on the Left Bank (closed Sun afternoon and Mon). *Denfert Rochereau* Ⓜ

# Bars/Beer Cellars/Pubs/Tapas

Cafés are Parisian, bars are not, except for the old working-class watering holes that have completely disappeared from the city landscape. Therefore almost all the bars you will find in this city have one sort of angle or another: immigrant bars, gay bars, beer bars, music bars or whatever (for those offering entertainment, see p.426). Beer is definitely trendy in this city, and more places devoted to it are opening up all the time; in recent years the institution of the happy hour has hit Paris in a big way; keep an eye out for signs in the windows; discounts on drinks can be spectacular. The biggest current fad is the 'Irish Pub', with Guinness, Irish music, and often a genuine Irishman in attendance. One gets the impression that what Parisians really want is English pubs, except for the fact that they are English.

## Right Bank *Bars*

**Arco**, 12 Rue Daunou, 2ᵉ. Some of Paris' tastiest and most authentic tapas, washed down with Spanish wines; expensive (til 1 or 2am, closed Sun). *Opéra* Ⓜ

**Le Baragouin**, 17 Rue Tiquetonne, 2ᵉ. Lively, affordable Breton bar (til 2am, closed afternoons). *Les Halles* Ⓜ

**Bar Belge**, 75 Ave de St-Ouen, 17ᵉ. Paris' oldest, friendliest and most extensive Belgian beer cellar, with Flemish snacks—moules and frites too of course (til 3am, closed Mon). *Guy-Moquet* Ⓜ

**Café Moustache**, 138 Rue du Faubourg-St-Martin, 10ᵉ. Relaxed gay bar popular with the international set; open til 1.30am. *Gare de l'Est* Ⓜ

**La Champmeslé**, 4 Rue Chabanais, 2ᵉ. Very intimate, very feminine and romantic bar; open 6–10pm (closed Sun). *Pyramides, Bourse* Ⓜ

**China Club**, 50 Rue de Charenton, 12ᵉ. In an old ice house, one of the trendiest bars in a trendy area; elegant atmosphere, Chinese snacks (til 2am). *Bastille* Ⓜ

**Le Comptoir**, 14 Rue Vauvilliers, 1ᵉʳ. Fashionable 1950s retro, serving beers, cocktails and very fancy tapas (until 2am, 4 am weekends). *Les Halles* Ⓜ

**Conway's**, 73 Rue St-Denis, 1ᵉʳ. One of the best American bars in Paris, run by the daughter of a New York boxer; Happy Hour 6–9pm, til 3am. *Les Halles* Ⓜ

**Le Duplex**, 25 Rue Michel-le-Comte, 3ᵉ. Where Paris' gay writers and Grandes-Ecoles graduates gather for *intello* chitchat; open til 2am. *Rambuteau* Ⓜ

**Flann O'Brien**, 6 Rue Bailleul, 1ᵉʳ. One of Paris' favourite Irish pubs; music most nights (rock or Irish traditional). *Louvre* Ⓜ

**Le Fouquet's**, 99 Ave des Champs-Elysées, 8ᵉ. A Paris instituion for the rich and famous. *George V* Ⓜ

**Gambrinus**, 62 Rue des Lombards, 1ᵉʳ. The 'God of Beer' offering 30 draught beers in a medieval crypt built by the Templars, T-bone steaks, country and rhythm and blues nightly. *Châtelet-Les Halles* Ⓜ

**Harry's Bar**, 5 Rue Daunou, 2ᵉ. Since 1911 the most famous American bar in Paris, home of the Bloody Mary and Side Car, where a big international business clientele gathers to discuss making more do-re-mi over one of 180 different brands of whisky or *Pétrifiant*—a slightly less lethal version of the Mickey Finn (daily til 4am). *Opéra* Ⓜ

**Kitty O'Shea's**, 10 Rue des Capucines, 2ᵉ. Popular Irish bar and scrum when Ireland plays France in the Five Nations; Guinness, good Irish coffees and beers (til 2am). *Opéra* Ⓜ

**La Micro-Brasserie**, 106 Rue de Richelieu, 2ᵉ. Serving 50 kinds of beer—including the house's own Morgane, brewed here since 1987; til 2am.   *Richelieu-Drouot* Ⓜ

**Le Moloko,** 26 Rue Fontaine, 9ᵉ. Currently the most *branché* place to see and be seen in on the Montmartre plain; male strippers some nights (til 6am).   *Blanche* Ⓜ

**Movida**, 14 Rue Marie-Stuart, 2ᵉ. Casual Spanish bar for lovers of flamenco, bullfights, and tapas (till 4am, closed Sun and Mon).   *Etienne Marcel* Ⓜ

**La Perla**, 26 Rue François-Miron, 4ᵉ. Laid-back California-Mexican, good margaritas, Mexican beers, flavoured tequilas (!) and snacks (til 2am).   *St-Paul* Ⓜ

**Le Sous Bock**, 49 Rue St-Honoré, 1ᵉʳ. Complicated cocktails and the best imported beers; snacks of mussels and frites at all hours. Includes a booze boutique that is a tippler's dream—180 varieties of whisky.   *Châtelet* Ⓜ

**Tigh Johnny's**, 55 Rue Montmartre, 2ᵉ. Bonhomie and Guinness with traditional Irish music, jazz and the occasional singsong and poetry (til 1.15am).   *Sentier* Ⓜ

**Le Vagabond**, 14 Rue Thérèse, 1ᵉʳ, ✆ 01 42 96 27 23. Paris' oldest and most serene gay bar (since the 50s); also an inexpensive restaurant.   *Pyramides* Ⓜ

**Académie de la Bière**, 88bis Blvd de Port-Royale, 5ᵉ. German beer specialists, with over 50 different varieties, mussels and frites (til 3am).   RER: *Port-Royal*

**Birdland Club**, 20 Rue Princesse, 6ᵉ. Castel's, the most exclusive nightclub in Paris, has moved St-Germain's sophisto-trendy nightlife scene to Rues Princesse and Guis-arde; stylish cocktails and good jazz records, open til dawn.   *Mabillon* Ⓜ

**La Closerie des Lilas**, 171 Boulevard de Montparnasse, 6ᵉ. Unchanged since Verlaine and Hemingway boozed here; great cocktails but at a price (til 2am).

RER: *Port-Royal*

**Le Crocodile**, 5 Rue Royer-Collard, 5ᵉ. Cosy, intimate night haunt for serious cocktail aficionados, with over 120 varieties—also Irish coffees (til 2am, closed Sun).

RER: *Luxembourg*

**La Gueuze**, 19 Rue Soufflot, 5ᵉ. A popular café with Paris' most impressive *carte des bières*—over 400 kinds from around the world.   RER: *Luxembourg*

**Mayflower**, 49 Rue Descartes, 5ᵉ. Popular but expensive drinks til 2am, two bars with a good selection of beers and wines and 100 whiskies.   *Cardinal Lemoine* Ⓜ

**Le Mazet**, 61 Rue St-Andre-des Arts, 6ᵉ. A serious beer cellar (15 kinds on tap) where you can also get a bowl of onion soup in the wee hours.   *Odéon* Ⓜ

**Le Merle Moqueur**, 11 Rue des Buttes-aux-Cailles, 13ᵉ. Workers' co-op for another side of Paris, French popular songs on Thursday; otherwise live bands and cheap beer (til 1am).   *Corvisart* Ⓜ

**Le Piano Vache**, 8 Rue Laplace, 5ᵉ. Relaxed, noisy and fun student bar, offering killer cocktails and less lethal beers and snacks (til 2am).   *Maubert Mutualité* Ⓜ

**Polly Magoo**, 11 Rue St-Jacques, 5ᵉ. Sleezy down at the heel fun in the modern equivalent to the old haunts of Villon, practically unchanged since it opened in 1970 (til 4 or 5am). *St-Michel* Ⓜ

**Pub Saint-Germain** (or Parrot's tavern), 17 Rue de l'Ancienne-Comédie, 6ᵉ. A popular non-stop Left Bank haven for beer connoisseurs, with over 100 varieties in bottles and some 20 on tap (open 24 hrs; ring the bell if it looks closed). *Odéon* Ⓜ

# Cafés, *Salons de Thé*, *Glaciers*

Nearly every crossroads in Paris has its café, an institution dating back to the 17th century, where people could shed most of their social and class distinctions and speak their minds about politics and (eventually) start revolutions. Since Haussmann's creation of the Grands Boulevards, cafés became what many remain to this day: passive grandstands of the passing throng, a place to meet friends and be at once private and yet public. A *salon de thé,* on the other hand, tends to be more inward looking, concentrating on light (and often overpriced) luncheons, but usually good for a quality cup of coffee, tea or chocolate and pastries.

## Right Bank                                                                 *Cafés*

**Angélina**, 226 Rue de Rivoli, 1ᵉʳ. A Viennese confection, vintage 1903 (when it was called Rumpelmayer), with a special rich African chocolate and the world's best *montblanc* (chestnut cream, meringue and chantilly). *Tuileries* Ⓜ

**A Priori Thé**, 36 Galerie Vivienne, 2ᵉ. Take a trip back in time over a cup of English tea and cheesecake under the glass-roofed passage. *Bourse* Ⓜ

**Au Rêve**, 89 Rue Caulaincourt, 18ᵉ. Old-fashioned Montmartre café, inexpensive and friendly. Lunch served. Open til 2am; closed Sun. *Lamarck Caulaincourt* Ⓜ

**Baggi**, 33 Rue Chaptal, 9ᵉ.The best homemade ice cream on the Right Bank, founded in 1850 and still going strong, using 100% natural ingredients. *Pigalle* Ⓜ

**Café Marly**, in the Louvre, facing the Pyramid, 1ᵉʳ. New, beautifully designed chic hangout in the old ministries vacated for the Grand Louvre project; also lunch and dinner for 200F and up. Especially pretty at night.
*Palais Royal–Musée du Louvre* Ⓜ

**Café de la Paix**, 12 Blvd des Capucines, 9ᵉ. A historic landmark; if you can't afford a ticket to the Opéra, you might manage the price of a coffee here; architect Garnier's second-best effort in the outlandish style he invented—Napoleon III.
*Opéra* Ⓜ

**Ladurée**, 18 Rue Royale, 8ᵉ. Exquisite and precious *salon de thé*, famous for its macaroons. Bring your laciest great aunt along for tea. *Madeleine* Ⓜ

**Ma Bourgogne**, 19 Pl des Vosges, 4ᵉ. Vortex of café life in the Place des Vosges; also a passable 185F lunch menu. *St-Paul* Ⓜ

**Mariage Frères**, 30 Rue du Bourg-Tibourg, 4ᵉ. Paris' best-known purveyors of tea; hundreds of blends to sample with a pastry. *St-Paul* Ⓜ

**Mollard**, 113 Rue St-Lazare, 8ᵉ. Beautiful Art Nouveau café-brasserie. *St-Lazare* Ⓜ

**Tea Follies**, 6 Pl Gustave-Toudouze, 9ᵉ. If chance finds you stumping in this dull quarter of insurance offices some afternoon, this tea room is a consolation; tasty scones, too. *St-Georges* Ⓜ

## Left Bank and Islands                                                    *Cafés*

**Berthillon**, 31 Rue St-Louis-en-l'Ile, Ile St-Louis, 4ᵉ. A long queue forms for Paris' best ice creams and sorbets with a list of flavours a mile long, but you can also enjoy them sitting down in most of the island's cafés. *Pont Marie* Ⓜ

**Le Bac à Glaces**, 109 Rue du Bac, 7ᵉ. Charming tearoom and delectable homemade ice creams and sorbets. *Sèvres-Babylone* Ⓜ

**Calabrese Glacier**, 15 Rue d'Odessa, 14ᵉ .The Leonardo da Vinci of ice cream inventions, home of the famous vanilla and cinnamon *soupe anglaise.*

*Montparnasse* Ⓜ

**Les Deux Magots**, 6 Pl St-Germain-des-Prés, 6ᵉ. A hoot for all its pretentions, and usually full of tourists, but the chocolate and ice cream are compensations. Note, however, if it's crowded, you may well be pressured into making a second order or leaving—inexcusable! *St-Germain-des-Prés* Ⓜ

**Le Flore**, 172 Blvd St-Germain, 6ᵉ. Fabled literary café, everything just so Parisian, but full of tired vampires trying to suck out your soul with their cool, discerning eyes. So popular with tourists that they've opened their own boutique.

*St-Germain-des-Prés* Ⓜ

**Le Flore en l'Ile**, 42 Quai d'Orléans, Ile St-Louis, 4ᵉ. Great view over Notre-Dame, great tea, great Berthillon ice cream (straight and in exotic cocktails).

*Pont Marie* Ⓜ

**La Pagode**, 57bis Rue de Babylone, 7ᵉ. Tea and cakes in a beautiful Japanese garden built in the 1860s. Also a cinema. *St-François Xavier* Ⓜ

**Le Loir dans la Théière**, 3 Rue des Rosiers, 4ᵉ. Tranquil and popular tea room in the Marais, 60F lunches too. *St-Paul* Ⓜ

**Le Pol'Noir**, 39 Rue Monsieur-le-Prince, 6ᵉ. Next to Polidor, a superb *glacier* serving fresh, homemade ice cream until 3am, 4 on Sat. *Odéon* Ⓜ

**Select**, 99 Blvd du Montparnasse, 6ᵉ. The last place to get a feeling for what Montparnasse was all about between the wars; open til 2am. *Vavin* Ⓜ

# Where to Stay

Anyone with student memories of Paris' old hotels—a Turkish toilet a mile down the hall, one neglected shower for the whole hotel, low-watt bulbs and shaky wiring, cheapskate timed lights that left you in pitch darkness on the 6th-floor stairway, smelly airless rooms and dingy brown flower wallpaper, and a grouchy *patron* who made you pay in advance—will be pleasantly surprised by the general mass upscaling down the line. Even one-star hotels have lifts, private bathrooms and lighter, airier rooms. Unfortunately, prices have risen as well, and draw ever closer to rates in London.

There are basically three kinds of hotels in the centre of Paris: big luxury and grand hotels, mainly on the Right Bank; business hotels, scattered everywhere; and small privately owned hotels, some very fashionable and some dogged dives, mostly concentrated on the near Left Bank. These small hotels have the most charm and character, but it's no secret they tend to fill up fast, especially the affordable ones. We haven't listed any hotels in the peripheral *arrondissements*; they aren't noticeably cheaper.

Advance bookings are essential in June, and in September and October when Paris is awash in salons and conventions. July and August are the low season, and some expensive hotels offer special discounts then. As a general rule, you'll be asked to send the first night's charge as a deposit. If you arrive without a reservation, **booking services** in the tourist offices will find you a room (see p.22).

**The figures listed below are 1996 prices for a double room.** Don't sue us if they're wrong, as they are always subject to change. In most places each room has its own price, depending on its view, plumbing, heated towel racks, etc. This is the French way of doing things, and it's also perfectly normal to visit rooms, or press the proprietor for details and negotiate. There are many admirable things about French hotels and this system is one of them—no imaginary etiquette; you tell them what you want, and if possible you'll get it. The one hitch is that there are few single rooms, and travellers on their own who don't book in advance often ending up paying for a double.

In the tip-top palatial hotels, add 18.6% luxury **tax** to the rate. Optional continental breakfast costs from 25F at the cheapie places to 180F a head at the Ritz. Many proprietors pretend not to know it's optional; hotels make extra profit on over-priced breakfasts the way restaurants do on wine—the same cup of coffee and croissant in the bar across the street will be more fun, and save you lots of francs. Parking will always be a problem. Even the luxury joints are not likely to have their own garages. But nearly every hotel can direct you to a nearby city garage, where overnight charges begin at 70F —or you can search for one of the precious spots on a side street, which will take an hour and ruin your day.

The annual **hotel list** for Paris available for 10F from the Office du Tourisme (127 Ave des Champs-Elysées, 75008) indicates all hotels with facilities for the disabled, as well as the most current prices. The Office du Tourisme rates hotels from five stars to none at all. Note that these ratings reflect plumbing and other amenities (lifts, bar, room telephones, etc.)—not intangible qualities such as tranquillity, ambience or good service.

## Ile de la Cité and Ile St-Louis

Islands have a certain magic, even in urban rivers; they are also conveniently central but quiet at night.

**★★★★**  **Jeu de Paume**, 54 Rue St-Louis-en-l'Ile, 75004, ✆ 01 43 26 14 18, ✐ 40 46 02 76. Paris' last real-tennis venue has been converted into the most enchanting little inn on the Seine, complete with a sunny garden; 840–1300F. *Pont Marie* Ⓜ

**★★★**  **Des Deux Iles**, 59 Rue St-Louis-en-l'Ile, 75004, ✆ 01 43 26 13 35, ✐ 01 43 29 60 25. In an 18th-century house, smallish rooms but decorated with period pieces and Provençal fabrics, and a late-night bar in the cellar; 850F . *Pont Marie* Ⓜ

**★★★**  **Lutèce**, 65 Rue St-Louis-en-l'Ile, 75004, ✆ 01 43 26 23 52, ✐ 01 43 29 60 25. Charming, tasteful and small, many rooms with beams; 850F. *Pont Marie* Ⓜ

**★★★**  **Saint-Louis**, 75 Rue St-Louis-en-l'Ile, 75004, ✆ 01 46 34 04 80, ✐ 01 46 34 02 13. Fashionable, antique furniture, but smallish rooms; 700–800F (no credit cards) *Pont Marie* Ⓜ

**★**  **Henri IV**, 25 Pl Dauphine, 75001, ✆ 01 43 54 44 53. 400 years old, frumpy flowered wallpaper, and toilets and showers down the hall, but visitors book months in advance to stay in all simplicity in the most serendipitous square on Ile de la Cité; 170–200F (no credit cards). *Pont Neuf* Ⓜ

## Right Bank: Place de la Concorde/Faubourg St-Honoré

Lap of luxury, as far as hotels go; few possibilities below the luxury threshold.

**★★★★★**  **Crillon**, 10 Pl de la Concorde, 75008, ✆ 01 44 71 15 00, ✐ 01 44 71 15 02. Behind the classic 18th-century façade stands the last luxury hotel in Paris to remain completely in French hands. Inside are some of the most exquisite and prestigious suites in town, and rooms, if not always grand, done up choicely with marble baths to match; 3200–3500F. *Concorde* Ⓜ

**★★★★**  **Intercontinental**, 3 Rue de Castiglione, 75001, ✆ 01 44 77 11 11. Built by Garnier nearly as lavishly as his Paris Opéra. Three of the seven grand imperial ballrooms have so much gilt and trimmings that they're listed as national monuments. The hotel takes up a whole city block, encompasses 390 rooms and 62 suites; 2000–2500F. *Tuileries* Ⓜ

**\*\*\*\*** **The Ritz**, 15 Pl Vendôme, 75001, ✆ 01 43 16 30 30, ✉ 01 43 16 31 78. One of the most famous hotels in the world. Keeping abreast of the times and the demands of its contemporary clientele, today's Ritz has not only sound-proof but bullet-proof glass on the ground floor, new tiled pool and health centre, free cookery classes that perpetuate the tradition of César Ritz's partner, the legendary chef Escoffier, business services and exclusive night-club; 3700F. *Opéra* Ⓜ

**\*\*\*** **Tuileries**, 10 Rue St-Hyacinthe, 75001, ✆ 01 42 61 04 17, ✉ 01 49 27 91 56. A quiet 18th-century *hôtel particulier* with antiques; 700–1200F. *Tuileries* Ⓜ

## Right Bank: Marais/Beaubourg/Les Halles

Your most likely abode on the Right Bank. Hotels in all categories, near lots of restaurants, sights and lively corners.

**\*\*\*** **Saint-Louis Marais**, 1 Rue Charles-V, 75004, ✆ 01 48 87 87 04, ✉ 01 48 87 33 26. An 18th-century Celestine convent offering romantic if monk-sized rooms. Five floors, but no lift—this is an historical landmark; 600–700F. *Sully Morland* Ⓜ

**\*\*\*** **Saint-Merry**, 78 Rue de la Verrerie, 75004, ✆ 01 42 78 14 15, ✉ 01 40 29 06 82. A stone's throw from the Pompidou Centre, this was once St Merry's presbytery and later a bordello. Its latest metamorphosis as a hotel stands out for the beautiful Gothic rooms; 400–1000F (no credit cards). *Hôtel de Ville* Ⓜ

**\*\*\*** **Hôtel de la Bretonnerie**, 22 Rue Ste-Croix-de-la-Bretonnerie, 75004, ✆ 01 48 87 77 63, ✉ 01 42 77 26 78. A very popular small hotel: Louis XIII furnishings *and* television; 630–750F. *Hôtel de Ville* Ⓜ

**\*\*\*** **Grand Hôtel de Champagne**, 17 Rue Jean-Lantier, 75001, ✆ 01 42 36 60 00, ✉ 01 45 08 43 33. Relatively quiet, near busy Place du Châtelet; originally decorated rooms, many with murals; fancy breakfast buffet; 640–800F. *Châtelet* Ⓜ

**\*\*** **Grand Hôtel Jeanne d'Arc**, 3 Rue de Jarente, 75004, ✆ 01 48 87 62 11, ✉ 01 48 87 37 31. Not so Grand any more—but ancient, cute and well run, close to the Place des Vosges; book far ahead; 390–460F. *St-Paul* Ⓜ

**\*\*** **Place des Vosges**, 12 Rue de Birague, 75004, ✆ 01 42 72 60 46, ✉ 01 42 72 02 64. Well restored, and just a few steps from the Place; 450F. *St-Paul* Ⓜ

**\*\*** **Vieux Marais**, 8 Rue du Plâtre, 75004, ✆ 01 42 78 47 22, ✉ 01 42 78 34 32. 510–550F with bath; most rooms with TV. *Hôtel de Ville* Ⓜ

★★ **Grand Hôtel de Besançon**, 56 Rue Montorgueil, 75002, ✆ 01 42 36 41 08, ✉ 01 45 08 08 79. Views over the Montorgueil market, 560–620F.

*Châtelet* Ⓜ

★★ **Sevigne**, 2 Rue Malher, 75004, ✆ 01 42 72 76 17. Nice place right around the corner from the nosher's paradise of Rue des Rosiers; 370–435F.

*St-Paul* Ⓜ

★★ **Andrea**, 3 Rue Saint-Bon, 75004, ✆ 01 42 78 43 93. Decent quiet choice near the Rue de Rivoli; 210F without bath, 350F with. *Hôtel de Ville* Ⓜ

★ **La Vallée**, 84–6 Rue St-Denis, 75001, ✆ 01 42 36 46 99. Excellent bargain choice, between Les Halles and Beaubourg; 200–290F. *Châtelet* Ⓜ

## Right Bank: Opéra/Palais-Royal

Quiet at night—a desert in fact, off the main boulevards—in daytime convenient to many sights; the streets around Palais-Royal have a discreet charm.

★★★ **Brébant**, 30–32 Blvd Poissonnière, 75009, ✆ 01 47 70 25 55, ✉ 01 42 46 65 70. Smart, stylish, crisply run hotel midway between the striped suits in the Bourse and the girlie shows at the Folies-Bergère; 750–900F.

*Rue Montmartre* Ⓜ

★★ **Cité Rougement**, 4 Cité Rougement, 75009, ✆ 01 47 70 25 95, ✉ 01 48 24 14 32. The best economy bet in the area, located in a traffic-free street off Rue Bergères, along with two other two-star hotels; 250–350F.

*Bonne Nouvelle* Ⓜ

★★ **Vivienne**, 40 Rue Vivienne, 75002, ✆ 01 42 33 13 26, ✉ 01 40 41 98 19. Very basic, near the *Bibliothèque* and arcades; 340–440F. *Bourse* Ⓜ

★ **de Rouen**, 42 Rue Croix-des-Petits-Champs, 75001, ✆ 01 42 61 38 21, ✉ 01 42 61 38 21. Old and comfortable, a good choice near the Palais Royal; 180–290F. *Palais Royal* Ⓜ

**Hôtel de Lille**, 8 Rue du Pélican, 75001, ✆01 42 33 33 42. A rare bargain hotel between the Louvre and Palais Royal. Old and plain; 220–270F.

*Louvre-Rivoli, Palais Royal* Ⓜ

## Right Bank: Champs-Elysées/Etoile

★★★★ **George V**, 31 Ave George-V, 75008, ✆ 01 47 23 54 00, ✉ 01 47 20 40 00. Stalwartly opulent, huge rooms furnished throughout with antiques, and recently outfitted with high-tech gizmos, including a bedside electronic control board to raise or lower the blinds; 2500–3900F. *George V* Ⓜ

★★★★ **Plaza Athénée**, 25 Ave Montaigne, 75008, ✆ 01 47 23 78 33, ✉ 01 47 23 78 33. Celebrated for its voluptuous luxury and superb service—there are twice as many staff as rooms, and more money spent on fresh flowers than lights. Mata Hari was arrested in its bar, but the spies have since given way to celebrities and corporate bosses—business services, stockmarket info, ticket agencies are only some of the services offered; 2500–3000F.

*Franklin D. Roosevelt ⓜ*

**** **Raphaël**, 17 Ave Kléber, 75016, ✆ 01 44 28 00 28, ✉ 01 45 01 21 50. Built in the 1920s, and like its namesake in Rome élite, intimate, splendid and artsy, plus an English bar and garden terrace with a view over Paris; 2100F.

*Kléber ⓜ*

**** **Vernet**, 25 Rue Vernet, 75008, ✆ 01 44 31 98 00, ✉ 01 44 31 85 69. Just off Place Charles-de-Gaulle. Handsomely furnished and air-conditioned each room has a marble bath with a jacuzzi. Guests have free access to the Hotel Royal Monceau's health centre and heated pool; the Vernet's *belle-époque* restaurant, Les Elysées, has a lovely crystal roof; 1900–2300F.

*George V ⓜ*

**** **De Vigny**, 9–11 Rue Balzac, 75008, ✆ 01 40 75 04 39, ✉ 01 40 75 05 81. Transformed in 1990 from a town house into one of Paris' most sumptuous small hotels, its bar evoking the Paris of the 1930s salons. Soundproof, marble bathrooms, library, cable TV; 2200–2600F double, suites from 2600F.

*George V ⓜ*

**** **Villa Maillot**, 143 Ave de Malakoff, 75016, ✆ 01 45 01 25 22, ✉ 01 45 00 60 61. Former Art Deco embassy of Sierra Leone, with many vintage 1930s furnishings. Air conditioning, mini-bars, cable TV, etc.;1700F.

*Porte Maillot ⓜ*

** **Flaubert**, 19 Rue Rennequin, 75017, ✆ 01 46 22 44 35, ✉ 01 43 80 32 34. North of the Etoile near Parc Monceau, a pretty hotel with plants cascading down the courtyard—modern baths, TV, mini-bar; 250–650F.  *Ternes ⓜ*

** **Villa d'Auteil**, 28 Rue Poussin, 75016, ✆ 01 42 88 30 37, ✉ 01 45 20 74 70. Pleasant tidy rooms; ask for one over the courtyard; 320F.

*Porte d'Auteuil ⓜ*

## Right Bank: Montmartre/Place de Clichy

Note that because of the steps, disabled access is very limited.

**** **Terrass**, 12 Rue Joseph-de-Maistre, 75018, ✆ 01 46 06 72 85, ✉ 01 42 52 29 11. Montmartre's most luxurious, overlooking the cemetery and rest of Paris. Also a good restaurant with—surprise—a terrace; 1100–1260F.

*Place de Clichy ⓜ*

** **Eden,** 90 Rue Ordener, 75018, ✆ 01 42 64 61 63, ✉ 01 42 64 11 43. Behind Sacré Coeur, pleasant, family run, and equipped with satellite TV.

*Jules-Joffrin ⓜ*

** **Ermitage**, 24 Rue Lamarck, 75018, ✆ 01 42 64 79 22, ✉ 01 42 64 10 33. A charming little white hotel under the gardens around Sacré-Coeur; 350–460F (no credit cards).  *Lamarck-Caulaincourt ⓜ*

** **Prima Lepic**, 29 Rue Lepic, 75018, ✆ 01 46 06 44 64, 📠 01 46 06 66 11. Pleasant and pretty rooms on the slope of the Butte; a trompe-l'oeil garden in the breakfast room; 320–370F. *Abbesses* Ⓜ

** **Régyn's Montmartre**, 18 Place des Abbesses, ✆ 01 42 54 45 21, 📠 01 42 23 76 69. A simple but good address in the heart of Montmartre, with good views over Paris; 435–455F. *Abbesses* Ⓜ

** **Timhotel Montmartre**, 11 Rue Ravignan, 75018, ✆ 01 42 55 74 79, 📠 01 42 55 71 01. Henry Miller knew it when it was called Paradis. It's still one of the most romantic hotels in Paris, overlooking delightful Place Emile-Goudeau—purchased and renovated by the Tim chain, with cable TV too; 550F. *Abbesses* Ⓜ

* **Prince Tholozé**, 24 Rue Tholozé, 75018, ✆ 01 46 06 74 83. Basic but respectable little hotel at the foot of the Butte; 180–250F, depending on plumbing. *Blanche* Ⓜ

## Left Bank: Latin Quarter

Very convenient, but apt to be noisy at night.

*** **Dacia Luxembourg**, 41 Blvd St-Michel, 75005, ✆ 01 43 25 34 53, 📠 01 44 07 10 33. On brash and bold Boul'Mich, very close to the Sorbonne and Jardin du Luxembourg, but sound-proofed, prettily-decorated rooms offer a quiet haven; 661F. *Odéon* Ⓜ

*** **Grands Hommes**, 17 Pl du Panthéon, 75005, ✆ 01 46 34 19 60, 📠 01 43 26 67 32. Earned a place in French literary history when resident André Breton defined Surrealism here in the 1920s. Furnishings, however, are more in the spirit of Voltaire and Rousseau, entombed in the Panthéon just in front—there's a small garden, cable TV, baby sitting, minibar and bath; 700–780F. *Cardinal Lemoine* Ⓜ

*** **Le Colbert**, 7 Rue de l'Hôtel-Colbert, 75005, ✆ 01 43 25 85 65, 📠 01 43 25 80 19. Elegant, peaceful hotel with tea room south of Place Maubert; 1010F. *Maubert-Mutalité* Ⓜ

*** **Panthéon**, 19 Pl du Panthéon, 75005, ✆ 01 43 54 32 95, 📠 01 43 26 64 65. Same owners as the Grands Hommes; but with more exposed beams, fewer four-posters; 700–780F. *Cardinal Lemoine* Ⓜ

** **Les Argonautes**, 12 Rue de la Huchette, ✆ 01 43 54 09 8, 📠 01 44 07 18 84. Perfect for Latin-Quarter nightowls and other urban creatures, on the corner of the narrowest street in Paris; 250–350F, not all with showers. *St-Michel* Ⓜ

** **Les Degrés de Notre-Dame**, 10 Rue des Grands-Degrés, 75005, ✆ 01 43 25 88 38, 📠 01 40 46 95 34. Ten charming rooms, many with prize views over Quasimodo's favourite perch. A quiet street, and a wine bar downstairs. All rooms with showers and WC; 430–500F. *Maubert Mutualité* Ⓜ

★★ **Familia**, 11 Rue des Ecoles, 75005, ✆ 01 43 54 55 27, ✆ 01 43 29 61 77. Comfort and frescoes in some rooms and great views of Notre-Dame from the top floors; 370–480F. *Cardinal Lemoine* Ⓜ

★★ **Grand Hotel St-Michel**, 19 Rue Cujas, 75005, ✆ 01 46 33 33 02, ✆ 01 40 46 96 33. Recently renovated, fairly quiet choice near the Panthéon with a garden; 360–500F. *Cluny-La Sorbonne* Ⓜ

★★ **Home Latin**, 15–17 Rue du Sommerard, 75005, ✆ 01 43 26 25 21, ✆ 01 43 29 87 04. Calm, well-kept, and friendly 430–495F.
*Maubert Mutualité* Ⓜ

★ **Delhy's**, 22 Rue de l'Hirondelle, 75006, ✆ 01 43 26 58 25. Modest choice on a quiet lane tucked near busy Place St-Michel; 230–350F. *St-Michel* Ⓜ

★ **Esmeralda**, 4 Rue St-Julien-le-Pauvre, 75005, ✆ 01 43 54 19 20, ✆ 01 40 51 00 68. Endearing, romantic hotel in a 16th-century building with a *classé* stairway and 19th-century furnishings; 320–490F, depending on the view.
*St-Michel* Ⓜ

★ **Marignan**, 13 Rue du Sommerard, 75005, ✆ 01 43 25 31 03. Friendly, informal and simple—pay showers down the hall; 220–270F.
*Maubert Mutualité* Ⓜ

## Left Bank: St-Germain

St-Germain has the highest density of smart and charming hotels, but prices tend to smart in another way.

★★★★ **L'Hôtel**, 13 Rue des Beaux-Arts, 75006, ✆ 01 43 25 27 22, ✆ 01 43 25 64 81. Besides seeing the last of Oscar Wilde (*see* p.277), this is one of the most romantic hotels in Paris; the honeymoon suite is outrageously furnished with a mirrored set once belonging to Mistinguett, the 1920s and '30s star at the Moulin-Rouge and Folies-Bergère; 1000–2300F. *St-Germain-des-Prés* Ⓜ

★★★★ **Relais Christine**, 3 Rue Christine, 75006, ✆ 01 43 26 71 80, ✆ 01 43 26 89 38. Luxurious, colourful rooms in a 16th-century Augustinian cloister, a quiet oasis; 1630–1720F. *Odéon* Ⓜ

★★★★ **La Villa**, 29 Rue Jacob, 75006, ✆ 01 43 26 60 00, ✆ 01 46 334 63 63. *Le dernier cri* in St-Germain, with precocious bathrooms of chrome, glass and marble and chi-chi piano bar; 1100–1400F. *St-Germain-des-Prés* Ⓜ

★★★ **Abbaye St-Germain**, 10 Rue Cassette, 75006, ✆ 01 45 44 38. One of the swankiest small Left-Bank hotels—originally a monastery—and despite the traffic on Rue Cassette, serenely quiet, especially if you get one of the bedrooms over the lovely garden courtyard; 880–1400F, four suites available.
*St-Sulpice* Ⓜ

★★★ **Académie**, 32 Rue des Sts-Pères, 75007, ✆ 01 45 48 36 22, ✆ 01 45 44 75 24. A converted 18th-century residence, with Louis XIV, Louis XVI and

Directory repros among exposed stone walls and beams that would have shocked the original owners; 690–890F. *St-Germain-des-Prés* Ⓜ

★★★ **Angleterre**, 44 Rue Jacob, 75006, ✆ 01 42 60 34 72, ✆ 01 42 60 16 93. A former British embassy, now a hotel with character. Some rooms have vertiginously high ceilings; huge double beds; 600–1100F.

*St-Germain-des-Prés* Ⓜ

★★★ **Crystal**, 24 Rue St-Benoît, 75006, ✆ 01 45 48 85 14, ✆ 01 45 49 16 45. Just around the corner from the church of St-Germain, a charming, cosy and lovingly cared-for little hotel; 550–820F. *St-Germain-des-Prés* Ⓜ

★★★ **Duc de Saint-Simon**, 14 Rue de St-Simon, 75007, ✆ 01 44 39 20 20, ✆ 01 45 48 68 25. In a 17th-century house in a quiet side street off Blvd St-Germain, one of the most fashionable little hotels on the Left Bank, all antiques, old beams, stone walls and snob appeal, its cellars converted into a string of bars and salons; 1100–1450F (no credit cards). *Rue du Bac* Ⓜ

★★★ **Lutétia**, 45 Blvd Raspail, 75006, ✆ 01 49 54 46 46, ✆ 01 49 54 46 00. Renovated early Art Deco palace, a favourite for honeymoons since Pablo and Olga Picasso and Charles and Yvonne de Gaulle canoodled here. When requisitioned by the Nazis, the staff walled up the prize wine cellars , and in spite of German interrogations never gave away the secret; 1500–2100F.

*Sèvres-Babylone* Ⓜ

★★★ **Luxembourg**, 4 Rue de Vaugirard, 75006, ✆ 01 43 25 35 90, ✆ 01 43 26 60 84. A small comfortable hotel by the Luxembourg gardens where Verlaine often stayed at the end of his life, at least when he was flush; 720–790F.

*Odéon* Ⓜ

★★★ **Marronniers**, 21 Rue Jacob, 75006, ✆ 01 43 25 30 60, ✆ 01 40 46 83 56. An enchanting little hotel at the bottom of a courtyard, with a garden at the back, but book well in advance; 750–850F (no credit cards).

*St-Germain-des-Prés* Ⓜ

★★★ **Université**, 22 Rue de l'Université, 75007, ✆ 01 42 61 09 39, ✆ 01 42 60 40 84. In a refurbished 17th-century town house, a few minutes from St-Germain-des-Prés—27 stylish, quiet rooms, each with a safe, bath and TV; 800–1300F, with reduced rates for kids sharing a room with parents.

*Rue du Bac* Ⓜ

★★ **Louisiane**, 60 Rue de Seine, 75006, ✆ 01 43 29 59 30, ✆ 01 46 34 23 87. Set amid the colourful Rue de Buci market, a celebrated favourite of Left-Bank literati. Most of the rooms are fairly plain and modern, but the friendly, good-humoured atmosphere makes all the difference. Reserve well in advance due to the slow turnaround, as some guests can't bear to leave—Simone de Beauvoir and Sartre stayed long enough to write several books; 510–710F.

*St-Germain-des-Prés* Ⓜ

**★★**  **Quai Voltaire**, 19 Quai Voltaire, 75007, ✆ 01 42 61 50 91, ✉ 01 42 61 62 26. A hotel since the 19th century, overlooking the Seine and the Louvre, a favourite of Baudelaire, Sibelius and Richard Wagner; 570–690F.

RER: *Musée d'Orsay*

**★★**  **Saint-Germain**, 50 Rue du Four, 75006, ✆ 01 45 48 91 64, ✉ 01 45 48 46 22. Rooms pretty, cosy and homey enough for a hobbit, who would appreciate the mini-bar, if not the French telly—baby-sitting available; 420–710F.

*St-Sulpice* Ⓜ

**★★**  **Welcome**, 66 Rue de Seine, ✆ 01 46 34 24 80, ✉01 40 46 81 59. Sweet, simple, soundproofed, and a warm welcome; 495–550F (no credit cards).

*Mabillon* Ⓜ

**★**  **Nesle**, 7 Rue de Nesle, 75006, ✆ 01 43 54 62 41. Slightly dilapidated but welcoming hotel of character that hasn't accepted reservations since it was an international be-in in the 1960s. Each room is in a different style: no.9 is Egyptian. Coin-operated washing machine, some rooms with shower; 260–300F.                              *Odéon* Ⓜ

**★**  **Saint-André des Arts**, 66 Rue St-André-des-Arts, 75006, ✆ 01 43 26 96 16, ✉ 01 43 29 73 34. A 17th-century musketeers' barracks, lively and often noisy until late at night; 440–470F.                         *Odéon* Ⓜ

## Left Bank: Rue Mouffetard/Jardin des Plantes

Pleasant, lively at night and cheaper than St-Germain.

**★★**  **Grandes Ecoles**, 75 Rue du Cardinal-Lemoine, 75005, ✆ 01 43 26 79 23, ✉ 01 43 25 28 15 (reserve weeks ahead). One of the most amazing settings in Paris, a peaceful cream-coloured villa in a beautiful garden courtyard; 350–600F.                              *Cardinal Lemoine* Ⓜ

**★★**  **Jardin des Plantes**, 5 Rue Linné, 75005, ✆ 01 47 07 06 20, ✉ 01 47 07 62 74. The best choice in the area, with its sauna, cheerful décor, and sunbathing on 5th-floor terrace overlooking the botanical gardens; 480–640F.

*Jussieu* Ⓜ

**★**  **Allies**, 20 Rue Berthollet, 75005, ✆ 01 43 31 47 52, ✉ 01 45 35 13 92. Simple place in a quiet street by the Val de Grâce; 200–300F.

*Censier Daubenton* Ⓜ

**★**  **Beauséjour Gobelins**, 16 Ave des Gobelins, 75013, ✆ 01 43 31 80 10, ✉ 01 43 31 30 03. Simple, serene lodgings near the foot of Rue Mouffetard; 230–290F.                              *Censier Daubenton* Ⓜ

**★**  **Le Central**, 6 Rue Descartes, 75005, ✆ 01 46 33 57 93. Conveniently located, family-run haven; 220–250F with shower. *Maubert-Mutualité* Ⓜ

**★**  **Port Royal**, 8 Bvld Port Royal, 75005, ✆ 01 43 31 70 06. Family-run, simple, immaculately clean; 196–25F.            *Les Gobelins* Ⓜ

## Left Bank: Montparnasse

A crop of big-business hotels, modern and low on charm, but a few stand-outs:

★★★ **Lenox Montparnasse**, 15 Rue Delambre, 75014, ✆ 01 43 35 34 50, ✉ 01 43 290 46 64. A large, elegant hotel, just off Blvd Raspail, opposite the seven cinemas; 590–650F. *Vavin* Ⓜ

★★★ **Orchidée**, 65 Rue de l'Ouest, 75014 ✆ 01 43 22 70 50, ✉ 01 42 79 97 46. Spanking new hotel with a jacuzzi, garden and sauna; 440–850F. *Gaîté* Ⓜ

★★★ **Villa des Artistes**, 9 Rue de la Grande-Chaumière, 75006, ✆ 01 43 26 60 86, ✉ 01 43 54 73 70. Where Samuel Beckett stayed, now given an Art Deco facelift—some of Montparnasse's best known artists had studios across the street; 520–800F. *Vavin* Ⓜ

★★ **Istria**, 29 Rue Campagne-Première, 75014, ✆ 01 43 20 91 82, ✉ 01 43 22 48 45. A charming, kind and cosy hotel that was a favourite of Man Ray, Aragon, Marcel Duchamp, Rilke and Walter Benjamin; 470–580F. *Raspail* Ⓜ

★★ **Parc**, 6 Rue Jolivet, 75014, ✆ 01 43 20 95 54, ✉ 01 42 79 82 62. A TV in each room, many overlooking sunny Square Gaston-Baty; 360–410F. *Edgar Quinet* Ⓜ

★★ **Stanislas**, 5 Rue du Montparnasse 75006, ✆ 01 45 48 37 05, ✉ 01 45 44 54 43. A well-kept, agreeable hotel in crêpe alley—TV, WC, shower and phones in each room; 330–350F. *Notre-Dame des Champs* Ⓜ

★ **Celtic**, 15 Rue d'Odessa 75014, ✆ 01 43 20 93 53. Simple, pleasant and convenient choice near Gare Montparnasse; 220–320F. *Montparnasse* Ⓜ

★ **Des Académies**, 15 Rue de la Grande-Chaumière, 75006, ✆ 01 43 26 66 44. Simple, unpretentious, family hotel near the Luxembourg gardens; 2555–310F. *Vavin* Ⓜ

## Faubourg St-Germain: Eiffel Tower/Invalides

Proust fans may want to sleep in the fabled Faubourg, but don't expect any life or spontaneity to put in your own album of remembrances.

★★★ **Bourdonnais**, 111–113 Ave de La Bourdonnais, 75007, ✆ 01 47 05 45 42, ✉ 01 45 55 75 54. Airy, elegant and comfortable, and breakfast is served in a sunlit indoor garden; 580–640F. *Ecole Militaire* Ⓜ

★★★ **Jardins d'Eiffel**, 8 Rue Amélie, 75007, ✆ 01 47 05 46 21, ✉ 01 45 55 28 08. Built at the same time as the 1889 Exposition. Rooms are cosy in an old-fashioned way, and there's a sauna; book a room on the top floors for a view of Mr Eiffel's flagpole; 660–960F. *La Tour Maubourg* Ⓜ

★★★    **Varenne**, 44 Rue de Bourgogne, 75007, ✆ 01 45 51 45 55, ✉ 01 45 51 86 63. An attractive converted town house with an interior courtyard in a peaceful corner of Paris; comfortable rooms all with bath and TV; 550–670F.

*Varenne* Ⓜ

★★★    **Verneuil Saint-Germain**, 8 Rue de Verneuil, 75007, ✆ 01 42 60 82 14, ✉ 01 42 61 40 38. Small for the price but pleasant rooms by the Musée d'Orsay and the antique dealers; 800–1100F.    *Solférino* Ⓜ

★★    **Centre**, 24bis Rue Cler, 75007, ✆ 01 47 05 52 33, ✉ 01 40 62 95 66. Recently refurbished old-fashioned hotel on Faubourg St-Germain's liveliest market street, and one of the cheapest in the quarter; 350–380F.

*La Tour Maubourg* Ⓜ

★★    **Kensington**, 79 Ave de La Bourdonnais, 75007, ✆ 01 47 05 74 00, ✉ 01 47 05 74 00. Pleasant and friendly, small and tidy; 385–480F.

*Ecole Militaire* Ⓜ

★    **Grand Hôtel Lévèque**, 29 Rue Cler, 75007. Friendly and pleasant and in the middle of Rue Cler market; 200–400F.    *La Tour Maubourg* Ⓜ

## Youth Hostels and Foyers

Low-cost accommodation for visitors between 18–30 years old comes under the august aegis of the **Acceuil des Jeunes de France**, for which you'll need a YHA card (they can sell you one). They have three agencies in Paris to help you find budget accommodation (and blithely consider everyone 'young'):

   **Beaubourg**, 119 Rue St-Martin (opposite the Pompidou Centre), ✆ 01 42 77 87 80, ✉ 01 42 77 70 48.

   **Quartier Latin**, 139 Blvd St-Michel, ✆ 01 43 54 95 86, ✉ 01 40 46 97 42.

   **Gare du Nord**, in the suburban station (June–Sept only), ✆ 01 42 85 86 19.

AJF's three top foyers are the superb *hôtels particuliers* in the Marais, all furnished with period pieces and immaculately maintained, where you can stay up to five days at only 120F per person, with breakfast. Too good to be true? The hitch is that they are often occupied by groups and take no individual bookings; to nab a bed come at 8am. The three hostels are:

   **Hôtel Maubuisson**, 12 Rue des Barres, 75004, ✆ 01 42 74 23 45, ✉ 01 42 74 08 93.    *Hôtel de Ville* Ⓜ

   **Hôtel de Fourcy**, 6 Rue de Fourcy, 75004, ✆ 01 42 74 23 45, ✉ 01 42 74 08 93.    *St-Paul* Ⓜ

   **Le Fauconnier**, 11 Rue du Fauconnier, 75004, ✆ 01 42 74 23 45, ✉ 01 42 74 08 93.    *St-Paul* Ⓜ

Other hostel options include:

**Y & H, or Youth's Residence Mouffetard**, 80 Rue Mouffetard, 75005, ✆ 01 45 35 09 53. The 'Young and Happy Hostel' on the 'Mouff' has been around since 1964; twin, triple and quad rooms and hot showers; 95F per person a night.

*Monge* Ⓜ

**Centre International de Séjour de Paris Kellermann**, 17 Blvd Kellerman, 75013, ✆ 01 44 16 37 38, 🖷 01 44 16 37 39. *Porte d'Italie* Ⓜ

**Centre International de Séjour Paris Maurice Ravel**, 6 Ave Maurice Ravel, 75012, ✆ 01 44 75 60 00, 🖷 01 43 44 45 30. *Porte de Vincennes* Ⓜ

**Fiap Jean Monnet**, 30 Rue Cabanis, 75014, ✆ 01 45 89 89 15, 🖷 01 45 81 63 91.

*Glacière* Ⓜ

**Maison Internationale des Jeunes**, 4 Rue Titon, 75011, ✆ 01 43 71 99 21, 🖷 01 43 71 78 58. *Faidherbe-Chaligny* Ⓜ

**Centre d'Accueil et d'Animation Paris 20e**, 46 Rue Louis Lumière, 75020, ✆ 01 43 61 24 51, 🖷 01 43 64 13 09. *Porte de Bagnolet* Ⓜ

There is a **city camp site**, nearly always full, in the Bois de Boulogne (Allée au Bord de l'Eau, ✆ 01 4524 30 00, 🖷 01 42 24 42 95). A bus links it to Ⓜ Porte Maillot.

## Bed and Breakfast

For listings, contact **Bed & Breakfast France**, P.O Box 55, Bell Street, Henley-on-Thames, Oxon RG9 1XS, ✆ 01491 578 803, or BAB France, 6 Rue d'Europe, 95470 Fosses, ✆ 01 34 68 83 15. For rooms in people's homes, try **Accueil France Famille**, 5 Rue François Coppée, 75015, Ⓜ Boucicaut, ✆ 01 45 54 22 39, 🖷 01 45 58 43 25.

## Short-term Rentals and Residence Hotels

If you plan to spend a week or more in Paris, a short-term let may save you money, especially if you're travelling with the family. Addresses to contact:

**At Home in Paris**, 16 Rue Méderic, 75017, ✆ 01 42 12 40 40, 🖷 01 42 12 40 48. Studios to six bedroom flats.

**France Lodge**, 5 Rue de Faubourg Montmartre, 75009, ✆ 01 42 46 68 19, 🖷 01 42 46 65 61. Studios to six-bedroom flats.

**Global Home Network**, reserve an apartment in Paris from the US, ✆ (703) 318 7081, 🖷 (703) 318 7086.

**Paris Apartments Services**, 69 Rue d'Argout, 75002, ✆ 01 40 28 01 28, 🖷 01 40 28 92 01. Studios and one room apts of character in the centre of Paris.

**Paris Séjour Réservation**, 90 Champs Elysées, ✆ 01 53 89 10 50, 🖷 01 53 89 10 59 or 645 N. Michigan Ave, Chicago, Il ✆ (312) 587 7707, 🖷 (312) 587 9887. Apartments, also viewable on a web page: http://www.qconline.com/parispsr.

Alternatively, there are a number of self catering **residential hotels**, among them:

**Citadines Paris-Austerlitz**, 27 Rue Esquirol, 75013, ✆ 01 44 23 51 51, 📠 01 45 86 59 76. Simple flats in a modern building, with a cafeteria and parking. Studios 2660–4130F a week, apts 4550–5705F. *Nationale* Ⓜ

**Citadines Paris-Montparnasse**, 67 Ave du Maine, 74014, ✆ 01 40 47 41 41, 📠 01 43 27 29 94. Studios 2772–3906F a week, apts 5957–6524F. *Gaîté* Ⓜ

**Citadines Paris-Trocadéro**, 29bis Rue St-Didier, 75016, ✆ 01 44 34 73 73, 📠 01 47 04 50 07. Studios 408–710F a day, apts 872–1590F a day. *Trocadéro* Ⓜ

**Flatotel International**, 14 Rue du Théâtre, 75015, ✆ 01 45 75 62 20, 📠 01 45 79 73 30. Studios 4270F a week, apts 6180F. *Charles Michel* Ⓜ

**Orion Paris Les Halles,** 4 Rue des Innocentes, ✆ 01 40 39 76 00, 📠 01 45 39 76 00. Studios 4130F, apts 6041F a week. *Châtelet* Ⓜ

**Pierre et Vacances Montmartre**, 10 Place Charles-Dullin, 75018, ✆ 01 42 57 14 55, 📠 01 42 54 48 87. Studios 3400-4990F, apts 5295-6300F week.

*Abbesses* Ⓜ

# Entertainment and Nightlife

When the last museums and shops close and the suburbanites catch their RERs to supper and television, the City of Light turns on the switch for a night of fun. There are several main circuits: from the Latin Quarter and across the Seine to Les Halles, the trendy new Bastille area, the Butte de Montmartre and Pigalle, St-Germain, Rue Mouffetard, Montparnasse and the Plaisance–Pernety area in the 14ᵉ. In a city as full of fashion slaves as Paris, the most *branché* ('plugged-in', i.e. trendy) clubs change fairly rapidly, but there are plenty of old reliables included below.

Besides the plethora of posters that cover the métro stations, cafés and Moriss columns, there are weekly guides that come out on Wednesdays, when the cinemas change their programmes: the 3 franc *Pariscope* (including everything from art exhibitions, museum hours to wife-swapping supper clubs, an English language section written by *Time Out*, a nightlife information hotline ℗ 08 36 68 88 55 and a Web site http://Pariscope.fr/ ), the similar but only 2-franc *L'Officiel des Spectacles*, and *7 à Paris* (same listings as *Pariscope*, but with articles and reviews on nightclubs and restaurants). The Wednesday *Figaro* has weekly listings; *Libération* has good pieces on art and music; the monthly *Paris Free Voice* has reviews in English.

## Ticket Agents

**FNAC** has ticket offices all over the city and a general number, ℗ 01 49 87 50 50; **Virgin Megastore**, 52 Champs-Elysées, ℗ 01 42 56 52 60 Ⓜ *Georges V*, is similar and open until midnight. Concerts, shows, plays, sporting events etc. may also be booked through the Tourist Office's Billetel ticket counter (127 Champs-Elysées, Ⓜ *Charles de Gaulle-Etoile,* ℗ 01 49 52 53 53, daily from 9am–8pm.

**Kiosque Théâtre**, near 15 Place de la Madeleine, 8ᵉ, Ⓜ *Madeleine.* Also on the Parvis de la Gare Montparnasse. Same-day, half-price theatre tickets, plus a 16F commission; expect a queue. Open Tues–Sat 12.30–8 and Sun 12.30–4 (closed Sun in July and Aug).

## Film

The Parisians may well be the biggest film junkies in the world, and chances are that in one of their 320 screens, one will show that obscure flick you've been dying to see for years. Along with politics and *les vacances*, films are the most common topic of conversation in the city—often bringing forth some curious and striking cultural differences. You can live in Paris for years and still not understand the city's lively appreciation for Jerry Lewis, or just what they find so alluring in Woody Allen: his 1991 film, *Alice* had a bigger box-office take in Paris than the whole United States. Paris' cinemas also offer a chance to see films rarely shown anywhere else—uncommercial films, Third World films (with French subtitles)—and sponsor a wide range of festivals and retrospectives throughout the year.

When perusing the listings (cross your fingers that you can recognize that film you've always wanted to see behind its French title), note that films dubbed in French or were originally made in several languages and are being shown in French are labelled *v.f.*; if shown in English, it will say *version anglaise*; if in the original language, with French subtitles, they'll say *v.o.* Average admission prices are between 25 and 50F and often you get 10 to 35 min of ads for free. Students and senior citizens are often eligible for discounts at weekday matinées. In some of the larger cinemas, the usherette should be tipped a minimum of two francs, a custom that has always annoyed some folks: 'Only a people in love with slavery would continue to endure the black bombazined harpies who turn the French theatres into infernos, first by their very presence, and secondly by their clamour for a *bénéfice*' as H. V. Lucas put it in 1909.

## Cinémathèques

A Paris institution, the Cinémathèque has one of the most extensive film libraries in the world. Tickets are only 28F (17F at the **Cinémathèque** in the Palais de Chaillot in two locations: by the Musée du Cinéma (but perhaps moving in late 1997 to the Palais du Tokyo) Ⓜ*Trocadéro*, and the Salle République, 18 Rue du Faubourg du Temple, Ⓜ*République,* both ✆ 01 47 04 24 24, closed Mon. The **Vidéothèque de Paris**, Porte St-Eustache in the Forum des Halles, ✆ 01 40 26 34 30 (closed Mon), Ⓜ*Châtelet-Les Halles*, shows films and documentaries daily from 2.30 to 9pm except Monday on changing themes; 30F adm for the day. The **Salle Garance** at the Pompidou Centre, ✆ 01 42 78 37 29 shows subtitled films from around the world with French subtitles, closed Tues; adm 27 and 20F.

## Commercial Houses

**Accatone**, 20 Rue Cujas, 5ᵉ, ✆ 01 46 33 86 86. Great for lesser-known classics from Russia, Eastern Europe and alternative films from just about everywhere else.
*Cluny-La Sorbonne* Ⓜ

**Action**, a small Paris chain of cinemas specializing in retrospectives of great old films, most on fresh prints drawn from the negatives. Their biggest showcase is **Grand Action** 5 Rue des Ecoles, 5ᵉ, ✆ 01 43 29 44 40, Ⓜ *Cardinal Lemoine*; nearby **Action Ecoles**, 23 Rue des Ecoles, ✆ 01 43 25 72 07 is rather smaller.

**Denfert**, 24 Pl Denfert-Rochereau, 14ᵉ, ✆ 01 43 21 41 01. Great repertory house in *v.o.*, although frequently films for children are dubbed.  *Denfert Rochereau* Ⓜ

**Dôme IMAX**, 1 Place du Dôme, La Défense, ✆ 08 36 67 06 06. 'Largest Wraparound Movie Theatre in the World'  *Grande Arche de La Défense* Ⓜ

**L'Escurial Panoramas**, 11 Blvd de Port-Royal, 13ᵉ, ✆ 01 47 07 28 04. Plush red-velvet movie palace, showing quality films in *v.o.*  *Gobelins* Ⓜ

**L'Entrepôt**, 7–9 Rue Francis-de-Pressensé 14ᵉ, ✆ 01 4540 78 38. One of the best: three rooms showing some of the best art and Third-World fare in Paris, also a bookshop, bar, satellite and cable TV from around the world.  *Pernety* Ⓜ

**UGC Cine Cité Les Halles**, 7 Pl de la Rotonde, Nouveau Forum des Halles, 1ᵉʳ, ✆ 08 36 68 68 58. 15 subterranean screens with Dolby sound, and the plush Grande Salle THX showing first-run *v.o.* films; at 10am only 25F.

*Châtelet-Les Halles* Ⓜ

**Gaumont Parnasse**, 82 Blvd du Montparnasse, 14ᵉ. Four high tech 'Gaumont rama screens' and eight others, showing mostly recent releases in *v.o.*

*Montparnasse Bienvenüe* Ⓜ

**La Géode**, 26 Ave Corentin-Cariou, 19ᵉ, ✆ 01 40 05 12 12. Extraordinary OMNIMAX cinema of the Cité des Sciences puts on shows with fish-eye-lens cameras that make you feel as if you were in the centre of the action. Hourly showings daily except Mon from 10am to 7pm of National-Geographic-type fare for 57F. Booking strongly suggested in advance for the 7, 8 and 9pm showings, same day only, ✆ 01 42 05 50 50.  *Porte de la Villette* Ⓜ

**Gaumont Kinopanorama**, 60 Ave de La Motte-Picquet, 15ᵉ. Very popular, 180° cinema, 70mm film, equipped for high definition Showscan (60 images per second) and extraordinary sound.  *La Motte Picquet* Ⓜ

**Le Latina**, 20 Rue du Temple, 4ᵉ, ✆ 01 42 78 47 86. Latin American film specialist.

*Hôtel de Ville* Ⓜ

**Max Linder Panorama**, 24 Blvd Poissonnière, 9ᵉ, ✆ 01 48 24 88 88. Most sumptuous and plush, state-of-the-art equipment; great for first-run films in *v.o.*

*Rue Montmartre* Ⓜ

**La Pagode**, 57 Rue de Babylone, 7ᵉ. Mme Boucicaut's Japanese folly has been a cinema and tea house since 1931, and thanks to Marcel Carné, an historical monument since 1982. The Grande Salle is lined with silk panels, although the Gaumont management shows mostly mainstream fare in French.  *St-François Xavier* Ⓜ

**Reflet Médicis Logos**, 3 Rue Champollion, 5ᵉ, ✆ 01 43 54 42 34. Art films in *v.o.*

*Odéon* Ⓜ

**Le Grand Rex**, 1 Blvd Poissonnière, 2ᵉ, ✆ 08 36 68 70 23. Films are all dubbed into French, but the Rex is a must for lovers of old Hollywood Busby Berkeley 1930s extravaganzas with one of the biggest screens in Europe, 2750 seats and a great ceiling.  *Bonne Nouvelle* Ⓜ

**Studio 28**, 10 Rue Tholozé, 18ᵉ, ✆ 01 46 06 36 07. Founded in 1928, charming, family run and still going strong. Films always in *v.o.*  *Abbesses* Ⓜ

**Studio Galande**, 42 Rue Galande, 5ᵉ, ✆ 08 36 68 06 24. Brave little cinema, with lots of old Fellini and Terry Gilliam, and *The Rocky Horror Picture Show* Fri and Sat nights, all in *v.o.*                                                                                                     *St-Michel* Ⓜ

**Studio des Ursulines**, 10 Rue des Ursulines, 5ᵉ, ✆ 01 43 26 19 09. Tiny but oldest art cinema in Paris (1926).                                                                                                                    *Luxembourg* Ⓜ

**Les Trois Luxembourgs**, 67 Rue Monsieur-le-Prince, 6ᵉ, ✆ 08 36 68 93 25. Very basic inside, but worth visiting for its great Dada sign, and innovative offerings on three screens.                                                                                                    *Odéon* Ⓜ

**Quartier Latin**, 9 Rue Champollion, 5ᵉ, ✆ 01 43 26 84 65. Small alternative cinema.
*Cluny-La Sorbonne* Ⓜ

## Opera, Classical and Contemporary Music

Paris has traditionally had an ambivalent attitude towards classical music. Paris must be the only great European capital without a proper symphony auditorium, not to mention a great orchestra to play in it; even the productions in its lavish opera house only seldom hit a high note of quality. Paris is, as one virtuoso put in, the only town in the world where people laugh at a man carrying a violin case. The great French composers of the early 19th century had the darndest time: one critic complained of Debussy's opera *Pelléas et Mélisande* that the orchestra never stopped tuning up, and Satie once prefaced a recital with some advice to the audience: 'Those who do not understand are asked to assume an attitude of submissiveness and inferiority.' Not a few people do the same at concerts of the experimental Ensemble Inter-Contemporain in La Villette's Cité de la Musique.

Thanks to the Ministry of Culture and reforms in education that have brought music into the schools, there is more interest in music than ever before: there are frequent lunchtimes concerts in the churches (listed in *Pariscope*), in medieval music and choirs at Sainte-Chapelle and chamber music at the Orangerie at La Bagatelle a number of music festivals throughout the year.

**Cité de la Musique**, 221 Ave Jean Jaurès, 19ᵉ, ✆ 01 44 84 44 84. Two high tech concert venues, one home to Pierre Boulez's Ensemble Inter-Contemporain.
*Porte de Pantin* Ⓜ

**Opéra de Paris Bastille**, Pl de la Bastille, 12ᵉ, ✆ 01 44 73 13 00. Opened by Mitterrand in 1990, the slugfest of controversy over its architecture, management, and obfuscating productions 'for the masses' has diminished to the occasional slap on the wrist. The acoustics, however, are great; tickets from 60–600F.    *Bastille* Ⓜ

**Opéra Comique**, 5 Rue Favart, 2ᵉ, ✆ 01 42 44 45 46. An older hall used by the Opéra Comique for a repertoire ranging from Lully to Carmen and the occasional operettas.                                                                                                              *Richelieu Drouot* Ⓜ

**Salle Pleyel**, 252 Rue du Faubourg-St-Honoré, 8ᵉ, ✆ 01 45 61 53 00. Larger than the Gaveau but just as old, where Chopin last played in public—although the stories of him coughing blood on the keys are an exaggeration; recitals and orchestral performances by the Orchestre Philharmonique de Radio France.     *Ternes* Ⓜ

**Théâtre des Champs-Elysées**, 15 Ave Montaigne, 16ᵉ, ☏ 01 49 52 50 50. The Paris equivalent of Carnegie Hall, where Josephine Baker first danced in Paris, and a favourite of big-name classical performers; also some opera.     *Alma Marceau* Ⓜ

**Théâtre du Châtelet**, Pl du Châtelet, ☏ 01 40 28 28 40. 130-year-old theatre that saw the first season of the Ballets Russes in 1909, and since 1980 very successfully run by the City of Paris, with better opera than the Bastille as well as a vast range of innovative music offerings.     *Châtelet* Ⓜ

**Théâtre de la Ville**, 2 Pl du Châtelet, 4ᵉ, ☏ 01 42 74 22 77. Excellent city-run theatre: every kind of music, from piano recitals to jazz to African songs.     *Châtelet* Ⓜ

## Jazz, Blues, Rock and World Music

In 1925, when *La Revue Nègre* appeared in Paris, it set off a craze for *le jazz hot*, Sidney Bechet, Mezz Mezzrow, the Charleston and Black Bottom so overwhelming that it undermined the old *bal musettes* and the French rewrote the rules saying that half the members of any band had to be French nationals—a problem the Americans got round by having the French musicians just sit there, holding their instruments. By the next decade France began to catch up by producing its own jazz, led by violinist Stéphane Grappelli and the three-fingered guitarist Django Reinhardt, while continuing to welcome and support black Americans, fleeing racial prejudice at home.

Still considered the jazz capital of Europe, Paris since the early 1970s has been in the forefront of the world music phenomenon, with its African, North African, Latin, Brazilian and Caribbean zouk clubs, where many modern stars found their first audiences. Paris is also the base of Cheb Khaled, the best-known raï singer, who some people call the Algerian Jim Morrison. Raï, derived from pre-Islamic Bedouin poetry, means 'opinion'; it is similar to rap in content and mostly about alcohol and sex, forbidden fruits easier enjoyed in Paris than in Algiers.

Clubs (most confirm to the smoky cellar stereotype) either charge admission or an exorbitant price for a first drink, averaging 100F, and many pester you to order more and not a few will bounce you out if they catch you with a flask.

### *Live Music Bars and Clubs*

**Arapaho**, Centre Commercial Italie 2, 30 Ave d'Italie, 13ᵉ, ☏ 01 53 79 00 11. Often interesting indie and Far Eastern music venue.     *Place d'Italie* Ⓜ

**Au Duc des Lombards**, 42 Rue des Lombards, 1ᵉʳ, ☏ 01 42 33 22 88. One of the best; popular, friendly dimly lit lounge, with jazz piano, trios and crooners ranging from excellent to competent; daily from 10pm–3am.     *Châtelet* Ⓜ

**Le Bilboquet**, 13 Rue St-Benoît, 6ᵉ, ℭ 01 45 48 81 84. St-Germain club, vintage 1947, on the main drag of cool jazz in the 1950s, and popular with tourists remembering those golden days. Pricey, average French jazz.    *St-Germain-des-Prés* ⓜ

**Caveau de la Huchette**, 5 Rue de la Huchette, 5ᵉ, ℭ 01 43 26 65 05. Since 1946, a home of traditional jazz and be-bop in its 14th-century cellar.    *St-Michel* ⓜ

**La Chapelle des Lombards**, 19 Rue de Lappe, 11ᵉ, ℭ 01 43 57 24 24. Some of the best, newest, affordable Caribbean and African music. Open Thurs–Sun only.
*Bastille* ⓜ

**Chesterfield Café**, 124 Rue de La Boétie, 8ᵉ, ℭ 01 42 25 18 06. Mostly rock groups made in America from 11pm on.    *Franklin D. Roosevelt* ⓜ

**Cithea**, 114 Rue Oberkampf, 11ᵉ, ℭ 01 40 21 70 95. Live soul, blues, jazz, funk etc. Thurs–Sat nights; attracts a lot of local musicians.    *Ménilmontant* ⓜ

**Divan du Monde**, 75 Rue des Martyrs, 18e, ℭ 01 44 92 77 66. Exciting club dedicated to a wide variety of world music and dance.    *Pigalle* ⓜ

**Les Etoiles**, 61 Rue du Château d'Eau, 10ᵉ, ℭ 01 47 70 60 56. Great Salsa and other Latin bands Thurs-Sat night, 100F dinner and music.    *Château d'Eau* ⓜ

**The Front Page**, 58 Rue St-Denis, ℭ 01 42 36 98 69. Best venue for blues, a large portion of the bands from the US.    *Châtelet-Les Halles* ⓜ

**Hot Brass**, Parc de La Villette, 211 Ave Jean-Jaurès, ℭ 01 42 00 14 14. Popular new space in a *folie* devoted to jazz and the blues.    *Porte de Pantin* ⓜ

**Jazz Club Lionel Hampton**, Hôtel Méridien, 81 Blvd Gouvion-St-Cyr, 17ᵉ, ℭ 01 40 68 30 42. Named after the wizard of the vibraphone, who plays a few weeks here every year; frequent gigs by big names when drinks become even more pricey. Dressy but relaxed—a modern version of an old Warner Brothers movie.
*Porte Maillot* ⓜ

**New Morning**, 7–9 Rue des Petites-Ecuries, 10ᵉ, ℭ 01 45 23 56 39. Not at all cosy, but plenty of room and fine acoustics—the place to find international all-stars of jazz and first rate world music.    *Château d'Eau* ⓜ

**Le Petit Journal Montparnasse**, 13 Rue du Commandant-René-Mouchotte, 14ᵉ, ℭ 01 43 21 56 70. One of best nightspots in the area, with enough space for big bands from France and abroad as well.    *Gaîté* ⓜ

**Le Petit Journal St-Michel**, 71 Blvd St-Michel, 5ᵉ, ℭ 01 43 26 28 59. Good jazz in a poky crowded club; closed-circuit TV in the alcoves.    RER: *Luxembourg*

**Le Petit Opportun**, 15 Rue des Lavandières-Ste-Opportune, 1ᵉʳ, ℭ 42 36 01 36. Small, intense bebop *à la française*, daily from 11pm–3am.    *Châtelet Les Halles* ⓜ

**Quai du Blues**, 17 Blvd Vittal-Bouhot, Neuilly-sur-Seine, ℭ 01 46 24 22 00. Pleasant riverside locations with live blues, boogie, and jazz.    *Porte-de-Levallois* ⓜ

**Slow Club**, 130 Rue de Rivoli, 1ᵉʳ, ℭ 01 42 33 84 30. The late Miles Davis's favourite jazz club in Paris, and a must for lovers of swing, New Orleans and traditional jazz.    *Châtelet Les Halles* ⓜ

**Le Sunset**, 60 Rue des Lombards, 1ᵉʳ, ✆ 01 40 26 46 60. Jazz, fusion, bebop, in the redecorated cellar cum tiled métro tunnel. *Châtelet Les Halles* Ⓜ

**La Villa**, 29 Rue Jacob, 6ᵉ, ✆ 01 43 26 60 00. Pricey, trendy, often jam packed and a bit posey, but some fine jazz on the Steinway piano. *St-Germain-des-Prés* Ⓜ

**Utopia**, 1 Rue Niepce, 14ᵉ, ✆ 01 43 22 79 66. Mostly made-in-France rhythm and blues; no admission charge and cheap drinks. *Pernety* Ⓜ

**Wait and See Café**, 9 Blvd Voltaire, 11ᵉ, ✆ 01 48 07 29 49. Live rock in the cellar especially popular with the young. *République* Ⓜ

## Major Concert Venues

**La Cigale**, 120 Blvd de Rouchechouart, 18ᵉ, ✆ 01 42 23 15 15. Nicely restored vaudeville theatre with the seats removed; plenty of rock. *Pigalle* Ⓜ

**Elysée Montmartre**, 72 Blvd de Rochechouart, 18ᵉ, ✆ 42 52 25 15. Where La Goulue first cancanned now hosts alternative and world music bands. *Anvers* Ⓜ

**Olympia**, 28 Blvd des Capucines, 9ᵉ, ✆ 47 42 82 45. Delightful Art Deco hall, where Piaf and other stars of music-hall France performed, and still do, with the likes of Tom Waits on other days. *Madeleine* Ⓜ

**Palais Omnisport Bercy**, 8 Blvd de Bercy, 12ᵉ, ✆ 01 44 68 44 68. The biggest, with 16,000 seats, expensive—and for music, obnoxious in almost every possible way, though it puts on more concerts than any other place in this list.

*Bercy* Ⓜ

**Grand Rex** (*see* cinemas, above), its 3000-seat capacity often used for concerts.

**Zénith**, 211 Ave Jean-Jaurès, 19ᵉ, ✆ 01 42 08 60 00. La Villette's inflatable, pop music hall decorated with a red aeroplane about to nosedive. *Porte de Pantin* Ⓜ

## Nightclubs, Discothèques and *Bal Musettes*

The French have a genuine wild and crazy streak that of late manifests itself in some funny neo-Dadaist pop videos, produced by groups who like to produce one or two videos, then break up like molecules and form other groups with different names. They compensate for an inability to produce any decent pop music, a problem former Culture Minister Jack Lang tried to solve by appointing a subminister of rock'n'roll. Unfortunately, most discos in Paris take themselves seriously and are full of uncool people posing for each other's benefit at the expense of having any real fun, in spite of the considerable sums of cash required. Your appearance tends to be all-important and the bouncers at the door picky if you're not their type; women have an easier time than men and at some of the best Afro-Caribbean clubs, the darker your skin colour the better. Others are so exclusive that getting in is one of the biggest steps a Parisian can make towards social and financial success. As a reaction to all this (very expensive) fuss, many Parisians are taking refuge in music bars. In the summer they like to waltz to the schmaltzy accordion tunes of their grandparents (*la bal musette*) especially at the festivals. Entrance fees and first drinks are usually 100F, 120F weekends.

**L'Alizé**, 14 Rue de la Croix-Nivert, 15e, ✆ 01 45 66 63 62. Great Caribbean sounds, with lots of reggae and ragga, open Fri–Sun.　　　　　　　　　　*La Fourche* ⓜ

**L'Aquarium**, 16 Rue Linois, 15ᵉ, ✆ 01 45 77 89 61. Very popular, young riversideclub that plays everything but techno; frequent theme nights.　　*Charles-Michels* ⓜ

**Les Bains**, 7 Rue du Bourg-l'Abbé, 3ᵉ, ✆ 01 48 87 01 80. Snooty club in an old bath house, the disco Parisians love to hate; closed Sun and Mon.　*Etienne Marcel* ⓜ

**Le Balajo**, 9 Rue de Lappe, 11ᵉ, ✆ 01 47 00 09 69. One of Paris' top retro monuments, with decor by the Moulin-Rouge's designer. A unique, occasionally surreal bastion of *bal musette*, swing and cha cha cha; women free Mon and Thurs.

*Bastille* ⓜ

**Au Bus**, 6 Rue Fontaine, 9ᵉ, ✆ 01 53 21 07 33. Large mix of Parisians; rock, funk, techno and soul, and free striptease night on Weds; closed Sun and Mon.　　*Pigalle* ⓜ

**Café de la Musique**, 242 Ave Jean-Jaurès, 19ᵉ, ✆ 01 42 40 24 13, by La Villette, in place among the city's movers and shakers, under the reign of Albert, Paris' cult DJ. Open daily until 2am.　　　　　　　　　　*Porte de Pantin* ⓜ

**La Casbah**, 18–20 Rue de la Forge-Royale, 11e, ✆ 01 43 71 71 89. Recreation of Rick's in *Casablanca*; Morocan cuisine in the restaurant (book), funk, house, acid and rock on the dance floor Wed–Sat.　　　　　　　　　　*Ledru-Rollin* ⓜ

**Elysée-Montmartre** 72 Blvd de Rochechouart, ✆ 01 44 95 45 45. In a hall designed by Eiffel, golden oldies, twist, disco, reggae every other Saturday night.　*Anvers* ⓜ

**L'Escale**, 15 Rue Monsier-le-Prince, 6ᵉ, ✆ 01 43 54 63 47. Small Cuban club, last hanger-on from the glory post-war days of St-Germain-des-Prés; open Tues-Sat

*Odéon* ⓜ

**Chez Félix**, 23 Rue Mouffetard, 5ᵉ, ✆ 01 47 07 68 78. Long established Brazilian nightclub in a medieval cellar, with samba and rum from 11pm until dawn. *Monge* ⓜ

**Le Gibus**, 18 Rue du Faubourg-du-Temple, 11ᵉ, ✆ 01 47 00 78 88. Long-standing club devoted to rock; techno, house, heavy metal during the week and with live bands Fri and Sat, ranging from future stars to utter nitwits (closed Mon).

*République* ⓜ

**El Globo** , 8 Blvd de Strasbourg, 10ᵉ, ✆ 01 42 41 55 70. Saturday Night Fever lives again in a huge disco under psycholdelic lights; Sat nights til 7am.

*Strasbourg-St Denis* ⓜ

**Le Hot Brass**, 211 Ave Jean-Jaurès, 19ᵉ, ✆ 01 42 00 14 14. Excellent alternative music, jazz, be-bop and R&B in one of the follies in the Parc de la Villette; with frequent special nights, films, live music and DJs.　　　　　*Porte de Pantin* ⓜ

**La Java**, 105 Rue du Faubourg-du-Temple, 10ᵉ, ✆ 01 42 02 20 52. A grand old music hall opened in the 1920s, where Piaf got her first break; Thurs and Fri live salsa, Sat *bal musette*. Sun night Brazilian.　　　　　*Goncourt, Belleville* ⓜ

**Keur-Samba,** 79 Rue de La Boétie, 8ᵉ, ℰ 01 43 59 03 10. The most fashionable African club in Paris; great music but hard to get inside. *S-Philippe-de-Roule* Ⓜ

**La Locomotive,** 90 Blvd de Clichy, 18ᵉ, ℰ 01 42 57 37 37. Next to the Moulin-Rouge and becoming an institution in itself; glitzy, three-storey nightclub with two dance floors: pop, techno and rock, and lots of boppers; weekdays 50F.
*Blanche* Ⓜ

**Mambo Club,** 20 Rue Cujas, 5ᵉ, ℰ 01 43 54 89 21. Oldest but still hot and shaking African club in Paris, with zouk, funk, salsa and more, and Sun nights live performance. Open Thurs–Sun. *Cluny-La Sorbonne* Ⓜ

**Le Neil's,** 27 Ave des Ternes, 17ᵉ, ℰ 01 47 66 45 00. Sophisto-sister disco of the one in New York, with books cases, plush sofas, and the occasional celebrity; good restaurant (250–350F) and disco after 12.30am *Ternes* Ⓜ

**Le New Raï,** 28 Rue de la Montagne-Sainte-Geneviève, 5ᵉ, ℰ 01 43 29 81 88. Authentic Arab club, specializing in the best of raï, closed Tues
*Maubert-Mutualité* Ⓜ

**Le Palace,** 8 Rue du Faubourg-Montmartre, 9ᵉ, ℰ 01 42 46 10 87. Two storeys, one of the best-known night haunts in Paris, with a variety of nights from good old-fashioned psychedelic to Motown, rap and gay (*see* p.431) *Rue Montmartre* Ⓜ

**Rex Club,** 5 Blvd Poissonnière, 2ᵉ, ℰ 01 42 36 83 98. Hyper trendy dancing under the cinema, with internationlly famous DJs; jungle muisc, goa, techno, et al; closed Tues. *Montmartre* Ⓜ

**Le Shéhérazade,** 3 Rue de Liège, 9ᵉ, ℰ 01 42 85 53 78. Exotic Ali Baba and the Forty Thieves interiors, left over from a belly-dancing club in the 1940s, where students flock to dance to grunge, Indie, pop and techno. *Europe* Ⓜ

**La Station,** 1 Ave de Clichy, 17ᵉ, ℰ 01 43 87 18 33. Bopping house music in Pigalle attracts crowds Thurs–Sat. *Place de Clichy* Ⓜ

**Le Tango,** 13 Rue au Maire, 3ᵉ, ℰ 01 42 72 17 78. Authentic Afro-Latino club; some of the best dancing and pounding rhythms in Paris, attracting mostly young workers in their mid 20s and 30s; Fri and Sat 11pm to 4am. *Arts et Métiers* Ⓜ

## Gay Music Bars and Clubs

**Banana Café,** 13 Rue Ferronnerie, 1ᵉ, ℰ 01 42 33 35 31. The trendiest music bar in Paris; put on your glad rags to get past the doorman. *Châtelet-Les Halles* Ⓜ

**Le Club 18,** 18 Rue de Beaujolais, 1ᵉʳ, ℰ 01 42 97 52 13. Lots of mirrors and techno in the basement disco, quieter upstairs in the bar and mezzanine. *Bourse* Ⓜ

**Le Duplex,** 25 Rue Michel-Le-Comte, 3ᵉ, ℰ 0142 72 80 86. Friendly artsy gay and straight music bar with affordable drink prices. *Rambuteau* Ⓜ

**Le Queen,** 102 Ave Champs-Elysées, 8ᵉ, ℰ 01 42 89 31 32. The hippest and most sophisticated gay disco draws a fair mix of stylish heteros as well; special Boy night on Thurs; Latin Wed, disco Mon. *Rue Montmartre* Ⓜ

**Le Palace,** 8 Rue du Faubourg-Montmartre, 9ᵉ, ✆ 01 47 70 75 02. Home of the celebrated gay tea dance on Sun from 4–11pm; also gay on Thurs nights, playing mostly house (*see* p.430) *Rue Montmartre* Ⓜ

**Le Piano Zinc,** 49 Rue des Blancs-Manteaux, 4ᵉ, ✆ 01 42 74 32 42. Predominantly but not exclusively gay and lesbian cabaret-bar; amusing, often high-spirited sing-alongs around the piano; open Tues–Sun from 10 pm. *Rambuteau* Ⓜ

**Les Piétons,** 8 Rue des Lombards, 4ᵉ ✆ 01 48 87 82 87. New cool music bar in the Marais with tapas and a Sunday brunch. *Hôtel de Ville* Ⓜ

**Le Quetzal** 10 Rue de la Verrerie, 4ᵉ, ✆ 01 48 87 99 07. Crowded bar newly done in an erector set decor, considered Paris' principal gay meat market. *St-Paul* Ⓜ

**Temple,** 9 Place Pigalle, 9ᵉ, ✆ 01 48 74 27 17. Mostly gay new club playing house music; open daily; Mon 100F with free drinks. *Pigalle* Ⓜ

**Toutim,** 4 Rue du Faubourg Montmartre, 9ᵉ, ✆ 01 42 46 22 20. New fun, mostly gay bar, a popular pre-club rendez-vous. *Rue-Montmartre* Ⓜ

**Le Vagabond,** 14 Rue Thérèse, 1ᵉ, ✆ 01 42 96 27 23. First gay bar-restaurant in Paris, with lots of regulars in a cosy atmosphere. *Pyramides* Ⓜ

---

### Lesbian Clubs

**La Champmeslé,** 4 Rue Chabanais, 2ᵉ, ✆ 01 42 96 85 20. Risqué decor and cheap drinks, and a cabaret every Thurs night; closed Sun. *Pyramides* Ⓜ

**Ego Club,** 50 Rue de la Chaussée-d'Antin, 9ᵉ, ✆ 01 42 85 20 38. Trendy women-only disco, free entry; open Thurs-Sun. *Chaussé d'Antin* Ⓜ

**L'Entreacte,** 25 Blvd Poissonnière, 2ᵉ, ✆ 01 40 26 01 93. Techno, funk and disco with different theme nights for the young. *Rue Montmartre* Ⓜ

**Entre Nous,** 17 Rue Laferrière, 9ᵉ, ✆ 01 48 78 11 67. Small, intimate women-only club dating from the 1940s; all ages; open Fri and Sat till dawn. *St-Georges* Ⓜ

**Le Scandolo,** 21 Rue Keller, 11ᵉ, ✆ 01 47 00 24 59. Fashionable youth-oriented rock'n'roll bar with a tiny dance floor. *Ledru Rollin* Ⓜ

## *Chansonniers*

Paris' own art form, first popularized by Aristide Bruant (*see* Topics, p.59), revived in the 1950s and '60s by Jacques Brel, Georges Brassens and Juliette Greco and currently being revived again—for both the Parisians and tourists.

**Le Bistro de la Gaîté,** 20 Rue de la Gaîté, 14ᵉ, ✆ 01 43 22 86 46. Reasonably priced bistrot in a theatre, with chansons Friday and Saturday night. *Gaîté* Ⓜ

**Canotier du Pied de la Butte,** 62 Blvd de Rochechouart, 18ᵉ, ✆ 01 46 06 02 86. Sit in romantic gloom and listen to favourite French songs and jokes; 10pm til dawn; the French come for the midnight show. Karaoke night on Wednesday. *Anvers* Ⓜ

**Caveau de la Bolée**, 25 Rue de l'Hirondelle, 6ᵉ, ✆ 01 43 54 62 20. 14th-century prison in a medieval alley, a place to evoke the old Latin Quarter and *les neiges d'antan* with its dinner-cabaret; 260F a head; 300F Saturday.  *St-Michel* Ⓜ

**Caveau des Oubliettes**, 11 Rue St-Julien-le-Pauvre, 5ᵉ, ✆ 01 43 54 94 97. French songs from the 12th to 20th centuries, a peek at a medieval dungeon, torture instruments (J F.K. as a senator is supposed to have put his head in the guillotine); open 9pm–2am exc Sun.  *St-Michel* Ⓜ

**Le Lapin Agile**, 22 Rue des Saules, 18ᵉ, ✆ 01 46 06 85 87. A valiant attempt at bringing old French traditional song back to life to busloads of Japanese tourists; show and first drink 110F (open 9pm–2am, closed Mon).  *Lamarck Caulaincourt* Ⓜ

## Cabarets, Drag and Ethnic Shows

Paris rivals Las Vegas as the world's epicentre of over the top kitsch-and-glitter-oozing, tit-and-feather spectaculars, invariably advertised as 'sophisticated', for fleecing tourists, provincials and businessmen.

**A Balalaïka**, 60 Rue de la Montagne Saint-Geneviève, 5ᵉ, ✆ 01 46 33 23 23. Russian cuisine by candlelight in a 13th-century cellar, to the tune of Russian songs and music. 500F; closed Wed; book.  *Cardinal-Lemoine* Ⓜ

**Club des Poètes**, 30 Rue de Bourgogne, 7ᵉ, ✆ 01 47 05 06 03. A treat for fans of French poetry, with a spectacle featuring the greats 'from Villon to Boris Vian'. Dinner and show from 140F. Closed Sun.  *Varenne* Ⓜ

**Crazy Horse**, 12 Ave George-V, 8ᵉ, ✆ 01 47 23 32 32. High temple of naked Barbie dolls with names like Bettina Uranium and Pussy Duty-Free dressed in leather straps; shows from 220F at the bar, 750F with dinner.  *Alma Marceau* Ⓜ

**Don Camilo**, 10 Rue des Saints-Pères, 7ᵉ ✆ 01 42 60 82 84. Biting Left Bank satirical songs—fun if your French is good. 250F dinner and show. *St-Germain des Prés* Ⓜ

**Douchka**, 6 Rue du Pont au Choux, 3ᵉ, ✆ 01 42 72 17 00. Delicious Russian cuisine and balilakas in charming setting; from 300F.  *St-Sébastien-Froissart* Ⓜ

**Lido**, 116 Ave des Champs-Elysées, 8ᵉ, ✆ 01 40 76 56 10. The best special effects perk up the act of the 60 Bluebell Girls; dinner and show 805F, show only 540 with champagne or 365F at the bar at 10 and midnight.  *George V* Ⓜ

**Michou**, 80 Rue des Martyrs, 18ᵉ, ✆ 01 46 06 16 04. Reserve for a place at Michou, a funny satyrical drag show that draws even the celebrities to see themselves being parodied. Dinner and show 550F.  *Abbesses* Ⓜ

**Le Monseigneur,** 94 Rue d'Amsterdam, 9ᵉ, ✆ 01 48 74 25 35. Arab cuisine, music and belly dancing from 11pm; from 150F  *Europe* Ⓜ

**Moulin-Rouge**, 82 Blvd de Clichy, 11ᵉ, ✆ 01 46 06 00 19. The most famous and the most Las-Vegasey of the lot, with its guest stars and cancanning Doriss Girls; dinner and show 750F; 10pm show and champagne only 510F, midnight 450F.  *Blanche* Ⓜ

**Le Paradis Latin**, 28 Rue du Cardinal-Lemoine, 5ᵉ, ✆ 01 43 25 28 28. In an old theatre built by Eiffel, the one music hall-cabaret of the genre with Parisian customers; count on spending at least 700F for dinner and the show.    *Cardinal-Lemoine* Ⓜ

**Pau Brazil**, 32 Ave de Tilsitt, 17ᵉ, ✆ 01 42 27 31 39. Brazilian meat feast, show, samba and lambada from 8pm–2am; menu 350–450F.    *Charles deGaulle-Etoile* Ⓜ

**Le Piano Show**, 20 Rue de la Verrerie, 4ᵉ, ✆ 01 42 72 23 81. Reasonably priced transvestite fun and laughs—only 200F for set meal with wine.    *Hôtel de Ville* Ⓜ

## Dance

There's a good range of dance to see in Paris, but little of it is home grown, thanks to the decision of the Culture Ministry to subsidize companies out in the provinces, and not in Paris. A Parisian 50 years ago would have been appalled to learn that France's best dance companies were Compagnie Dominique Bagouet in Montpellier, Compagnie Jean-Claude Gallotta in Grenoble, Compagnie Régine Chopinot, based in La Rochelle, Ballet National de Marseille Roland Petit and Compagnie Maguy Marin in Créteil. One of these is likely to be in town.

Many of the already listed theatres and concert halls put on dance performances, often by visiting companies, and each week's listings seem to bring forth new studios or theatre venues. Places especially dedicated to dance in Paris are:

**Opéra de Paris-Garnier**, Place de l'Opéra, 9ᵉ, ✆ 01 44 73 13 00. It's a bit sad that a building that's an opera in itself should be set aside for dance only, but that's how it is. Home of the Ballet de l'Opéra de Paris.    *Opéra* Ⓜ

**Café de la Danse**, 5 Passage Louis Philippe, 11ᵉ, ✆ 01 47 00 01 79. A good place to see contemporary and innovative small companies.    *Bastille* Ⓜ

**Studio Regard du Cygne**, 210 Rue de Belleville, 20ᵉ, ✆ 01 43 58 55 93. Devoted to international innovative companies.    *Place des Fêtes* Ⓜ

## Theatre and Performance Arts

The first theatre in Paris was built by Cardinal Richelieu in the Palais Royal in 1641, and the trickery of the stage machines played as big a role in the performances as the music and dance. Over the last 350 years, Paris has come full circle: the blockbusters in its theatres are multimedia extravaganzas with extraordinary special effects. Enjoying or watching them with mouth agape requires little if any French. The only serious contemporary drama are translations from the West End in London; new French playwrights are as rare as good French rock bands. Otherwise, French speakers can still find plenty of Racine and Molière from the excellent Comédie-Française and frequent revivals of Ionesco, Anouilh, Genet and company, not to mention Paris' perennial bland boulevard comedies, inevitably about marital hanky-panky. But the big draws are translations of West End and Broadway hits—Cats, etc.

**Les Bouffes du Nord**, 37bis Blvd de la Chapelle, 10ᵉ, ✆ 01 46 07 34 50. Former neighbourhood music hall that has become Peter Brook's baby; now a venue for some of the city's most acclaimed experimental productions. *La Chapelle* Ⓜ

**Cartoucherie Théâtre du Soleil**, Rte du Champ-de-Manouvre, 12ᵉ, ✆ 01 43 74 24 08. In a former ammunitions depot Ariane Mnouchkine's five-stage complex, home of perhaps the most thought-provoking theatre in Paris, including plays in their original language. Phone ahead to reserve at the three theatres: La Tempête, ✆ 01 43 28 36 36; L'Epée de Bois, ✆ 01 48 08 39 74; Aquarium, ✆ 01 47 99 61; Le Chaudron, ✆ 01 43 98 20 61. Ⓜ *Château de Vincennes*, linked with a free theatre shuttle bus.

**Théâtre National de Chaillot**, Pl du Trocadéro, 16ᵉ, ✆ 01 47 27 81 15. Formerly the playground of Antoine Vitez, frequently the stage for lavish, productions of Brecht and the like. *Trocadéro* Ⓜ

**Comédie-Française**, 2 Rue de Richelieu, 1ᵉʳ, ✆ 01 40 15 00 15. Founded in 1680 and playing in the beautiful Salle Richelieu in the Palais Royal; excellent productions of the old classics by Molière, Beaumarchais, Marivaux and Racine, also foreign classics in translation; seats at ticket office sold two weeks in advance.
*Palais Royal* Ⓜ

**Comédie Italienne**, 17 Rue de la Gaîté, 14ᵉ, ✆ 01 43 21 22 22. The old Comédie Italienne was an intense rival of the Comédie-Française until Louis XIV banished the Italians for calling Mme de Maintenon a prude and the king Monsieur de Maintenon. In a poky theatre amongst 'live sex' shops, the revived company puts on Goldoni, Commedia dell'Arte and Pirandello in French. *Edgar Quinet* Ⓜ

**Maison de la Culture at Bobigny**, 1 Blvd Lénine, ✆ 01 41 60 72 72. One of the most exciting, innovative, risk-taking companies. *Bobigny-Pablo Picasso* Ⓜ

**Odéon Théâtre de l'Europe**, 1 Pl Paul-Claudel, 6ᵉ, ✆ 01 44 41 36 36. Shares resources with Comédie-Française, its fellow state theatre; Grande Salle is often the stage of the Théâtre Populaire National; Petit Odéon sees alternative theatre and foreign companies' productions in their own language. *Odéon* Ⓜ

**Palais-Royal**, 38 Rue de Montpensier, 1ᵉʳ, ✆ 01 42 97 59 81. Loveliest place to take in a boulevard comedy. *Palais Royal* Ⓜ

**Théâtre de la Huchette**, 23 Rue de la Huchette, 5ᵉ, ✆ 01 43 26 38 99. They've been doing Ionesco's *La Cantatrice Chauve* and *La Leçon* for 40 years. *St-Michel* Ⓜ

**Théâtre National de la Colline**, 15 Rue Malte-Brun, 20ᵉ, ✆ 01 44 62 52 52. Two stages dedicated to contemporary European works. *Gambetta* Ⓜ

**Théâtre de Nesle**, 8 Rue de Nesle, 6ᵉ, ✆ 01 46 34 61 04. Often hosts performances the city's English language companies. *Odéon* Ⓜ

**Théâtre de la Porte St-Martin**, 16 Blvd St-Martin, 10ᵉ, ✆ 01 42 08 00 32. Often sparkling, very Parisian productions and one-man shows in a crummy neighbourhood. *Strasbourg St-Denis* Ⓜ

# Shopping

*All the visible universe is nothing but shops and signs.*

Baudelaire

People who think shopping is an art have long regarded Paris as Europe's masterpiece when it comes to consumption; throughout its history, the city has enjoyed an enviable reputation for craftsmanship, especially in luxury goods. Paris also invented the idea of fashion as we know it—one of the spin-offs of the Revolution, which upset the age-old codes of dressing to show one's social status or occupation at a glance. During the Second Empire, just as Haussmann divided Paris into good and bad addresses, a clever English dressmaker named Worth whetted the desire of wealthy women to set themselves visually apart from the less fortunate by the cut of their clothes (and the colour of their clothes—until 1900 working women stuck to black, as it best hid the inevitable, indelible Paris mud).

With the advent of department stores (*see* Au Bon Marché, Walk X, p.287), industrial-made imitations of couturier designs became available to a much wider public. The race began for the wealthy to remain a step ahead of the plebeian department-store crowd—distracting women, as Walter Benjamin noted, from life itself: 'For fashion was never anything but the parody of the gaily decked-out corpse, the provocation of death through the woman ... the bitter whispered *tête-à-tête* with decay. That is fashion. For this reason she changes so rapidly, teasing death, already becoming something else again, something new, as death looks about for her in order to strike her down.' Fearing the natural changes of their bodies, the fashionable end up imitating mannequins. That so many Parisians are fashion's slaves lends the city its curious weightlessness, forgetfulness, or as many long-time residents have noticed, a tangible restlessness in its eternal hellish pursuit of novelty.

But if you think you can beat the Devil, the pitiless death-cult of Parisian fashion discreetly awaits. You can have your own *haute-couture* garment hand-sewn to your measurements beginning at around 50,000F. Despite all the hype, the big 'designers' only show *haute-couture* collections to get free media attention for their worldwide chain outlets. Size up the current vogues and modes by stumping through the exalted **prêt-à-porter** (ready-to-wear) fashion zone in the 8e, specifically along Rue du Faubourg-St-Honoré, Avenue George-V, Rue François-1ier and

Avenue Montaigne, but beware that you'd better have similarly pricey gladrags on your back to get a friendly acknowledgement from the boutique employees that you exist on the same planet.

If you find designer **prêt-à-porter** too dear, there are a number of shops that sell last season's or earlier clothes and accessories, or you can tackle Paris' walloping huge department stores listed below. For shoppers who prefer more intimate safaris, Paris has endless little speciality shops tucked into nearly every *arrondissement*; for the bargain hunter there are mega flea markets and some interesting second-hand shops. No place on the planet has more sensually gratifying food markets and food shops.

A couple of other **shopping notes**. If in one place you fork out over 2000F (non-EU resident) or 4200F for EU residents, you are entitled to a rebate on the VAT you've paid. The shop or store gives you the form (the magic word is *détaxe*), which you present to French customs as you depart. A few weeks later they post you the rebate. The big sales take place nationally during the first two weeks of January and the first two weeks of June, when prices on seasonal goods are cut, often by half. Remember, most Paris shops **close** on Sundays and Mondays.

**Shopping Tours**: Contact Shopping Plus, 99/103 Rue de Sèvres, 6ᵉ, ✆ 01 47 53 91 17. Walking tours in various quarters on various themes: high fashion, art, antiques, food, crafts, etc. 180F a person.

## Antiques

There are four very pricey strongholds for antique dealers in Paris, where you'll find a Louis XIII chair but never a bargain:

**Louvre des Antiquaires**, next to the Louvre, the poshest, biggest and after the Marché St-Ouen the best place for browsing, 1ᵉʳ          *Palais Royal* Ⓜ

**Village St-Paul** in the Marais, Rue St-Paul, 4ᵉ.          *St-Paul* Ⓜ

**Village Suisse**, 6 Avenue de Champaubert, 15ᵉ          *La Motte Picquet* Ⓜ

**Carée des Antiquaires**, just west of Rue des Saints-Pères, 7ᵉ.          *Rue du Bac* Ⓜ

The keen-eyed arrive very early at the flea markets—still by far the best place for antiques (*see* pp.353–4) or haunt Drouot. Other suggestions:

**Derrière les Fagots**, 8 Pl des Abbesses, 18ᵉ. Affordable bric-à-brac and clothes from the '30s–'50s.          *Abbesses* Ⓜ

**Art Depot**, 3 Rue du Pont-Louis-Philippe, 4ᵉ, lots of fun (and packable) Art Déco pieces.          *Saint-Paul* Ⓜ

**La Fouinerie**, 141 Blvd Volaire, 11ᵉ, Great place to rummage for treasures from the 1850s–1930s.          *Voltaire* Ⓜ

It made all the art mags when Colnaghi, the famous London and New York dealer in Old Masters, opened a branch in Rue du Faubourg St-Honoré in May 1992—not far from where the firm was originally founded—before being forced by the Revolution to move to London. Apparently Old Masters are easier to pick up in France than anywhere else (one reason is that most French collectors buy only French painting). This is especially true at the auction house **Drouot**, which sells anything from Impressionists to junk glass lots that go for 10F—all sales are listed in the weekly mags under *Vente aux Enchères*. What Drouot fails to auction off ends up at **Drouot Nord** (64 Rue Doudeauville, 18ᵉ, ⓜ Château Rouge).

*Pariscope* and other entertainment magazines, and the monthly guide *Association des Galeries*, free at the larger galleries, will give you the lowdown on what's showing throughout the city. Commercial galleries are concentrated in certain areas, and unless one of your favourites is showing at a certain address, it's more fun to window-shop (*leche-vitrines*, 'lick the glass') and pop in when something catches your fancy. From Quai Voltaire to the Institut de France is the place to hunt up an Old Master; St-Germain, on all sides of the lower Rue de Seine, is nothing but galleries, mostly specializing in artists still living or fairly warm in the grave; in the 8ᵉ, west of the Palais de l'Elysée is the area for established artists, while the Marais, Beaubourg and Bastille are the hot spots for contemporary new artists. Also try the **Sunday art market** (10.30–4.30) in Place Ferdinand-Brunot, 14ᵉ, ⓜ*Mouton Duvernet*. Below are some addresses for art-related items most mortals can afford; other good place to check out are the **museum shops**—Orsay, Louvre, and Art Moderne de la Ville de Paris.

**L'Ami des Artistes**, 48 Rue Vavin, 6ᵉ. If Paris inspires you to take up the brush yourself, this shop has the most reasonably priced paints, easels and canvases.    *Vavin* ⓜ

**Antares**, 218 Boulevard Raspail, 14ᵉ. Reasonably priced prints and etchings, many by artists still trying to make a name for themselves, and the attendant cash benefits.    *Raspail* ⓜ

**Art Prestige**, 47 Quai de la Seine, 19ᵉ, for frames, posters and lithographs.    *Stalingrad* ⓜ

also 8 Rue du Faubourg-Montmartre, 9ᵉ, with cinema posters.    *Rue Montmartre* ⓜ

Paris, especially the Left Bank, is a paradise for book lovers, even if you don't read French. The *bouquinistes*, who unlock their picturesque green wooden stalls along the Seine on fair-weather afternoons, make good browsing, where the persistent are often rewarded with second-hand gems.

**Abbey Bookshop**, 20 Rue de la Parcheminerie, 5ᵉ, ✆ 01 46 33 16 24. Genial Canadian-owned bookshop, with a good selection of new and used English and North American titles. *St-Michel* Ⓜ

**Album**, 6-8 Rue Dante, 5ᵉ. Best shop for comic-book collectors. *Maubert-Mutualité* Ⓜ

**Artcurial**, 9 Ave Matignon, 8ᵉ. Largest collection of glossy art and coffee-table books, in French and English. *Franklin D. Roosevelt* Ⓜ

**Atmosphere**, 7–9 Rue Francis de Pressensé, 14ᵉ. Has the most extensive collection of books, rare posters, and stills—paradise for all film fetishists. *Pernéty* Ⓜ

**Brentano's**, 37 Ave de l'Opéra, 2ᵉ, ✆ 01 42 61 52 50. New books and magazines in English, American interests; novels, guides, children's and art sections too. *Opéra* Ⓜ

**La Chambre Claire**, 14 Rue St-Sulpice, 6ᵉ. Grand specialist in photography; posters, manuals, books and more. *Odéon* Ⓜ

**Cinédoc**, 43 Passage Jouffroy, 9ᵉ. Great for cinema books, posters and memorabilia, also antique sex literature—perhaps a weakness of the owner's. *Rue Montmartre* Ⓜ

**Ciné Reflets**, 3bis Rue Champollion, 5ᵉ. Films books, posters and a large library of stills. *Cluny-La Sorbonne* Ⓜ

**Librarie de l'Ecole Supérieure des Beaux-Arts,** 17 Quai Malquais, 6ᵉ. Architecture books from around the world. *St-Germain-des-Prés* Ⓜ

**FNAC**, a Paris institution—the city's biggest and fullest book chain (including some titles in English). Outlets in the Forum des Halles, Rue Pierre-Lescot, Ⓜ *Châtelet-Les Halles*; at 26–30 Ave des Ternes, 17ᵉ, Ⓜ *Etoile*; at 136 Rue de Rennes, Ⓜ *Montparnasse Bienvenüe*.

**Fourmi Ailée**, 8 Rue du Fouarre, 5ᵉ. Feminist bookshop and tea room. *Maubert Mutualité* Ⓜ

**Galignani**, 224 Rue de Rivoli, 1ᵉʳ, ✆ 01 42 60 76 07. Cosy place founded in 1802—the oldest English bookshop on the Continent; new titles, children's and glossy art books. *Tuileries* Ⓜ

**Institut Géographique National**, 107 Rue La Boétie, 8ᵉ. Paris' *Stanford's*, with superb collection of maps, ordnance surveys, guidebooks and everything else you need to venture off the beaten track. *Miromesnil* Ⓜ

**Gilda**, 36 Rue du Bouirdonnais, 1ᵉʳ. Huge collection of secondhand books and records in French. *Châtelet* Ⓜ

**Librairie des Gourmets**, 98 Rue Monge, 5ᵉ. Books on food and cooking in French and English. The most popular Parisian cookery book? *La Cuisine de Madame Saint-Ange*, which first appeared in 1923. *Censier Daubenton* Ⓜ

**L'Introuvable**, 35 Rue Juliette-Dodu, 10ᵉ. As the name suggests, if you haven't been able to find it elsewhere, you may come across it here. *Colonel Fabien* Ⓜ

**Parallèles**, 47 Rue St-Honoré, 1ᵉʳ. Media and source centre of alternative Paris, underground publications, books on music, records and more.

*Châtelet-Les Halles* Ⓜ

**Tschann**, 125 Blvd Montparnasse, 6ᵉ. Classic address for French literature and poetry. *Vavin* Ⓜ

**Shakespeare & Co**, 37 Rue de la Bûcherie, 5ᵉ, ✆ 01 43 26 96 50. Just what a bookshop should be—a convivial treasure hunt, crammed full of inexpensive second-hand and new books in English (*see* Walk VIII, p.238). *St-Michel* Ⓜ

**Tea & Tattered Pages**, 24 Rue Mayet, 6ᵉ, ✆ 01 40 65 94 35. A blessing for paupers: English tearoom with stacks and stacks of old paperbacks at low prices.

*Duroc* Ⓜ

**Librairie Théâtrale**, 3 Rue Marivaux, 2ᵉ. Vast selection of librettos, plays, scenarios and anything having to do with the performing arts. *Richelieu-Drouot* Ⓜ

**Le Verre et L'Assiette**, 1 Rue du Val de Grâce, 5ᵉ. Best selection of books and accessories for wine lovers. *Port Royal* Ⓜ

**The Village Voice**, 6 Rue Princesse, ✆ 01 46 33 36 47. Where Odile Hellier carries the banner of American literature in Paris, hosting scores of readings by contemporary writers; has anglophone Paris' most discriminating collections of books.

*Mabillon* Ⓜ

**W. H. Smith**, 248 Rue de Rivoli, 1ᵉʳ, ✆ 01 44 77 88 99. Especially good for their English-language magazines; fiction, children's and travel sections.

*Concorde* Ⓜ

## Clothing

**A. Sulka**, 2 Rue de Castiglione, 1ᵉʳ. Luxuriously tailored menswear classics, custom-made shirts and more at luxury prices. *Tuileries* Ⓜ

**A la Bonne Renommée**, 26 Rue Vieille-du-Temple, 4ᵉ. Beautiful, richly-coloured satins, silks and velvets with a folkloric touch. *St-Paul* Ⓜ

**Pierre Cardin**, 59 Rue de Faubourg St-Honoré, 8ᵉ. Classic Parisian couture.

*Madeleine* Ⓜ

**Chanel**, Rue Cambon,1ᵉʳ. Probably the most famous house in Paris, now under the design wand of Karl Lagerfeld. *Madeleine* Ⓜ

**Evolutif**, 139 Rue d'Alésia, 14ᵉ *Plaisance* Ⓜ and 57 Ave de Gral-Leclerc, 14ᵉ. Current Yves-Saint-Laurent and Kenzo styles for men at 20 per cent off.

*Alésia* Ⓜ

**Jean-Paul Gaultier**, 6 Rue Vivienne, 2ᵉ. *Bourse* Ⓜ; also 30 Rue de Faubourge St-Antoine, 11ᵉ, Bastille *Bourse* Ⓜ. The kilted doctor of Eurotrash's shops are fun for his more extraordinary than usual efforts to create a mystique around the clothes.

**Hermès**, 24 Rue de Faubourg St-Honoré, 8$^e$. Pay a month's rent for a scarf.

*Madeleine* Ⓜ

**Magic circle**, 25 Rue Etienne-Marcel 1$^{er}$. Over the top '70s styles for cool chicks and drag queens. *Etienne Marcel* Ⓜ

**Patricia Louisor**, 16 Rue Houdon, 18$^e$. Affordable clothes and jewellery from trendy young designers. *Abbesses* Ⓜ

**Saint-Laurent Rive Gauche**, new flagship of the designer's worldwide chain in Rue du Faubourg-St-Honoré (on the Rive Droite), and don't let anyone fool you—the latest shows have confirmed YSL as the king of Paris fashion; Catherine Deneuve and his own mom say so. *Concorde* Ⓜ

**Tati**, 2–30 Blvd de Rochechouart, 18$^e$. While the pampered few swan in the boutiques, the masses of every nationality swarm to the incredible Tati for women's, men's and children's clothes. *Barbès Rochechouart* Ⓜ

**Versace**, 62 Rue du Faubourg-St-Honoré, one of first and most opulent 'mega-boutiques' in Paris that must be seen to be believed; Versace's fashion-as-theatre approach in a glass-domed Roman temple with changing rooms resembling ancient baths or the Paris Opéra. Clothes for men, women and children. *Madeleine* Ⓜ

**Au Vieux Continent**, 3 Rue d'Argout, 2$^e$. Described as 'a 15-year-old French boy's dream of America'—motorbikes, cars, jeans, Mexican beer, records from the 1950s. *Sentier* Ⓜ

## Clothing: Accessories

**Anthony Peto**, 12 Rue Jean-Jacques Rosseau, 1$^{ier}$. Superb selection of men's hats from bérets to panamas. *Palais-Royal* Ⓜ

**Divine**, 39 Rue Daguerre, 14$^e$. Jewellery, masks and hats for men and women, in modern styles and styles from the 1920s. *Denfert Rochereau* Ⓜ

**Franchi**, 15 Rue de la Pépinière, 8$^e$. Men's and women's French and Italian shoes at half-price. *St-Augustin* Ⓜ

**Marie Mercié**, 56 Rue Tiquetonne, 2$^e$. For the kind of hat you see in films and have always dreamed of on your own head. *Etienne Marcel* Ⓜ

**Philippe Model**, 33 Pl du Marché-St-Honoré, 1$^{er}$. Paris' top glove, hat and shoe designer. *Pyramides* Ⓜ

**Sidonis**, 42 Rue de Clignacourt, 18$^e$. Vast selection of designer bags, ties, umbrellas and scarves at some of the cheapest prices in Paris. *Anvers* Ⓜ

**Stéphane Kélian**, 13bis Rue de Grenelle, 7$^e$. *Sèvres Babylone* Ⓜ; also 6 Place des Victoires, *Sentier* Ⓜ. Perhaps the most extraordinary and certainly the most expensive women's shoes in Paris.

**Testoni**, 25 Rue Marbeuf, 8$^e$, *Franklin Roosevelt* Ⓜ also 267 Rue St-Honoré, 1$^{er}$, *Palais Royal* Ⓜ. Beautiful and dear men's and ladies' shoes and bags from Bologne.

## Clothing: *Dépôts-Ventes*

*Dépôt-Ventes* are places where designers dump last season's unsold clothes, where prices are a third to half off.

**Anna Lowe**, 35 Ave Matignon, 8e. One of the oldest high fashion discount houses in Paris, selling Chanel, Escada Lacroix, YSL, etc. at 50% off.    *Miromesnil* Ⓜ

**L'Astucerie**, 105 Rue de Javel, 15e. Especially good for accessories by Chanel, Hermès and Vuitton for women and children.    *Félix Faure* Ⓜ

**Chercheminippes**, 109–111 Rue du Cherche Midi, 6e. Last season's fashions and quality second hand for men, women and their offspring.    *Duroc* Ⓜ

**Chlorophylle**, 2 Rue du Sabot, 6e. For 30–50 % off fashions by Alaïa, Yamamoto, Commes des Garçons and more; Tues–Sat pm only.    *St-Germain-des-Prés* Ⓜ

**Dépôt des Grandes Marques**, 15 Rue de la Banque, 2e. Big discounts and a good selection of larger sizes by Ungaro, Cerruti, Valentino, etc. for men.    *Bourse* Ⓜ

**Half and Half**, 28 Ave des Gobelins, 13e. Only the biggest designers, at half-price; where the dresses used in the fashion shows often end up.    *Gobelins* Ⓜ

**La Marelle**, 21–25 Galerie Vivienne, 2e. One of the nicest *dépôt-ventes*, for women's and children's designer goods.    *Bourse* Ⓜ

**Le Mouton à Cinq Pattes**, along Rue St-Placide, 6e. Great deals on French and Italian designs (Gaultier, Vivienne Westwood, Byblos, Ferré). No. 8 is for women, 14 for men and women, 18 is for big discounts, 48 is for men only.

*Sèvres-Babylone* Ⓜ

**Réciproque**, 92, 103 and 124 Rue de la Pompe, 16e. Biggest and best known *dépôt-vente* in Paris, with clothes by Chanel, Lacroix, and company, for men and women (including some in larger sizes); also coats, raincoats, hats, bijoux.

*Pompe* Ⓜ

**Unishop**, 40 Rue de Rivoli , 4e (men) *Hôtel de Ville* Ⓜ and 61 Rue de la Verrerie 4e (women). High fashions, minimum 20% off the original price.

## Clothing: Second-hand and Antique

In French this is called *la fripe*, whence our word 'frippery'. Retro garments tend to be the kind that have sat unsold in a warehouse for 30 or 40 years.

**L'Apache**, 45 Rue Vieille-du-Temple, 4e. Great, reasonably priced second-hand clothes and fedora hats from the 1930s and '40s; open every pm.    *Hôtel de Ville* Ⓜ

**La Bonne Aventure**, 14 Passage des Panoramas, 2e, Atmospheric shop in an atmospheric arcade, with antique clothes, accessories and bijoux.    *Rue Montmartre* Ⓜ

**Diableries**, 65–67 Pl du Docteur Lobigeois, 17e. Excellently restored retro fashions for men and women.    *Rome* Ⓜ

**La Halle aux Fringues Rétro**, 16 Rue de Montreuil, 11ᵉ. One of the most interesting, especially for men. *Faidherbe Chaligny* Ⓜ

**Rag**, 83 Rue St-Martin, 4ᵉ. Everything from tails to kimonas, for all taste. *Châtelet* Ⓜ

**Vertiges** , 85 Rue St-Martin, 4ᵉ . Especially good for the wilder styles from the 1940s–'70s. *Rambuteau* Ⓜ

## Department Stores

Because you can shop till you drop for just about anything in one of these monsters, they are the biggest purveyors of *détaxe*.

**Au Bon Marché**, 38 Rue de Sèvres, 7ᵉ. The only one on the Left Bank, but the grand-daddy of every department store in the world (*see* Walk X, p.287) still puts on a pretty good show of desirable stuff—its extraordinary food halls are an unrivalled gourmet cornucopia, and its prices for clothes and other goods tend to be a bit lower than its big-name rivals across the river. *Sèvres Babylone* Ⓜ

**Bazar de l'Hôtel de Ville**, 52 Rue de Rivoli 4ᵉ. BHV has been around since 1854 and lacks the pretentions of other department stores. A good bet for practical items often not easily found in the golden centre: brake fluid, electric outlets and mixing bowls. If you're fixing up a flat, its tool rental is indispensable.
*Hôtel de Ville* Ⓜ

**Galeries Lafayette**, 40 Blvd Haussmann, 9ᵉ. A bit of Art Nouveau splendour has survived the current philistine management. But better than anyone, they know what the Parisiennes like. Every Wednesday morning, the store puts on its own free fashion show, with selections from its various designer boutiques; make reservations, ✆ 01 42 82 34 56. *Chaussée d'Antin* Ⓜ

**Printemps**, 64 Blvd Haussmann, 9ᵉ. Squares off with the Galeries Lafayette like the Hatfields and the McCoys. On the whole Printemps is a wee bit posher, stuffier and nearer the cutting edge of fashion for women's designer clothes and accessories.
*Havre-Caumartin* Ⓜ

**La Samaritaine**, 19 Rue de la Monnaie, 1ᵉʳ. The most beautiful department store in Paris, with its Art Nouveau façade, skylight and balconies (in the old building)—though the present management thinks more like Woolworth's than Harrod's. The café on its 10th-floor terrace, open April to September, has one of the most gratifying of all views over Paris, across the Pont Neuf. *Louvre Rivoli* Ⓜ

## Fabrics and Lace

**Fuschia Dentelle**, corner of rues de l'Ave Maria and St-Paul, 4ᵉ. Large selection of antique lace. *Pont Marie* Ⓜ

**Marché St-Pierre**, 2 Rue Charles-Nodier, 18ᵉ. Four huge floors of silks, velvets, cottons and wools for your body or house. Many other fabric shops nearby. *Anvers* Ⓜ

**De Gilles**, 13 Rue des Tournelles, 4ᵉ. Huge choices of old and new fabrics. *Bastille* Ⓜ

**La Masion du Bouton**, 12 Rue de Cotte, 12ᵉ. Any button you could possibly want, and every other conceivable ribbon and geegaw. *Place Clichy* ⓜ

**Wolfe et Descourtis**, 18 Galerie Vivienne, 2ᵉ. Beautiful, exotic fabrics and flannels. *Bourse* ⓜ

## Home Design and Furnishings

Some 60 artists and artisans, including men involved in traditional French crafts, have shops and ateliers in the **Viaduc des Arts** along Avenue Daumesnil (see p.367).

**Au Bain-Marie**, 8 Rue Boissy d'Anglas, 8ᵉ. Paris' best-known address for anything you could possibly want for the kitchen or table; also books and antique tableware. *Concorde* ⓜ

**Autour du Monde**, 8 Rue des Francs-Bourgeois, 4ᵉ. Trendy, colourful home furnishings, with everything in pretty patterns. *St-Paul* ⓜ

**La Chaise Longue**, 20 Rue des Francs-Bourgeois, 3ᵉ, *St-Paul*; ⓜ 8 Rue Princesse 6ᵉ, *Mabillon* ⓜ. Reproductions of items big and small from the 1940s to '60s.

**En Attendant les Barbares**, 50 Rue Etienne-Marcel, 2ᵉ. The name 'Waiting for barbarians' comes from a poem by Cavafy, in which the Romans, bored of civilization, all come out to greet the barbarians who fail to come; furniture in the same spirit. *Châtelet-Les Halles* ⓜ

**Kitsch**, 3 Rue Bonaparte, 6ᵉ. They're not kidding; glorious and expensive one-of a kind ceramics. *St-Germain-des-Prés* ⓜ

**La Licorne de Cluny**, 25 Rue du Sommerard, 5ᵉ. Tapestries and pillows woven on medieval designs in the Musée de Cluny. *Cluny-La Sorbonne* ⓜ

**Limoges-UNIC**, 12 & 58 Rue de Paradis, 10ᵉ. Rue de Paradis is lined with porcelain, crystal and glass shops; this one has works from Lalique, Baccarat, Meissen, Lladro and more. *Gare de l'Est* ⓜ

**D. Porthault**, 18 Ave Montaigne, 8ᵉ. For the *crème de la crème* of table linens, sheets and towels. *Franklin D. Roosevelt* ⓜ

**La Tisanière**, 21 Rue de Paradis, 10ᵉ. White porcelain from Limoges and Berry. *Gare de l'Est* ⓜ

## Food and Wine

Besides the splendid food halls in Au Bon Marché and the markets, you can scatter buckets of francs in the following speciality food shops.

**Arietis**, 73 Blvd St-Germain, 5ᵉ. *Fois gras*, *confits* and wines from southwest France. *Maubert-Mutualité* ⓜ

**Barthélemy**, 51 Rue de Grenelle, 7ᵉ. The *ne plus ultra* of *fromageries*: only the most refined classic French cheeses. *Rue du Bac* ⓜ

**Brûlerie de l'Odéon**, 6 Rue Crébillon, 6ᵉ. One of Paris' oldest coffee roasters, still providing fresh roasted coffees and teas for picky java junkies. *Odéon* Ⓜ

**Bootlegger**, 82 Rue de l'Ouest, 14ᵉ. Huge selection of beers from around the world. *Pernéty* Ⓜ

**La Cave du Moulin Vieux**, 4 Rue Butte-aux-Cailles, 14ᵉ. One of the last places in Paris where you can buy good loose wine from barrels. *Place d'Italie* Ⓜ

**Caves Taillevent**, 199 Rue du Faubourg St-Honoré, 8ᵉ. Some 2500 different perfectly cared for French wines, in all price ranges. *Ternes* Ⓜ

**La Cigogne**, 61 Rue de l'Arcade, 8ᵉ. Delicious products and dishes from Alsace, starring tempting tortes and tarts and meaty sausages. *St-Lazare* Ⓜ

**Debauve et Gallais**, 30 Rue des Saints-Pères, 7ᵉ. Oldest and most beautiful *chocolatier* in Paris; the unusual displays (recently, chocolate passports) are worth a trip in themselves. *St-Germain-des-Prés* Ⓜ

**Fauchon**, 26 Pl de la Madeleine, 8ᵉ. The most famous and snobbish grocery in Paris, with the best of everything you can imagine, a huge wine cellar and a self-service to try some of the goodies on the spot. In 1970, Leftists looted the shop to bring caviar to the masses in the *bidonvilles*, or suburban shanty towns.
*Madeleine* Ⓜ

**Fromagerie Cler**, 31 Rue Cler, 7ᵉ. Has 250 to 300 of France's official list of 400 cheeses on offer. *Ecole Militaire* Ⓜ

**Goldenberg's**, 7 Rue des Rosiers, 4ᵉ. Paris' best Jewish deli and a godsend to any New Yorker living in Paris. *St-Paul* Ⓜ

**Gosselin**, 123 Rue St-Honoré, 1ᵉʳ. Voted best baguette in Paris in 1996. *Louvre-Rivoli* Ⓜ

**Hédiard**, a tiny chain of grocers nearly as extensive and highfalutin as Fauchon: 126 Rue du Bac, 7ᵉ, Ⓜ *St-Germain-des-Prés*; 70 Ave Paul Doumer, 16ᵉ, *La Muette* Ⓜ; and 106 Blvd de Courcelles, 17ᵉ, Ⓜ *Ternes.*

**Izraêl**, 30 Rue François-Miron, 4ᵉ. Good for exotic imports from Brazil, China, North Africa and just about everywhere else. *St-Paul* Ⓜ

**Jean Danflou**, 36 Rue du Mont-Thabor, 1ᵉʳ. Great selection of traditional French high-octane spirits—Armagnacs, Cognacs and eaux de vie. *Concorde* Ⓜ

**Ladurée**, 16 Rue Royale, 8ᵉ. Maker of heavenly chocolates. *Madeleine* Ⓜ

**Marie-Anne Cantin**, 12 Rue du Champ-de-Mars, 7ᵉ. A hundred finely ripened cheeses from farms and small producers. *Ecole Militaire* Ⓜ

**Mariage Frères**, 30 Rue du Bourg-Tibourg, 4ᵉ. 400 different types of tea and tea-flavoured goodies. *St-Paul* Ⓜ

**Maison du Chocolat**, 8 Blvd de la Madeleine, 9ᵉ; *Madeleine* Ⓜ; 225 Rue du Faubourg St-Honoré, 8ᵉ, *Ternes* Ⓜ. Sensational variety of chocolates; enter at your own risk.

**Maison de la Truffe**, 19 Place de la Madeleine, 8ᵉ. Truffles and other costly delicacies from the southwest of France. *Madeleine* Ⓜ

**A la Mère de Famille**, 35 Rue du Faubourg-Montmartre, 9ᵉ. Chocolates, home-made sweets, jam in every flavour from rhubarb to eglantine; this charming shop, dating from 1793, could be a picture postcard of old Paris. *Cadet* Ⓜ

**Petrossian**, 18 Blvd de La-Tour-Maubourg, 7ᵉ, ✆ 45 51 70 64. Paris' top address for beluga, oscietre, and sevruga caviar, vodka, smoked salmon, *foie gras*, truffles.
*La Tour Maubourg* Ⓜ

**Poilâne**, 8 Rue du Cherche Midi, 7ᵉ. Tasty sourdough country bread, the most famous in Paris; used in the best sandwiches across the city. *Sèvres Babylone* Ⓜ

**Point Saumon**, 262 Rue de Charenton, 12ᵉ. Smoked, marinated, and other forms of salmon from Ireland, Scotland and Norway. Also Iranian caviar. *Michel Bizot* Ⓜ

**Poujauran**, 20 Rue Jean-Nicot, 7ᵉ. The second most famous bakery in Paris: *pain de campagne* of stone-ground flour, baked in a wood-burning oven; great olive and walnut breads too. *La Tour Maubourg* Ⓜ

**Vins Rares Peter Thustrup**, 25 Rue Royale, Cité Berryer, 8ᵉ. Old wines, rare wines, collectors' wines, none under 100F. *Madeleine* Ⓜ

## From the Provinces and Beyond

**Anaitis**, Rue du Bucherie, 5ᵉ. Egyptian inspired trinkets, jewellery chess sets and inlaid wood. *Maubert-Mutualité* Ⓜ

**Andines**, 24 Rue André-del-Sartre, 18ᵉ. Imports from all over South America. *Anvers* Ⓜ

**Les Artisans du monde**, 20 Rue Rochechouart, 9ᵉ. Food and crafts from Third World co-operatives, all profits going towards good causes. *Cadet* Ⓜ

**La Boutique Tibetaine**, 4 Rue Burq, 18ᵉ. Lovely things made by Tibetan refugees, in all price ranges. *Abbesses* Ⓜ

**Breiz et Norway**, 33 Rue Gay-Lussace, 5ᵉ. Books, spirits, gifts and more from Brittany and other Celtic lands. *RER Luxembourg*

**Cocody**, 1bis Rue Ferdinand Duval, 4ᵉ. Colourful fabrics and ornaments from East Africa; reasonable prices. *St-Paul* Ⓜ

**Galerie Urubamba**, 4 Rue de la Bûcherie, 5ᵉ. American Indian crafts and books.
*St-Michel* Ⓜ

**Le Monde Sauvage**, 82 Rue Rambuteau, 1ᵉʳ. Popular arts and crafts from around the world. *Châtelet* Ⓜ

**La Route d'Alexandre**, 6 Rue des Grands-Degrés, 5ᵉ. Central Asian boutique with rugs, cushions and wall hangings; also jewellery. *Maubert Mutualité* Ⓜ

**Kimonoya**, 11 Rue du Pont-Louis-Philippe, 4ᵉ. Superb Japanese shop. *Pont-Marie* Ⓜ

**Souleiado**, 78 Rue de Seine, 6ᵉ. Paris branch of the sunny Provençal prints made according to hundred-year-old designs. *Mabillon* Ⓜ

## Music

Compared to Britain or the States, recorded music is very expensive in France (often over 100% more—because of luxury taxes!), but if your ears wander along currents beyond the mainstream, try some of these addresses:

**Afric' Music**, 3 Rue des Plantes, 14ᵉ. All kinds of African music. *Alésia* Ⓜ

**Blue Moon**, 7 Rue Pierre-Sarrazin, 6ᵉ. Imported tapes and discs from Jamaica and Africa, specializing in reggae. *Odéon* Ⓜ

**Budin**, 14 Ave Carnot, 17ᵉ. One of the world's greatest specialists in harps—it takes 10 years to finish one. *Etoile* Ⓜ

**Crocodisc**, 42 Rue des Ecoles, 5ᵉ. Rock and pop, but also good selections of African, Caribbean, reggae, folk, country and funk. *Maubert Mutualité* Ⓜ

**Crocojazz**, 64 Rue de la Montagne-Ste-Geneviève, 5ᵉ. Sister of the above, with jazz, gospel and blues. *Maubert Mutualité* Ⓜ

**Disques Sannino**, 123 Rue Oberkampf, 11ᵉ. Rock, garage, British '50s and '60s and lots of vinyl. *Parmentier* Ⓜ

**Disc' Inter**, 2–4 Rue des Rasselins, 20ᵉ. African, Haitian, Jamaican, Antillaise, Cuban and funk. *Porte de Montreuil* Ⓜ

**FNAC Musique**, 4 Pl de la Bastille, 12ᵉ, is devoted to music. The other addresses, listed above under books, have huge selections of records as well. *Bastille* Ⓜ

**Hamm**, 135 Rue de Rennes, 6ᵉ. New and used instruments, sheet music and scores. *St-Placide* Ⓜ

**Librairie Musicale de Paris**, 68bis Rue Réaumur, 3ᵉ. For all kinds of sheet music and books about music. *Réaumur Sébastopol* Ⓜ

**Librairie Théâtral**, 3 Rue de Marivaux, 2ᵉ. Opera scores. *Richelieu Drouot* Ⓜ

**Oldies but Goodies**, 16 Rue du Bourg-Tibourg, 4ᵉ. Specializes in rare jazz, blues and rock recordings hard to find anywhere else. *Hôtel de Ville* Ⓜ

**Papageno**, 1 Rue de Marivaux, 2ᵉ. Oodles of ballet and opera records, some rare. *Richelieu-Drouot* Ⓜ

**Virgin Megastore**, 52 Ave des Champs-Elysées, 8ᵉ (closed Sun). *Franklin D. Roosevelt* Ⓜ

**Carrousel du Louvre**, 99 Rue de Rivoli, 1ᵉʳ (closed Tues). A huge success ever since it opened, with every conceivable tape, record, CD and book under the sun. *Palais-Royal-Musée du Louvre* Ⓜ

## Sport

**Budostore**, 34 Rue de la Montagne-Ste-Geneviève, 5ᵉ. Everything for the martial arts—swords, kimonos, books, videos, etc. *Maubert Mutualité* Ⓜ

**La Gazelle**, 47–49 Blvd Jean-Jaurès, Boulogne-Billancourt. Beloved of all bike enthusiasts in the Paris area, with everything from custom racers on down.

*Boulogne-Jean Jaurès* Ⓜ

**Passe-Montagne**, 95–102 Ave Denfert-Rochereau. Everything you need for a mountain holiday : clothes, gear, boots, ski, etc. *Denfert-Rochereau* Ⓜ

**Planete Sport**, 207 Rue des Pyrénées, 20ᵉ. Name brand sport clothes, shoes, equipement etc. especially for tennis; also golf, ping pong, football, rugby.

*Gambetta* Ⓜ

**Repetto**, 22 Rue de la Paix, 2ᵉ. The top supplier of dance outfits and shoes in Paris, from the littlest ballerina on up. *Opéra* Ⓜ

**Au Vieux Campeur**, 48 Rue des Ecoles, 5ᵉ. Everything you need for dealing with mountains—camping, climbing, skiing and mountain-bike gear.

*Maubert Mutualité* Ⓜ

## Unusual

The gift shops in Paris' **museums** are often excellent and full of surprises: marine and meteorological gifts at the Musée de la Marine, books about Paris at the Carnavalet, copies of the seals of all the kings of France at the Archives Nationales, genuine art prints from original plates at the Louvre. The **Boutique Paris Musée**, 29bis Rue des Francs Bourgeois, 4ᵉ, rounds up items from all the museum shops in Paris (Ⓜ *Chemin Vert*).

**Les Alizés**, 12 Rue Henri Desgrange, 12ᵉ. Ships' models in all sizes, sextants, and other pretty things from or related to the sea. *Bercy* Ⓜ

**Anna Joliet**, no.95 Jardin du Palais Royal, 1ᵉʳ. The best shop in the universe for music boxes, from kid trinkets to 5000F monsters in inlaid wood cases that play twelve different tunes. *Palais Royal* Ⓜ

**Au Chat Dormant**, 31 Rue de Bourgogne, 7ᵉ. Cat-obsessed arts and crafts. *Varenne* Ⓜ

**Chronopassion**, 271 Rue St-Honoré, 1ᵉʳ. For Paris' most extraordinary clocks and watches, astrolabes, planetary timepieces and golden cufflinks that tell the time.

*Concorde* Ⓜ

**Cusinophile**, 28 Rue du Bourg-Tibourg 4ᵉ. Kitchen gear from your (or your mother's) childhoood. *Hôtel-de-Ville* Ⓜ

**La Galcante**, 43 Rue de l'Arbre-Sec, 1ᵉʳ. Old newspapers, books, magazines and posters from as far as China; pick up the front page of a French paper on the day of your birth. *Louvre Rivoli* Ⓜ

**Instant**, 17 Quai aux Fleurs, 4ᵉ. If you've left your main squeeze at home while you've painted Paris red, you can make up with a bust of yourself, a model of your hand or an imprint of your smile so he or she won't feel so lonely next time you slip off. Made with lasers; from 3000 to 15,000F. *Cité* Ⓜ

**Madeleine Gély,** 218 Blvd St-Germain, 7ᵉ. Since 1834 the most imaginative cane and umbrella shop in Paris. *Rue du Bac* Ⓜ

**Marie Stuart,** nos. 3 Galerie Montpensier, Palais Royale. Military trinkets as well as medals and decorations from around the world (comes in handy when you're invited to a diplomatic reception) *Palais-Royal* Ⓜ

**La Maison de l'Astronomie,** 33 Rue de Rivoli, 4ᵉ. Everything for the astronomer in your life; also alarm clocks that keep track of the position of the moon. *Hôtel de Ville* Ⓜ

**Paris Magic,** 18 Rue Brillat-Savarin, 13ᵉ. Where Paris magicians shop for manuals, vidoes, and illusions. *Maison-Blanche* Ⓜ

## Flea Markets

**Les Puces de Saint-Ouen,** the mother of all flea markets; open Sat, Sun and Mon—*see* Peripheral Attractions, p.353 for a tour. *Porte de Clignancourt* Ⓜ

**Puces de Montreuil,** great junky flea market; open Sat, Sun and Mon (*see* Peripheral Attractions, p.354). *Porte de Montreuil* Ⓜ

**Puces de Vanves,** the most humble, and potentially most exciting market for the eagle-eyed, with many amateurs; open Sat and Sun (*see* Peripheral Attractions, p.354). *Porte de Vanves* Ⓜ

## Special Markets

**Marché aux Fleurs:** Parisians love flowers and flower markets. **Place de la Madeleine** 8ᵉ (daily except Mon), **Place des Ternes,** 8ᵉ (daily except Mon) and **Place Lépine** 4ᵉ, (open Mon–Sat).

**Marché du Livre Ancien et d'Occasion,** Rue Brancion, Parc Georges-Brassens, 15ᵉ. Second-hand book market on Sat and Sun. *Porte de Vanves* Ⓜ

**Marché aux Timbres,** the stamp market (the same one that co-starred in *Charade* with Audrey Hepburn and Cary Grant) north of Théâtre Marigny, near the intersection of Avenues Gabriel and de Marigny, 8ᵉ. *Champs-Elysées* Ⓜ

**Marché aux Vieux Papiers de St-Mandé,** Ave de Paris, 12ᵉ. One of the more obscure markets—old books, postcards and prints; open on Wednesdays. *Porte de St-Mandé Tourelle* Ⓜ

## Food Markets

The permanent street markets listed below are intoxicating to visit, even if you're just picking up the ingredients for a park picnic. Most are lined with shops that spill out into the street—seafood markets where the employees have to wear sailor outfits, white-aproned matrons bustling over their lovely displays of cheeses or pastries, ruddy-cheeked butchers ready to tell you how to prepare the mysterious cut of meat you've just purchased. These markets are open daily except Sun afternoons and all day Mon, and many shops close for lunch. The most captivating are listed below—for a complete list of all the **covered markets** and the 60 **travelling street markets**, open one or two days a week, ask at the tourist office.

**Place d'Aligre**, 12ᵉ. One of the most colourful, with a strong North African presence.

*Ledru Rollin* Ⓜ

**Buci**, 6ᵉ. One of the liveliest, with a good selection; best on Sunday mornings.

*Mabillon* Ⓜ

**Rue Cler**, 7ᵉ. The market of the aristocratic Faubourg, noted for its high quality. Closed Mon.

*Ecole Militaire* Ⓜ

**Rue de Lévis**, 17ᵉ. Similar to the above, the *haute bourgeoisie* equivalent of Rue Cler.

*Villiers* Ⓜ

**Montorgueil**, 1ᵉʳ. On the street of the same name, north of Rue Etienne-Marcel, convivial and fun, a whiff of the old atmosphere of nearby Les Halles.

*Etienne Marcel* Ⓜ

**Mouffetard**, 5ᵉ. Lower end of Rue Mouffetard, with lots of character and characters.

*Censier Daubenton* Ⓜ

**Poncelet**, 17ᵉ. Begins at Ave des Ternes.

*Ternes* Ⓜ

## Farmers' Markets

These in French are called **Marchés Biologiques** and are open to farmers in the Ile-de-France countryside who bring in their organic fruits and vegetables, nuts, free-range chickens, homemade breads, cakes, cider, sausages, goat cheeses, etc. The suburban ones have métro or RER connections.

**Boulevard Raspail**, 6ᵉ, Sunday mornings.

*Rennes* Ⓜ

**Marché Boulogne**, 140 Route de la Reine, Boulogne-sur-Seine; open 8am–4pm the first and third Sat of each month.

*Boulogne-Porte de St-Cloud* Ⓜ

**Marché Joinville-le-Pont**, Place Mozart, Joinville. The same market, open the second and fourth Saturdays.

RER to *Joinville* and then bus 106 or 108N.

**Ave Jules-Guesde, Sceaux**, Rue des Mouille-Boeuf; open Sundays 8.30–1.

RER: *Robinson* (Line B2)

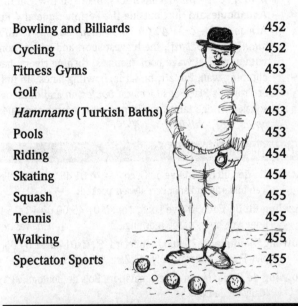

# Sports

A typical Parisian's idea of recreation is smoking and drinking in a café. One reason for this is, outside of a few municipal pools, gyms and the odd tennis court, they have to travel to the old city gates and beyond to keep fit, and even then sports are more of a privilege than a right. To find out what's feasible try ringing the municipal sports line **Allo Sport**, ✆ 01 42 76 54 54 (*Mon–Thurs 10.30–5, till 4.30 on Fri*). For the average short-stay visitor, the three best places to go if you crave some exercise and want to avoid all the falderal are the **Bois de Boulogne** (*see* p.349 and **Bois de Vincennes** (*see* p.365) both with jogging tracks, bike and rowboat hire and **Aquaboulevard**, just outside the Périphérique at 4 Rue Louis-Armand, 15ᵉ, ✆ 01 40 60 10 00 (*daily 8am–10pm, Fri and Sat till midnight;* Ⓜ *Balard*), the biggest sport and leisure complex in Paris with a tropical wave pool, jacuzzis, rushing rivers, hammams, climbing wall, funfair, billiards, bowling lanes, an indoor repro of St-Tropez's Place des Lices for *boules*, in and outdoor tennis, squash, bridge tables, boutiques, restaurants and cafés (*adm for four hours, 68F, children 3–12, 49F*).

## Bowling and Billiards

**Académie de Clichy**, 84 Rue de Clichy, 9ᵉ, ✆ 01 48 78 32 85. French and American billiards and snooker; always packed.                    *Place Clichy* Ⓜ

**Bowling-Etoile Foch**, 8 Ave Foch, 16ᵉ, ✆ 01 45 00 00 13. 15 lanes open daily until wee hours of the morning.          *Charles de Gaulle-Etoile* Ⓜ

**Bowling Mouffetard**, 73 Rue Mouffetard, 5ᵉ, ✆ 01 43 31 09 35. Roll the rock or play French billiards daily (till 2am, Fri and Sat till 4am).          *Monge* Ⓜ

**Bowling de Paris**, Jardin d'Acclimatation, Bois de Boulogne, ✆ 01 40 67 94 00 (daily till 2am).                    *Sablons* Ⓜ

**Bowling Montparnasse**, 25 Rue du Commandant-René-Mouchotte, 14ᵉ, ✆ 01 43 21 61 32. Bowling, pool tables and other games (till 2 am, Fri and Sat till 4am).                    *Montparnasse Bienvenüe* Ⓜ

## Cycling

After being paralyzed by mass public transport strikes in December 1995, Paris decided it was high time to create 50km of cycle-only zones (*couloir vélos*) in the city. Although these may add something to the joys of pedalling in one of western Europe's most polluted cities, you'll have more fun cycling in the Bois de Boulogne or Bois de Vincennes, or in one of the forests beyond the suburbs (especially

Fontainebleau). See p.9 for bike hire and the increasingly popular tours of Paris on two wheels.

## Fitness Gyms

A handful of chains control the American-style fitness centres in Paris and all require at least a month's membership if not a year's. The biggest groups, Gymnase Club and Garden Club, are only worth while if you're living in Paris and intend to buy a year's membership for around 2800F, around 1500F for students. The best is:

**Espace Vit'Halles**, 48 Rue Rambuteau, 3$^e$, ✆ 01 42 77 21 71 with aerobics, weight training, gym, sauna, etc. Monthly or yearly subscription.

*Rambuteau* Ⓜ

## Golf

Golf is increasingly popular among Parisians, but very expensive and incredibly enough, you may well be asked to produce your golf insurance policy to play the links. Pick up information from Mon–Fri at the **Fédération Française de Golf**, 69 Ave Victor-Hugo, 16$^e$, ✆ 01 45 02 13 55, Ⓜ *Victor Hugo*. The most accessible course for visitors is the 27-hole **Golf Disneyland Paris**, RER: Marne-Le Vallée, open year round from 9am (8am Sat and Sun); ring ✆ 01 60 45 68 04 for information.

## *Hammams* (Turkish Baths)

**Alésia Club**, 143 Rue d'Alésia, 14$^e$, ✆ 01 45 42 91 05. *Hammam*, sauna and gym, etc. Daily rates.

*Alésia* Ⓜ

**Hammam de la Mosquée**, 39 Rue Geoffroy-St-Hilaire, 5$^e$. ✆ 01 43 31 18 14. Eucalyptus vapours offer the perfect antidote for stress in Paris. Tues and Sun men only; women only all other days, 85F.

*Jussieu* Ⓜ

## Pools

Besides the aforementioned Aquaboulevard complex, there are 35 municipal and private swimming pools in Paris. Admission for an adult is 13F; 6.50F for children. Note that on Wednesdays and Saturday afternoons you'll have to share the water with crowds of kids. Opening hours change, so ring ahead.

**Piscine des Amiraux**, 6 Rue Hermann-Lachapelle, 18$^e$, ✆ 01 46 06 46 47. Designed by Henri Sauvage in 1930 and recently renovated.

*Simplon* Ⓜ

**Piscine Buttes-aux-Cailles**, 6 Pl Paul-Verlaine, 13ᵉ, ✆ 01 45 89 60 05. The indoor pool is a tiled Art Deco landmark from 1924; there is also a small outdoor pool in the summer. Both are filled by artesian wells.

*Place d'Italie* Ⓜ

**Piscine Emile-Anthoine**, 9 Rue Jean-Rey, 15ᵉ, ✆ 01 53 69 61 59. Newish pools, gym and outdoor running track, by the Eiffel Tower.    *Bir-Hakeim* Ⓜ

**Piscine Georges-Hermant**, 4 Rue David d'Angers, 19ᵉ, ✆ 01 42 02 45 10. Picnic on the lawns by the largest pool in Paris, with a sliding roof.    *Danube* Ⓜ

**Piscine Georges-Vallerey**, 148 Ave Gambetta, 20ᵉ, ✆ 01 40 31 15 20. Recently spruced up Olympic-sized pool with a sliding roof.    *Porte de Lilas* Ⓜ

**Piscine des Halles**, Forum des Halles, 1ᵉʳ, ✆ 01 42 36 98 44. Vast new municipal pool, with skylights and a junge touch; open late most eves.  *Les Halles* Ⓜ

**Piscine Henri-de-Montherlant**, 32 Blvd Lannes, 16ᵉ, ✆ 01 45 03 03 28. Two indoor pools, one especially for kids, sunning terrace, gym, tennis.

*Porte-Dauphine* Ⓜ

**Piscine Jean Taris**, 16 Rue Thouin, 5ᵉ, ✆ 01 43 25 54 03. Unchlorinated pool near the Panthéon, with a pretty Japonese sunning garden.

*Cardinal Lemoine* Ⓜ

**Piscine de Pontoise**, 19 Rue de Pontoise, 5ᵉ, ✆ 01 43 54 06 23. Attractive skylit pool with squash courts, jacuzzi and sauna, and nude swimming on Mon and Thurs after 8pm.    *Maubert Mutualité* Ⓜ

## Riding

Getting on a horse in Paris means often bringing your own crop and boots and all, and buying a riding permit, a *Carte Nationale de Cavalier* from the Fédération Equestre Française, at 164 Rue du Faubourg-St-Honoré, 8ᵉ. To ride in the Bois de Boulogne, contact the **Centre Hippique du Touring Club**, Rte de la-Muette-à-Neuilly, 16ᵉ, ✆ 01 45 01 20 88; in the Bois Vincennes, contact Bayard UCPA Centre Equestre, 12ᵉ, ✆ 01 43 65 46 87; at La Villette, **Centre Equestre**, ✆ 01 40 34 33 33.

## Skating

**La Main Jaune**, Place de la Porte-de-Champerret, 17ᵉ, ✆ 01 47 63 26 47. Roller-skating rink open Wed and Sat 2.30–7pm; roller-disco Fri and Sat 10pm to dawn, Sun 3–7.30. Skate hire available.    *Porte de Champerret* Ⓜ

**Patinoire Edouard Pailleron**, 30 Rue Edouard-Pailleron, 19ᵉ, ✆ 01 42 08 72 26. The only ice-skating rink in Paris, with skate rental available.    *Bolivar* Ⓜ

## Squash

**Squash Club Quartier Latin**, 19 Rue de Pontoise, 5ᵉ, ℗ 01 43 54 82 45. Gym, pool, sauna, jacuzzi, martial sports, and squash. *Jussieu* Ⓜ

**Squash Montmartre**, 14 Rue Achille Martinet, 18ᵉ, ℗ 01 42 55 38 30. Sauna, gym, restaurant and squash. *Lamarck* Ⓜ

## Tennis

There are roughly a hundred times as many tennis players as courts in Paris, so competition for space is stiff and reservations essential—if you live in Paris and have a Carte Paris Tennis (get one from your *mairie*), book a week in advance.

## Walking

Within an hour of Paris is a network of trails to explore; for maps and information contact the *Comité régional de la randonnée pédestre d'Ile-de-France*, 64 Rue de Gergovie, 14ᵉ, ℗ 01 47 66 55 92. The Randonneurs d'Ile de France, ℗ 01 45 42 24 72, offer a wide variety of guided walks of varying degrees of difficulty.

## Spectator Sports

There are plenty of sports to watch (check listings in the Wednesday *Le Figaro* or the sports-only paper, *L'Equipe*) but you have to scramble for tickets for the major events in the calendar: the French Open, the last leg of the Tour de France (round the Arc de Triomphe, the third week in July), the Five Nations rugby matches, and horse races—the *Prix du Président de la République* steeplechase in April at Auteuil and the *Grand Prix de l'Arc de Triomphe* flat race, the first Sunday in October at Longchamp. Note that the race courses close from mid-July through August, and information on all may be had by ringing ℗ 01 49 10 20 30; off-track betting (even the little old ladies do it) takes place in any bar with the sign PMU. Major venues are:

**Hippodrome d'Auteuil**, Bois de Boulogne, 16ᵉ. Steeplechase (hurdle) race track.
*Porte d'Auteuil* Ⓜ

**Hippodrome de Chantilly**, in Chantilly (*see* Day Trips, p.476). Prettiest race course in France; site of the prestigious Prix du Jockey Club (second Sunday in June) and the Prix de Diane (third Sunday in June).

**Hippodrome de Longchamp**, Bois de Boulogne, 16ᵉ. Flat races.
*Porte d'Auteuil, then shuttle bus* Ⓜ

**Hippodrome de Vincennes**, Bois de Vincennes, 12ᵉ. Trotting (harness racing).
RER: *Joinville*

**Palais Omnisport Paris-Bercy**, 8 Blvd de Bercy, 12ᵉ, ✆ 01 43 46 12 21. A distinctive stadium with slanted walls that require the attention of a lawn-mower; designed to host 22 sports from hockey to motorcross.

*Gare de Lyon* Ⓜ

**Parc des Princes**, 24 Rue du Commandant-Guilbaud, 16ᵉ, ✆ 01 53 21 15 15. Big concrete stadium home to Paris' two soccer teams—St-Germain and Racing-Paris I—its rugby union team and other rugby events.

*Porte de St-Cloud* Ⓜ

**Roland Garros**, 2 Ave Gordon-Bennett, 16ᵉ, ✆ 01 47 43 48 00. Site of the presti-gious French Open last week May and first week June; reserve by Feb in writing to FFT, Service Réservation, BP 333-16, 75767 Paris Cédex 16.

*Porte d'Auteuil* Ⓜ

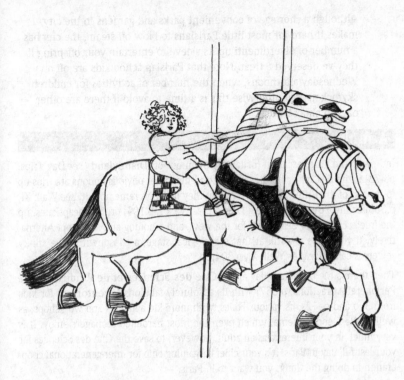

# Children's Paris

Although a shortage of convenient parks and gardens in the city makes it hard for most little Parisians to blow off steam, the city has a number of divertimenti up its sleeve to entertain your offspring if they've deserved a treat. Note that Parisian schoolkids are off on Wednesday afternoons, when the number of activities for children skyrockets, but otherwise this is a time to avoid if there are other days to choose from.

## Activities

Indulging the little rascals in (or talking them out of) **Disneyland** (*see* Day Trips, p.478) is the first major hurdle for most parents; other obvious options are trips up to the top of the **Eiffel Tower** (corny but they'll always remember it, *see* Walk XI, p.305) or the **Towers of Notre Dame** (*see* Walk I, p.109) or, for cheapskates, up the free escalators of Beaubourg for the view, and a hotdog and soda pop. Alternatively, if your kids are still at that scatological stage, a trip down to the stinky sewers is called for (*see* Walk XI, p.304).

Then there's the obligatory day at the **Cité des Sciences et de l'Industrie** (*see* Peripheral Attractions, p.357) with its absolutely fabulous **Inventorium** for kids from 3–6 and 6–12s, its various Folies, with more kid activities and workshops, as well as the Géode cinema, which even the most hardened teenagers enjoy. It is very much in your interests as an adult, however, to save the Cité des Sciences for your last full day in Paris. It's your chief bargaining chip for inter-generational cooperation in doing the things you want to in Paris.

Another sure winner for younger kids is the **Jardin d'Acclimatation** in the Bois de Boulogne, with lots of participatory activities (*see* Peripheral Attractions p.350); **Parc Astérix**, a theme park with mock-ups and characters from the comic, and rides—often scarier than Disneyland's, especially the roller coaster (*in Plailly, 38km north of Paris off the A1, linked every 30 min by Courriers Ile-de-France shuttle bus from RER B Charles-de-Gaulle 1; open Apr–Sept, 10–6, Sept and Oct Wed, Sat and Sun only; adm 160F adults; adm 3–11pm 110F*); or take the rug rats to one of the biggest sandboxes in Europe, **La Mer de Sable** at Ermenonville (*see* Day Trips, p.478).

Many city parks put on traditional **marionnette** (*Guignol*) performances on Wednesdays, Saturdays and Sundays (listings in the back of *Pariscope* along with children's theatre and circuses under the heading '*Pour Les Jeunes*').

There are the **zoos** at the Jardin des Plantes (*see* Walk IX p.258) and the Bois de Vincennes (*see* Peripheral Attractions, p.365), the latter of which could be easily combined with a few hours at the delightful **Parc Floral**, a lower-key version of the Bois de Boulogne's Jardin d'Acclimatation (Rte de la Pyramide) or the aquarium and ethnographic exhibits at the **Musée des Arts d'Afrique et d'Océanie** (*see* p.364).

Other kid pleasers include the gadgetry in the **Palais de la Découverte** (*see* Walk VI, p.205); the ships in the **Musée de la Marine** (*see* p.309), the aeroplanes and spaceship at the **Musée d'Air et de l'Espace** at Le Bourget (*open Tues–Sun, 10–6, summer till 6; adm; take bus 350 from Gare de l'Est or Porte de la Chapelle or bus 152 from Porte de la Villette*), the dinosaur bones in the **Galerie d'Anatomie Comparée et de Paléontologie** and the stuffed beasts in the **Grande Galerie d'Evolution** in the Jardin des Plantes (*see* Walk IX, p.258).

Even young children enjoy the hoaked up wax people at the **Musée Grevin** (*see* p.179), the magic tricks at the **Musée de la Curiosité et de la Magie** (*see* p.317) and the old fashioned funfair at the **Musée des Arts Forains** (*see* p.380).

For an extra-extra-extra special treat for kids of any age, reserve (weeks in advance) a day at the circus at the **Cirque de Paris**, 115 Blvd Charles-de-Gaulle, Villeneuve-la-Garenne (bus 137 from Ⓜ *Porte de Clignancourt,* ✆ 01 47 99 40 40). It takes place on Wednesdays and Sundays, and daily during school holidays (except July–Oct, when the circus is on the road). The performers put children through the fundamentals of their art as they rehearse, have lunch with them and from 3–5pm the children attend the circus itself. A day for a child ranges from 195–230F (depending on the seat for the performance), for adults 235–395F.

The Centre Pompidou encourages creativity in its arty **Atelier des Enfants**, ✆ 01 44 78 49 17 (*ages 6–12; Wed, Sat, Sun and school hols 2–6, adm 30F*); its special children's library and videothèque (**Salle d'Actualité Jeunesse**) has masses of books, including some in English, that kids over 6 are welcome to browse through (*open Wed 12–7 and Sat and Sun 1–7*).

Incurable video game heads can easily blow all their pocket money at the **Centre Sega**, 5 Blvd des Italiens, Passage des Princes, 2ᵉ, Ⓜ *Richelieu Drouot, open 10am–midnight.*

Kids used to running around like banshees and kicking a ball around a field will get ants in their pants in Paris. Grass is a sacred herb not to be walked on—in the **Jardin du Luxembourg** only toddlers and their handlers are permitted onto the specially designated lawn (it also has a playground, sandpit, pony rides, carrousel, puppet show and roller-skating rink). **Parc des Buttes-Chaumont, Parc Georges-Brassens, Jardin du Ranelagh** and **Parc de la Villette** offer most activities for squirmy youth. Skateboarding teenagers hang out at the Jardins du Trocádero and at La Défense. If the weather's good, you can park your 7–11-year-olds for a couple of hours in the delightful fantasy playground (especially in the

Labyrinth) of the **Jardin des Halles**, 105 Rue Rambuteau (**M** *Châtelet-Les Halles; open Tues, Wed, Thurs, and Sat 10–7, Fri 2–7, Sun 1–7; adm*). If you've brought swimming costumes, the tropical pool complex **Aquaboulevard** (*see* Sports, p.452) should keep kids of all ages happy.

Lastly, if your fussy eater is suffering severe culture shock at the thought of eating real food in French restaurants (note that these are usually good about doing children's portions), some 50 McDonald's and other fast-food clones wait to ward off starvation. Once the little dears are pumped full of junk food, get a babysitter (several hotels offer the service, or call one of the addresses below) and have a romantic night on your own.

## Babysitting/Child-Minding Services

Most of the places listed below charge an agency fee (from 35 to 50F) in addition to the hourly rate (around 30F) that goes to the sitter. If you're out after the last métro, you'll be expected to drive the sitter home or pay for a taxi.

**Ababa**, © 01 45 49 46 46. Good for a pinch, usually able to get a sitter to you within an hour; has many English speakers.

**Allô! Maman Poule**, © 01 47 48 01 01. One of the biggest agencies, and certain to have an English-speaker available (3 hours minimum).

**Allô Service Maman**, © 01 42 67 99 37. Excellent 24 hour service. Usually can get a sitter to you within two hours.

**CROUS**, © 01 40 51 37 53. University student babysitters; call © 9.30am–7pm the same day or day before. No agency fees; some English speakers.

**Kid's Service**, © 01 47 66 00 52. Call between 8am and 8pm or 10am–8pm Saturday; they also have specially trained nannies for babies.

## Shopping for Children's Clothes

In France, these tend to be discouragingly expensive, but there are some possibilities. Among the *Dépôt-Ventes* (end-of-line designer discount shops listed in Shopping, p.442) **Chercheminippes** and **La Marelle** have large sections of children's clothes. Other shops that won't soak you too badly for quality clothes that the squirts are just going to grow out of anyway are:

**Bambini Troc**, 26 Ave du Bel-Air, 12ᵉ. Nearly everything a kid needs from birth to age 16. *Nation* **M**

**Baby Troc**, 16 Rue de Magdebourg, 16ᵉ. End-of-line famous name clothes. *Trocádero* **M**

**Le Bisou de la Sorcière**, 136 Blvd Vincent-Auriol, 13ᵉ. Amusing original fashions that aren't outrageously dear. *Place d'Italie* Ⓜ

**Bois de Rose**, 30 Rue Dauphine, 6ᵉ. Adorable handmade smocks and embroideries for little girls and infants. *Odéon* Ⓜ

**Maman Troc**, 14 Rue Laugier, 17ᵉ. All labels of clothes, shoes, accessories, games and toys for up to 16 years old. *Ternes* Ⓜ

**Le Mouton à Cinq Pattes**, 10 Rue St-Placide, 6ᵉ. Affordable classics and designer duds for fashion slaves up to age 14. *Saint Placide* Ⓜ

**La Taquinerie**, 23 Rue Poncelet, 17ᵉ. Fashionable boutique for clothes and shoes for the 12–18s, and 30 per cent off for their parents.

*Ternes* Ⓜ

**Tout Autre Chose**, the biggest and most affordable children's clothing chain in Paris: there are one or two in almost every *arrondissement*.

**Troc Mioch**, 26 Rue Malar, 7ᵉ. Designers' second-hand clothes and shoes in perfect condition. *Ecole Militaire* Ⓜ

**Troc Lutin**, 6 Rue des Cinq-Diamants, 13ᵉ. Last and this year's designer wear for babies and to age 14s, at half-price; special ski section; toys.

*Place d'Italie* Ⓜ

## Shopping for Games, Books and Toys

**Au Nain Bleu**, 406 Rue St-Honoré, 8ᵉ. Since 1836, with all kinds of toys, especially the classics, and an amazing array of dolls. *Concorde* Ⓜ

**Chantelivre**, 13 Rue de Sèvres, 6ᵉ. A wonderland of children's books in French and English, cassettes, videos and educational toys of all kinds.

*Sèvres Babylone* Ⓜ

**EOL**, 62 and 70 Blvd St-Germain, 5ᵉ, ✆ 01 43 54 01 43. Paris' biggest selection of models of all kinds. *Maubert Mutualité* Ⓜ

**Le Ciel est à Tout le Monde**, 10 Rue Gay-Lussac, 5ᵉ. Europe's best and biggest collection of kites, frisbees, etc. RER: *Luxembourg*

**Les Cousins d'Alice**, 36 Rue Daguerre, 14ᵉ. Charming old-fashioned toys and books. *Denfert-Rochereau* Ⓜ

**Jouets & Cie**, 11 Blvd de Sébastopol, 1ᵉʳ. At the surreal sign of the elephantine baby doll, an elephantine toy store. *Châtelet-Les Halles* Ⓜ

**Jouets Extraordinaires**, 70 Rue d'Auteuil, 16ᵉ. Educational and quality toys from around the world. *Porte d'Auteuil* Ⓜ

**Pintel**, 10 Rue de Paradis, 10ᵉ. Huge selection of name brand toys.

*Château d'Eau* Ⓜ

**Si Tu Veux**, 62/68 Galerie Vivienne, 2ᵉ. Great selection of old-fashioned toys.

*Bourse* Ⓜ

**Tous les Trains**, 73 Rue de Charenton, 12ᵉ. Model trains and all the accessories you need.

*Bastille* Ⓜ

*To live anywhere else, is to exist in the relative sense of the word, secundum quid; to live in Paris is to exist in the absolute sense, simpliciter.*

The 14th-century scholar of Senlis

If you find yourself saying 'Hear, hear!' to the good scholar of Senlis, your first task is to accumulate several barrels of money and an oil tanker full of patience; the French, after all, invented bureaucracy and even if your French is immaculate, finding a place to live will drive you buggy. For some clues as to what 'existing in the absolute sense' involves, pick up a copy of *Paris Inside Out*, published by Parigramme and available in Paris's English-language bookshops.

## Living and Working in Paris

## Basic Bureaucracy

If you're not an EU national and you mean to stay longer than three months in Paris, the first thing is to make sure you get a residence visa (*visa de long séjour*) *before* you come to France, from the nearest French consulate in your home country (or country of residence). You can't get a visa once you're in France, and there's no way around it. Students or au pairs are eligible for a special visa that will keep them from having to get a residence permit (*carte de séjour*) once in France. For any visa, you'll need lots of papers and photos, including proof of financial support. Phone your consulate first to see what they require .

Once in France, EU member or not, the law says you have three months to get a *carte de séjour* from one of three Centre de Réception des Etrangers listed below, or outside Paris from the local *mairie*. In practice the only reason to get one is if you want to work in France legally. Here again, phone ahead to find out what you'll need. Every office has its own interpretation of the requirements, but in addition to your visa you will need several photos, *timbres fiscaux* (government stamps, purchased at tobacconists), proof of means (even EU nationals have to have a minimum sum in the bank) etc. They may or may not force you to have a medical examination, reputed to be an exceptionally degrading experience.

### Adressess of the Centres de Réception des Etrangers:

1ier–7e and 13e–15e *arrondissements*: 114–116 Ave du Maine, 14e, Ⓜ *Gaîté*

11e, 12e, and 20e *arrondissements*: 163 Rue de Chartenton, 12e, Ⓜ *Reuilly Diderot*

8e–10e, 16e, 17e *arrondissements*: 19–21 Rue Truffaut, 17e, Ⓜ *Clichy*

## Studying in Paris

Enrolling is the easy bit and not expensive. The cultural bureau at your French consulate can give you a list of addresses and tell you how to go about it. Anyone under 30 enrolled for a year-long university or similar course can apply for a single or double room at the Cité Universitaire (19 Boulevard Jourdon, 75014 Paris, ℂ 01 45 89 68 52); prices depend on facilities (the *Maison Américaine* is the cosiest and costliest at 2400F a month for a single room).

## Finding a Job

Once you've sorted out your *carte de séjour*, you can try to crack this nut. EU nationals have a legal right to work in France but do make sure it says so on the back of your *carte de séjour*. Teaching English (especially if you have a TEFL certificate), nanny/au pair work and working in bars are the standbys; language schools run ads for teachers nearly every day in the *International Herald Tribune*, or you can ring around once you arrive in Paris.

With sky-high unemployment in France, a *carte de séjour* with a work permit for non-EU citizens is nearly impossible to get unless you already have a job waiting in Paris; and in a typically *Catch-22* situation, you can't apply for most jobs unless you already have the priceless papers in your hand. Au pair jobs are the exception to the rule, and unless you're lucky these can be real stinkers—long hours, low pay and bossy *madame mères* who haven't heard that slavery is out of style. The only other solution is to make enough money to support yourself as a freelance self-employed worker (*travailleur indépendent*).

Foreign students in France have the right to work 20hrs a week or less to support themselves, with an *autorisation de travail* from the Ministère du Travail, Service de la Main d'Oeuvre Etrangère, 80 Rue de la Croix-Nivert, ✆ 01 40 56 60 00. There are often adverts for temporary jobs on the bulletin board at CROUS, 39 Avenue Georges-Bernanos, 5ᵉ.

If you want to set up your own business in Paris, start the ball rolling with the *Greffe et Régistre du Commerce*, 1 Quai de la Corse, 4ᵉ, ✆ 01 43 29 12 60. The Chambre de Commerce et d'Industrie de Paris, ✆ 01 45 08 36 00, has many offices, and along with the Chamber of Commerce in your national consulate can tell you everything you need to know about imports and exports. The *Paris-Anglophone* business directory, available in most English-language bookshops (or on Internet at http: www. paris-anglo.com) may prove useful. Note that in France very little business can be transacted over the telephone; the French like to file papers, and they like to have written words to mull over, and to keep for records. If you're applying for a job, both your skill at written French and your handwriting will be as important to employers as anything else about you (the pseudo-science of 'graphology' is big business here, and firms actually use it to evaluate candidates).

## Finding Somewhere to Live

Like London, Paris is in a nasty property slump just now. Anybody looking to buy a luxury apartment will find real bargains—but the rest of us might not notice any difference. Avoid dealing with agents and their lofty fees if you possibly can. Of the newspapers, only *Le Figaro* has extensive rental listings, but there are several weeklies of classified ads (*J'Annonce, De Particulier en Particulier*) where landlords and renters can cut out the middleman. The *Paris Free Voice* also has some listings, as does the *Herald Tribune* (but luxury only here). Other possibilities are the bulletin boards at:

**American Church**, 55 Quai d'Orsay, 7ᵉ, ✆ 01 47 05 07 99, Ⓜ *Invalides*

**British Institute**, 9–11 Rue de Constantine, 7ᵉ, ✆ 01 45 55 71 99, Ⓜ *Invalides*

**France-USA Contacts Bulletin Board**, 3 Rue Larochelle, 14ᵉ, Ⓜ *Gaîté; open Mon–Fri 10–7, Sat 12–5.*

Also try a rental company that gathers lists of properties let by private parties:

**Euro Location**, 19 Rue de Reuilly 12ᵉ, Ⓜ *Reuilly-Diderot*, Ⓒ 01 40 24 05 99; also 366ter Rue de Vaugirard, 15ᵉ, Ⓒ 01 48 56 05 05 Ⓜ *Porte de Versailles.*

Any halfway decent-looking ad for a flat will draw scores of would-be tenants, leaving it to the landlord to pick and choose. Most will demand a payslip (*fiche de salaire*) or some other proof that you have the means to pay up; students should bring a *porte-garant* (a letter from a parent or employer guaranteeing payment should you blow the rent money at the races). Because tenants have so many rights in France, as a foreigner (obviously wealthy and temporary, to the mind of the landlord) you have a slight advantage over the French. The painful part comes when you have to dole out two months' rent in advance, plus a security deposit (*caution*), plus any agency fees, plus another 500F to have the joint inspected by a *huissier* (bailiff) for a document confirming the state of the property (*état des lieux*) to prevent fights over the return of the security deposit. The minimum lease for a furnished flat is a year, and three for unfurnished, during which your rent cannot legally be raised beyond the official inflation index (some 5% or so a year). Prices are by the square metre which sounds more alarming than it usually is because most flats are definitely in the poky department, although in prime areas (St-Germain and its Faubourg, the 16ᵉ, the Marais and now the Bastille area) 200F a square metre adds up to a pretty penny pretty fast.

Deciphering the adverts requires an extra year of French, but in a nutshell: m² (sq metres); 3 p. (3 *pièces*)—three rooms not counting bath; *conforts* means amenities (maybe wall-to-wall carpet, balcony or extra baths); *asc.* means lift/elevator—a very important consideration here; *meublé* or *vide*—furnished or unfurnished; *ref* (refait) remodelled; *charges*, extra money on top of rent; *partage* means sharing. The cheapest accommodation besides sharing is a *studio*, *garçonnière* (bachelor flat) or converted *chambre de bonne* (maid's room).

## Addresses

**Alcoholics Anonymous**: Meetings in English (*daily*, Ⓒ *01 46 34 59 65*).

**All-night bakery**: Boulangerie de l'Ancienne-Comédie, 10 Rue de l'Ancienne-Comédie, 6ᵉ.

**All-night tobacco**: Old Navy, 150 Blvd Saint-Germain, 6ᵉ. Also, Le Weekend, 3 Rue Washington, 8ᵉ; Le Terminus, 234 Ave de Versailles 16ᵉ; and La Favorite, 3 Blvd St-Michel, 5ᵉ (*all open every night till 2*).

**American Club of Paris**, 34 Ave New York, 16ᵉ, Ⓒ 01 47 23 64 36.

**Astronomical evenings**: Société Astronomique de France, 3 Rue Beethoven, 16ᵉ, Tues and Sat nights; call Ⓒ 01 42 24 79 00 for reservations and the latest news on comets and novas.

**Bee-keeping courses**: Hundreds of kilograms of honey are produced in the Luxembourg gardens every year. Courses are offered by the Société Centrale d'Apiculture, 41 Rue Pernety 14e, ✆ 01 45 42 29 08.

**British Community Committee**: 9 Rue d'Anjou 8e, ✆ 01 42 65 13 04.

**Canadian Cultural Center**: 5 Rue du Constantine, 7e, ✆ 01 45 51 35 73.

**Deceased pets**: For cremation, Cremadog, ✆ 01 30 57 31 29; an expert taxidermist will stuff for 3000F (more if you want your cat immortalized holding a golf club or smoking a cigar) at Deyrolle, 46 Rue du Bac, ✆ 01 42 22 30 07.

**Electrical breakdown emergencies**: EDF Dépannage, ✆ 01 43 46 15 26.

**French lessons**: Paris has billions of **language schools** ready to perfect your French. Some of the more respected institutions: Alliance Française, 101 Blvd Raspail, ✆ 01 45 44 38 28; British Institute, 11 Rue de Constantine, ✆ 01 45 55 71 99; Cours de Civilisation Française de la Sorbonne, 47 Rue des Ecoles, ✆ 01 40 46 22 11.

**Gas breakdown emergencies**: GDF Dépannage, ✆ 01 48 87 61 70.

**Groceries**: Peanut butter, Rolling Rock, homemade brownies and other American essentials at The General Store, 82 Rue de Grenelle, 7e, ✆ 01 45 48 63 16, Ⓜ *Rue du Bac*, and 30 Rue de Longchamp, 16e, 01 47 55 41 14, Ⓜ *Trocadéro*.

**Lost Property**: 36 Rue des Morillons, 15e, ✆ 45 31 14 80 (*open Mon–Fri 8.30–5*).

**Minitels**: You don't have to be in Paris for long before you notice half the ads invite you to *tapper 36 15* on the Minitel, the national telephone computer. For as little as 20F a month you can have your very own, and for 2.23F minimum per minute you can do everything from talk dirty or make dates (3615 CUM, GAY, etc.), test your knowledge of the French traffic code (3615 AUTOTEST), practise your Arabic (3615 LINGUATEL), play chess (3615 ROQUE), or see where the wind is up in Brittany if you feel like windsurfing (3615 WIND).

**Newspapers and magazines**: The biggest selection in town (over 10,000 titles) is at La Galcante, 52 Rue de l'Arbre-Sec, 1er; all-night kiosks can be found 16 Blvd de la Madeleine, in Place d'Etoile, 33 Champs-Elysées, 2 Blvd Montmartre.

**Paperwork**: Hire someone else to stand in those long queues for you. Assistance Démarche, Rue Choron, 9e, ✆ 0 800 01 40 77, Ⓜ *Notre-Dame-de-Lorette* for a visa, VIP Visa Express, 3 Rue Lebouis 14e, ✆ 01 44 10 72 72, Ⓜ *Gaîté*.

**Pest control**: Rats, roaches, ants whatever, the city's Laboratoire d'Hygiène will know what to do; ✆ 01 45 82 80 50.

**Pick your own**: One cure for the urban blues is to harvest your own strawberries or beans at one of seven **Les Chapeaux de Paille** farms in the Paris area. For the one nearest you, ✆ 01 64 41 81 09.

**Pizza home delivery**: Pizza Hut and Domino's are taking over: try **Zap Pizza**, ✆ 01 43 20 43 20, for something tasty and different. Other home-delivery numbers when you just can't face another shop or restaurant: **Cactus Charly**, ✆ 01 45 67 64 99, for Tex-Mex or Indian; **Fruits de Mer Express**, ✆ 01 43 27 20 50, for fresh shellfish and all the trimmings (minumum order 250F); **Allô Paella**, ✆ 01 43 74 80 56; **Allô Sud-Oeust**, ✆ 01 45 57 00, for *foie gras*, *cassoulet* and duck dishes.

**Poodle essentials**: When little Toutou looks frumpy, visit **La Boutique du Chien**, in La Samaritaine, 19 Rue de la Monnaie, ✆ 01 40 41 28 61, for the latest doggie trim or hairdo *la coupe New Look* (they also sell poodle clothes, matching collars and coordinated bags and pooper-scoopers); have a hand-painted pet portrait by Patricia Anceau, ✆ 01 47 36 81 37; and when you go on holiday, dump your darling off at a four-star canine and pussy-cat *pension*, the **Ferme du Bel-Air in Charmentray**, 77410, ✆ 01 60 01 90 28, where your pet can undergo the same rigorous training as animals used in commercials; and if it's time for romance, arrange a date on the Minitel 3615 FIDO.

**Rent a Chauffered Bugatti**: Rétromobile, ✆ 01 48 25 88 33. Over 1000 antique cars to choose from.

**Rent a billboard**: Impress your sweetie, or make your prejudices public from 2000F: Affichage Dauphin, ✆ 01 40 82 82 82.

**Rent a camel**: SAPA, ✆ 01 39 82 90 29; daily and weekly rates.

**S.O.S. Help**: Crisis hotline in English, from 3pm to 11pm, ✆ 01 47 23 80 80.

**Tux/formal-wear rentals**: From shoes to hats available at Au Cor de Chasse, 40 Rue de Buci, ✆ 01 43 26 51 84.

**Video Rental**: For home delivered films in English, try Reels on Wheels, ✆ 01 45 67 64 99; also Prime Time Video at Tea and Tattered Pages (also second hand books) 24 Rue Mayet, 6ᵉ, ✆ 01 40 56 33 44, Ⓜ *Duroc*.

**WICE**: (Women's Institutute for Continuing Education), 20 Blvd du Montparnasse, 15ᵉ, ✆ 01 45 66 75 50; originally founded by wives of American businessmen in Paris and extremely active, sponsoring lectures, courses in the humanities, support groups for women and new residents.

*Versailles*

# Day Trips from Paris

Beyond the tentacles of the metropolis are enough attractions to fill another book. Most notable of all are the forests—all former hunting reserves of the king and nobility, and one of the few things Parisians can't thank the crown enough for; the forest of Fontainebleau alone is bigger than intramural Paris. Then there's the constellation of châteaux of all shapes and sizes, from dinosaurs such as Versailles to the newest synthetic number belonging to Sleeping Beauty in Disneyland. And further afield, but well worth the effort, are genuinely magical places such as Chartres or Monet's colour-drenched gardens at Giverny.

This list of day trips begins southwest of Paris with the mother of all suburban excursions and Paris' first artificial satellite town: Versailles. From there excursions are listed more or less clockwise.

## Southwest of Paris: Versailles

> *Don't copy my liking for war or my taste in building.*
>
> Louis XIV to Louis XV, on his deathbed

Versailles' name comes from the clods that the farmer turns over with his plough, referring to the clearing made for a royal hunting lodge. And so Versailles remained until the young Louis XIV attended the fatal bash at Fouquet's Vaux-le-Vicomte (*see* p.479), which turned him sour with envy. He would have something perhaps not better but certainly bigger, and hired all the geniuses Fouquet had patronized to create for himself one of the world's masterpieces of megalomania—123 acres of rooms. They are strikingly void of art; the enormous façade of the château is as monotonous as it is tasteful, so as not to upstage the principal inhabitant. The object is not to think of the building, but of Louis, and with that thought be awed. It is the shibboleth of France, the albatross around her neck. You can almost hear the slight shriek of hysteria in the words of Academician Henri de Montherlant: 'Versailles must be ranked very high. It must be defended against all comers. We are on Versailles's side; what am I saying? we are *a part of it*'. Voltaire had the clearer vision: *un chef-d'oeuvre de mauvais goût et de magnificence* (a masterpiece of bad taste and magnificence).

Versailles contributed greatly to the bankruptcy of France: Louis, used to overawing his subjects, began to hallucinate that he could bully nature as well. He ordered his engineers to divert the Loire itself to feed his fountains, and when faced with the impossible, settled on bringing the waters of the Eure through pestilent marshes to Versailles by way of the aqueduct of Maintenon, a ten-year project that cost 9,000,000 livres and the lives of hundreds of workmen before it was abandoned. Too much sacrifice and money has been concentrated here for the French to shake the albatross loose; they are *a part of it.*

If there's no art in Versailles, there is certainly an extraordinary amount of skilful craftsmanship. Besides its main purpose as a stage for Louis (Versailles and its gardens were open to anyone who was decently dressed and promised not to beg in the halls; anyone could watch the king attend Mass, or dine), the palace served as a giant public showroom for French products, especially from the new luxury industries cranked up by Colbert. As such it was a spectacular success, contributing greatly to the spread of French tastes and fashions throughout Europe. Today, Versailles's curators haunt the auction houses of the world, looking to replace as much of the original decoration as possible—a bust here, a chair there. Even the gardens have been replanted with Baroque bowers, as they appeared in the time of Louis XIV. One thing the restorers don't care to recreate is the palace plumbing—a mere three toilets for the estimated 20,000 residents, servants and daily visitors to Versailles.

> *After Louis XVI and Marie-Antoinette were evicted by the Paris mob on 6 October 1789, Versailles was left empty, and there was talk of knocking it down when Louis-Philippe decided to restore it as a museum. The result is excruciating to visit, not only because of its size, but the enormous crowds who come to marvel at the myth. Getting there is easy by RER:C or train from the Gare Montparnasse or, most pleasantly, by train from Gare St-Lazare to Versailles-Rive Droit followed by a 15-minute walk from either station. The château is open Tues–Sun 9–6.30, closed holidays;* **Grands Appartements** *(entrance A) adm 45F; 35F after 3.30pm and all day Sun. Another 25F at entrance C will get you into the* **Apartments of Louis XIV** *and the* **Apartments of the Dauphin and Dauphine** *with an audioguide in English; unfortunately the* **Opéra Royal**, *the latter a gem designed by Gabriel for Louis XV in 1768—all wood, painted as marble, but designed 'to resonate like a violin'—is currently off limits. Gardens free except Sun and hols from May–mid-Oct when* **the musical fountains are turned on** *(all still using their original plumbing); 25F adm. Four summer Saturdays occasion the extravagant* **Grandes Fêtes de Nuit**, *fireworks, illuminated fountains and an 'historical fresco' (book with FNAC or the Versailles tourist office ℭ 01 39 50 36 22, ✆ 01 39 50 68 07). There are also frequent concerts of Baroque music, ℭ 01 39 02 30 00 for information. For a royal lunch or dinner in Versailles, try Le Potager du Roy, 1 Rue du Mal. Joffre, ℭ 01 39 50 35 34, excellent menus 125 and 175F.*

The Grands Appartements are the public rooms traditionally open to all in Louis XIV's day—although in the crowds you may feel as squeezed as toothpaste in a tube. There's the elliptical, two-storey **Chapelle Royale**, architecturally the high-light of Versailles; a historical gallery of rooms lined with portraits of royal relatives and views of Versailles; the **Grands Appartements**, a series of tiresome gilded drawing rooms, each dedicated to a Roman deity; the **Salon d'Hercule**, designed around Veronese's *Repas du Christ chez Simon le Pharisien*, the one good painting in the palace. The **Salon de Diane** has the gusty bust of Louis by Bernini. Louis's throne, naturally, was in the Salon d'Apollon, where the Sun King would have done well to recall Montaigne's words: 'On the highest throne in the world, we still sit on our own bottom.'

Beyond are the **Salle de Guerre** and **Salle de Paix**, linked by the famous 241ft **Hall of Mirrors**, still crowned with Lebrun's paintings of the first 17 years of Louis XIV's reign, but minus the original solid-silver furniture, which Louis had to melt down to pay his war debts. The famous 17 mirrors with 578 panes are post-1975 copies, put in place after a disgruntled Breton blew up the originals; facing the win-dows, they reflect the sunlight into the gardens, a fantastical conceit intended to remind visitors that the Sun himself dwelt within. He would have become decid-edly overcast had he known that on 18 January 1871 another empire—and one that had just completely humiliated France—would create its first kaiser here. On 28 June 1919 the allies, with a fine sense of irony, ended the horrific Act Two of the conflict, by staging the signing of the peace treaty in the same spot.

Beyond the Salle de Paix are the formal apartments of the queen; their current appearance required a colossal reconstruction—shreds of fabric were found and rewoven in the original designs, and Savonnerie carpets copied from old designs. The *Chambre de la Reine* was used for the public birthing of Enfants de France. In the Antechamber, note the portrait of *Marie-Antoinette and her children* by Madame Vigée-Lebrun. The Salle du Sacre was created by Louis-Philippe to receive a copy of David's painting of Napoleon's coronation in the Louvre—a copy David preferred to his original.

Then there are the gardens, last replanted by Napoleon III, with their 13 miles of box hedges to clip, and the 1100 potted palms and oranges of the Orangerie, all planted around the 'limitless perspective' from the terrace fading into the blue horizon of the Grand Canal. Not by accident, the sun sets straight into it on St Louis's day, 25 August, in a perfect alignment with the Hall of Mirrors. On either side, Le Nôtre's original garden design—more theatrical and full of surprises than any of his other cre-ations—is slowly being restored while hundreds of trees have been sacrificed in the name of new vistas of the château, inspired by Louis XIV's guidebook to the gardens, the *Manière de montrer les jardins de Versailles*. In it he devised a one-way route for his visitors to take, for even at their best Le Nôtre's gardens are essentially two-dimen-sional; to appreciate them they must be seen from just the right angle.

Louis kept a flotilla of gondolas on his Grand Canal, to take his courtiers for rides; today the gondoliers of Venice come to visit every September for the *Fêtes Vénitiennes*. The rest of the year you can hire a boat to paddle about or a bike to pedal through the garden, or even catch a little zoo train to a building far more interesting than the main palace, the **Grand Trianon** (*adm 25F*). An elegant, airy Italianate palace of pink marble and porphyry with two wings linked by a peristyle, it was designed by the staff of Hardouin-Mansart in 1687 for Louis XIV ('I built Versailles for the court, Marly for my friends, and Trianon for myself' he said). After his divorce, Napoleon brought his new Empress Marie-Louise here, who did it up quite attractively in the Empire style; in 1966 the then Culture Minister, André Malraux, subjected it to a thorough restoration.

The gardens in this area were laid out by Louis XV's architect, Jacques-Ange Gabriel, who also built the Rococo **Pavillon du Jardin des Français** and the refined **Petit Trianon** nearby (*adm 15F*), intended for Louis XV's meetings with Madame de Pompadour. Louis XVI gave the Petit Trianon to Marie-Antoinette, who spent much of her time here. On a torpid afternoon around 5pm on 10 August 1901, two Englishwomen, Miss Moberly and Miss Jourdain, were wandering through the wood near here when they went into an uncanny time warp: through the trees they saw a woman in white, dressed in the 18th-century fashion, a man running urgently, a gardener and ladies playing a 'Chinese ring' game. Feeling increasingly uneasy, the two women withdrew; when no one could explain what they had seen, they researched the site, and came to the conclusion that the woman in white was none other than Marie-Antoinette and the man running was a messenger warning her that the Parisians were marching on Versailles; the Chinese ring game, long forgotten, was rediscovered by archaeologists, who confirmed other details as well. The story draws a crowd of wannabe time travellers to the same spot every 10 August. Beyond the Petit Trianon is the **Hameau de la Reine**, the delightful operetta farmhouse built for Marie-Antoinette, where she could play shepherdess.

Nothing escaped Louis XIV's attention, and even his carrots and cabbages were planted in geometric rigidity in his immaculate vegetable garden, **Le Potager du Roi**, arranged to please all five senses (*entrance at 6 Rue Hardy, on the left side of Place des Armes, the square in front of the château; guided tours with fruit and jam tastings 3 Apr–15 Nov at 2.30pm, Wed–Sun; adm. Book © 01 39 24 62 62*). The visit includes the adjacent **Parc Balbi**, a romantic park planted by the Comte de Provence (future Louis XVIII) for his mistress. As an antidote to Versailles, you can try to visit the nearby **Salle du Jeu de Paume**, 1 Rue du Jeu-de-Paume (*rarely open; ring © 01 30 84 76 18*), where the Third Estate made its famous Tennis Court Oath to give France a constitution on 29 July 1789.

*From Gare Montparnasse, the same train that passes through Versailles continues through **Rambouillet** (52km from Paris)—near the 16th-century picture-book castle with pointy turrets where François I died, where Louis XVI raised Spanish merino sheep to improve the French strains, and where the President of France comes to get away from Paris— to **Chartres** (89km from Paris). Near the cathedral, Le Pichet, 19 Rue du Cheval Blanc, © 01 37 21 08 35 is a good bet for lunch (75–150F).*

A world away in spirit, Chartres lies at the edge of the Beauce, a flat, pleasant country that has always supplied the capital with much of its grain. But the famous photo view of France's greatest cathedral, with its Gothic towers rising over the horizon from a field of wheat, is becoming harder to find these days, as the growing town spreads out over its countryside.

The Romans found this part of Gaul inhabited by a tribe called the *Carnutes*, after whom Chartres is named. The village, built around a sacred well, was an important religious site from the earliest times. As such it was a key target for the Christians. They may have taken it over as early as the 4th century, substituting the worship of the Virgin Mary for that of the ancient mother goddess, who always ruled over wells and underground springs—a primeval wooden statue of the goddess, recycled as Mary, was worshipped here as late as 1793. The first Christian basilica was built in the 4th century and rebuilt several times after fires.

Don't wonder that such a small town should have managed such an impressive cathedral. Medieval Chartres, about the same size as the present version, was relatively much more important; in the 11th century its cathedral school was an internationally known centre of learning, a rival to Paris itself. The current building took form after a fire in 1194 destroyed a brand-new cathedral. Rebuilding commenced immediately and contributed much to the legend of pious community participation in cathedral building. Everyone pitched in with labour or funds to complete the inspired new design for the 'Palace of the Virgin'—even Kings Philippe-Auguste and Richard the Lionheart, who were then fighting over the area.

By 1260 the building was nearly complete; the rapidity of the work allowed Chartres to have a stylistic unity seen in few other medieval cathedrals. And its construction shows many advances in the new Gothic architecture: carving the thick pillars into apparent bundles of slender columns, to accentuate the verticality and lightness of the building. Also, Chartres perfects the concepts of roof vaulting and the flying buttress, allowing it to be the widest of all Gothic cathedrals, while letting in more light with big windows in the clerestory and especially in the magnificent apse, nearly all glass.

In the words of Emile Mâle: 'Chartres is medieval thought in visible form'. More than 10,000 figures in stone or glass complete the encyclopedia in stone, which would take a thorough knowledge of Scripture and medieval philosophy, and a lifetime's work to decipher properly. The **west porch** survived the 1194 fire, and is the oldest part of the cathedral. Besides the exquisite statues of saints that flank the doors, note on the left door the *zodiac signs and works of the months*, one of the loveliest of the Gothic 'stone calendars'. While the tympanum of the central portal is dedicated to Christ (in an almond-shaped mandorla, surrounded by the symbols of the Evangelists), those on the sides belong to Mary: an *Annunciation* (left) and *Assumption* (right). The façade's south tower is original; the northern one was struck by lightning and rebuilt in the flamboyant style in the 1300s.

The **south porch** honours the saints: the martyrs (right door), apostles (central door) and confessors (left door), surmounted by nine choirs of angels—seraphim, cherubim, thrones, dominations and all the rest. The *north porch*, less extravagant, includes a tympanum of the Adoration of the Magi.

Inside, your attention will be caught between the brilliance of the architecture and the finest stained-glass windows ever: 173 of them, mostly originals. In Chartres it was the custom for the city guilds to supply these; look at the bottoms of the windows along the nave, and in many you will see scenes of the contributing guild's members at work: goldsmiths, bakers, weavers, tavern-keepers, furriers, money-changers, blacksmiths and many others. Especially good are the tall windows in the apse, picturing the life of Christ (a *Tree of Jesse*, etc.) and the great rose windows, especially the *'Rose de France'* in the north transept, celebrating the Virgin; the rose in the south transept represents Christ in glory, as in the Book of Revelations.

On the floor of the nave, the famous **labyrinth** (sometimes covered by chairs) is now almost unique in France; many other Gothic cathedrals had similar ones, but most were destroyed in the vapid 18th century. A large exhibit erected off the nave attempts to explain the Christian meaning of the maze—but it's an utter fabrication; there simply isn't any. The symbolism of labyrinths since the remotest times has always had something to do with the passage of the soul and with astronomy; here it possibly also reflects the patterns of a dance, a survival of pre-Christian times. Originally, there was a bronze relief of Theseus and the Minotaur at the centre. Below the choir, in the *crypt*, the ancient sacred wells still survive.

Just behind the cathedral, to the left, the **Musée des Beaux-Arts** contains few artworks from the cathedral, but a fine collection of tapestries and Renaissance paintings (*open daily except Tues, 10–12 and 2–6, till 5 in winter; adm*). The oldest part of the town, the *haute ville*, conserves a good many medieval buildings, though it seems a little over-restored. Some of the prettiest corners are around Place de l'Etape-du-Vin and Place de la Poissonnerie.

## West of Paris: Maison de Monet in Giverny

*Open 10–6, closed Mon and Nov–Mar; adm. The nearest train station is 6km away in Vernon (35 min from Gare St-Lazare), with bus or taxi connections to Giverny. For lunch try Les Jardins de Giverny (140–200F) or less expensively the Restaurant de la Poste, 26 Ave Gambetta in Vernon. Beware that most of the tour buses pull in right after lunch.*

The Impressionists' impressionist Claude Monet moved out to this charming house in 1883 and stayed until he died in 1926, immersed in his Japanese prints and the gorgeous chromatic gardens and waterlily ponds he designed, each section arranged to bloom in a predominant colour. A subterranean passage links the ponds and gardens, separated in Monet's day only by a seldom-used railway line. The huge studio he designed for his waterlily canvases is now a boutique. May, June and July, the best months to visit, are simply drunk with colour. To see what Monet's American co-Impressionists were up to, visit Giverny's **Musée d'Art Américan**, 99 Rue Claude-Monet (*open 10–6, closed Mon; adm*).

## North of Paris: Ecouen and Chantilly

Trains on the same line from the Gare du Nord penetrate beyond suburbia into the former domains of the Montmorencys, a pretty piece of real estate picked up by these wealthy counts through marriage. Two of the family châteaux are now museums: the first, the 16th-century **Château d'Ecouen**, provides the perfect setting for 16th-century art in the **Musée National de la Renaissance**.

*19km from Paris and a short walk from the Ecouen-Ezanville station; open daily except Tues 9.45–12.30 and 2–5.15; adm, half-price Sun.*

On display are painted Florentine wedding chests, glass from Venice, Limoges enamels, automata, tiles, astrolabes, *objets d'art*, a bronze statuette of sexy satyrs from Il Riccio and the magnificent 246ft of tapestry panels on the story of *David and Bathsheba*, woven in Brussels in 1515.

### Chantilly

*38km north of Paris and a 2½km walk from Chantilly station; **Château Musée Condé** open 10–6, closed Tues; adm. Chantilly's best restaurant is Le Relais Condé, 42 Ave du Mal. Joffre, © 01 44 57 05 75 (160–300F).*

Chantilly, birthplace of whipped cream, has long been rich and coveted. It began as an island in a bog topped with a Roman fort, which in feudal times the Montmorencys made into a castle with a moat. This was rebuilt in the Renaissance by a boy named Anne, the Grand Connétable Anne de Montmorency, who had 29 other estates to live in while work progressed. His granddaughter Charlotte caught the roving eye of Henri IV, who thought the best way to have his evil way with her would be to marry her off to a complaisant husband, Henri de Bourbon-Condé; the plan backfired when the groom refused to recognize the king's *droit de seigneur*, and the old skirt-chaser showed his displeasure by exiling the young couple. They were able to return to Chantilly in 1643, after the king's death, and left the estate to their son, the Grand Condé, who brought the château its greatest fame, commissioning gardens and fountains from Le Nôtre. And like the ill-starred Fouquet at Vaux-le-Vicomte (*see* p.479), the Grand Condé thought to show off his remodelled estate with a bash, with Louis XIV at the top of the guest list. The victuals were prepared under the legendary maître d'hôtel Vatel, who had begun his career with Fouquet. Trouble began the first day, when more guests arrived than expected (enough to seat 60 tables, with 80 people each) and Vatel was caught short of roasts. His despair was complete the following day, when the fish for supper failed to arrive on time; Vatel ran himself through with a sword, the first but hardly the last French chef to commit suicide over an *affaire d'honneur* (losing a Michelin star pushed one Paris chef over the edge in the 1960s).

The grandson of the Grand Condé, who knew he would be reincarnated as a horse, built for his future self the Grandes Ecuries, one of the most palatial stables in the world. These have endured (before the château, near the edge of Chantilly's prestigious racecourse), while the Renaissance château was destroyed in the Revolution, rebuilt and destroyed again in 1848. What you see today is the fifth in the same spot, overlooking the former bog—now a mirror of waters.

## Musée Condé

Inside the château, the art collection of the Musée Condé is one of the best in France outside the Louvre: a fine if somewhat dottily hung selection from the Italian Renaissance, with works by Annibale Carracci, Palma Vecchio, Raphael, Andrea del Sarto, Filippino Lippi, Mazzolino, a sad sweet *Virgin* by Perugino, a very linear *Autumn* by Botticelli, a surreal Sassetta and from oddball Piero di Cosimo a *Portrait of Simonetta Vespucci*, wearing a viper around her neck. There are exceptional French works: François Clouet, Watteaus, Poussins, Jean Fouquet's *Les Heures d'Etienne Chevalier* (1460); beautiful monochrome windows in the Galerie de Psyche on the *Legend of the Golden Ass*, made by a follower of Raphael for Anne de Montmorency; Ingres's *Antioches et Stratonice*, a famous piece of neoclassical kitsch; and portraits—of the 'Big Bastard of Bourgogne' (Flemish, 15th century), of Talleyrand (who does look like a 'living corpse' as one Englishman described him), of Molière about to cock a brow and laugh (by Pierre Mignard), of Louis XIV daintily lifting his fleur-de-lys skirts (by Hyacinthe Rigaud), of Bonaparte, First Consul (by Gérard), the only picture covered with glass, as if the administrators expected someone to spit on it and a

*Déjeuner de Jambon*, by Watteau's follower Lancret, a typical scene of gluttony, enjoyed by French nobles as much as the petite bourgeoisie of the Dutch genre painters. The jewel of the collection, the *Très Riches Heures du Duc de Berry*, that unparalleled masterpiece of early 15th-century illuminator's art, is hidden in the library, where you have to go with a guide, and even then all you are permitted to see are well-made facsimiles. Still, whenever the French drive you crazy , there's nothing like these magical pictures with their precise detail and charming naturalism to remind you why you learned to conjugate the imperfect subjunctive in school.

## Musée Vivant du Cheval

> *Open daily except Tues, 10.30–5.30; three dressage demonstrations daily; © 01 44 57 40 40 for hours; adm.*

So much for great art; the Condé's horse palace up the road gets most of the visitors and schoolkids these days, now that it's the Living Museum of the Horse. There are 30 beautifully groomed horses of nearly every conceivable breed, some 31 rooms of horsey artefacts and toys, audiovisuals and models of everything Old Paint or Black Beauty is useful for—except those Parisian horseburgers.

Chantilly has one of the most beautiful forests in the Ile-de-France, divided by the A1 from the **Forêt d'Ermenonville**, where Rousseau spent his last months, a guest of the Marquis de Girardin, and where he died and was originally buried before being Pantheonized. If you have a car and children, consider the forest's 50-acre **Mer de Sable** on the N 330—a sea of sand dunes left over from the Tertiary Age, fitted out with all the usual kid activities—rides, train, shows, and camel excursions (*RER B3: Charles-de-Gaulle I and then bus to Ermenonville, © 01 44 54 00 96; open Apr–Sept, 10.30–6.30, Sun 10–7; adm 78F*).

## East of Paris: Disneyland

> *32km east of Paris at Marne-la-Vallée; RER: Marne-la-Vallée/Chessy. Open daily, although hours change according to season and school holidays; © 01 60 30 60 30 for all information, events schedules, and hotel/bungalow reservations. High season adm 195F; 150F for children 3–11; 'multipass' good for two or three days available.*

Back in the 1930s, Walt Disney put out a cartoon version of *Pinocchio*, where at one point the naughty wooden puppet and other truants end up in an amusement park for bad boys, where they have so much mindless fun they turn into donkeys, and are then captured and sold by the evil owners. The idea must have put a seed in old Walt's brain; the results may now be seen in California, Florida, Tokyo, and since 12 April 1992 in the far suburbs of Paris.

'A cultural Chernobyl at the heart of Europe,' snarled theatre director Ariane Mnouchkine although, as the French themselves have pointed out, culture in Europe must be pretty thin gruel if threatened by a cartoon mouse. The French government helped bring the fox into the chicken coop—an RER line and TGV line linked up to Marseille, Lyon, Lille, Charles de Gaulle airport and eventually London, and land made available on very favourable terms. Although the first three years were characterized by a brutal baptism in red ink and farcical Franco-American misunderstandings, Disneyland Paris appears to have settled down under French management; the new regime has none of the brash, hip-shooting swagger of the first American-run years, and no one frets any more about cultural pollution leaking out of Marne-la-Vallée.

The park is a fifth the size of the city of Paris—1943 hectares (4800 acres), protected from the outside world by 30ft sloped dikes. Six large theme hotels are run with that guaranteed 'Have a nice day' friendliness and chocolates on the pillow approach (no fake concessions to European culture here). Besides the rides, the corporate-processed fun includes infinite 'shopping opportunities', special shows, food (American, Mexican, Italian and other European) and discothèques and weird American nightlife at the Festival Disney complex. If you go in summer, bring a good book: Tinkerbell herself must have designed the enchanted queue routes for the rides that curl in and out, up and down, all the better to keep you believing you're almost there when there's still the population of Zambia waiting in front of you. For more chills and thrills and less mouse, try Parc Astérix, with Europe's most terrifying roller-coaster (p.458).

## Southeast of Paris: Vaux-le-Vicomte and Fontainebleau

If you're considering hiring a car for a day trip, make it this one: that way you can combine both châteaux and the sights around the forest of Fontainebleau.

### Vaux-le-Vicomte

*Get there by train from the Gare de Lyon to Melun (61km), then take a taxi 6km to the Château de Vaux-le-Vicomte. Open daily 10–6 from 1 Apri–1 Nov; for other times by appointment, © 01 64 14 41 90. Fountains play the 2nd and last Sat of each month from 3–6; romantic candlelight tours Sat 8.30–11pm from June to Sept; adm).*

Vaux was the prototype for Versailles but is much prettier: designed by Louis Le Vau and decorated by Charles Lebrun, it is set in the first true *jardin à la française* by André Le Nôtre, who for the first time had a scale vast enough to play with vanishing points and perspectives to his heart's content. The whole shebang was paid for and masterminded by Nicolas Fouquet, Louis XIV's minister of finances, who adopted Hercules as his patron, just as Louis fancied himself as Apollo.

Even if Fouquet aped a decorative mythology on the level of Disney's *Fantasia*, the concept of Vaux was undeniably Herculean. Not only did Fouquet unite the greatest talents of his time (Madame de Sévigné and La Fontaine were among his other 'discoveries') but he created this country palace and gardens in only five years, employing 20,000 masons, decorators and gardeners, all with one aim in mind: to form a suitable stage for a grand fête to impress one single person, the king, on 17 August 1661. It was, by all accounts, the most splendid party in the history of France. The choicest dishes were prepared on gold and silver plates by Vatel, the famous maître d'hôtel; the great Lully composed music for the occasion, the *comédie-ballet* was by Fouquet's friend Molière, 1200 jets of water danced from the fountains, elephants decked in jewels lingered among the orange trees, while Italian fireworks wizards astounded all with their artistry. The 23-year-old Louis was certainly impressed—and so miffed that he refused to sleep in the *chambre du roi* built just for him.

Vaux was used as lavish proof of Fouquet's graft and cited in his embezzlement trial three years later, but it wasn't the expense that got Louis's goat that famous night—after all, limitless graft by treasurers was built into the still feudal system, and Cardinal Mazarin had filched much more. What niggled Apollo was that Hercules, a mere mortal, had upstaged him not only in extravagance but as an arbiter of taste (Vaux suggests that *style Louis XIV* should really be called *style Fouquet*). And like Apollo, who was often cruel, Louis punished Fouquet's hubris, personally intervening in his trial to insist on a sentence of solitary confinement for life (the unfortunate judge who had merely condemned Fouquet to exile was himself sent into exile). The king confiscated all Fouquet's property. Then he confiscated Fouquet's ideas to create Versailles, hiring Le Vau, Lebrun and Le Nôtre to repeat their work at Vaux, but on an appalling scale; Fouquet's tapestry weavers and furniture makers were employed to form the nucleus of the Gobelins factories; Louis hired Fouquet's firework makers to light his own fêtes; he even carted off Fouquet's 1200 orange trees for his Orangerie at Versailles.

In the 19th century, Le Nôtre's gardens with their clipped hedges, statues and elaborate waterworks were restored. Period furnishings and tapestries from the Gobelins and Savonnerie complement the surviving decorations, which include Lebrun's portraits of Fouquet in the **Salon d'Hercule** and his poignantly unfinished ceiling in the **Grand Salon**. Another salon honours La Fontaine, who wrote *L'élégie aux Nymphes de Vaux* for his fallen patron, a touching tribute from one of the Classical Age's sweetest characters, if the most absent-minded (once he walked past his own son, and asked, with a puzzled air: 'Haven't I seen that young man somewhere before?') Vaux's stables contain the **Musée des Equipages** full of beautiful antique carriages. Lastly, look for the carved squirrels—Fouquet's family symbol (because they hoard all their goodies).

---

## Fontainebleau

*The train to Melun continues to **Fontainebleau**, 65km from Paris; get off at Fontainebleau-Avon, where bus A or B from the station will whisk you to the centre. The **Tourist Office**, at 31 Place Bonaparte, hires out bikes, an ideal way to explore ancient forest paths (they also sell a detailed map). The **Château de Fontainebleau** is open 9.30–12.30, 2–5, closed Tues; adm. For lunch in Fontainebleau try Le Caveau des Ducs, 24 Rue de Ferrare, © 01 64 22 05 05 (100–175F).*

At weekends half of Paris seems to be here; the **forest**, with its wonderful variety of flora—including 2700 species of mushrooms and fungi—oak and pine woods, rocky escarpments and dramatic gorges is the wildest place near the metropolis. It was always exceptionally rich in game and by 1150 had already been set aside as the royal hunting reserve of Louis the Fat. The medieval kings managed with a fortified castle-hunting lodge, but along came François I, who chose Fontainebleau to be his artistic showcase; down went most of the old castle and up went an elegant **château**, fit to be decorated by the artists the king had imported from Italy, especially the great Rosso Fiorentino, a student of Michelangelo, but a man so badly shaken by the brutal sacking of Rome in 1527 that he was half-mad, and ended up committing suicide. Rosso and his fellow Mannerist Primaticcio (Primatice, in French) had a decisive influence on the French artists of the first Ecole de Fontainebleau (led by Jean Goujon, Jean Cousin and Antoine Caron), who were best known for their extreme refinement and eroticism. Work on the château continued under Henri II and the exquisite Philibert de l'Orme. Henri IV added two courts decorated by Flemish artists, who influenced a second, if less original, Ecole de Fontainebleau. Every subsequent ruler to Napoleon added to the place; the Revolution destroyed most of its furnishings, while Louis-Philippe hired ham-handed restorers, who left much of the art a shadow of itself.

With contributions from so many monarchs, the château de Fontainebleau makes an interesting style book. Enter through the **Cour des Adieux**, where Napoleon bid farewell to his Imperial Guard after his abdication on 20 April 1814 and Louis XIII built the magnificent horseshoe staircase. The tour of the **Grands Appartements** includes the famous **Galerie François I** (1533–37) with Rosso's repainted frescoes framed in the original stuccoes; the Michelangelo-influenced **Chapelle de la Trinité** and the extraordinary, sumptuous **Salle de Bal**, both built under Henri II; the **Chambre de l'Impératrice**, with Marie-Antoinette's elaborate bed; and the **Salle du Trône**, designed for Napoleon. Other rooms, under restoration, were used by Pius VII during his stay in Paris. The **Petits Appartements** are less grand, but just as interesting *(tours only, at 10, 11, 2.15 and 3 from June–Aug)*; also to see in the château is the **Musée Napoléon I**), concentrating on the daily life of a self-made emperor.

Fontainebleau's gardens, notably the Parterre, were first laid out by François; Henri IV added the water, dubbed the Tibre, and Le Nôtre rearranged the whole into geo-metric gardens, although his urge to create the illusion of infinite perspectives was checked by the plans of his predecessors. In 1812, Napoleon ordered English gardens planted around the Fountaine Belle-Eau.

The most dramatic drive in the forest is just north of town, a circuit called **Les Hauteurs de la Solle**, where weekend rock climbers dangle like exotic insects over the boulders.

| | |
|---|---|
| **Abbaye** | abbey |
| **Arrondissement** | a city district |
| **Auberge** | inn |
| **Banlieu** | suburb |
| **Bidonville** | shanty town |
| **Carrefour** | crossroads |
| **Caryatid** | column or pillar carved in the figure of a woman |
| **Cave** | cellar |
| **Château** | mansion, manor house or castle |
| **Chemin** | path |
| **Chevet** | eastern end of a church, including the apse |
| **Cité** | originally a village, later a row or small compound of house used for artists' studios now often used by property developers |
| **Cloître** | cloister |
| **Cour d'Honneur** | the principal central courtyard of a palace or large hôtel |
| **Couvent** | convent or monastery |
| **Ecluse** | canal lock |
| **Eglise** | church |
| **Faubourg** | area |
| **Gare** | train station (SNCF) |
| **Gisant** | a sculpted prone effigy on a tomb |
| **Guinguette** | a tavern with a garden for dancing outside, from a certain Guinguet who opened the first in Ménilmontant in the 1670s |
| **Halles** | covered market |
| **Hôtel** | originally the town residence of the nobility; by the 18th century more generally used for any large, private residence or building |
| **Jeu de Paume** | Real Tennis. In the Middle Ages it was played with the palm of the hand, in the 15th century a glove was used, and later a racket. The first professional players date from 1687 |
| **Mairie** | town hall of an *arrondissment* |
| **Marché** | market |
| **Pays** | region |
| **Pont** | bridge |
| **Porte** | gateway |
| **Poubelle** | rubbish bins, named after the Préfet who organized Paris's municipal trash collection in the 1890s |
| **Retable** | a carved or painted altarpiece, consisting of a number of scenes |
| **Rez-de-Chausée (RC)** | ground floor |
| **Tour** | tower |
| **Transi** | in a tomb, a relief of the decomposing cadaver |
| **Tree of Jesse** | Christ's family tree, often painted or carved in churches |
| **Tympanum** | sculpted semicircular panel over a church door |

# Glossary

| | |
|---|---|
| **Villa** | a detached house in the suburbs, or in Paris, a small cul de sac lined with small houses and gardens |

## Language

### Deciphering French Menus

#### Hors d'oeuvre et Soupes

Assiette assortie

Bisque
Bouchées
Bouillon
Crudités
Potage
Velouté

Vol-au-Vent

#### Starters and Soups

Mix cold hors d'oeuvres
Shellfish soup
Mini vol-au-vents
Broth
Raw vegetable platter
Thick vegetable soup
Thick smooth soup, often fish or chicken
Puff pastry case with savoury filling

#### Poissons et Coquillages

Aiglefin
Anchois
Anguille
Barbue
Blanchailles
Brème
Brochet
Bulot
Cabillaud
Calmar
Carrelet
Coques
Coquilles St-Jacques
Crabe
Crevettes grises
Crevettes roses
Cuisses de grenouilles
Daurade
Ecrevisse
Escabèche

Escargots
Espadon
Flétan
Friture
Fruits de mer

#### Fish and Shellfish

Little haddock
Anchovies
Eel
Brill
Whitebait
Bream
Pike
Whelk
Fresh cod
Squid
Plaice
Cockles
Scallops
Crab
Shrimp
Prawns

Frogs' legs
Sea bream
Freshwater crayfish
Fish fried, marinated, and served cold
Snails
Swordfish
Halibut
Deep fried fish
Seafood

Gambas
Gigot de mer

Hareng
Homard
Huîtres
Langouste
Languoustines
Limande
Lotte
Loup (de mer)
Maquereau
Merlan
Morue
Moules
Oursin
Pageot
Poulpe
Raie
Rouget
Saumon
Saint-Pierre
Sole (à la meunière)

Thon
Truite

Giant prawns
A large fish cooked whole
Herring
Lobster
Oysters
Mediterranean lobster
Dublin Bay Prawns
Lemon sole
Monkfish
Sea bass
Mackerel
Whiting
Salt Cod
Mussels
Sea urchin
Sea bream
Octopus
Skate
Red mullet
Salmon
John Dory
Sole (with butter, lemon and parsley)
Tuna
Trout

#### Viandes et Volaille

Agneau
Andouillette

Biftek
Blanc
Blanquette

Boeuf
Boudin blanc
Boudin noir
Brochette

Canard, caneton
Carré

#### Meat and Poultry

Lamb
Chitterling (tripe) sausage
Beefsteak
Breast or white meat
Stew of white meat, thickened with egg yolk
Beef
Sausage of white meat
Black pudding
Meat (or fish) on a skewer
Duck, duckling
The best end of a cutlet or chop

| | | | |
|---|---|---|---|
| Cervelles | Brains | Steak Tartare | Raw minced beef, often topped with a raw egg yolk |
| Châteaubriand | Porterhouse steak | | |
| Chevreau | Kid | | |
| Civet | Stew of rabbit | Suprême de volaille | Fillet of chicken breast and wing |
| Confit | Meat cooked and preserved in its own fat | | |
| | | Tête (de veau) | Head (calf's) |
| Contre-filet | Sirloin steak | Tournedos | Thick round slices of beef fillet |
| Côte, côtelette | Chop, cutlet | | |
| Cuisse | Thigh or leg | | |
| Dinde, dindon | Turkey | Tripes | Tripe |
| Entrecôte | Ribsteak | Veau | Veal |
| Epaule | Shoulder | Venaison | Venison |
| Estouffade | A meat stew marinated, fried, and then braised | | |

## Légumes, herbes, etc. — Vegetables, herbs, etc.

| | |
|---|---|
| Ail | Garlic |
| Artichaut | Artichoke |
| Asperges | Asparagus |
| Aubergine | Aubergine (eggplant) |
| Avocat | Avocado |
| Basilic | Basil |
| Betterave | Beetroot |
| Céleri (-rave) | Celery (celeriac) |
| Cèpes | Wild dark brown mushrooms |
| Champignons | Mushrooms |
| Chanterelles | Wild yellow mushrooms |
| Chicorée | Curly endive |
| Chou | Cabbage |
| Choufleur | Cauliflower |
| Concombre | Cucumber |
| Cornichons | Gherkins |
| Courgettes | Courgettes (zucchini) |
| Cresson | Watercress |
| Echalote | Shallot |
| Endive | Chicory |
| Epinards | Spinach |
| Estragon | Tarragon |
| Fenouil | Fennel |
| Fèves | Broad beans |
| Flageolets | White beans |
| Fleur de courgette | Courgette blossoms |
| Frites | Chips (French fries) |
| Haricots (rouges, blancs) | Beans (kidney, white) |
| Haricot verts | Green (French) beens |
| Laitue | Lettuce |
| Maïs (epis de) | Sweet corn (on the cob) |

| | |
|---|---|
| Faisan | Pheasant |
| Faux filet | Sirloin |
| Foie | Liver |
| Foie Gras | Goose liver |
| Fricadelle | Meatball |
| Gigot | Leg of lamb |
| Graisse | Fat |
| Grillade | Grilled meat |
| Jambon | Ham |
| Jarret | Knuckle |
| Langue | Tongue |
| Lapin | Rabbit |
| Lard (lardons) | Bacon (diced bacon) |
| Lièvre | Hare |
| Maigret (de canard) | Breast (of duck) |
| Merguez | Spicy red sausage |
| Noix de veau | Topside of veal |
| Oie | Goose |
| Os | Bone |
| Perdreau (perdrix) | Partridge |
| Petit salé | Salt pork |
| Pieds | Trotters |
| Pintade | Guinea fowl |
| Porc | Pork |
| Poularde | Capon |
| Poulet | Chicken |
| Poussin | Baby chicken |
| Ris (de veau) | Sweetbreads (veal) |
| Rognons | Kidneys |
| Rôti | Roast |
| Sanglier | Wild boar |
| Saucisses | Sausages |
| Saucisson | Dry sausage, like salami |
| Selle (d'agneau) | Saddle (of lamb) |

| | | | |
|---|---|---|---|
| Marjolaine | Marjoram | Crème fraîche | Sour cream |
| Menthe | Mint | Crème pâtissière | Thick pastry cream |
| Mesclum | Salad of various leaves | | filling made with eggs |
| Morilles | Morrel mushrooms | Dattes | Dates |
| Moutarde | Mustard | Figues (de Barbarie) | Figs (prickly pear) |
| Navet | Turnip | Fraises (de bois) | Strawberries (wild) |
| Oignons | Onions | Framboises | Raspberries |
| Oseille | Sorrel | Fromage (plateau de) | Cheese (board) |
| Panais | Parsnip | Fromage blanc | Yogurty cream cheese |
| Persil | Parsley | Fromage frais | Similar to sour cream |
| Petits pois | Peas | Fruit de la passion | Passion fruit |
| Piment | Pimento | Gâteau | Cake |
| Poireaux | Leeks | Glace | Ice cream |
| Pois chiche | Chickpeas | Groseilles | Redcurrants, goose- |
| Poivron | Bell pepper | | berries |
| Pomme de terre | Potato | Madeleine | Small sponge cakes |
| Radis | Radishes | Mandarine | Tangerine |
| Riz | Rice | Marrons | Chestnuts |
| Salade verte | Green salad | Merise | Black cherry |
| Thym | Thyme | Miel | Honey |
| Truffes | Truffles | Mirabelles | Greengage (plums) |
| | | Mûres | Mulberry, blackberry |

## Fruits, Desserts, Noix

## Fruits, Desserts, Nuts

| | | | |
|---|---|---|---|
| | | Myrtilles | Bilberries |
| Abricot | Apricot | Noisettes | Hazelnuts |
| Acajou | Cashew | Noix | Walnuts |
| Amandes | Almonds | Oeufs à la neige | Meringue |
| Ananas | Pineapple | Pamplemousse | Grapefruit |
| Banane | Banana | Parfait | Frozen mousse |
| Bavarois | Mousse or custard in | Pastèque | Watermelon |
| | a mould | Pêche (blanche) | Peach (white) |
| Bombe | Ice cream dessert in | Petits fours | Tiny cakes and pastries |
| | mould | Poire | Pear |
| Brebis | Sheep cheese | Pomme | Apple |
| Brugnon | Nectarine | Prune | Plum |
| Cacahouète | Peanut | Pruneau | Prune |
| Cassis | Black current | Savarin | A filled cake, shaped |
| Cérise | Cherry | | like a ring |
| Charlotte | Custard and fruit in | Truffes | Chocolate truffles |
| | almond biscuits | | |

## Cooking terms, miscellaneous, snacks

| | | | |
|---|---|---|---|
| Chausson | Turnover | | |
| Chèvre | Goat cheese | Addition | Bill |
| Citron | Lemon | Aigre-doux | Sweet and sour |
| Citron vert | Lime | Aiguillette | Thin slice |
| Clafoutis | Berry tart | A l'Anglaise | Boiled |
| Compôt | Stewed fruit | A l'Arlésienne | With aubergines, |
| Corbeille de fruits | Basket of fruit | | potatoes, tomatoes, |
| Coupe | Ice cream | | onions, and rice |
| Crème Anglaise | Trifle | A la Périgordine | truffle and foie gras |
| Crème Chantilly | Sweet whipped cream | | sauce |

| | | | |
|---|---|---|---|
| A la Provençale | Cooked with tomatoes, garlic, olive oil | Médaillon | Round piece |
| A point | Medium steak | Mijoté | Simmered |
| Beignets | Fritters | Mornay | Cheese sauce |
| Béarnaise | Sauce of egg yolks, shallots and white wine | Nouilles | Noodles |
| | | Oeufs | Eggs |
| | | Pané | Breaded |
| Beurre | Butter | Paupiette | Rolled and filled thin slices of fish or meat |
| Bien cuit | Well done steak | Pavé | Slab |
| Bleu | Very rare steak | Piquante | Vinegar sauce with shallots and capers |
| Bordelaise | Red wine, bone marrow, and shallot sauce | Poché | Poached |
| | | Poivre | Pepper |
| Chaud | Hot | Quenelles | Dumplings of fish or poultry |
| Confiture | Jam | | |
| Coulis | Strong clear broth | Raclette | Toasted cheese with potatoes, onions and pickles |
| Couteau | Knife | | |
| Crème | Cream | | |
| Crêpe | Thin pancake | Sanglant | Rare steak |
| Croque-monsieur | Toasted ham and cheese sandwich | Salé | Salted, spicy |
| | | Sel | Salt |
| Croustade | Small savoury pastry | Sucré | Sweet |
| Cru | Raw | Tranche | Slice |
| Cuillère | Spoon | Vapeur | Steamed |
| Emincé | Thinly sliced | Vinaigrette | Oil and vinegar dressing |
| En croûte | Cooked in a pastry crust | | |

## Boissons     Drinks

| | | | |
|---|---|---|---|
| En papillotte | Baked in buttered paper, foil | Bière (pression) | Beer (draught) |
| | | Bouteille (demi) | Bottle (half) |
| Epices | Spices | Café | Coffee |
| Farci | Stuffed | Démi | A third of a litre |
| Feuilleté | Flaky pastry | Doux | Sweet (wine) |
| Fourchette | Fork | Eau (minérale) | Water (mineral) |
| Fourré | Stuffed | Eau de vie | Aquavitae |
| Frais, fraîche | Fresh | Gazeuse | Sparkling |
| Frappé | With crushed ice | Glaçons | Ice cubes |
| Frit | Fried | Infusion (or tisane) | Herbal tea |
| Froid | Cold | Lait | Milk |
| Fumé | Smoked | Moulleux | Semi-dry |
| Gallette | Flaky pastry case or pancake | Pichet | Pitcher |
| | | Pressé | Fresh fruit juice |
| (au) Gratin | Topped with crisp browned cheese and bread crumbs | Pression | Draft |
| | | Sec | Dry |
| | | Sirop d'orange/ de citron | Orange/ lemon squash |
| Grillé | Grilled | Thé | Tea |
| Fromage | Cheese | Verre | Glass |
| Hachis | Minced | Vin blanc/ rosé/rouge | Wine white/ rosé/red |
| Hollandaise | Sauce of butter and vinegar | | |
| Huile (d'olive) | Oil (olive) | | |

# Further Reading

## Culture and History

Ardagh, John, *France Today*, Penguin 1988. A look into all aspects of contemporary France.

Brassai, *Le Paris Secret des Années 30*, Thames & Hudson, 1976. Magnificent collection of photos of a completely different city from the one occupying the same space today.

Carlyle, Thomas, *The French Revolution*, hundreds of editions. Pick this hallucinatory classic up at the next secondhand booksale; it's cheap, legal, and the only dangerous side effect is the urge to read it out loud.

Cronin, Vincent, *Napoléon Bonaparte*, William Morrow, 1972, well-written (and one of a thousand) biographies on France's bugbear.

Culbertson, Judi and Tom Randall, *Permanent Parisians*, Chelsea Green, 1986. Witty guide to the star stiffs in Paris's cemetery, with maps and photos.

Goncourt, Edmond and Juiles de, *Pages from the Goncourt Journal*, Oxford 1962. The abridged English version of the extraordinary 19th-century diary of life in Paris kept by the Goncourt brothers (after whom the literary prize is named).

Gramont, Sanche de, *The French: Portrait of a People*, Putnam, 1969. One of the funnier attempts at the favourite French pasttime: national self-analysis.

Guérard, Albert, *France in the Classical Age*, Harper & Row, 1956. The great classic on the classical age, and intriguing for the non-French reader to see what contortions the author goes through to avoid pounding Louis XIV.

James, John, *Chartres*, Routledge & Kegan Paul, 1982. Intriguing account of the building and design of the most beautiful of Gothic cathedrals.

Hibbert, Christopher, *The French Revolution*, Penguin, 1982. Compared to Carlyle, an easily digestible and concise account.

Horne, Alistair, *The Fall of Paris: The Siege and the Commune 1870–71*, Macmillan, 1965. Enthralling, anecdote-filled account of the momentous events you scarcely study in school; the amazing stupidity on all sides is a lesson for all.

Littlewood, Ian, *Paris: A Literary Companion*, John Murray, 1987. A juicy selection of writings both famous and obscure on the capital; good maps and pictures.

Marx, Karl, *On the Paris Commune*, Lawrence & Wishart, 1971. Typical meaty Marx, with a history by Engels.

Maurois, André, *Victor Hugo and His World*, Viking 1966. A member of the Académie takes on the dinosaur.

Restif de la Bretonne, *Les Nuits de Paris*, Random House. The classic translated into English by Linda Asher and Ellen Fertig.

Rudorff, Raymond, *Belle Epoque: Paris in the Nineties*, Hamish Hamilton, 1972. The colourful politics and culture of Paris's mythic decade.

Salvadori, Renzo, *Architect's Guide to Paris*, Butterworth Architecture, 1990. Not only for architects, with maps on the growth of Paris, building plans, and black and white photos.

Seward, Desmond, *The Hundred Years War*, Constable and Company 1978. A good read about some of the more unwelcome English visitors to Paris.

Wiser, William, *The Crazy Years: Paris in the Twenties*, Thames and Hudson 1990. A lively, annecdote-filled account of the Parisians and expats in Paris in *les années folles*; good photographs, too.

Wyndham Lewis, D. B., *François Villon*, Sheed & Ward, 1928. The authorative biography of the rascally poet.

Zeldin, Theodore, *France 1845–1945*, Oxford 1980. Five well-written volumes on all aspects of the period.

---

## Modernism

Baudelaire, Charles, *Les Fleurs du Mal*, good translation by Marthiel and Jackson Mathews, New Directions, 1962; *The Painter of Modern Life* and *Art in Paris*, translated by Jonathon Mayne, Phaidon Press, 1965.

Berman, Marshall, *All That Is Solid Melts Into Air*, Verso 1987. A necessary 'remembering' of the affirmative, creative forces of modernism, with a large chapter devoted to Baudelaire in Haussmann's Paris.

Buck-Morss, Susan, *The Dialectics of Seeing: Walter Benjamin and the Arcades Project*, MIT Press, 1989. A fascinating 'picture book of philosophy' that brings to life the ideas in Benjamin's unfinished *Passagen-Werk* with a minimum of jargon. Highly recommended.

Chevalier, Louis, *Labouring Classes and Dangerous Classes: Paris in the First Half of the Nineteenth Century*, translated by Frank Jellinek, Howard Fertig, 1973. Louis Chevalier is Paris's best known historian; if you read French, you may want to dip into his latest, a damning account of the ruling technocracy, *L'Annihilation de Paris*

Evenson, Norma, *Paris: A Century of Change 1878–1978*, Yale, 1981. Excellent, well-illustrated account of Paris' physical and social upheavals.

Macchia, Giovanni, *Les Ruines de Paris*, Flammarion, 1988. An essay on Paris the autophage by a worried Italian lover of the city.

Miller, Michael, *The Bon Marché: Bourgeoise Culture and the Department Store 1869–1920*, Princeton 1981. Scholarly account of the growth of consumers and their commodity fetishes.

Sennett, Richard, *The Fall of Public Man*, Vintage 1978. Excellent, thought-provoking book on the social devolution, mostly about 19th-century Paris; intriguing account of the Dreyfuss Affair and Zola's *J'accuse!* defence.

# Paris in Literature

Abélard, Peter, *The Story of My Misfortunes*, The Free Press, 1958. Abélard's autobiography in English. Also see *The Letters of Héloïse and Abelard* (Penguin).

Aragon, Louis, *Le Paysan de Paris*, Gallimard, 1953. Surrealist masterpiece.

Balzac, Honoré de, *Père Goriot* and *Cousine Bette*, trans. by Marian Ayton Crawford, Penguin, two of the best by the author of Paris's Human Comedy.

Beauvoir, Simone de, *The Prime of Life*, André Deutsch, 1962. An evocative account of intellectual life on the Left Bank by author of *The Second Sex.*

Breton, André, *Nadja*, another Surrealist classic, but translated in 1930, so you may root it out of the library. Fairly easy to find in French.

Gysin, Brion, *The Last Museum*, Faber & Faber, 1986. What happens when Burroughs, Ginsberg, Kerouac and company decided to be Americans in Paris.

Hemingway, Ernest, *A Moveable Feast*, Panther 1977. Not as amusing as Stein's accounts, but more readily available.

Hugo, Victor, *Les Misérables*, Penguin 1982. Four rousing volumes of social injustice, revolts, and everything else, including Paris's sewers.

Miller, Henry, *Tropic of Cancer* (1934) *Black Spring* (1936), *Quiet Days in Clichy* (1955), often reprinted. Among the most evocative, as well as sex-obsessed, love letters to Paris.

Orwell, George, *Down and Out in Paris and London*, Penguin 1989. Orwell's first book, an artless but moving account of bare survival in Depression-era Paris (which seems delightful compared to Depression-era London). Just don't read it before a fancy meal in a fancy hotel.

Proust, Marcel, *Remembrance of Things Past* (three volumes, Penguin). The ultimate meandering journey through Marcel's amazing involuntary memory, mostly set in Paris; readers either find it compelling or a load of fuddle-duddle.

Simenon, Georges, *Maigret at the Crossroads*, Penguin 1986. Paris's crime classics, with fascinating descriptions of the underworld.

Stein, Gertrude, *The Autobiography of Alice B. Toklas*, first published in 1933, one of the classics of ex-pat life in Paris.

Sterne, Laurence, *A Sentimental Journey*, Penguin. Account of a 1768 trip to Paris by the dying but ever delightful author of *Tristram Shandy.*

Verne, Jules, *Paris in the Twentieth Century.* Recently rediscovered work reveals that Verne was spot on, predicting everything from the fax machine to the homeless.

Zola, Emile, *Nana* (1880, about a courtesan in the days of Napoleon III) and *L'Assommoir* (1876, about working class life in Paris) Penguin, 1972. Two of the master of Realism's best novels, with extraordinary detailed descriptions of Paris.

Main references are marked in **bold**.

# Index

Orly airport 2–3
Orsay, Musée d' 335–44
architecture (1850–1900) 337–8
Art Nouveau 344
Ballroom 344
Barbizon School 338
Café des Hauteurs 341
caricatures 338
Classicism 337
decorative arts 337
Fauvism 343
Galerie Bellechasse 342–3
Impressionism 339–41
Nabis 343
Orientalism 339
Postimpressionism 342–3
precursors of the Impressionists 338
precursors of symbolism 337
Realism **338**, 339
Romanticism 337
Salle de l'Opéra 337–8
Salle Redon 342
Salle Toulouse-Lautrec 342
sculptures **336–7**, 344
Symbolists 344
Synthetism 342–3
Tour Guimard 344
*View of Paris* 338
Ott, Carlos 125

Pagode, La 301–2
Palais Abbatial 285
Palais Bourbon 294
Palais de Chaillot 307
Palais de la Découverte 205–6
Palais de l'Elysée 191
Palais Galliera 310
Palais de l'Institut de France 275
Palais de Justice 95, **99–102**
Palais du Luxembourg 67, **280–1**
Palais Omnisports de Paris-Bercy 367
Palais Royal 173–5
Palais de Tokyo 310
Panthéon 83, **249–50**
Panthéon Bouddique 309–10
Parc
Astérix 458
de la Bagatelle 351
Balbi 473–4
de Belleville 361
Bois de Vincennes 365
des Buttes-Chaumont 361
du Champ de Mars 302–3
Georges-Brassens 379
de Monceau 193
Montsouris 369
de la Villette 357–60
*Parisii* **24**, 94
parking **8**, 408–9

Parvis 210
Parvis-Notre-Dame 103–4
Pascal, Blaise 33, **248**
Passage
Brady 164
du Caire 165
Choiseul 177–8
Jouffroy 178–9
des Panoramas 178
Ste-Anne 177–8
St-Paul 135
Verdeau 180
passages 84
passports 4, 14–15
Passy 346–8
Pasteur, Louis 379
Pater, Jean-Baptiste 70
Pâtisserie Lerch 261
Pavillon de l'Arsenal 137–8
Pei, I.M. 323
Pénaud, Alphonse 54–5
performing arts 433–4
Perrault, Claude 82, **321**, 371
Petit Luxembourg 281
Petit Palais 205
Petit Pont 238
Petit Trianon 473
Philipe-Auguste, King of France **26**, 233
'Philippe Egalité' (Duke of Orléans) 36
Piaf, Edith 361
grave 364
Picabia, Francis 78
Picasso, Pablo 77, 159, **274**
museum 130–1
Pigalle, Jean-Baptiste 225
Plaisance 376–7
Planétarium 358
Poilâne 287
police 14–15
Pompadour, Madame de 34
Pompidou Centre 88, **156–60**
Pont
Alexandre III 205, 293, **294**
de l'Alma 305
des Arts 96
au Change 99
au Double 236
d'Iéna 306
Marie 115
Neuf **95–6**, 97, 170
Notre-Dame 102
de la Tournelle 116, **260–1**
Porte Dauphine 351
Porte St-Denis 163
Porte St-Martin 163
Post Office (Rue Castex) 126
post offices 19–20
Pottier, Eugène, grave 364
Poussin, Nicolas 67

Pré Catelan 350
Préfecture de Police 102
*prêt-à-porter* 436–7
Proust, Marcel, grave 363
Prud'hon, Pierre-Paul 72
Puces de Montreuil 354
Puces de Vanves 354

Quartier
Dauphine 351
Goutte d'Or 225
Gros Caillou 303
de l'Horloge 160
Javel 380
Latin *see* Latin Quarter
du Parc 210
Quatre Temps 210

Racine **248**, 278
radio 18
Rambouillet 474
Ray, Man 78
Redon, Odilon **76**, 342
Réseau Express Régional (RER) 7, 498
restaurants 384–401
prices 384–5
Restif de la Bretonne 236
Revolution (1789) 35–7
and art 71
Revolution (1830) 38
Richard the Lionheart 95
Richelieu, Cardinal **30**, 280–1
Rigaud, Hyacinthe 69
Robert, Hubert 71
Robespierre, Maximilien de 36
Rodin, Auguste 75–6, **295–6**
Roissy (Charles de Gaulle) airport 2–3
Roman baths 240
Roman Empire 24
Rotonde barrière 193
Rotonde Félix Potin 165–6
Rotonde, La (café) 377–8
Rotonde de la Villette 359
Rousseau, Henri 75
Rousseau, Théodore 73
Rubens, Peter Paul 331
Ruche, La 379
Rude, François 72

Sacré-Coeur 222, **223–4**
Sade, Marquis de 123
St-Augustin 193
St Bartholomew's Day Massacre 30
Sainte-Chapelle 65, 80, **99–101**
Ste-Clotilde 84, **295**
St-Denis 24–5, 65, **355–7**
St-Etienne du Mont 248–9
St-Eustache 81, **151–2**
St-Germain 268–88

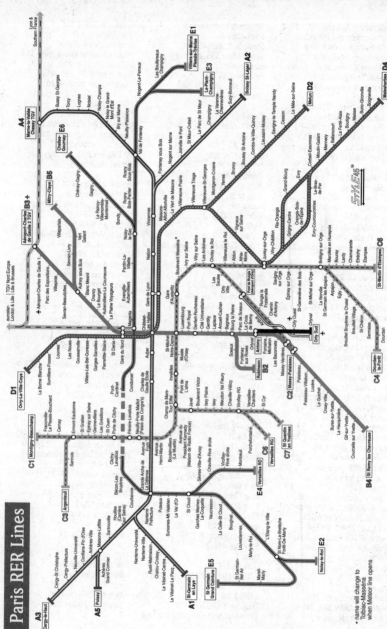

# Paris RER Lines